The ABC's of ABC Ware

Davida and Irving Shipkowitz

4880 Lower Valley Road, Atglen, PA 19310 USA

Frontispiece

The small grey plate on the left, shaped by hand of a coarse clay, is the oldest alphabet plate in the collection. Its companion is a newer version . . . a brighter copy. Neither of their histories is known, but both carry a mythological griffin, the eagle-headed lion who has, for thousands of years, been a winged symbol of protection in ancient tombs and sanctuaries. May this trusted motif of Middle Eastern lands guard our glimpse into the past.

Figure Frontispiece 1 - "Griffin." 3.5 in. Late 18th century. No mark.
Figure Frontispiece 2 - "Griffin." 3.5 in. 19th century. No mark.

Dedication

"Old China for Sale. Job Lot." "Well," soliloquized the old china maniac, "Job and Lot lived a long—a very long time ago; it really must be very antique china! I shall endeavor to get some."
—*Pottery Gazette,* page 795, December 2, 1889

To all those who endeavor to get some china from a very long time ago, this book is fondly dedicated.

"Small Flower." Creamware. 1.75 in. No mark. $350+

Library of Congress Cataloging-in-Publication Data

Shipkowitz, Davida.
The ABC's of ABC ware / Davida and Irving Shipkowitz.
p. cm.
ISBN 0-7643-1537-4 (hardcover)
1. Tableware--United States--History. 2. Tableware--England--History. 3. ABC ware (Tableware)--United States--History. 4. ABC ware (Tableware)--England--History. I. Shipkowitz, Irving. II. Title.
NK8725 .S54 2002
738.3'0973'075--dc21
2002001109

Designed by Bonnie M. Hensley
Cover design by Bruce M. Waters
Type set in Americana XBd BT/Korinna BT

ISBN: 0-7643-1537-4
Printed in China
1 2 3 4

Published by Schiffer Publishing Ltd.
4880 Lower Valley Road
Atglen, PA 19310
Phone: (610) 593-1777; Fax: (610) 593-2002
E-mail: Schifferbk@aol.com
Please visit our web site catalog at **www.schifferbooks.com**
We are always looking for people to write books on new and related subjects. If you have an idea for a book, please contact us at the above address.

This book may be purchased from the publisher.
Include $3.95 for shipping.
Please try your bookstore first.
You may write for a free catalog.

In Europe, Schiffer books are distributed by
Bushwood Books
6 Marksbury Avenue
Kew Gardens
Surrey TW9 4JF England
Phone: 44 (0) 20 8392 8585
Fax: 44 (0) 20 8392 9876
E-mail: Bushwd@aol.com
Free postage in the UK. Europe: air mail at cost.

Contents

After-colored ink print by Peter Lobban, Stoke-on-Trent, Staffordshire.

Acknowledgments

It would not have been possible to complete this text without the assistance of so many individuals. Kindness after kindness expanded our world as we worked secluded in a small suburb of Los Angeles. Our heartfelt thanks to all those who gave of their time and expertise to further the research without which this book would not have become a reality. Listed in alphabetical order, they are: Ilene Abramson of the Children's Room of the Central Library, Los Angeles, for her encouragement and research assistance; Amazon.com for their fabulous help in finding every long-ago published text we ever wished into Warrillow Photo Collections; Paul Eugene Camp, librarian of the Special Collections Department at the University of South Florida for lyrics; Lori A. Carson, Interpreter, Museum of Ceramics in East Liverpool, Ohio, for securing needed information; Susan Casey for completing an elusive patent search; the Concord, New Hampshire, Chamber of Commerce for old post office history; Jackie Chamberlain, for reference books; Wilfred and Dolli Cohen of Antique & Art Glass for friendship and acquisitions; Nancy Cooper of Cross Country Antiques for her spelling skills, her loving care, and acquisitions; Marcia DeFilipps,

 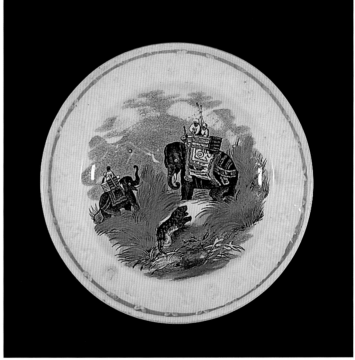

for; Gail Bardhan of Corning, New York's Corning Museum of Glass for pressed-glass research; Margaret Beard of the Archive Service, Hanley Library, for her cheerful assistance; Irwin Becker for his German geography; Monty Berna for making house calls to heal our always ailing computer; Michael Berry of Berry & Company for finding flatware; Steven Birks, whose incredible Web sites and personal communication have provided much essential information as well as the photo of the Eagle Pottery; Helen Burton of Special Collections and Archives, Keele Information Service, Keele University Library, for her investigations Historian of Holley, New York, for her updates; Martin Durrant, of the Victoria and Albert Museum, who worked very hard to provide us with a rare transfer of hunting elephants; Elizabeth Fairman of the Yale University Library Special Collections for her assistance; Melissa Gold, Assistant Museum Registrar of the Yale Center for British Art, for her provision of a rare print; Bill and Donna Gray of East Liverpool, Ohio, for their encouragement and photos of Hotel China; Bob and Cletha Hale of Simi Valley, California, for their "heavenly" attentions to religious content; Tom Harrington of the Gallaudet University Library for information concerning the development of sign language; George (and his parrot) of George's Antiques for his interest; Susan Harris, Librarian at the New Bodleian Library at Oxford, for her exhaustive searches; Jeongsook Heo for her patient mapmaking; Wayne and Lola Higby of Ventura, California, for their encouragement and loan of pressed-glass items from their personal collection; Librarians Jerry Husfeldt and Marcia Dellenbach of Chicago Public Library's Computer Assisted Research Center and CPL's Librarian Marc Conrad, who found the "WB over W" trademark to conclude a three-year search; Ian Ingham of The Royal Pavilion for "royals" and research; Dr. Peter and Christine Jacob for translating information secured from museums in Germany; John Jaros, of the Aurora, Illinois, Historical Society, for recalling Aurora's high school days; Basil Jeuda, Lecturer in Transport History at Keele University, Keele, Staffordshire, for his contribution of words and photographs of railroads; Bernard Kalban, of Carlin American Inc., for information concerning the publication of Hattie Starr's lullaby; Genevieve Krueger for her unique storehouse of books from which so much of the original transfer material was so graciously given; Sunny Lenzner for significant transfer histories; Lisa Libby for special permissions at the Huntington Library; ABC authors Ralph and Irene Lindsay of New Holland, Pennsylvania, for their generous encouragement

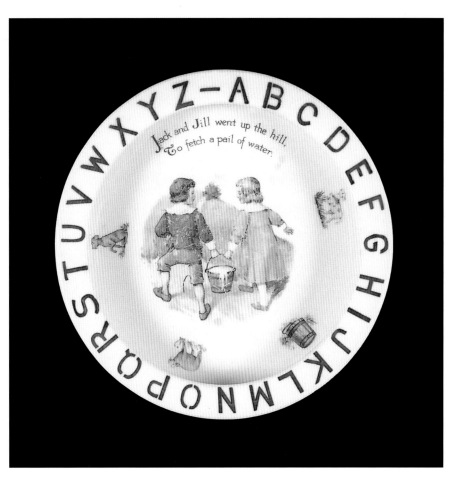

and photos; Jennifer Luna and Laura Wong, of the Photo-Duplication Department of the Library of Congress, for their "spirited" assistance; the Newport, New York, Chamber of Commerce for village information; Tony Lehner and Frank Nguyen, who performed the content analyses of the Shipkowitz-Berard metal collection; New York Public Library's Tom Lisante; Radames Suarez and Anne Lauder for their help in assuring prints of the Enoch Wood Pottery; Peter Lobban of Longton, England, for his masterful watercolor of the bottle ovens; Judy and Sara Mandel, whose research contributed to Chapters E and J; Roz Mass for the loan of her treasured book about Coney Island; the invincible team of Charles and Marilyn McClellan of Green Valley, Arizona, whose rapid research skills and love of railroads worked many miracles; Lynn Miller, Information Officer of the Wedgwood Potteries, for providing a marvelous line drawing of the famous factory; R. S. and Carolyn Machtolff, of Machtolff's Mercantile Antiques of Southern California, for kind support and many acquisitions; Mary Mills, Christine Brown, and Tracey Williams of Wolverhampton's Local Studies Research Library, for research; Sharon Morris, at the Los Angeles Public Library, for her "good-humored" investigations; Muriel Motola for her provision of historic infant food recipes; "Aunties" Ruth Mover and Beatrice Zimmerman for information gathering at local libraries in the Chicago area; Harley Munger for an extended loan of his library on lustre; the C. L. Nelsons, of Spring Park, Minnesota, for their knowledge and ceramics; Ben and Marcia Omessi for their support, love, and encouragement; Doris Orenstein for her rapid research into Judaica; the Pennacchios of Penn's Landing Antiques in El Cajon, California, for their serious interest; Amy Presser and Shirley and Melvin Sandler for acquisition of prints at the Special Collections Department of the Milton S. Eisenhower Library, Johns Hopkins University, Baltimore, Maryland; Richard Roberts (and his staff) of the Connecticut State Library, Hartford, Connecticut, for assistance; Harald Rosmanitz of the Keramikmuseum in Höhr-Grenzhausen, Germany, for his enthusiastic help; Marilyn Z. Ross of Worthington, Ohio, for her long-time loan of the Metal Patent Dial Plate; Cindy Rust, of Just Everything Silverplate, for her Hollywood history; Jean Rutter, of Quakertown, Pennsylvania, for sharing her "Great Expectations"; Joe and Libby Sanes for their selective shopping; Joel Silver, of the Lilly Library at Indiana University, Bloomington, for permission to reproduce the *Alphabet of Virtues*; Judy and "Bernie" Simon of Ventura, California, for their patient assistance with German language texts and personal contacts with German museums; Gary Shutlak of Nova Scotia Archives and Records Management for digging into the history of Cleverdon & Company; Donald Snoddy, Union Pacific Railroad historian, for his background knowledge of the Railway Station at Omaha, Nebraska; Kathleen Strang, director of Local History at the Willard Library for Post Cereals, Battle Creek, Michigan, for information concerning the evolution of breakfast cereal products; the Thomases (The Linen Merchants) for their continued support; Sean D. Thompson, Assistant Manager of Technology at Kinkos, for technical support; the Tomasini family of Petaluma for their memories; Ted and Janice Tytell for their technological wizardry and creative talents; Sandra Wassa for miraculous finds at Connecticut's flea markets; Mr. and Mrs. Richard Watson of Medford, New Jersey, for lending us their colorfully dressed Zouaves; Allan Weathers of the Meriden Historical Society, Meriden, Connecticut, for his kind help in securing catalogue photos; Mrs. O. Werner and the staff at the Deutsches Porzellanmuseum in Hohenberg/Eger, Bavaria, for their research into German potteries and their trademarks; Hamish Wood and Angela Lee of the Gladstone Museum for their continuous assistance and kind permission to reprint information from their printings; and last, but not least, to Sheila Williams, of the Arcade Hotel in Arcade, New York, who added colorful insights into the history of Buffalo Pottery.

It is impossible to thank all the members of every visited library staff. Extraordinary thanks go to the staffs, in alphabetical order, of: the Berlin-Peck Memorial Library in Berlin, Connecticut; the British Library Reading Room and Reader's Services; the Libraries at Burslem and Tunstall, Staffordshire; Hartford Historical Society Library, the Print Room at the Victoria and Albert Museum, London, and many more.

Without the searches, the sharing, advice, encouragement, and love of Ann and Dennis Berard of Fitzwilliam, New Hampshire, there would have been no book. Items from their collections and their informative contributions are sprinkled throughout the text. They have been our partners in this project. And, as knowledgeable East coast dealers, they have suggested much of the pricing as listed in Chapter "W Is for Worth."

Thanks also to: Nancy Cooper, of Cross Country Antiques in San Francisco, who contributed the values of mixed-metal mugs; *ABC Collectors' Circle Newsletter* editor Dr. Joan George of Old Bridge, New Jersey, who assisted in all categories; the Grays of East Liverpool, Ohio, who priced the Hotel China; author Joyce Johnston, of Johnston's Antiques in Monroe, Ohio, who assisted in the pricing of pressed glass; and Michael Berry, of Berry & Company, who concurred in the values listed for alphabet flatware. There were others as well, from all areas of the country, who chose not to be named. The text of Chapter "W Is for Worth" was reviewed by the esteemed Pasadena appraiser Bill Novotny, whose suggestions were gratefully incorporated.

Special thanks to three individuals for their extraordinary dedication. First, to Lois Smith, for her enduring vigilance in eradicating this manuscript's every dangling modifier; to Kath Bromage, Office Manager of the Centre for Continuing and Professional Education at the Keele University Library in Keele, Staffordshire, for her love, her generous counsel, and rapid research; and to the notable Kathy Niblett, of Stoke-on-Trent, for her respected research, advice, consent, and perseverance.

Ringing kudos to two singularly important persons. First, to John Peter Hayden, Jr., of Hayden & Fandetta, Rare Book Dealers, New York, who gave us both the courage to begin and the tools with which to ensure our accuracy; his humor was our strength. And to our photographer, Jacob Mikaili (Advanced Photo, Canoga Park, California), who said, "No problem!" to our request for hundreds of "re-dos," our esteemed appreciation for his extraordinary equanimity, interest, care, and creative talents.

Of course, most gratitude goes to Peter Schiffer of Schiffer Publications, Ltd. and to our editor, Donna Baker, who endured, with infinite patience and trust, our everlasting changes and continuous modifications. It has been a privilege to write under her intelligent editorship and we are thankful for her good humor, constructive advice, and scrupulous care.

Special love to Irene Lowy for her strength and counsel, and, most affectionately, our continuing reverence to the memories of Rosalie Shipkowitz, Hannah Greenfield, and Rabbi Martin Lowy, for their everlasting love.

Before We Begin

Alphabet-encircled earthenware plates absorbed their succulent gravies on warming racks and were slowly "greased" brown. Metal plates were hammered by infant spoons, thick Bavarian porringers were chipped by falling mugs, and frosted glass dishes were shattered after tumbling from pressed-back highchairs. The late 18th, 19th, and 20th centuries produced thousands of children's ABC plates, but few relics remain to reward their collectors' efforts both here and on the Continent. Soaring over the last decade from $8 to $800, each plate design serves as a glimpse of what our "then" parents selected as age-appropriate.

Whether for use or decoration, dinner-large to silver-dollar-sized, elegantly lettered rims encircled transfer views of everyday 19th-century living, which pictured not only the work ethic of the times but the era's vigorous change in attitudes toward children. From having been seen only as small, disciplined adults, the young were now, with new insights, being cherished as a unique and coddled age group with special needs of their own. A chronological view of the collection displays this evolution and establishes children as an authentic "target group" of its own, by and large, for whom potters could design.

With appetizing backgrounds for foods, plates offered hundreds of designs, which, when gathered together, can be grouped into subject categories that both rival any contemporary curriculum area and present intimate insights of the Victorian childhood. A favorite table setting might offer bites of letter sounds, bits of prose between swallows, names of animals from far-away jungles, or the difference between weight and distance. Other scenes might champion a cause, build patriotism, or inspire a prayer. With each plate goes the tale behind the transfer that was told at mealtime. Each transfer was chosen to deliver a message. *It is to these messages, which together make a portrait of a period, that we devote this book.* Even the structure of this book, with its text preceding its illustrations, is presented in the style of the times. Though text and graphics might have been two books, about 1860, it is here combined into one, more efficient, edition.

The plates themselves, if arranged chronologically, would tell some of the story of the century's industrial history. The intimacy of the English transfer ware lies in the infancy of industrialization. Factories with a slowly emerging sense of mass production allowed for hand-made pieces of earthenware—their

THE PRETTY CHILD ON TIPTOE STANDS, TO REACH THE PIANO WITH HER HANDS.

underglaze decorations applied at a worker's whim. More recent productions boast of the gleaming sameness accomplished by new machinery and the pride of quality control.

Examples of metalware and glassware can be seen as well. Metal products became popular with the start of metal-stamping, while enameled metal slowly gained acceptance after Frederick Walton created that process. Brightly colored lithographed metal presided at dollies' tea parties, while silver and silverplate wares enhanced damask cloths everywhere. Light reflected from beads of clear glass that rivaled fine crystal highlighted the frosted designs that enlivened the glass industry, and played on amber carnival glass cereals at the breakfast table.

Displaying and discussing the production of all types of alphabet plates, this book is divided into categories from A through Z, with each lettered chapter telling part of the story. A begins the tale with a bit of American history. B tells of the early bonfires and 19th-century bottle ovens that fired the glazes. C, for commercialism, brings with it the new railroads, the burgeoning markets across the seas, and our familiar red and white cans of Campbell's soups along with the Disney dishes from which to eat them. D displays deep dishes, most of them made in Bavarian potteries. E discusses the role of the plates in educating the young, the children of both the well-to-do and the poor. It was the poorest of the poor who, while helping to produce the plates, gained little from their messages. F describes flatware, etc. More traditionally, the volume does include a category-by-category "plate

5. WHY WOULD THIS PASTRY COOK
MAKE A GOOD SOLDIER?

SACRED HISTORY of JOSEPH and his BRETHREN

JOSEPHs BRETHREN
Applying to him for CORN in time of FAMINE

CRUSOE MAKING A BOAT

finder." Chapter "W Is for Worth" lists each plate and its estimated value. These categories tie closely with those as presented in the books by the Chalalas (1986) and the Lindsays (1998). Included in the Appendices are complete texts of quoted lyrics, clarifications of historical data, and recipes for both bleaching greasy glazes and combining the curdling contents of 19th-century infant foods.

Gathering information for this book was, at times, a euphoric experience. We searched references in zealously protected archival collections and dusty stashes in homes of passionate collectors of ephemera and books. The helpfulness of research librarians and the passions of those who shared our excitement were a joy. Yahoo.com has helped to make delightful friendships that have grown through the steady barrage of questions and answers directed to patient librarians here and abroad. And always respected was the companionship of definitive authors through old volumes with cracked bindings and brittle pages: the devoted and patient Alice Bertha Gomme, the venerable if not caustic O. Moore, the inexhaustible Opies, the spiritually reminiscent Charles Shaw, the gracefully dramatic Bernardin De Saint-Pierre, and more.

But the search, from England to New England and all points west, had its frustrations as well. Though all plates have a tale to tell, the search for the exact sources of published pictures that matched transfer illustrations proved only occasionally rewarding. Retrieval systems in archival libraries are logical. It was difficult, at best, to find reprintable items when well-meaning librarians required exact titles . . . the search for prints, aside from the few referrals in other texts, is totally random. Sources quoted in Riley's *Gifts for Good Children* (1991) were invaluable, and we are positive that extended research would add significantly to the documentation of designs and trademarks.

Most industrial catalogues have fallen prey to fires; most firms in failure felt little need to keep what remained of their demise. Merging companies found new identities with few remaining records of their roots. But through the search for industrial histories that often provided little but dates and verifications of changing partnerships were revealed the creative, the aggressive, the compassionate, the leery, the lecherous, the lazy, and the scandalous personalities that created them. Their footsteps still sound through their fading trademarks.

Aside from traditional types of sources, careful research and background by the esteemed Kathy Niblett, Ceramic Historian of Stoke-on-Trent, and Basil Jeuda, of the Keele University at Keele, Staffordshire, have provided some of the research that makes this volume both a catalogue of many of the alphabet plates produced and an industrial history of the firms that produced them. Certainly there are many areas that need further exploration. The collection of background material expands with each new acquisition . . . this effort just scratches the surface.

Of course, we don't have all of the plates ever made; some of our outstanding examples have been found "mysteriously missing." Our losses are grievous. And some items that we do own have not been included. It is the joining of all of the material presented in this and other texts, along with the *ABC Collectors' Circle Newsletter,* edited by Dr. Joan George of Old Bridge, New Jersey, which will begin to provide an adequate idea of how many plates were actually produced.

Not being able to include late acquisitions will always be a source of frustration! As Ebay proves hour by hour, the search never ends . . . but this book needs now to begin.

A Is for Americana

They were made in England, but so many Staffordshire alphabet plates told the tale of the beginning of America. **Figure A1** takes us back to 1741 when Europeans first made contact with the northwest U.S. Native Americans; it was 1812 when England established many posts on the Northern Pacific coastline that would be named British Columbia.

The Tsimshian people, according to information from the Royal British Columbian Museum, were one of the Native American peoples whose rights to the fishing for the coveted candlefish, known also as *eulachon* or *oolakan,* were both highly prized and scrupulously monitored. Trade routes, known as "grease trails," were established; surpluses were sold by those who had more than they needed of the smelt that could be burned like a candle or used as a torch when a thin strip of bark was inserted into the body of the smoke-dried saltwater fish. The oil was both a food and a commodity, and rights to it were willed, through maternal lines, from generation to generation, as was the land those Indians owned. The peoples of the Northwest had plentiful resources. Plants provided meals and medicines. Salmon, shellfish, pelts, and whale oil were traded. Sophisticated homes of cedar protected their families while they maintained councils and practiced self-fulfilling religions. The complex societies of the Northwestern Indians were sensitive to wealth, inheritances, and each individual's achievement. Their civilization was firmly established until the colonization of the English about 1812.

Two hundred years earlier than the building of British forts in British Columbia, the English, seeking gold and a passage to the Orient, had come to the shores of North America, far to the east and somewhat south of the Tsimshian lands. This east coast, too, would become a land of British colonies. Spain had failed to establish two colonies someplace between Chesapeake Bay and the Savannah River about five hundred miles to the south. The French would call all the land between what would become the thirteen colonies and the unexplored western borders, New France. It was England's James I who set his sights upon the eastern shores of the faraway land. It was 1607 when the London Company's Captain Newport and his three ships of adventurers set anchor to found the colony called Jamestown (Virginia). After placing a cross at their landing spot, they proceeded up the justly named James River to raise a three-sided fort and trading post, a church, a storehouse, and a row of "wattle and daub" huts to protect them from the wind. With trunks of fine clothes rather than tools for turning the soil, they began their search for gold.

But finding none wasn't the worst of their grief; having been told there was gold for the getting and not inclined to physical labor, most lacked both the skills and the spirit for survival. Even worse, they had contracted malaria from the pesky mosquitoes, dysentery from the drinking water, and poison darts from the Indians whose lifestyle had been interrupted. The gold seekers who survived knew they owed their very lives to the tough-love leadership of red-bearded John Smith, who kept the group intact until he left for England. In his absence, the Powhatan laid siege to the fort. And with the siege came the "Starving Time." Desperate, the settlers ate their boots and shoes and, some historians say, remnants of the slaughtered. All but sixty starved to death. Their buildings had been burned for warmth and were, like the remaining settlers, mere shadows of their former selves. But sails were seen on the horizon . . .

Some began planting tobacco, as did the Indians. In 1612, John Rolfe, with imported seed from the West Indies, began to cultivate the entrancing varieties that became popular in Europe; luckily the climate and soil of the Chesapeake Bay Colonies were perfect for growing the easily exported crop. In 1619, a Dutch ship docked at Jamestown, bringing twenty black slaves who had been kidnapped from their African homes by traders and sold to the captain of the ship that brought them; help was needed to plant and harvest the broad-leafed plants. And that year saw the arrival of nearly one hundred women, each of whom could be had for a mere 120 pounds of the sweet-smelling weed; the economic importance of the "cash crop" was immediately established. It was in that year, too, that the House of Burgesses first met to begin representative government in America. The settlers, now allowed to own land, built homes around the original settlement; small villages grew along the banks of the James River and the small streams that flowed into it. But mortality interrupted so many "happily ever afters." The population dropped despite the landing of over a thousand; by 1620 the number fell to 843.

1620 also saw the arrival of the *Mayflower.* To half the Pilgrims who filled its meager spaces, Christianity was more important than land. The Pilgrims were Christians but different from the followers of the King's Anglican Church of England. As Separatists, they spoke directly to their Maker and had no need for intervening bishops or other clergy even remotely connected with the Roman Catholic ritual; the King demanded they join the Church of England or choose between jail or exile. Believing more in God's sovereignty than the King's, the Pilgrims left England for Holland and Holland for Virginia. The navigation of Captain Christopher Jones ended their journey at Cape Cod rather than at the more southern tobacco-growing community. The fear of winter storms and the misery of sixty-six days of foul living on the "vast and furious ocean" sent them round the cape to a place on John Smith's map called Plymouth **(Figure A2)**. They wrote the Mayflower Compact and went about building homes on Indian-cleared land until they could abandon ship. Most died of scurvy; the local Indians proved no threat, as they too had been victims of an unknown plague. Fortunately they weren't alone; without the Indians, the newcomers may very well have perished. A few Indians spoke English, one of whom was Squanto, who had been kidnapped to England and returned by a sympathetic merchant. Being of a sympathetic nature himself, Squanto, whom the Pilgrims believed had been sent by God, helped the newcomers to find and cultivate food and to explore their surroundings safely. He was there to welcome his brothers to a Thanksgiving Day feast and to welcome new Pilgrims as well.

By the autumn of 1630, one thousand of these Puritans had graced the shores of the Massachusetts Bay Colony in search of the freedom to worship in their own way. Like them, the Quakers were persecuted in England, and, even in New England, severe laws provided for their whipping and imprisonment. Stepping on Puritan territory earned the "cursed sect" a thrashing, the loss of their ears, or a noose. It would be a long sixty-one years after the *Mayflower* before these peacelovers would find safe haven in a colony yet to be named . . .

In 1623, New Hampshire was settled, and two years later the Dutch West India Company "bought" Manhattan island from the Indians. Since the Native American forefathers did not believe that individuals could possibly own land, they probably considered the trade of beads and trinkets for land a hoax, but the Dutch had the last laugh. They traded sumptuous furs for European gold and began a city called New Amsterdam, where the wolves were kept from the town by a wall that would remain "the" place for trading for all time. And like New York, other colonies were settled—Maryland, Connecticut, Rhode Island, Delaware, North and South Carolina, and New Jersey in 1664. In 1681 (2?), William Penn founded Pennsylvania, where, at long last, the Quakers were allowed a place to live **(Figure A3)**.

The Quakers' Religious Society of Friends was founded to protest the 17th-century formalism of religious doctrine, the elaborate church rituals, and the domination of the church by the English aristocracy. In spite of his incarceration, William Penn, the quiet-natured son of a wealthy Anglican English sea captain, became a convert, having heard his God's calling at the tender age of ten; Penn's remaining sixty-four years were devoted to ensuring that he, and others who worshipped as he did, would no longer be threatened. His ecclesiastic spirit inspired the founding of a new American state, "a holy experiment," where his plainly dressed sect, along with others of any belief, could self-govern and uphold their unique belief styles as well.

Actually it was an old debt that paved the way. Charles II had borrowed a considerable sum of money from Penn's father, and His Majesty paid the debt with a massive land grant west of the Delaware. Penn named the land Sylvania (or forest), to which the good king prefixed Penn as a lasting memorial to William's father and to which Penn invited English Quakers as well as those from Scotland, Ireland, and Wales. He encouraged farmers and craftsmen from the Rhine Valley, Switzerland,

and Sweden to make their homes on new lands in this idyllic setting.

Later, in 1732 or 1733, as varied sources would have it, Georgia became the thirteenth colony, and soon after, in spite of the British warnings to stay out of western territories so the militia would not have to protect them, pioneers, strong and independent, moved westward on their own. Many traveled in wagons named for the Conestoga Valley in the heart of Pennsylvania's Lancaster County, where the wagons were made by hand. Famous for their curved oak floors, designed to prevent their cargoes from rolling around within the wagon's generous spaces, they were equipped with brakes and pulled by special draft horses that announced their comings "with bells on." It is more than likely that many ABC plates crossed the plains deeply buried in barrels of cornmeal, secure beneath their beeswax-covered linen seals. Thanks to Quaker Daniel Boone and a few dozen others who widened the Indian trail, the wagons could travel the Wilderness Road, the 300-mile path through the Appalachian Mountains that thrust them into Kentucky and all points westward **(Figure A4)**.

The year 1732 also saw the birth of George Washington **(Figure A5)**. Though he served in the French and Indian War as a colonel in charge of the Virginia troops, it was his appointment as commander in chief of the Continental Army by the Continental Congress that proved his strength and commitment to the separation of the Colonies' governing bodies from the whims of the king's governors on this side of the Atlantic and the relentless schemes of taxation from the other. His forces were volunteers . . . ragged, freezing, dying of typhus, succumbing to smallpox, and constantly planning mutinies to be freed of their miseries. Thanks to Ben Franklin, the French joined the fracas to finally outnumber the British. At Yorktown the French army of the Comte de Rochambeau and the ragtag army saw the last of it all, and Washington returned to Mount Vernon. The Revolutionary War was over **(Figure A6)**.

It was six years after the Boston Massacre that delegates from all thirteen colonies met in Philadelphia to draw up a formal document declaring, in Thomas Jefferson's words, that "these United States are, and of right ought to be, free and independent states." The American Eagle flapped its wings to celebrate its adoption on July 4, 1776. The anniversary of this event was celebrated with two glass plates issued in 1876 **(see Figures G4 and G5 and Figures A7 and A8)**.

The Constitution provided that an electoral college was to elect the first president and all who should come after him. Washington, unanimously elected to the first presidential term, had to borrow £600 to attend his own inauguration. All of Philadelphia turned out to greet him with parades and fancy balls, quiet showers of rose petals, and awesome roars of cannons. Floating choruses accompanied his crossing of the Hudson as he found his way to the balcony of Wall Street's Federal Hall, where he took the oath of office on the 30th of April, 1789.

Three years later the newspapers of March 14th ran Washington's plan: "A premium of $500 . . . will be given to a person who . . . shall produce the most approved plan for a Presidential House to be erected in this city." "This city" was Washington, D.C., named after both our first president and Columbus (as in District of). The president was to supervise the construction; he chose the plans of a two-story house fronted with a columned portico. Its architect was James Hoban, an immigrant from Dublin who sent for six stonecutters from Scotland to bring his drawings to life. The early stages of construction were completed by slaves hired from nearby owners; facing the portico was the workers' city, complete with sleeping quarters, mess halls, woodworking shops, sawmills, and stone yards. Sadly, George lost his life after a bout with Quincey Disease (or a strep infection of the tonsils). Adams moved into the unfinished and drafty structure, its rooms serving the laundress more than its honoree. Before retiring for the night, he asked "heaven to bestow the best blessings on this house, and all that shall hereafter inhabit it. May none but honest and wise men ever rule under this roof." But the blessing didn't prevent the British from burning the house down in the War of 1812, during which Dolly (or Dolley) Madison saved Gilbert Stuart's portrait of our first president. Thank heaven for that **(Figure A9)**.

At the same time, the design of the Capitol became the focus of another contest. Ultimately under the direction of four architects, it was first designed by amateur architect Dr. William Thornton, who won $500 and a parcel of city land for his conception of a low dome and two wings, one for each branch of government. After George Washington laid the cornerstone of the building on the 18th of September, 1793, the Senate met in the North wing in November 1800. The South or House wing was finished in 1807 under the direction of Benjamin H. Latrobe. After the fire in 1814, the building was occupied once more in 1819 under its central copper-covered dome, which was completed in 1829 by Charles Bullfinch. Its present wings and iron dome were designed by Thomas U. Walter between 1851 and 1865 **(Figure A10)**.

On the other side of the Mississippi, western towns were thriving with new arrivals in groaning wagons; herds of cattle raised the dust, saloon gates swung, and overloaded donkeys were pulled by exhausted miners. Violence confronted the Indians as the pioneers trampled the land that had been the beloved home of flourishing tribes. Trail bosses often refused to pay the "beef tax" imposed on them to ensure safe passage of their herd; they provoked many unnecessary encounters **(Figures A11 and A12)**.

From eight million people in 1800 to thirty-one million when Lincoln became our sixteenth president, our country grew rapidly. Trains carried thousands of immigrants farther west, and wagons carried them even farther. All across the North, skies were darkened with the smoke of factories making the steel that built the overcrowded cities and the bridges that connected them. Millions came from faraway shores to work in the mills or man the new ingenious machines that mass produced far more than the bare necessities. New technology created ever-expanding opportunities for burgeoning industry and bulging Northern pockets. The noisy cities, the babble of many tongues, and the hurried pace of this industrial society was not the Southern lifestyle. Life was different on the sprawling plantations that rose and slept with the warm Southern sun. Slaves made substantial profits for their owners and none for themselves. The North said the Southerners were backward; the South shouted, "miserable Yankees" in return. Though they scoffed, they depended upon each other; the North needed Southern cotton to process in its mills so Southerners could buy it back by the bolt **(Figure A13)**. Plantation rice, sugar, or tobacco was exported from Northern ports, which charged smartly for their services. And of course the issue of slavery boiled beneath the surface.

Hendrik Van Loon, in his *Story of Mankind* (1938), stated it quite simply:

Slavery had been introduced into the American continent by the Spaniards. They had tried to use the Indians as laborers in the fields and in the mines, but the Indians, when taken away from a life in the open, had laid down and died and to save them from extinction a kind-hearted priest had suggested that Negroes be brought from Africa to do the work.

It was a kindly suggestion that was taken by so many who were unkind. Tales of incredible cruelty followed the slave trade from place to place, and, with some kindness from agitators (and a bit of conscience as well), laws were passed that put an end to slavery in the British colonies, the French possessions, and in the Netherlands by midcentury. But in the United States, an unending battle simmered in the respected halls of Congress. Southern states wanted to hold fast to slavery; by keeping the blacks ignorant, owners could keep them "in their places," and those places were not "created equal." It took the Civil War to end the conflict.

In 1850, there were millions of savagely undernourished slaves who worked the fields by the light of the moon, who were cruelly tortured for not having "picked enough" in the scorching heat, and who endured the awful pain of seeing their kith and kin sold into the diaspora, which the Southerners had hoped would extend all the way to the Pacific shores. Though there were hidden pockets of resistance on both sides, rebellions were picking up, and the voices of the abolitionists were being heard above the lashings and over the scratching of pens.

Even the alphabet became a Unionist strategy. The Huntington Museum's treasure, *The Anti-Slavery Alphabet* (printing by Merrihew & Thompson for the Anti-Slavery Fair in 1847) begins, "A is an Abolitionist—A man who wants to free . . ." **(Figures A14 and A15)**.

With more style than the clever picture book, Harriet Beecher Stowe's scratching pen spoke for freedom through the cast of women who walked upon her pages, women who had not yet found their voices but who she knew were as sensitive as she to the social injustices in the world around them. Until the 1850s, few women had broken the barriers of convention that forbade women to write about anything brutal or real. *Uncle Tom's Cabin* (Stowe, 1852), published first as a serial in the *National Era* (June 1851), was purchased by hundreds of thousands and translated into about forty languages. The influential novel presented a picture of slavery through a series of images so vivid and compelling that even a child could understand them. The brutality of slavery, Stowe believed, was contrary to the law of God, and abolition must then be God's will. With two million copies sold before the war, the book perforated indifference and readied the Northerners for battle. When introduced to the author, Lincoln said, "So this is the little lady who wrote the book that made the great war." And the theme of the book soon became the single, poignant issue of the bloody struggle **(Figures A16, A17, and A18)**.

If Lincoln **(Figure A19)**, elected in 1860, had let the South create its own Confederate States of America, there may have been no great war, but the South, young Abe said, had no "morally justified cause." Men were willing to die to protect their principles, and the need to protect themselves began when Southern guns fired on Fort Sumter at Charleston, South Carolina, on April 12, 1861. Southern ladies watching from telescopes and boys standing on rooftops were not disappointed . . . after thirty-four hours of continuous bombardment, Union Major Robert Anderson surrendered with no casualties to count. The first big battle, also watched with picnic baskets and pointed scopes, was a bloody one; the dream of a short and sweet skirmish dissolved near the muddy Bull Run River three months later. And it didn't stop there. Eventually, though estimates will never be certain, more than 620,000 very young Americans died and at least 471,000 were wounded; family members fought in both blue and gray, plantations were destroyed, and cities were incinerated. For four years, the stench of death was everywhere (Figure A20).

Laments of the manufacturers whose shipments to the United States were interrupted by the Civil War are found in the Stoke-On-Trent Library's microfilm records of many issues of *The Pottery Gazette*. The English called it a foolish and fratricidal war, that war across the Atlantic. While trains transported troops and seaports were blockaded in the United States, English exports to the Americans were curtailed. Nevertheless, the Civil War generals were immortalized on ABC plates. Items picturing Union generals were probably produced about 1865 and show only Union or Federal Army personalities. Tales of their successes and their surrenders tell but a few fleeting moments in the time line of great trial (Figure A21).

Using the time line in Hakim's text (1999), the major events of the war will "connect" the short vignettes highlighted with ABC portraits of Civil War heroes.

Sumter and the defeat of the Union at Bull Run in July 1861 were long over. The Confederates had defeated the Union at the battle of Wilson's Creek in Missouri (August 1861). Major General George Brinton McClellan had replaced the aging Lieutenant General Winfield Scott as the U.S. Army commander in chief (November 1861). Though General Ulysses S. Grant's army had missed the battle, the Confederates surrendered Fort Henry, and the loss of Fort Donelson, in Tennessee, was a catastrophe for the South (February 1862). The Battle of the *Monitor* and the *Merrimack* (March 1862) was history, and, by April of 1862, General Robert E. Lee had become the military advisor to Confederate President Jefferson Davis. Richmond was the Confederate capital.

April 10-11, 1862

It was April of 1862, and one Brigadier General Quincy Adams Gillmore's performance was a rousing success. He was a structural engineer whose unique approach to artillery operations resulted in the 1862 capture of thick-walled Fort Pulaski, which, from Cockspur Island, guarded the sea approach to Savannah. Gillmore deployed heavy artillery from Tybee Island across the Savannah River facing the fort. Rifled guns with long range and penetrating shells were used against the enemy. For two days, April 10-11, 1862, Fort Pulaski was bombarded, and in the afternoon of April 11, young Colonel Charles H. Olmstead surrendered. Over 5,000 shot and shells had been fired, but only one Union death was suffered; Gillmore's victory strengthened the Union blockade of Confederate ports (Figure A22).

Major General Thomas "Stonewall" Jackson had driven the Union forces from the Shenandoah Valley (May 1862); at the Battle of Shiloh, Grant defeated the Confederate forces, though Union casualties were extremely high (April 1862), and New Orleans had surrendered to the Union Navy under Captain David Farragut (April 1862).

May 30, 1862

It was May of 1862, and Major General Henry Wagner Halleck was put to the test. In spite of Halleck's gigantic intellect and superb administrative abilities, his "people skills" allowed him only an aloof, forbidding manner that earned him more enemies than friends. After an impressive career as a teacher and writer of legal and military subjects, Lincoln's appointee tarnished his stars with his poor grasp of field affairs and strategies. Dubbed "Old Brains," Halleck was remembered as one who "plans nothing, suggests nothing and is good for nothing." He did win victories at Pea Ridge and Shiloh, but his performance at Corinth, Mississippi, was slow—so slow that he allowed the Confederates (whose army was much smaller) to vanish while they actually pretended, with purposeful noises of trains and shouting of troops, to be welcoming incoming reinforcements. Perhaps the "dubbers" were right, after all (Figure A23).

June 1862

The superb transfer (Figure A24) of General McClellan, looking much the hero on his horse, Dan Webster, establishes his place in this ceramic saga of the Civil War. McClellan brought order, skill, and pride to the 100,000 men of the Union Army. With 2,500 supply wagons, 300 cannons, and herd after herd of cattle, the forces were ready at the southern tip of the Virginia Peninsula to march north to Richmond. Perhaps Figure A25 is a good picture of how they stood at attention for their leader. But there they sat with McClellan soliciting permission to follow his own plan for the attack rather than following Lincoln's War Order No. 1. Overly cautious and continually overestimating the strength of the Confederates, McClellan not only hesitated, he lost. He advised his president, after fighting for seven days, that the army's failure was due to being overwhelmed by larger forces when, in fact, he was fighting an army smaller than his own.

And the war went on. Both sides suffered terrible losses in September at Antietam, where McClellan moved too slowly and failed to put newly arrived men into action. Lee's army withdrew. In November 1862, he was finally removed from command. Lincoln presented the preliminary Emancipation Proclamation to his Cabinet on Monday, September 22, 1862.

December 13, 1862

Winter was coming (Figure A26). Reluctantly Major General Ambrose Everett Burnside, a tailor's apprentice who attended West Point, superseded McClellan as general of the Army of the Potomac. On a foggy December morning, Burnside's Federals, in spite of Confederate sharpshooters, constructed five pontoon bridges across the Rappahannock River and crossed to attack Lee's well-entrenched forces at Fredericksburg. Burnside failed miserably. The cost was hideous; 1,284 were killed, 9,600 wounded, and 1,769 missing—12,653 casualties to the Confederates' 5,309. The Union Army remained in the city . . . the Confederates remained on the hills (Hakim, 1999).

The Confederates won at Chancellorsville, but Stonewall Jackson died. It was Sunday, May 10, 1863, when pneumonia, which followed the amputation of his arm, conquered its tragic victim of friendly fire.

July 4, 1863

The bloody battle at Gettysburg took more than 20,000 men from both sides; the air carried the stench of rotting flesh. Lee led the seventeen mile wagon train of wounded and exhausted men southward from Seminary Ridge at Gettysburg. To seize the opportunity for an easy capture, Lincoln ordered the victorious Major General George Meade to pursue the weakened militia, but the steady rain that drenched their blood-soaked bandages probably dampened the fighting spirit of General Meade as well. The men were tired . . . and the irascible, hot-tempered general allowed the Southern gentlemen their trudge toward the Potomac and Virginia. The general himself may have been the victim of an untimely attack of charity **(Figure A27)**.

With the surrender of Vicksburg, the Union now controlled the Mississippi River. Grant was named the U.S. commander in chief and Sherman began his march.

Late April and Early May 1864

To provide much-needed raw materials for Northern mills, a plan to capture cotton-growing Texas had evolved, sending Major General Nathaniel Prentiss Banks and his troops to enter Louisiana's Red River region, where he was to join Brigadier General Frederick Steele's forces marching south from Little Rock, Arkansas. Together they were to take over Texas. At the Battle of Jenkin's Ferry, the third of the major skirmishes of the Red River Expedition, Steele's starving army, plagued by torrential rains, dense fog, and the hideous specter of bodies mangled in the mud, was driven back into Arkansas. Banks' soldiers, suffering the lack of Steele's support, tried hard to maneuver between waterfalls, rapids, and the reedy swamps and shallows now filled with the mines of harassing troops invisible behind the stagnant black smoke. The first days of May saw the campaign come to a close. Though he was involved in many phases of the war, Banks remains long-known for this unsuccessful effort to win the critical cotton-growing state for the North **(Figure A28)**.

The End Is Near

Grant, who suffered the ridicule of being caught by surprise at the Battle of Shiloh (1862), went on as U.S. commander in chief to prove his military worth by directing the military campaigns of the Civil War in its final year. In May, General Sherman cut a path through Georgia, cruelly ravaging miles of Southern fields and factories. Heavily fortified Petersburg, Virginia, fell to Grant and Richmond fell to the Union Army in April of 1865.

Palm Sunday, April 9, 1865

And on a day that April, Lee surrendered to U.S. General Ulysses S. Grant in the comfortable sitting room of Wilmer McLean at the tiny village of Appomattox Court House, Virginia. In a moment of compassion, Grant **(Figure A29)** allowed General Lee his magnificent side sword, his horse, and his baggage; the cavalrymen and artillerists, too, were allowed their horses for spring plantings and the Confederates were fed from Federal stores. With General Robert E. Lee's parting words, it was just about over: "I have done for you all that it was in my power to do. You have done all your duty. Leave the result to God. Go to your homes and resume your occupations. Obey the laws and become as good citizens as you were soldiers"

(Long, 1971). Grant himself felt "sad at the downfall of a foe who had fought so long and so valiantly" (Hakim, 1999). (Chalala's 1980 book pictures other luminaries from the war: General Windfield Scott and Commander A. H. Foote, Category G1.)

Good Friday, April 14, 1865

It was a Good Friday that was everything but good. The Grants were to join the Lincolns that night at the Ford Theater, but they were called away; Lincoln went along grudgingly, obliged to please Mary. John Wilkes Booth had a grudge, too, as he made his way to the entry of the president's box and carefully took aim. Despite the efforts of Lincoln's physicians, Old Abe succumbed the next morning to his assassin's whim . . . and the tears of a nation fell with him. Perhaps this plate was made soon after that fateful day to pay homage . . . perhaps it was made to celebrate an inauguration . . . perhaps it was made at some time during the war to support his cause. . . perhaps it is ours, now, to cherish **(Figure A30)**.

May 23, 1865

In spite of the deep mourning, the Grand Armies of the Republic passed in a last review from the Capitol to the White House. Children sang, men marched, and the flag was raised for the first time since Lincoln died. Through misty eyes they cheered as the regiments passed, divisions paraded, the Irish Brigade with green plumed hats marched by, cannons and ambulances lumbered along, and the Zouaves, in their dazzling uniforms, might have run through their display singing,

"Oh we belong to the Zoo-Zoo-Zoos,
Don't you think we oughta?..."
(Smith and Younghusband, 1996)

Their dazzle marked them clearly for targets and for their reputation of precision drilling as well. Originally, the Zouaves had been natives of Algeria's Zouaoua tribe mixed with French settlers. Their native dress—baggy trousers, short jacket, and fez in exquisite varieties—were replicated by the Americans, who owed the craze to one Elmer E. Ellsworth, whose fascination with militia began at an early age. Sadly, Elmer was killed early in the war after removing a Confederate flag from a tavern in Virginia. His volunteer infantry regiment of New York Fire Zouaves, which fell to the command of Noah L. Farnham, the 11th New York's lieutenant colonel, assumed their place in the first battle at Bull Run in July of 1861; their uniforms were colored as, coincidentally, they are shown on **Figure A31**. The participation of Zouave brigades from all over the North was honored in the *Union ABC*, printed by Degen, Estes and Co. (1864) **(Figures A32 and A33)**.

"We're going down to Washing-town
To fight for Abraham's daughter . . . "
(marching song)

Tuneful too was an openly derogatory message still a part of the American scene, and the Staffordshire ceramic—with its reference to the children's dolls as "Alabama coons"—was certainly destined for the American market. It quotes the first four lines of the chorus of a lullaby written by Hattie Starr, a popular American ragtime composer of no less than six ditties for daddy

(Mom had songs . . . why not Dad too?) and "coon songs," songs with now offensive terms that were part of the genre of popular comic songs that poked fun at every ethnic group. The sheet music cover **(Figure A34)**, fortunately designed without the typical black caricatures, promoted "Little Alabama Coon" as it was sung by Miss Frankie M. Raymond in Broadway's *Aladdin, Jr.*, which opened at the Broadway Theater in New York in April of 1895. Originally published for voice, piano, and chorus by Willis Woodward & Co. New York, 1893, the publication is housed in the Sheet Music Collection of the John Hay Library (presented here with the permission of Brown University, Providence, Rhode Island). The words are reprinted in Appendix AA1, having been retrieved from both the Library of Congress Online and The University of South Florida Library's Special Collections.

Along with the text on **Figure A35** is a circle of children, each with a sleepy doll. The word "picaninny" on the plate does not include a "k," which is part of the spelling in the poem as it is written on Poem Finder (http://www.poemfinder.com).

Certainly our twentieth head of state should have enjoyed a front-row seat at the Broadway show, but one Charles J. Guiteau, a disappointed office seeker, ended the four-month presidency of James Abram Garfield; Guiteau lay in wait for his target at Washington, D.C.'s Pennsylvania Railroad Station with a well-aimed firearm. A supporter of the newly organized Republican Party, Garfield had been elected to the Ohio Legislature, after which he saw action in the Civil War and a seat in the U.S. Senate. Winning by less than 50,000 votes, he served a term that was sadly short-lived, as he died of his wounds on September 19, 1881. Children are reminded of the tragedy with two alphabet-rimmed dishes; a ceramic blue transferred portrait shown here and a glass plate, seen later in "G Is for Glass." We bid him fond farewell **(Figure A36)**.

From 1607 to 1893 . . . our plates represent 286 years of our nation's short history. How many more plates could be found to help complete the story is unclear. How many plates complete the set of generals is at least predictable . . . they can tell more of the tale, more of the bloodshed, and more of the victories, though no sources of any portrait transfers could be identified in a search through the archives of the Gettysburg National Military Library. And there are sets of plates that picture each of our presidents; someone owns them, as evidenced by one commander's image with a darkly scribbled background that claimed an impressive sum on an Internet auction. Surely the collection of transfers that tell the tale of the United States is, as will be others to follow, a most significant collector's category of its own.

B Is for Bottle Ovens

From bonfires to bottle ovens . . . a tale beginning sometime after ancient man had, by divine chance, discovered fire. Suppose a soft clay shape, dropped too near a blazing fire, was transformed into a hard vessel that waited patiently to cradle the rain. Fast-forward to nomadic peoples who grew grain and raised livestock. Perhaps it was they who planned the placing of vessels over an open fire. Upside down, ancient pots were dried by heated embers; covered with twigs, they were quickly enveloped by flames to miraculously turn black.

With passing years firing became more efficient below ground. Round walls of deep pits held the heat more evenly, and with slower cooling came fewer cracks and less breakage. Iron bars placed over the pits allowed the fire's glowing embers to fall and gently coddle the ware below.

Early potters refined the process to raise firing temperatures by raising the kiln to ground level, upon which circular walls of bricks and mud were constructed. Through fireholes at the base, fuel could be easily added. Replaceable mud-and-straw dome roofs insulated the kilns.

New developments by Egyptians, Greeks, Mesopotamians, and Romans brought the open-top updraft kiln, which, with a major advance in design, housed a lower chamber of burning fuel. Above it, the firing chamber, with a perforated floor, held pots covered with shards of broken pottery, straw, and clay to contain the heat; holes above allowed the warm gases to escape. Advances in engineering added a fixed roof and joined the small holes to become a chimney while a flue, which drew air through the firebox, also pushed the heat upward, allowing temperatures to be raised.

From 1700, highly combustible coal fueled the kilns that fired European ceramics. The industry in the English Potteries used readily available coal to keep their fires hot; the need for better air circulation and more efficient ways of retaining the heat led to building the kinds of "bottle ovens" that distinguished the Potteries' skyline from the 18th century through the 1960s **(Figure B1)**. More than two thousand were built around courtyards, set in rows behind large factories, or, when built into the workshops, sprang from

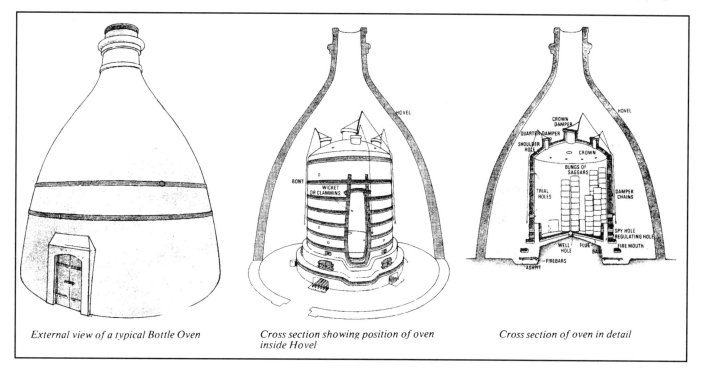

External view of a typical Bottle Oven

Cross section showing position of oven inside Hovel

Cross section of oven in detail

Figures Diag. 1 (left), Diag. 2 (center), and Diag. 3 (right) - Diagrams from *Bottle Ovens* (leaflet), Wooliscroft, Terrence, contributor. Gladstone Working Museum. Longton, Staffordshire. n.d., Page 1. *Courtesy of the Gladstone Working Museum, Longton, Staffordshire.*

their rooftops. Few looked alike . . . rings and borders were designed as the bricks were set.

Our glimpse into the days of the dark brick giants has been graciously assisted by the Gladstone Working Pottery Museum's eight-page leaflet, *Bottle Ovens*. With the help of Gladstone's three comprehensive diagrams **(Figures Diag. 1, Diag. 2, and Diag. 3)**, a tall brick oven is reconstructed for us.

Large wooden doors **(Diag. 2)** opened into the bottle oven, a hollow brick *hovel* whose narrowed neck rose ten fathoms into the toxic sky. Within the bottle-shaped hovel was the crown-topped **(Diag. 3)** *firing chamber*, its foot-thick walls banded by iron straps or *bonts* **(Diag. 2)**, which, set a foot apart, strengthened them as they expanded and contracted during firing. Into the crown were set the *dampers* **(Diag. 3)** or flap-covered holes with easily reachable pulley systems. As Gladstone says:

> By opening different ones the draught was accelerated in different sections of the oven allowing the fires to burn more fiercely raising the temperature. Likewise, by closing the dampers the temperature could be kept steady or lowered (Wood, 1999).

At the floor around the exterior of the firing chamber were *firemouths* **(Diag. 3)** onto which coal was added every few hours. Connected to each firemouth was both a *flue* **(Diag. 3)**, designed to carry the heat beneath the floor to evenly warm the interior, and a *bag* **(Diag. 3)**, or small chimney, which carried heat directly into the chamber at the wall side. In the center of the oven floor was the *well-hole* **(Diag. 3)**, where all the underfloor flues met. Over this hole was placed a stack of bottomless saggars through which the oven's smoke and gases escaped; that chimney formed the *pipe-bung of saggars* **(Diag. 3)**.

Photos found in varied sources reveal differently shaped saggars atop the *placers'* heads **(Figure B2)**. Selected by size and shape to best fit the type of ware to be loaded, the round, oval, square, or banjo-shaped (for stacking two bungs of small plates or saucers) ceramic "boxes" were placed in the firing chamber, taking optimum advantage of the space available for a maximum and efficient fill. Each packed saggar was carried on a placer's head, balanced over his hat, into the front of which had been placed a hard, doughnut-shaped roll of stockings that made a flat area on which to rest the load.

Placers entered the oven through the *clammins* or *wicket* **(Diag. 2)**, the iron-edged doorway of the firing chamber. From ladders called *horses*, or *'osses*, ovens were skillfully filled with as many as two thousand saggars **(Figure B2)**. The *cod placer* was responsible for siting the heavy boxes correctly as placers brought them into the firing chamber. Critical to the method of *placing* was the cod placer's knowledge of the variability of temperatures within the firing chamber and the appropriate placement of specific kinds of ware to be fired. Because the

floor of the oven sloped up to the pipe-bung, the stack had to be leveled with fragments of broken house bricks. With the placing completed, the responsibility of the kiln was handed over to the fireman, who, once the wicket was built up with bricks, lit the firemouths.

The temperature rose slowly, and from time to time the oven was *baited*—coal was added to each firemouth in turn. Trials, small pieces of pottery or specially made ceramic samples, were retrieved from the firing chamber to tell of the load's progress **(Figure B3)**. When appropriate, the load was allowed to soak at peak temperature, after which the dampers were opened and part of the wicket was broken. Bricks tumbled from the open door, allowing the kiln to cool **(Figure B4)**. Many times, workers assigned to **"draw"** or empty the ovens, had to clear the rubble to enter a still scorching interior. Or, in the words of one Enoch Bradshaw (Hanley, February 16, 1844):

> [T]he individual who refuses must lose his situation. Therefore he has to cover his hands with flannel, or with something that will not hold heat. His head and shoulders must be covered likewise . . . and . . . his breath will be almost taken away . . . A man . . . has to suffer extreme torment; his ears begin to smart, and just under his finger nails there is such an uncommon pain which he cannot describe. This is not all, for he feels at times as if his nostrils were bleeding and as though his eyesight were almost gone from him . . . and . . . there is the perspiration which he loses in thus drawing these heated ovens. This is one way to shorten the days of ovenmen (Lewis, 1981b).

With a more lenient schedule, men could enter easily into a cool oven to remove the weighty saggars and ready the oven for its next cycle.

Different kinds of ovens were needed for different kinds of processes. Bottle-shaped muffle kilns were used to fire enamel and/or gold at lower temperatures. Their interior shell protected their shelved pottery from the flames of firing in temperatures up to 800° C. "Calcining kilns operated in an entirely different way to the traditional bottle kilns, but so strong was the tradition for bottle ovens that they too were built in the bottle shape. They tended to be a more narrow shape than the squatter glost and biscuit kilns" (Wood, 1999).

Most of the two thousand bottle ovens are gone now; new structures cover their memories. The Clean Air Acts of 1956 cleared the black skies as factories were forced to power furnaces by electricity, gas, or oil. At present only forty-seven of the brick icons stand, protected by law, to majestically retell the dazzling history of the clay shapers. Narrowly rescued from the bulldozers, a group of five structures stand at Longton's Gladstone Pottery Museum to quietly fire the imagination of those who still hear the fragile clatter of activity in its small cobblestone courtyard and feel the blistering heat from the tall ovens, cold against the clean, blue sky.

C Is for Commercialism

The discussion of commercial products and their manufacturers, when known, continues chronologically from the building of the railroads **(Figure C1)** at the conclusion of "P Is for Potters and Their Potteries." With lengthening track and mushrooming factories, time became money. And with the coming of the workday and the transportation necessary to get to it, "railroad times" became critical; trains needed to be met, wages by the day were measured, pieces completed by the hour were counted, and even the Monday factory holiday disappeared as the hours it wasted killed capital gains **(Figures C2 through C6)**. More than likely, the children gaining a sense of time from a deep dish of shirred eggs at breakfast were not those stumbling to early dawn work hours, but the emerging industrial society was keeping pace with Franklin's proverb, "Employ time well if thou meanest to gain leisure; God gives all things to industry" **(Figures R94 and R95)**.

It must have been God, then, with the help of the railroads, who provided the way to deliver those who had given their all to industry onto the lap of leisure. "Pampering" became the Victorians, both at home and in the United States. Holidays abroad, with travel made easy, were the new sensation. New York's Long Island, once a five-mile patchwork of sandy wildlands, undulating dunes, and curling marshes, now had its station to welcome the occupants of long strings of velveted railroad cars to the gardened portals of the three glitziest resorts on the North American Atlantic Coast.

We owe the phenomenon, the finery, and the fun to William Engeman and August Corbin, who, after acquiring titles to Brighton and Manhattan beaches, determined, with a backing of investors and the blessings of the Sun God, to build two luxury hotels. Railroad tycoon Corbin immediately saw the potential of his New York and Manhattan Beach Railway as a door-to-door delivery service; the mogul's Manhattan Beach Hotel opened to the dedication speech of Ulysses S. Grant appropriately on the Fourth of July of 1877; it was ready for occupancy by fashionable society **(Figures C7 and C8)**. The "wooden temple," built for "worship of the sun and sea . . . (was) bristling with towers and turrets and dormers, boasting a front on the ocean no less than one-eighth of a mile" (McCullough, 1957). The hotel took particular pride in its cuisine; $3.85 bought courses then unique to American fare. By 1880, the hotel provided 2,350 single bathhouses and 350 larger rooms for teeming crowds of bathers who filled the beaches by day and the bandstands by night; they thrilled to the spirited themes of John Philip Sousa and Victor Herbert while spectacular showers of glimmering color burst into starlit skies.

Engeman's Brighton Beach Hotel opened a year later to sleep 500 and feed thousands each day **(Figures C9, C10, and C11)**. It catered to wealthy salesmen, "well-knowns" from the stage, and the least crooked of the politicians. But in spite of its fastidious interior, the exterior was particularly subject to the whims of nature; the bathing pavilion had to be moved back beyond the tides, and "the entire hotel, a several-storied structure more than five hundred feet long, had to be jacked up on railroad cars and eased six hundred feet inland. Six locomotives in two teams of three each hauled the building so gently that not a pane in a window and not a mirror in a room was cracked" (McCullough, 1957).

Farthest east on the island was the fortress-like Oriental Hotel **(Figure C12),** which, since 1880, was home to the families that could afford to stay the summer—theater folk and respected politicians. In complete safety they could stroll along the seashores to the faraway strains of Admiral Neuendorf's Naval Band.

The American market opened as quickly as the waiting barrels were uncrated at Eastern ports. Bought by European visitors, plates advertising the Coney Island properties made return visits home to waiting youngsters. Like travel brochures, these alphabet plates nourished memories for American travelers as well and encouraged a quick return to the therapeutic value of the climate, the relaxation of sea bathing in the peaceful rhythms of the ocean currents, the love and laughter with newfound friends, whispers of crooked politicians, honky-tonk sideshows, fortune tellers, succulent hot dogs, rumors of houses of prostitution, and those sumptuous meals served leisurely on silver platters.

For those interested more in sightseeing than in self-indulgence, there were travels to historic sights where Staffordshire earthenware or German lustred novelties were made available as souvenirs or fund-raising mementos.

Four places to visit, Washington's Capitol, the White House, Philadelphia's Independence Hall, and Public Buildings are seen on Staffordshire-produced plates in Chapter "A Is for Americana." In this chapter, a German lustred edition pictures our capitol's Congressional Library **(Figure C13)**. Founded in 1800 to assist the members of Congress, it lost its books to a fire set by the British in 1814; the purchase of the 6000 volume library of Thomas Jefferson revived its collections. The library was moved from the Capitol into the John Adams building, with its wondrous dome, in 1897. The addition of the newer James Madison Building, in 1980, makes it the largest library in the United States. Its classification system is used by major libraries around the country, and it is, with over 115 million acquisitions, one of the foremost libraries of the world.

German lustres also picture The Union Station (or "Cow Shed") at Omaha, Nebraska, built in 1899. According to railroad historian Donald Snoddy, the station, torn down in 1927 and replaced with an Art Deco building, served not only the Union Pacific but the Missouri Pacific, the Chicago and Northwestern, the Illinois Central, the Chicago, Minneapolis, St. Paul and Omaha, the Wabash, and the Milwaukee lines as well. The plate may have been distributed along with advertisements of several other turn-of-the-century businesses in Nebraska's capital **(Figure C14)**. And the dignified statue of Roswell Pettibone Flowers (1835-1899), which stands on Washington Street in Watertown, New York, commemorates Flowers' governorship of New York from 1892 to 1895 **(Figure C15)**. The last of the three figures pictures the dignified post office and courthouse building in New Hampshire's capitol, Concord. Opening in 1889, it was vacated by the post office in 1967 and renovated into legislative offices by 1975. It too was celebrated by ceramic whatnots **(Figure C16)**. Another of this series, not shown, might have been purchased near the Lincoln Monument, in Springfield, Illinois.

A wonderful Staffordshire series of graphics remembers the magnificent buildings of the Columbian Exposition, which opened in Chicago on the first of May in 1893 in celebration of the 400th anniversary of the landing of Columbus. It took three years of frantic preparation to create a world of dazzling structures, only one of which remains. The Palace of Fine Arts was recreated by Julius Rosenwald (1862-1932), philanthropist and chief executive of Sears and Roebuck (1895-1932), into the present-day Museum of Science and Industry. The Administration Building **(Figure C17)** is grand with its exquisite dome, which is included in the background of the Electrical Building **(Figure C18)**. Many more complete this series. (Noteworthy is the backstamp on C17, which refers to a trademark registered in the U.S. Patent Office. See "U Is for Undersides" for further information.)

Far away from the big windy city is the village of Holley, New York, immortalized by the West End Pottery Company of East Liverpool, Ohio **(Figure C19)**. Their souvenir plate **(Figure C20)**, which spells the village name as H-O-L-L-Y, is a product of a firm which was founded, in part, by the Burgess family in 1892 (3?). The start of the company was the finish of the long-time controversy over the awful stench caused by the boiling and burning of animal bones needed for the manufacturing of bone china. The East Liverpool Board of Health met on the 8th of September, 1891, to explain that Burgess and Company, rather than purchasing already calcined bone from Baltimore, was, as it had been before, the source of the terribly offensive odors that threatened the community's good health. To end the problem, the Burgess' bone china plant, claiming the high costs of production, merged into a joint-stock firm incorporated as the West End Pottery Company, which was to be a producer of only white ironstone (or white granite). By 1927, the firm offered an impressive line of semi-vitreous dinner, hotel, toilet, and tea wares along with hospital and pharmacists' utensils. Despite the volume of complaints, the East Liverpool city council had remained unwilling to censure this local pottery which closed in 1938.

The next two souvenir plates, **Figures C21 and C22**, re-call visits to Quebec, Canada (the firm name could not be verified) and the small village of Newport, New York, which, established in 1857, still stands proud of its historic buildings.

Like those village souvenirs, the two snapshots on each plate of the Brownhills travel series kept merry memories of just about everywhere else ready for the reverie. Of course, many English items, like the Brownhills Pottery, found their way back home with grandparents who presented gifts of dinnerware to whet the appetites of the next generation to travel abroad **(Figures C23 through C27)**.

Especially appealing were the transfers that stirred the subconscious to promote a getaway: a distant gaze came a little closer on plates that nourished the soul with Staffordshire's "idyllic and romantic" landscapes, designed as much for export as for local utility china. Harry Rinker (in *Romantic Staffordshire, The Perfect Reflection of Victorian Taste*) writes of the "romantic Staffordshire's highly imaginary, almost romantic patterns that graced the pieces' surfaces with scenes from the esoteric to the exotic. Scenes of far away places, mountains, lakes and pools, twelfth century ruins covered with hanging vines, strange flora and fauna, and strolling lovers were common. Pattern names evoked a strong sense of the romantic—Caledonia, Japonica, Millennium, and Venus."

Perhaps these transfers evolved from paintings to evoke a sense of the perfect, the peaceful, the pastoral, and the pleasuring; the low-bending boughs of the luxuriant forest, stone bridges, and wide, gentle stairways transported the traveler from one bucolic fantasy to the next in boats that serenely passed over slowly rippling waters . . . **(Figures C28 and C29)**. (Some texts do refer to romantic landscapes as having been replicated from identified paintings.)

But travel incentives, real or fanciful, weren't the only ABC plate commercials. There were soaps and soups and cereals and shoes, and more. Commercialism reached new heights with the birth of the mail-order catalogue by John Durant Larkin's Soap Company. Larkin featured many offerings from his Buffalo China company catalogue, some of which were the Campbell Kids Bowls **(Figures C30 through C33)**. David and Micki Young's book *Campbell's Soup Collectibles* (1998), pictures the items as china food-warming dishes and dates them all as 1917, at which time they sold from 60¢ to 75¢. **(Figure C34** is a Campbell "Kid" look-alike and is not seen in Young's book or noted in other sources. The mark is green, smudged, and illegible.)

Larkin's idea of selling directly from "Factory to Family," through catalogues, eliminated the traveling salesman and laid the foundation for contemporary marketing. "The money saved by selling directly to the users was given back to them in the form of premiums equal to the amount of their purchases" (Heaivilin, 1981). And to reduce his costs even further, Larkin established the Buffalo Pottery Company. He could produce his own premiums, only a few of which were ceramic, rather than purchasing products from worldwide potteries.

Chartered on October 23, 1901, the company elected John Larkin as president, a position he held until his death in 1926. Set next to the tracks of the Pennsylvania, Lehigh and Lackawanna Railroad in Buffalo, New York, the company fired its first kiln two years after its founding under the direction of William J. Rea, who recruited ceramic artists of ultimate quality and skilled craftspeople from around the world. Among them was a relative of the illustrious Gilbert Stuart, painter of the forever famous portrait of George Washington. Ralph Stuart, whose ancestors were pottery decorators, became head of the Art Department; he leaves his wall murals (which picture the four seasons) and the exciting scenes of a fox hunt in the pub of Arcade, New York's Arcade Hotel for us to admire. The hotel was founded by the Aldus family of Staffordshire.

Run entirely by electricity, Buffalo's fireproof pottery imported clays from other states and other continents, which were processed in its ultra-efficient factory. The firm boasted of a superior semi-vitreous porcelain before 1915 and vitreous china after that date. Three new buildings accommodated the massive production of tableware for World War I bases, hospitals, and merchant ships. All other production was proudly discontinued until after the war, when the company turned its focus exclusively to hotel and institutional ware; now, if chipped, every item's interior showed the same color as its glaze. The factory continued production of custom-made hard-use ware for railroads, steamship lines, restaurants, and so forth until the 1940s, when it limited its output to a few "appealing-to-all" designs. Becoming Buffalo Potteries Incorporated in 1940, the firm modernized and, after supporting the World War II effort, changed its name to Buffalo China, Inc. in 1956. In 1983, the firm was acquired by Oneida Ltd. of Oneida, New York.

Offered for five years (1913-1918), plates advertising Campbell's Soup are marked Buffalo Pottery, as the company mark was changed in 1915 when vitrified china was introduced. Plates featuring the Campbell's Kids were made of both vitreous and semi-vitreous china and guaranteed not to craze. Though the soap company introduced the concept of premiums, the Campbell Kids alphabet bowls were not premiums themselves but were to be sold for 50¢ each; the purchase of one did entitle the buyer to 50¢ credit toward a premium. Without the credit, the cereal bowl was sold for 25¢. Although the words "Campbell's Soup" never appeared on a plate, they rang familiar as Campbell's Kids were easily identified by magazine readers through the company's prolific ad campaigns.

Those chubby, rosy-cheeked youngsters were the brainchild of Philadelphia illustrator Grace G. Drayton, who brought them to life in 1904 for a set of streetcar advertisements. They popularized the company that began thirty-five years earlier as Anderson and Campbell in Camden, New Jersey; it had been best known for placing a single can-size tomato in a hand-wrought tin. Even after their soup won the Centennial Exposition medal for quality, Anderson left the firm, which then became Joseph Campbell & Company. In 1905, the first magazine advertisement, released in *Good Housekeeping*, boasted twenty-one kinds of soup. A different soup each night for three weeks at only 10¢ a can.

A far cry from the burgeoning saddlebags on the backs of beasts of burden is the high-tech advertising dished out by the more current makers of Campbell's Soup; the more current alphabet plates still carry the friendly warmth and comfort of the "old days." Like tricycle license plates, rubber stamps, toothbrushes, and ceramic mugs, personalized items still keep gift

shops turning fast profits. Certainly Virginia could hardly wait to eat a bowl of hot, chunky chicken soup from a bowl made especially for her **(Figure C35)**.

Plates rather than bowls advertised a gritty gray soap that promoted an unlikely product for children, but a likely purchase for their hard-working fathers. Appearing on a "tin" series of at least five, the illustrations, which had little to do with the industrial-strength cleaner, were accompanied by very small typeset messages on dark-colored metal backgrounds. The fine layer of graphics is easily scratched, and most examples show evidence of less-than-careful handling. This set, currently owned by Ann and Dennis Berard of Fitzwilliam, New Hampshire **(Figures C36 through C40)**, recalls the start of the Lava Soap Company in 1904 as a small firm within Proctor and Gamble. The sandy-textured soap was used by car mechanics, plumbers, steel workers, gardeners, and millions of others whose grimy work required Lava Soap to scrub them clean for dinner—which just may have been eaten from any one of its "tinny" advertisers.

Breakfasts, too, required clean hands . . . a favorite fast-breaker might well have been eaten from ABC-edged Beetleware bowls of red plastic seen here. With Donald Duck and Mickey Mouse to make them soooo appealing were the 1935 cereals **(Figures C41, C42, and C43)** manufactured by Hemco Moulding, a division of the Bryant Electric Company of Bridgeport, Connecticut, for Post Cereals. The company featured children's cocoa mugs, divided feeding dishes, and cereals in a shiny, stiff plastic of red, white, light blue, cream, "depression green," and yellow (more about Disney later).

To be enjoyed in those "Beetle" bowls were the two cereals named on the backstamp: Grape-Nuts and 40% Bran Flakes. The bowl was a 10¢ premium with the purchase of Grape-Nuts, which was perfected in the fall of 1897, but not placed on the market until January of 1898. Mr. Post loved the nutty taste, which came from "grape sugars," and thus the crispy nuggets were christened. Post's 40% Bran Flakes appeared in 1922 and became the largest-selling bran cereal in the world. Cellophane-wrapped packages of Post-Tens appeared in 1939; each box offered a different cereal already in its own paper bowl . . . they didn't need our plastic alphabets.

Buster Brown shoes, too, were advertised on plates with and without ABC-cast borders. The Buster Brown shoe first appeared at the 1904 World's Fair and quickly became a household name in children's footwear. The Brown Shoe Company of St. Louis introduced this shoe and heavily advertised it using the colorful comic strip character created by Richard Fenton Outcault (1863-1928) for the *New York Herald* in 1902. Two years after its debut, the strip's characters, which included Buster's dog Tige and his sister Mary Jane, were licensed to more than two hundred consumer products. For decades, young boys wore Buster Brown haircuts and suits and girls wore Mary Jane shoes. Today the Brown Shoe Company operates the Famous Footwear and Naturalizer chains of retail stores while it continues to market Buster Brown along with Life Stride, Night Life, Naturalsport, Dr. Scholl's, and others **(Figures C44 and J3)**.

Plates with other company names were awarded to children (and their parents) for purchases. This kind of commercialism can easily be a focus of collecting; sometimes accompanied by a short poem, the "thank you" is often printed on the reverse (Figure C45). Seen in this figure is a nurturing message from A. F. Tomasini, owner of the largest hardware store in the Petaluma, California, area. It reads, "To the baby with our best wishes. May it always relish what is on this dish." From 1920 to 1940, Grandpa T. distributed many different children's dishes, which are carefully collected by the family today; our Figure D83 will eventually reside in the Tomasini collection. A less personal message, found on Figure C46, clearly pictures both the ancient Coat of Arms of Nova Scotia and the name of a local firm, Cleverdon & Co. The Cleverdon family owned several firms in the area. From 1859 through the 1870s, W. H. Cleverdon owned a china and gift shop. In 1890, he advertised Royal Watches and diamonds and in 1895 W. H. was listed as a jeweler and watchmaker. His bicycle shop thrived from 1902 to 1904 after which he might have retired. Cleverdon died in 1912; the elegant black and white plate might have been a thank-you for purchases at his china shop until 1866 for, in 1867, a new Coat of Arms was adopted when Nova Scotia (New Scotland) joined Canada.

A great market for plates and mugs on both sides of the Atlantic rested on the premise that quality rewards will foster new energies. They were offered as gifts to little ones on their birthdays, to special relatives for good behavior (Figure H97), and to the winners of spelling bees (Figure C47). Plates and mugs that carried religious transfers rewarded deserving students at Sunday School and provided reinforcement for learning bits and pieces of religious verse at home, as well. Sometimes transfers or decals bore the name of the school as an honor, a commemorative, or perhaps as a fund raiser. A fairly recent German edition made for The Old West High School in Aurora, Illinois, pictures one of two secondary schools built in 1906; the town fathers commemorated several city sites on ceramic items at the start of the 19th century. That school became a middle school, and the building now houses a privately owned institution (Figure C48).

And there was a substantial commercial market for china that was stamped "HOTEL." HOTEL china experts William and Donna Gray of East Liverpool, Ohio, assure us that the line was made by Harker Pottery of East Liverpool, Ohio, sometime between 1890 and 1920, though the mark does not appear in the replications of Harker backstamps in Lehner (1988) or in DeBolt (1994). It is listed on page 83 of The East Liverpool, Ohio, Pottery District: Identification of Manufacturers and Marks by William C. Gates, Jr. and Dana E. Ormerod (1982). Burford Brothers Pottery (1879-1904), also of East Liverpool, displays a nearly identical mark.

The start of it all was in 1839, when Benjamin Harker endured the sailing from England to buy fifty acres from Abel Coffin in the startup town of East Liverpool, Ohio. With the help of his mules, Harker removed clay from the hill and sold it to nearby potter James Bennett, as well as to other small firms in the Pittsburgh area. At first determined to farm his property, Benjamin, inspired by Bennett's business, opened pottery number two in East Liverpool; a beehive kiln, built next to a defunct log-cabin distillery, made the yellow ware, which was soon carried by boat and wagon to nearby cities. The date of Benjamin's death is uncertain but it was not long before the venture fell to his sons, Benjamin Jr. and George S., who were trained by a former partner, one John Goodwin. Housed in a three-story brick building called Etruria, it was reminiscent of England's leading firm and produced doorknobs, ceramic tiles, and hound-handled pitchers (1844-1847). In 1846 (7?)-1851, James Taylor entered the firm which was, from 1851-1854, called the Harker, Taylor and Company.

The history continues, though facts remain "fuzzy." Taylor, it seems, left to form a firm with one Henry Speeler, making way for Ezekiel Creighton and Matthew Thompson to join Ben Jr. and George S. at Etruria in the production of yellow-glazed ware until Creighton died about 1853. The firm, which had been called Harker and Thompson, continued as George S. Harker and Company. (References used do not account for the whereabouts of Mr. Thompson.) Ben Jr. left the Harker firm to join William Smith and operate as Harker and Smith in the making of yellow ware when, from 1853 to 1857, the firm became Foster and Garner. Benjamin then joined the Union ranks of the Civil War.

Brother George S. continued to manufacture yellow ware at Etruria until his death in 1864. Sister Jane Harker Boyce's husband, David Boyce, took over as George's sons were not yet old enough to manage the firm; the Boyce family continued its leadership in the firm throughout its history.

Harker began production of white ware in 1879. Only five years later a disastrous flood drowned all but the employee's love for the firm. To save the company, many long-time workers held their paychecks until the firm recouped its losses. After Ben sold his remaining interest in 1877, George's sons continued as Harker Pottery with W. W. Harker its president in 1890. The sons of David Boyce were executives of the firm in the 1940s and, in 1949, Robert E. Boyce became president of the company upon the death of ninety-year-old H. N. Harker, one of the industry's most respected and talented individuals. In 1969 (70?) the pottery was purchased by the Jeanette Glass Company, but it continued to operate under its own name until its death knell was sounded in 1972. The firm had produced a very large variety of kitchenware under an array of trademarks; its HOTEL ware was made to endure the continuous, rapid, and noisy stacking of the restaurant trade. The Lindsays (1998) note the plates' graphics as decals, whether placed by Harker or by other firms dedicated to decal decorations.

Most photographs of the Harker Pottery HOTEL collection have been graciously provided by the Grays of East Liverpool, Ohio (Figures C49 through C52, Figures C55 through C71, and Figures C73 through C76). The third in the "Baby Buntings" series, which is not owned by the Grays (Figure C54), is a William Brunt Pottery "Harker look-alike." It is nearly identical on its face but lighter in weight than the Harker's HOTEL line; its mark dates its manufacture between 1900 and 1911.

The first William Brunt Pottery Company was established by William Brunt the Elder from 1847 to 1856; his son Henry joined him from 1856 to his retirement in 1895. A second son, William Brunt, Jr., was involved in the Phoenix Pottery and the Great Western Pottery as well as in the William Brunt Son and Company with his son from 1879 to 1894. In 1894 (92?), the firm was incorporated once more under the name of the William Brunt Pottery Company. According to W. A. Calhoun, after William Brunt, Jr. retired, the plant went into decline due to "reckless expenditures." Calhoun gives no closing date; DeBolt provides the year as 1911.

Continuing with Harker Pottery Hotel ware, the mysterious "Great Expectations" (Figure C72), is shown courtesy of Jean C. Rutter of Quakertown, Pennsylvania.

Figures **C73 through C81** are Sunbonnet Kids, but not all of them are Harker Pottery products. **Figures C77 through C81** were manufactured by the National China Company. That firm, incorporated in June of 1899, was noted for its porcelain-like translucent pottery and decorative decals. In 1911, the pottery moved from East Liverpool to Salineville, Ohio, seventeen miles to the east, where items of lesser quality were produced as works made after 1920 have been found to show crazing. In 1929, National China merged with seven other firms to found the American Chinaware Corporation until its close in 1931.

All the National China products in this collection are found on shallow soups that might have been included in "D Is for Deep Dishes." The simple HOTEL mark (**Figure C77**), accompanied by N. C. Co., dates its plate as a 1900-1911 product. The more complex mark (**Figure C78**), similar to a British Coat of Arms, combines the shield and its lions with the firm's monogram; it is dated (by DeBolt from Ormerod) from 1911 to 1920. Collectors might look for products other than "Sunbonnets" made by this firm (see two other examples in **Figures N111 and N113**).

Harker and National were not the only users of "Sunbonnet" decals. "The Sunbonnet Kids at Work" is seen in **Figure D98**; the soup shape was made by D. E. McNicol of Clarksburg, West Virginia, and is severely damaged. Another collectible, not found in this collection, shows the "kids" making a piecrust. Captioned as AP-1 on page 194 of the Lindsays' publication, the dish is attributed to the Smith-Phillips China Company founded in 1904. In 1929, this was one of the firms that formed the American China Corporation, which closed because of the Depression. Smith-Phillips made hotel china and semi-porcelain tableware; the ABC plate was probably made in the 1920s. (Smith-Phillips is sometimes listed in references without its hyphen.)

All the Sunbonnet Kids illustrations were rendered by Bertha Corbett Melcher (AKA Bertha L. Corbett, Bertha L. Corbett Melcher, 1872-1950), who spent most of her life in Colorado. The Sunbonnet Babies appeared when she illustrated a children's book authored by Eulalie Osgood Grover, with figures immediately recognizable by their large-brimmed bonnets. The story is told that Corbett and a friend were discussing the fine art of illustration when the friend stated that emotion could be expressed only through facial expressions. Corbett asserted that she could, in fact, convey feelings through body language showing *no face at all*. The result was a series of at least six books still listed in the Library of Congress online catalogue; all were published by Rand McNally (New York) from 1902 through 1929. Some say Melcher was influenced by the beloved illustrator of Victorian children's literature, Kate Greenaway. With or without Greenaway's influence, Corbett-styled designs still contribute to the quilter's art; her "kids" will adorn prize-winning coverlets as long as the fine art of stitching survives.

As readable as Grover's primers were the cartoons of "Felix the Cat," whose popular purr was first heard on November 9, 1919. Released through *Feline Follies* produced for the Pat Sullivan Studios, Otto Messmer's Felix the Cat (**Figures C82 and C83**) became Charles Lindbergh's chosen mascot and the focal point of RCA's first television transmission. The two 8-inch plates were produced as Holdfast Baby Plates, also made by D. E. McNicol of East Liverpool in the 1920s.

Another overnight sensation was *Steamboat Willie*, whose animated cartoon opened at the Colony Theater on November 18, 1928. Those plates and hundreds of other Mickey Mouse products facilitated the organization of Mickey Mouse Clubs; as worldwide commercial ventures, they boosted sales in banks, bakeries, dairies, and department stores. The clubs promoted moralities and self-care as well—the 1930s Depression voices of Watts and Franklin (see "R Is for Religion, Reform, and Reason"). A Disney trademark backed the older cereal bowl (**Figures C84 and C85**), dated c.1930, which was probably imported by the Carl Schumann China Company of Bavaria (whose story is included in "D Is for Deep Dishes"). The mark on the newer edition (**Figures C86 and C87**), dated c.1935, assured its purchaser that the Mickey Mouse trademark had been registered and authorized by Walter E. Disney, himself.

Certainly many lettered items may have been manufactured, as were these, to prompt adult purchase. It was, after all, the adult who had to provide the lamb chops along with the learning and those ever-present letters. More mature topics, such as the rather foolish tale of John Gilpin, the patriarchal poetry of *The Cotter's Saturday Night* (see "I Is for Infant to Infirm") and the kitschy items (see "K Is for Kitsch") were presumably not children's choices; perhaps they recalled memories for Scottish nannies who chose either to dish out their long-suffering wisdom or to set the dishes on dresser scarves to hold hatpins. Not too different from today's packaging, items for children are visually addressed for the adults who impulsively reach for their credit cards . . . with a smile.

Then, as now, many designs are targeted for children's attention, as are Sesame Street editions and others that come boxed in sets and are often made of plastics . . . many are inexpensive and found in hotel gift shops, supermarkets, toy marts, and mail-order catalogues. More costly recent editions, some inspired by designs of long past issues, can be purchased in the finest of china shops, such as Tiffany of New York, Herrods of London, and Geary's of Los Angeles. Three-quarter-inch dinner ABC plates with their salads and mugs are available for small dolls picturing a Teddy Bear, Raggedy Ann and Andy, and six familiar animals; they are charming additions to dollhouses for very tiny ones who live in teeny spaces. A chapter for R might well have been for "Recent Editions" found easily in current mail-order catalogues.

Antiques are now big business, and ABC plates are no longer dependent upon their traveling donkey peddlers. Each is now a commercial venture in itself. Prospective owners do the advertising . . . collectors fill their closets by transfer categories, by manufacturer, by material, by country of origin, or simply by the fine art of fascination itself. Each plate has unique characteristics of its own, carried by the currents of hunter-gatherer traders to the waiting arms of their clients always eager to plunder the overflowing containers. And plates are sold before the ink is dry. Cross-country advertising is frustrating for the faraway consumer, who knows full well that pictured items are stored in new cellars long before the mail carrier has lightened his load. No one need hawk them . . . they advertise themselves.

In addition, appealing graphics can be quickly acquired on the unseen information highways; contemporary marketing requires only the pressing of keys. Prospective buyers may access bookmarked antique auction locations by computer; search "abc plate"; survey the items available; open a sleepy eye to those that magically appeared overnight; bid or rebid on current offerings; and rush off to work only to worry about the fate of those hopeful dollars sent off to tenaciously fight quiet wars against gavels that silently close the contests. Auction prices depend upon the grouping of plates available and the sweaty palms of the operating bidders; prices are sometimes far below the norm and, just as often, outrageously high.

But the auctions have something else to say aside from "Highest bidder" or "Auction closed." With fifty or more offerings daily, it is obvious that more plates have been produced than collectors might ever have imagined. The infinite numbers of varieties and the extensive numbers of plates within each set soon challenge the best of fortunes. In short, a complete and definitive source for these curiosities is nearly impossible as new items are quickly found, and with them, new volumes will, in the near future, be written.

D Is for Deep Dishes

It is commercialism that introduces this "D" chapter as well . . . there is no better prelude to the subject of deep dishes than the huge poster of Sampson Bridgwood's deep dish at the entry to London's Museum of Childhood on Bethnel Green. What more appropriate symbol of education and its connection to alphabet ware could ever be chosen to advertise the name of this most respected institution! The actual bowl, a colorful porringer manufactured by Sampson Bridgwood & Son about 1920, was on display in the museum's upstairs gallery (1998). Its continuing role in the educating of young diners is now assured **(Figures D1, D2, and D3)**.

Manufactured in Germany, Czechoslovakia, England, and the U.S., infinite varieties of these high-walled dishes offered a safe haven for mouth-watering meals, whether Irish frish-frash, English pap, thick oatmeal, lamb stews, or thick soups of chicken or beef (see Appendix AR8). Often showing signs of wear, the bowls were hard used but resisted breakage from falls and spoon strikes by the strength of their fabric.

The Czechoslovakian, English, and German products were made of hard paste and gleamed with the perfection of fine china, not subject to earthenware's crazing or seepage by liquids. Where some American products allowed the seepage of foodstuffs through their surfaces, German ceramics are, says Röntgen, with few exceptions, nonporous, hard-paste ceramics. Unlike them, American-made bowls manufactured by D. E. McNicol of East Liverpool, Ohio, or by Buffalo Pottery of Buffalo, New York, do show signs of crazing and evidence of "peeling." Altman (1987) alludes to oven warming as a possible cause of cracking. But there might have been other causes as well, as the surfaces of virtually all of these dishes, despite the pottery's guarantee, have shattered.

Unlike the traditional Staffordshire products, transfers had been replaced by full-color decals that "used the same method of chromolithography found on postcards of the period. Of course, since the decals were mechanically reproduced, the German china of a specific pattern has a cookie cutter sameness, unlike the handmade English product" (Lindsay and Lindsay, 1998). Some dishes show heavily "spoon-scraped" decals, suggesting that the decorations might have been applied as "overglaze decorations" after the dish's second firing **(Figures D46 and D47)**.

Pre- or post-1900, designs reveal the styles of the times. As the century turned, bowls were meant to entertain rather than instruct. Their subjects were fun and fantasy, often with clowns, cartoons, and charismatic animals. Some characters were featured in several designs; sets were available for the collecting. But not all plates that use graphics of the same series can be assigned to the same maker; to confuse the collector, several identical designs bear differing backstamps.

Some letter styles on unmarked pottery may, therefore, be more reliable as hints indicating country/factory identification than their illustrations. McNicol's "fuzzy" sprayed blue stencil-style edges along with their Clarksburg factory's gold letters set in groupings, the Schumann factory's well-defined black ABCs, the Crown Pottery's interspersing of small bows between letter sets, the National China's title "Baby Plate," and other unique border characteristics are hints to makers. And the very shapes of the bowls themselves, their unique and sometimes lustrous surface types, may also allow a cautious assigning of provenance.

Unlike the Staffordshire plates, fewer than a dozen bowls in the collection were not marked. Some are stamped solely with country names; they announce only their points of origin. Some marks include the country name along with the potter's identification designs. All photographs in this chapter are arranged by countries and by factory names within those countries in alphabetical order. Plates follow their trademarks.

The only dish made in Czechoslovakia **(Figures D4 and D5)** echoes the design and shape of a country-marked dish identical but for its border edge in *Czechoslovakian Pottery: "Czeching" Out America* by Bowers, Closser, and Ellis (The Glass Press, Marietta, Ohio, 1999). Most deep dishes are German made and postdate World War II; records of some potters may no longer exist. George W. Ware, author of *German and Austrian Porcelain* (Crown Publishers, 1963), assures his readers that the approximately two hundred potteries in the whole of Germany suffered less than 10% damage and practically all of them resumed full operation soon after the war. Some manufacturing histories were provided in Robert Röntgen's *Encyclopedia of Marks on German, Bohemian and Austrian Porcelain* (Schiffer Publishers Ltd., 1997). Additional data were provided with the generous help of Ms. Petra Warner, M.A., along with the Deutches Porzellanmuseum staff at Hohenberg a. d. Eger. They verified six of the potteries. The histories of several British potteries and the histories of American potters are easily gathered in current "encyclopedia-style" publications which can be identified in the Bibliography.

The list of identified German potteries begins with the Arzberg Porcelain Factory. Stamped as Bavaria, Germany, the mark was used from 1927 through 1981. The factory was absorbed into the Hutschenreuther Pottery Group in 1972 **(Figures D6 and D7)**.

The stylized H **(Figure D8)** was attributed by the staff of the Porzellanmuseum to represent the factory of Rudolph Heise of Berlin. The translation of an article, *Hersteller heute*, by Stephanie Ludwig in *Puppengeschirr in Vergangen und Gegenwart* (Doll Dishes, Past and Present) tells the story of a tableware firm that began in 1919 with a wholesale and retail glass and porcelain business in Berlin. Heise's son added a line of ware known for its especially hard, stonelike finish. The firm's salespeople, in order to lighten their loads, requested miniature editions of the varied ware they carried to sell; the small dinner sets evolved into a line of doll dishes, each piece of which is stamped with the company's trademark **(Figure D9)**.

Figure D10 follows the configuration of the Hutschenreuther marks. In this mark, the lion is enclosed in a round shape with a crown immediately above. The lion standing on four feet, with initials beneath them, are descriptive of marks from this pottery. In 1857, the firm, founded by C. M. Hutschenreuther in Hohenberg, was managed by his son Lorenz. After becoming a joint stock company in 1902, Hutschenreuther absorbed many, many other potteries, making table, household, hotel, and decorative porcelain; coffee and tea sets; gift articles; and figurines **(Figure D11)**. Since 1975 the firm has owned distributing companies in France and the United States; it is housed in North Branford, Connecticut.

According to Robert Röntgen (1997), **Figure D12** is a mark of the C. A. Lehmann & Son Company, which existed in the city of Kahla from 1895 to c.1935; Röntgen's listing is number 1883. It pictures the castle Leuchtenburg, Light Mountain's fortress, which belonged to the noble family of Leuchtenburg. After the feudal wars, the castle was given to the town of Kahla, which is located just north of Rudolstadt, home of the pottery that produced ABC ware seen in "K Is for Kitsch."

Franz Bauer Porcelain Manufactory merged with Lehmann and Son in 1935 to make Bauer and Lehmann, which existed until 1965. The firm, after several other mergers, ceased to exist in 1990 **(Figures D13, D14, and D15)**.

A flower inside a triangle surrounded by the initials R. C. W. on three sides points to the Retsch & Co. Porzellanfabrik of Wunsiedel **(Figures D16, D17, and J12)**. It is now Porzellanfabrik Retsch GmbH & Co. KG (Porcelain Factory Retsch Ltd. & Co.), which has been maintained from 1884 to the present making household and decorative porcelains. The mark seen is dated 1919; the plate pictures children with a goat, a favorite pet in the Victorian years. A detail of this plate, and other deep dishes whose borders show exclusions of the letter J, are also pictured in "J Is for J, the Last Letter of the Alphabet."

The two lions **(Figure D18)** on the back of the silhouette **(Figure D19)** *may* be the mark of the Royal Bayreuth factory, as it is known in America. Though other European marks include lions, shields, and crowns, Royal Bayreuth is the only factory found to have designed two lions whose heads are turned toward their thin and crooklike tails. The mark reads "Royal Bavaria" and the lions' paws rest on an oval coat of arms topped with a crown. The oval on a 1968+ mark of the factory has changed to a shield, and there is no crown. Since 1957, the Royal Bayreuth factory has been named the "Royally Privileged Porcelain Factory at Tettau." A possible second identification, suggested by the museum staff of the Deutsches Porzellanmuseum in Hohenberg/Eger, is the Joseph Rieber & Co. of Selb. The two lions in this mark are silhouettes and face

each other, but the oval shape and its crown are part of the design.

One deep dish, pictured in **Figure K4**, is part of a series of Kewpie table settings produced by the Royal Rudolstadt Pottery (also known as the New York & Rudolstadt Pottery) of Thuringia, Germany. The firm was founded in 1882 and was maintained until 1918. Additional information can be found in "K Is for Kitsch."

The mark of Carl Schumann's Porcelain Factory, Bavaria (1881-1996), is Röntgen's listing number 92 **(Figure D20)**. Founded by Heinrich Schumann in Arzberg (1881), the firm produced decorative household and giftware **(Figures D21 and D22)**. Schumann was also the maker of the Walt Disney deep dishes that can be found in "C is for Commercialism" and "Z is for Σ and Other Reversals." Both deep dishes pictured are clearly authorized by Walter E. Disney **(Figures C84 through C87)**. Heide and Gilman's *Disneyana* (1994) gives credit to the "Shumann" factory as these ABC bowls are fine examples of collectibles that cross interest lines. They are highly sought after by both ABC collectors and Disneyana devotees. The ever-dwindling supply has skyrocketed the value of Disney bowls; sixty-year-old "Mickies" now approach $1000.

The circle design of the Three Crown Pottery **(Figure D23)** was found as #45 on page 969 of Ludwig Danckert's German Edition of *Handbook of European Porcelain Marks* (1992) **(Figures D24 through D27)**. The mark, also found on page 227 of Warman's *English and Continental Pottery and Porcelain* (2nd edition), dates the mark c.1930 but does not, like Danckert, assign it to any currently known manufacturer.

Country of origin script marks come in green, reading Bavaria **(Figures D28, D29, and D30)**; green, reading Germany **(Figures D31 and D32)**; and blue, reading Germany **(Figures D33, D34, and D35)**. Ten plates are stamped with one orange word reading GERMANY in capital letters **(Figures D36 through D47)**. (The last two plates in this 10-plate series are good illustrations of "condition." The effects of extensive use are obvious even on these beautifully made ceramics.)

One script mark, blue, is accompanied by a circle upon which the green capital letters E(B or R)PHILA can be read **(Figures D48 and D49)**. A lowercase mark in shiny gold reads "Germany" in an up-arching half circle **(Figures D50, D51, and J13)**. Another lowercase mark reads "Made in Germany" in an orange circular pattern **(Figures D52 and D53)**.

GERMANY in capital letters, enclosed between circles, is found several times in the collection; in Röntgen, listing number 548 is listed in the text as "unknown." One circle mark is printed in pink on one plate **(Figures D54 and D55)**, an orange mark is printed on two plates **(Figures D56, D57, and D58)** along with an orange mark with a central numeral on **Figures D59 and D60**. A green circle mark **(Figure D61)** is found on the underside of **Figure D62**. (**Figure D63**, a mug matching both **Figures D60 and D62**, is shown, though there is no alphabet incorporated into the design.) **Figures D64 and D65** carry orange circles reading Austria as the country of origin. Circles have been noted, in Ebay auction information, as being used before World War I (pre-1914).

And there are other marks that could not be found in any of the available texts or by the German research staff: L. O. Co. N. Y. in combination with a script blue Germany is probably the mark of an exporter, N Y standing for New York **(Figures D66 and D67)**; O (or D) G Germany **(Figures D68 and D69)**, and

G. W. Co. of Germany (Figures D70, D71, and D72) were also not identified. An additional green circular mark that is too indistinct to decipher is pictured on Figure D73 along with its deep dish, Figure D74; a mark with this configuration could not be found.

There are three potteries of deep dishes whose chronicles are integrated into British ceramic history. First is the Sampson Bridgwood & Son Potteries (Figure D75), opened in 1805 and creator of the now-famous deep dish at the chapter opening (Figures D1, D2, and D3). Of the nine potteries that involved one Bridgwood or another, it was Bridgwood of Longton that absorbed the Anchor Pottery of Longton c.1853 in order to become the largest exporter of ware to North America. Though the name was retained, the firm was managed, from 1879, without the inclusion of any Bridgwood. The partners were Martha Napier (wife of George Webster Napier of Aldersley Edge) and Mary Walker (wife of Reverend James Harold Walker of Foxearth). After Martha's retirement, Mary Walker continued the factory's management. In 1939, the company was bought by James Broadhurst & Sons and, in 1984, was named Churchill Hotelware. The firm is still in business as part of the Churchill China Group, owned by the Roper family, with main offices in Stoke-upon-Trent. The celebrated plate looks similar to the German variety, snowy white and free from blemishes.

A second pottery known by its mark, C & F over G, over England (Figure D76), was Cochran and Fleming, 1896 to 1920, of Glasgow. The firm continued as Britannia Pottery Co. Ltd. from 1920 until 1935 (Figure D77).

The third pottery, the Swinnertons of Hanley, Staffordshire, has occupied several premises. It began in 1906; Ltd. was added to the name five years later. The mark seen on the deep dish (Figure D78) is clearly Swinnertons but is not pictured in Godden's references or Kovels' New Dictionary of Marks (1986). The two dishes (Figures D79 and D80) are similar but for the blackening of some areas in the line drawing and the erratic placement of the designs. In 1959, the company was taken over by The Lawley Group Limited. It functioned until 1970 (71?).

Four American potteries produced deep alphabet dishes in this collection. The first is a firm in Evansville, Indiana, which began in 1882 with A. M. Beck, who opened a majolica pottery (Figures D81 through D85). Following Beck's death in 1884, the firm was sold to Bennighof, Uhl and Company, which began the making of white ware. Seven years later, the firm was renamed the Crown Pottery by the Flentke family. Later, after absorbing the Peoria Pottery Company to make dinnerware, toilet ware, semi-porcelain, and white granite dinner sets, the company was renamed Crown Potteries. Unable to expand within its small property, the firm closed between 1955 and 1958. Figure D85, though heavily damaged, serves as the only example of the airbrush-stencil technique in the collection.

Other bowls by the American McNicol recall the history of the well-known East Liverpool McNicol factory. Daniel Edward McNicol became president of the firm after the former McNicol, Burton and Company was dissolved; the D. E. McNicol Pottery Company was incorporated in East Liverpool, Ohio, in 1892. The firm produced yellow-glazed ware Rockingham and "semi-granite." In 1902, a second plant opened, followed by a third factory at Clarksburg, West Virginia, in 1914. The last facility opened in East Liverpool five years later.

Until 1925, the East Liverpool plant produced hotel, dinner,

and toilet ware as well as yellow-glazed ware, making it the last firm in the area to use local clays. McNicol's specialties were souvenir and calendar plates; undoubtedly the semi-vitreous ABC bowls were among them. The Clarksburg plant specialized in ware specifically designed for railroads and steamships, hotels, hospitals, clubs, and restaurants; to diners, signature ware provided a sense of intimacy and importance. In c.1928-1929 the Ohio operations closed, allowing the West Virginia plant to remain busy until 1954, when the McNicol Pottery closed its doors forever.

Too heavy for small hands to hold are the dishes with the familiar Holdfast Baby Plate (Patented) shield (Figures D86 through D92). (Also made was an 8.37 inch edition of Figure D91.) Figures D93 through D96 bear the McNicol, East Liverpool, mark, while Figures D97, D98, and D99 were produced at the Clarksburg factory, being the more traditional soup bowl shapes. These were probably made before the 1920s; after that year production dates appeared beneath the logo. Along with Figure D98 are other small dinner plates in the collection of Harker's Hotel china and National China, which also feature the Sunbonnet Kids; they can be seen in "C Is for Commercialism."

Another Ohio-area firm, ELPCO China, is an abbreviation for the East Liverpool Pottery Company of East Liverpool (Figures D100 and D101). Easily confused with the East Liverpool Potteries Company of East Liverpool, the firm began about 1894 making good quality semi-porcelain ware. They were one of the potteries that gathered to form the East Liverpool Potteries, which existed from 1900 through 1903.

Also made by ELPCO are two high-quality semi-porcelain china dishes (Figures D102 and D103) shown here courtesy of Sunny Lenzner, noted Southern California expert on flow-blue and children's china. These plates tell the story of a transfer that crossed the Atlantic from Selb, Germany, to East Liverpool, Ohio, sometime around 1900. The baseball player on the European deep dish (Figure D11) is also seen on the Ohio-made Figure D102. On Figure D103, a plate of the same series, is a coordinating graphic of a football player, a similar rendering of which made its way to the Dresden China Company of East Liverpool, a maker of lesser-quality alphabet ware (Figures D104 and D105).

Lehner's 1988 Encyclopedia of U. S. Marks on Pottery, Porcelain & Clay reveals that the initials in the 1916 mark, T. P. C-O. Co. (SEMI-VIT) (Figures D106 and D107), stand for The Potters Co-operative, founded in 1882 in East Liverpool. The factory's history began when, in 1875 (76?), William Brunt Jr., his brother Henry Brunt, an in-law, William Bloor, and a man named Martin started the Dresden Pottery Works of Brunt, Bloor, Martin and Company to make, among other types of ceramics, hotel ware. The firm continued until 1882 when it and seven other manufacturers founded The Potters Co-operative (T. P. C-O.). By 1925, the firm was once again called Dresden Pottery and remained so until c.1927, when the business was forever closed. A William Brunt Pottery is mentioned in "C Is for Commercialism" as well.

Not all deep dishes are pictured in this chapter, and not all deep dishes are ceramic. There are "deep dishes" found in "K Is for Kitsch" that feature the images of Kewpies, the signature characters of Rose O'Neill, noted above as products of the Royal Rudolstadt Company in Germany. Others are the products of McNicols of East Liverpool. And "C Is for Commercialism" turns its attention to the Sunbonnet Kids' hotel-quality cereals, made by the McNicols Pottery at Clarksburg and the Harker and National China Companies at East Liverpool. That chapter also features Felix the Cat, Campbell's Kids, and Disney items of both clay and plastic. But three glass bowls, described in "V Is for Variations on a Theme," are the deepest dishes of all. Products of an unknown manufacturer, the glass dishes hold molded images of Bo-Beep on clear and frosted glass circles. To see the kids or the cats, the cute teeny chicks, or any of the colorful designs which made those feeders so appealing, they had to be cleaned . . . the food had to be finished.

The most clearly motivating message is found on Crown China's **(Figure D119)** last of the porringers. Here the friendly duck **(Figure D120)** encourages the youngster to eat that lunch before it does . . . thank Heavens it's a small soup bowl made by Crown Hotel China whose factory mark has not yet been identified. A display of Crown Pottery marks does show the word "Hotel," but, according to DeBolt (1994), it is followed by "Ware" rather than "China."

Becoming easier to find than the older Staffordshire pieces, and with their alphabets more easily read than on their cast counterparts, the deep dishes nurture a rich history sadly incomplete with the destruction from two world wars. But, from within their rimmed walls, children can continue to enjoy their cereals as the enduring and nonpermeable surfaces of these pieces, usually found in excellent condition, will beckon to breakfast for many years to come.

E Is for Education

To understand the role of ABC plates in the education of 19th-century children, a brief summary of the schools of the time will be helpful. Those who *needed* to learn from those ceramic "teachers" were children with few opportunities to have owned them. The letter-encircled ceramics were there for the comfortable, who most probably were provided with adequate classrooms beginning with a well-stocked library in a children's wing and a nanny to present its treasures. Like the books on classroom shelves, ABC plates carried transfers that can be categorized into curriculum areas as we know them today: basic reading skills, short rhymes, nursery tales, fables, fiction, basic arithmetic, science, and social studies, though transfers that taught what would have been called "current events" are found in "N Is for 19th Century." Many plates (see "R Is for Religion, Reform, and Reason") were religious in nature and could easily have been used to teach lessons or reward excellent progress in home schools, Sunday Schools, or the day schools where religion was often the path through which reading was taught.

There were many forms of education in Victorian times; to each child was given or not given the opportunity depending upon his or her gender, class, religion, parent's financial position, and attitude toward its necessity. And Parliament was reluctant to say just who had the final say of whether or not a religious or nonreligious education or any education at all should or would be provided. Additionally, there was little agreement as to what should be taught, how to teach whatever was agreed upon, how to pay for educational institutions, and to whom to offer its learning. "Education not only varied among classes but also helped determine class. Some historians consider that improved education was the reform on which all other Victorian reforms rested; schooling made democratic elections possible and supplied the training to both develop the economy at home and rule an empire abroad" (Mitchell, 1996).

Ultimately, religion guided the hand of progress . . . the independent reading of the Bible became a "right," and many persuasions claimed the right to teach it. In The Potteries the rights belonged to the Old Connexion Methodists, the New Connexion Methodists, the Catholics, the Church of England, and so many other affiliates (see "R Is for Religion, Reform, and Reason"); sometimes the right of learning had to be accepted from the school within walking distance **(Figure E1)**.

The Society for Promoting Christian Knowledge began its work in the very last years of the 17th century; it set up charity schools with an eye toward teaching poor children to read, first from the New Testament and then from the Old. The Church of England, with funding from voluntary subscriptions and the "charity" collected at church services, had set up more than 1,000 schools in Britain by 1729. The completion of the Testaments and rote memorization of prayers and catechism were the goals, strengthened by church services and weekly duties. In some schools, girls were taught needlecrafts, and a sprinkling of industrial schools helped some boys to realize occupational stability. But promoting regular attendance and parents' support was, in the words of Mr. Thomas Cheadle of the Fenton Park Company's Colliery, "very ignorant and low" (Scriven's interview No. 163, 1975, p. 73). Regular attendance would remain a problem for years. In the Staffordshire area, there is mention of a Charity School in Eccleshall, but few attended.

Dame schools followed . . . rooms in homes set up to seat students under the tutelage of the "Dame" who owned them. For a few pence a week, students in these early private schools learned no more than what the Dame could teach. Students may have learned to read but not to write. Young students of supportive parents might attend such schools as a "head start" before they began to work at age six or seven. Charles Shaw's vivid description of Miss Betty W.'s Dame School in Tunstall proves the worth of these one-room "shelters from ignorance." For those like Mr. Shaw, who were entranced with reading as a three-year-old, learning was a lifelong love in spite of those fast-maturing days of employment in The Potteries.

Later in the 18th century, Robert Raikes, a Gloucester newspaper owner, started a Sunday School and, in 1780, promoted the idea in his newspaper. A large number of Sunday Schools became a reality **(Figure R57)** under the guidance of both the Church of England and Methodist John Wesley. Again, writing was rarely taught and biblical reading was the focus. By 1803 there were 7,125 schools and nearly 900,000 students in the country. It was hoped that once-a-week learning was better than none at all; some delighted in its benevolence, while others believed a little education could encourage only criminal pursuits. Perhaps the doubters weren't all wrong; one William Brick, an ex-pupil of the good founder, tells of students delivered to the classroom with 14-pound weights and heavy logs tied to their legs. In spite of it all, an 1840 list of schools proved that of the 29 schools in the Staffordshire area, 20 were Sunday schools.

Perhaps the first Sunday Schools were really "Ragged Schools," as they were inspired by the wretched dress and bare feet (as well as the cursing and swearing) of the urchins who noisily played and rioted in the streets on the Sabbath. Usually Ragged Schools were set up by benevolent souls . . . sometimes cobblers nestled the poorest ones around them, for they were too ragged and filthy to attend anywhere else. Less benevolent at one Ragged School were the students whose "object . . . was to have a lark." Lewis, in *Education since 1700* (1984), describes a long afternoon in October of 1844 when terrorizing behaviors and great violence erupted. The teachers endured, as did the schools, a concept furthered by Lord Shaftesbury, longtime president of the Ragged School Union. Most noteworthy was the Hanley and Shelton Ragged School, which opened in 1851. Admittance was refused when the earnings of the family amounted to more than two shillings a day for each of its members, and no boy was admitted if he had been to day school during the preceding year. The students were "grossly ignorant," and few could read. Mr. Glass taught Bible and catechism, and a library that focused upon moral training was at the students' disposal. The inauguration of the Longton Industrial Band of Hope Ragged School proves there was a Ragged School in Longton as well.

The reports of one Samuel Scriven, Assistant Commissioner of Education, recorded hundreds of interviews with children employed in both the mines and the manufactories. Often, students such as seventeen-year-old Minton Pottery worker George Bragg told of their attendance at Sunday School, of their forgetting everything they learned, and of their having been called away too often to mind the cows. Even the availability of weekday school hours didn't help students, whose exhaustion defied their will.

A far different kind of school was created sometime around 1815; the Monitorial School was inspired by a system developed in an orphanage in India. The Reverend Andrew Bell's design was a progressive one: a teacher taught a small group of older students, each of whom would then teach a small group of younger children. If students could answer the weekly questions orally, it was a success. Adding a current strategy of behavior modification to the scheme, Quaker Joseph Lancaster introduced merit marks, which were collected to purchase prizes for good work in reading, spelling, writing, and rote mathematics. But good attendance was rarely the reason for a reward . . . children attended sporadically, and parents were not rigorous proponents. The system, however, was encouraging to Wedgwood when he planned his school in Etruria for the children of his working families. Regulated Monitor scripts, taken from the Staffordshire Record Office, read: "Show Slates . . . Lay Down Slates, Clean Slates, Show Slates Clean, etc." Progressive perhaps, but the script's busy antics worked wonders only for rote memories and social control.

The Reform Bill of 1832, which ensured large numbers of middle-class men the voting privilege, signaled a rise in arguments for and against compulsory education. But it was the approval of compulsory half-time education which was most important to working children. Also good for students was the Revised (education) Code, issued by Parliament in 1862, that laid the government regulations for grants. It was the system known as "payment by results," whereby the school received its funding and the teachers earned their salaries. Log books validated attendance and specific numbers of students had to pass Her Majesty's yearly "standard" examinations in Arithmetic, Writing, and Reading. Anxious students, six years and older, were either rewarded with colorful certificates or quickly ushered out with their howls and whimpers. Pass or fail, at least standards were being set.

But Her Majesty's Inspectors could do little about **attendance.** It took the (Liberal Party's) Forster's Education Act (1870) to do two things. First, students attending a British school would not have to attend for even minimal exposure to religious verbiage as those readings were given at the very start and the very end of the school day. Separation of Church and State had taken root. And, the act provided that the School Boards, in every community, could make attendance compulsory. Lord Sandon's Act, which followed in 1876, mandated that each area have either an established School Board or an Attendance Committee. Even more wondrous, it made certain that no child, below the age of ten, could be employed and that all children, from ten to fourteen years of age, had to attend school at least part-time.

It is here, with attendance now mandated, that we can leave out pottery children who could now, hopefully, read the titles under the transfers they were required to paint.

Of course, there were Grammar Schools (having derived their name from the hours of Latin grammar required). And there were the larger Grammar Schools, which were called Public Schools, or schools open to anyone of the public whose parents had the means. The latter of these had been providing a more adequate education than other schools for young British children of upper-class and well-to-do middle-class homes since time began. In a contemporary sense, they were "private schools," as devoted to the fees they charged as they were to the floggings they inflicted. As the years went on, curriculum was examined, technical instruction and the inclusion of sciences in secondary education gained support, and schools were opened for boys who exhibited "troublesome behaviors." Oxford and Cambridge offered "exams" even to those who had not attended a Public School. But these aspects apply only to the children of the potters rather than to the children of the potters' employees. The substantial contrast of the workers' situations to that of the pottery owners was equivalent to the contrast in their children's education. The intellectually supported students were those who most likely enjoyed the early introduction of alphabet plates at long lunches, while the uneducated, who needed them most, were undoubtedly denied the privilege.

Perhaps it was this head start at home that helped to ensure the success of the wealthy Horace Mann, author of the education report on the 1851 Census (1853), who concluded that no matter what the financial status of the family, the education of the 50,000 middle-class children who were being educated at home would probably last no more than six years (Jordan, 1987). And not all of that time was spent in study **(Figure E2)**.

But home-schoolers were well-meaning. A governess might have begun with the alphabet letters. At the very first step of reading development, students might have been asked to match shapes . . . to see that an A here is the same as an A there. Many plates have double alphabets **(Figures E3 through E7)**, an ideal place to start the reading process. Eaters could match one F to the other, an N to an N, and so forth. This very primary skill was easily accomplished when what was on the alphabet was remembered for its tempting taste!

Then ceramic letters, displayed on plates and/or mugs, were introduced along with items that began with that letter. Little ones could practice the letter sound between bites, and pictures of items that begin with that sound could be chosen while chewing; the images tempted young tastes for primary language.

The next steps were to choose one letter from the mugs and plates that displayed three large letters on their transfers and to find the items pictured that began with that letter. The hunt is now called a *symbol-sound process*. Picking the letter shape is selecting a *symbol*. Saying the *sound* of the letter in order to match an item that begins with that sound completes the match. Of course, reversing the process was just as profitable; *saying* the name of a pictured object to hear its sound and then *selecting* the letter that begins it is called a *sound-symbol process*. Both processes require early skills in sound discrimination and basic vocabulary **(Figures E8 through E23)**.

Of course, the alphabet may have begun with the names of the letters as they were sung to popular tunes of the time. Among so many others, the simplest version of English alphabet rhyme, still popular today, was sung to "Twinkle, Twinkle, Little Star." The last two lines will vary somewhat from region to region.

ABCDEFG,
HIJKLMNOP,
Q AND R AND S AND T,
UVWXYZ,
Now I've said my ABC's,
Tell me what you think of me.

And what was thought then is what is thought now. When a youngster accomplishes that milestone, when he or she can independently sing that song, the rite of passage into the intellectual kingdom of man has been earned. Singing that song from memory did not then, and does not now, indicate understanding; it is a rite of passage.

Ruth Baldwin's masterpiece, *100 Nineteenth Century Rhyming Alphabets in English* (Southern Illinois University Press, 1972) lists very old English alphabet rhymes. Any of them could be sung to these plates; the many rhymes, in varying levels of difficulty, have countless variations.

One such alphabet song is a cumulative rhyme (noted in 1671) and is republished in Baldwin's book (1972) as having been published in *The Picturesque Primer* (see Appendix AE1):

A was an apple-pie;
B bit it;
C cut it;
D danced for it . . .

There are a great number of variations of this chant (see Appendix AE2): "C cried for it, F fiddled for it, G gobbled or got it, H hid or had it, etc."

Some early rhymes showed little discrimination in subject matter. Lines such as "D was a drunkard, and had a red face," "U was a usurer took Ten per Cent," or "Y was a youth, that did not love school" were later considered to have a harmful effect on children. They were replaced by the widely taught alphabet rhymes of the *New England Primer* published by Benjamin Harris in the late 17th century, which combined moral messages with the learning of letters, such as, "In Adam's fall / We sinned all." Or as *Arthur's Alphabet* (1877), "T is for Toys, with which he must not play, / For in well-earned disgrace is poor Arthur today."

After the popular chants came the transfers that presented short titles or rhymes and the letters that began them **(Figures E24 through E29)**. The next level of difficulty would be found on plates that presented three letters at a time; diners might be asked to find objects that began with any one of the three **(Figures E30 through E35)**.

Many plates presented nursery rhymes (see Appendix AE3), which might be memorized to increase the student's awareness of the rhyming sounds . . . a precursor to spelling. Fun to recite over and over, each rhythmic tale had its social history! By no means is this history of children's poetry complete, as it briefly touches only the rhymes in this collection **(Figures E36 through E 55)**.

Jean Harrowwen, in her *Origins of Rhymes, Songs and Sayings* (1979), has classified children's rhymes in the chronological order of their well-researched origin. They begin with the Pre-Christian period, then to the time of the Romans, the Norman time to 1154, Plantgenet to 1399, Lancaster to 1461, York to 1485, Tudor to 1603, Stuart to 1714, and, last, Hanover to 1910, which includes the Victorian time of manufacture. Some rhymes evolved to simply amuse children; many were satiric comments on political/religious issues set into culture's memory by tiny chapbooks or wandering minstrels. For many there are several possible explanations; the chronology is maintained by presenting the earliest first in each case.

Rhymes on deep dishes have been included here and are so noted by their references to Figures that begin with the letter D. References to rhymes can be found in "M Is for Metal" and in "C Is for Commercialism" as well.

The series begins with an ancient Scandinavian myth that tells us to search the moon, Mani, for the images of "Jack and Jill," with their buckets and shoulder poles, who, to this day, continue their search for water. Another explanation carries the origin far ahead to Tudor times, when, according to James Christiansen (1942), Cardinal Thomas Wolsey and Bishop Tarbes, in the service of King Henry VIII, failed in their attempt to mediate a peace agreement between the Holy Roman Empire and the French. To make matters even worse, Wolsey raised the poor peoples' taxes to finance the British troops caught in the clash. The rhyme might be a charade of their "fetch" for peace and their unfortunate fall. Usually recited as a four-line tale, the poem has been extended in an 18th-century chapbook series to fifteen verses. But the source of the poem begins long before chapbooks that featured Jack's head wound bandaged and Jill's spanking for "grinning" at his plastered nob **(Figure E36 and Figures D21 and D34)**.

In less ancient times **(Figure D95)**, we see one socially dysfunctional Georgie Porgie, who lived when Emperor Charlemagne reigned (A.D. 800 to 814). It appears the reasons for his being "celebrated" are as elusive as Georgie's runaway behavior. Or perhaps G. P. was better known as King Charles II (1660-1685), in Stuart times, who did more than kiss the girls. Since his wife could not provide an heir, the good king spared her concerns with at least fourteen "un-heirs" to his throne!

From Norman times, three hundred years later, comes Jean Harrowven's (1977) answer to "Who Killed Cock Robin?" The stray arrow that pierced the breast of the not-too-popular William Rufus II assured his brother Henry I's seat upon the throne in early August of 1100. William's death, according to the fourteen-stanza poem, was seen and sung by the creatures of the New Forest from which Rufus' blood-soaked body was carried on a hand barrow. Was it the pagan sacrifice of "a sacred king" at Lammastide to ensure good crops?

"Little Boy Blue" **(Figure D111)** comes to us from Tudor times (1485 to 1603). Perhaps the rhyme recalls a boyhood moment of Cardinal Thomas Wolsey, the young son of an Ipswich butcher. Back then, butchers kept their own herds, which required watching, but the young Wolsey, the watcher, had a habit of falling asleep on the job. Thankfully, he outgrew his lazy days and became Lord Chancellor and chief adviser in foreign affairs to King Henry VIII. But Henry didn't consent to all of his good advice. Wolsey was neither able to convince the King not to destroy his marriage for political reasons nor successful in obtaining Pope Clement VII's permission for Henry's royal divorce from his tiresome marriage to Catherine of Aragon sometime around 1529. Catherine was banished from the bedroom, the Lord Chancellor was banished from the court (and eventually accused of treason), and Catholicism was banished from the kingdom.

"Little Jack Horner" **(Figures E37 and E38, Figure D117, and Figure S7)** tells the rest of the story. Henry VIII wed Ann Boleyn (1533), the Church of England was established, and with that, the very powerful King Henry became the head of all things religious and secular. Catholics were no longer allowed to hold positions of leadership; their authority, their properties, and their very lives were doomed. Fine Gothic buildings were razed, religious jewelry was melted down, and libraries were sacked. The wealth of the monasteries became the wealth of the monarch.

Richard Whiting, the Abbot of Glastonbury in Somerset, the richest abbey in the kingdom, was the last, in 1539, to go on trial. Some say he angered the king by building a kitchen more splendid than the royal cookery. Sensing his offense, the Abbot sent a gift to the king at Yuletide, a pie beneath whose crust lay hidden one title deed for each of twelve manors, one perhaps for each day of Christmas. Thomas Horner, trusted steward to Whiting, was the courier and, goes the legend, the puller of a "plum" for himself—a deed to the Manor of Mells. Some sources say the inheritors of one British manor can trace their owners back to a Thomas Horner. Other sources say that relatives insist they have bills of sale with no Horners listed, but it's a tasty tale that ends when Whiting, a stubborn proprietor of church property, was hanged, drawn, and quartered; for him the bell tolled.

It nearly tolled, too, for the kitty who was put down the well but, thanks to the kindness of little Tommy Stout, the feline was saved. The bell sounded first in 1580 when John Lant, an organist of Winchester Cathedral first sang,

> Jacke boy, ho boy newes,
> the cat is in the well,
> let us ring now for her Knell,
> ding dong ding dong Bell.

This poem, perhaps a poor suggestion to youngsters with a tendency toward mischief, has been recited with numerous aliases for Johnny Green (1765), that nasty boy who tried to torture the feline. He's been called Tommy O'Linne (1797) or Tom a lin or Tommy O'Lin and Tommy Quin (1840). A 20th-century version has it as Tommy Flinn . . . perhaps he's still "wanted" **(Figures E39 and E40)**.

Though all authors are not convinced, "(Little) Bo Peep,"

like the tale of the lucky cat, may have originated in the 1500s as well. Lost, or led away to pasture for their inevitable tail-bobbing, the quadrupeds reappear in the seldom-recited fifth stanza when, to the reader's surprise, the shepherdess tries to reattach their trimmed-off appendages! There is some chance that the stanzas tell the tale of Mary, Queen of Scots, who, imprisoned for many years, was accused of plotting both her husband, Lord Darnley's, demise and the earthly end of England's Elizabeth I (1558-1603). She lost both her Scottish throne and her head at Fotheringay Castle in February of 1587; her search for them continues with every repetition of the rhyme. **(Figures E41, E42, and E43, Figures D22, D34, D72, and D112, and Figures V21, V22, and V23)**.

Only three years later came the release of a new *Haggadah*, the Prague edition of the liturgy recited at the Passover Seder meal. It just might have been the source of the accumulative rhyme that told of the forlorn damsel **(Figure E44 and Figures D24 and D74)** who was "kissed by the man, all tattered and torn, who was married by the priest all shaven and shorn." The conclusion of the Seder service recalls the Holy One, who "slew the angel of death / That killed the *schochet* that slaughtered the ox / That drank the water that quenched the fire / That burned the stick that beat the dog / That bit the cat that ate the goat / My father sold for two zuzim" (Goldberg, 1973). Typical of the English rhymes pictured here, and others that followed it, are the phonetic "-orn" phrase endings.

> This is the cock that crowed in the morn,
> That waked the priest all shaven and shorn,
> That married the man all tattered and torn,
> That kissed the maiden all forlorn,
> That milked the cow with the crumpled horn . . .
> that lay in the house that Jack built.

An 1820 version (Opie and Opie, 1997) reads, "who swept the Stable snug and warm, that was made for the Horse of a beautiful form, that carried Jack with his Hound and his Horn, that caught the Fox that lived under the Thorn . . ."

And it was soon after, in this Tudor age of Elizabeth I, that the believers rode to Banbury. Adorned with bells on their long, tapered shoes and the finest of jewelry, they came to see the cross on the hill and a fine lady (perhaps Queen Elizabeth or Lady Godiva) upon a white horse. The residents at Banbury felled the cross when anti-Catholic feelings were popular (1602), but our alphabet ware insists upon inviting its diners to mount their steeds and ride away once more to see the modern cross at Banbury . . . perhaps one of those fine ladies will still be there to welcome them **(Figure C22 and Figure D90)**.

Elizabeth's castle, that great, drafty place, welcomed lots of cats to catch those pesky rats that came running in when the great gates open. . . and what better place for "Pussy Cat, Pussy Cat" **(Figure C21 and Figure D94)** to hide than beneath the chair of Tudor Queen Elizabeth herself! It's an old tale told by the cat, who, with obvious respect to Her Majesty, refrained from "the kill."

Some say a few public houses remain from 1603, the time of the charming spinster queen's death. And perhaps they're still called "The Cat and the Fiddle," where the good queen's ghost might yet be joyfully dancing to sprightly tunes. The cow, too, springs easily over the moon (was it the Earl of Walsingham?) and the dog (was it the Earl of Leicester?) who laughed to see such silliness before he asked to serve in France, waved aside by the gracious monarch. "Hey Diddle Diddle" has been published with some interesting variations: "and the dish lick't up the spoon," and "the goats jumped over the moon," "and the Maid ran away with the Spoon," and others (Opie and Opie, 1997). Time is sure to diddle-up some even more unique differences in the centuries to come **(Figure E45, Figures D34 and D49, and Figures M38 and M39)**.

About fifty years after the publication of the ritual Passover Seder service came the printing of two volumes concerning insects written by Dr. Tom Muffet. Written in Latin and published forty years after his death, it was dedicated to King James I. It was about 1590 that Miss Muffet, actually Patience Muffet, Doctor Tom's daughter, was frighted by a spider, though she must have been highly familiar with the eight-legged creatures. That tuffett may have been the traditional stool upon which young ladies patiently sat waiting for their knights in shining armor. Perhaps the pretty miss wasn't ready for the match **(Figure E46 and Figure C57)**.

Though the next poem, "Simple Simon" **(Figure E47 and Figure M41)**, was first published in the Stuart period (1665), the name of the poem's character was the dictionary's term for "simpleton" or "silly fellow." The poem, which shows Simon fishing for a whale in his mother's bucket, still proves the point.

Figure E48 pictures "The Milk Maid," who responds to the question of where she is going with "I'm going a-milking, Sir, she said." The poem is a 19th-century rewrite of an old song heard in 1698:

> Whither are you going pretty fair maid, said he . . .
> Shall I go with thee pretty fair maid, he said . . .
> Do it if you will, sweet Sir, she said . . .

The complete tale of the milk maid, soon with child, can be found in **Appendix AE3**.

She should probably have run, as did Tom Tom, the Piper's Son, when he ran away with a pig, but did anyone hear the snouty thing protest? Made by a pig-pie man, the delectable sculpture was made of paste deliciously filled with the finest of candied fruits. Its eyes were currents quickly devoured by Tom along with the rest of the 18th-century treat. The stomachache he undoubtedly got for hurriedly gobbling his loot was punishment enough for his crime **(Figure E49)**.

Since 1760, this real Little Pig (and the countless renditions of it) has been the big toe of countless infants who have been counting to three to describe the satisfied "piggie," to four to find the impoverished oinker, and to five to find the incompetent porker that couldn't even find its way home. Opie and Opie (1997) say, "'This Little Pig' is the most common toe-rhyme today and it has been for a century" **(Figure E50 and Figure D87)**.

Twenty-four years later, in 1784, "Goosey Goosey Gander" was found in his lady's chamber with a man who "would not" (or in some editions "could not") say his prayers. Taking things under its own wings, the goose, with little judicial sense, pulled the gentleman by his left leg and threw him down the stairs **(Figure E51 and variant Figure S10)**; in some versions he followed the directives to "throw him up again."

In 1821, the rhythm of the two-handled saw was sung to "Margery Daw" **(Figure E52 and Figure S5)** when Jacky's (or Tommy's) salary could have been but a penny each day be-cause he was a bit slow. Surely a bit more interesting is the surprising conclusion, found in Opie and Opie (1997):

> See Saw, Margery Daw.
> Sold her bed and lay upon straw;
> Sold her bed and lay upon hay,
> And pisky came and carried her away.
> For wasn't she a dirty slut
> To sell her bed and lie in the dirt?

It is interesting for two reasons: most important, very few nursery rhymes include mention of a fairy, and second, the definition of "slut" meets the Scottish definition of an "untidy person" rather than that unsavory meaning inferred in American slang.

Twenty-two years later, in 1842, a rhyme about a crooked man emerged. With grueling effort, he is seen here making his way down the crooked road. A seldom-seen second verse makes his plight less painful as he is given a crooked wife, Joan, with whom to share his miseries **(Figure E53)**.

Used in Edinburgh to determine who would begin a game, the "Hickory, Dickory, Dock" rhyme has had several endings. Opie and Opie (1997) cite two: "(1846) The clock struck three, The mouse ran away," and "(1846) The clock struck ten, the mouse came again." The rhyme probably encouraged finger play that tickled the tummy of the listener **(Figure D89)**.

About fifty years later, the complete 14-verse tale of "Old Mother Hubbard" was printed in a toybook, *The Comic Adventures of Old Mother Hubbard and Her Dog*, published on June 1, 1805, by J. Harris of London. The first three stanzas were probably written long before sweet, smiling Sarah Catherine Martin was born (1768-1826). Sarah completed it with eleven additional posies and possibly illustrated the saga. The starving dog never seemed to enjoy a meal, as the reader of the poem on this alphabet plate was expected to do **(Figures E54 and E55)**. In a different poem, "There Was an Old Woman Who Lived in a Shoe," the old woman's shoe-house clearly represented her commitment to "too many children," but when they became too much to handle (in the 1797 version), she tried to kill the poor darlings. Strikingly similar are the third stanza of Mother Hubbard and the fifth and sixth lines of this poem: after both elderly matrons bought coffins for their near and dear ones, both found their "dead darlings" quite alive and loudly laughing.

Surely Victorian darlings were expected to be the ultimate statement of Victorian propriety **(Figure D71)**; their clothes were simply small adult outfits. Even for the well-to-do, clothing was expensive and hard to keep clean. The value system encouraged perfection, and Victorian-age Americans were faster than their English cousins to press for labor-saving devices. Bishop and Coblentz (1979) quote the Beecher sisters of Hartford, Connecticut, who rushed to produce volumes of housekeeping advice. Evidently Polly Flinders never read the book; she was either unconcerned about the need to launder her frock or unaware of the monumentally laborious and cumbersome process needed to do the job. The sisters said,

> Two wash forms are needed, one for the two tubs in
> which to put the suds and the other for blueing and starch-
> ing . . . Aside from the four tubs, also needed was a large
> wooden dipper, two or three pails, a grooved wash-board, a

clothes-line, a wash stick to move clothes when boiling, and a wooden fork to take them out. Provide, also a (double flannel) clothes bag in which to boil clothes . . . a starch strainer, a bottle of ox-gall for calicoes, a supply of starch, a bottle of gum arabic, two clothes baskets; a copper kettle for boiling and a closet for keeping all these things.

Last but not least is the very short rhyme of the "Old Woman Who Lived Under a Hill." It's a few lines of just plain fun (Figure D67). A second version found on *Ask Jeeves* (Dreamhouse Nursery Bookcase) reads,

> There was a maid on Scrabble Hill,
> And, if not dead, she lives there still.
> She grew so tall, she reached the sky,
> And on the moon hung clothes to dry.

The next step of instruction went from rhymes to fables; not much longer than the rhymes, they were short tales with long lessons. The most noted writer of fables was, of course, Aesop, the author whose ancient biographies seldom agree. Aesop has been described as having lived in various centuries, as having been a slave, an adviser to a king, and a riddle solver to the ruler of Lycurgus. Aesop may have been only a name given to someone else's set of bestiaries, tales that focused on beasts given human interests and emotions. Though animals are unreal as they talk people talk, the fables describe realities in short, concrete vignettes designed specifically to teach. Nothing is left to the imagination. Because the moral (or the principle of conduct) is embodied in the fable's plot (or the specific example of the behavior), an explicit statement of the moral need not be given, though it sometimes is; it is the moral of the tale that is far more important than the story built around it.

Before Aesop came Poggius (1380-1459), a humorist who wrote original morality tales and copied forgotten or abandoned manuscripts in his most elegant handwriting. One such tale, also found in old Persian (Iranian) literature, was exquisitely printed in a 16th-century volume of fables and appears in Aesop's tales as well. The two plates (Figures E56 and E57) tell the story of "The Man, The Boy and the Donkey," who were traveling together in harmony. Each traveler they met had a different idea of which of the three should be walking or which of the two should be riding the donkey or if the quadruped should, in fact, be relieved of his usual task and carried. With his feet bound, the donkey, being carried, fell into the water and drowned. The moral of the tale is still timely . . . please all and you will please none, especially yourself.

Ten tales of Aesop provide morals with meals. Beginning with "The Dog and the Shadow," the moral tale tells of a dog so greedy that he grabs at everything without looking to see if what he has taken is good or evil (Figure E58). The "Fox and Goose," too (Figure E59), is about temptation and greed. The moral of the tale, not included in common collections of Aesop's works, is clearly stated in a short poem on the first page of a small, blue, gold-imprinted volume found in the archives at the University of California, Los Angeles. It read,

> Mankind has an enemy whom they will know,
> Who tempts them in every way;
> But they, too, at length shall o'ercome this foe,
> If wisdom's right law they obey.

It must be Goosey locked in Mr. Reynold's jaws, for the sly fox had already eaten her sister Gobble but had not yet met the persistence of sister Ganderee's wisdom. Mother Goose warned her three offspring of the sly one's hunger, but, as in "The Three Little Pigs," it took three strikes to knock out the intruder.

"The Fox and the Grapes," the tale of the hungry fox who couldn't reach the grapes and left the arbor disgruntled, proved that it is easy to despise what one cannot get (Figure E60). Like that tale, "The Dog in the Manger" (Figure E61) also reveals the common truth that often people begrudge others what they cannot have themselves.

"The Travellers and the Bear" (Figure E62) teaches that any friend who deserts another when the going gets rough is not a friend at all.

And "The Leopard and the Fox" proved that intelligence is as beautiful as a finely decorated exterior when the fox matched his "brains" with the big cat's spots (Figure E63).

"The Hare and the Tortoise" and "The Fox and the Tiger" are both tales of inner strength. The first (Figure E64) is the old favorite written to prove that he who works diligently will, most certainly, succeed. The second (Figure E65) is a tale of warning . . . no one, no matter how confident, can be so certain of his talents or strength that he does not to judge the strength of others around him.

The last two fables are tales of judgment. In the illustration of "The Cock and the Fox," the dog is not pictured in the transfer (Figure E66). The tale, like "The Fox and the Tiger," is a warning; no matter how cunning, even the most clever can be outwitted. "The Shepherd's Boy" certainly was outwitted (Figure E67). He played the game of truth or consequences and lost.

From fables to fairy tales, plates picture golden-haired Cinderella and tell the story of Little Red Riding Hood and her anxious encounter. The transposition takes the youngster from very short stories that provide stern instruction in morality, to longer tales that encourage the young adolescent's first independent journeys.

The child relates to animals and people in both fables and fairy tales. However, the fairy tale depends upon the "fluff" and sparkle of magic and imagination. Bruno Bettelheim's *The Uses of Enchantment* (1977) reminds us that the child may choose only to enjoy the fairy tale, passing up the opportunity to accept its real meaning. Pictures of characters on plates enlivened the retelling of stories that build eaters' memories, nourished their imaginations, and nudged them into a land of enchantment where clues to reality really do hide in flights of fancy.

"Cinderella," the best known of all the fairy tales, was first recorded in Egypt; some historians point to Cinderella's diminutive slipper as evidence of its Eastern, or Chinese, roots. Rewritten by Frenchman Charles Perrault and then by Jacob and Charles Grimm, the tale is a reprieve from the guilt that accompanies a youngster's hate of his/her sisters or brothers while in the throes of sibling rivalry. Cinderella's station among the ashes is a sign of debasement and of feeling unworthy no matter what the effort—feelings that parallel a lonely youngster's agony. Winding its way through tangled pumpkin vines and scurrying vermin, Cinderella's magical independent journey carries her from the dusty hearth to the luxurious safety of the royal throne; the uncompromised romantic venture ends, as do all authentic fairy tales, happily ever after (Figure E68).

Though the tale does challenge the imagination, "Red

Riding Hood," written by Perrault, was first a cautionary tale; certainly Little Red Riding Hood, eaten by the wolf, should have been more cautious. In later editions, the wolf needs first to get rid of grandmother in order to more easily "seduce" the youngster. The rescuing father figure is the fast-acting hunter who solicits his daughter's love by his supreme act of kindness, as well he should. The end? Both gentlewomen are safe while the beady-eyed antagonist gets his just desserts, a fitting end to this tale of an independent journey taken a bit too soon **(Figures E69 through E72)**.

From short to longer stories, ABC graphics lead to more descriptive tales or novels. The character of Robinson Crusoe, whose story is the subject of a great many transfers, was inspired by a real experience. Not originally written for children, the tale quickly became available in less difficult editions, which were an immediate success! Crusoe's tale focused upon the adventures of disgruntled Scottish sailing master Alexander Selkirk (also spelled Selcraig [1676-1721]), who, after a dispute with his captain, asked to be put ashore onto what is now Robinson Crusoe Island, of the Archipelago Juan Fernandez, off the coast of Chile. Rescued after four years by one Captain Rogers in 1709, Crusoe was the subject of Daniel Defoe's acclaimed narrative. Produced by different manufactories, ceramic pictures plotted the course of Crusoe's survival in the simplest terms. The saga began with the torrential waves that cast Crusoe upon an island where, with only his dog for companionship and the rescued refuse from the ship, he built a comfortable home, harvested his plantings, and cared for his goats. A prisoner brought to the island as a tasty meal for visiting cannibals was rescued by Crusoe and named Friday, for it was on that day that his life was saved. After many years of resourcefulness, the two finally returned to England aboard a ship they miraculously reclaimed from a band of mutineers. The saga became a "forever" classic of courage and determination; it defended the strength and perseverance of an individual of the middle class who, up to this time, had never been the subject of a narrative **(Figures E73 through E82)**. The exotic setting represented England's colonial expansion; though the surroundings were strange and often foreboding, it was there that Crusoe experienced his religious awakening. Like other tales of its day, it too could be considered a morality tale; it taught readers that an intelligent approach to survival and a solid work ethic could conquer all (see two versions of Crusoe Making a Boat in "V Is for Variations on a Theme").

As in any curriculum, in addition to literature is the study of mathematics. A memorable series, now known for its possibly prejudicial character rather than its value for teaching number concepts, presents cartoons of black characters demonstrating basic number operations **(Figures E83 through E88)**. Did the Victorians interpret these cartoons as prejudicial? If so, Victorians must have viewed the "bias" as a "value" to be cemented during formative years. Certainly they were not targeted toward the black community; the Victorians judged the purchasing power of the Black community to be extremely limited (Cheadle, 1997). Whether these scenes were designed primarily to be Black bashing rather than instructive can only be surmised.

"The Rule of Three" **(Figure E83)** demonstrates that it takes three quantities to determine any one missing quantity of a proportion. The two refreshments raised high represent one fraction, while the third represents one numeral of the second. The rule is also called the Golden Rule; as gold transcends all other metals, so is this rule the most important in arithmetic. In the same setting, the three composed drinkers have fallen onto the floor, their legs in the air and their chairs overturned. **Figure E84** is titled "The Sum Total," and the transfer is perhaps an illustration of addition as a commutative operation; the sum total of objects will be the same no matter what their position in the sequence.

The Lecture in Arithmetic demonstrates linear and quantity measurement **(Figures E85 and E86)**. "Interest" is simply presented by the girl selling her flat-iron to the pawnbroker, who would, at some later time, sell her property back to her with an added cost of interest **(Figure E87)**. And "Decimals," the last of this incomplete collection of mathematical transfers, is taught by a figure walking hurriedly with one pig under each arm. It just may be their last breath of fresh air before the butcher sections them for sale **(Figure E88)**. Page 119 of Riley's *Gifts for Good Children* (1991) features "Division," on which a poor eligible soul is being tugged at by two sweet young lovelies, each determined to have a share of his attentions.

Of course, the telling of time was a crucial skill. Clocks are included in "C Is for Commercialism," as it was the coming of the factories that made the "new" skill necessary **(Figures C2 through C6, Figures G12, G16, and G39, Figures M12 through M15 and M49, and Figure S16)**. And the ability to determine the months and seasons, seen here by examples from three existing sets, was also crucial **(Figures E89 through E105)**.

The study of peoples of the world is best accomplished through the Brownhills series of plates, which picture twenty-four countries (U and X are not included) and the typical costumes worn within their borders. Those pages, which are included in this chapter, are found in "T Is for Transfers and Toybooks" as the original source of the plate illustrations **(Figures T35, T36, T40, and T42)**. They have been reproduced from a childrens' book, published by T. Nelson & Sons of London & Edinburgh, in 1847 and titled *Picture Alphabet of Nations of the World,* each accompanied by a romantic four-line poem not found on the ceramics. The series here is replicated, with permission of the Southern Illinois University Press (Carbondale, Illinois, 1972), from a book edited by Ruth Baldwin. All but one in this collection **(Figures T37, T38, T39, T41, T43, T44, and T45)** are easily recognized and there are subtle differences between the originals and the ceramic views. In his first *ABC Collector's Newsletter,* dated January 1982, Joseph Chalala explained that the Turkish lady, in the 1847 publication, has her face covered; the engraver of the pottery transfer imagined how she appeared beneath her *rooband.*

Of all the countries represented in the collection, mysterious to most is the country called Wallachia (also correct with one l) and pronounced Wal-ak-i-a. After centuries of Turkish rule and Russian guidance, the tiny European country of Walachia, along with its northeastern neighbor, Moldavia, joined to form the single state of Romania in 1859. The principality may be best remembered for the 15th-century fortress of Poenari, which, resting majestically atop 1400 steps, still overlooks the densely forested Arges River Valley. Built by Vlad III the Impaler (prototype for Bram Stoker's 1897 tale of the vampire Dracula), the castle walls still hum with lurid tales of the ruler who dined in the forest amid thousands of upstanding arrows, each draped with the speared body of a Walachian peasant. It was warfare without an army; by annihilating the population and eliminating all food sources, the invading Turks were certain to turn away under the gaze of their enemy king, who dined savagely on blood-soaked bread. Perhaps the unassuming gentleman on the Brownhills plate is not yet unaware of the ghosts of Vlad's 40,000 victims, who lurk quietly in the mountain shadows behind him.

Another series focuses on China **(Figures E106 through E111),** while others look at children from Holland and their native dress **(see Figures L15 and L16, Figure C56, Figures D27, D32, and D42, Figures E40, E152, E153, and E174, and Figure G2).**

The social sciences included the chronicles of the Crimean War, which are presented, through ABC plates, in the discussion of that current event in "N Is for 19th Century" **(Figures N69 through N72).** Though pictures appear on plates made for children, the details of the war, with its causes and consequences, was more easily digested by adults.

After a humorous introduction to the fictitious animal kingdom on a doll plate **(Figure E112),** topics focused upon real animals and birds from near and far. The serious study of all but one of the pictured animals **(Figures E113 through E130)** abounds thoughout general texts, but the lifestyle of the Wild Dog **(Figure E117)** is not usually included in common sources. With greyhound-like legs, the dogs travel in packs; the lead dog is ready to lock its jaws onto a prey's snout to keep it at bay while the pack attacks the victim's hindquarters. Dogs of this kind cannot live without their pack . . . and the pack takes good care of its pups. They are brought to eat when the pack makes a kill. If the puppies eat it all, the pack leaves to find another; adult wild dogs never compete with their children for nourishment. (At least some part of the story carries a good lesson to the dinner table.)

Tales of the birds that could be identified by the child when outdoors were worth repeating with every meal. Birds, with their colorful plumage, were common subjects of late-19th-century Victorian illustrations. As on some alphabet plates, the birds were realistic and could be named; others inhabited faraway lands **(see Figures E131 through E149).**

One Brownhills plate presents the little-known Pica Vagabuuda. According to *Knight's Pictorial Museum of Animated Nature* (c.1850), this bird **(Figure E131),** unlike the other members of the pie family who forage for food only in one neighborhood, "wanders," as does a vagabond, from place to place in its search for fruits and berries. A long, gray, graceful bird with a beautiful thirteen-inch black-tipped tail, the Wandering Pie **(Figure E132)** is a native of the Himalaya Mountains of India.

A better-known pie, the magpie **(Figure E133),** builds a massive basket-like domed structure for its home, mud-plasters its walls thickly, and lines the deep, cup-like nest with fibers to keep its blue-green freckled eggs warm and safe. If a mate is killed, a large gathering of birds appears on the scene, a new papa or mama is chosen, and the bird "remarries" within a day or two. This cousin of the crow was abundant in England; admirers even brought it indoors to languish in wicker cages, where its shiny black and white plumage quickly faded (as did its vibrant population).

Not faded were the feathers of the Bird of the Gods, the *manukdewata,* found in the Molucca Islands (north of Australia) in 1522 **(Figure E134).** With a throat of brilliant shining green, a glowing purple breast, and iridescent back plumes of

bright red-orange, this ornamental creature was a gift of Captain el Cano to Spain. The plumed birds were said to have come from the unknown; they were of unearthly beauty, as were the hats adorned with their feathers. In 1910, 100,000 male birds were extracted from the jungles of New Guinea, a hunt that nearly exterminated forty-two species. The birds were saved by laws passed to halt the feather traffic, but the natives nearly starved to death when the jungle economy was suddenly plucked away. "Proud as a Peacock," the male bird will draw attention by showing his courtship display as he lifts and spreads his 20-foot-long train into a giant fan. Gold and green feathers are adorned with blue eye-spots, or *ocelli,* which rivet the attention. Also quite riveting are the loud, shrill, piercing calls of this large bird, which prances about, lifting his large ugly feet while performing for his plainly colored mate. Those clangorous cries still make him a particularly good "watch-bird" on the manicured lawns of wealthy lords and ladies.

Worn by the wealthy lords and ladies, too, were hats made with the feathers of the birds of paradise. Hunted by the natives of New Guinea and nearby islands as well as Australia, the birds' "touchy-feely" feathers were frequently exported to Europe. The transfer **(Figure E135)** represents about forty species of forest birds known for their magnificent ruffs and tails, some measuring over 100 magnificent centimeters.

Other islands 620 miles west of the South American mainland were the settings for the discoveries of Charles Darwin, who brought the *HMS Beagle* to their shores. There the good doctor was amazed to find so many species of finches **(Figures E136 and E137),** who were so much alike and yet so very different. Darwin concluded that, over many years, each species had adapted to its unique sources of food. Time, he said, had shaped their beaks to best gather their "goodies," be they fruits, nectars, seeds, or insects. Known as Darwin's Finches, these unassuming birds began the research that inevitably called to order the Scopes trial, where they and the hallowed text of Creation fought for the last word in the chronicle of life.

Not so remote were the city dwellers of Europe and America who depended upon their large populations of horses. **Figure E138** pictures the sparrow, a native European, which was brought to Brooklyn in 1852 and, like all European immigrants, spread, over the century, to all parts of the country. Family birds, both male and female sparrows build the nest . . . though it's untidy at best. Large sparrow populations were fed by waste grain from horses' feed. As the quadrupeds were replaced by automobiles, the population of urban sparrows declined significantly.

Dependent upon the presence of horses, too, were the thick populations of swallows; farm yards provided meals of blowflies and hover flies that gathered over piles of manure. With the number of farms decreasing and the use of insecticides shrinking the insect population, the number of swallows has been reduced as well. But the enthusiasm of the visitors from all over the world who wait patiently in mid-March for the swallows to return to California's Mission San Juan Capistrano hasn't declined. Legend says the swallows **(Figure E139),** seeking sanctuary from an innkeeper who destroyed their nests, took up residence at the old mission. They return to the site each year knowing their young will be safe within the mission walls.

And inside those mission walls were reminders of the religious legend, according to Christensen (1997), that colored the robin's orange-red plumage **(Figures C70 and Figure S9).**

The crown, seen resting round the head of Christ, was a reminder of when, according to some, a drop of His blood fell upon the saintly bird as it plucked a thorn. Another tells of the bird's kindness as it brought drops of quenching dew to souls in Hell; its feathers still reflect the blazing fires.

Like the robin, the tits **(Figure E140)**, also represented by Brownhills, are the best-known of all European birds and, being "people friendly," are always willing to dine at feeders in gardens and farmlands. They are small birds with beaks built to probe beneath tree bark in search of insects. In a unique pattern, the bigger birds will feed on the larger, upper branches; the smaller birds on the lower, shorter limbs. They may live in holes in old trees or, like the kestrals, take up residence in a variety of settings.

The kestral is the only type of scavenger **(Figure E141)** in the collection; it might nest on high mountain cliffs, in hollows of rocks, ledges of buildings, old tree trunks, or long-abandoned homes of other species. Wherever they are, Mom and Dad are attentive for one month, after which the little ones are given their first and final freedom to go house hunting on their own.

Inappropriate to the kestrals is the inland water habitat of the reed warblers, which live on the edges of rivers and lakes and whose nests are supported by the reeds that grow there. Unlike its vocally talented cousins, the reed warbler **(Figure E142)** has a creaking, wheezing, angry-sounding song; a lengthy kerra-kerra-krik-krik-gurk-gurk-gurk that is comforting only to nestlings awaiting their dinner of insects and small water animals. Simon and Schuster's *Guide to Birds* notes that one reed-warbler family in Hungary was observed feeding its youngsters small fish . . . appetizers, perhaps, before the crunchy crickets.

Perhaps **Figure E143** is a skylark. And perhaps the plates that follow, embellished with fluid designs of birds and flowers, were designed to provide an appreciation of our feathered friends and their flights of fancy.

Before a hearing-impaired child could use a set of letters to spell or signify "bird," he had to learn the signs that signified the letters that spelled the word b-i-r-d. It is to the credit of H. Aynsley & Company, Ltd., which opened its doors in 1864, that hand-sign plates **(Figures E150 through E158)**, with their signs for "Good" and "Bad" between each Z and A, were made for children who could share concepts only through the art of signing and their hearing communicators. With the hand-sign plates, some decorated with Louis Wain-inspired cats, the pottery took a stand in the history of special education . . . a history complete with still-standing debates and doubts.

Among its pioneers were Pedro Ponce de Leon (1520-1584), who might have invented the earliest manual alphabet, and Juan Pablo de Bonet, who, in 1620, published the first book concerned with the teaching of sign language. Contrary to the one-sign-for-one-word system was John Bulwer's 1648 edition of *the Deafe and Dumbe Mans Friend*, which enabled anyone with "an *obſervant Eie,* to Heare what any man ſpeaks by the moving of his lips."

In 1775, Abbe Charles Michel de L'Epee of Paris opened the first free school for deaf individuals, knowing that any group of the nonhearing anywhere naturally develops a unique sign language of its own. But there was another way. Samuel Heinicke (1778) of Leipzig, Germany, developed the oral system that influenced the teaching of the deaf around the world.

The British Braidwood family, highly secretive about their procedures, taught oral strategies through the last years of the 18th century. Both were very concerned about the "essential" normality of appearance, insisting that any form of signing bore the characteristics of the less cultured, inferior "savage" and mimicked the actions of the lower animals. Alexander Graham Bell, along with Samuel Gridley Howe, director of the Perkins School for the Blind, were on their side . . . the unending war between the oralists and the manualists raged.

It was the American Thomas Hopkins Gallaudet who, interested in helping his neighbor's deaf youngster, left for Europe in 1815 to study at the Paris National Institution for Deaf-Mutes of Abbe Roche Ambroise Sicard. Hoping to be trained in both oral and manual styles, he was rejected by Braidwood. Gallaudet returned to the states with Laurent Clerc, a French hand-sign teacher, to found, in 1817, The American School for the Deaf at Hartford, Connecticut. It taught only manual communication, which was enthusiastically supported by parents of adolescents.

But the pendulum was swinging back, and with it came Horace Mann's endorsement of the oral method after his visits to Germany and the United Kingdom. Although no purely oral schools were established until 1867 (Strong, 1988), his support motivated teachers from the American schools to scurry off to witness success for themselves; they returned having seen things other than Mann described. Communication in the European school was actually sign-based, especially in the living quarters, though oral techniques were somewhat successful for those with residual hearing. The "combined system" originated in the 1860s and 1870s, which meant that children would begin instruction in oral classrooms, and if enough progress was not observed, they would be transferred to manual classrooms (which really meant manual spelling). At the same time, advocates for the art of signing pleaded for its employment through the college curriculum . . . the battle raged.

The Aynsley Pottery was in business through the heat of the debate. The plates might have been produced as a way of supporting the teaching of hearing-impaired students in a visual medium . . . of taking a position in the continuing controversy giving little ones a head start at spelling m-e-a-t or p-u-d-d-i-n-g. With a two-handed manual alphabet, the plates were not designed for import to the states, which employed one-handed ABCs. Perhaps they were designed for export to support schools in France or the Netherlands; Dutch dress is pictured on several designs. Or perhaps research will reveal a member of the Aynsley family who would have benefited from hand-sign instruction.

The two-hand sign alphabet is the system of choice in Australia, India, Indonesia, and other areas that have been influenced by Great Britain. The BBC Online and its subgroup, the BBC Learning Zone, has a Web site that teaches the two-handed signing used in the British Isles, which has not only signs for words but its own grammatical structure. Drawings of the signs on plate borders show the signs nearly identical to those taught today, though the visual descriptors are not drawn continuously from the same position of observation.

Alphabet ceramics also present the Braille alphabet **(Figures E159, E160, and E161)** for the significantly visually impaired. The system of reading and writing for the blind was the ingenious modification of a soldiers' silent- and night-writing system by Louis Braille (1809-1852) who became blind, himself, at three. At the age of ten he went, as a foundling, to the only school for the blind in Paris. He died at forty-three, leaving his language to be adapted into almost every known language. The signs for the blind, read with sensitive fingertips, are not presented on plates for eating; dot arrangements, signifying letters, appear, in this collection, on ash-trays and can easily be found, in a wide variety of colors, at minimal expense.

It is suspected that these smoking receptacles have been made recently. They do, however, remind us that blindness was a substantial disability in 19th-century Britain. The first years of that century saw the beginning of specialized medicine with the founding of the London Dispensary for Curing Diseases of the Eye and Ear by John Cunningham Saunders. Though incidents of visual impairments receded dramatically after about 1870, diagnostics were in their infancy; treatment was not very effective for ocular venereal infections and insect-borne corneal scarring. Irritations from airborne pollutants, especially in the potteries, could not be alleviated.

More commonly thought of as "second languages" are languages of other countries. With ABC rims, earthenware plates taught simple Spanish names and French vocabulary. Easily interpreted graphics presented words quickly learned at lunch **(Figures E162 through E174)**. All plates but one in this collection are self-explanatory. **Figure E173** pictures those who lived in Kabylia, on the coast of northeastern Algeria. An area of wild terrain with high mountains and deep valleys, it isolated its Muslim people, who produced a Berber dialect called Kabyle; French was the people's second language. The last of the series **(Figure E174)** wishes a Dutch child a happy day of his birth, with good wishes for all time to come.

It is unreasonable to assume that any one child, with or without home teaching or with or without a need for special systems of education, benefited from the entire scope and sequence of the ceramic curriculum. It is reasonable to assume that only one or two alphabet-bordered plates were on hand to dish up dinner and that plates were provided, often as gifts, to youngsters by adults whose interests promoted the purchases. Each curriculum category had many lessons to teach; a complete listing of all plates in any one subject grouping does not yet, and perhaps will never, exist. Hundreds of plates might remain to complete any one of the small subject areas reviewed in this or any other chapters and years of collecting may not begin to connect the missing links. But every collection teaches an important lesson. Each graphic deserves its share of research; it is the purpose of each to teach, and it is our pleasure, as collectors, to learn.

F Is for Flatware

A spoonful of sugar or a forkful of mashed potatoes—both came with a mouthful of letters that adorned the sterling silver, silver plate, or small-scaled flatware of varying alloys that graced the nursery table. Their histories began, like the beginnings of glass and clay vessels, somewhere in the gray awakenings of man's beginning.

Using the flake of flint that had cut his foot, Stone Age man hacked pieces of savory meat from a fresh kill; early man could feed himself with the help of sharpened stone. Waiting patiently for him, the flint had formed millions of years before when the glassy skeletons of sponges were caught in an upheaval of the earth's crust. Flint was early man's survival tool. He learned to chip it away, to grind and polish it, to turn fragments into spear points and knives, and sometimes to set it into wonderfully carved wooden or ivory handles, making the first flatware known to humankind.

Of course, early man ate with his fingers with the help of a cutting tool. And many peoples do still eat in that fashion, dipping three fingers of the right hand *only* and some, as in southern India, never beyond the first knuckles.

But metals made it easier. The history of iron began at least six thousand years ago, when early man possibly learned to use the iron in meteorites that had fallen to earth. By chipping and hammering this metal, the ancients made crude weapons and tools. But metal came from down under as well, to be fortuitously found in the ash of fires that had been started atop outcroppings of red iron ore called paint rock. And a fortunate accident taught the ancient Turks how to smelt copper ore, to make their bowls and weapons of the shiny but too-soft pink metal. Somewhat later, tin, probably because copper ore was found near tin ore, was added to that copper and it fused, creating very hard bronze; stone molds for casting bronze knives have been found in the Middle East as far back as 3800 B.C. But tin was scarce back then; it was easier to find iron.

Iron ore was common, and by 1400 B.C. the Chalybes, a Hittite tribe, had the secret of forging it. For their own military advantage they tried to keep their process secret. After the destruction of their Asian empire in the 12th century B.C. by the dominating Phrygians, the Hittites were swept out of their homeland, and their secret was no secret anymore. Enlightened metalworkers in Asia and southern Europe soon found other elements, which, when fused, made an even harder metal we now know as steel. Steel swords were the best for battle . . . and steel knives, the making of which became a thriving industry, were the best knives for every stage of the capture and consumption of food.

Sharpened blades were set into handles of precious metals and carved bone. Some were designed and colored to be used on special religious occasions. Especially prized were knives whose handles were fashioned from the tusks of mythical unicorns, which, it was said, protected their owners from bad luck. Actually those handles were bad luck for the narwhals, which were massacred to provide them.

So many treasured cutting tools were laid at once that rules, reminiscent of the old Roman Sumptory Laws (see spoons, ahead), were set to ensure every diner's safety. One French college required that all students draw them out at the same time, focusing everyone's attention on the process. When on the table, the knife's cutting edge needed to face its owner, and taking it from its place when not in use was as intimidating as handing it to another with the blade facing him . . . decidedly disrespectful. To end this Gothic performance, all utensils were returned to their cases as they were removed, in unison. (A different kind of safety was assured when a French "Rule of Civility" asked that knives not be wiped on bread or on the tablecloth but on a napkin provided for this purpose.)

Knives became personal items carried everywhere, some in embellished leather cases and some stashed between a hairy leg and its slippery sock. Innkeepers of the Middle Ages didn't provide them, nor did the hostesses of Saturday night soirees. Though it is not clear if "ordinary" women carried knives as well as men, it is known that among nobility only males carried the utensils; gentlemen were expected to cut food for the women. It was even better if two accompanied the diner, as eating with a knife in each hand was the very height of refinement—though a risky skill it had to have been. Even riskier was the practice of flossing one's teeth with the point of the coveted tool; Erasmus's 16th-century edict took a stab at halting that "picky" habit.

But it was the 17th-century knives of Puritan America that were given the most sophisticated function of all. After a knife was wiped clean with one's napkin, it could be used to carry salt very carefully from its dignified station at the father's head of the table back to the diner's place . . . salt shakers, at first called *casters*, designed for sprinkling sugar and pepper, were yet a century away. And salt was not the only food balanced on the blade . . . Rose Bradley (1912) mentions a lady of "excessive gentility" who was accomplished at balancing a pea upon the blade. It took five hundred years for folding and "take-apart" knives to be designed for travelers, but by that time forks and spoons accompanied them in tooled carrying cases.

As forks were added to table settings, knives no longer needed their points. Food was more gently lifted with sharpened tines, and table knives were redesigned with rounded tips by the last years of the 17th century. To give energy to the trend, France's King Louis XIV, in order to restrain increasing violence, forbade the making of pointed knives, the carrying of steel-sharp tools, or the provision of cutlery at innkeeper's tables. In addition, he ordered that the points of all eating knives owned by anyone needed to be rounded off. Europe got the point, and the new style spread quickly . . . so quickly that enterprising designers overextended the rounded tips of the blades, twisting them crook-like to the right to accommodate to the knife users whose food slipped between the two too-wide tines of the newfangled forks.

After knives came the spoons that early man formed in a bowl-shaped receptacle from fired clay. It was three thousand years before Christ that a spoon was buried in an Anglo-Saxon grave near Lucerne, Switzerland. The word spoon was *spon*, the Anglo-Saxon word for chip or splinter of wood; evidently a flat, splintery fragment of wood was used before the idea of carving a bowl was born. A thousand years later the horns of sheep or goats were used to make oval spoons fastened to stems of wood or another bit of horn. Horns were boiled as well and pressed into spoon shapes, with their handles attached, to harden. Hands cupped water for drinking in coastal lands until someone noticed that seashells, nestled in the sand, held liquid, too. Found in Egyptian tombs are seashells polished and shaped into spoons. The cowrie shell, used as a spoon fifteen hundred years before Christ, had handles of gold and ivory. By 1000 B.C., bronze spoons were being made in Egypt . . . long incense spoons served at ceremonials, and triangular spoons, with sharp points at the far ends of the bowl and stem, were undoubtedly designed to coax a tasty snail from its tunneled home.

The Romans cast their spoons. A utensil cast of clay perhaps stirred the soup but was never used to eat it. Or spoons might have been cast by the inefficient lost wax method (pouring molten metal into a shape of wax surrounded by clay); the model had to be resculpted each time. Two bronze spoons have been discovered, one or both of which had been made by either one of those methods. One had a round bowl, called a *ligula,* and the second was close in appearance to the long and pointed Egyptian design. The handles of each were sharp enough to pierce the shells of eggs, letting the evil spirits slip away from these symbols of the life cycle before they were consumed!

Of course, the Romans loved their banquets and set their tables with as many silver and bronze articles as possible. They stole their cache (even held communities at sword point until they coughed up their treasures) and, with excess the rule of thumb, soon found themselves subject to a Sumptory Law limiting the display of precious metals to be used on any one tabletop at any one meal—so much for the show-offs. The law didn't affect the bone spoons, crafted with small holes in the bowls . . . perhaps precursors of today's slotted servers. After Rome fell, all of its newly refined table manners (like washing hands between courses and wiping them on clean, white linen napkins) fell away with them, returning the world to early man's sharp knife and greasy fingers; the silver fell away as well, into the melting pot, which turned finely crafted ornaments into heavy coins owed to weary soldiers.

Romanesque days saw hearty morsels set on boards, as tables and chairs were not yet part of the castle inventory. One side of the covering cloth reached to the floor, preventing waiting canines from gobbling goodies hiding under pointed shoes as the diners sat on long benches before bowls of soup (each one sipped by two invited guests). A rosewater pitcher (called an *aquamanile*) and towel sat for all to see . . . each diner eager for his neighbor to wash his hands before reaching (perhaps with a knife) into the common pot. Hardened bread served as plates; with fingers extended to keep them clean for the next course, meat was piled on the four-day-old trenchers that would be given, gravy-soaked and nibbled on, to the poor at meal's end.

By the 1200s spoons were willed to the next generation, carved from rare woods, or made of bronze, gold, or silver. But just how gold or just how silver were they? Were the markings real?

Few implements of the Middle Ages remain today. What does remain began with the start of the Guilds, which developed in England to ensure the absolute truth of metal assays without a destructive process. Assay stamping had already been apparent on French silver to certify the content, date of manufacture, and maker, but in England there was no such guarantee. Items could be made with excesses of copper, which went unseen, as the pink-toned metal did not change the color of the silver; the gold standard could be easily violated as well.

In 1300, Edward I took action. He gave the members of the Worshipful Company of Goldsmiths the right to set up a single standard for English money and "the right to mint this money" (Chase, 1969). And a mark was introduced—the head of a leopard, pressed into the metal, was to confirm that the item was made from 925 parts of silver per thousand (92.5%) to 75 parts of copper (7.5%). On March 30, 1327, a charter bestowed upon the Worshipful Company of Goldsmiths the obligation of enforcing compliance with the assay laws. Since the assay was to be conducted at the Guild Hall and the mark placed upon the piece by the yearly elected "master of touch" or "touch warden," the term "hallmark" was born.

But the trip to London was long for far-off metalsmiths and fraught with robbers who would kill for less. Most ignored the edict. Choosing not to ignore the difficulty, mayors of residential areas were granted the power of "touch" in 1363, and the sterling marks could then be locally affixed along with a maker's mark as well. A picture-mark allowed illiterates to identify the smith without having to read his name. But that was not enough. The masters themselves did not stay in close enough touch with set standards, and a new mark was added in 1478 to enforce their obligation to honesty. They were required to use a letter of the alphabet to personally denote their dating. When the cycle was completed, a letter of another type style restarted the twenty-six-year rotation. The letter that served as their signature was set into the metal for all time.

In 1697, the government once more stepped in to ensure honesty. The practice of clipping reduced the side of a coin by the area of a small chord; it was sold to a silversmith. Forged currency was made from the shards until the "powers that were" raised the standard of sterling to 95.84% and the higher quality became the norm. But the new standard did not allow the production of highly decorated ware, and because too many artisans went belly-up, the old standard was resumed in 1720 when many makers' marks were letters . . . as more buyers by then could read.

So spoons were marked and remembered from that 15th-century England when marks were letters that denoted the year of the mayor's approval. There were the famous Apostle spoons whose figured stems gave comfort to those offering thanks to the Almighty for their portion. But designs were not always created for ornament. With the styling of the stiff, round collar ruffs, the stems of spoons needed to be longer, and soup spoons were critical as anyone "ruffed up" at the table could hardly get the bowl to his mouth. Also, the bringing of tea from the Far East and coffee from Turkey by Italian seamen created the need for much smaller bowls.

Cultures were merging. Cities were growing, trade was flourishing, and self-scrutiny encouraged refining changes: some people were no longer lifting their lice-ridden cloaks in the streets, blowing their noses in their sleeves, or passing 'round a single cup from which all the group could sup. Table manners were coming into their own, and civility was called upon to keep filthy fingernails from fishing in the common pot for the biggest share with that nosy "fishing finger."

However, things were gaining civility a bit more slowly on the more recently settled side of the Atlantic. The Colonists used a "spike and spon," or a knife and spoon, which gave them clean fingers and us the expression (as well as the pulverized cleaning product), "spic and span." Eating spoon meat meant eating food of any sort with a spoon that was also used as a fork when turned upside down to hold the meat for cutting. But they resorted to spoon forms that hearkened back to man's beginning. They fastened shells to sticks, fashioned animal horns, and carved spoons from wood because few had brought pewter or silver utensils with them. Wiping hands before meals was adequate . . . washing was not required before helping oneself out of the cooking pot while standing in front of the fire. Dripping juices were absorbed by huge napkins "draped over the shoulder" that doubled as hot mitts as fiery food was lifted from boiling pots. When a meal was enjoyed around boards balanced on barrels, the pot sat in the middle while stale bread doubled as trenchers that were consumed. Wood slabs as trenchers, lovingly shared with a neighbor, were wiped clean first by the eater and then by his/her napkin. Set into "voider" baskets, trenchers awaited another wiping before being shelved for the next meal.

As the numbers of Colonists grew, the newcomers brought as much money in coin with them as they could. Reversing history's trend of committing exquisite metal art to the melting pot to create coin, the new Americans melted their coins to make easily identifiable silver objects of distinction, perhaps made by Paul Revere himself, should they be robbed. Actual coins were turned into spoon bowls; debts could be paid with objets d'art.

It was after the spoon and the ever-faithful knife that the most commonly used utensil, the fork, began, like the others, at the start of man's triumphs. Huge bronze two-pronged forks lifted the flesh of offerings from Egyptian fires of religious sacrifice. The Greeks, using a hand-shaped utensil modeled after their "flesh fork," lifted sacrificial offerings and carcasses from boiling pots. The Romans actually did use their large, two-pronged bronze forks to hold the meat while it was carved and quickly eaten with the fingers. (Unlike the Romans, the English, through the 1600s, were expected to hold the paper-covered roast with one hand while they cut a chunk off with the other; the paper frills that adorn our lamb chops are possibly the remnant of this practice. See Appendix AF1.)

But it is history's first diner's fork that vies for first in the literature. Perhaps the prize should be given to the bearer of those small, flat silver forks found in the ruins of Pompeii and Herculaneum . . . marks of refinement long buried by the ashes of Vesuvius in A.D. 79. And it is known that 7th-century royal table settings in the Middle East boasted forks, but they didn't emerge into "modern Europe" until about four hundred years later.

Perhaps the tale begins with the 11th-century Venetian doge who, on a journey to the Middle East, wed a beautiful Turkish princess. Together they journeyed to her new home with her "baby forks," only to enrage the church leaders of Venice, who claimed that only God's natural forks could feed. Or perhaps the trophy for who owned the first fork belongs to the fastidious Greek wife of Doge Domenico Silvio (Selvo) of Venice in 1100. Her quick demise was blamed on her pretentious use of these scandalous tools.

A 1361 inventory listed silver forks as belonging to the city of Florence, and the French Charles V (c.1370) owned a few, but, in an apologetic tone, he declared they were used only for tasties that just might have stained his fingers. In 1463, a silver fork was mentioned in the will of John Baret of Bury St. Edmunds, and the Italian Catherine de' Medici, daughter of the Florentine Medicis, wed King Henry II of France in 1533 with a dowry that included the tined utensils, which she set for each diner at the French court. The times were more accepting; by 1560, most Italians were fork-lifting their pasta to their mouths and eating the "stuff" in soup with a fork while the liquid was drunk from the bowl.

England, however, did not receive the gift with charity. The author Thomas Coryate (Coryat), a Somersetshire squire, was berated as a "Furcifer" (a fork bearer or gallows bird) for having introduced the pointed tool to England in 1611. The English Church saw, as an insult to God, eaters denying His gifts by using manmade metal fingers, and Thomas was forced to endure the irksome reputation of being enthralled with an effeminate bit of finery.

By the end of the 1600s, all of Europe began using the flat, sterling "split spoons," which at first had been given only a slight curve. A most distinct curve soon followed, making the "scoop" easier and enabling it to fit more easily into the shape of the receiving lips and mouth. But forks were still luxuries that lovely ladies used as elegant jewel-handled toys to "pick at their sweetmeats" (Bradley, 1912). In 1630, the fork had crossed the Atlantic; Massachusetts Bay Colony's Governor Winthrop owned what was assumed to be the only fork in America.

Though the first carcass forks, with their two long, thick tines, changed to the shortened and much thinner tines of the 17th century, eating was still not a comfortable task; the knife was still employed to do the work of the trident-shaped tool. In time, since small pieces of food fell between the tines, a center tine was added. By 1700, German craftsmen offered four-, five-, and six-tined utensils; looking more like they belonged on a dresser top than a dining table and being far too wide for most diners' mouths, the five- and six-tined tools were cast aside, and the four-tined fork became the standard.

Thanks to Louis XIV (1638-1715), a new standard was set that inspired all the royal courts to follow suit. There is no doubt that it was Louis who was the first to provide each royal dinner guest with a full table setting of flatware. No longer did his visitors need to "bring their own" or share a goblet. Each ate with an embellished setting of royal silver, while the Sun-King, in his radiant glory, sliced his chops with a solid gold knife. In their search for fancy and formalism, European royal courts designed unique utensils to fit every foodly function. There were long-handled spoons for tall glasses, smaller-bowled spoons for teeny bits of rich desserts, very large bowled-spoons for heavy soups, etc. By the time the Victorians were the designers, sets were housed in massive carved chests and included as many as 140 pieces, each with its own form and often exaggerated function. The dining experience was becoming more and more elaborate. For the wealthy there were infinite varieties of silver- and gold-washed tableware. For the farmer and the poor there were a few forks of common metals and scarcely enough dinner . . . the dining experience was unfulfilling.

But the Industrial Revolutions in England and America brought forks to everyone's table. Steam-powered factories replaced the metalsmiths; knives, spoons, and forks, once made by hand, were now cut mechanically into strips from sheets of metal and fed into presses, where they exited as unfinished but recognizable table tools. Dies gave the utensils their dimension and the patterns their selectability.

Sterling silver utensils can be found without difficulty on the antique market today. After 1840, they might have been plated with silver by an electroplating process . . . an electrical current that facilitated the deposit of an even coat of silver onto copper or nickel. The vast majority of flatware was silver plated after 1890. Shiny souvenir spoons were all the rage at midcentury, with ABC sets considered to be "favored items" by their manufacturers. But silver or silver plate was not the substance of all children's utensils. Alloys of other metals were used for flatware as well, and the components of those alloys accompany each graphic. Notable is the boxed set, packaged as beautifully as a set of finer metal service.

All flatware shown has at least some, if not all, the letters of the alphabet. They can be found on both the facing and the undersides of the utensil stems (or handles) and/or spoon bowls. Identical designs were manufactured on straight-stemmed and toddler spoons, the latter possibly loop-handled for easier grasp. A fork, fairly flat and without sharply pointed tines, and possibly two spoons make up a set, though today's collectors seldom find these childhood "tools" in their original groupings. Most infant tools measure about four inches, and there are larger "junior" sets as well . . . more like the size of modern-day children's editions of both sterling and silver plate that accompany so many flatware patterns. Blunt-tipped knives were included only in the longer sets for older eaters.

The items pictured in this chapter have been identified by maker and dated, when possible. The only patent found to date follows the photo of its item. A thorough search of patent records might reveal other included designs, but because patent records are often listed by their design originators rather than by the companies that produced them, they are most difficult to locate.

The utensils shown in **Figure F1** are stamped **Sheffield**, England, and are possibly replications. The authentic Sheffield company began in 1742 when Thomas Boulsover discovered that copper and silver would bond when pressed together. Matthew Boulton founded a manufactory in Birmingham, England, to produce objects of the bonded metals until, in 1800, it was discovered that electric currents would transfer layers of silver onto a metal, ensuring its quality. Sheffield silver has been pro-duced by many companies, each with its unique mark. Because the stamp of the flatware pictured has not been found to be a metalsmith's stamp within the Sheffield community, it has been suggested that the children's set is probably a copy of an item produced at some time during the 20th century and stamped with Sheffield's illustrious name.

Reed & Barton—1840

The story of Reed & Barton of Taunton, Massachusetts, began with the firm of Babbitt and Crossman in 1824. Starting with the manufacture of Britannia ware and pewter, the enterprise flourished until November of 1834, when only three in the floundering firm remained: Benjamin Pratt, a company agent; Henry Reed, a spinner; and Charles Barton, the solderer. Enduring partnership changes and the depression of 1837, the team of Henry Reed and Charles Barton claimed the name Reed & Barton in 1840. Production of silver plated ware began in 1848. Charles Barton passed away in 1867 with Reed at his side. One year later, Henry Fish and George Babrook, both of whom had been a part of the company, joined Henry Reed in a new partnership. The three began the production of solid silver services in 1889, and by 1904, sterling was becoming more popular than plated ware. In the 1940s, with defense requirements, the production of stainless steel flatware brought a product to the market that is still enormously popular. Known for its graceful tableware, the firm, continuing under the management of the Reed family, has "the same sense of unity and dedication to craftsmanship as their founding fathers" (Rainwater and Redfield, 1998). **(Figure F2.)**

Meriden Britannia—1852

D. Wilcox, H. Wilcox, I. Lewis, J. Frary, L. Curtis, and W. Lyman founded The Meriden Britannia Company in 1852 for production of large quantities of Britannia hollowware. According to Rainwater and Redfield (1998), Britannia was a silver-white alloy of tin with added antimony and copper as hardeners. With more tin than in pewter and with no lead, Britannia also contained small amounts of bismuth and zinc: 140 parts of tin, 3 of copper, and 10 of antimony. More brilliant, harder, and longer lasting than pewter, Britannia was taking its place in American homes.

By 1855, Meriden Britannia produced silver-plated hollowware and flatware with German silver articles as well. German silver was a silver-white alloy of copper, zinc, and nickel; World War I sentiments changed the name of the alloy to nickel silver, also indicated as N.S. In 1867, the company developed a system whereby the metal content of an item was noted in a number code stamped on each item . . . silver types were immediately recognized. Also developed by the firm was its unique area plating; a patent dated March 10, 1868 would ensure extra silver plate on the areas of flatware that sustained the hardest wear.

The Rogers Brothers (of Hartford, Connecticut) combined with Meriden Britannia in 1862. Their 1847 Rogers trademark significantly contributed to the reputation of the firm. By 1879, Meriden Britannia had become an international company with a branch in Ontario, Canada. **Figure F3** is a detail from an engraving of the plant from Meriden Britannia Co.'s "Electro Gold and Silver Plate, Nickel Silver and White Metal" catalogue published in 1882. An M. B. product, napkin ring number 293-4, sterling, is also stamped with its date of patent issue, July

15, 1919 **(Figure F4)**. Located in the Los Angeles Central Library by author Susan Casey, the patent for its design was applied for on March 19, 1919, with a seven-year term. Filed by George Ohl, Patent Number 53603 is pictured in **Figures F5a, F5b, and F5c**.

In 1898, the firm's administrators recognized the wisdom of combining with other small firms to form one giant organization; all could work with more efficiency to meet the varying demands of the purchasing public. Meriden Britannia was the one of the initiators of the movement, which encouraged about twenty-five firms to become the nucleus of the International Silver Company in November of 1898.

William Rogers Manufacturing Company—1865

Of the thirty or so sterling silver and silver plate firms that bear the name of Rogers, the William Rogers Manufacturing Company of Hartford, Connecticut, was one of the twelve companies that formed the International Silver Company in 1898. William Rogers and his son, William Henry Rogers, Jr., were two of the five who founded the company in 1865, but by 1872, when the company was incorporated, the Rogers father and son were no longer part of it. A long string of trademarks, most of which carry the anchor as it is seen on each end of the name Rogers, is stamped on the back of the alphabet set **(Figure F6)**.

G. K. Webster Company—1869

George K. Webster founded G. K. Webster Company in 1869 in North Attleboro, Massachusetts. As time passed, George K. purchased his partners' interests and supervised the firm until his death in 1894, when it was renamed the Webster Company. The sterling product line focused on baby goods, picture frames, and dresser items. Before the purchase of the Frank W. Smith Silver Company of Gardner, Massachusetts, the Webster trademark became the property of the Webster Company Division of Reed and Barton, silversmiths, of Taunton, Massachusetts in 1950 **(Figure F7)**.

The Watson Company—1874

In 1874, Clarence Watson and others founded Cobb, Gould and Co. of Attleboro, Massachusetts, to manufacture a line of gold-plated jewelry. The partnership dissolved, leaving Watson and Fred Newell, who continued to operate under Watson & Newell; the firm, from 1880 through 1886, made thirty different ladies' name pins and sleeve buttons. After new partnerships were formed, the product line expanded to lace, cuff, and shawl pins. Silversmithing began when the renamed Watson & Newell Company opened new quarters in 1896. Nearly fifty flatware patterns and many more varieties of souvenir items were designed. In 1904, the firm restructured; the sleeve and collar button division became the Standard Button Company, and their production of hundreds of souvenir designs was administered by Watson and Newell until Newell's death in 1910. In 1920, the company was incorporated, becoming The Watson Company, which regularly introduced new flatware designs. Like Milton Hershey of chocolate fame, Clarence Watson cared intensely about the welfare of his workers. The firm built homes and created social and relief agencies to assist in times of illness. And like his father-in-law, Grover Richards reliably cared for the company after Watson's death in 1930. R. Wallace and Sons purchased Watson in 1955 and employed Richards in an executive position. Nine years later the souvenir spoon dies were

sold to Whiting and Davis of Plainville, Massachusetts **(Figures F8, F9, and F10)**.

Manchester Manufacturing Company—1887

The mark on the fork pictured in **Figure F11** is a variant of the mark of Manchester Silver of Providence, Rhode Island. A descendant of a family of English silversmiths, Providence's William H. Manchester founded the W. H. Manchester and Company in 1887. The firm became Manchester Manufacturing Company when the Baker family became involved; with the withdrawal of William H. from the firm about 1915, Baker continued on Chestnut Street under the Baker-Manchester Company name even though the founder had bowed out. Manchester had moved to Pavilion Street in about 1914. The firm was owned solely by one Frank S. Trumbull in 1947 when E. B. McAlpine and son George purchased an interest, and it was they who assumed complete ownership upon the death of Frank S. "If it's Manchester, it's Sterling," they said, and the company's production shone until 1980, when the cost of silver escalated and the firm disclosed its liquidation. Manchester Silver was absorbed in 1985 by J. C. Boardman of Wallingford, Connecticut.

Wilcox & Evertsen Company—1892

Wilcox & Evertsen began as Rowan and Wilcox in 1889. Three years later Evertsen joined Wilcox as a partner, making sterling silver hollowware. In 1896, the company was absorbed by the Meriden Britannia Company, and the plant was moved from New York City to Meriden, Connecticut. After joining the International Silver Company, the flatware division was moved to Wallingford, Connecticut. Its trademark, an Indian head, is prominent on the catalogue page shown in **Figure F12**. The three-piece alphabet set, undoubtedly manufactured after the merger into International Silver, is the only one found to date that incorporates a "pusher." In this salesman's photo, the letters are etched only onto that piece and the knife; the spoon is stamped with a graphic called "Rocking Horse" while "Humpty Dumpty" decorates the fork. Perhaps the sets were available in each design in both baby and child sizes. This photo, from page 20 of Catalogue Number 135 of the Wilcox & Evertsen Company, is included thanks to the efforts of curator Alan Weathers, with permission of the Meriden Historical Society at the Andrews Homestead, Meriden, Connecticut.

Wallace Brothers—Mark Patent Date 1895

The tin-alloy articles are called Malabar Plate and were made by The Wallace Brothers of Wallingford, Connecticut. According to research completed at the Chicago Public (Main) Library, the trademark, WB over W, was filed for on the 17th of June in 1895 and registered on the 6th of August (#0026912). The flatware **(Figures F13 through F16)** was listed as table service made of steel and tinned. It was first offered for sale on May 1 of the same year; its metal components are listed at the photo site.

The firm began as The R. Wallace Co. on May 1, 1855. In 1865, the corporation, Wallace Simpson & Co., was organized. Wallace bought most of Simpson's interest, and in 1871, the corporate name was changed to R. Wallace & Sons Mfg. Co., as his sons and sons-in-law had joined him. The firm, which was renamed Wallace Brothers in 1875, manufactured flatware on a base of cast steel. In 1924, a Canadian plant was opened, and in 1944, sterling flatware was added to the line. In 1934,

William S. Warren, a designer for the firm, conceived of the idea of three-dimensional flatware patterns, for which the company has since been noted. The Watson Company of Attleboro, Massachusetts, was bought by Wallace in 1955, after which the firm became known as Wallace Silversmiths. Purchased by the Hamilton Watch Company in Lancaster, Pennsylvania, Wallace became a subsidiary of The Katy Industries, Inc., of Elgin, Illinois, in 1983. It was bought by the Syratech Corporation in 1986.

Paye and Baker Manufacturing Company—1896

A student at the Rhode Island School of Design, Charles Paye, with engraver Jessie O. Simmons, founded the Simmons and Paye Co., a souvenir spoon house (possibly in Providence, Rhode Island); its products advertised seven hundred North American memorable geographic places and immortalized ten thousand buildings on their stems. Forget-me-nots of current events were quickly created . . . timely interest was the key. In 1900, Frank Baker's purchase of Simmons' share brought with it a name change to Paye & Baker Manufacturing Company (1901) and a move to Attleboro, Massachusetts. A new steam engine ran the machinery, and Paye and Baker ran the marketing and design. For the next twelve years the company produced hundreds of spoons, mesh bags, gold and sterling silver pins, charms, bangles, links, and any other items that would sell, including ideas inspired by others here and abroad; the firm's ideas were copied by others as well. The sudden death of Charles Paye changed all that; Frank Baker drastically modified the line from items designed to stimulate bandwagon buying to the serious design of medical and dental tools. When Baker too died suddenly, back again came the novelties and hollowware, silver plated. In 1928, the firm was listed as a manufacturing jeweler until the passing of one Henry Paye in 1952, at which time the company was taken over by the Bishop Company, makers of photo frames. The firm's ABC baby and dog design is the most beautiful stem pattern in the collection (**Figure F17**).

USA Maker (Unidentified)—1900+

Some designs are marked "Made in USA." No manufacturers have been identified for either of the two patterns, but the wording of the stamp helps to determine a starting age of the piece as 1900 (**Figures F18, F19, and F20**). The undersides of both stems hold the alphabet. The cascading flow of the letters is the same on both Peter Rabbit and the dancing toddler, but the distribution is different. The entire alphabet is presented on the rabbit spoon . . . perhaps an indication of its never having had a companion fork. The other set divides the sequence: A through M are found on the spoon, with the remainder of the alphabet on the fork.

Weidlich Sterling Spoon Company—1915

Bridgeport, Connecticut's Weidlich Sterling Spoon Company manufactured sterling flatware and souvenir spoons marked with the Weidlich owl (U.S. Mark Patent 103,304, dated March 30, 1915). In business from 1915, the close of the firm was marked by the sale of the patterns and dies to the Web Silver Company of Philadelphia thirty-seven years later (**Figures F21, F22, F23, and F24**). The "stork spoon" whose bowl advertises the "Helmet Dam in Helmet, California," has been engraved in error—it should have read, the Hemet Dam in Hemet, California. The engraving pictures the Lake Hemet Dam in California's Riverside County, which dams water from the San Jacinto River. Owned by the Lake Hemet Municipal Water District, it was built in 1895.

Unverified Firm

Items from an uncertain maker are found in a boxed set and are clearly marked "Standard." The set is over 75% tin and probably produced by a stamping company . . . the "standard" may be confused for a mark of Victorian coin silver, but an assay proves it an alloy of tin. Because a nonsilver item (see Malabar Plate, **Figure F13**) was made by a silver manufacturing company, "Standard" may also stand for the Standard Manufacturing Company of Winsted, Connecticut; or Standard Silver of Toronto, which merged with International Silver in 1912; or The Standard Silver Ware Company of Boston, Massachusetts, which was last listed in 1921 (**Figure F25**).

The history of flatware extends over an enormous span of time. Resistance, it seems, prolonged the development of the unnatural leap from fingers to forks. Using a utensil is a learned skill, and a difficult one at that . . . watching a toddler clutch a spoon with one hand while he pushes food into its mouth with the other begs the question of real need. It was in the name of civility that those metal wonders were devised to keep phalanges and faces clean while putting industrial designers to work creating vast arrays of patterns to meet every taste and using varieties of metals to meet every budget. Despite a resurgence of finger foods, the use of flatware is still here and here to stay . . . gracing our tables with shining accoutrements that entice our appetites for finesse as well as for food.

G Is for Glass

It's a giant step from the artisans who created a small Egyptian lion's head to the Polish and German glassmakers sent to America's Jamestown to produce glassware for Puritan homes. Sadly, those 18th-century artisans bickered more than they blew, and nothing much remains from the site of their beehive-shaped beginnings. Fortunately, however, more ambitious souls picked up their blowpipes, and by the 1750s, a small industry was producing American-blown glass. Maturing to a crude pressed glass trade, the technology was soon refined; a rapid series of innovative patents was spurred by swiftly growing villages that nestled into the landscape along America's waterways. Small towns grew into cities, and with new homes came the call for mass-produced window glass and kitchenware, along with glass products needed by other growing industries. Emergent factories expanded with ingenious technologies and the investments of competing industrial revolutionaries; the hand craft became a power-driven giant, challenged at times with the issues of modernization and survival.

Before 1820, glass was free-blown. The basic components of glass have not changed over the centuries: sand and alkali such as lime, soda, or potash. They were combined in heavy ceramic pots that sat on shelves within a beehive-shaped brick furnace and heated to melting by a central wood or coal fire. Through openings called "glory holes" a gaffer inserted a hollow tube into one of the clay pots to pick up a gather (or a glob) of molten glass. With strong puffs, the gaffer blew through the blowpipe, transforming the glob into an oval or a spheroid bulb. A punty rod was affixed to the opposite side of the hollow ball, and, while rolling it to keep its desired shape, the gaffer transformed the piece with the help of holding tongs, pucellas, or other tools designed to style the slowly cooling object before it was placed in a lehr, or annealing oven.

Later, two processes were combined when glass was removed for finishing after it had been blown into a patterned mold, which was first a hollowed-out block of wood and, in time, improved with hinges. Molds were later constructed of clay, stone, or metal or, reportedly, even dental plaster of paris.

Crude pressing had been prevalent in English and Dutch manufactories in the late 18th century, which provided nicely weighted vessels for frothy brown ales. Following in their footsteps, John P. Bakewell (then of Bakewell, Page & Bakewell, Pittsburgh) seems to be the first given a patent, in 1825, for a mechanical improvement in the making of glass furniture knobs. His firm, founded in 1808, produced free and mold-blown glass of such high quality that a service was presented to then President James Monroe.

Because the machine could hold only small molds, the early presses made glass items one at a time. With two people at the machine, the first had to gather the molten glass on a punty rod, and his partner, estimating the amount exactly, cut a glob from the gather and let it fall into an open mold. The mold was immediately closed by means of a long lever handle. The plunger then forced the molten glass (also called "metal") into all parts of the design. The trick, of course, was to get just the right amount of glass and just the right pressure on the lever so that the piece was neither underfilled nor overthick, not too filled with bubbles, nor lopsided, nor . . . The hope was that it would not crack before it was set to rest in the annealing oven, where cooling was controlled.

With the use of the brass or iron molds came a change in the chemistry of the molten material. Since soda-based glass was found to be too stiff for molding, lead oxide was substituted for soda in the batch. Called flint glass because the lead had originally been refined from burnt and ground flint stone, the glass proved an excellent medium for pressing (as well as for cutting and engraving).

Soon came the changes that revolutionized the industry. As Welker and Welker tell it,

> In the early days of mechanical pressing the force was transmitted to a plunger by a hand-operated lever as the plunger entered the mold cavity. Later mechanical power was employed to activate the plunger. This is the basic process by which all pressed glass has been made (Welker and Welker, 1985).

Following close behind the first patent for furniture knobs, other early inventions from 1825 to 1829 refined both the mechanics and the products. The names behind the inventions were New England Glass (Cambridge), Stourbridge Flint Glass Works (Pittsburgh), George Dummer and Co. (Jersey City), and the Boston and Sandwich Glass Co. (Sandwich, Massachusetts). Various sources agree that it was Deming Jarves, at his Boston Sandwich factory, whose efforts significantly furthered the industry. It was there, on April 20th of 1827, that Jarves noted the start of cup plate making and the start of tumbler production six weeks earlier.

Two years later, the cap ring, a patterned metal ring that fit around the mold plunger, made its debut. According to Husfloen (1992), when the mold was closed, the ring sealed its edges, ensuring the even distribution of liquid glass at the edge of the piece. The rim of the cup, no longer under- or overfilled, was now a perfect testimonial to this 1829 stroke of genius.

And Deming Jarves again energized the industry with his 1830 patent, which eliminated the need to fuse molded pieces to form a single unit. In 1831, John McGann of Philadelphia was issued a patent for the machine manufacture of a hollow vessel with a neck opening smaller than its interior; the neck and body of the vessel were pressed at the same time, the plungers were removed, and the two parts were fused . . . bottles were born.

While these patents and others were documenting the fast-paced history of pressed glass, many tableware factories were producing the increasingly ornately designed "pinging" tableware. From c.1825 through 1850, the Lacy Glass Period ensued. The Boston and Sandwich Glass Company (later to become Libbey Glass Co.) would soon be one of the most prominent Eastern firms to produce Lacy Glass, while some miles to the west, many, many others were producing pieces that carried the delicate and colorful designs, as well.

Some dainty Lacy Glass molds became casualties of a short-lived economic depression. Designs became less intricate; simpler geometric designs lowered production costs to save many in the industry. On the upside, coal replaced wood as fuel in most factories, and the new pressed pattern glass was manufactured more economically along with bar glasses, produced to meet increasing demands. In 1840 came the bold designs of pressed pattern glass and the start of fire-polishing to improve its surface. In 1841, the first multiple mold for pressing glass was devised by Hiram Dillaway and in 1845, Joseph Magoun was issued one patent for a glass-press that could be easily adjusted to fit molds of varied sizes and designs and another for a mold that left no "marks."

By the late 1840s and early '50s, an exciting variety of items were being produced to accompany basic table settings pressed to look like cut glass. Ensembles of serving objects were included in sets; spoon holders and spill holders, egg cups, decanters, pitchers, nappies, compotes, celery vases, and honey dishes were only part of the entourage. By the 1870s, sets might include nearly seventy unique pieces of one pattern.

From 1840 to 1860, the industry swelled to meet the needs of a rapidly growing economy. Along with the westward trails that cleared the way for quickly gentrifying communities and rapidly refining tastes came the unceasing parade of immigrant workers arriving ready to begin their journeys from America's golden shores. The railroads that pushed toward the Pacific and the extensive river transport system carried the sparkling dinnerware and the glass lamps (along with the furniture to put them on) that furnished the fast-growing American cabins and castles.

The glass industry was invigorated by the 1859 discovery of petroleum and the consequent need for kerosene lamps. And natural gas, a new source of energy found in Pennsylvania, fueled the melting of sand and an ongoing flood of new patents, quickened by industrial genius; ovens were enlarged, cooled plungers no longer stuck to the glass, preheated molds reduced heating time, and . . . much more. In 1860, the government needed money and set a 25% duty on imported glass, which stimulated domestic sales—it was an economic energizer. Frederick McKee and Charles Ballinger from McKee & Brothers of Pittsburgh, Pennsylvania, were issued an 1864 patent for a revolutionary steam-operated press, and that same year, William Leighton, Sr., of the Hobbs, Brockunier and Co. in South

Wheeling, West Virginia, perfected a new formula for glass, ensuring its luster with bicarbonate of soda in place of soda ash. Lighter, less expensive, and no longer incorporating the lead so critical in wartime, William Leighton's glass brought with it an unexpected and unique advantage—workers had to work faster because this new material hardened more quickly.

With the Civil War calming in the late 1860s, tableware could once more assume its importance in daily living. By the 1870s, the start of the late period of pressed glass, the geometric (then waning in popularity), naturalistic, and/or classical designs fed diners in all thirty-nine United States and were soon exported to South America, Europe, and the Far East. The early 1870s were colorless, though milk glass **(Figures G1, G2, and G3)** was popular. (A painted Santa Claus, not shown, has also been found.) By 1875, caramel, custard, and marble glass took center stage while "a mania for color developed" (Welker and Welker, 1985). An 1871 patent carried William O. King's design for the processing of multiple molds in successive rotation. And, says Welker, four years later one Washington Beck, of Pittsburgh, was issued a patent for a pneumatic power-operated press. The Centennial Exhibition of 1876 inspired patriotic offerings **(Figures G4 and G5)**. These two plates, the Emblem Plate (the Eagle) and the Independence Hall Plate, are pictured in Bessie Lindsey's unique *American Historical Glass* (1980) with no mention of their maker. But Lindsey does tell of the creation of the emblem by Thomas Jefferson, Ben Franklin, and John Adams; the Eagle with the shield on its breast, thirteen arrows in its right talon, and the motto "Out of many, one" stands alone to assure its reader that the United States of America relies on its own virtue. And, as seen in Gillinder's ABC 1876 plate series **(Figures G8, G9, and G10)**, relief molding and new techniques using hydrofluoric acid were evidence of a now more sculptured style introduced by the firm's 1876 frosted designs.

In the '80s, geometric designs lost the trendy races in the Midwest; fruits and flowers won the trophies. Designs that could not be produced in cut glass, such as thistles and blossoms, leaves and grapes, and lions and dragons, sat serenely upon tabletops. Soft colors along with strong blues, greens, and rubies returned to all Pittsburgh factories (but Ripley), and cut glass imitations were readily available. Steam-operated presses turned out sculpted bears and birds and designs that showed the influence of Japanese art on the industry. By 1882, natural gas was the fuel of choice, and by 1885, the pattern-glass industry was explosive. According to the Welkers, "Items were produced in astronomical quantities, as 5-10¢ stores sold it, and it appeared on the shelves of every country store. National wholesalers purchased by the carload, and resold by the barrel."

The time was remembered, too, for its commemorative plates. A memorial plate to honor the tragic assassination of 20th President James Garfield **(Figure G17)** was produced; it is interesting to note here that Husfloen (1992), in a list of "Important Patterns of the 1880s," includes a pattern titled "Jumbo" which honors a star attraction of P. T. Barnum's circus. No certain information is given concerning the manufacturer of the design (Aetna or Canton Glass?), but its popularity is proof enough of its celebration of the Greatest Show on Earth, the subject of a mixed-metal plate **(Figure M18)** said to have been produced (or reproduced?) by a Central Stamping Company in 1920. The location of the stamping company remains, as does the maker of the glass, elusive.

By 1885, the increased production stimulated competition, which eventually lowered quality, slashed prices, and sowed the seeds of industrial collapse. Machines in 1886 replaced the need for hand finishers; workers, with the coming of compressed air and, later, electricity, had even less to do. The more technology advanced, the less the labor market required skilled artisans. Costs were lowered, and with the depression of 1893, many factory doors slammed shut. New companies that opened up with the availability of natural gas in Ohio and Indiana closed or relocated by the end of the 1880s with the depletion of that fuel source. Unions became stronger, and to ensure their survival, the first combine or cartel of eighteen glass factories, under a unique superstructure (The United States Glass Company, 1891), allowed the workers to meet union demands with a unified front. Factories that joined the U.S. Glass Co. combine were given a letter of the alphabet. For example, Factory A was originally Adams Glass. Factory B was Bryce, McKee, F was Ripley, K was King, etc. But even joining hands for protection did not guarantee protection against competition. In 1899, a second combine, The National Glass Co. (which included some factories that had left U.S. Glass and other yet independent firms), presented competitive pressures until its closure in 1904. Some of its members (Fenton Art Glass, Imperial Glass, Federal Glass, etc.) continued on successfully; U.S. Glass continued production into the 1960s.

The last chapter of our tale, though a sad close to the era, is set in the happy years of expanding electricity, silent movies, noisy motorcars, and soot-covered trains, all of which needed the glass industry to grow along with them. Despite the depression, the combines allowed for the production of massive amounts of pressed glass (including the newer chocolate glass, the recipe introduced by one Jacob Rosenthal). Older pressed patterns were 1895 giveaways for special purchases, while many were sold to catalogue houses for rapid dispersal. Exquisite patterns of cut glass found favor, and for those who couldn't afford to set Libbey Glass' brilliant designs atop their mission oak tables, new lines of "imitation cut" were there for the asking. Competition was fierce, and lookalike designs jumped from one manufacturer to another. Art glass was becoming an industry of its own. In 1898, Victorians, who hated empty spaces, had plenty of colorful "whimseys" to fill their shallow shelves.

In a giant effort to distract customers from suddenly appealing china, vast arrays of novelty items appeared: bonbon dishes, rose bowls, footed jelly compotes, spoon trays, and cigar, pomade, and cracker jars begged for attention along with ice-cream sets (see the ABC ice-cream set platter and dish, **Figure G38**). Added to the menagerie was the 1907 introduction of Fenton's carnival glass, which sparkled in spite of its resting places in dreary, dust-layered Victorian parlors. Reheating after a spraying of metallic salts on freshly pressed forms brought an iridescent shine of glowing purples, greens, blues, and, most commonly, a clear golden "Marigold" orange. From a Marigold bowl shines a radiant stork surrounded by the alphabet, a deep dish **(Figure G11)** that was made, like all carnival glass, to imitate the very expensive glass developed by Louis Comfort Tiffany. Carnival glass has, in fact, been known as the "poor man's Tiffany."

By 1915, imitation cut glass was no longer offered, and the simpler patterns recalling Colonial times were popular; Fostoria began the American pattern, which lasted longer than any other pressed tableware. The Fenton Art Glass, Imperial and Federal Glass Companies were established in the 1920s and remained successful for many years. Many older patterns were reintroduced, and very popular were the historically important moments fixed for all time in glass trays . . . some bread platters continue giving thanks for the daily bread now fresh from the supermarket. Still, nonautomatic factories continued such novelty items, although, by the 1920s, the bulk of the manufacturers had turned their interests, with Prohibition's severe reduction in calls for bar service, to the needs of rapidly expanding technologies. The fast-growing field of motion pictures and advances in the automobile and rail industries provided new directions for glass production.

The early history of the glass factories, their innovative geniuses, their products, their fluctuating economics, the expansion of their markets, and the tides of tastes and turmoil constitute an authentic history of the Industrial Revolution, as glassmaking is our country's oldest industry. There are volumes devoted to the development of factories, the most complete of which is John and Elizabeth Welker's *Pressed Glass in America* (1985). With their help it is appropriate to conclude this "highlight summary" with thumbnail accounts of the industries that produced ABC ware, ordered here by the year of their founding. (The reader is urged to view notable omissions from this collection in Lechler's *Toy Glass*, 1989, pages 159 and 161-163.)

Adams and Company—1851

Founded in 1851 by John Adams and Mr. Macklin, the Adams, Macklin & Company gave way to Adams and Company when Macklin left the firm. In 1882, the plant, on other property, began the manufacture of lamps and planned a unifying move to a newly constructed facility, but the plan was never realized. The firm did, however, build a new plant with new partners after the partnership of Adams and Co. was dissolved in 1883. In 1886 (or 1887?) J. A. died, and, about five years later, the plant became U.S. Glass Company's Factory A. The factory had established a large export trade, producing both fine tableware and lamps. Two items from the collection are attributed with certainty to Adams and Company: the very rare ABC mug **(Figure G6)** and the amber plate with 1000 Eyes **(Figure G7)**, one of a dinner-set with a large range of items. The letters are visible on the face of the mug.

Gillinder and Sons—1861

The Gillinder and Sons factory, famous in glass history for its origination of the frosted glass process in 1875, was the largest glass factory in America in 1879. The company began as Franklin Flint Glass Works in 1861. Founded by William Thynne Gillinder in Philadelphia, Pennsylvania, the firm began production of pressed glass in 1863, when it was renamed Gillinder and Bennett. Bennett left to start a new pottery in Baltimore, and the company, under the leadership of Gillinder and his two sons, James A. and Frederick R. (1867), became a landmark in the history of commercial glass as Gillinder and Sons. William Thynne died in 1871, and James A., as president, moved the pressed glass division (1888) to Greensburg, Pennsylvania, employing the natural gas resources; Lechler dates the ABC plate in the 1880s, probably at this location. After purchasing molds from the bankrupt Belmont Glass Company, the pressed glass division joined U.S. Glass as Factory G with an 1891 agreement that pressed tableware was never to be produced again. The ABC plates **(Figures G8, G9, and G10)** are fine examples of the frosted technique that made Gillinder glass so famous.

Belmont Glass—1861 (1866 in some sources)

The Standard Encyclopedia of Carnival Glass, by Edwards and Carwile, Edition 7 (2000), identifies Belmont Glass as the maker of the ABC carnival glass gem. Stippled and embossed numbers encircle the flying stork on the floor of the plate. Straw lines are prominent, and the plate glistens in hues of marigolds and ambers; Edwards, in his text, wonders if the item, made in crystal, pink, green, frosted green, and the amber pictured here, may have gone to U.S. Glass for the "Carnival-effect finishing." Conflicting sources say that Belmont was founded in either 1861 or 1866 in Bellaire, Ohio, as Barnes, Faupel and Company. Regardless of its start, a second furnace was added in 1872, and the flourishing plant now employed 125 employees. About 1885, colored glass was introduced, but in spite of many changes in leadership, the firm's success dimmed, and by 1890 the factory's molds were sold to the Crystal Glass Company of Bridgeport, Ohio, and the Central Glass Company of Wheeling, West Virginia. The stack, dynamited in October of 1892, ensured Belmont's demise. The heavy carnival glass piece **(Figure G11)**, reportedly one of a set of two, was produced sometime between 1885 and 1889.

Ripley and Company—1865

The history of Ripley and Company begins in October of 1865 with a group who purchased property from the Ihmsens, a long-established glass family; they called the Pittsburgh property the Tremont Glass Works. Through changes of shareholders and the death of Daniel C. Ripley, Sr., Daniel Jr. inherited a share of the establishment and he joined with a new partner (John Stevenson) to build a new Ripley and Company in 1875. This became the very last of the major Pittsburgh factories to include colored glass in its catalogues. Following the industry's trend, the company became Factory F of the U.S. Glass Company in 1891; Daniel C. Ripley became the first president of U.S. Glass. (It was here that the Roman Key-edged clock plate, **Figure G12**, was manufactured.) Ralph Baggeley succeeded Ripley in 1893 but resigned after his attempt to restructure the firm in the name of economy. Back again came Ripley in 1895, but he resigned in 1909, determined to form a new Ripley and Company in Connellsville, Pennsylvania.

The three Ripley Glass ABC plates, as seen in **Figures G13 through G17**, are dated by Doris Lechler (1989) at somewhere between 1880 and 1890. But there is some disagreement as to the maker of **Figure G17**, the President Garfield memorial. According to Edwards and Carwile (2000), the plate was made by Campbell, Jones and Company, makers of many commemoratives, to memorialize Garfield's assassination. That Pittsburgh-based firm was founded in the 1860s, making plates bearing messages in Spanish for the South American market.

King Glass Company—1869

A seriously fragmented cover begins the catalogue, dated 1890-1891 (Microfiche T-434, card 1 of 4, Library of Congress), which shows two plates: The Hen and Chicks, without its frosted variant; and the Sitting Dog, a 4-inch Toy 1,2,3 plate **(Figures G18 and G19)**. There are rope-edged versions of **Figures G20,** G21, and G22 not seen on card 4 of the microfiche photo; the floor graphics are reversed on the drawings.

It was King, Son & Company that gave birth to these items. Amid conflicting and complex reports of its 1869 start, it is clear that David King died in 1875 and that, four years later, a fire destroyed the plant. It was immediately rebuilt. In 1884, a second fire destroyed the company, and that same year the partnership was dissolved and reorganized as King, Son & Company, Ltd. In 1885, the rebuilt factory was operational. Three years later the partnership was again dissolved and reorganized as King Glass Company. The same year, McKee and Brothers was acquired, but growth was short-lived; the last ad for King Glass was seen in March of 1891. The United States Glass Company took over as Factory K. Son William King had been the inventive one, and many patents on glassmaking machinery remain as his legacy.

Crystal Glass Company—1869

An article in the *Glass Collector's Digest* (Vol. 1, No. 4., Dec./Jan. 1988, pp. 48-51), by author and collector Joyce Johnston, displays the special offerings of Pittsburgh's Crystal Glass Company for the Christmas season of 1879. Johnston quotes a visiting reporter to the sales room and the *American Pottery and Glassware Reporter* dated Thursday, December 11, 1879, as saying,

> Among new things offered for the holiday trade are some very handsome goods now being made by the Crystal Glass Company, Southside. These consist of . . . four patterns of ABC plates for children, etched bottoms, one bearing the figure of a lion, another of a stork, a third of a rabbit running, and the fourth with a rabbit at rest . . . . The . . . children's plates . . . are the prettiest things of the kind we have seen, and ought to sell well.

The entire set is not included here **(Figures G23 and G24)**. An additional stork, one with a raised leg, and a purple-red glass duck (or dove in some texts) was evidently produced after the 1879 season **(Figures G25 and G26)**. That second stork, found by Sandra Wassa in Southbury, Connecticut, is assumed to be one of the collection because of its size, design, style, and technique; the item has not been seen or mentioned in texts found thus far.

The Crystal Glass Company began when the Birmingham Pottery, which had been in business since 1848, sold its premises to Crystal Glass in 1869. In business until 1884, King, Son and Company, a victim of fire, leased the premises as Crystal was getting rid of its inventory. The firm faded about 1887. Though a leader in the making of early jelly glasses and tableware, the company advertised little. Glass histories advertise more prominently for the firm today; its glass plates are featured in several volumes of children's tableware.

Bryce, Higbee & Co. / J. B. Higbee Glass Company / New Martinsville Glass Manufacturing Company—1879

The stories of the three plates shown on the page of the New Martinsville catalogue **(Figures G27 and G28)** are included with the permission of the Library of Congress from the microfiche records of trade catalogues of the Corning Museum of Glass. They begin with the tale of Bryce Higbee and Company, whose closing led to the opening of the J. B. Higbee Glass

Company and its ties to the Martinsville Glass Company and Viking Glass; the plates trail through them all. The histories of the companies have been thoroughly researched by Wayne and Lola Higby, authors of *Bryce, Higby and J. B. Higby Glass* (The Glass Press, 1998). Their text is a study of the Higbees (Higbys) and their family's remarkable place in the history of American pressed glass.

The Bryce, Higbee and Company (also called the Homestead Glass Works) was founded in 1879 on the southeast side of Pittsburgh in Homestead, Pennsylvania. Its first advertisements boasted the employment of one hundred men, a sizable workforce to produce the new lines of clear, amber, and blue tableware, which were displayed at the 1881 Glass Show. Many novelties and vast quantities of dish sets were offered by Montgomery Ward's and Butler Brothers' catalogues.

In August of 1888, cofounder John P. Bryce died; John B. Higbee and Charles K. Bryce were to continue the leadership of the firm. In spite of some workers' discontent, the factory was busy with successful older issues and new patterns. An 1899 edition of imitation cut glass announced the coming century with the new Paris 1900 pattern, a set of 125 pieces. The set included oil cruets, individual egg holders, tiers, berries, and salvers, along with several sizes of vases.

The year 1904 brought the resignation of Charles K. Bryce, superintendent of the factory, among accusations of scandal. Charles was declared "incompetent," but it was the death of J. B. Higbee in December of 1906 and the devastating fire and the flood of the Monongahela River that laid the company to rest for all time. Ollie Higbee assumed responsibility of the firm, which was, amid suits and squabbles, sold to Carnegie Steel in 1908. Whatever could be carried off from the abandoned site (molds, machinery, and equipment) was sold back to the J. B. Higbee Glass Company by Carnegie for $8,500.

J. B. Higbee Glass Company was founded by Oliver "Ollie" Higbee and R. G. West in June 1907 in Bridgeville, Pennsylvania. Since plans had been made for the new venture before J. B. died, the firm was named in his honor. The plant was in operation by October 1907, making colorless pressed glass. With most items bearing the identifying design (a bee with an H on the left wing, an I on the abdomen, and a G on the right wing), business boomed with 100-piece patterns for sale. In 1911 and 1912, seven patents were issued to Ollie for a vacuum bottle, which, after demonstrations of its amazing feats at the Pittsburgh 1912 Exposition, sold by the thousands. The last of twenty-eight new patterns (ABC plates included) continued until, in February of 1918, the doors mysteriously closed. With rumors that Ollie, who died soon after, had robbed the piggy bank, the half-acre plant was sold to General Electric for $90,000. As had occurred in so many other glass plants, its products had changed from tableware to lighting paraphernalia.

The New Martinsville Glass Manufacturing Company in New Martinsville, West Virginia, opened in 1900. Rebuilt after a 1901 fire, a 1907 flood and fire, and a third fire caused by lightning, the bar glass factory made tea, lemonade, and berry sets, along with lamps and novelties. Ira Clark of the then-bankrupt J. B. Higbee Glass Company took the position of manager about 1918. The enterprise was lively until the Depression and Clark's sudden death. The firm was declared bankrupt in 1937, and the factory went into receivership. A year later, a group from Connecticut restarted the company, calling themselves The New

Martinsville Glass Company. They continued until 1944, when one member of the team purchased all of the stock and renamed the firm Viking Glass. Viking closed its doors in 1986, only to be reincarnated as Dalzell-Viking.

Is "Emma" (or "Emmas" or "Boy") a girl or a boy **(Figure G29)**? Is it named after both the wife and daughter of Charles K. Bryce (foreman of the mold department of Bryce, Higbee & Company)? Why was it originally called "Boy" and looked more like a girl? Minnie Watson Kamm, in her *Eighth Pattern Glass Book*, shows "Emmas" on a page from an 1880s Bryce, Higbee & Company catalogue; it was made then in clear, blue, and amber. It also appeared in an 1893 Butler Brothers catalogue for 75¢ a dozen or, in singles, for 10¢ each. J. B. Higbee named it "Boy" and continued its production in 1907 in clear glass only. The Higbee "bee" was incorporated into the design **(Figure G30)**, which was removed by New Martinsville Glass before the firm reproduced the plate from c.1921 to c.1928. (Since then, Clay Crystal Works has reproduced an 8-inch edition in bright colors with the child's head in satin finish.)

On the reproduced picture of "Emmas" in the New Martinsville catalogue, the alphabet surrounding "Emmas" begins with A at about 12:30. Also "Emma's" head is placed to the right of the floor center. On this plate, with head centered, A begins at 6:30. On page 174 of Lola and Wayne Higby's (1998) *Bryce, Higbee and J. B. Higbee Glass*, the alphabet begins at 12:00 over Emma's head.

The Dog ABC Plate was named "Rovers" in a Bryce, Higbee catalogue from the mid-1800s. The 6.5-inch plate appeared in an 1893 Butler Brothers catalogue for 75¢ a dozen in clear, blue, and amber. (Please see the plate on the catalogue page.) Featured in the J. B. Higbee General Catalogue as "The Dog ABC Plate," the 1907 edition was made with a smooth-headed dog in clear glass adorned with the trademark bee in its jowls **(Figure G31)**. New Martinsville Glass removed the bee and sold it as a 6.25-inch item. One edition of the plate displays SI letters between the letters T and U; undoubtedly the plate was reproduced for the Smithsonian Institution with the dog's head textured in a pebbled effect **(Figure G32)**.

"The Plain Star" **(Figures G33 and G34)** was found, like the "Emmas" and "Rovers" plates, in a Bryce, Higbee catalogue from the mid-1800s and in an 1893 Butler Brothers catalogue for 75¢ a dozen in clear, amber, and blue. Also featured in the 1907-1917 J. B. Higbee General Catalogue, the 6.25-inch plate with its sometimes beaded and scalloped border was made in clear glass with the signature bee. In the early and mid-1920s, New Martinsville produced the plate in a greenish-yellow with an "M" aside the "bee" **(Figure G35)**. A black light reveals the "Vaseline"-colored glass to be just that . . . the glass that glows vibrantly in the dark with the addition of uranium before it was known to be lethal **(Figure G36)**. Though no Higby molds were supposedly used by the Viking Glass Company, it did make the Plain Star ABC Plate in 1944 and again in 1983 in tinted amethyst with the V for Viking placed aside the Higbee trademark bee. A plate marked in this manner is owned by the Wayne Higbys of Ventura, California.

Hazel-Atlas Glass Co.—1885

A firm, founded by Charles Brady and C. H. Tallman in Wellsburg, West Virginia, had only one tank, and that, used for opal glass, produced the liners of Mason fruit jars in 1885. One year later, after a move to Washington, Pennsylvania, the firm was renamed Hazel Glass Co. because the furnace, following the industry's tradition of naming its furnaces for curvaceous females, had been christened Hazel. The year 1894 saw the development and installation of the Blue Machine, which made the production of wide-mouthed jars a semiautomatic process. Jars and bottles were no longer hand blown, and the design by one Charles E. Blue of Wheeling, West Virginia, became a commercially sound procedure. Two years later, the Atlas Glass Company was founded, a firm solely devoted to the making of glass containers, at Washington, Pennsylvania. But its singleness of purpose was short-lived. With a string of mergers, Hazel Glass, Atlas Glass, Republic Glass, Wheeling Hinge Co., and Wheeling Metal Co. combined to become, in 1902, the Hazel-Atlas Glass Company. Along with bottles and jars, the firm produced metal lids and pressed tableware. By 1930, Hazel-Atlas had thirteen plants producing much of the Depression glass. In 1956, the tables turned; Hazel-Atlas was absorbed by the Continental Can Company, which sold out to Brockway Glass in 1964.

The pristine ABC ware **(Figure G37)** clearly marked Hazel-Atlas is unique and contemporary. The 1934 catalogue #35 (Wheeling, West Virginia) named the white ware "Platonite." To quote,

> Platonite is the name we have given to this line of new hard-bodied, smooth white tableware, designed to meet the demands of the most fastidious hostess. Platonite is slightly translucent—a quality formerly found only in very expensive tableware. Yet in spite of its grace and delicacy Platonite will withstand more than ordinary usage. In the artistic new Moderntone design Platonite Ware has met with an especially hearty reception from everyone.

In spite of the parallels to the enduring truths of its namesake, that ABC ware is rarely found today, and when it is, the print is usually smudged and peeling.

Federal Glass Company—1900

Lechler (1985) lists the Federal Glass Company, Columbus, Ohio, as the creator of the charming clear toy ice-cream set. Founded in 1900, the company produced bottles for the first five years of its history. Pressed glass was added to the line in 1906, just at the time when berry and ice-cream sets became popular. Packers' jars and tumblers were produced before the company's momentous 1916 development of the Tucker-Reeves-Beatty "gob feeder," a device that fed uniform measures of molten glass into the hungry pressing machines. In 1925, the majority of the production line was tableware; packers' jars were no longer made. In 1958, the 55-acre plant became a division of Federal Paper Board Co. Inc. and operated at full tilt until its closing in 1980. The ice-cream set **(Figure G38)**, c.1906, included a central oval platter, with its non-ABC

leafy patterned border, along with six small, round ABC dishes. The pattern was also named "Wabash" and is dated 1914.

No less beautiful than the others, the remainder of the glass plates **(Figures G39 to G45)** are orphans as there are no identifiable sources of their production. There are, however, identifiable sources of their designs researched by Carl G. Liungman and published in his *Dictionary of Symbols* (1991).

Figures G40 and G41 show repeated opposing wave designs that stand for Aquarius, the zodiac sign representing the period between the 21st of January and the 18th of February. Despite their look of water, the waves are an air sign and the circles between their rises represent the point of watching that rain from a place (or station) on the planet. Somehow the drops fall close to but never upon the watcher.

Figure G42 presents a repetitive design of impressed pyramid shapes on its reverse. As one looks down through the face, the design appears as an "eye of the dragon," a combination of a triangle, which stands for danger, and an inset Y, which represents the choice between good and evil.

The next plate design, **Figure G43**, is formed by repetitions of the hexagram, the ancient symbol of the Jewish kingdom or the Shield of David. During the Middle Ages, it was a general symbol of alchemy; as a combination of the sign of fire (upward pointing triangle) and water (downward pointing triangle), it also meant "fire water" or alcohol. With or without "spirits," the six-pointed star also stood for the command, DRINK!

Figure G44 is called the "Eight Pointed Star," though it appears made of diamond-shaped petals joined at the center. Once a mythological symbol for the Roman goddess of beauty, the shape was also used to signify the planet Venus when it appeared in the east, just before sunrise, as the "Morning Star," or when it was seen in the west, shortly after sunset, as the "Evening Star."

The last of the series, "Christmas Eve" **(Figure G45)**, has been provided by Ralph and Irene Lindsay of New Holland, Pennsylvania. The photo has been computer enhanced to complete its shape. A partner to the plate is titled "Christmas Morn" and can be seen on Page 161 of Lechler's *Toy Glass* (1989).

Painted drinking glasses are rare, indeed. **Figure G46**, a 12-ounce tumbler, was purchased for pennies in a cluttered Vancouver antique shop. The others pictured **(Figure G48)** are members of a series shown on page 82 of *Collectible Drinking Glasses* by Mark Chase and Michael Kelly (1996). They are marked, as are the products pictured in **Figure G37**, as products of Hazel-Atlas **(Figure G47)**.

The history of glass in the United States parallels the growth of its industry. Bessie Lindsey's book, *American Historical Glass*, ties all manner of glass designs to the human history that inspired them. It is intriguing reading and accomplishes the task that this collection of ABC glass could only begin.

H Is for Hollowware

Originally designed with wide-eyed faces, they quietly watched their diners sup and slobber. Gentrified, those handcrafted "mugs," or "cans" as Godden calls them, were replaced by transfer-designed vessels. Designed to instruct, monochrome or overpainted engravings presented alphabet letters and illustrations that prompted their diner to say the letter sound and to identify one or more objects that began with it. This brightly illustrated hollowware also reinforced values and virtues, prompted the re-reciting of nursery rhymes, encouraged "table talk," and authenticated tasteful design while providing serviceable tableware hardly scaled for small hands (see Appendix AH1). And those small hands had, most often, to rotate the mug in order to see-and-say it all, which is what our photographs attempt to do. With three images and computer technology, we have attempted to rotate every vessel.

Mugs in this chapter are presented, first, in alphabetical order by identified manufacturers. The durations of each firm's activity gives some indication of the item's age. But because so few of the collection carry potters' marks, it is helpful to note that mugs decorated with a single transfer were probably made before 1830; later mugs usually carried two. The placement of those designs may be a clue to age as well; centering was given more attention before the half-century. With an expanded market, quantity won over quality.

Some certainty in judging age may be achieved by the coordination of a mug with a matching plate that has been dated. It is not always accurate, however, as similar transfers were used by many firms, both in the United States and abroad. Just as fragile are attempts to date transferred ceramics by corroborating the potter's years with the dates of printed matching graphics, as so few of the era's books were dated. It is often impossible to determine, with certainty, if the printing preceded the potter.

So many of these designs were "lifted" from printed sources (see "T Is for Transfers and Toybooks"). Interesting are the variations from the published engravings to their applications on alphabet mugs. Subtle changes in shadows and line backgrounds, differences in cloud formations, modifications of scale or complete simplifications are indicative of engravers' efforts to skirt copyright obligations. Good examples of "simplifications" are found when comparing **Figures H27, H31, and H33** with others in the series. These graphics coordinate with those found in the alphabet set originally published, undated, as the *Child's Treasury of Knowledge* by Wier & White of Boston. They are presented here, with publisher's permission, from their reprint in Ruth Baldwin's *100 Nineteenth-Century Rhyming Al-*

phabets in English (**Figures H15 through H48**).

Most of the time the letter and its picture are an obvious set, but focus letters and their illustrations are sometimes mismatched. The comparison of the "E" on **Figure H57** with the "E" on **Figure H58** provides an excellent example of transfer error. Perhaps they were the last transfers remaining at the end of the day. More likely, the transfer placer could not read.

A second type of error, a letter placement clearly out of sequence, can be seen in **Figure H60**. Like **Figures H57 and H58**, they were originally published in the *Alphabet of Virtues* (London: Darton & Co., June 20, 1856) and are reprinted here with the permission of the Lilly Library of the University of Indiana, Bloomington. Other examples of sequential errors are seen in **Figures H32, H34, H111, and H112.**

In some instances, a prominent alphabet letter may seem to have little to do with its image until the original text is located. Illustrations, like these two editions of "C for Charity" **(Figures H53 and H54)**, prove this need for validation. Other titles may be assigned to the graphic until the authentic narration proves its connection.

A scrutiny of the "E" mugs **(Figures H57 and H60)** reveals another discriminating factor as well . . . they are different in shape. Frustrating the set collector are coordinating engravings that appear on mugs of different structures, sizes, and handle designs. Additional variants appear when differently colored line border(s) are found at the tops or bases of those venerable lookalikes.

An additional factor in mug design is letter style. The format of the large capital may signify a member of a particular set. An excellent example of contrasting styles is pictured here, also from the *Alphabet of Virtues* (**Figures H62 and H63**). At least two sets are represented in this one alphabet sequence.

A third alphabet set of major importance includes mugs decorated with three letters and a scene, within which a set of matches is to be found. Perhaps manufactured by the same pottery that produced their four matching plates (see "S Is for Sets"), they represent a step further on the road to good reading. These designs offer multiple opportunities to find three symbol-sound agreements, making the process one of logical selection rather than one of simple identification **(Figures H94 to H103)**.

Two graphics from the alphabet seen in Baldwin's book (and from that same series published in the *Object Lesson ABC* [Chicago: Donohue. n.d.]) are not represented in this collection: the transfers for the letters M and O are pictured, however, for reference. Every letter of the *Alphabet of Virtues* is represented. The series that pictures three letters at the rim of each mug is complete but for the first in the set, A B C. In that series particularly, varieties of illustrations provide somewhat difficult opportunities to not only match graphics to beginning sounds (as is the match of "wicket" to the VWX mug, **Figure H102**), but to conjure up a verb, such as "pull" for the girl with her wagon, pictured on **Figure H100.**

On Brownhill items, with nonspecific phonetic emphasis, alphabets were placed as running background designs **(Figures H4 through H13)** and were manufactured to match or coordinate with luncheon plates, though now they are almost never sold as "sets." On mugs made by other manufacturers, single letters that decorate the face of the vessel are easy to see and sing with. Harder to follow are letters found along the inside of the rim **(Figure H127)**, and the most difficult of all to read are letters on **Figures H106 and H126**, which are faintly cast around the outer edge.

The remainder of the collection includes items gathered from many sets and some mugs made as "singles." German issues are found at the conclusion of the chapter, though they are not the least cherished of the treasures. Two of these show alphabets cast upon the face of the mugs **(Figures H135 and H136)** while the incomplete alphabet of gold letters decorates the outer rim of **Figure H137**. On snow-white, egg-shaped German cups, the alphabet letters are often molded and overpainted in smooth, shiny gold. Decals are the "ornaments" and typically picture chickens, animals, or toys. German-made cups are easily found today with their lustre-saucers, and complete arrays can be assembled with little searching; Lindsay and Lindsay (1998) include several pictures of fairly complete German lustre sets in their text. Matching (or harmonizing) pitchers can be acquired, with and without added lustres.

Sometimes the alphabet on cups, plates, or saucers has been designed to be divided. The alphabet will begin on the cup and conclude on its mate. Two such examples are the plate **(Figure O16)** and the tiny cup **(Figure O17)**, both pictured in "O Is for Ornamental Borders." The search for their "other halves" continues.

Loop and spurred loop handles **(Figures H126 and H130)** helped tiny hands to hold the mugs close. A few drinking vessels carried ear-shaped **(Figure H128)** or flat-topped, ear-shaped holds that provided even firmer grips **(Figures H27, H37, and H41)**. Most ends of handles, as they attached to their vessels, were undecorated, while other *terminals* were shaped like leaves **(Figures H57, H87, H94, H95, H99, H100, etc.)**. The vast majority were not painted; some bore dainty sections of transfers **(Figure H128)**. Most vessels were simple cylinders that small hands could clutch, but their weight, when filled, made them vulnerable. Some were slightly oval, purposefully or through a production error. Other vessels were tapered or designed with "bracelets" at their bases for added support. And, of course, some were large and some were small. Because they fracture easily at their delicate handles and their thinned rims, they are less available for purchase than plates, and most remaining items carry chips, cracks, and/or injured or missing handles. Damage does reduce their value but does not, in any way, diminish their charm.

Both German and English mugs and cups are included in chapters other than this: "C Is for Commercialism," "K Is for Kitsch," "L Is for Lustreware," "M Is for Metals," "S Is for Sets," and "V Is for Variations on a Theme." A rarely found French-made lustred cup and saucer can be seen in "O Is for Ornamental Borders" as well.

The pictures in this chapter include those lent from the private collection of Ann and Dennis Berard, as noted in the caption of each item. The Berards of New Hampshire have assumed this century's task of reassembling the lettered sets. We wish them well.

(Footnote: Most mugs are valued at $250+. Seldom are they offered, on either coast, for less. It is often thought that a mug with one transfer should be less valued than one with two; actually, the single transfer may indicate an older item. And unpainted transfers usually do command less. Of course, damage will lower the value. The prices listed are appropriate when the vessel's condition is good. Some sets are more rare or some manufacturers more coveted, making their mugs more worthy. Scenes that describe royalty, railroads, baseball, etc. may be priced over the suggested worth given at plate sites. The more special the item, the more spectacular the asking price.)

I Is for Infant to Infirm

Seven chapters ahead, "P Is for Potters and Their Potteries" tends to the plight of the desperately poor youngsters who were put to work, often to be put to death, so much before their time. But with or without work, death was the reality . . . about one third of all conceptions aborted in the months before delivery, and about the same number died between birth and the fifth year. Statistics are few and data may be flawed; suffice it to say that the "burying club" dues, at a penny a week to avoid the pauper's grave, was some proof of an accepted inevitability. Deaths in poorer neighborhoods were extremely high, and death insurance offered financial benefits to poor, mourning parents. When the deaths of children enrolled in insurance clubs doubled, reformers accused uninformed mothers of neglect.

But prenatal care was unavailable to low-income mothers-to-be, most of whom continued at their strenuous employments through their pregnancies. Unbalanced diets lowered resistance to disease; low-income mothers were more likely to bear children from a pelvis deformed by rickets. Poor nutrition produced children of low birth weight whose hunger was satisfied by unrefrigerated milk, which brought diarrhea. Tuberculosis was rampant; diseases that spread in epidemic proportions through crowded communities (as was typhus, carried by body lice) devastated the lower classes but were not confined to them. Prince Albert died of typhoid in 1861, and cholera was everywhere that the residues of rotting garbage and infested manure piles seeped into the water supply.

Sally Mitchell, in her *Daily Life in Victorian England* (1996), tells of reformers who claimed that "maternal feelings were so blunted that (mothers) drugged their infants" to death; the white poppy eased every infant's pain. The best of all physicians had little else to prescribe. Well-meaning apothecary Ambroise Hackwitz popularized his Godfrey's Cordial to soothe, with a "composing bottle," all those complaining children into eternal complacency. It was a boon to ladies hired for child care . . . large groups under their watchful eyes were dead quiet. Perhaps those complaining cries were hunger pangs that sugar water and crumbled bread did not satisfy. Death by diet was ill-understood, and the watery mixture might well have been lethally contaminated by migrating rats, unsavory sewage, and industrial wastes. Gloomier still were deaths brought by diseases contracted from the long-departed bodies that continued their squalid, earthly residence until funds could finance their final resting places. Many took formal photos of the deceased in frilly smocks; some charged a coin or two to view them.

The black clothes worn to respect a "passing" made not only for black couture but for the creative design of black-stoned jewelry, paintings of the mourners sobbing against sculpted headstones, and treasured artifacts made of the deceased's hair, so avidly collected today.

In this chapter, we will attend to the developmental steps of the child who is lucky enough to survive . . . one who is pictured on most transfers in classic Victorian dress consumed with the glorious days of childhood. Through transfers in this chapter and others, the life cycle of the Victorian can be seen from infant to infirm.

Children with sparkling eyes and rosy cheeks perpetuated the image of perfect progeny flourishing in the most bountiful and serene of homes . . . a promise of better things to come began with a snug, ideal childhood. Few homes matched the reality, but the dream lingered on **(Figures I1 and I2)**.

Living more like their good Queen Victoria, middle-class mothers who did not leave the home to work maintained a constant focus on their children. Middle-class families depended entirely upon Pa-pa's income. The boys were given enough education and experience to follow in their father's footsteps, but girls were not yet encouraged to join the workforce (see "E Is for Education"). If young ladies were needed elsewhere or if nearby rural areas did not provide age-appropriate bachelors, they might leave to reside with other family members, providing elder or child care or assisting with the education of little ones. Well-to-do middle- and upper-class families were larger, with plenty of food and more controlled sanitation. But they were quick to learn that education was expensive, and new methods of birth control preserved the profits. By 1900, the laboring classes had twice the number of children as those of the middle-class professionals.

It was Pa-pa's authority that was final, while mother ran the home morally and practically **(Figures I3, I4, I5, and I6)**. "Children, obey your parents in the Lord," charged St. Paul's text. "Obedience was one of the first of many duties expected of a child by parents, and it was a virtue highly prized throughout society by those who considered they had a right to demand it" (Reader, 1973).

But the death of a parent was not uncommon, and single parents were hard-pressed to make ends meet. Children were often split among the families of relatives and friends. Whole families moved in with others, second and third marriages twisted the boughs of family trees, and, as a last resort, the poorhouse door was always open.

In working-class families, a six-year-old might have charge of a very young sibling, a popular excuse for being absent from school. In very secure homes, children were first cared for by "monthly nurses" and then by a nurse, with or without a cadre of under-nurses who washed and scrubbed and swept and ate and slept in the nursery, who was ever watchful of her charges **(Figure I7)**. When caring for their children nurses were the parents as well, toddling after them or tying them to their aprons. Mothers and grandmothers spent only a few precious hours with their youngsters, reading aloud and teaching through games, finger songs, and simple rhymes **(Figures I8, I9, and I10)**. Volumes such as Friedrich Fröbel's *Mother's Songs, Games and Stories* (William Rice, London, 1890) still provide minutely detailed instruction for infant teaching. The work is a masterpiece, accompanied by sign language, songs, and piano scores intended to fully educate both parents and children by *doing* rather than just listening or reading. The volume begins with separate introductions to cottage mothers, rich mothers, unmarried women, religious people, the materialists, and academic minds; Friedrich Fröbel's teachings could energize all. Curiously, the text does not directly address nannies, whose task, as viewed by parents, was the effective separation of their children from the mainstream of a "sordid society." Fröbel's aim was the integration of the child into the family . . . being taught by all adults without Godfrey's Cordial and without the opiate of many moralistic books, which, he felt, would only prompt the youngster to talk of duty and never do it.

The teaching of personal responsibility and diligence to the work ethic was the job of the nanny, and the work of the child was play. Books in library archives show a great deal of evidence that water-painting the black and white pictures in beautifully bound volumes was an elegant pastime. Dolls were dear **(Figures T52 and T53)**, puppets became skillfully operated, horse-headed sticks and rocking horses were nursery furniture. Symbols of reality were the stamped tin toys that furnished the doll houses as were the tin and glass tea and ice-cream sets **(Figures M79, M80, and M82 through M93, and Figure G38)** that recreated formal tea parties at small wicker tables. Building model ships and stacking taught the rudiments of construction **(Figures I11 and I12)** while clangorous noises and comparable weights developed discrimination skills **(Figures I13 and I14)**. Wagons and carts became popular toward the end of the century . . . often homemade, their lives were quickly ended **(Figures I15 and I16)**. Girls were always busy with needlecraft, but no plates exist in this collection to honor the craft.

As the techniques of stitchery were passed from one generation to the next, so were the rules of games passed on from child to child as schooling began. As maturing years signaled life changes, games reflected the benchmarks. There were divination games, harvest games, sport games with animals, trade and occupation games **(Figures I17 and I18)**, military games **(Figures I19 and I20)**, courtship **(Figure I21)** and lovemaking games (see "K Is for Kitsch"), marriage games, funeral games, and so forth. As in real life, games brought chances to develop self-esteem through winning, acceptance of loss as an unavoidable part of life, consequences for breaking the rules, gains and losses of material wealth, opportunities to risk inventive strategies, the experience of being both empowered and shunned, and, in the dramatic games, they gave the pretenders a chance to recreate their observed reality.

In **Figures I22, I23, and I24**, the youngster happily identifies with the actions of her father; the smallest details of an elder's behavior are quickly observed through the dramatic play of six- to eight-year-olds, who love to dress-up in costumes, put on messy makeup, make all their world "their stage," and command the complete attention of every available adult. The boots our "star" is wearing are her papa's boots, the chair in which she is sitting is her grandmother's chair, and the hat, being placed upon her head, is that which is worn by her grandpa. She is the typical eight-year-old, beginning to penetrate deeply into the world of the adult, looking a bit more mature and beginning to detach. (There are, in others' collections, several other plates of this series that reinforce the importance of dramatic play.)

At age five, children of the upper class spent the mornings in the schoolroom **(Figures I25 and I26)** with their governesses until the boys went to boarding school and left the girls at home to enjoy a more secluded education. Even newspapers were guarded . . . the issues of the day were off-limits. And so the growth of children's literature exploded with suitable tales of moral virtue and vicarious excitement between ornate covers **(Figure I27 and Figure T5)**. After sheltered school hours, the garden swing offered relaxing rhythmic activity; when one tired of play, it was time for conversation **(Figures I28 through I32)**.

And of course for those with governesses and those who lived on the streets, there were the seasonal games, which evolved as the year brought the months of changing weather . . . it was all as predictable as the ice-cream jacks or the carolers. Some said the calendar began with marbles, traditionally played on winter pavements but especially, says Jean Harrowven (1980), played on Good Friday, as the game was linked with the dice-throwing games played by the soldiers at the foot of the Cross. Variations of games rolled across the smooth mud and rougher surfaces, as difficult weather conditions often added to the excitement and challenged the players' skill. Boys, according to Norman Douglas (1931) played at Knucks and Marble-Board, at Skittles, Glascow, Three Holes, Nixy's In the Hole, and I Take, Gutterspan, Row Marbles, and Up the Alley. And there was Spick and Span, Dob 'em, and Tip, Four Holes, Nearest the Wall, Picking the Plums, and Going Up. Bowling in the Hole, Hit It-Leave It, Hit It-Have It, Throwing It and Stays were names of other marble games. And let us not forget Hits, Spans, Five Ten, Picking Numbers, Bagatelle, In the Ring, Pitching, Follow On, Killing, Porky, Throw the Farthest . . . and hosts of others **(Figure I33)**.

Mud-pies kept children busy as the snow thawed and the first buds of the coming spring signaled the whirring of the tops; there were more than a few opportunities for the ancient amusement to entertain **(Figures I34 and I35)**. There was Chippings and Hoatie and Pig-In-The-Ring, Peg Top, Pegging, Scurran-Meggy and Whigmeleerie, and so many more. Top-Football and Skating and Growling Keeps and Getting In the Ring and Sending Messages and Hully-Gully and Fly Dutchman and Boat Race kept the sport alive. Even in Virgil's *Aeneid* can be found, "As young striplings whip the top for sport, On the smooth pavement of an empty court; . . .They lash aloud, each other they provoke, And lend their little souls at ev'ry stroke" (Gomme, 1898). The whips were dried eelskins or willow wood and were perhaps kept by towns to ensure that the peasants had enough exercise in winter; they were even held to have been part of a choir-boys' ritual in France.

Skipping began on Good Friday when the fisher folk, ten at a time, jumped to a single rope at Brighton Beach. And there was Shuttlefeather or Battledore and Shuttlecock **(Figure I36)** or Badminton, which, first mentioned in the 14th century with the hitting of a tied ring or "posty" of flowers with the palm, absorbed the townsfolk on the second Sunday in May or on Shrove Tuesday. Kites appeared when the winds rocked Summer into place **(Figures N114 and T20 and T21)** while the seasons cooled for snowball fights **(Figure I37)** and hoops at Christmas **(Figure M83)**.

There were games played with foils or sabers **(Figure I38)** and races with stilts **(Figure I39)**, and games were played when there were no marbles or tops or shuttlecock racquets. Hats or shoes or jackets pulled over the head became tools of the game; sticks were grabbed, flower-heads were decapitated, nuts were thrown against stone walls, peach pits were rattled in old tobacco cans, and more. For hundreds of years old knives carved the dirt or floor stones into checkerboards on which sticks and stones were counters for chess and checker-like contests.

And that ain't all . . . there were body games in which running, skipping, hopping, or jumping over something or someone made some kind of game that entertained all before the sun went down. The game of Leap Frog **(Figures I40, I41, and I42)** is described by Lady Gomme from information given her by her dearest friend and mentor, the good Reverend Dr. Gregor. The boy who stooped his back was called the *bull* (pronounced "bill"). The line of leapers took their turns jumping over his bent body, periodically extending the leaping line behind until the floundered one became the bull himself. Varieties of the games had names: Bung the Bucket, Cat Gallows, Half Hammer, Hop Frog, Saddle the Nag . . . and more. (For fascinating reading about traditional games, see the writings of Lady Alice Bertha Gomme, 1898.)

Perhaps the game of Touch (and its variants) sprang from a time when those suffering from specific diseases were to be isolated as taboo **(Figures I43 and I44)**. In a circle, players are able to avoid the touch of the blinded . . . he or she, chosen by luck, became a victim of certain diseases or one subjected to a special punishment for some very good, but unexplained, reason.

Other games, ball games particularly, led to the development of big business entertainment. While those stories can be found in "N Is for 19th Century," it is the younger child's play at ball—thrown, hit, or kicked—that concerns us here. Gomme (1898) says that "games played with a ball are remains of divination" **(Figures I45 and I46),** the belief in ghosts and charms that leads to the worship of wells and trees. The "ball games played by two opposite parties with bats and sticks, the origin of our modern cricket and baseball, have been developed from those early contests which have played such an important part in parish and town politics" **(Figures N124 through N127)**.

And there were playgrounds **(Figure I47)** with equipment that, besides building muscles, built concentration and coordination. But it is those very well-equipped playgrounds, or the well-meaning teachers who still mandate the rules of the game, and the ever-glamorous advertising of toy stores that encourage hoards of parents to purchase fancy packaged tools that have dampened the world of pretend. The teeming activity and amazing creativity of the English street games has all but disappeared. Chroniclers of the times describe the Bobbies who banished the marble games from blocking the pavement, the "fussy" moms who were annoyed with pants worn through at the knees, and the shop vendors who no longer stocked the

vast array of marbles with less demand. The lists of games are extraordinary . . . the creativity that fashioned them remains remarkable, and the prolific verses to ring- or line-games and their inevitable variations, extinct or thriving, are, thanks to Alice Gomme and other patient historians of folklore, safely stored in dusty volumes.

Along with transfers of children at game playing are many graphics of children with their dogs. The English love for dogs was, some historians say, symbolic of the yearning to return to the soil and the simpler life of the farmer. So many feeding vessels pictured children and their "status symbols," which, with the growth of industry and better-paying jobs, could now be afforded. Many were absorbed in the breeding and care of exotic breeds . . . members of kennel clubs were particularly impressed by unique appearances and distinguished pedigrees **(Figures I48 through I52, Figures C59, C63, C64 and C65, Figure D108, Figures L4, L13, and others)**. The canines were favorites of mothers, who saw the animals as a way of inculcating responsibility. Happy, healthy animals came alongside their well-dressed masters or mistresses with promises of adoration and an air of sophistication as well **(Figures I50, I51, and I52, Figure D108, and Figures L4 and L13)**.

A frequent gift to children from their wealthy parents around the 1860s was a cart pulled by a large dog or a small horse or pony. Children were introduced to horsemanship by learning to ride an animal they could call their own **(Figures I53, I54, and I55)**.

By the dress of the children on **Figures I56 and I57** it is evident that cages of rabbits and the exotic "pollies" might have been pets of children of upper-class families. But the transfers also illustrated the responsibilities of the farm children to their animals (see "N Is for 19th Century"). Often the youngest children were forced to sit in the fields screaming at the crows or to herd Bessie into the barn at milking time. The essential care of the animals was usually left to the youngsters, which included the feeding of the ducks, the prideful gathering of eggs **(Figures I58 through I62)**, and the nurturing of the donkeys.

Rewarding, too, were the gardens planted on farms and on the fancy grounds of wealthy families. Prince Albert loved to garden, watching his creations grow by the hour. It was both a science and an art for him, as it was for J. C. Loudon, deemed the father of Victorian gardens. For the very rich, glass greenhouses provided year-round fruits and vegetables and kept tropical plants thriving through cold English snows. Thousands of plants from every continent were introduced into conservatories built to keep the temperatures and humidity perfect for entire rooms of the many species of orchids, mushrooms, shiny green melons, varieties of grapes, strawberries waiting for heavy cream, and ferns growing in bottle gardens. Illustrated paper plans and do-it-yourself pattern books were available for those whose purse looked more like the sow's ear or whose land was restricted. How gardens were arranged was the grower's passion . . . some were absolutely geometric, some were punctuated with urns and vases which "married the house to the lawn" (Burton, 1972a), some were designed with flowers that opened at appointed times to keep a daily vigil of color, some were tall in the center with surrounding plants in gradually diminishing sizes, and some were planned to appear wild and tangled as they matured. Gardens grew as did their caretakers; maturity brought its joys **(Figures I63 through I67)**.

Maturing children brought with them the promise of new

families who guaranteed the flowering of the family tree. While upper-class entries into adulthood were marked by dance cards signed by the socially elite, the less fortunate held parties where they welcomed their guests in flowing gowns and ornate hairdos; special guests were enjoyed only in the company of family or friends. Most marriages in the middle classes were late; the groom was required to have enough steady income for a home and all its fixings. Papa's permission was essential . . . a letter usually asked the question; the exchange of gifts could then follow an affirmative reply. On the farm, the personal introduction, so beautifully described on **Figures I68, I69, and I70**, recalls the melodic lines of Robert Burns's *The Cotter's Saturday Night,* written in 1785-86. In spite of the poet's affinity for alcohol and the ladies, his poem shines upon his love for his God-fearing father, who, with a station beneath that of a lowly tenant farmer, put his family's care and his love of God first. The tale of daughter Jenny and her new love presents not only the familiar awkwardness of the introduction (Verse VIII) and parental fears for her protection but the beauty of the moment within the simple graces of the thatched cottage (see Appendix AI1 and AI2).

The cheerfu' supper done, wi' serious face,
They, round the ingle, form a circle wide;
The sire turns o'er with patriarchal grace,
The big ha'-Bible, and his father's pride -

. . . from which tales are read that shine a "heaven-ward flame" (Verse XIII), by which his "warmest wish is sent" (Verse VII).

And warm wishes tied the family together, especially on the holidays. The Dickens' Christmas began with church hymns and the feast followed; stuffed fowls, legs of pickled pork, plum pudding, and mince pies waited while fires gleamed into warm velvets and dark, rich woods. Branches of pine, honoring the ancient tree worship, sent a spicy fragrance to mingle with aromatic gravies and sugared fruits. Christmas cards, the ingenious inspiration of Sir Henry Cole, who didn't have enough time to write individual greetings, adorned the mantle. Reading aloud was the long-awaited pleasure, while short plays and humorous pantomimes were illuminated by snow-white candles set upon boughs of fresh fir. The retold tale of Harlequin, invisible to all but his desired Columbine, was told with colorful costumes and the brandishing of wooden swords. It was a splendid day for young and old alike; gifts waited for the New Year. Certainly each of the grandchildren **(Figure I71)** was to be given a silver spoon with the ABC's on its handle and a picture-plate with lustred letters.

The portrait of the grandparent is seen both with laughter and with love; four engravings parody the coming of those final years. The first, titled "Gaping," shares an unflattering and very private moment before a mirrored check for wrinkles or a hurting molar **(Figure I72)**. **Figure I73** boasts a fair damsel who, after attending to her glorious hair with a curling iron, proudly proclaims, "O How Handsome." And contentment, with its surrounding cloud of black smoke, would surely bring the pleasures articulated on tobacco advertisements; every smoker, the ads said, would experience an improvement of his disposition and the quieting of his nervous personality and stomach **(Figure I74)**. Snuff, too, with its quick nicotine high, appears to have provided the perfectly satisfying state **(Figure I75)**.

A more serious, and certainly more sensitive, look at our last years concludes this chapter. Four lines from Burns's *John Anderson, My Jo,* describes a woman's full acceptance of her husband's snowy locks and their inevitable sleep, side by side, at the foot of life's "hill." Hand in hand, the Andersons lead us to life's reward (see Appendix AI3).

Of course, education was explored in "E Is for Education"; spiritual awareness in "R Is for Religion, Reform and Reason"; and occupations, adult recreations, and cultural trends in "N Is for 19th Century." No plates, mercifully, are given to our last moments of mortality. (Though not an ABC edge, one plate on pages 39 and 40 [#103] of Riley's 1991 book does recall a grandfather's love after his passing, and there is a "Symptoms of Grave-Digging" mentioned in Riley as well.) These many plates do, however, celebrate the fun and frolic of youth, the building of the work ethic, the maturation of the adolescent into young parenthood, a comedic look at the inevitable emergence of maturity's last laughs, and Burns's tribute to our inevitable end. The cycle is complete **(Figure I76)**.

J Is for J, the Last Letter of the Alphabet

The old order of the Roman alphabet (H, I, K) is dished up on many ceramic ABC flat plates and deep dishes. The 10th letter of our alphabet, J, follows the I, which not only looks much like it but holds the key to its origin. The entwined histories of the two began about 2000 B.C. with the formation of the 24-symbol Egyptian consonant alphabet.

But the language of the Egyptians began long before that. At least 5,000 years before Christ, the language of hieroglyphs (thing-pictures such as a shape of a man to signify "man") began its evolution to idea-pictures (such as a setting sun to tell of "death") and then to sound-alike word pictures (drawings of things that sounded like the word to be used). The next phase was the development of a 24-picture alphabet, simple hieroglyphs or pictures that stood for two-letter sounds (such as a worm for a DJ) or single sounds (such as owl for the sound of M), both of which could be strung together to spell words. It was the second symbol in this 24-letter set of this first Egyptian alphabet that began the history of the 26th chronological letter of our alphabet; the J would stand 10th in line.

The letter J began as a sound picture, a drawing of a quill or a thin leaf that, even then, had two sounds: the EA as in "eat" and the J as the first sound in "jump." But after the transition to a sound-picture came another change. About 3500 B.C., a new kind of writing developed. It was called *hieratic* writing; hieratic meant "priest," for the writing was used only by priests to record the sacred word. The alphabet was built of flowing forms derived from the stoic, patiently drawn basic shapes of each of the alphabetical hieroglyphs. For instance, the quill (or leaf) shape was simplified to a straight line with a short serif (an introductory stroke), first facing left and then, as the language evolved, facing right; both looked somewhat like our modern J.

The alphabet of hieratic shapes was simplified by the Phoenicians, who, freed at last from subjugation by the Egyptians, became the Mediterranean's most successful merchants. Dropping the Egyptian word pictures completely, the traders cared only for the ease of recording their fast-paced dealings. Sometime between the 12th and 11th centuries before Christ, they combined some shapes from other Eastern languages along with Egyptian hieratic writing to make an alphabet of straight, deliberate strokes that could be written rapidly and read with clarity; the efficient twenty-two-letter sequence formed the basis from which was derived all other Western alphabets.

The Phoenician version of the hieratic quill was an angular figure looking much like a backward modern F with a slightly tailed staff, which brought the figure to resemble a modern Z. It

appeared to be a *yadh* or a hand with its fingers facing left, and was pronounced as the Y at the end of the word toy. The letter was called a semiconsonant, which means it could be read either as a vowel or as a consonant. Charts of Egyptian and Phoenician alphabets show only consonants. Oscar Ogg (1971) says it was the reader who made the decision as to whether a letter was to be read as a consonant or a vowel; the pronunciation of the vowel sound was at the discretion of the decoder.

But the Greeks didn't much like guesswork. They added symbols for vowels to keep reading consistent, and because the alphabet was a work in progress, Greek scribes took the liberty of dropping a few vowels they had added as the people and their written language evolved to an alphabet that included 24 characters. In its place, the yadh might have been approached in sequence from right to left, left to right, down to up, or up to down. Even the directionality of reading and writing was not established until the 6th century, when only left to right was "right."

Time passed. About 900 B.C., the Greek scribes first elongated the Z shape (on some charts shown in reverse), which evolved, with the culture's penchant for making things look more perfect, into a classic, straight line. With the addition of vowels to the alphabet, the semiconsonant status was transposed to the vowel E as in we. And because it became a very small letter (it rose just above the baseline), it was appropriately named *iota*, which was the very smallest letter of all.

In the hands of the Romans, some alphabet letters were discarded, some were discarded and recaptured, and some were simply redrawn; happily, with the development of new writing tools, graceful curves could replace harsh angles. But the fate of the iota was again subject to whim. Once more it was demoted to semi-consonant . . . it could be read as an I as in "index" or Y as in "maior" (pronounced "mayor"); the seeds of confusion were firmly planted for centuries to come.

Hand-sharpened quills recorded the passage of centuries as both the sounds of letters and the peoples evolved. Sometime before the 6th century, the consonant (or nonvowel) I passed through a sound something like the DI or DE in "odious" or "hideous". . . it was on its way to being symbolized as DZ when, as years passed, it evolved, with French influence, to a soft G as at the start of "judge." From the 11th century, then, the I represented both the vowel sound of I and the sound of DZ.

But more than the confusion of the sound variants, the two sounds both looked like each other and might appear as the approaching strokes of adjacent letters as well; various modifications were initiated sometime around the 13th century to keep them distinct. It took the frustrated scribes to orchestrate the final stages of the J's evolution.

Early in the medieval Latin period (beginning in A.D. 700), a dot was added over the short, simple line to prevent its confusion with the approaching strokes of adjacent letters and with the N (which was then written with two short vertical strokes) or the M (which was written with three short vertical strokes).

The process of graphically differentiating between the I and J began with the turning of the 17th century. An I occurring at the start of a word, or an initial I, was given a new look as it was prolonged either above or below the baseline; the initial letter might have been either the vowel sound of I, which was prolonged upward, or the more often used initial nonvowel (consonantal) sound of J, which was prolonged downward. An I in the final position was undoubtedly read as J and so was drawn below the baseline. Centuries later, calligraphers flourished the end of that plunging line with a graceful curve along with the dot, called a tittle, which had given such beauty and balance to the minuscule I. The lovely, flowing cursive J was born.

The old French sound now had its ornamental form, and about 1630, one Lazarus Zetzner, a typesetter in Strasbourg, gave the J an uppercase design; Johann zum Gansefleisch Gutenberg's *King James Bible* could now be reprinted resetting the type for "iudge" to read "judge" and for "Iesus" to read "Jesus." Thus it was in the 17th century that the two forms of the letter, each with its own shape and unique sound, were finally differentiated; one symbol for the vowel I and another for the consonant J. (Of course, there were exceptions. In certain words, especially in proper names, or in words from the German, the J retained the Roman value of Y as in "yellow.")

But good news doesn't always travel fast. A few knowledgeable souls recognized the differences in the letters, but the general feeling remained that I and J were simply two forms of the same letter; most asked, "Who needs both?" Even the astute lexicographer Dr. Samuel Johnson (1709-1784) treated them as one. Though he recognized each for its own unique sound and shape, he combined the two listings in his dictionary: "jabber, jam, iambic, jangle . . . juxtaposition, ivy and jymold." And he wasn't alone. Geoffrey Godden (*Encyclopaedia of British Pottery and Porcelain Marks,* 1991b) reminds us that the initial J may appear as an I on 18th- and 19th-century potter's marks. And the old order of the Roman alphabet was retained in the alphabet lists of many 18th- and 19th-century primers. To add to the confusion, I and J words were blended in dictionary lists down through the start of the 20th century.

The addition of the J was a latecomer to the German alphabet, as the "missing Js" on German plates indicate. Even now, some German dictionaries show only a handful of words beginning with the letter, while others present several pages of words beginning with the consonant sound of Y. According to Kaiser Walker, Ph.D., of Germanic Studies at Cornell University, Ithaca, New York, the I and J were used interchangeably for some time. In texts and grammar books, the distinction between I as a vowel and J as a consonant was heard in the late 16th and early 17th centuries, but not all texts acknowledged the difference that early.

The maker of the pictured dark green majolica plate **(Figure J1)** reverses the trend and leaves the alphabet without its I. One of only two examples of Victorian majolica in the collection, the plate represents the industry's response to the 1850 majolica craze on both sides of the Atlantic. The Kovels (1986) remind us that this majolica was made in quantity by factories in England, the Netherlands, Italy, France, and the United States. On the underside of this flowered plate is a small, shallow circle that might be a clue to its origin.

Another variant on the "-I-J-" sequence is seen on the Disney deep dish, whose black-lettered border reverses the order of the two letters **(Figure J2)**. The collectible is also shown (along with its mark) in "C Is for Commercialism" as **Figures C86 and C87**.

Aside from the elimination of the J **(Figure J3 and all plates following)**, the elimination of X/Y is found on the next seven German-made pieces **(Figures J5 through J11)**. But that's another story.

All dishes in this chapter (except perhaps the majolica, **Figure J1**) are of German origin. Though 90% of the German-made deep dishes in the entire collection are marked, these flat plates are not.

The concluding photos **(Figures J12 through J16)** are details of bowls showing the exclusion of J in their alphabets. Each is shown in full face in "D Is for Deep Dishes" and their figure numbers are provided in the captions for cross reference.

Produced as the century changed, these alphabet edges reflect the old order, perhaps a quiet hold on the past. With languages and their peoples ever-evolving, there just might be another change.

K Is for Kitsch

Trash . . . the definition of *Kitsch* from the German dictionary is clear and simple. No doubt it's correct, but trash is a subjective noun. Every antique dealer knows full well that what is trash to one is treasure to another.

A more comprehensive definition of Kitsch is described in Georg Brühl's *Porzellan-figuren* (1989), which might translate to a theme from the popular culture represented by a decorative item produced in mass quantity and targeted for low-cost impulse buying. Trash to some, perhaps, but an art form nevertheless. The production of Kitsch was designed to draw large profits as the quick sellers were produced in materials of common quality. No harm in that . . . it was not meant to deceive the buyer; it had a purpose. Items sold as treasures from trips or small gifts of fondness or humor have their place on our shelves and often in our hearts. European and American Victorians were known to fill their homes with the Kitschy stuff to mimic the parlor displays of the wealthy. Taste was, and still is, a civil right.

The writings of Fritz Karpfen discuss the manufacture of Kitsch-Art. Among several categories of these products, Karpfen highlights Hurra-Kitsch (hurrah, joyous, fun, or entertaining) and Erotic-Kitsch (sexually awakening). Made at the end of the 19th century, Kitsch-Art was considered to have little authenticity as art because it needed no interpretation and transmitted nothing but the most superficial messages. Sometimes silly or foolish, sometimes purely sentimental, and oftentimes sexy, many items projected a feeling of "wildness." A translation from the German assures the reader that it took guts to create them and guts to display them. Sometimes the sexy was cleverly combined with the humorous; irresistible, it "winked" at its buyer.

Kitsch-Art helped to release the body form into the public eye in Germany as gymnastics was becoming a national phenomenon; through Kitsch-Art the body was revealed both in its most provocative forms and in the "cutsie" and more comic form of the Kewpie. Offered in the Shäfer & Vater Porzellanfabrik (1890-1962) catalogue (November 1914) as smiling winged Cupids that brought to all a symbol of hope, the figures were sculpted with hats of cowboys and firemen and the chapeaus of other occupations. Also wearing uniform hats and red hearts to assure their owners of their love, Kewpies were given to World War I wounded; the sweet, protective angels brought a moment of joy to their frightened comrades.

Thanks to Berlin's George Borgfeldt, thousands of the small, winged, three-dimensional guardian angels were also exported to the United States from Ohrdruf's J. D. Kestner & Company and other firms. From one inch to toddler tall, these children's companions were conceived by Rose O'Neill in 1909; her children's book introduced the naked and smiling figures to youngsters in the United States. From 1912 through the 1920s, consumer fascination with this bisque spirit soared.

Kewpies adorned baskets, lamps, vases, pincushions, and a host of other household items, including alphabet tableware. Kewpies on plates and cups **(Figures K1 through K6)** were made in Germany by the Royal Rudolstadt Porcelain Factory (otherwise known, according to Kovel and Kovel [1986] as New York & Rudolstadt Pottery, 1882-1918, Thuringia, East Germany). Lewis Straus & Sons of New York, co-owners (or owners) of the factory, were its sole importers of goods to the United States.

In America, Kewpie-decorated deep dishes bearing the Holdfast "Baby Plate" shield were produced during the 1920s by the McNicol Potteries **(Figures K7 and K8)** at its East Liverpool, Ohio plant. The "Three Kewpies" cream-colored bowl bears the mark of Dresden China **(Figures K9 and K10),** whose firm began as Brunt, Bloor, Martin and Co. in East Liverpool. (They are noted also in "D Is for Deep Dishes" as **Figures D106 and D107**.) The firm was organized as the Potters' Cooperative in 1882, and from 1916 through 1925 items were marked T. P. C-O. The "casually manufactured" feeder was produced about 1926, as the mark is dated one year before the firm's closing in 1927. Whether edged by the McNicol's stenciled blue letters or the gilt hand-placed letters on Dresden China's dog-dish-shaped feeder, scenes of Kewpies will undoubtedly continue to protect and nourish their hungry mortals with spoonsfull of smiles (See "D Is for Deep Dishes" for additional firm histories).

Also, within the category of Hurra-Kitsch are the English humorous drawings, probably the creations of one Cromek, an apprentice in a school of illustrators run by Thomas Bewick (1753-1828), who, famous for his unique wood engravings, is considered to be the father of modern book illustrations. Bewick, always up to mischief and a truant from school, drew in the margins of his schoolbooks and often chalked on the churchyard flagstones; it took his apprenticeship with Newcastle's engraver, Ralph Beilby, to teach him the rigorous discipline and patience for long hours of work. Noted for his volumes of quadrupeds and birds, the illustrator was an extraordinarily happy individual whose sense of humor was reflected in the work of his students as well. The satire titled "Drolleries of the Steam Engine" was found in *Banbury Chap Books* (Pearson, 1890), which presented a selection of woodcuts by Bewick, Cruikshank, Blake, and other noted illustrators of the 18th and 19th centuries **(Figure K11)**. Published in London in 1890 by Arthur

Reader, the original drawings, a collection of "naked" spoofs on the uses of the new steam engine, appear at first glance to be Hurra-Kitsch indeed. On second thought, perhaps their creator was not cheering at all, for the invention of steam power would inevitably rob the worker of all that was dear to him. In the pen-and-ink rendering at the center, top row, the gentleman's natural mobility is unnecessarily hampered with an engine on his back to fuel his newly steam-powered legs. The message was clear . . . technology would replace what the individual could already do for himself! But inventiveness, early on, outran human endurance. The Industrial Revolution could no longer be argued with; the final brown ceramic transfer attempts to restore what remains of the worker's dignity with a fine, tailored suit. Caustically titled "Symptoms of Walking Made Easy," it is sad humor, at best **(Figure K12)**.

But not all notions of German or English Victorian Kitsch were humorous or benign. Karpfen's category of Erotic Kitsch applied not only to his country's naughty little sculptures but to items seen in this collection, which reflect the darker side of Victorian sexuality. Prudery prompted Miss Sewell, educator and most militant champion of innocence, to suggest that sharp and instant punishment be given to children who did or said anything that lacked refinement or modesty. Like all "Podsnappians," she was determined to stifle any female's most remotely sexual (or evil) thought. Curiously, she may not have recognized the centuries of children's games drawn from replications of courtship and marriage. Though children were to be kept away from any suggestion of playing at romanticism, it is the list of "suggestive" playground games that is the most extensive in Lady Alice Bertha Gomme's two-volume set, titled *A Dictionary of British Folk-Lore* (1898). The books examine the histories of 19th-century games that were danced and sung in the round with clasped hands or played in lines to recall all the milestones of growing maturity. So many amusements focused on courtship and love **(see Figure I21)**. Some games recalled the old tribal custom of paying for and carrying off a bride with no manner of courtship played out. But there were games that did perform courtship rituals. One, called "Babbity Bowster," called upon the boy to obtain a kiss with an expected struggle. Another expects a marriage bond while the door is locked and the bride's reluctance is announced. Suggestive titles such as "Here Comes a Virgin" and "Hear all! Let me at her," are common. Ring-me-rary sings, "As I go round, ring by ring, A virgin goes a-maying," and another chorus chants, "Stand and face your lover. . . Give me a kiss, my darling," and there are many, many more. Could these self-perpetuating relics of ancient culture be slain by Sewell's efforts?

Innocence, Sewell said, needed shielding; parents had a duty to safeguard the innocent from any suggestion of sexuality with strong doses of fear and hatred. Only innocence, she railed, was the respectable state of conscience, and such naiveté led to practices as desperate as covering furniture legs lest they be seen as muscular and seductive (Vicinus, 1972) to either girls or boys. Until a young daughter was safely brought to maturity, her virtue was the responsibility of her also respectable mother; boys too were protected by horn-shaped coverings lest they be seduced into naughty nights. But rest assured, their father knew well the dangers of life. The wife he lovingly adored was undoubtedly the carrier of a stylishly repressive childhood. Papa may well have sought the exciting cocoon of a porno-advertised brothel. "(M)en," wrote William Acton, "con-

sidered the sin a thing that everybody practices, though nobody talks too much about it, until to abstain is looked upon almost as a mark of want of manhood" (Fisher, 1997).

From the bizarre to the more bizarre . . . some mothers protected their daughters from the least crack in the pod of "wombandly revelation," while other mothers, poor and not so poor, sold their offspring into wretched slavery until the insidious spread of venereal disease loosed their bonds. Thousands of youngsters were lured away from homes where unsuspecting parents were grateful to receive gifts of support earned by prostitution. Hordes of orphaned or runaway children searched the river mud for things to sell; some, crowded twelve to a vermin-ridden bed, played and danced naked till dawn. It was the great social reformer, Lord Shaftesbury, who brought to the House of Lords the truths of frightfully common reprehensible crime. "It is impossible," he said, "to exaggerate the physical and moral evils that result from this state of things" (Wohl, 1978).

Secret solicitations were widespread. The factory girl, employed for long hours in hot and airless areas, often fell prey to "overtime" tasks (Vicinus, 1972). Statements abound of how household servants serviced their masters in attic niches and crooked stairwells. At least the respectable women in sedentary occupations, desperate for cash, were lucky; they could sometimes choose their company. Indeed, there was an underside in spite of Victoria's virtue, and it took the Good Queen's Parliament many years to challenge it.

Since it was the duty of the parent—particularly the nourisher, or the mother—to protect her child from "the dark side," would the "suggestive" table ware seen in this chapter be appealing to parents? Graphics of children and animals actually promoted erotica. The scene of the invasive Tom Cat **(Figure K13)** can be viewed with more than a hint of harassment. Four scenes of interacting mustached youngsters raise issues of role play and immature sexuality. Three are seen in **Figures K14, K15, and K16**. A fourth member of the set can be found on page 41 of the Lindsays' (1998) text which pictures two children whose facial features are mature; one is caressing a rabbit, a mythological symbol of fertility with the ability to change its sexual identification as the moon does in its phases.

The mug **(Figures K17 and K18)**, titled "The Meeting" or "The Rendezvous," is graphically lecherous. An elderly gent, looking everything but gentlemanly, reaches from behind a bush for a sweet young thing undoubtedly in mourning for her recently lost love. A large letter R stands between them. . . for "rendezvous" or "romance" or "rape"? Perhaps there were pornographic alphabets as well.

The second mug displays an invasion of privacy **(Figure K19)**, which ties the letter W to a (literally) embarrassing whipping. Perhaps the act's appearance on everyday china is a clue to its common occurrence. Traditionally, parent-delivered punishments, spankings, or floggings for breaches of behavior were common. It didn't hurt a child, the Victorians said, to be beaten once in a while. Even in church, boys might often experience a rap on the head with a wand or a stick by the beadle or the verger. But the transfer on this mug describes infliction of pain to children by children. In Karpfen's terms, was that too a "theme from the popular culture?"

Though items of 19th-century Kitsch were inexpensive, like all collectibles, their values have grown. Once bought for a paltry sum, "Innocence" now wears a prohibitive price tag **(Figure**

K20). Its startling engraving has made it perhaps the most "worthy" item of ABC ware collected to date. In the engaging transfer, a smiling youngster has covered his "Tommy" with only a full-skirted gown which he has coyly lifted for our "invasive view."

Has he successfully invited an unsuspecting viewer to share in his fantasy? Is he enjoying an early adventure into cross-dressing? Or shall we ask the ghost of Ms. Sewell to simply wink at a bizarre incident of prepubescent sport?

L Is for Lustreware

The shine of glowing metal or the changing of hues in the firelight added a "touch of class" to one's tableware. It took only a thin line of the shiny stuff to qualify a ceramic mug, a pitcher, or a butter pot as a coveted item of lustreware. To retell the history of the "magical paint" we turn to John Bedford, author of *Old English Lustre Ware* (1968); to Margery Clinton's *Lustres* (1991); to editor Robert Charleston's *World Ceramics* (1968); to an entertaining and beautifully photographed printing titled *19th Century Lustreware* by Michael Gibson (1999); and to the ultimate text by Godden and Gibson, *Collecting Lustreware* (1991). All are recommended reading.

Because so many names are used to describe the subtle differences in lustres, Clinton, in an effort to minimize the confusions, begins her book with a reference to M. L. Rancher, the French chemist who, in 1926, explained the two basic processes of creating lustred ware. To create them, he said, the potter works with two kinds of fires. Chemically different, the two processes create lustres that look different . . . and, to complicate their histories, sometimes appear much alike.

One type of fire, burning with reduced or restricted air, is a reduction fire. When the air is withheld, the "hungry atmosphere takes the oxygen from the metal oxides in the kiln, reducing them to actual metal" (Clinton, 1991). This reduction fire produced *iridescent reduction lustres* first seen in pre-Islamic Egypt and in Mesopotamian and Persian (Iraqi and Iranian) pottery centers from the 12th through the 14th centuries. Iranian artisans probably migrated to southern Spain, where portions of large wing-handled vases were conceived in kilns at Malaga, then fitted together, refired, and decorated with opalescent shimmers applied with quills and brushes. As Spain expelled the last of the Moors and waved farewell to Columbus, potters continued production of their famous Hispano-Moresque lustreware. By the 1500s, Italy became famous for the gold-on-blue-and-white ware of Deruta and the red ruby ware of Gubbio. After a 17th-century revival in Persia, the shiny stuff waited for 19th-century England to glow again. In 1873, London's William DeMorgan, while subjecting both his glazes and his roof to fires, refined Gubbio's red ruby lustre by adding sawdust and wood chips to his kiln. He achieved a strong ruby red from copper, a yellowish gray from silver oxide (which gave a blue-silver iridescence), and more; others after him picked up the flame, and the lights of Persia were forever rekindled. But it is the oxidation lustreware, not the reduction lustreware, that is represented in this chapter.

The second kind of fire burns "with plenty of air [and] what is being burnt combines with the oxygen in the air making oxides i.e. it is an oxidizing fire and there is no smoke" (Clinton, 1991). *The aim of oxidation lustreware is the reproduction of metallic effects.* Oxidation lustreware began in Persia along with the reduction processes, but the gold leaf was not very durable. The refinement of the process waited patiently until the end of the 18th century, when all-over lustres were produced to imitate the more costly metal products.

The six types of lustres—silver, steel, gold, copper, purple and pink—were applied in different ways. The English earthenware items seen in this chapter are not coated by a metallic to resemble any other material. This pottery carries brushwork, albeit not too meticulous. When on white or nearly white, thinly applied coats of "a gold recipe" produced an exciting shiny pink that glowed in contrast. With or without added tin oxide to deepen their color, the renderings of rural cottages, houses of worship, public houses, and castles did not include human or animal forms, as replications of these anatomical wonders would exceed the prowess of their painters. Christened "cottage designs" by lustre enthusiast Atwood Thorne, the renderings were childlike creations by those who were very young or those with limited talents; with the simplest of techniques the ware was quickly produced by the hundreds and sold for a few pence a dozen **(Figures L1, L2, and L3)**. "(T)here is something in their very crudity," says Bedford (1968), "which makes a gathering of them attractive on one's shelves."

Unfortunately, these plates are not marked, and few, pictured in notable texts, carry factory identifications. There is one ABC lustre on record. It can be found on page 143 of Chalalas' *A Collector's Guide to ABC Plates, Mugs and Things* (1980), and that plate is (mistakenly) captioned, "transfer with lustre on scene and edge." (The very same plate is found in the Lindsays' book as well.) It seems valuable, then, to first establish a list of Staffordshire firms that produced both ABC plates and lustreware: William Adams (Stoke and Tunstall), Charles Allerton (Longton), Herbert Aynsley (Longton), Bailey and Ball (Longton), Davenport (Longport), Hackwood (Hanley or Shelton), Wedgwood (Etruria), and J. F. Wileman (Longton). All of these firms produced ware using lustres, but only the firm of Bailey and Ball at Hanley is associated, in references, with "cottage designs."

Very similar designs to the Chalala plate and to the examples pictured here are found on non-ABC products made in the Out-Potteries, far from Staffordshire. Usually "type-cast" as Sunderland, the ware may have been made in that area or in just about any other ceramic center in the north of England, Scotland, or Wales (Gibson, 1999). North of London is Sunderland, and Newcastle-upon-Tyne, Cardiff, and Swansea are west of London, in Wales. From listings in Bedford's book and *Collecting Lustreware* (1991) come mentions of the rustic scenes as they were known to have been produced by the major potteries in those areas.

As noted, Sunderland is north of London, on the eastern coast, and is now synonymous with the mottled or splashed pink lustre made by spraying droplets of oil on wet lustre. The Garrison Pottery, among others, made the pink-lustred cottage ware; "primitive" cottage designs (as seen on page 36 of Bedford's text), displayed at the Sunderland Museum, are said to possibly have been made at that firm. Cottage ware was also produced when the factory was known as Dixon and Austin. Sunderland's history also recalls Dawson's (or Ford or Low Ford) Pottery, which made the primitively designed pink-painted teaware. And worthy of note is a significant cottage teapot pictured on page 216 of *Collecting Lustreware* (1991).

North and west of Sunderland is Newcastle-upon-Tyne. Here, Thomas Fell and Company (St. Peter's Pottery) is noted as maker of a cottage line. Tyne or Sheriff Hill Pottery of Patterson & Company sold large quantities of a more exacting cottage pattern, as well.

Far to the south of Sunderland, to Cardiff in Wales, comes mention of a cottage-designed mug that, according to Bedford (1965), displayed a darker and more iridescent pink.

West of Cardiff is Swansea. Among its lustre-producing firms was the Cambrian Pottery opened in 1783 by one Mr. George Haynes. In 1802, the firm was sold to Mr. Lewis Weston Dillwyn, whose botanical interests influenced the themes on Swansea ceramics. A plate, similar to **Figure L1** with its crossed and peaked roof, is labeled "very primitive" and pictured on page 252 of Godden and Gibson's book (1991); the plate is marked by the Dillwyn & Co., Swansea. Other painted cottages have flat roofs **(Figures L2 and L3),** with trees and grass clumped alongside the hastily drawn fences that protect them.

Very different from the hand-painted ware is the black-transferred alphabet plate, **Figure L4**, without a letter edge. The dish, which pictures a child teaching the letter sequence to a puppy, has a traditional half-inch lustre-edge as seen on many items in Gibson's text. The charming scene, offered for sale as a French Limoges, has no mark of either French or English origin.

The religious mugs that follow in **Figures L5, L6, and L7** show a combination of decorative techniques. These three outstanding vessels display three transfers of the Historical Scripture Alphabet (no bibliographical listing has been located). They display typical use of pink lustred, immaturely applied broad-brushed highlights around black transfers; the technique is typical, but not provable, of Sunderland manufacture.

The darker "blackberry juice" purple border edges the rim of **Figure L8**, also featured as the spectacular frontispiece of Noël Riley's *Gifts for Good Children* (1991). We are privileged to picture the well-known vessel from the collection of Ann and Dennis Berard of New Hampshire.

Though these items may not all have originated from the Staffordshire area, it seems that the contenders for the "who lustred first in England" honor were area professionals. Godden and Gibson's definitive text notes the types of lustres and the names of those individuals who are associated with them.

So many writings on lustre begin their narratives with the "obituary challenge." Was it Hanley's John Booth, the first manufacturer of china in the Staffordshire potterie, who was responsible? Bedford quotes a letter from an 1846 edition of the *Staffordshire Mercury* that challenges the accomplishments of the recently deceased Booth, whose obituary credited him with being "the inventor of lustre for earthenwares." That letter, written by John Hancock (b. 1757[8]), begs "to state that this is incorrect, as I was the original inventor of lustre, which is recorded in several works on Potting, and I first put it into practice at Mr. Spode's Manufacuty . . . long before Mr. Booth or any other person attempted to do so" (Bedford, 1965). And Bedford also reveals that Hancock, in partnership with William Henning, "launched" gold and copper lustring on a commercial scale in 1823 at a factory owned by one Mr. Wolfe at Stoke-upon-Trent. (In the spirit of contradictory research, Michael Gibson warns that there is little indication that Hancock ever worked for Wolfe. And Godden and Gibson, after putting some often-quoted dates and data into perspective, find that Hancock probably did not invent lustre at the tender age of twelve.) Leaving the doubts and the details to the documented texts of the experts, suffice it to "name drop," knowing that, along with the name, there was not always a clear explanation of the type of lustre "invented" or "revived."

Perhaps loudest applause goes to Richard Horobin of Tunstall (1765-1830), an organ builder who received credit in an 1830 Staffordshire *Advertiser* as "The reviver of gold lustre on china and earthenware." And, reminds Bedford, there is John Aynsley (Simeon Shaw spelled it Ainsley) of Lane End, whose 1829 notice of death honors him as "the first lustrer." There are two mentions of the origin of a rich, deep purple lustre, the color of ripe blackberry juice. Bedford gives credit to David Wilson of Hanley. In addition, Bernard Hughes (1959) writes of one Dr. Fothergill, who had suggested to Josiah Wedgwood that a purple Powder of Cassius, used for enameling, might be prepared to make a commercially profitable metallic lustre. Thomas Lakin, too, must be remembered for his recipes for gold and silver lustres. One of the technique's earliest specialists, Lakin produced his own lustreware until the end of the 18th century, and after his death, his wife produced an 1824 edition of his valuable "brews."

Simeon Shaw's text, *History of the Staffordshire Potteries* (1829), lists a Mr. John Gardner (of Stoke); one Mr. G. Sparks of Slack Lane, Hanley; a James Daniel of Pleasant Row in Stoke, who discovered the technique of gold lustre application by "the pencil" (which is really a "brush"); and a Burslem artist by the name of "Hennys." (Godden and Gibson [1991] take exception to the naming of Hennys as it cannot, after extensive research, be verified.)

First or foremost makes little difference. At least most of these gentlemen, and surely others, contributed to the fine art of lustre design, each to his own type and each in his own unique way. With processes and techniques so coveted by each company, the secrets of the ingenious contributors to the fine art of pottery decoration often remained unknown until the printing of their glowing obituaries (or the swiping by talented thieves).

But the English sheen is not the only lustre in this collection. A great deal of soft-finished lustreware is seen in the photos of later German alphabet editions. Some, like the English lustre, have a very shiny and iridescent quality that causes shimmering purples to dance across their surfaces. Other rounds are decorated with lustres that appear to have been powdered with glittery dust. The last type, seen in this collection, presents a smooth, silk-like matte finish that gives the china the soft, velvety look of satin glass. The rich pastel pink, blue, blue-green, and yellow-green colors **(Figures L9, L10, and L11)** are seen on crisp rims and as wide borders that reach toward the plate's center **(Figures L12 through L16)**. A smooth, satin glass type finish is found on a great many English commemorative items and in children's toy ware as pictured in Mary Gaston's *Collector's Encyclopedia of R. S. Prussia* (Collector Books, Fourth Series, 1998). In the style of the Schlegelmilch factories' decorations, the three elegant and sensuous pink-rimmed portraits **(Figures L17, L18, and L19)** were offered for sale as R. S. Prussia alphabet ware. Matching images have not been found in books on R. S. china, which typically show repeated transfers on varied shapes, nor are the items marked. But the paintings do clearly reflect the illustration style of the R. S.-marked pottery and the deeply rooted Victorian appreciation of the delicate and fragile, always "to-be-protected" sex.

Typical of the German ware are decals of hens and roosters shown here (and in "S Is for Sets") with shiny gold painted over each molded letter. Deep dishes often display a wash of shiny yellow-gold seen, for instance, in **Figure D72**. And there are lustred items in "C Is for Commercialism" that were commissioned by communities, such as Concord, New Hampshire, and Aurora, Illinois, to be fund-raisers and/or souvenirs to commemorate events that are now remembered with pride. Historical societies are delighted to find safe havens for these items, long away from home.

A lustred cup and saucer, **Figure C48**, advertises a "place to visit," and two pink-lustred cup and saucer sets are shown in **Figures L20 and L21**. The second is the only backstamped French-produced pair in the collection. Its primitively painted letters are gritty, dull, and somewhat green in appearance. The service was made by Delinieres & Company of Limoges, France, sometime in the last quarter of the 19th century; its mark can be seen on **Figure U20**. Lustred flat dishes advertising places to visit can also be seen in **Figures C13 through C16**.

Less often seen than the traditional pink and blue tones is the nearly fluorescent orange that surrounds a red transfer graphic from The Diverting History of John Gilpin **(Figure L22)** titled, "From and Return Home." Contemporary in its coloring, this startling border includes letter reversals featured in "Z Is for Σ and Other Reversals."

Lustres of all types have a charming quality with genuine collectible interest. English lustred ABC ware is very rare and becoming quite costly, while the German "sparkle dust" and satin finishes are more easily purchased and do not yet command rising prices. Both, however, reflect the radiant repasts of long-ago years . . . their warmth and glow still light our lives.

M Is for Metals

Becoming more collectible than ceramics, metal plates, especially the smaller pieces, are rapidly increasing in value. Perhaps it is their secretiveness. A few, which might be called English or American commemoratives, help us to determine their possible dates of issue, but there is scant evidence of makers and dates of other designs; relentless research has been rewarded with little success.

Even more secret is the combination of elements that have remained well hidden behind the word "tin" . . . impenetrable until now. With the newest of high-tech machines (the X-MET 2000 Metal Master, advertised as the world's most accurate and versatile portable alloy analyzer and produced by Metorex International in Finland), the combinations of elements that constitute the core of each plate can now be measured. Coatings found on some items, such as tea trays, would prevent the analyzer from going beyond the outer skins . . . only discs that are no longer coated or those that have never been treated have been assayed, as no destructive process was needed to authenticate their "recipes."

Thus the combinations of metals within ABC "tins" are "unknown quantities." Assays of metals find that tin, in spite of its pervasive use as a categorical title, is an infrequently found component. Metallic breakdowns of all specific elements are found with chapter photographs . . . and with those lists come the disclaimers that accompany all assays. No analysis, says the disclaimer, is perfect. Though all analyses have been performed on the same machine, various contaminants on antique surfaces will always skew the outcomes. And even with the most sophisticated equipment in laboratories today, second and third assays on ultra-clean material performed by the same equipment and completed concurrently will vary with normal variations in the distributions of the metals within the item; averages become official. Though the decimals are often to the thousandths, metal scientists consider the results to be "rough figures." Rough, perhaps, but acceptable for our purposes.

Each of the metal items has been given individual attention by Jacob Mikaili of the Advanced Photo Lab in Canoga Park, California, in order to ensure the most detailed view. Because some metal surfaces are very worn, highly polished, or lightly stamped, or show evidence of rust or fire damage, the true color of the item may have been distorted in order to reveal the minute elevations in the surface. The many items contributed by Ann and Dennis Berard of Fitzwilliam, New Hampshire, have generously enriched this chapter.

Since ABC plates are products of metal stamping, the "tin

tale" begins with **Figure M1**, a fine portrait of the Alderman W. H. Jones (Esq., J.P.), whose writing opens to tales of the brawly tin workers—"a free and easy sort." At day's end they gathered at Wolverhampton's Red Lion or The Woolpack to pass their snuff boxes through rounds of cards, jugs of dark ales, and the curling fragrances of their long clay "church wardens." Bawdy conversations were of local gossip, the victories at Waterloo, the wins of mighty boxers, or the planning of good-humored stunts while boastful choruses of "The Battle of the Nile" were heard over trudging steps home by the midnight moon.

Young followers were hired at age ten for years of punishment at the tin workers' hands—a month in jail a just reward for even a few hours of absence. Too soon were these children introduced to the quenching foams after a clock round of feeding the hungry fires or shouldering the heavy sheets of dark metals in the noisy, black-smoked workshops dimly lit by foul-smelling whale oil. Slowly each apprentice, though short and slight for his years, became a skilled craftsman who knew well how to extort an excellent performance from both his tools and his own "child" maturing under his tutelage.

And genius flourished in the tin shops. Fine paintings adorned the trays that were first displayed in 1851 to shoving crowds at the Mechanics' Institute on Queen Street in Wolverhampton. The new art of tin-stamping was shown too in this spectacle, which made its way to Prince Albert's Great Exhibition in London's Crystal Palace. With the new patent of one Mr. Nasmyth's steam hammer and an alteration suggested by one John Pinson, a device was born that "ultimately revolutionized the trade." Nasmyth himself introduced his "machine which [would] strike a blow with the force of two tons weight, or [could] be let fall so gently as to crack a nut without injuring the kernel" (Jones, 1900). Thus the new art of tin stamping produced the tea trays adorned with alphabets and ornate swirls. Collectors still search for the trays that both taught and toted at the afternoon repasts of the well-to-do **(Figures M2 through M9)**. Most interesting of the collection is the rare Patent Dial Plate, courtesy of Marilyn Ross, which features the time in twenty-seven cities around the world when the clock strikes noon at the Parliament Building in London **(Figure M10)**; it's always time for lunch.

The turn of the century brought the emergence of gas cooking, and with it came a need for light utensils, such as those made of enameled steel. With peddling ironmongers believing that tinware, copper, and cast iron were superior, the sheet-iron enamel ware, patented by one Mr. Frederick Walton, remained difficult to find. Somewhat subject to chipping but far less time consuming to produce than pottery, each iron shape was spread evenly with a compound of flux (silica, minimum, and potash) together with carefully measured proportions of pulverized metal compounds to color it and a dash of calx (or stannic and arsenious acids if white) to turn it opaque. Carefully introduced into the muffle of the furnace, the article was quickly heated to a bright red and, when shining, was removed from the heat **(Figures M11 through M14).** One resulting item was found in an October 1926 catalogue of items produced by Orme, Evans and Co. Ltd, Wolverhampton, England. The Prince of Wares wrought iron enameled ware item "Alpha Clock Plate," No. 1050, was 8 inches in diameter and sold for 12 shillings, 9 pence a dozen **(Figures M15, M16, and M17).**

The Orme, Evans and Co. was founded about 1790. In 1902, at the Jeddo Works in Jeddo Street, the firm was involved in tinsmithing, enameling, and japanning. The catalogue of 1932, with its forward-looking Crown Prince, bragged that the firm used only English steel and employed only English workers (never mind the Irish and Welsh who lived in the area). Also situated at the Elgin works on Great Brickkiln Street, Orme Evans manufactured coffee and canning pots, table-serving and food-heating articles, coal storage units, trunks, hot water cans, colorful trays for serving children and adults, and supplies for the milking barn. Many illustrations of their products can be found on their Web site: http://www.localhistory.scit.wlv.ac.uk/Museum/metalware/general/orme.htm.

The carriers of metal ware were the tin peddlers of whom Margaret Coffin (1968) writes with such passion . . . most with horse and cart and many, before the building of the highways, carrying their wares slung over shoulders fixed with a webbed harness or a leather strap. It is the ghostly, ghastly peddlers' folklore of murders and mayhem that keeps the jangling sounds of their decorative ware riding on the soft winds of the dark, lonely roads east and west of the Mississippi. Killed for their purses, slashed and stashed in old wells or beneath basements or barns, many never returned to the family hearth, at least in an earthly form. But not all tin-toters were driven onto heavenly highways.

The peddler (or pedlar, as it was spelled then) carried lively news and gossip along with long-delayed personal messages to faraway families. To the youngsters, the peddler was a voyager from the great beyond . . . a bringer of a tiny toy or an ABC dinner dish. To the peddler, every stop brought a welcome sale of the tinware that was cut and soldered and pierced or gloriously painted with oils, bronze powders, or gold leaf. That tin ware, made of English sheets of tin-coated iron, was the work of tinsmiths who first learned their craft in Europe and, after settling in the Colonies, taught their trade to apprentices, to whom they were bound to impart not only the standards of their craft but their (high?) moral standards as well.

Most notable were those trained by the Pattison (or Patison or Paterson or Patterson) family (Anna, Jenni, Edward, and William), who had emigrated, with a few sheets of tin, to the "perfect village" of Berlin, Connecticut. They came from Tyrone County, Ireland, having run from religious persecution in Scotland with their father, who had planned to accompany them. Skilled at their trade, the brothers built the first tin shop in America across the street from their two-story clapboard home on Hart Street (some sources say it was a "backyard" shop). Rumor had it that the two worked quickly, and, with baskets full of shiny stuff strapped to his horse, Edward became the first tin

peddler in America. He approached the good housewives of Berlin and then, accompanied by his brother, trotted on to New Britain and all points west. They hired new hands; their apprentices became accomplished, opened their own establishments, and trained their own apprentices . . . the jangle of the "Bang-alls" rang throughout the land. By 1860 there were nearly 550 peddlers operating out of Connecticut, many spending six to eight months away from home; there were many colorful characters like Sidney Thomas, who had a tin foot crafted to look like his own, or Frank Bresee, who called at customers' doors by day and at barn dances by moonshine, or Carter and Fisk, whose silver-belled steeds drew gorgeous circus-wagon stores of hard-to-resist merchandise. Often they stayed in a town for two or three days, settling on a main street, to which clients hurried for the needles and pins, clocks and axes, books and spoons, and round tin plates that were often traded for rags to take back to the mills for the making of paper.

Authentic tinware was not a stamped product, as were the ABC plates that hung among the handcrafted ware. But they jangled just the same . . . as did the poem found in *The Posy Ring*, a book of children's verse co-edited by Kate Douglas Wiggin (b. 1856), founder of the first free kindergarten in the West and author of *Rebecca of Sunnybrook Farm*. The third verse of the poem, "The Pedlar's Caravan," (see Appendix AM2) reads:

> Chairs to mend, and delf to sell!
> He clashes the basins like a bell,
> Tea-trays, baskets ranged in order,
> Plates with the alphabet round the border!

But not all metal plates were selected from those well-remembered horse-drawn carts drawn by John Jacob Astor, the richest man in America when he retired in 1834, or by Amos Bronson Alcott, father of the famous Louisa May, who, along with his brother, Chatfield, were employed by the Upson Tin Company of Stonington, Connecticut. Much tinware was sold for purchase through country stores, one of which, a small establishment in Connecticut, was clerked by the future circus magnate, P. T. Barnum. Perhaps it was while working here that P. T. imagined that advertising through tin plates was an ingenious idea, but it was long after his three-ring success story that plates were made to honor his three most important stars. They might have been included in "C Is for Commercialism," as they were certainly made to promote the most historically important stars of the circus, but their dates of manufacture are uncertain.

The Jumbo plate, which immortalized the enormous pachyderm, was said to have been produced by the Central Stamping Company (location unknown) in 1920 (twenty-nine years after Barnum died and thirty-five years after Jumbo's unfortunate collision with the unscheduled train). The animal **(Figure M18)** was as big as Barnum's dreams for him. Jumbo, the largest bush elephant (or so they say) to be held in captivity, was a $10,000 purchase in 1881 from London's Zoological Society. Standing nearly thirteen feet high and weighing seven tons, he was loved by the British until, in spite of Queen Victoria's protest, the gentle beast was sold to P. T. Barnum. Jumbo's short-lived circus life brought P. T. more than $2 million until, as he and a baby elephant were being led across a railroad track, the lights of an unscheduled freight train ended his earthly performances. Some say he died a hero, saving the little one from the same deadly fate. Crushed between a boxcar and a flatcar, he remains, to this day, the namesake of jumbo hotdogs, jumbo snow-cones, jumbo jets . . .

Barnum's General Tom Thumb, a most profitable sensation of the 19th century, is immortalized in his typical thumb-in-vest stance **(Figure M19)**. The tiny, perfectly proportioned Charles Stratton was a midget, the victim of a malfunctioning pituitary gland. Barnum brought other midgets to play, with Tom, before the public. Among them was Mercy Lavinia Warren Bumpus, who became Tom's wife in a "genteel and gracious" ceremony on February 10, 1863, at Hartford's fashionable Grace Church. While being accused of having arranged the romance to capitalize on the sexual curiosity surrounding the wedding, Barnum accompanied Tom and Lavinia to meet President Lincoln, only to face further accusations of conspiring with Old Abe to "ease the melancholia caused by the disasters of the Civil War" (Harris, 1973). Barnum seems to have ignored the turmoil . . . the Strattons retired a bit but returned to the stage under Barnum's management. Mildred Chalala, in her December 1986 article for the *Antique Trader*, presumes that the metal plate was made in 1844 to commemorate the occasion of Tom's visit to entertain Queen Victoria.

Even more profitable was the voice of Jenny Lind; Jenny arrived from Scandinavia at the Canal Street dock to the wild enthusiasm of thousands, some of whom fell overboard in their effort to get a glimpse of the Swedish Nightingale. Her image, stamped into a metal plate **(Figure M20)**, is after the prototype engraving by P. O. Wagner. The lovely soprano thrilled burgeoning audiences for only ten months under Barnum's guidance. Having been convinced that she would be received with greater dignity away from P. T.'s circus attitude, Jenny Lind remained in America for only one more year, earning less but enriching her life with her marriage to a young pianist, Otto Goldschmidt, with whom she raised their children in their English home. (Neither the Circus World Museum in Baraboo, Wisconsin, nor the Barnum Museum of Bridgeport, Connecticut, could provide any information concerning the plates that featured any one of the Barnum luminaries.)

ABC metals with no stamped design on the plate floor were undoubtedly made by several companies. Distinctions are:

The alphabet may encircle the rim with no interruption, as in Figures M21 and M22, which are made mostly of aluminum. **Figure M23** shows the attached clamp designed to fasten the dish securely to the high chair or table.

An "&" (ampersand) separates the Z and the A, as in **Figures M24 and M25.**

An "&" and a five-pointed star separate the Z and the A, as in **Figures M26 and M27.**

An "&" and a pointing hand separate the Z and the A, as in **Figure M28.**

An "&" and a horizontal diamond separate the Z and the A, as in **Figure M29.**

An "&" and a period separate the Z and the A, as in **Figures M30 and M31.**

A five-pointed star alone separates the Z and the A, as in **Figure M32.**

A six-pointed star separates the Z and the A, as in **Figure M33.**

Two dog-dish-style vessels are pictured in **Figures M34**

and **M35. Figure M34** bears an alphabet block design and is stamped "Underwood's Patent"; there is no listing of this firm in Rainwater and Redfield (1998). **Figure M35** is beautifully engraved with flourishes and figures. The item was made and guaranteed by the Van Bergh Silver Plate Company of Rochester, New York (1892-1926), which merged into Oneida Community Limited.

Figure M36 is encircled by two sets of letters, one in capitals and one in lowercase.

Type styles and/or their sizes may differ subtly, and the "swing" of the ampersand may be the defining clue of difference. It is often necessary to do rubbings of the letters and superimpose them to be accurate. In this study, we must rely not only upon what is seen but on what can't be seen.

Plates identical to **Figures M24 and M25,** with only an ampersand between the Z and A, were offered by Sears and Roebuck (Chicago) in an 1897 catalogue (6 inches, 2¢ each or 20¢ per dozen). No manufacturer was listed. (No reproduction of the page is included as the image was indistinct.) In addition, a reprint of Boston's Dover Stamping Company's *1869 Illustrated Catalog* features a similar plate. Founded in 1833 and already on its third catalogue by 1869, this leading distributor of housewares pictures the plate on page 7 with a barely discernible drawing along with squash-pie plates, "scallop" plates, and Washington pie or jelly-cake pans. Whether Sears obtained this item from Dover is unknown.

A plate featuring an ampersand and a five-pointed star **(Figures M26 and M27)** was also featured in the 1902 Sears Catalogue. (Again, no reproduction of the Sears catalogue page has been included.) Two manufacturers of this design were identified from the Winterthur Museum collection of metal housewares items (on microfiche available at the Library of Congress). The design was found on a catalogue page featuring shallow stamped ware from a Republic Metalware Company (Buffalo, New York and Chicago, Illinois) catalogue of 1907. The item was 6-3/4 inches in diameter and sold for $2.25 a gross. The same design was labeled "plain" and made by Shepard, Sidney and Company of Buffalo, New York, in 1873. Plate images on these two findings were very small and difficult to interpret.

As in "E Is for Education," plates that introduce only the alphabet letters are followed by plates that feature rhymes; **Figure M37** features a well-worn "Little Jack Horner." **Figures M38 and M39** dish out "Hey Diddle, Diddle," with two different edges, one rolled and one flat. The whimsical stamping was offered by Butler Brothers, 1899-1920. **Figure M40** sings "Mary Had a Little Lamb," **Figure M41** is Oneida's "Simple Simon," and **Figures M42 and M43** continue to ask "Who Killed Cock Robin?" Most unique is **Figure M42**, which has been painted and dated 1897 on its reverse. This plate was also pictured in an 1899 Butler Brothers Catalogue. A rare find by Ann and Dennis Berard of Fitzwilliam, New Hampshire, is seen in **Figure M44**; the design answers the question and completes the set.

The next mixed-metal plate illustrates one adventure of Palmer Cox's Brownies **(Figure M45)**. The mischievous creatures were featured in the 1883 *St. Nicholas Magazine* and in books such as *Brownies at Home, Another Brownie Book, Many More Nights, Brownies at the Race Track*, etc. The cheerful imps were housekeeping fairies; they lit the morning fires and cooked sumptuous breakfasts ready for waking families.

The complicated plate design of this Brownie stamping, patented on February 11, 1896, is also featured on Plate 60 of Powers and Floyd's *Early American Decorated Tinware* published by Hastings House of New York (1957); the photograph pictures an overpainting of the Brownies' scene in terra-cotta, cream, and old blue surrounded by gold letters.

In addition, four other familiar mixed-metal plates are included on Plate 61. Its black and white photo of "Miscellaneous Articles" presents a decorated "Cock Robin," a colored "Mary Had a Little Lamb," a gilt-enhanced "Jumbo," and a simple alphabet plate edge (Z/&/A) highlighted in gold. Text notes describe the retouching of decorations as "restoration," though, aside from the "Cock-Robin" plate, which had been overpainted and dated by its 1897 owner (**Figure M42**), only lithographed metal items have been found showing evidence of coloration.

Not associated with time-honored tales are plate designs such as the iron or the brass horse (**Figures M46 and M47**), the patriotic eagle (**Figure M48**), or the aluminum clock (**Figure M49**), the trademark of which was the subject of a long and unrewarding search in spite of its point of origin, "Wolverhampton," so clearly stamped.

Places to go were well represented in the history of "tin" plates: a mostly aluminum Niagara Falls (**Figure M50**) and many issues of varying sizes keep the memory of 1851's Great Exhibition (**Figures M51 through M54**) from fading from our memories. The four plates (spanning the mini-plate size range) present a stamped impression of the Crystal Palace, which was designed by Sir Joseph Paxton in only ten days. Its million feet of glass held more than 13,000 exhibits, which were seen by more than 6,200,000 visitors, who enjoyed concerts from the world's largest organ and a circus that featured thrilling performances of the world-famous tightrope walker, Blondin. When the Great Exhibition closed, the palace was moved to Sydenham Hill in South London and reconstructed in what was, in effect, a two hundred-acre Victorian theme park. The new Crystal Palace Park at Sydenham was opened by the Queen on June 10th, 1854 (http://www.victorianstation.com/palace.html). Two editions, **Figures M51 and M52**, which measure 4.25 inches each, are identical except for the placements of the interior designs with respect to the rotations of the letters surrounding them. The larger plate, celebrating the relocation at Sydenham, completes the set (**Figure M55**).

And there were people to see; stalwarts, loyal to their causes, were committed to metal memories. Father Theobald Mathew (or Matthew or Matthews) (**Figure M56 and Figure R20**), a young Capuchin friar, founded the Irish Abstinence Movement in 1838. With his hand raised in commitment, he continues to fight the war for abstinence. Sir Colin Campbell (**Figure M57**) was remembered for his bravery in the War of 1812, waged against the United States; the Opium War against China; the Sikh War of 1848; and the Indian Mutiny. Always concerned for the well-being of his men, he was called "Old Careful," and, like the Civil War generals recalled in "A Is for Americana," he was criticized for overcaution in time of battle. The memorials to General George Washington and General Ulysses Grant, in two sizes each (**Figures M58 through M61**), remember steadfast leadership in the Revolutionary and Civil Wars.

Another leader of liberty brought his cause to our shores, having traveled aboard the steam frigate *Mississippi*. Two metal stampings of General Lajos (Louis) (Kussuth) Kossuth (**Figures M62 and M63**) honor this great Hungarian exile's plea for assistance in his struggle to secure independence for his country. Despite his passionate speech to the U.S. Congress at the capitol's National Hotel on January 7, 1852, George Washington's advice, according to author Bessie Lindsey, suggested that America not get involved in quarrels beyond its shores. Faithful to his cause, Kossuth returned to his homeland without diplomatic or military support from the U.S. government, but he did have some satisfaction for having seen the wearing of his high-crowned hat become a fad. Copies of his chapeaux, with its large feather, were worn by hundreds of young men before he left America. Kossuth's hatless image is encircled by words on both plates that cannot all be deciphered. Stamped in capitals, it reads: KOSSUTH, GOVERNOR OF HUNGARY AND GUEST OF AMERICA THE FRIEND OF____ L (O or I) VE ____ FREEDOM.

Easier to decipher is a spectacular plate pictured as number 1207 in *Gifts for Good Children* by Noël Riley (1991). That transfer was taken from a daguerreotype by Claudet; when Kossuth visited the great city the Hungarian general posed with his family for an account to be printed in the *London News*.

A more familiar influence was the family of Queen Victoria, well documented in metal souvenirs. Four designs salute the Queen (**Figures M64 through M67**) and her beloved Albert. The first busts rest within a frame of upper- and lowercase alphabets. The second, third, and fourth are surrounded by capitals whose A and Z are separated by four dots, which, if connected, would form a plus sign. **Figure M66** is framed by a floral surround. **Figures M68 and M69** present handsome portraits of the Prince and Princess of Wales, who also rest comfortably in their carriages on **Figures M70 and M71**.

But not all plate designs were stamped. Some bore the signature of the Ohio Art Company in the 1920s. The "Girl on the Swing" tea set, as seen in Kerr and Gilcher's *Ohio Art - The World of Toys,* was produced from 1918 through about 1925. It was a seven-piece set with only the plates encircled with letters; Kerr's comments attribute a lyrical quality to the litho art. The second series, the "Kittens," was first seen at the 1920 New York Toy Fair. Displayed by H. S. Winzeler, founder of Ohio Art, the set was manufactured throughout the 1920s. Again, neither the cup, the coffee pot, nor the smaller plate includes letters in its designs (**Figures M72 through M75**).

The "Girl on the Swing" was the Bryant, Ohio, company's first toy. Other lithographed metal, colorful lithographed tea sets and trays, pails, shovels, and sand molds continued until 1923, when there were two hundred employees working hard to accommodate the firm's growing production, which expanded with the installation of new machinery in 1927. An ABC wagon was added to the line in 1928, as well as boldly colored drums, tops, and watering cans, bringing the company to 1930, when it absorbed the Mutual Novelty Manufacturing Company (makers of Christmas tree icicles) as well as other houses with diversified products.

Now known for the vibrant color on its toys, which have survived beautifully over the years, Ohio Art used a process of chromolithography that began at the end of the 18th century. German map inspector Alois (also Aloys) Senefelder (1771-1834) experimented with acids, inks, and stone in an effort to be his own publisher. In 1798, after thousands of trials, he prepared a stone so that a print could be pulled using a process based on the chemical reactions between oil and water. He found that when a picture was drawn in reverse on smooth, porous limestone with a grease crayon, water would stick to the stone's surface but not to the crayon marks. When an oily ink was spread over the stone, it would stick to the crayon marks and not to the water-protected stone surface. Paper pressed against the stone would be printed with the picture on the stone, only it would be printed in ink instead of crayon. Because the images were drawn rather than etched or engraved on copper, fine details could be reproduced easily. Artisans used as many stones as needed; each stone contributed one color to each print. Each print had to be carefully registered; each print had to be placed exactly over the other to create the full and accurate effects of the colors. Once steam presses had been manufactured, thousands of lithographs could be printed each day.

It was not until 1875 that the basic process was adapted to tin printing. Robert Barclay and John Doyle Fry patented an offset process that was eventually adopted by the entire industry. Their tin process transferred a design from the stone onto a large rubber roller, which rolled the design onto a large tin sheet. After each color was laid, the metal was sent through an annealing oven to fix the paint. The printing process was repeated with the registration, or fitting of each color crucial to the process, the key to the glowing pictures of cats and kids on the tins of Ohio Art, the advertisements of Lava soap **(Figures C36 through C40)**, and the red Canadian plates **(Figures M76 and M77)**. At least the latter are known to have been made by the Kemp Manufacturing Company of Toronto, Canada, though none of the plates noted have maintained the smooth, vibrantly colored surfaces of the Ohio Art products. In his 1926 edition of *Tin and the Tin Industries* published by Sir Isaac Pitman and Sons, London, Alfred Mundey warned that because the film of ink was so thin, only the highest-quality inks should be employed. He also cautioned against a rapid drying process, necessary to retain the film's elasticity and reduce the chance of cracking or chipping, as seen so clearly in **Figure C38**.

In 1914, continuous ovens for drying inked tin-plate were introduced, speeding the lithograph process along. Recent developments, according to Lisa Kerr and Jim Gilcher (1998), include ultraviolet lithography machines by which "six colors can be laid down and baked on in sequence in one process. This speeds up the process considerably."

Also lithographed is the vibrant red toy bank (by Burnett of London), which might have sat upon a table awaiting generous contributions before the Jewish Sabbath meal **(Figure M78)**. Also painted is the very smallest collectible of all, included courtesy of William and Sandra Wassa of Southbury, Connecticut; the brown table candlestick is pictured trimmed with a hardly legible alphabet border **(Figure M79)**.

Not painted are the last two toys, a teeny table and a rattle, both embellished with alphabet letters and numerals **(Figure M80)**. Ready for tea, perhaps the three-legged casting furnished the doll house garden. The rattle, pictured on page 41 (plate VII, item number 32) of Harry Weiss' *American Baby Rattles from Colonial Times to the Present* (1941), was manufactured about 1825 with a drum-shaped head; 5-inch handles had two "fife" holes in the side of the hollow cylinders if made of metal (or whistles in the ends if they were wood). The drum sides carried the letters of the alphabet, but, as they were too tiny to be read and beyond the "reach" of the shaker, the poorly impressed toy functioned best as a noisemaker or a mallet-shaped instrument built to clamor for second helpings **(Figure M81)**.

More valuable to collectors than the toys are the very small, uncolored servers. The proverbial "Good things come in small packages!" holds true, as the wee plates, 3 inches or less in diameter, carry giant price tags. The little ones may have been manufactured to be doll-ware, romantic remembrances, or decorations to put upon the "whatnots." Easily lost and damaged, these "smalls" seem less and less available; finding them encourages growing investments.

The deepest of the miniatures is the pie plate **(Figure M82)**, whose rim, with an "&" and a dot between its A and Z, bears a tiny hole from its hanging; uniquely, the letter baseline is the outside rim of the plate and is seen in **Figure O4** to highlight this border oddity. The Boy and Girl With a Hoop has recently been restamped **(Figure M83)**; seldom seen are the Lion **(Figure M84)**, the Baby's Head **(Figure M85)**, and a prancing horse **(Figure M86)**, as are the three unique roosters **(Figures M87, M88, and M89)**, which made handy chewables for teething gums.

Two unique smalls hold borders with incomplete alphabets—the first **(Figure M90)** reaching only from A through V and the second **(Figure M91)** ending at Q but shouting "Eureka," for it alone is made partly of gold. These two miniatures can be seen in greater detail as **Figures O11 and O12** in "O Is for Ornamental Borders."

A most unique small is titled "Grinding Old into Young." To the believer, the message may be read as a less divine and somewhat humorous process of reincarnation. To others, it is but a melancholy reminder of man's inevitable termination **(Figure M92)**.

An additional miniature, "Man on a Horse" **(Figure M93)** and a full-sized mixed-metal plate titled "Liberty" **(Figure M94)** can also be seen in "Z Is for Σ and Other Reversals." Both illustrate examples of letters that have been rotated or flipped horizontally.

Aside from letters right side up, hollowware mugs of metal brought thirst-quenching nourishment. Metal mugs, like those typically found crossing the plains in Conestoga wagons, were chromolithographed with black alphabets on red background or stamped with borders that twined around the vessel. More "classy" were the silver-plated mugs still cherished as gifts for newborns or toddlers. Manufacturers have been determined only for the silver-plated/sterling mugs that are clearly marked with trademarks easily matched in Rainwater and Redfield's *Encyclopedia of American Silver Manufacturers* (Schiffer, 1998).

Two very fragile metal lithographed drinking cups read "For A Good Boy" and "A Good Girl" **(Figures M95 and M96)**. Three mugs, made mostly of iron, have distinct designs. **Figures M97 and M98** display three design lines each. The third of the less fragile grouping, **Figure M99**, has a four-line stamping.

The first of the silver-plated cup designs was produced by the Forbes Silver Co. of Meriden, Connecticut. Begun in 1894 as a division of the Meriden Britannia Co. for hollowware silver-plating, the firm eventually formed part of the International Silver Company **(Figure M100)**. The novelty item was pictured in two catalogues, the Forbes Silverplate catalogue, page 58 (no date) and the Wm Rogers Silverplated Hollowware publication hand-dated 1937. **Figures M101 and M102** picture the cover and one page of the printing; they are included with the permission of the Historical Society Library at Hartford, Connecticut.

A second silver-plate cup **(Figure M103)** is stamped W. A. Rogers 470. The firm (c.1894-1929) was an Ontario corporation with factories in Niagara Falls, New York, and North Hampton, Massachusetts. The last item **(Figure M104)** was acquired at the 1983 Bing Crosby (1904-1977) auction in Oakland, California, and brings with it a sad note of Hollywood history. It was a gift to Bing Crosby's daughter, the middle child by his second wife, Catherine Grant, who married Bing in 1957; Harry was born in 1958, Mary Frances in 1959, and Nathaniel in 1961. The silver cup was a gift from Lindsay Crosby (1938), the fourth child of his first marriage, who died on December 12, 1989 of a self-inflicted gunshot wound. The sterling cup, made by Lebkuecher & Co. of Newark, New Jersey (1896-1909), brings with it a measure of misery.

There are other items of metal in this text in addition to those seen here. Referred to in this chapter are the Lava Soap advertisers found in "C Is for Commercialism." Magnified rims of several plates included here are also found in "O Is for Ornamental Borders." "Z Is for Σ and Other Reversals" presents a second look at the full image titled "Liberty," a photo of the same plate with a reversed letter stamping, and a magnification of each.

Certainly there are other objects of sterling, silver plate, and mixed-metals to be collected. One mixed metal plate, stamped with the image of a beehive, was seen in a national advertiser and another mixed metal, listed as Figure TP-1 on page 181 of Lindsay's *ABC Plates and Mugs* (Collector Books, 1998), is a fine addition to a collection of royal commemoratives. Of course, the "Peter Rabbit" found on the cover of the Lindsays' book is the quintessential collectible of all decorated metals.

There is little question of the components of sterling mugs and plates; silver-plated/sterling items should conform to manufacturing standards. All other items contain unique combinations of elements . . . varieties of "recipes" whose secret ingredients, once revealed, give more reliable definitions to the term "tin." Like other categories, the collecting of metals, both plates and mugs, is assuredly a lifelong search with a ringing promise of profit.

N Is for 19th Century

Dickens was right. It was the best and the worst of times. There was contentment and contempt, pride and poverty, ingenuity and indifference, riches without righteousness, propriety alongside pornography, and more. The period is best remembered for its change from a seasonal agrarian to a fast-paced industrial society, some of which can be revealed through our accumulated ceramic records.

Romantically, the Victorian Era carries with it a sense of infinite order, the peace of piety and unquestioned standards of right and wrong. People went about their work with a great sense of individual purpose, and what God, the Queen, and the Social Order said was correct was, indeed, just that. Social standards carried an air of authority . . . each class conformed to its standards. The aristocracy and the landed gentry kept the tills filled with profits from lands and investments. The aristocracy held titles as well, from Dukes to Barons and from Duchesses to Ladies. Like the land, titles were inherited, and along with those and the 19th-century reforms came the obligation to sit in Parliament or on local councils to improve the quality of life in his/her community. The middle class did the "clean" work . . . the thinking jobs were theirs; it was that middle class that grew significantly during the Victorian period, and it was this self-motivated, hard-working, churchgoing, family oriented, virtuous group of individuals that encouraged the reforms for which the century would be known. The working class did the dirty work . . . they were permanently relegated to the hard labor of the potters and the miners and the builders and the fishermen, and, most of all, the farmers. Without them there would have been no progress. At the start of Victoria's reign (Mitchell, 1996) there were more than a million farm laborers and another 364,000 indoor farm servants (including the dairy maids who milked cows and churned the butter).

The landed gentry, who enjoyed inherited property, rented sections of their thousand acre estates to farmers who paid for the privilege of working its soil; property owners could farm thousands of acres by the hands of others, and those hands never held enough. Though the cost of rent was little or less, it was often "paid" in potatoes or milk. Cash for clothing was rare, and care in times of illness was beyond expectation; the farmers were often doomed to very long months of hard physical labor **(Figures N1 through N12)** and the farm women, pictured with a sense of strength and purpose on so many transfers, did their fair share of field labor as well. Especially important were their long hours of labor at harvest time, when, after the grain was cut by scythes, they gathered the sheaves and followed behind the wagons to glean the leftovers. So many

beautiful plates ensure these hard-working women their well-earned immortality **(Figures N13 through N18)**. It is possible that **Figure N9** represents a meeting of the top-hatted landowner and a farm femme . . . a commercial conversation, to be sure.

Those landed gentry dressed in the spirit of George Bryan ("Beau") Brummell, the trend-setter of the country gentleman's wardrobe; he was the authority to court society on all manner of dress designed by him and executed by the venerable Mr. Weston, tailor, of Old Bond Street. They wore the top boots, the buckskin breeches, the blue coats cut away at the waist and the light buff waistcoats. They wore the clothes, these gentry, that befitted their station as they considered hunting and shooting, "the only proper life for a man" (Reader, 1973). It was in their outdoor life that they marshalled their animals to find their game as one would engage a battalion of soldiers in pursuit. The land-owning class was quite content; it maintained its estates, enjoyed its leisure, loved its comfort and relished its social positions. Packs of well-fed hounds, the sleekest of horses and newest of beautifully designed weapons, were ready to gather at the sound of the horn. Blood sports, especially the shooting of foxes, were the elaborate rituals of the rich, though the high cost of the game often shot the family fortune along with its elegant prey **(Figures N19 through N23)**. Plates also present "cartoons" that tell the tales of horses and riders around a central diamond **(Figures N24 through N29)**. Each tale depended upon the horse, of course, and most often the horse was in command. Throwing its rider, the horse let the eater laugh while he lingered over his lamb chop. Set apart from other transfers for their humor, these graphic illustrations are clear examples of those aspects of Victorian humor that found hazardous situations humorous **(Figures N30 through N33)**. Three scenes, **Figures N34, N35, and N36,** ask whether man or beast is truly the hunter! Perhaps they were self-congratulatory . . . allowing the viewers, with some indifference, to compare infirmity with their own well-being.

And there seemed to be an indifference to the balance of nature as well; the threat of extinction was not yet a popular cause. The wilds were just being explored, too often to excess. **Figures N37 through N40** are scenes of hunts that today would kill the appetite along with the buffalo and the seal pups. From a very small collection of pottery transfer, or "pulls," in the print collection at London's Victoria and Albert Museum, emerged a unique transfer scene, presented here with the museum's permission. Strikingly similar to the colorfully painted ceramic scene, **Figure N41**, **Figure N42** is one of a precious few designs that remain from The Potteries' past. This "reversed" view of hunting on elephants remains from the manufactory of H & C or Hope and Carter of the Fountain Place Pottery in Burslem (1862-1880). The firm was formerly Pinder, Bourne and Hope from 1851 to 1860 and subsequently G. L. Ashworth and Brothers from 1880 to 1968. Riley (1991) says that this is one of a set of hunting scenes supplied by Elisha Pepper to the Dutch factory of Petrus Regout, Maastricht, Holland, 1836-1870. Regout was determined to compete with the English in their production of transfer-printed designs. He not only employed English craftsmen in his factory, he also purchased copper plates from firms in The Potteries.

Like India's elephants, England's sleek and often cropped-tail horses were vehicles for the hunt but provided transportation as well. Horses delivered commercial goods and services in magnificent stagecoaches overburdened with packages and people, provided the opportunity to show off their owners' finery in a carriage ride around the town, and jumped over short walls or raced around a track, with or without an attached buggy. So many plates paid homage to the importance of these beauties; youngsters could lope gracefully through lunch (Figures N43 through N52).

For the very lucky squires and landowners, stables, manicured gardens, and velvet-lawned grounds surrounded the elegant and spacious manor houses. Whole wings were given to the children, the laundresses (Figure N53), the nurses, undernurses, and teaching governesses. (More about that in "I Is for Infant to Infirm," "R Is for Religion, Reform, and Reason," and "E Is for Education").

Near the manor houses were villages with their wells, as important to "cacklings" as they were to the kitchens. Village greens were settings for festivals and entertainment (Figures N54 and N55). Larger villages had their small cathedral; smaller towns their churches, their schools, shops, and those who provided services for the town's citizens: a few of England's 25,000 blacksmiths, Mr. Fix-its (Figures N56 and N57), the pub owners, shoemakers, clothing makers, as well as those who paid attention to the more personal side of life . . . the midwives, the nurses, and those who cared for the ones who passed on. And there were the thrashers (Figure N58), the grain grinders, and the bread sellers (Figures N59, N60, and N61), all of whom were central figures in the controversy over the Corn Laws.

In 1846, Britain had adopted free trade; all levies (or duties) on products coming into the country from other shores had been done away with, which helped the flow of British trade at the time. The duties that had been imposed on the import of all grains since the 12th century by the Corn Laws were designed to protect the British landed gentry against the import of cheaper foreign grain; they ensured a stable and sufficient supply of grain while allowing for imports if needed. But with poor crop conditions and an influx of people from elsewhere, bread became more and more expensive. The poor were hungry. Two Manchester manufacturers, Richard Cobden and John Bright, led the fight in Parliament to establish free trade and abolish the Corn Laws; they won the support of Sir Robert Peel, who knew that if the starving were to be fed, grain must cost as little as possible. Peel led the final repeal of the Corn Laws at mid-century (Figure N62). Sadly, he died from injuries sustained as he fell from his horse. In the 19th-century tradition of paying homage with ceramic images, this circular portrait of the Prince Consort Albert's dear friend reminds its diners of not

only his efforts in Parliament but of his founding of London's "Bobbies," the city's Metropolitan Police, who were justly named for their founder.

It wasn't long before the rural farmers began their migration to the cities. In the early 1800s, most males were farm dwellers. At the half-century, 25% of all males were tillers of the soil and by 1871 the number was reduced to about 12%, each earning about 12 shillings a day. The women did less and machinery did more. In the 1880s, with the import of wheat from the United States, many farmers and their families turned from milling to machines. Now toiling in manufactories or working as domestics, they sought shelter in horrific urban slums which offered too many to a mattress and too little sanitation in crude dwellings that were too damp and too dark. Even the air was dirty; the mud, the dust of the granite ground by iron shod hooves, the soot from a thousand black chimneys and the airborne particles of horse-droppings seeped onto every surface. There was too much crime which gave rise to new prisons; unions were the natural outgrowth of so much despair with too many incidents of violence.

Parliament moved at a snail's pace to regulate industry's inhumanities. But slowly the nation's conscience came alive. The Reform Bill of 1832, five years before the ascension of the young Queen Victoria, was the start of the democratic process. It redefined the vote, and by secret ballot, the voices of the middle class were heard. Investigations into the conditions in the factories provided laws to protect the working masses and humanize child labor (see "P Is for Potters and Their Potteries"), and soon, with ravaging epidemics, the need for a public health system was conceived. "R Is for Religion, Reform, and Reason" describes the role of the Evangelical Revival as it actively brought remedies to social ills; the virtues of work and worship were tied to lift the spirits and the lifestyle of the middle and working classes. Slavery was abolished in the British Empire, and a Poor Law brought charities to help those who could not help themselves, especially during a depression which, at the start of the '40s, raised the percentage of those dependent to nearly one-fifth of the population. And at long last, in 1862, the government began its support of a free education for all (see "E Is for Education").

It was of this England that the 18-year-old niece of King William IV became queen in on June 20, 1837, her reign crossing the centuries from 1837 to 1901. Leaving her overprotective mother's bedroom, Alexandrina Victoria soon proposed to her charming Prince Francis Charles Augustus Albert Emmanuel of Saxe-Coburg-Gotha; the royal couple's blessed event (1840) was commemorated on plates, both metal and ceramic, some of which have been gathered here and in "M Is for Metals," to bless the union. Neither of them, Lytton Strachey (1949) quickly convinces us, were immediately struck by cupid's arrow. But, with a royal flourish (hers faster than his) Albert became the "supreme political influence over Victoria" (Strachey, 1949), and the two were THE moral influence over their subjects, adding to their royal homes more than a dash of domestic tranquility and middle-class vigilance (Figures N63, N64, and N65, Figures M64 through M67, and Figures O18, O19, and O20). The marriage of only one of their nine children was commemorated on plates with molded borders in this collection—the 1863 union of their second child, Albert Edward (1841-1910), Prince of Wales (subsequently King Edward VII), to Princess Alexandria of Denmark (Figure N66 and Figures M68 through M71).

Eight other children were born to them: Princess Victoria Adelaide Maria (1840-1901), the Princess Royal, who married Frederick III, Emperor of Germany; Alice Maud Mary (1843-1878), who married Louis IV, Grand Duke of Hesse-Darmstadt; Alfred Ernest Albert (1844-1900), Duke of Edinburgh and Saxe-Coburg-Gotha, who was married to Grand Duchess Marie Alexandrovna of Russia; Helena Agusta Victoria (1846-1923), who married Prince Christian of Schleswig-Holstein; Louise Caroline Alberta (1848-1939), who married John Campbell, 9th Duke of Argyll; and Arthur William Patrick (1850-1942), Duke of Connaught, who married Louise Margaret of Prussia. The Queen's innovative use of chloroform helped to make the birth of her eighth child easier for her and consequently for all women who had the courage, as did the Queen, to ask for it. Leopold George Duncan was born in 1853 to become the 1st Duke of Albany and to marry Helene of Waldeck and Pyrmont. The youngest, Beatrice Mary Victoria, was born in 1857 (58?), to marry Prince Henry of Battenberg. Victoria's descendants eventually became members of nearly every royal family in Europe. Victoria sustained nine pregnancies in about eighteen years; in spite of her flares of temper, she maintained both motherhood and monarchy.

An integral part of both her lives, the Queen's love of letter writing might well have inspired the institution of the Penny Post. On the sixth of May in 1840, thanks to Mr. Rowland Hill's perseverance, inexpensive postage went on sale in London for the first time. He rightly insisted that a low rate would dramatically increase the volume of mail and everyone could write, not only the rich. And those who couldn't write, learned **(Figure N67)**.

Two years later, with the opening of the railway from Manchester to London, the mail could be carried by train. By 1845, the people movers were saving the lives of the unemployed, with booming opportunities to construct their bridges, tunnels, and tracks (see "P Is for Potters and Their Potteries"). The ragged image of the undernourished factory worker was slowly changing to that of the 250,000 muscle-bound, beer-drinking "navvies" who built, without the help of modern earth movers, the 80,00 miles of track that by 1848 connected the major cities. Rapid growth continued through 1914. The coal and iron industry built the trains that carried the goods to the ports where the great vessels waited.

Steel was produced with the Bessemer process; power looms were driven by Watt's engines. The raw materials that the Colonies produced were changed by enterprising factories into finished products to be exported back to the Colonies and to the rest of the world. To show off their worldly goods, the 1851 First World's Fair was planned under the direction of the good Queen's Consort, whose passion for science and the arts led to the celebration of England's place as the crown of the world market. Built in only six months, Joseph Paxton's prefabricated iron and glass Crystal Palace housed the Great Exhibition **(Figure N68)**, which was divided into four groups: machines, fine arts, raw materials, and the manufactured goods made from them. Thirteen thousand exhibitors added to the colossal display of objects from around the world . . . rococo Victorian objects sat uneasily against the clean lines of the transparent structure; nearby stood an American McCormick reaper, soon to change the agrarian lifestyle; a massive twenty-four-ton block of coal from a mine owned by the Duke of Devonshire; and, most wonderful of all, a doctor's walking stick, complete with test tubes and an apparatus built to hold an enema at the ready (Priestley, 1972). Although Charles Babbage, the father of the computer, suggested an elevated railway to move people effortlessly through the exhibit, 6,063,986 wide-eyed visitors managed to walk the long halls absorbing the spectacle's messages of the values of free trade, the brilliance of technological advancement, and the glory of the English work ethic. Surely Sam Smiles smiled (see "R Is for Religion, Reform, and Reason").

It was only three years later that the Queen watched, with her best wishes and prayers, the solemn pageantry as the last battalion of cheering men went off to a war that some could find absolutely no reason for joining and others demanded. And the most magnificent spectacle ever witnessed in The Potteries took place only three years after that; Edward Stanton (severely wounded at the battle of the Alma), John Walker (wounded at the attack on the Mamelon), Robert Blake (wounded before Sebastopol), and William White (wounded in the Redan) and others rode in a festooned carriage to the cheers of 20,000 people amid the shiny flags and banners borne by the proud workers of the thirteen nearby potteries. The muskets roared, and cheers for the Queen, the Chief Bailiff, and Chief Marshall rose from the joyous throngs while the Fire Brigade slowly flaunted its engine, resplendent with allied flags and pine boughs, as it passed the dusty buildings dressed, for the day in ribbons and sashes. Mounted Heralds, who strode to the beat of the Etruria Juvenile Drum and Fife Band, were followed by Captain Steel's one-hundred-member cadre of uniformed Royal Pensioners. A solid red banner that boldly declared, "WAR IS EVIL" was soon followed by a white flag that wrenched salty tears with its reminder to "Honor the Brave." The memories of Robert Edge and George Turner would linger in the hearts of the twenty thousand who celebrated the return of the pottery men.

Many pottery transfers presented information as would a newspaper photo; ABC plates offered "sterile" scenes of the Crimea as the conflict waged on the Black Sea coast of Southern Russia to prevent Russia from expanding her influence into Turkey on the Mediterranean Sea. Under Queen Victoria, Britain had stayed out of European wars until Turkey invaded Russia in 1853. Britain, France, and an army of 10,000 from Sardinia came to the aid of the Ottoman Turks. But the war was strategized badly on both sides, and aside from military killed in needless battle, 250,000 were lost to disease. So shocking were the accounts of the savage conditions in the Crimea that Florence Nightingale escorted thirty-eight women, who, in spite of the misery, organized critical care to reduce fatalities. Though the Russians managed to rid Sebastopol of its ships, its forts, and its population, their cause was ultimately lost. It was, however, a great victory for shipping, as Russia surrendered Southern Bessarabia at the mouth of the Danube and the river was opened to the shipping of all nations. It was a great victory for humankind as well, for, as the peace treaty was signed the end of the hostilities, women's role in nursing was sealed for all eternity.

Tennyson's poem imprints the war's most famous battle at Sebastopol. It was October 25, 1854. Russian General Prince Menshikof's huge army stormed the rear of the British flanks, but the 93rd Regiment, under Sir Colin Campbell **(Figure M57)**, kept the cavalry at bay. General Scarlett, with the English Heavy Cavalry Brigade, skirmished with yet other Russian troops. At this time, a message was received by Lord Cardigan, who commanded his Light Brigade of Cavalry to overcome an enemy battery positioned at "the other" end of the long, narrow valley.

To attack, his men would need to pass between facing lines of the Russian men and machines, and if they did reach their destination, would meet enemy fire, "head-on." Of the 673 who braved it, 195 returned unhurt.

> Cannon to right of them,
> Cannon to left of them,
> Cannon in front of them
> Volley'd and thunder'd;
> Storm'd at with shot and shell,
> Boldly they rode and well.
> Into the jaws of Death,
> Into the mouth of Hell
> Rode the six hundred.

Perhaps the ABC plate transfers were inspired by historic sketches from the front **(Figures N69 through N72)**, as this was the first war ever covered by telegraph, newspaper photographers, and reporters. How much of the political reality could a youngster really learn? Perhaps it was enough to present images of those who exhibited bravery against great odds . . . courage and croquettes were nourishment enough.

Aside from skirmishes in the Colonies and the Crimean War, the Boer War was the only other reportable conflict, but no "transferable" information appeared. There were other scenes, however, of the military **(Figures N73 through N77)** as the British Empire had expanded to Africa, Asia, North America, Australia, New Zealand, and more (see list of British Colonies in Appendix AN1.)

Soldiers were stationed in far-off places where the British flag flew high, though the local governments, to prevent another revolution "American style," were allowed self-rule alongside the Queen's governors. Many military personnel spent time away from home . . . the prospect of life in uniform was alluring to the "genteel" offspring of the landed gentry and aristocracy.

For these upper-class sons, "head-hunters" sought openings in socially regulated regiments **(Figure N78)**; the higher the prestige, the higher the price. Most illustrious were the guards who protected the Queen and the horse-riding cavalry who paid dearly for their spiffed-up steeds and socialites at fancy dress balls. Promotions of officers living in less comfortable tropical zones were less expensive but more expedient . . . and open to trade. For the poorer, the common soldier's lot was not a happy one; the populace suspected Their Majesty's gatekeepers to be those who might just as well have languished in jail. With dim futures ahead, boys barely beyond boyhood drummed, bugled, and burned the beans before the regiment could call them soldiers at eighteen. Paid less than a shilling a day they were flogged for the least mishap. Artillery and engineer commissions were granted for schooling rather than for sale. One wonders if the "drilling scenes" might have been found in training manuals **(Figures N79 through N83)**.

While some dug trenches in the Crimea, others worked feverishly at digging an under-river tunnel; a project baptized, by the *London Times*, as "precarious grubbery." Its danger was ever-present; its grubbery came in explosive waves of black gravel, maddening rushes of foul muck, torrents of fire, and noxious escapes of sulfur gasses that made the diggers feeble, brought tremors to their limbs, dimmed their vision, and wasted their flesh. Those who stayed filled sacs with mud to clear a tunnel beneath the Thames from Rotherhithe to Wapping (now in use as part of the Metropolitan Line of the London Underground). On three levels of an ingeniously constructed platform, they faced the earth to clear about twenty inches, the week's progress measured meticulously by its tireless and ingenious mastermind, Marc Isambard Brunel (some sources include his son, Isambard Kingdom Brunel, as well). Though knighted by the queen as the tunnel celebrated its grand opening in 1843 **(Figure N84)**, Sir Brunel may have had a more profound impact upon the world with the building of The Great Eastern. (For a superb essay on the tunnel, find *Marc Isambard Brunel* by Clements, 1970.)

Samuel Morse's dots and dashes (1843) were the forerunners of the technology that inspired the laying of a cable under the sea. Several unsuccessful attempts had been made; the elaborately wrapped copper wire cable had either snapped or was broken by the ice. **Figure N85** commemorates the third attempt, the completion of a path of electricity from Valentia, Ireland, to Heart's Content on Trinity Bay in Newfoundland. This well-painted graphic pictures Brunel's *Great Eastern*, the most massive ship afloat, "paying out" more than one thousand miles of cable from huge reels stored in its enormous water-filled tanks. This third and successful effort began by the splicing of two cables, one from an American ship and the other from Brunel's marvel, in midocean. Without accident, the *Great Eastern* arrived in Ireland at nine o'clock that morning. His message, "Thank God, the cable is laid, and is in perfect working order," was received on July 27, 1866 with cheers on both sides of the Atlantic. Though the current was too weak to last, the possibility of more efficient transmission systems was firmly established. The life of the vessel, too, was short. It wasn't too many years before Brunel's magnificent ship was laid to rest. Perhaps our commemorative was produced shortly after 1866 to secure the *Great Eastern's* place in the history of communication; certainly it taught determination and strength.

With the transatlantic cable, the expansion of Western Union and the growth of the school system came the rise of the news industry. More news was gathered more quickly from wider areas for a growing number of newspapers. Battalions of six- to sixteen-year-olds, fiercely competitive "entrepreneurs," hawked them to the public. At daybreak, each newsboy bought one hundred papers and, if he sold them all, enjoyed a piteous profit. Orphans all, they slept, homeless and ragged, in filthy alleys after warming their bodies with an evening's snort of whiskey . . . wicked comforts for young boys **(Figures T22, T23, and N86)** whose energies and determination educated the masses. Even alphabet rhymes honored the "newsies." The Railway A.B.C. (found in *Childhood's Happy Hours*, published by London's Frederick Warne and Co., Kronheim in 1865) wrote:

> N is the News-boy, who cries "Here you are!
> Punch, Times, Daily, Telegraph, Standard and Star.

The Mother's Picture Alphabet (S. W. Partridge, 1887), begins its eighteen line rhyme with:

> N begins News-boy, with papers to sell,
> What a good thing it is to learn to read well!

But one didn't need to read to enjoy the swell of alphabet books that began in the early 18th century. Early ABC rhymes, for example, recited from the *New England Primer*, battledores and tiny books brought simple poetry and postulates to the young ones. As the 19th century dawned, the rhymes became instructive and even, as the years passed, absurd and silly. Tales of morality filled books and popular magazines, many with hand-colored woodcuts or engravings, and by the 1870s, some color prints filled one side of a page. Transfers with rhythmic verses can be seen in "T Is for Transfers and Toybooks." Most of the transfers found both in children's books and on ABC plates in this collection can be seen in that chapter. Replications of graphics from sources other than children's literature are sprinkled throughout the text.

One such source is the high-spirited tale of John Gilpin, who, displaced in his carriage by a relative accompanying John and his good wife on their anniversary junket, was left to ride a horse to join his beloveds (**Figures N87 and N89, Figure L22, and Figure Z4**). The humorous ballad, written by William Cowper (pronounced Cooper, 1731-1800), recounts the tale of the real Mr. Beyer, a draper of Paternoster Row; the tale was published as *The Diverting History of John Gilpin* by Charles Tilt of London in 1828 (see Appendix AN2). The well-known illustration in **Figure N88**, a George Cruikshank creation, documents **Figure N89**. The signature of the illustrator is somewhat hidden in the print, used here courtesy of the Beineke Books and Manuscript Library, Yale University.

Strictly for adults was the story of *Paul and Virginia* (**Figure N90**), very romantic and immensely popular at the time. The curtain rises on the birth of Paul and Virginia in the solitude of the island where the Fan-Palm River shimmers between the high encircling cliffs of purple rock. Bonded by circumstance, each mother is mother to both, uniting the children even in infancy to eternal bonds of love. Idyllic and maturing, the pair's growing adoration is interrupted by the contentious designs of the maiden's great aunt. Rich, old, and pious, she lures the lass away to be schooled in France and chosen for marriage by a match suited to her newly inherited station. The final act begins when Paul, paralyzed by the contest between free will and the acceptance of Heaven's command, is quickly renewed by the prospect of Virginia's return. A white flag announces the vessel's arrival, but Nature, whose kind raptures had nurtured his very soul, now, in anger, cast his love from the railed deck of the *Saint-Geran* into a grave beneath the sand. Within days Paul too is quickly summoned through the shadows of death . . . a tragic Wagnerian end to an opera of unfulfilled love.

Romantic too were the Queen's musical evenings at Buckingham Palace; the Victorian mark of refinement became the polished piano in the parlor! The fashionable parlor recital proved the family's "high-end" status to visitors, who could admire the instrument (if not the voices or the performance). Governesses needed enough competence in music to inculcate their charges with the basics, as every young lady who desired to be a "lady" needed a tolerable proficiency at the keyboard (**Figure N91 and Figure T34**) to accompany singers (**Figures N92 and N93**) or flautists. Family sing-alongs provided entertainment and spiritual bonding at holidays and celebrations. The instrument and its talented performer shared the center of attention; mastery was the indisputable proof of cultural grace.

Children received musical training in piano or (the less expensive) organ and were encouraged to sing in church choirs or glee clubs and to march with bands. Ballet and folk dancing were popular as were the new "square" dances, jigs, horn pipes, and country dances (**Figures N94, N95, and N96**). Organs were played in the streets of the big cities (**Figure N97, Figure E27, and Figures V14 and V15**); ballad singers strolled, and fiddlers begged for trifles. Alphabet plates mixed songs with salads, keeping meals in perfect harmony (**Figures N94 through N99 and Figure T56**).

Punch and Judy entertained at fairs where, from flag- and bunting-festooned tents, hot mutton pies and sweetmeats were sold (**Figures N100 and N101**). Samuel Pepys recorded what was probably the first presentation of the humpbacked, hooknosed figure at Covent Garden in May of 1662. One wonders how many innocent diners knew just how evil this character of the Italian *Commedia dell'arte* really was; Punch first killed his noisy infant, then beat his wife, tricked the hangman (who then hung himself), and finally vanquished the devil. This uncommonly ugly and guiltless "hero" proved, once and for all, that crime did pay. And audiences paid, too, for grand performances of the full array of Punch and Judy puppets staged by Punchmen, who also strolled among the noisy street entertainers. The few dozen puppeteers of the century trained live dogs to participate as the dog Toby and used a mouthpiece called a "swazzle" to make Punch's "squalk" come alive. The (possibly) first Punch and Judy script was published in 1828 embellished with Cruikshank's illustrations, and as the bawdy character became more gentrified, his spirit of cleverness was celebrated in the pages of *Punch*, the enduring testament to British satire.

Animals (**Figure N102**), jugglers, tumblers, actors, and acrobats entertained thousands who flocked to the spectacles, enchanted with pleasure. And circuses were the rage . . . Philip Astley, the first clown, created the first circus in England (1768). His act told the tale (as it continues to do today) of Billy Buttons the tailor, who remained better at sewing than at staying astride his horse. Astley impersonated the clothier attempting to ride to Brentford to cast his vote in an election; the funny man tried hard to remount the beast after it bolted forward . . . without him (**Figure N103**).

A less humorous look at the animal kingdom was entertaining as well . . . a scene of children at the zoo was exciting, as the London Zoological Gardens had opened in Regent's Park in 1828 (**Figure N104**), and people were beginning to establish their own menageries; references to the often maddening antics of dogs and the perpetual hijinks of monkeys are found in the famous folktales of the Staffordshire area. Plates with entertaining references to the agile beasts are further proof of the fondness of their keepers (**Figures N105 through N109**).

As the curious flocked to see the zoo animals living in quiet captivity, so they flocked to events where slaying an animal was the name of the game. The Roman urge to watch animals kill one another hadn't yet diminished, and English gentlemen, who "would lay odds on anything from a horse-race to the gambols of a couple of flies on a window-pane" (White, 1969), gambled voraciously on savage sport. In the early years of the 19th century there were at least forty rat-pits in London, where hundreds of caged rats would be let loose to be viciously terminated by terriers in a grizzly siege (**Figure N110**). Or two dogs of equal weight were set for bets, washed in milk to be certain that no revolting paste was smeared on one to discourage the fangs of the other before being released for battle. Bulls, bears, badgers, and cocks waged war till the bloody end, and the end did not come soon enough. Cockfighting was banned in 1849 but did not dwindle for many years to come. Though the birds were bred to draw blood, owners treated them kindly in indoor cages while allowing them very solitary yard exercise should they be tempted to practice their art. The illustration on **Figure N112**, looking very much like the pen-and-ink and pencil drawings in the portfolio of Harrison Weir (1824-1906) held at the Victoria and Albert Museum, London, boasts of the prize fowls. The scenes on either side of that ceramic **(Figures N111 and N113)** are polychrome decals of a bitter battle, made by the National China Company, an Ohio firm. They could only have inspired a feeding frenzy.

The fights were as much a child's recreation as a collier's. A bouncing-ball ballad begins,

Come all ye colliers far and near,
I'll tell of a cock-fight, when and where,
Out on the moors I heard them say,
Between a black and our bonny grey.
(Fish, 1975; see Appendix AN3 for completion of the ballad)

The call has since quieted but is not yet still. Three states in the United States still champion the sport as brutal, but not cruel. Admission remains free for those under twelve.

The transfer of the dog seller is the closest the collection comes to honoring London's street-folk. They represent the street sellers who, aside from offering live creatures, sold sweet-smelling stuff to eat, things to read and write with, shirts and snuff and worn-out old shoes. There were those who bought what the sellers sold to sell it once more, and at the bottom of the heap were pickers who picked up just about anything from the gutter to sell it back to those who lived in it. There were fire-eaters and fortune-tellers and fine players of musical bells, stilt dancers and singers of psalms; spoon makers and umbrella fixers worked among makers of frilly nightcaps and great wire cages to imprison singing canaries.

Transfers also picture some of the less competitive pastimes, such as kite flying **(Figure N114)**, archery **(Figure N115)**, rowing **(Figure N116)**, ready to sail **(Figure N117)**, punting **(Figure N118)**, ice skating **(Figure N119)**, or leisurely walking **(Figure N120)**. And there were the noisy ball games for boys that would grow into seasonal adult entertainment, now known as football and baseball, which would become big business.

Football **(Figure N121)**, then, was any one of many games played by kicking a ball. Ancient football had been a game played by the poorer classes, who did not seem to care about the mortal danger the game could bring; "fractured skulls, broken arms, legs, jaws, noses or copious bloodshed, crept into the wealthy man's public schools where the boys (who had been used to individual sporting skills at home) . . . happily initiated the rowdy play of the skull bashers" (Burton, 1972b). Perhaps the noisy weekend game we know owes its start to the Danish soldier whose captured head was kicked about to celebrate a Roman victory or to the poor goat that generously offered its bladder to serve as a gruesome ball. Those medieval bladders were leather covered just in time for the team of thoroughly modern married ladies to play the spinsters of Midlothian, Scotland, and beat them handily. But most women had a greater sense of maternal protection and stayed out of the insidiously violent game, which, until the 19th century, had no rules for judiciously getting the ball to the opponent's goal posts behind them.

The rules and "ordered play" of "old" football, or rugby **(Figures N122 and N123)**, were developed in 1863 and prohibited carrying the ball. In 1823, William Webb Ellis, a student at England's Rugby School (famous for its setting of Thomas Hughes' novel, *Tom Brown's Schooldays*), caught the ball from an opponent's kick; he astonished (and delighted) the crowd by running with it—by either accident or design—in the direction of the opponent's goal (Burton, 1972b). The common code of play was broken. The ball could be caught, not just kicked. This startling innovation, or violation, was not recognized until 1841. Ellis became a hero; rugby gave birth to a new game. It took John Heisman's forward pass (in 1906) and new rules to make the contemporary game of football as we know it now safer and more captivating . . . a far cry from the bloody chill of kicking a poor Dane's head.

The second ball game, the one "played by two opposite parties with bats and sticks, has been developed from those early contests which have played such an important part of parish and town politics" (Gomme, 1898). Cricket **(Figures N124 and N125)** and baseball plates help to tell the story; the series of "American Sports" plates **(Figures N126 and N127)** that feature baseball might well have been placed in "A Is for Americana." Those plates, which call to cross-category collectors, have escalated in value and are rarely found for sale.

The rules of the "old" sports were now cast in stone, and "new" games established professional teams. The roots of the newest game had been cricket and rounders, a children's stick-and-ball game brought to these shores by the early Colonists; even Lewis and Clark tried to teach the Nez Perce Indians the game! Like marbles, it had many names: Old Cat, One Old Cat, Two Old Cat, Three Old Cat, Goal Ball, Town Ball, Barn Ball, Sting Ball, Soak Ball, Stick Ball, Burn Ball, Round Ball, Base Ball, Base-Ball, and, at long last, Baseball. From town to town, from some rules to others, the game finally settled in New York City in 1842, when the future members of the New York Knickerbocker Baseball Club refined the rules, took over the Elysian Fields, and lost the first official match to the New York Base Ball Club. As the last decades of the 19th century passed, "fun" became "fads," and stores in America sold out of bats and balls. Uniformed team members were paid to play; the banking of baseball had begun (Ward and Burns, 1994).

Away from the noisy weekend competition, there was the quiet sport of fishing. Kathleen Lawrence-Smith (1992) memorializes Staffordshire's Izaak Walton, the ultimate angler. Angling, he said, "is an art worthy of the knowledge and practice of the wise man . . . a rest to his mind, a cheerer of his spirits, a diverter of sadness, a calmer of unique thoughts, a moderator of passions, a procurer of contentedness." Isaak, grieving over the death of his wife, Rachel, and his seven infant children, over time found solace in the sport and, in 1653, wrote the book that brought the charm of Staffordshire's rivers and their bounty to the reading public. In 1676, *The Compleat Angler* reached its fifth edition, just seven years before the world's most famous fisherman caught his last breath **(Figures N128, N129, and N130)**.

One wonders how Walton would have faced the industrialization of Staffordshire's countryside and the invasion of his beloved waterways; the story of the Victorian century of change provides long hours of reading in vast numbers of texts. This scant summary, tethered here by collected transfers, retells only fragments of the century's passing. In spite of vast collections of china that celebrate 1897's Diamond Jubilee, no ceramic souvenirs in this ABC collection exist to pay homage. And whether or not the plates that picture the good Queen Victoria in her younger years were issued before or after her passing is uncertain.

What is certain is that, in the china room at Windsor, there remained unchanged by her edict a special table that held every one of the mugs of her childhood and those of her own children as well; what of our treasures it held we may never know. But we do know that, as the Queen's chronologically stored royal wardrobes, permanently cupboarded dolls, crowds of family photos, and relics of the dead that surrounded her were the absolute proof of her reverence of the past, we, too, must keep the spirit of the century's grandeur alive and its ultimate lesson clear. In the words of Samuel Smiles, "Even the humblest person, who sets before his fellows an example of industry, sobriety, and upright honesty of purpose in life, has a present as well as a future influence upon the well-being of his country; for his life and character pass unconsciously into the lives of others, and propagate a good example for all time to come" (Smiles, 1882).

O Is for Ornamental Borders

"Plates with the alphabet round the border."

The English poet William Brighty Rands noted the lettered borders of ABC plates in his poem (see Appendix AM2), "The Pedlar's Caravan." It is an ABC plate's identifying charm. Though some plates do have the alphabet set across them, the vast majority of letters are found on rims. Each hand-painted, transferred, molded, or stamped letter is an example of 19th- or early 20th-century design. Lettered rings enclose their "art" with complementary frames, the most alluring of which, in this collection, is seen in **Figure O1a and O1b**. The circle of characters gives each plate its purpose; each alphabet brings to each diner the links to literacy.

Transfer letters are easiest to see and make irresistible potpourris of patterns and shapes **(Figures O2 and O3)**. In various colors, letters, with their baselines encircling the plate center, were in their upright positions farthest from the reader. At the table edge they were, of course, upside down. To read a letter in its correct position, the diner would rotate the plate. Conversely, on one tiny metal toy plate **(Figure O4 and Figure M82)**, as well as on a variety of ceramic editions, the alphabet is set with baselines toward the outside rim; readability is then closest to its dolly-diner. And at least one manufacturer thoughtfully set the letters on the outside rim so that all the letters, in order clockwise with A at the table edge, would face the user and are, consequently, the most easily read. One example of this "fan" series is seen "upside-down" among the borders in **Figure O3**.

There are some interesting positional variations when glass plates are compared from one catalogue page, text, or sample with another. Though it is assumed that glass plates are formed in a static mold, scrutiny reveals that the letter order around the designed floor does rotate. On each of different plates, the A might be found at various angles to the picture's baseline. Higbee Glass author Lola Higby (*Bryce, Higbee and J. B. Higbee Glass*, 1998) responds to the concern with possible answers: the same basic design may have been produced by different manufacturers or at different sites belonging to a single maker; a manufacturer might have repositioned the border for deliberately different editions; or the replacements of parts of molds might have been attached with their positions at random.

Cast borders may vary in their depth and clarity as well. Sometime in the 1740s, one Ralph Daniel of Cobridge brought the first plaster of paris casts to Staffordshire, replacing molds of metals and clay. Castings could be taken more quickly from them, but clarity faded as they eroded with use. As the "Figures" show, some borders are nearly imperceptible.

Borders of all depths held more than letters. Boldly colored paint and/or lustres were brushed over them **(Figure O5)**. Hazy blue puddles, which gathered in their ridges, identified their glazes **(Figure O6 and Figure N92)**. And sometimes letters were transferred over already molded nonalphabet rims.

When describing the differences among cast borders, it is the letter styles, backgrounds, and interior and exterior edge variations above and below the letter border that can help to define provenance. With careful comparison, an infinite variety of details help to establish sets, may help to determine makers, and may even hint at years of manufacture. Varying fonts, backgrounds (plain, lined, or stippled), and styles of edge decor (vitruvian twists, scallops, rococo shapes, etc.) may be identical to plates that carry manufacturers' marks. And the unique use of secondary alphabets **(Figure O7)**, letter reversals (see "Z Is for Ƨ and Other Reversals"), as well as colors and placements of lined edges can be clues to makers.

On some transfer alphabets, bowers of flowers are placed between the A and the Z **(Figure O8)**. On metal plates, separators may be diamonds or stars or pointing fingers; on deep dishes they may be "Baby Plate" or dots in different configurations. Rarely do cast alphabets show motifs between the A and the Z but this collection affords a unique example of the very rare **Figure O1**, "Flowers That Never Fade Series—Liberty."

Some rims separate one letter from the next with encircling vines or enchanting circles of beasts found in blue, green, and orange of various hues on German deep and flat dishes **(Figures S14 and S15)**. In "D Is for Deep Dishes" are examples of transfer or decal borders that are constructed of sets of letters with intervening spaces or small bows. An excellent example of letter groupings points quickly to the McNicols Pottery of Clarksburg, West Virginia **(Figures D97, D98, and D99)**. On **Figure O9**, small decals are the magical connectors among the random series of capital letters; alphabet borders are not always totally inclusive.

And there are unique glass and ceramic shaped edges into which the alphabet is set—beaded scallops, key shapes, bubbles of glass, octagon-shaped forms, and more. Other alphabet plates have no letter borders at all. They feature a focus letter graphic, leaving the rim to decorative florals, leaves, and dots **(Figure O10)**. These overpainted cast-surrounds add a distinctive energy to what may become a collector's category of its own.

Some alphabets are too big for their plates . . . on transfer rims a careful search will find that some letters or parts of letters which have been removed to make the series fit. More planned are the sequences around two tiny metal plates that stop just short of the end **(Figures O11 and O12)**. Then there were rims too large for single sequences . . . workers added random sets of letters to fill the voids **(Figure O13)**. Other evidence of difficulties are seen in **Figures O14 and O15.** The first shows an effort to self-correct a runaway line while the second is a splendid example of letter placement by inexperienced hands. Too small for the entire alphabet, some articles carry only part of the A-to-Z series. As mentioned in "H Is for Hollowware," the remaining letters wait for a matching cup or saucer **(Figures O16 and O17)**.

Some dishes include numerals along with their letters **(Figure D71)**, and some plates in this collection have been included though they are encircled only with numbers **(Figures D60 and G22)**. Of course, clock plates, included in "C Is for Commercialism" and "G Is for Glass" may include both Roman and Arabic numbers as well as names of the days of the week and the months. All were good teachers.

Cast alphabets, especially on German plates and mugs, are most often expertly overpainted with shiny gold. On the lustred French item cup, the letters are poorly overpainted with a dull, grainy metal **(Figure L21)**. Many alphabets surrounding milk glass items can also be found overpainted with a "gritty gold," which buyers are often seen scraping away as bits of the remaining paint are annoying.

This chapter has sent readers searching through the text to cross-referenced points of interest. It is appropriate, too, that collectors search their inventories for border details. Purchases of plates are usually influenced only by their transfer designs . . . buyers might expand and categorize their collections of varying perimeter treatment, as well. There are multitudes of unnoticed details quietly waiting, on the edge of discovery.

Authors' Note:

As this book was going to press, a plate was purchased from Ian Ingham of the Royal Pavilion, which provided a border so unique it begged inclusion. Though every cast border is not absolutely perfect in its spacing of letters, this piece of early Victoriana is an exciting example of highly irregular spacing. **Figures O19 and O20** clearly show border segments with uneven letter placements. In addition, the print of Queen Victoria is a rare example of a cartoon-like portrait which, quite unflatteringly, describes the royal in riding habit. Though she was already a noted horsewoman, the tilted crown might represent an artist's suspicion of the young queen's possible insecurities as she began her monarchy. If this article **(Figure O18)** had been included in the collection earlier, it would have been placed as **Figure N63** along with other transfers that picture the queen in "N Is for 19th Century."

P Is for Potters and Their Potteries

There were other potteries in Britain, but none rivaled the inventive genius of the small industries that shone through the black, suffocating smoke of North Staffordshire's ragged communities. It was in any one of those midland hamlets, in any one of their village potteries, that the primitively painted, alphabet-encircled transfer ware was created. In that geologic space there just happened to lay a remarkable variety of clays alongside the continuous supply of coals that would change the colored muds into a new material. They would become the products of a thriving industry nestled in littered landscapes of black, looming ovens, deep muddy holes, mine dumps, heaped mountains of "sherds," and the refuse-filled potholes that pockmarked the river banks and footpaths. Each shovel interrupted the continuous cycle of the land as it, over hundreds of millions of years, was built up, worn away, and rebuilt once again.

The start of "The Potteries" was the start of the earth, fiery and unformed. Earth's inner core emerged of heavy nickel and iron surrounded by a molten outer core of liquid iron. Over that core formed a mantle of solid rock with pockets of molten material that often found its way to the surface through fractures in the earth's crust. At the upper mantle, the rock is soft and slushy, nearly melted, and, heated from below, slowly flowing. Its currents carried with them the cooling crust above, a layer six miles thick beneath earth's oceans and at least six times that beneath its land. The plates, once a solid continental mass called Pangaea, were torn apart and pushed to collide, reshaping the continents as we know them today. When forced beneath one another, earth's plates buckled and belched upward into islands with volcanic futures, continents of jagged peaks, and the extensive outcroppings typical of England's Midlands. Sometimes hot magma pitched up from below remained trapped and cooled beneath granite domes. Converted by hot gases to china clay, the soft material remained at places like Tregonning Hill on the Land's End peninsula, where William Cookworthy first discovered the massive deposit about 1746.

Gases that exploded through the crust expanded, shrank, and weakened the surface stone. Hot lava rising through the breaks to seal the wounds flowed over the surface, squeezing the land below. Moist air assaulted the exposed surfaces as well. Water seeped between the mineral grains, and chemical reactions destroyed the hard surfaces. Pieces of weathered rock were washed away by rain, blown by the wind, or carried by ice. Some of the decomposing sediment, along with its organic particles, was the soil in which, over tens of thousands of years, trees rooted and plants grew. Some of the sediment was swept away, eroded by currents of rivers and glaciers that ground at the rock, carrying its fragments to settle beneath slowly spreading rivers, lake beds, or, ultimately, ocean basins. Layers of sediment became layers of clay.

It is the disintegration of the rock that determines the chemistry of its clay . . . decomposing and remaining at the site of the "mother rock," the clay is called a "primary" or "residual" clay because it has formed and remained there. Its particles are large, and the clays are therefore almost nonplastic. Most clay is secondary clay, formed from accumulations of the miles of mixed minerals and organic matter that are carried from the mother rock by the forces of weathering. With the heavier particles settling first below the river beds and lakes, the resultant clay is finely ground and, therefore, highly plastic. In each area there may be a number of pits, and each pit might house ten or more differentiated clays lying in veins or pockets. Tertiary clays vary in color . . . the fortunate commingling of two or more already comminuted settlings.

What minerals the muddy stuff carried along with it made it the clay it became . . . its color helping to indicate its mineral content. White clay, a primary or nearly pure on-site clay, is composed only of silica, alumina, and water, the basic ingredients of all clay. Secondary brown clays combined with manganese, and reds with iron. Ball clays, or very dark clays adjacent to mine deposits, were named for their propensity to curl while being dug . . . the mining process heaped balls of it onto carts or the backs of donkeys or bent-over boys. Ball clays were the dark browns and blacker clays combined with carbons and sulphur. According to Dr. Robert Plot, first curator of Oxford University's Ashmolean Museum, there were brick clays that, when fired, became blue, providing the famous Staffordshire Blue Brick. Between Burslem and Hanley, a two-foot band of yellow clay lay seven feet below the surface above a fathom of red clay. Red clays (colored by iron) were the basic clays used for most early pottery. Deep pits, from which was dug the red clay, were called "marl holes" **(Figure P1**; see also Appendix AP1). Plentiful were the dull white hard-fire clays, used as bricks for firemouths because they withstood intense heat without warping or cracking. A white clay streaked with yellow was called *bottle clay* and burned white. A blue-white material burned yellow, and there was clay of blue, which burned white, found between Shelton and Hanley Green. And there were more.

How much mineral was in each required analysis, as the results of sedimentation were uneven. An article in the *Pottery Gazette* (February 1, 1882) quotes Mr. Maw clarifying the variable analyses of clay content from the mine at Teignmouth Hill: "the mines there produce clays containing silica and alumina in every proportion, from 95 to 50 per cent. of silica and from 50 to 4 per cent. of alumina." Clearly there are some clays not useful to the industry. Mr. Maw's catalogue listed 123 clays through all of the geologic formations in Britain, including all of their colors, plasticities, strengths, purities, chemistry, degrees of contractions in the kiln, and more.

It took an energy source to turn these clays into an entirely new material. At first it was wood that fired the kilns; with a shortage of wood becoming a national problem throughout 17th-century England, coal was mined to fire-bake the clay. The start of that combustible rock began 300 million years ago, when Britain was a low-lying swamp of dense trees and giant ferns. The leafy giants died, slowly becoming thick layers of peat that sank into the muds of inland lakes and seas; as the land rose once again, with its flourishing vegetation, the mud was turned to rock. Layers of peat compressed by layers of rock and subjected to great heat from below were miraculously turned into coal. The layers are the seams from which coal was mined as early as 1282. By 1467, the coal was used for the firing of pottery. In the late 18th century, owners of the potteries joined together to form mining companies to mine the long flame coals needed for firing the kilns.

The first shards of pottery long predated the mines; found where Staffordshire would rise, they fell from pots built by Neolithic man. Representing the early and middle Bronze Age (1900-1000 B.C.) were food vessels, tiny religious items, and cinerary urns formed with walls of ringed clay. The potter's wheel appeared in Staffordshire about 75 B.C., and with the Roman militia in command, mid-1st-century remains of a circular kiln and fine gravel-coated ware using a variety of clays have been unearthed: flagons, cinerary urns, platters, storage vessels, and lamps. Though little other than rough, bag-shaped items have been found from the Saxon period, large quantities of fragments and the Middle Ages custom of naming persons for their occupations proved that much ware was potted at what would become the pottery towns. A mid-14th-century William le Potter and a Robert Potter were probably of Tunstall. Records show an obituary for Robert Potter in 1405; perhaps they were one and the same. In 1363, John Pottere was fined for fighting in Burslem, and in 1372, one Thomas the Througher bought land but soon came upon hard times and was fined for nonpayment of debts. Perhaps it is to these gentlemen and the seven brethren potters who closed the Burslem monasteries at Hulton and Rushton that we look for the start of the pottery towns, soon to emerge.

And emerge they did. Along the outcrops of coal and clay, the brooks and the rivers, grew the villages. The towns, from north to south, were called Tunstall, Burslem, Hanley, Stoke-upon-Trent, Fenton, and Longton. By the 1600s, both the northern and southern areas were involved in pot making, with Burslem remembered best for its tall, cylindrical butter pots used by farmers to transport fresh-churned butter to markets at Leek, Cheadle, Stone, Uttoxeter, and Newcastle. Also remembered was the act of Charles II's Parliament that regulated the size and weight of the butter pots after false-bottomed vessels and water-absorbing pots proved useful in cheating the public; some still call the yellow stuff "pot-butter."

As the village borders widened, small pot-works, with their attached farmhouses, grew into small manufactories. At first the pot-banks were small farms, boosting their incomes with each firing. Clay was dug from roadside pits to avoid using planting land, but soon turning pots proved more profitable

than turning the soil; the time was right to expand the kilns. As the midland's industry grew, potters enlarged each oven, and when safety became a factor, they built other ovens. Slowly the number of kilns per factory grew, along with the opening of new sites per manufactory, which encouraged the talented to found new establishments. The 1710 manuscript collection of Josiah Wedgwood lists forty-seven pot-works with never more than six workers, usually family members, to work them. By 1802, Hanley's T. Allbutt published a map of expanding town borders, and the number of pot-banks tripled Wedgwood's count.

And with their growth came their uniqueness. One Richard Pococke, after traveling through the district in 1750, wrote his description of the industry. "He noted the specialties of each village, Stoke made white stoneware; Shelton was 'famous for the red china'; Hanley made 'all sorts' of pottery; Burslem produced 'the best white and many other sorts'; and Tunstall made 'all sorts' and was 'famous for the best bricks and tiles'" (Haggar, Mountford, and Thomas, 1981). Although Pococke does not mention it, porcelain was being made at Longton Hall.

But there were commonalities as well. As time went on, all towns suffered the contrast of outrageous fortune to the misfortunes of the working class. All towns shared the woes of smothering smoke, deaths and diseases from polluted streams, insufficient and contaminated drinking water, filthy privies, and rotting refuse; all eventually built sewage systems and switched from gas to electricity, some well into the 20th century. Some towns provided more health services than others, but all eventually had postal facilities, scheduled coach connections, commercial transport by canals, and a railway station with both industrial and passenger service. Every town built churches, some more than others, to soothe their hard-working souls, and all tried to inspire their citizens, too, through libraries, reading rooms, institutes, art schools, and small museums. Their theaters, built for dramatic offerings, orchestral concerts, or circuses, did not always succeed, but cadres of spooks and specters hung around to haunt the mines, perhaps to warn of accidents or to create havoc unless a miner found an old shoe or said The Lord's Prayer to avert the danger. All towns had their casts of scamps and scholars who took center stage in their captivating stories and ghostly yarns. And within all towns grew an industry that shone through its suffocating smoke (see Appendix AP2).

From those Staffordshire towns, hand-drawn carts and overloaded asses carried plates and prattle down soft. muddy roads **(Figure P2)**. Thanks to these house-to-house hawkers, 18th-century housekeepers, miles away from The Potteries, no longer needed to create their own ceramics, for with clay in abundance and areas of coal hugging the pottery towns **(Figure P3)**, the industry grew steadily and the villages thrived.

But each village, with its clusterings of farmsteads, had its uniqueness. The town of **Burslem** (or Barcardeslim, meaning a solitary dwelling near a wood) was called the "Mother of the Potteries," as it was the first to feel the thrust of the Industrial Revolution. Two kilns and fragmentary remains have been found dating from the 13th century. The Adams family began potting with brothers William and Richard, who were taken to court for illegally digging clay on a common road in 1448. And there was the Daniels family, who were accused of butter-pot fraud at the end of the 16th century. Burslem saw the Wedgwoods in operation by the 1650s. The Malkin's Knowle Works dates from

1651, having passed through many capable hands before its demolition by the end of the 19th century. The works attached to the Brick House are traced to potter John Adams (1657-1687) and were let to Josiah Wedgwood in 1762. And it is said that in 1693, Gilbert Wedgwood and sons Thomas and Richard were in some way associated with the Elers Brothers (David and John Philip), then of Bradwell Wood. Early Burslem could also boast of the Fountain Place Works, a grand manufactory built in 1789. Its high walls and castellated parapets, which included the sites of four older potteries, may have given "a distant view of the works in its heyday . . . the impression of a hillside fortification" (Greenslade, 1983a). The well-known, gracefully designed entrance arch and domed bell turret (**Figure P15**) welcome the reader to Wood's *Representation of the Manufactoring of Earthenware . . .* (1827; **Figure P4**). And there were more.

About 1710, there were about thirty-five potteries at Burslem (two of them not then worked). Names of families and their early establishments weave through the 18th century of Burslem's history and continue on the undersides of 19th-century ABC plates; the Adams family; the Wedgwoods; the John Davenports; Edge, Malkin and Company; and the Brownhills Pottery are all frequent producers of alphabet ware.

Some potters built their homes of saggar chips mortared with mud, and some, like Thomas and John Wedgwood, influenced the well-to-do with their grand mansion built in 1751; its extravagance brought the curious from near and far. Other estates of potters whose names remain within our focus, nestled into the landscape. They included Hadderidge, house of the Adams family; Ivy House, owned by John and Thomas Wedgwood (distant relatives of Josiah); and an estate at Jackfield built by the Malkin family.

The number of potteries multiplied, commercial establishments flourished, and with them came substantial increases in residents. In 1801, the population was documented at 6,578; thirty years later the town registered 12,714 persons; and by 1851, 18,000 individuals inhabited the area. With ever-increasing schedules of mail and city-to-city travel by coaches from 1790, increasing canal transport, and the completion of the Potteries Loop Line railway to Burslem in 1873, the 19th century was a period of rapid urbanization

In 1869, the Wedgwood Institute opened, replacing the first art school, which might have served the creative skills of the pottery painters if it hadn't been situated above the pig stalls; it closed in 1858 thanks to the filth, the fragrance, and the frustration of its instructor, the talented Mr. Muckley, who was seldom paid.

And Burslem became famous . . . by 1910, "Bursley" was the subject of an Arnold Bennett novel, *Anna of the Fire Towns*, whose words colorize our description (see Appendix AP3):

> . . . on a little hill in the vast valley was spread out the Indian-red architecture of Bursley—tall chimneys and rounded ovens, schools, the new scarlet market, the grey tower of the old church . . . the crimson chapels, and rows of little red houses with amber chimney-pots, and the gold angel of the blackened Town Hall topping the whole. The sedate reddish browns and reds of the composition, all netted in flowing scarves of smoke, harmonized exquisitely with the chill blues of the chequered sky. Beauty was achieved and none saw it (1975).

That golden angel watched from the top of the old Town Hall through the 1890s, when there were seventy working potteries, some of which were producers of alphabet ware. M. W. Greenslade (reprint, 1983a) presents detailed accounts of the potteries and their natural transitions, with copious references for further reading to enhance and expand this compressed view.

North of Burslem is **Tunstall,** the town of market stalls where there was no church until well after the start of the 19th century. With the establishment of churches and mission centers came bell towers, and with the coming of the manufactories, the sounds of the hourly bells (which first sounded in 1833) were welcome. The railways, too, depended upon the clock.

Tunstall was said to have been the most pleasant village in the Potteries. It developed, with its market center, from forty small houses in 1821 to more than fifty times that fifty years later. There were sturdy homes, many with oval plaques above their arches bearing the street names and the dates of construction. More modern than construction in the other Pottery Towns, each four-roomed dwelling was provided with an ash pit and a privy in its walled rear yard; a wash-house and a water closet followed in later years. Providing more gracious living, grand Tunstall's estates were held by some whose names were familiar in the potteries: Adams, Meir, Malkin, and others.

With the growth of the manufactories and the building of new homes for its workers, sanitation was problematic in Tunstall, especially with the rules preventing the "Commissioners of Drainage" from correcting the pollution already coming from the factories and mines that abused the water supply despite bringing prosperity to the area. Polluted drainage, an inadequate water supply, and inadequate cemeteries threatened the public health until a pumping station was built in 1854 and new lands for cemeteries were established.

Water mills dated from the 13th and 14th centuries. Corn and flint mills were active, especially that of Thomas Baddeley of Newfield, who employed the illustrious James Brindley to fit the mill with machinery for grinding flint and pumping water out of a neighboring mine!

The development of the potteries was slower in Tunstall than in other areas. Following William le Potter of 1348 and Robert the Potter, who died about fifty years later, there was a 16th-century pottery at Goldenhill and a dish maker at Ravenscliff in 1603. At the start of the 19th century there were only three potteries in the town, with several in outlying areas. By 1818 there were ten in the township, by 1834 the count was thirteen, and nineteen by 1863. Of importance to ABC ware is the Greengate Works, which grew out of a pottery owned by one George Booth in 1745; it was sold to William Adams (of Burslem), who rebuilt it and sold it to John Meir (1882), who worked it for fourteen years and sold it back to the Adams family in 1896. One other firm, which stood on a road north of Greengate, began exchanging hands from about 1800 until 1918, when it was trading as Alfred Meakin of Tunstall.

The growing potteries needed the coal from the many small mines surrounding Tunstall, some of which had been active since the 13th century. And there were ironstone mines as well, which began long, long before the Middle Ages. The making of bricks and tiles was a significant part of the industrial complex in 1890, along with chemical plants, which produced crystallized salts and sulfuric acid.

To educate the town's workers, the Tunstall Athenaeum and Mechanics' Institute provided intellectual activities along with reading rooms and a free library. Schools of art refined the talents of ceramic painters, and a museum, the collections of which were eventually moved to Hanley, opened in 1897.

Jenny Lind, with her very refined voice, sang in recital at the covered market of **Hanley** (or Hanbridge, meaning the place at the high clearing), the town south of Burslem. Aside from cockfighting and horse-racing, Hanley provided its citizens with a cultural life that, from 1790, included subscription libraries; a Pottery Philosophical Society before 1835; a Mechanics Institute, which promoted worldly knowledge; a natural history museum; schools of art and design; and a school of science and technology. Theater began in 1824; in 1878, the Theater Royal, among others, became a music hall, home of the Imperial Circus and the gathering place for Hanley and Shelton's Philharmonic. Choral societies had performed since 1824; music festivals featured Sir Edward Elgar (1857-1934), and the Meakin family (of the Eagle Pottery) endowed concerts at Victoria Hall in the late 1880s.

Perhaps there were other potters who supported the arts as well. Their industry began in 1540 with Richard Broke's kiln. According to Greenslade (*A History of Hanley*, 1983b), it is possible that the famous Thomas Toft (d. 1689) worked at Hanley and that Joshua Twyford (1640-1729) worked at nearby Shelton in partnership with John Astbury (1688-1743), who just may have introduced Devonshire clay and built the flint mill. The tale of that 1720 "discovery" sounds a bit suspicious. In summary, while on a journey to London, Astbury stopped at an inn seeking care for his horse who was rapidly losing its vision. Hoping to remedy the situation, the hostler of the inn burnt a flint stone till quite red, ground it finely, and blew the dust into each eye of the animal. Astbury was taken by the whiteness of the powdered stone and the claylike nature of the residue; taking the hint, he added ground flint to his clay, achieving considerable advantages. Earthenware was now harder and whiter.

A stellar procession of potters followed, among whom were producers of alphabet ware; their histories are included in "U Is for Undersides." Familiar names include the Wedgwood Factory at Etruria (1769); the Meakin Brothers (of the Eagle Works from 1859); Powell and Bishop (which became Powell, Bishop and Stonier by 1880 and Bishop and Stonier by 1896); and the factory of Joseph Clementson. There were the tile and brick works, too, which undoubtedly produced the blue brick that paved the city's walkways. Circumstances closed some of Hanley's potteries; new firms were built at the turn of the century. Most of the inhabitants of Hanley and Shelton then worked in the potteries and subsidiary businesses that extensively employed women and children.

In addition to potteries, there were mills for grinding bone, flint, glazes, and colors. And a few ironworking mills along with the famous G. H. Fourdrinier Paper Company, founded in 1827, produced paper by the piece rather than by the sheet. The firm also produced tissue paper for pottery transfers as well as ordinary paper for packing and general use. A short-lived silk mill significantly increased the midcentury population. And there were the collieries' pits, deep ones, and the consequent slippage from above, which swallowed an unsuspecting soul in 1904 and challenged the foundations of St. John's Church one hundred years before.

Beginning as a triangular spread of small dwellings in an early 13th-century agricultural setting, Hanley reveals a collection of various architectural designs with many reconstructions over aging dwellings and public buildings. Along with the pastoral settings of well-kept homes on wide streets and bricked pavements, there was serious overcrowding; moats filled with decomposing filth and open ditches met the blackened skies. Some water closets were installed in 1887, thirty years after water of questionable quality had become available to some homes on some days of the week. "Hanley was said to have been the worst and most evil spot in all the towns" (Warrillow, 1960). Accounts of six to a sodden mattress, the foul-smelling remains of squashed vermin on the walls, and children, black with filth, living in the most abysmal of squalor dates as late as 1900 . . . tenants left their filth behind for new tenants, who rarely cleaned it away. Was it a lack of enthusiasm that kept the Housing of the Working Classes Act Committee from visiting local slums only once in two years? But it wasn't all bad. . . . there was the infirmary, the many churches, and the bustling shops with goods far above the standards of every other town in the string.

South of Hanley is **Stoke-upon-Trent,** where a cup, possibly from prehistoric days, was found along with evidence of 1st- and 2nd-century (A.D.) Roman pot works. The *Domesday Book* of 1066 (William the Conqueror's survey of the lands of England) does not attest to a village here but does tell of a church; the word *Stoke* stems from the Old English term for a holy place. There are items remaining from 1600, and butter pots date from the 1680s. The Cliff Bank Works, documented from the early 18th century, was owned by one Thomas Alders. Josiah Wedgwood, after leaving his brother's Burslem Churchyard Pottery, was in partnership with Thomas Alders and John Harrison the elder from 1752 to 1754 before he joined with Thomas Whieldon in Fenton. The Adams family began production in the area about 1818, and the litany continues with names of the ingenious who made significant contributions to the development of the industry: Daniel Bird, who is said to have discovered the correct proportion of flint and clay needed to keep ware from cracking in the kiln; Josiah Spode, who helped to develop underglaze transfer printing; and Josiah Spode II, who developed bone china and helped to perfect the use of steam power to grind flint, installed by the Mintons in 1819. Minton's works soon produced tiles, and by 1890, there were fourteen brick and tile companies, some near the Trent and Mersey Canal.

The written history of this pottery town began auspiciously with a parish church of the Middle Ages. A few farms constituted the village, with some pottery-making in evidence about 1600; by 1750, the church stood a bit east of three pot banks that took root. The industry escalated with the turnpiking of the road from Derby and the opening of the Trent and Mersey Canal in 1777. Dwellings mushroomed along with a new church, wharves, and warehouses to service the earthenware factories. Proof enough of the industry's success was the population growth to nearly 20,000 by 1871. To accommodate the town's needs, shops and public buildings rose alongside new roads to meet the clouds already darkened by pottery fires.

Plaques honoring the memories of the families of Spode, Wedgwood, Adams, and others adorned the walls of the new church, begun in 1826 to replace the original medieval parish church, St. Peter ad Vincula, which was demolished in 1830.

Along with other churches that followed, the spired, bell-towered church of the Holy Trinity was built by the Minton family in Hartshill in 1842, surrounded by its residence, school, and churchyard.

The responsibility of influencing behavior belonged to the appointed chief bailiff and his watchmen and beadles. The Chartist riots of 1842 (and the damage to the home of the chief bailiff's house at Penkhull) led to an acute awareness of the inadequacy of the police force, and thus it was significantly augmented. An inspector of nuisances was appointed in 1845, whose responsibilities were the suppression of bothersome things, the watering of the streets, and the supervision of the lighting of the town. A scavenger was appointed four years later, for the problem of drainage had, as it had in all pottery areas, become serious. Polluted waters from the mills, muddy streets, flooded cellars, overflowing privies, and accumulations of rotting sewage brought fevers and disease. Eventually the filth summoned the cleaning of the sewers and the start of improvements to prevent contamination. As part of the Herbert Minton Memorial Scheme, public baths were opened, water closets eventually became the norm, and modern means of sanitation, along with new cemetery grounds, were in place. The design of the North Staffordshire Infirmary incorporated the advice of the illustrious Florence Nightingale. Medical facilities seemed to have thrived in Stoke-upon-Trent more than in other towns, including a short-lived hospital dedicated to smallpox and a new expertise in eye disease. The North Staffordshire Blind and Deaf School took shelter within the magnificent mansion of Josiah Spode II (1803); it was appropriately named The Mount. A home for those with skeletal deformities opened in 1911.

In 1872, the local government attributed a sudden rise in mortality to an inadequate and unfit water supply, which quenched neither thirst nor building fires . . . all pumps were closed with more than an ounce of prevention and many a prayer for rain. But rain was the last thing prayed for on days when the horses raced or the football club proved its worth. Indoor recreation could be enjoyed at the music hall (from 1880), the theater (c. 1880), at performances of the Stoke Philharmonic (founded in 1877), at lectures of the Socratic Society, at the library, in classes at the old school of design (which opened in 1847), at the new school in the Minton Memorial Institute in 1860, or at dinner at the Noah's Ark Inn or at the Wheatsheaf. The town was much more than Dickens's description of a "heap of houses, kilns, smoke, wharfs, canals and a river." Stoke-upon-Trent offered its citizens what seems to have been a life of lively interests, employment opportunities, and services to help prolong their years.

South of Stoke is the **Fenton** Free Library, to which Andrew Carnegie contributed £5,000 . . . the lone survivor of the town's cultural offerings. But it would serve a growing population. From a hamlet of 33 hearths in 1666, 3,710 homes were documented in 1831, 5,767 in 1851 and twice that number only twenty years later. Established in the 13th century, the area was but a community adjacent to Longton. It did not have an agrarian start, as did the other pottery towns. One mill on record had, by 1782, become a flint and color mill used at least through the 1870s. And records of the start of the pottery industry do not occur here until 1710 with one William Poulson, who died in 1746. It is said that the famous Thomas Whieldon took over Poulson's pot-works. Whieldon opened his own establishment in 1740, after which he bought Fenton Hall from John Peate.

After a five-year partnership with Josiah Wedgwood, continuing until 1759, Whieldon, famous for his realistic fruit-and-vegetable-shaped ware and unique branch-handled teapots, waxed rich producing knifehafts, snuff boxes, salt glaze earthenware figures, and more. Whieldon's formula led to Wedgwood's production of his famed Queen's ware.

In the 1760s, there were about six potters in the area, and thirteen more twenty years later. Among the many manufactories that followed in Fenton, the firm of Henry Wileman is included in the summaries of those associated with ABC ware. Energy for the potteries came from the coal mines, first documented in 1695, with a substantial number of coal and ironstone mines opening in succeeding years.

As in the other pottery areas, there were sanitation problems in Fenton, with areas of crude housing, communal privies, and standing drainage to prove it. Wisely, the town's fathers were first in The Potteries to set building standards to reverse the poor conditions, but it took the sewers, laid in Fenton's most crowded areas, to remove the filth. An outbreak of typhus in 1866 again clearly signaled a need for better utilities, one of which was the provision of clean water; Fenton, more than the other pottery towns, had been deprived of water before 1850. But the town did have gas in the early 1840s, and because of it, electricity was considered to be unnecessary until well into the 20th century.

The building of many potteries and dwellings established a town with two subdivisions, Great Fenton and Little Fenton, which eventually grew together and were served by coaches that provided transport throughout the villages. As early as 1802, with about 2,000 homes to serve, mail was delivered by carriage. More efficient were the railway lines, three of which crossed through the area. On potter Thomas Whieldon's land were erected the massive sheds and the elephantine, 200-foot Round House, which cradled the engines. The North Staffordshire Railway Company's engine works grew from the sheds that opened there in 1848; twenty years later and onward, it became economically feasible to manufacture the engines, as well as carriages and wagons, on site. By 1892, the California Engineering Works to the south produced the locomotives that carried the history of Fenton rapidly into the 20th century.

Longton, or long village, is the southernmost member of The Potteries, covering about 1,000 acres. Like the others, Longton's first recorded populations quickly increased. The Hearth Tax in 1666 was paid from thirteen homes, and in its Lane End region (the northern section of the town), from twelve. With the coming of roads, the village grew, adding a church in 1761, a school one year later, and a market in 1789. A town hall, a new market in 1814 (with others following in 1844 and 1863), a second school in 1822, a drapers, Mr. Walker's famous toffee, and more appeared with the coming of the brickworks, coal mines, and a substantial iron industry. Soon came scheduled coaches to London and Manchester, The Potteries' first refuse destructor in 1877, the railway, and, by 1901, electricity. The population soared from 25 to 4,930 in 145 years. By 1851, Longton boasted 15,149 residents; this number more than doubled forty years later in spite of the disease-laden air thick with the stink of smoke from the ovens and the town's appalling drainage **(Figure P5)**.

But the darker the air, the brighter the economy. An article from the *Pottery Gazette* (n.d.) records, "It is believed, indeed, that the city fathers are rather proud of their smoke, and regard it as a very reliable barometer indicating the condition of trade in the town . . . . [The] visitor had better make up his mind to it, and get to business." It was the town's "firm belief that business is business. The business of the Longton manufacturer is to produce that which will sell, to get it made as cheaply as possible and to utilize every legal means to make a profit . . . . In Longton the principal has been elevated into a system of morality, and even religion." Perhaps it was the work ethic that built so many churches in Longton, and perhaps it was the church music that satisfied the residents' souls as the Longton Sax-horn Band gradually lost its audiences.

It was the famous Longton Hall Pottery for which the town was first noted; a Publick auction on Tuesday the 16th of September, 1760, was held to dispose of that pottery's remaining "profusion of useful and ornamental porcelain articles" (Watney, 1957). *Aris's Birmingham Gazette, The London General Evening Post,* and *The London Public Advertiser* had announced the sale of 90,000 objects, which was held in the Great Sale Room at the Sun at Fisherton, adjoining the city, from 10:00 to 5:00. The partnership at Longton Hall was duly dissolved.

But other potters followed; thirteen were listed in 1784 and twenty-seven at the turn of the century. By 1851, there were forty-one pot-works in Longton, more than in any other pottery town. Those factories included some that added alphabet borders to their ware and whose stories are found in "U Is for Undersides": H. Aynsley (c.1873), Sampson Bridgwood (1805), and the Charles Allerton and Sons factory (1890), which produced many pieces of this text's collections.

The coal mines had provided the fuel at Longton Hall and for all the china and earthenware industry that grew around it—The Golden Hill, Foley, Speedwall, Meir Hay, Woodhouse, Swingle Hill, Land End, Stone Row, Anchor, Cinderhill, Longton Hall, Florence, and more, some in connection with iron works. Generous seams provided the eight tons of coal consumed in the firing of only one ton of earthenware.

The most noted of the ironworks was the Land End, leased from the Duke of Sutherland by one William Sparrow from the Wolverhampton area. The works kept three furnaces at full blast at least as long as 1912. Brickworks were part of the industrial complex, and breweries contributed to the smoke-filled air. Mills ground flint, bone, and corn with water power until after World War II.

Providing respite for the workers of the mud-infested community were railway excursions. Known as "People's Trips," annual railway getaways were popular. Encouraged by Baptist missionary Thomas Cook (1808-1892), the first "Cook's Tour" (1841) was to a temperance meeting in another city; these newly exciting "pleasure trips" soon included hotel accommodations and planned activity. The working classes could take advantage of increasingly available railway track and get away for a day, even to the different smoke and grime of another city (Burton, 1972b). But those trips weren't their only getaways. Gambling, which followed the bloody animal contests and the other "detestable sports," provided raucous recreations fed by more pubs than found in any other pottery town.

The Potteries, as developing towns anywhere, grew essentially by the labors of their people and the salability of their products and services. Each town in The Potteries grew by the innovations of its geniuses, the artistry of its talented, and the sweat of its laborers; it is the unique age range of a segment of the laborers in proportion to the enormity of their task that is important to the history of The Potteries. It is the contrast of the magnificent artistry of the ware against the exhausting efforts of the half-starved, tubercular bodies of the young children employed in its production, that dims our vision. But employment of the underaged was not conjured up by the Victorian tycoons as a creative cost-cutting option. As in any preindustrial society, children had been part of the family workforce; their contributions to the family economy were vital to survival itself. The majority of the population was very young. Samuel Scriven, an assistant commissioner to the House of Commons Commission, testified in his report to the House of Commons, on January 30, 1843, that indifferent parents cared only that "protective" legislation might restrict their offspring's working hours (and salaries); no concern was given to the need for legislation that might reduce the threat of bodily harm or terminal ignorance.

Traditionally reluctant to interfere in the sacred covenants between employers and their workers, Parliament left the conditions of employment to the conscience of the business owners; the use of child labor was completely unregulated. Large numbers of children were "available." At least 50 percent of the population were children; many had been orphaned by rampant diseases, some had run from home, and others had been sold into employment by poverty-stricken parents to live in factory dormitories . . . or worse. With few parental instincts, factory owners exploited their charges until Parliament, albeit slowly, recognized the need for intervention in specific areas of employment, one by one. Victorian reform took a giant step for mankind.

The first efforts of Parliament were directed toward orphans under the age of twelve, who could no longer be required to work more than twelve hours each day. That Factory Act of 1802 also made provision for a little education as well. Though reports on child employment in the pottery industry in 1816 and 1825 brought no legislation to foster change, in 1833, a Factory Act banned the employment of children under the age of nine in the mills and limited their hours of work to forty-eight per week. Pertinent to the subject of this text was the 1842 addition of coal mines to the list of regulated industries. At last females and boys under ten could not be sent underground. Attention was slowly being turned to the abysmal effect of early employment on the young.

The reports of the House of Commons Commission instituted to investigate the conditions of child labor in the mines reveals that, though we are led to believe that both boys and girls were a part of every mine, only boys, typically from age six up, were employed in the Staffordshire area. The inquiries, published in 1842, were solicited from clergy, doctors, teachers, mine administrators, and the workers themselves. Though feelings of fear and reluctance are a common thread throughout workers' responses, Staffordshire county council's Advisory Officer R. A. Lewis (1975) does state, "the practices which aroused most public indignation were unknown, or at least uncommon, in Staffordshire. For example, [the investigative process revealed that] women and girls were not found underground in pottery mines. In parts there was even a strongly held opinion that a woman below ground in the mine brought bad luck."

But stories abound of sordid images of young, nearly naked girls working as harriers among naked men and strapped to

500-weight corves that they pulled, on hands and knees, along tracks . . . falling into slush or cold-water ditches in the solid blackness of the narrow, yard-high tunnels. Before they were harriers, boys sat in darkness waiting, one on each side, to open and close the traps for passing cargo, to catch the mice, or to sweep the rails and passages facing oncoming teams of horses. Tenth birthdays signaled their rites of passage to full-time pullers and pushers of the coal-loaded wagons or corves. Dressed only in shoes and a *byat*, a leather harness with a chain and hook attached, children pulled the corves on hands and knees or pushed them with their heads. Interviews reveal injuries due to falling coal, breaking ropes, swinging chains, and collisions with tunnel roofs and sharp-cornered skiffs. Fractures of the skull, cervical vertebrae compressions, and spinal cord injuries could easily result from hyperextended neck positions thrust against massive weights. A general concern was added to the findings at Longton . . . the unfenced pits of worked-out mines waited below the twinkling stars to swallow innocent lives (see Appendix AP1).

Child labor in the potteries was investigated by Samuel Scriven Esq. as well; the second report, dealing with employment in the potteries, was presented in 1843. Again, information was gleaned from the reports and testimonials of teachers, clergymen, and supervisorial adults. Some workers refused to provide information "on the grounds that it might incriminate them" or that their answer might "lead [them] to express a prejudiced, and therefore incorrect, opinion of the people in general." In spite of their honest fears, the words of the workers are revealing and the conclusions, written by Scriven and his core of researchers, are wrenching. Of the seventy-five manufactories subject to investigation, a dozen names of ABC ware manufacturers appear on the list of factories investigated. But it is an impossible task to accurately correspond disparaging conditions with their providing factories, as not all interviews included factory names. Suffice it to say that, at least in some of the factories, at some of the time, for a period of some years, disparaging conditions did exist.

And Scriven, more interested in the welfare of the workers than in identifying ruthless factory owners, merged his findings. Of his rationale he wrote,

> When first I began my inspection of the several works, it was my intention to report on each separately, but I found there was so great a similarity in their character, that it would have occupied my time uselessly. . . . I determined, therefore, to divide the whole into three distinct classes, not according to their magnitude or extent, but to their merits as to drainage, ventilation, and convenience. (Lewis, 1975, p. 11)

Interviews told the story. Samuel Littler, then age ten, had already worked for three years as a painter. Sue Wilcox, also age ten, had been bound a year. John Cooper, age thirty-eight, had been employed in the dipping house thirty years. Jesse Gordon, age forty-seven, had been a potter for forty years.

From five years old, children, Scriven said, were required to do work in damp, dark, ill-ventilated cellar rooms or sheds often heated beyond endurance. Charles Shaw, the eloquent pottery autobiographer, remembered them thick with wasted clay and "stinking of the most objectionable refuse of which little, if any, notice was taken." But the premises and the potters were spick, span, and sober for visitors . . . surely they knew when to shine.

And just as surely, the visitors noticed the children toting unbearably heavy baskets of wet clay, dragging flat wicker baskets of coal from the rucks to the ovens, removing the iron tubs of oven ash, and carrying the molds to and from the drying sheds on planks longer than the children were tall. General discomfort aside, young children were found in areas where dipping, scouring, dish making, and painting were the tasks at hand, making this phase of the process ultimately fatal. The formed and fired plates needed to be glazed, and for that they were dipped and handed to young boys dripping with a mixture of borax, soda, potash, carbonate of lead, and sometimes arsenic and water. In saturated clothing children carried them to drying shelves; G. Bernard Hughes, in his *English and Scottish Earthenware, 1660-1860* (1961), estimated that an experienced workman with two boys could dip about 700 dozen plates each day. But it didn't take as many as 840 dips into the poisonous concoction each hour to reward its handlers with neuropathy, anemia, epilepsy, kidney failure, and varieties of other bowel diseases.

The 1925 *Cox's Potteries Annual and Year Book* included an article titled, "New Departure in Suspected Lead Poisoning Case," which described the first microscopically investigated death conclusively declared to be caused by lead poisoning. From the wisdom of one Dr. F. Shufflebotham came the start of a real foundation for change.

But lead and arsenic weren't the only killers. More ominous and more difficult to control than lead in solution was the dust created by the bedding of china in the silica dust and the scouring away of the ground flint that attached itself to bisque ware in firing. The flint powder, when airborne, nestled in respiratory tissues, eventually weakened the workers' voices, and caused silicosis (also called "potters' rot" or "potters' asthma") and other lung diseases similar to those encountered by the miners. Tuberculosis signaled demise. From the Daniel and Sons China Factory in Stoke comes the testimony of thirty-three-year-old Fanny Wood. "I have been a scourer seven years. . . . The work does not agree with us very well, because it is so dusty it makes one short of breath; every one that works in this place suffers more or less with coughs, and we are all stuffed up; we have known a great many deaths from it; . . . William B . . . knows five women who have died from it and numbers that have been obliged to leave it; he now says he couldn't enumerate the number, there have been so many" (Lewis, 1975, p. 43).

Angela Lee of the Gladstone Pottery Museum (June 2000) gives us the likely recipe of that earthenware: 25% ball clay, 25% china clay, 15% china stone, and 35% flint. Fortunately, a patent for grinding that 35% flint replaced the iron mortars with underwater grinding furthered by the genius James Brindley. The Factory and Workshop Act of 1891 began the difficult process of control, which did not become effective until 1933.

And there were other threats to health and safety. Some children interviewed spoke of being beaten for slowing their tedious turning of the wheel. Bill Morland's rag-dressed children (see the *Staffordshire Magazine*, "Kid Cogs," February 1980) had no regular time for sleep; they could be called upon at any time of the day or night to walk a mile or more in any weather to serve their time elsewhere. Ordinarily the privies they used were in a disgusting state and not separated for the sexes. Food was most often eaten irregularly; some reports say time was not always given, food was insufficient, or, if eaten, was consumed alongside or covered by toxic materials. The testimonials are tales of terror.

But it was not only undeveloped bodies that so disturbed Samuel Scriven. He was saddened to find that children who had attested to years of Sunday School attendance and to literacy were found to know little more than the names of the letters and that, quoting #35, "from the whole body of evidence it appears, however, that there are at present in existence no means adequate to effect any material and general improvements in the Physical and Moral Condition of the Children and Young Persons employed in labour" (Lewis, 1975, p. 10).

Scriven concluded that because the children were paid by the workmen, their hours might be severely prolonged and irregular . . . Charles Shaw knew that well. His grotesque descriptions of mismanagement tell of the loosest daily or weekly supervision of the work people in their separate "shops"; accountable only for the number of pieces they produced, they could work or play very much as they pleased. Employees wallowed in the refreshment of smuggled beer from dawn to dusk while staging brutal and often bloody brawls for the rousing and sadistic enjoyment of all. Degrading indulgences were witnessed by the innocent; forced to consume unholy quantities of poor liquor, young women, adjusting their torn, clay-soaked clothing, continued their overnight toil with downcast eyes by the dim morning's light. Without the use of machinery to guide production, there was little accounting for time . . . hours or days could net little or nothing while children worked like galley slaves, often spurred on by beatings to make up the deficits by Friday, for each man began his day as he wished, often at three or four in the morning.

The abuse of time and materials fell not only upon the shoulders of the pottery owners. Shaw's tales of abuse, with some contempt, echoed the ill-treatment among workers themselves, who chose power over responsibility in a self-determined class system devoid of dignity or direction. And with pervasive sadness he describes the profound chasm between the employer and the employed . . . the wealthy versus the grossly underpaid, who were completely cheated and terminally plagued by managerial indifference and the abject poverty that engulfed them. Echoing this message are the words of Jordan (1987), who writes of the "degeneracy problem"—with children looking like little old men, deformities and distortions the result of opposition to reform by unscrupulous men who would circumvent the law for profit.

In spite of the efforts of the report writers, it took a rise in the numbers of children employed from 1851 to 1861 to prompt Lord Shaftesbury's motion in Parliament (August 1861), which requested renewed inquiries into the employment of the underaged. Evidence presented acknowledged the condition of the children and the state of education in the district. But the means by which those "evils" might be arrested—or at least reformed—were elusive. Sources say the meetings were publicized, but Marguerite DuPree (1995) assures her readers that the inquiry was, in fact, not brought to the attention of the public.

The wrangling of manufacturers against this plan or that plan was caustic, with the intensity of the opposition in direct proportion to the numbers of children the towns employed. Tunstall, Hanley, and Stoke had low numbers. Fenton and Burslem had higher numbers, but Longton topped the list at 33% child laborers. DuPree has painfully summarized the minutes of the gatherings of pottery owners whose self-protective interests conscientiously postponed child labor reform. Among her notes was the argument, expressed at a meeting chaired by Francis Wedgwood, that one intention of educating the underaged was a political-religious tool to inculcate the ideologies of the Church of England in a highly Wesleyan area . . . clearly a distortion of intent. Meetings ended by forming committees rather than commitments, and diversionary tactics took center stage until July 24, 1864, when the House of Lords, with a royal nod, settled the matter for the factory owners who knew reforms were needed but could not bring themselves to a consensus. Now there was legislation that had special implications for the children involved in the production of low-cost earthenware; it was only in the best interest of the factories to keep their costs of cheap items at a minimum. At least some of the abuses, described so well by Samuel Scriven twenty years before, were now illegal. By August of 1898, no person under fourteen could be involved in cleaning ware after the dipper, in glaze blowing, china scouring, color dusting, and other processes that, in time, offered deadly consequences. By 1899, the solubility of lead was decreased by law, but because the law was hard to enforce, this abuse might have continued. It is only since 1949 that no deaths have resulted from contact with lead substances.

Of course, there were producers of materials who supported the pottery industry; there were industries not remembered for their involvement with child labor. Lead, originally the most costly of materials, mined as lead sulphite, was brought from Derbyshire, Cumberland, and North Wales. One William Jenkinson patented and produced an engine to remove water from the mines. Not related to the production of ABC plates but pertinent to the history of The Potteries was the need for salt. Mined at Cheshire in the form of brine, salt was brought to the towns to use in glazing. And the building of mills to grind grain for growing populations and to produce materials for the pottery industry showed real growth from the 1700s, along with crate making, saggar making, and the manufacture of kiln furniture.

There were smaller industries as well, sparked by a rush of growing technologies. Brought to England from France by Ralph Daniel of Cobridge in 1745, plaster molds reduced the potter's dependence upon the potter's wheel and the lathe. No longer were the old casts of brass, fired clay, and stone used, as they did not absorb water as quickly as molds made of gypsum (calcium sulphate), a substance formed with clay by the evaporation of salty water. Burnt and then ground, the plaster of paris expanded when mixed with water to make precise forms. Drying quickly, the molds quickened and standardized the process of bulk production.

From trees came the raw materials for paper, which was critical to the industry as well. William Adams knew that, and at the end of the 18th century, he opened a paper mill at Cheddleton to process thin papers for transfer printing. Then there was the Ivy-House Paper Mill at Hanley, which, besides making the heavy papers for packing, made more of the tissue paper used in the printing of the copperplate engravings. It was M. Fourdrinier, in 1827, who perfected and patented the machine that so beautifully made the perfectly thin paper from pulp; four years later a patent was granted to John Potts of

Burslem, whose new invention printed the thin paper designs onto continuous rolls of tissue (see "T Is for Transfers and Toybooks"). It was about twenty-five years later that an article in the *Pottery Gazette* (d.?) announced the invention of a "dissolving tissue" that must have made the removal of the used transfer far easier (see Appendix AP2).

The early history of transfer printing (see "T Is for Transfers and Toybooks") brings us to Liverpool in 1756 to the firm of John Sadler & Guy Green, where John Sadler experimented with transfer printing after seeing children sticking waste prints onto broken earthenware to make doll's tea sets. Josiah Spode helped to develop underglaze transfer printing in Stoke when he persuaded Thomas Lucas, an engraver, and James Richards, a printer, to leave the Caughley Works in Shropshire and join him in the production of blue-underglaze transfer ware. From Liverpool came the perfection of onglaze printing. "Those influences, too, can be seen on the vast quantities of print decorated 'Cream Ware' produced by Josiah Spode as well as Josiah Wedgwood and William Adams" (Freeman, 1977).

Actually, Hanley and Shelton became the centers of transfer making, where designs were created and copied onto the copper plates that held the color that printed the tissue that was cut by the girls that were placed on the plates . . . the tune was repeated from firm to firm. A light firing to drive off the oil in the colors took place after the transfers were applied to the plates. They were then dipped in glaze and fired once more. And alphabet ware, if overpainted, as so many were, was then placed into the kiln for the fourth firing. It would be reasonable to assume that, being (then) of questionable quality, additional firings for "delicate" colors were not common practice.

Firms that make the paint still carry the names of generations past. By 1818, there were more than a dozen paint shops, twice that in 1822. Though they kept their formulas secret from one another, in a spirit of goodwill they did combine their powdered color with pigment from other firms in order to fill large orders. The colors they made were not new finds. The metallic oxides, applied by hand thousands of years before Christ, have changed little; iron and manganese provide the blacks, browns, and yellows of the ancients. Copper greens and turquoise blue were legacies of the Egyptians. The expensive blue of Staffordshire fame came from the refining of cobalt, known by the 10th century of the Common Era. And there were pinks and roses and maroons and purples and lustres, some of which are evident in this text's collection.

As time went on, growing numbers of establishments provided the packing crates, the engines and machinery, the glazes, and other materials essential to plate making. Floods of patents followed . . . among them Ralph Shaw's improvement in the kiln and Alsager's string throwing wheel. Kathy Niblett, Staffordshire ceramic historian, reminds us of the architects who designed model factories that took into account the needs of production and employees—A. R. Wood and A. A. Longden being two important examples. Improvements to the machines used in factories were made by engineers like William Boulton. Famous chemists who developed colors and glaze effects included Francis Emery, Thomas W. Harrison, William Burton, and the noted A. F. Wenger, whose special interest was the use of gold. Rope makers like T. R. Hinde and A. T. Robson were invaluable to the burgeoning trade, and the wheels of industry were lubricated by Sampson Walker, who refined and sold oil. Raw materials were prepared and improved by potters' millers,

Jesse Shirley being one of the most famous.

But without the early vision of Josiah Wedgwood, there would not have been as rapid a development of those factories . . . the transportation system of water and roads that facilitated the coming in of materials and the going out of products with uncommon ease. Exceptionally skilled at the potter's wheel and totally committed to experiment and research, he created new and ambitious pottery techniques, but it was not only the creation of unique wares that intrigues us. Wedgwood's vision extended far beyond his factory walls.

In 1750, the roads in Britain were worse than they had been when the Romans left. Deep ruts, grooves, and gullies were left by wagon wheels through the icy muds of winter; holes dug for clay and filled with refuse of all manner eroded their banks, while overturned wagons and carriages were reminders of unfortunate journeys. Over these ravaged and often impassable arteries, raw materials had to be transported to the factories and fragile merchandise from them. Wedgwood, as were other potters, was desperately concerned about the safety of fragile wares in transport, as losses and breakage in carriages were very expensive. More globally, Wedgwood understood that the infrastructure was crucial to the survival of the 150 separate Potteries in Burslem and its neighborhoods. He was instrumental in bringing a petition to turnpike the roads and subsequently became one of the Committee of Trustees who approved contracts for their construction. The passage of an act of Parliament in 1763 began the slow process of improving the roads, with special permissions to keep the toll gates at reasonable distances from the potteries. By 1800, soil-covered layers of stones and pebbles designed by Scottish engineer John Macadam reliably facilitated the delivery of clays and coal to the manufactories despite inclement weather.

But there was a smoother way to transport goods to come. In the second half of the 18th century, England was enjoying substantial trade; a more rapid transit of raw materials than the new roads could accomplish was needed. A network of transit canals, first built in the area by the Romans, was the answer **(Figure P6)**. The wealthy young Third Duke of Bridgewater was the first to have a waterway built to transport coal from his mines at Worsley to Manchester. With more efficient transport, the cost of coal became affordable. The engineer of that Bridgewater Canal was the inventive genius who conceived the great system of canals that connected England's four main navigable rivers, the Mersey, Trent, Severn, and Thames. James Brindley named the plan "The Grand Cross," which included a route from the Mersey to the Trent that he called The Grand Trunk. The plan for The Grand Trunk was backed by Josiah Wedgwood, who, supported by the potters, presented a bill to Parliament requesting the building of the link. The act of Parliament was granted on May 14, 1766; Josiah turned the first sod two months later, placing the spade into the competent hands of his engineer friend. Sadly, Brindley, chilled after being caught in a rainstorm, died on the 27th of September in 1772. His brother-in-law, Hugh Henshall, completed the 93-mile waterway in 1777.

The Grand Trunk and hundreds of miles of other broad and narrow canals throughout lowland Britain made it possible to move the clays, coal, stone, iron and copper ores, lime, sand, manure, and agricultural produce that earlier could not support the cost of transport. Over the waterways one canal boat could easily carry up to fifty tons of cargo, hardly a match for a pack horse. But horses were needed to pull the narrow boats whose services and isolated families were too soon threatened by the coming of the steam engine.

The Trent and Mersey carried goods from all the potteries as well as to and from Wedgwood's new Etruria, which opened on the banks of the canal in 1769. Close to the factory he created a village for his workers and a grand mansion for his family, which he proudly named Etruria Hall. The new facility produced his neoclassical figured Jasper ware and the forever-remembered black basalt made from clay stained with iron. But it was Josiah's invention of the pyrometer that earned him commendation as a Fellow of the Royal Society, and thanks to the encouragement of his dear friend, scientist Erasmus Darwin, the factory at Etruria was the first to install a rotary steam engine from James Watt, a pioneer in the use of steam power, in 1782. Perhaps it is to this grandfather of Charles Darwin that we owe the unforeseen tumultuous growth of the industry. But could he ever envision the justifiable terror of the workers when the great rolling monsters, the machines, invaded the livelihoods of the workers? Their very existence hung in the balance.

The potteries did not explode with the installation of new-fangled machinery, as did other industries of the era . . . the workforce quickly revolted. Excerpts from *The Pottery Examiner* of 1844 and 1845, as reprinted in R. A. Lewis's school curriculum, carve deep images. "And the cries of hungry children are pleasurable sounds to the ears of tender-hearted parents whose hearthstone is desolate and . . . whose cupboard is empty. MACHINERY is your deadliest enemy. To obstruct its introduction into any branch of your trade should now be the one great principle of your lives . . . [as] it was a battle for bread, and home, and life, for mother, child and wife. . . . It was the duty of any worker, whose . . . manufacturer . . . may have attempted to introduce the curse . . . to close his works, and to inscribe thereon, CLOSED FOR EVER!" (Lewis, 1981b, p. 36).

Traditional methods changed slowly. A masterpiece of early engraving by Enoch Wood best tells the traditional process in sequence. Smiling, well-dressed men and women carry on the work of the pottery, perhaps deceptively appearing most healthy, wealthy, and wise (Figures P7 through P15).

As in the process pictured, ABC ware with raised letters on its rim was relief-molded around the plate rim. The three rough marks on the glaze indicate where the "stilts" or small tripods were placed to keep them from fusing in the kiln. Because most were made before the technology of color transfer processing, the color appears in childlike or primitive style, certainly not the work of exquisitely talented crews of the factories. Likely done by children, the painting very often occluded the transfer, or simply edged the ground with a grassy green swish!

And swish they did . . . right onto boats for export—brought by narrow canal boats and later by the railways. Delays on the canals created an impatience for a faster and more economical delivery system. Because of heavy tolls and pressure to meet the more accelerated pace of industry, the building of railways was demanded by industries that were ready to carry their commerce into the 20th century; the steam-powered iron horse needed to reach from the Main Line to the Potteries, connecting them to the world. In the words of Basil Jeuda, Lecturer in Transport History at Keele University in Keele, Staffordshire:

The promoters of the early passenger railways in England envisioned schemes linking, for example, London with Birmingham and Birmingham with Liverpool and Manchester. Industrialists in the Potteries pinned their hopes on one of these schemes passing through, rather than near, the Potteries and Stoke; the 1836 proposals of the Manchester South Union Railway, from Manchester through Stoke towards Birmingham, and then to London, would have achieved this, but the national railway politics of 1839 frustrated the plan. The North Staffordshire Railway Acts of 1846 led to the establishment of two railway routes passing through Stoke (both of which still survive) from Macclesfield to Colwich and Crewe to Derby, and these were opened in 1848/49 as part of the creation of a national railway network. With the completion of the Loop Line (1873-1875) Stoke would connect to the other Pottery towns (July, 2000).

The famous "loop" (the west side of which was the main line) was designed to serve the towns of Etruria, Hanley, Cobridge, Burslem, and Tunstall (and on to Kidsgrove). Conceived in 1847 and reinvented in 1854, it was estimated to replace the yearly services of 150 men and 300 horses (Figure P16). After much controversy and the relocation of the North Staffordshire Infirmary from Hanley to Hartshill due to the noise and emissions, a commercial northeast-southwest line from Etruria to Hanley opened in December of 1861, and a "people mover" carried its first passengers on July 13, 1864. Citizens from Burslem and Tunstall pressed for the completion of the service. A year later, on July 5, 1865, the Potteries Loop Line Act allowed three years for the purchase of land and two years more for the finish of 7-3/4 miles of track.

The first locomotive was put on rails at Turnhurst Hall, a fitting honor to its one-time resident, engineer James Brindley. A second line was laid between Etruria and Hanley to take out the "kinks," and a new station was opened at Hanley when the loop reached Burslem on November 1, 1873. Exactly one month later, Tunstall was opened for business. The final cost of the loop to Kidsgrove was £493,976, significantly over the original prospectus but worth many times its investment to the Potteries it served for twenty years.

Though not as famous as the Loop Line, the expansions of the North Staffordshire line to serve the coalfields and ironworks; the Apedale line in 1853; the Biddulph Valley line, which opened in 1859; and the Audley and the Market Drayton lines, which opened in 1870, all owed their viability and longevity to the vast coal deposits around Stoke (Jeuda, 2000). But change was not too far down the track. In 1882, the North Staffordshire Tramways bought the service from Burslem to Hanley, converted it to a steam tramway, and extended it south to Stoke, Fenton, and Longton. Serving so many Potteries, it carried four million passengers between 1896 and 1898. With the founding in 1898 of the Pottery Electric Traction Company, trains became available in 1899, and by 1905, 115 electric trams were racing, as was time, into the 20th century. Basil Jeuda allows us a glimpse into a time early in the 20th century with rare photos (Figures P17, P18, and P19) of a station at Stoke on some autumn midmorning about 1905 and a train yard at Burslem (1912). The North Staffordshire Railway Company (NSR) lasted until 1923, when it was incorporated into the London, Midland and Scottish Railway (LMS) by way of the Railways Act of 1921; with its consolidation, the NSR disappeared. Many portions of the original tracks have been abandoned, a similar fate of railroads around the world (McClellan, 2000).

Like the North Staffordshire Railway, the making of Staffordshire alphabet ware has disappeared, but interest in the unique contributions of the children who created it for those more fortunate than they is a most poignant chapter in the story of the Potteries and a most significant force behind the Industrial Revolution. The trail from the indiscriminate and often inhumane employment of youngsters to laws that guaranteed them a more healthful existence and an appropriate education parallels the progress of technological advances. Machines, those monstrous threats to the pottery worker, also allowed his children the opportunities to shatter the cycle of back-breaking and dehumanizing poverty. The expanding world of commercialism offered alternatives that required an education and mandated that the parent, caught in the long-continued lifestyle of the preindustrial society, not only allowed but supported it. Though the discourse concerning education argued about where to teach, what to teach, and how to teach it, the question of whom to teach became more apparent. Without reforming the educational system to include all children, there could be no real Victorian reforms to support a rapidly growing and democratic economy. Our relics of the old days must be cherished to honor the painful efforts of those little ones who helped to create them—especially to those whose physical health was so cruelly sacrificed. And they are, on the upside, symbols of change as well; their tale might have been told under a chapter called, "R Is for Religion, Reform, and Reason."

Q Is for Queries

Children's books of "Queries" might well have inspired the production of the "query plates" which, with their riddles and conundrums, were perfect servers for jelly-cakes at parlor games where the powers of intellect were tested. Awards and applause were bestowed upon the unrivaled contestants who most conscientiously devoured the printings; books of Enigmas, Charades, Rebuses, Puzzles, Anagrams, and Puns were to be studied for great performances at social gatherings. Riddles and their cousins, the conundrums, were written at first for adult entertainment. "Uncle George," editor of *Parlour Pastimes for the Young* (Blackwood, 1857), described the conundrum as the simplest and most amusing of all kinds of riddles. It is, he said, a sort of riddle, an ambiguous description "in which some odd resemblance between things quite unlike was proposed for discovery."

On a series of alphabet plates **(Q1 through Q7)**, any one of these six conundrums could be practiced three times a day; those questions might always be answered correctly for, when the meal was done, the answer could be found on the overturned plate. The questions read:

1. Why is this poor little rabbit so terribly frightened?
2. Why is this geometrical fishing?
3. Why is the gentleman in cap and gown the better logician of the two?
4. Why are these boys wrong in their arithmetic?
5. Why would this pastry cook make a good soldier?
6. What fruit does our sketch represent?

This time the solutions can be found in Appendix AQ1.

More complex conundrums, or riddles, were sets of clues to be combined, with inventive skill, with a definition of a single object or condition. They appeared in a 1765 issue of *A New Riddle Book or a Whetstone for Dull Wits,* (McCulloch, 1979). Later books included a question-and-answer section alongside more challenging formats; answering queries quickly became a popular pastime, and soon publishers of toybooks ran regular issues of extraordinarily compiled and wonderfully illustrated question-and-answer books. Chapbooks with woodcut illustrations were released in the 1820s, and by 1850, Peter Puzzlecap (really Samuel G. Goodrich) and others published hundreds of "Q and A"-style titles. Titles, says McCulloch, such as Thomas Hood's *Puzzledom - An Original Collection of Charades, Conundrums, Puzzles and Games,* made their appearance in Philadelphia about 1866. Problem-solving exercises were included in *Our Young People's Post Office Box* and the *St. Nicholas'*

Letter Box, which not only provided pages of entertainment but also allowed children to have a voice in the selection of materials presented in each *Harper and Century* weekly issue. Finally, the books provided merriment without moralities or messages to memorize; they exercised critical thinking skills, as sorely needed now as then.

Mrs. Pullan's *Book of Riddles,* published in London (1855), is an extraordinary collection of queries, exquisitely illustrated with intricate woodcuts and written in levels to suit the capacity of its listeners. Mrs. P's protective (and pedagogically sound) introduction describes the pitiful look in children's eyes when they have "given up" with overchallenge. Most important, she says, is that youngsters *like* to find the solutions, and they cannot like what they cannot comprehend . . . solid good sense and an important step in the 19th century's new definition of childhood.

Noël Riley's *Gifts for Good Children* (1991) lists one of several transfer sources of **Figure Q8** as *The Girl's Own Book* (Thomas Tegg, 1832) and titles the graphic "The Graces" or "The Flying Circle." Typical of the Victorian tendency to join unrelated themes in print is the transfer of the game "La Grace" and its "wormy" riddle.

> I ever live man's unrelenting foe
> Mighty in mischief though I'm small in size
> And he at last that seeks to lay me low
> My food and habitation both supplies.

The game challenges one player to catch the opponent's thrown hoop on his/her crossed sticks. Imported from Germany to France and from France to England, the game, when played artfully, is most graceful.

The second riddle **(Figure Q9)**, whose answer is a clock, reads:

> Tis true I have both face and hands
> And move before your eye
> But when I move I always stand
> And when I stand I lie.

The game that accompanies it challenges one player to miss the shuttlecock once it is hit over the net by his/her opponent. The game was then (and is now) called Badminton (see "I Is for Infancy to Infirm" for additional history).

The last riddle **(Figure Q10)** reads:

Pray tell us ladies if you can
Who is that highly favoured man
Who though he has married many a wife
May be a bachelor all his life.

Again, the activity of the young women has little to do with the riddle other than giggling over the eligible clergyman while playing what appears to be a round dance similar to "Ring-a-Ring o' Roses." Gomme says the source of this game is simple—the making of a circle of flowers, the turning of the group around those blossoms with joined hands, and the bowing or curtsying of each member of the ring toward the garland's center. Evidence of the activity's mythical origin was seen in the long-past inclusion of sneezing, as that bodily function has, since ancient times, been regarded as a supernatural event in everyday life. The song, titled "Ring by Ring," found on page 111 of Gomme's *Dictionary of British Folk-Lore* (1898), is short:

Here we go round by ring, by ring,
As ladies do in Yorkshire;
A curtsey here, a curtsey there,
A curtsey to the ground, sir.

At least one figure on the transfer appears to be in deep curtsey (or curtsy) . . . the others about to follow along. But the words of this ditty make no reference to sneezes or snapdragons, as traces of mythical and early forms had long since eroded when Gomme alluded to them over a century before.

Other puzzles, riddles, and charades are transfer subjects of plates pictured on page 83 in Riley's book, though they are examples without alphabet borders. With so popular a trend, it was no wonder that intriguing riddles and conundrums were featured on ABC ware, some silently encouraging a clean plate before the answer could be found. But with so few items in this collection, we are left with a query. Just how many other plates of this nature might eventually be found?

R Is for Religion, Reform, and Reason

The table for the Sabbath's High Tea would be best set with plates that offered Old Testament tales along with the obligatory breads and butter. Tasty finger food could be quickly eaten to reveal the moral messages that kept Victorian children thinking good thoughts on Sunday while herding Noah's wooden animals on and off their handsomely painted ark. Pious observance of the Lord's Day was revived after the turn of the century in a wave of conscience, perhaps, to unbalance the flourishing social vices; Sabbatarianism kept its participants sitting quietly in church (Figure R1) or at home reading the Bible (Figure R2), religious novels, moral parables, or those inexpensive, messianic printings of The Religious Tract Society that sanctioned only the perfect reverence of the day's sacred hours. With amazing grace, a quiet Sabbath crossed the lines of religious difference; there were quiet hours in homes of Anglicans and their splintered Dissenters.

But everyone paid some tax to keep up the royal, established Church. That Anglican Communion had three divisions: the high, the broad, and the low. The high were the Orthodox, strict and stoic with no liberal leanings. The broad church brought less sermonizing. Its sanction was Royal, as Victoria and Albert allowed no finger-shaking threats of hell and damnation to encourage the devotion of their children. It was, in fact, the broad church that courageously suggested that perhaps, just perhaps, science and religion could coexist. And practical schools, adult schools, and late-evening colleges for the working man were designed to raise the level of education even for the less advantaged.

From the low Church came the doers who went directly into the homes of the less fortunate to do good. But they weren't the only self-helpers. Evangelicals rose from the ranks of the Nonconformists or Separatists, which represented all those "other" Christians who were called Baptists, Congregationalists, Presbyterians, Wesleyan Methodists, Independent Methodists, Armenian Methodists, Welsh Methodists, Unitarians, Plymouth Brethren, English Moravians, members of the Churches of Christ or the New Jerusalem Church, the Salvation Army . . . and lots more. The splinters, as a total group, represented about 60% of the believers. As the 19th century progressed, Evangelicals, whether Anglicans or Dissenters, looked for converts . . . high-spirited and determined, they sought to rid society of its social sins.

Forever remembered will be Isaac Watts (1674-1748), an early Dissenter and Evangelical who served his Independent Congregation gloriously with an astounding list of original hymns. One extraordinary record of his genius was found in pocket-sized tract publications of Philadelphia's American Sunday-School Union; in one anecdote his mother rewarded him for writing a couplet (Figure R3):

> I write not for a farthing, but to try
> How I your farthing writers can outvie.

Less appreciative, his father nearly whipped him for his continually rhyming speech, to which Isaac answered,

> O father, do some pity take
> And I will no more verses make.

He lied, thank Heavens. First published in 1707, his cautionary poetry was nearly monosyllabic, making it easy for youngsters to read and memorize, though it remains doubtful that little persons could comprehend the theology. But Watts' intent was clear. A morass of statistics does provide differences in the death rates of children by dates, classes, and areas of the United Kingdom. But whether children lived with family or with foundling home peers, the death rate was at least one third or more of all children from birth to age five. Industrial abuse was rampant, medicine was in its infancy, and sanitation just medieval. So many children perished that the unthinkable was commonplace; children were enrolled in one or more burial clubs, which, for a penny a week, would cover the cost of their interment, and with that promised money, the rate of death club enrollees was twice the national average. And bodies were held for viewing . . . to the tune of entrance fees to soothe the sorrows (see "I Is for Infant to Infirm").

With the high rate of mortality, Watts devoutly believed that the vulnerable young needed a swift education of religious truths. They needed to know how "to behave so well" so they would "Not be afraid of dying" (moral song, "Good Resolutions").

Under the guise of saving little ones from idleness and using child labor to maintain profits in a highly competitive industry (see "P for Potters and Their Potteries"), labor-class children were painfully disfigured with twisted knees, bowed chests, spinal flexures, and losses of limbs while being subjected to deplorable, slowly debilitating toxins. Others drank the unseen poisons of rotting refuse and infested waters. Eight-year-olds began their work in the black, black coal pit before four in the morning. Death's angels loosened the shackles of four-year-olds chained sleeping at their machines. Thin young souls, recruited from orphanages, were soaked in brine and sent up chimneys to extinguish the fires or scrape the soot. Even in the middle and upper classes, mortality from diseases was high, while epidemics slew mercilessly in the squalor of the slums. Many perished from wholly preventable fluid depletion, and thousands succumbed to the feeding of infant formulas of ales, milk, flour, and sugars called pap or posset served in inadequately cleaned vessels (see Appendix AR1 for recipes). The most caring of nannies murdered their charges with offerings of the sweet stuff, which was teeming with bacteria. With a high rate of mortality, God and the hereafter were close to those with religious convictions. Watts's popularized praises were touching comforts in tragic times.

The good reverend helped to shape the lives of millions of youngsters in Britain and America, but his intense love for children was not always expressed in terms of endearment. Reflecting his passionate desire to swiftly save each soul, many verses grimly warned against encroaching evils. Like England's 19th-century newspapers, Sunday School tracts and hymnals rang with tongue-lashings against the follies of being wicked. Watts reminded his songsters that God "writes down every fault," "gives no repentance in the grave," and provides only a hell for devils, "In darkness, fire and chains." *Divine Songs*, first published in 1707, thanked God for His gifts, stated clearly that Christians were luckier than Heathens and Jews, and, rather than "love thy neighbor," Watts suggested pity to those who lived in non-Christian lands while extolling the superiority of British ground, "Where streams of heavenly mercy flow."

In spite of English loyalties, Isaac's hymns, first published in America by Ben Franklin in Boston in 1739, were sung by those of the Revolutionary period and are found today in contemporary hymnals. A goodly number of alphabet plates carried verses from Watts' *Divine and Moral Songs for Children*. Some of these are pictured, beginning with the first verse of "A General Song of Praise to God," Song I **(Figure R4)**. (Verses are complete in Appendix AR2.)

> How glorious is our heavenly King
> Who reigns above the sky!
> How shall a child presume to sing
> His dreadful majesty!

The second transfer was inspired from the painting of the *Resurrezione* **(Figure R5)** by Piero della Francesca; the work is now at the Museo Civico in San Sepolcro, Tuscany, Italy. Different from the transfer **(Figure R6)**, the flag in the painting becomes a cross in Christ's right hand. Three guards, not four, attend; the "sleeping figure" is animated rather than still; the diagonal direction of the center sentry is reversed, and the engraver chose not to include the fourth, probably to firmly end possible complications of copyright. (Verses are complete in Appendix AR3.)

> Behold him rising from the grave:
> Behold him rais'd on high:
> He pleads his merit there to save
> Transgressors doom'd to die.
> (Verse five: Praise Be to God for Our Redemption . . . Song III).

(Figure R7 - Verses are complete in Appendix AR4.)

> At twelve years old he talk'd with men
> (The Jews all wondering stand;)
> Yet he obey'd his mother then,
> And came at her command.
> (Verse three: Examples of Early Piety, Song XIV)

(Figure R8 - Verses are complete in Appendix AR5.)

> How doth the little busy bee
> Improve each shining hour!
> And gather honey all the day
> From ev'ry op'ning flow'r!
> (Verse one: Against Idleness and Mischief, Song XX)

Not only was this song reprinted by the American Tract Society, but Lewis Carroll parodied the verse for Alice (in Wonderland) when she sang,

> How doth the little crocodile
> Improve his shining tale,
> And pour the waters of the Nile
> On every golden scale!
>
> How cheerfully he seems to grin,
> How neatly spreads his claws,
> And welcomes little fishes in
> With gently smiling jaws.

True, both sing of natural behaviors . . . the bee in literature has long been the symbol of serious industry. And because the crocodile eats fish, though more cruel than taking nourishment from nectar, he is not under Satan's spell. Because he smiles, he is not up to mischief . . . he is simply acknowledging the fish's place in the food chain, though perhaps, with the inference of claws and grin, we might give in to a little less than "saintly" satisfaction.

(Figure R9 - Verses are complete in Appendix AR6.)

> The tulip and the butterfly
> Appear in gayer coats than I:
> Let me be dress'd fine as I will,
> Flies, worms, and flowers exceed me still.
> (Verse four: Against Pride In Clothes, Song XXII)

(Figure R10 - Verses are complete in Appendix AR7.)

> I lay my body down to sleep
> Let angels guard my head,
> And through the hours of darkness keep
> Their watch around my bed.
> (Verse three: An Evening Song, Song XXVI)

Presumably there are other plates that illustrate the good works of this soulful songwriter. An exhaustive list of titles can be found at http://www.ccel.org/w/watts/psalmshymns/TOC.htm.

Sounding much like Watts in meter and matter, a verse on a product **(Figure R11)** marked with a capital W sings, "I thank the goodness and the grace / Which on my birth have smiled, / And made me, in these Christian days, / A happy English child." And who could not be happier than the father teaching biblical verse; **Figure R12** is an exemplary transfer of Victorian ethic, while Wedgwood & Co.'s **Figure R13** assures the little ones that their prayers will indeed be heard.

Like many other similar transfers on early English pieces, the brown transfer plate introduces a second renowned dissenting Evangelist, the honorable Reverend Richard Jordan, Minister of the Gospel in the Society of Friends, which began in England by one George Fox (as the Seekers) seeking to protest the religious hierarchy and formalism of doctrine, the elaborate church rituals, and the domination of the Church by the English aristocracy. Inmates of English jails and the targets of mob abuse, the believers were harassed in the New World by the Puritans (themselves runaways from religious persecution), who promised the Friends the loss of their ears (and then of their lives) should they not keep their distance.

The anonymous biography written two years after Jordan's death on November 14, 1826, tells the tale of a man born in Norfolk, Virginia, in 1756, who spent his days in the service of Gospel missions on the Eastern seaboard and abroad **(Figure R14)**. In his early years he was a vocal Abolitionist. A roving evangelist in his later years, he moved his residence several times, always to be among strangers. His simple lifestyle imparted, with power and clarity, the need for service to the Divine Master. The excessive quiet of the Quakers gave way to reform; new energies established mental hospitals, changed prison conditions, opened schools, and provided food and poverty relief. Quaker managed businesses, like Cadbury Chocolates, still add comfort and sweetness to our lives. For the remainder of his forty years, Richard Jordan traveled from Meeting to Meeting, "a preacher of righteousness . . . ; being concerned, by a circumspect walking, to keep himself unspotted from the world" (Anonymous, 1828; see "A Is for Americana" for the story of William Penn and the Quakers).

The Evangelicals were expanding their focus, tying rewards in the thereafter to the betterment of life in the here and now as technology was rapidly improving ways to do everything. Inventions lit the streets, carried the mail, controlled diseases, penetrated the watery depths, pierced the clouds, and more. Geologists and anthropologists were uncovering ancient truths, disturbing the fundamentalists' absolute literal interpretation of the Bible. And an energizing wave of humanitarianism fostered the zealots to eliminate crime and squalor. Their hugely successful efforts did away with ghastly public hangings, flogging in the military, and most "blood sports." The vast list of organizations founded to cure the world's ills named even a protective society for the faraway Aborigines; closer to home, there were societies for the Suppression of the Opium Trade, Anti-Slavery, Children's Aid, Distressed Gentlefolks, Discharged Prisoners, and more. On the home front, Evangelicals addressed issues of the mentally and socially challenged, with schools

and new treatments for the disabled and orphanages for children left alone after epidemics took parents from their earthly homes.

With the Rescue Society, the Society for the Protection of Young Females, the Society for the Prevention of Cruelty to Children, and others, it was evangelical intervention that stood strong to change the lifestyle of those who entertained themselves with drunkenness and the deaths caused by "overlaying," abandonment, and beating by dead-drunk parents. As many as one beer store per every twelve dwellings was enough to tempt youngsters as well. Before 1839 there were no restrictions on the sale of liquor to children. Wages were given to workers who quickly exchanged them for refreshing ales that robbed their children of any hope of nourishment. Meager earnings were passed out to twelve-year-olds once inside the pub; they would soon be drunk for a penny or dead drunk for twice that. Of more than 202,000 visits to pubs on a single Sunday (Manchester, 1854), more than one-fifth were calls by children (as young as four and five), and Joseph Livesey felt the call to arms for each and every one of those squalid souls. Infuriated by the vagaries of alcohol, he knew that a pledge of total abstinence would be not only innovative but England's last chance. Livesey gathered believers—in 1834, one John King was the first to sign his pledge. About eight years later in Leeds, seventy-two-year-old temperance motivator Mrs. Carlisle addressed a gathering of hundreds of unscathed youths with the immortal words, "I think we ought to call the present meeting a Band of Hope," and thus the organization was born and the transfers, under its banner, still carry the message of abstinence as good today as it was then (Tayler, 1946). "Raise your right hand and repeat after me . . . . We solemnly pledge ourselves to abstain from the use of all spirituous and malt liquors, wine and cider, as a beverage; from the use of tobacco in every form, and from all profanity. We also promise to honor our parents, to obey the laws, and to be loyal to the government and constitution of our country" **(Figures R15 and R16)**.

It was a big promise, inclusive of every opportunity for wrongdoing, and it turned the tide to the tune of "God Save the Queen" (for the entire text of the "Ode of Welcome," see Appendix AR8).

> Welcome to join our Band,
> Welcome with us to stand,
> In this pure cause . . .

And there were other plates that helped to wage the war. A set that introduced the morality tale of "The Bottle," taken from engravings attributed to George Cruikshank (1792-1878), can be seen in Riley's *Gifts for Good Children* (1991). The end of that series reads, "The bottle has done its work—it has destroyed the infant and the mother, it has brought the son and the daughter to vice and to the streets and has left the father a hopeless maniac." The transfers could be a chapter of their own; "P Is for Polemical" would picture those transfers that pull for abstinence. There are no plates that tug for the tipplers. **Figure R18**, which promises to keep the Band of Hope Pledge, is one of a versed set **(Figures R17 and R18)**, illustrated in a more "cartoon-like" style. The message, however, is the same. And the Drunkard's Progress is most probably one of another set; this time the final message tells of "The Ruin'd Family" out in the cold, their faces frozen in sadness **(Figure R19)**.

With some compassion, Father Theobald Mathew of Cork understood the grim reality **(Figure R20)**. It was warm in the pub, and the house was cold. It was friendly there, and the house rang with the crying of little ones and the leavings of daily living. There were chairs to sit on, and most homes had little, if any, furniture. The pub offered neighborhood friends and quenching drinks to the overworked poor. Water was usually contaminated; the rivers and streams were possessed by "The Great Stink," and teas and coffees were too expensive. Beer, then, was the obvious choice and sought more as addictions dictated. But as the century passed, alternative gathering places became accessible, more recreational drinks were available, and the water supply could be trusted. With the resurgence of religious values it was not only the Band of Hope that clamored for sobriety. Other temperance societies were vocal and joined the Roman Catholic Father Mathew, always pictured with his right arm raised and his left holding his hat. He issued the pledge while the audience, always a group on its knees, was drawn around him **(Figure M56)**.

But not all efforts of the Evangelicals were on home soil. Purchase of handiwork from the baskets passed among the congregants supported the work of Evangelical missionaries abroad, and speeches by those returning from their fieldwork rekindled the generosity. They were brave souls, the missionaries; perhaps they were inspired by the likes of David Livingston, who, in 1856, crossed darkest Africa. His medical reports portrayed the people of Africa as helpless and in need of both religion and remedies. Tireless Evangelicals learned remote languages, translated biblical texts, and trained the converts to nurse and to heal. With the Victorians' sense of superiority, the English, from the 1860s on, spread the kingdom's knowhow with an air of confidence fueled by their certainty that since the Anglo-Saxons had evolved furthest from their animal roots, they had, like a good parent, the responsibility of improving the character and culture of others. Imperial expansion and the consequent deterioration of indigenous societies followed the good Queen's dictate that England's duty was the protection of the poor natives and the advancement of civilization **(Figures R21 and R22)**.

Tales of the Old Testament were taught to the new converts just as they were taught to Victorian youngsters. Pictures on ABC plates made the learning easier for those little ones, especially as the images were tied to the tastes of satisfying dinners by warming fires. Tales of the Old Testament, retold here only to highlight the transferred graphics, were commanding.

Though **Figure R23** illustrates the commandment, "Thou shalt do no murder," the scene is assuredly reminiscent of Chapter IV of Genesis in which the story of two brothers is told, only one of whom was obedient. Abel's sacrifice to God was acceptable, while Cain's was not; in a jealous rage, Cain slew his brother. With the Bible's first mention of sacrifice and first quoted sarcasm as well, "Am I my brother's keeper?" remains the quotable quote from the tale that branded Cain a murderer for the rest of his days. Perhaps Watts's Divine Song "Love Between Brothers and Sisters" might be sung at the end of the meal . . .

And 'tis a shameful sight,
When children of one family
Fall out, and chide, and fight.

Now it came to pass that, as men began to multiply, the wickedness of man was great; outraged, God put an end to everyone but Noah. To be the lone survivors in a world of violence, Noah **(Figure R24)** and his family entered the dark, wooden ark along with pairs of clean and unclean creatures, mates of every kind. For forty days and nights it rained . . . and all but those with Noah perished. As the ark gently rested upon the mountains of Ararat, a raven was released and returned after fourteen days with an olive branch, a sign of dry land and freedom for all. The rainbow promised no further floods, and with the seed of Shem, Ham, and Japheth, the Old Testament promised in Chapter III of Genesis the continuation of humankind.

Two chapters forward we meet Abraham, first patriarch of the Jewish people, whose son was Isaac; Isaac's son Jacob was followed by Joseph, the beloved son of his old age. Each of Joseph's brothers was destined to begin one tribe of Israel— but for now each of them hated Joseph, as they saw him both to be the greatest rival for his father's affection and the son of Jacob's beloved wife. Favoritism, no stranger to the household, soon brought resentment and brutality. To make matters worse, Joseph told his brothers of his dreams, one of which foretold of eleven sheaves of wheat bowing down to Joseph's, which stood straight and tall; it was a sure sign of some yet unknown power to be **(Figure R25)**.

It soon came to pass that the brothers planned to kill Joseph. It was Reuben who changed their minds from worse to bad. To throw him into a pit seemed torment enough, and so it was done **(Figure R26)**. A passing band of Ishmaelites promised a profit. For 20 shekels of silver Joseph was gone; the dreamer was sold into slavery, and his coat of many colors was dipped into the blood of a goat to convince Jacob of his son's demise.

Sold again, this time to the Egyptians, Joseph began life anew as the trusted overseer of the army Captain Potiphar's entire realm. And it was here that Potiphar's beautiful wife tried repeatedly to seduce him; as pictured, it was here too that she accused him of "insult" **(Figure R27)**. Curious, this selection; this is no savory table talk for toddlers!

Joseph entered a new phase of life, as he was now jailed for a crime he did not commit. But with an enduring spirit he again was given the task of looking after the others. When asked to interpret a dream for the head butler (who, as all Egyptians, looked upon the dream as a message from God), he did so **(Figure R28)**. The butler was released from prison in three days, as Joseph's dream foretold. Two years later and still showing no signs of despair from his thirteen years in prison, Joseph interpreted the Pharaoh's dreams and was once again elevated to the role of caretaker—this time as viceroy of the ruler's treasury and all his realm.

The distribution of Egyptian food to all who were hungry **(Figure R29)**, the reestablishment of Joseph's family ties, his marriage and rearing of a son of his own conclude the account. After being the brutalized victim of sibling rivalry, slavery, false accusations, and imprisonment, Joseph became a revered caretaker; the transition taught lasting lessons of patience, courage, and the benefits of a positive attitude, no matter what the odds. It is thought that Joseph was embalmed and buried somewhere in the Valley of the Kings . . . a stranger from a foreign land lifted to prominence. (Two additional plates from this series can be found in the Lindsays' text, 1998, p. 134.)

When the Israelites became too numerous in Egypt, the Pharaoh ordered every newborn son drowned in the Nile, but the boy-child, born to Levites Jochebed and Amram, was hidden **(Figures R30 and R31)**. At three months, the infant was lowered into a basket of papyrus reeds sealed with mortar and pitch. Set among the bulrushes under the watchful eye of his sister, the youngster was rescued by the Pharaoh's daughter and tenderly relinquished to his mother, who posed as a wet-nurse for hire. Adopted by his rescuer, he was named Moses, the one drawn out for, as she said, "I drew him out of the water."

The Brownhills plate pictures the Pharaoh **(Figure R32)**, whom, as the story is told in the book of Leviticus, the Egyptians worshipped as one god of many. He built great temples and added his pyramid to the others; here he could rest, in a universe beyond, surrounded by his earthly treasures. For the hauling of the stones the Hebrews were enslaved until the Lord brought nine plagues to torment the land—blood, frogs, flies, gnats, cattle diseases, sores, hail, locusts, and darkness. But it was the tenth, the destruction of the first-born of the Egyptians, that broke the Pharaoh's resolve. He let those people go but changed his mind and went after them with horses and chariots until his army, mighty as it was, was drowned by the Reed (also known as the Red) Sea. And thus is described The Destruction of the Pharaoh. The tale is retold each year around the Passover table.

Our transfers pick up again past the first Five Books of Moses. In the fourth book of the Prophets, Samuel, we find the tale of the birth of Samuel to Hannah, who sent him to live at the Temple under the guidance of Eli, the priest. The Brownhills print shows Samuel before Eli revealing his first vision; the house of Eli would be brought down because his sons were wicked and he, their father, chose not to influence their character. Thus Eli learned that Samuel would take his place when his house was destroyed **(Figure R33)**—the lesson of parental guidance is directed this time to the teller of the tale. Samuel designated David, the youngest of his family, to be king after Saul, the inheritor, was disobedient. Soon after that David, sent to bring nourishing cheeses to his brothers, encountered a sudden challenge.

He saw them, standing ready for battle—the Philistines and the Israelites on opposite sides of the hill. From the line of Philistines swaggered forth the ten-foot giant, clothed in weighty bronze armor and protected by a "shield runner" not far ahead. For many days Goliath did taunt the men of Israel, plying them to choose one who would go against him. If he won, the Philistines would serve Israel. If the giant lost, all of Israel would be the Philistine's slaves. Having just arrived in his simple garments of the sheepherder and armed only with shepherd's weapons, David stood the challenge. While running toward the onslaught, he took a smooth stone from his bag, fixed it into his sling, and slung it to strike the giant's forehead **(Figure R34)**. Goliath fell forward, and David, brandishing the giant's sword, severed his

opponent's head while the Philistines withdrew, taking their promises with them. The message? Swindall (1997a) points out that with faith in his own power, the young shepherd did not give way to intimidation; it was David, indeed, who could be called the giant.

From tales of David in the book of Samuel, we go forward to the Book of Kings, where, in about the 9th century B.C., we find Elijah, the Tishbite, living in hiding from King Ahab, son of Omri (King of Israel). His Phoenician Queen Jezebel sought to make Baal, with all its cruelties, the religion of the Royal Court. Elijah knew no danger, either from the King or from an ongoing drought and famine. Protected by God, he hid by the brook Kerith (a small tributary east of the Jordan halfway between the Sea of Galilee and the Dead Sea), where twice each day the ravens brought meat and bread **(Figure R35)**. Many years later it was a chariot, bathed in fire, that carried Elijah, in a great and swirling rush of wind, to Heaven. His return is eagerly awaited as a silver cup of wine stands ready for its visitor on every Passover table.

Further in Kings is the epic of Hezekiah, The Good King of Jerusalem, who reigned, it is said, for twenty-nine years. Hezekiah's miraculous recovery, sometime about 700 B.C.E., is the subject of many notable works of art, oratorios, and contatas. The plate, **Figure R36**, also recounts the event of God's extraordinary gift of good health. The sign was seen on the sundial. Miraculously the sun had moved back ten degrees; fifteen years of a goodly life were bestowed upon Hezekiah, who begot Manessah whose kingly role was everything but good.

Near the conclusion of the Old Testament we find the story of Daniel in the lion's den. It began with a law that prevented anyone but King Darius from petitioning any deity for thirty days. Knowing that Daniel would never turn from the Law of his God, the chief officials, jealous of his impending promotion by the King, designed the decree to ensure that Daniel, his faithful servant, would fall into disrepute. As expected, Daniel, discovered faithfully calling upon his Lord, was quickly sealed into a den of hungry lions with a stone laid at the entrance **(Figure R37)**. The scenario ends with the king's gladness that the angels closed the mouths of the golden beasts. He declared that all must have reverence for the God of Daniel and ensured Daniel's protection through the remainder of his reign and the subsequent reign of Cyrus, the Persian.

Following the Book of Daniel came Ezra-Nehemiah, which completes the Old Testament; the New Testament begins with the Gospel of Matthew, which recalls the Nativity, pictured in what may be the first in the series of Incidents In The Life Of Our Blessed Savior in this Nativity scene **(Figure R38)**. Mary, Joseph, and Jesus are accompanied by the shepherds. It is remarkable that no others of this series are offered in other ABC texts. Included in the Gospel of Matthew as well is the "Lord's Prayer," part of the Sermon on the Mount. The lines are simple ones that ask for guidance **(Figures R39 and R40)** and are good reminders of long-learned tales.

Many plates, not biblical, came with spoonfuls of nourishing words that strongly encourage choices that develop moral character.

Let Brotherly Love Continue and Keep Within Compass **(Figures R41 and R42)** are two of a series. The circle of the Moral Compass cautions to keep behavior within the confines of set parameters or within the circle of influence, as is inferred by the inner circle of the Band of Hope signature design that encloses the cross and its anchor, or the compass circle in the insignia of the masons. A quotation found in J. Child's *The Staffordshire Potteries as an Empire Asset and Illustrated Souvenir of the Royal Visit* (1913) mentions "a piece of Aynsley pottery [which] bears the following distich: Keep within compass and you shall be sure to avoid many troubles which others endure." Unfortunately, neither of these two plates is marked.

Larger sets, such as the beautifully designed Flowers That Never Fade, The Importance of Punctuality, and others, reinforced the most virtuous qualities of the 19th-century Victorian **(Figures R43 through R56)**. Together they provide a steady stream of homilies that might reward "good achievement" or "most positive attitude" or "regular attendance" in any school.

Charles Shaw, in his 1903 autobiography, *When I Was A Child,* provides us with a cherished testament to his Methodist Sunday School's Bible class teacher: "His name," he says, "is written in 'The Book of Life,' for the Recording Angel never passes by deeds like his. I cannot tell all this 'saintly' young man was to me. . . . He lent me books. He gave me counsel. He breathed his prayers for me."

Sunday Schools were a practical offering for working-class children like Charles Shaw. It was the one day they didn't have to work; volunteer teachers were available; they were the only educational opportunity for working kids. A summary of statistics reveals that somewhat more than 10% of the working-class children attended Sunday School just after the start of the century. Thirty years later the number had more than tripled, and by the half-century, three-quarters of all working-class children had attended classes sponsored by one church or another. To seat them all, the numbers of Sunday Schools mushroomed; for example, the Primitive Methodists, according to the 1851 Census of Great Britain, had four schools in 1811 and 542 in 1851. The Bible Christians began with one school in 1811 and enrolled 115 by 1851. A phenomenon popularized by the printer-publisher Robert Raikes of Gloucester in 1781, Sunday Schools promoted his organized Sabbath-School instruction augmented by cautionary tales of goodness and punishment: Sarah Trimmer (1741-1810), daughter of landscape artist John Kirby of Ipswich, and Hannah More (1745-1833) of Bristol were determined to realize as much literacy through readable religion as the short hours would allow **(Figure R57)**.

Not everybody bought the "Do unto others" precept. **Figure R58** vividly depicts a justly deserved flogging for torturing a cat, not an uncommon subject in Victorian prints. The case would probably have been dismissed by a long-wigged Magistrate, as it did not fit into a "police class of offenses"—crimes against animals included only cattle, horses, and sheep. But it most certainly did cry out for the well-being of all unfortunate creatures who might suffer from the violent nature of a great number of young criminals we do not usually tie to the "angelic and oh-so-proper" image of the young Victorian. Jordan (1987) recalls Turner's study of 1851, which counted 14,569 male and 2,557 female "angels" under the age of seventeen in prisons, two-fifths of whom were in London jails. **Figure R59** is a lesson in kindness, this time from a peer . . . it is hoped the lesson will be learned before "the striker" becomes a statistic. Animal abuse is a well-documented first step in a lifestyle of violent pathology. The FBI lists cruelty to and mutilation of powerless animals as a trait that consistently appears in its personal histories

of those who commit abusive, violent, and murderous acts against others. **Figure R60** pictures an even younger abuser of property . . . again it is hoped stealing apples will not be the start of a long and not very illustrious career.

Combined with the lessons of virtue are those many alphabet plates that clearly reflect the self-help movement. Victorians believed in progress, trusting that people could change their lives and rise in the world through self-help (Mitchell, 1996). Samuel Smiles was the best-selling 19th-century author of self-help books; he believed that success was recognized through hard work and perseverance while demanding both discipline and impeccable ethics. Work was the moral good and financial gain only a reward. Smiles's writings broke through the confines of social class (1859 through 1887) with proverbial truths much like those of our Son of Liberty, whose words became immortal on both sides of the "Pond."

Published first in *Poor Richard's Almanack* (1732-1758), written under the pseudonym of Richard Saunders, the ceramic quotable quotes titled "Dr. FRANKLIN'S MAXIMS," "FRANKLIN'S MAXIMS," "POOR RICHARD'S MAXIMS," or "FRANKLIN'S PROVERBS," were not all Franklin's creations. His inspirations were the hallowed words of Rabelais, Bacon, and others. Essentially self-taught, he catalogued the moral virtues he had "met" while reading. Each of the thirteen—Temperance, Silence, Order, Resolution, Frugality, Industry, Sincerity, Justice, Moderation, Cleanliness, Tranquility, Chastity, and Humility—stood in the order of "acquisition," as accomplishing one would contribute to the acquiring of the next. The maxims facilitated the virtues . . . they were the rules by which the virtues were achieved. Franklin kept a chart to guide his actions with a week given to his performance of each; only history can judge his success. But his message was loud and clear—in order to get ahead in this world, one had to keep one's nose to the grindstone. His autobiography tells us he did just that.

A memorial 19-6/16 (H) x 24-1/4 (W) printing of Franklin's maxims **(Figure R61)**, published by T.O.H.P. Burnham of Boston (1859), and registered at the District Court of Massachusetts in 1859, was the template for many plate transfers. The source of that work was Robert Dighton's engraving of *Bowles Moral Pictures: or Poor Richard Illustrated. Being LESSONS for the YOUNG and the OLD, on INDUSTRY, TEMPERANCE, FRUGALITY & c. By the late Dr. BENJ. FRANKLIN.* which, published by Bowles and Carver of London, 1795, is pictured on page 309 of Noël Riley's *Gifts for Good Children*. There are major differences between the two engravings; the portraits, the typesetting style, and the backgrounds that surround the oval frames are the most prominent.

Obvious differences are found in the placement and style of the portraits of Mr. Franklin. An aged profile graces the top center of the London edition, while a more viewer-friendly portrait is found in the center of the Boston printing, engraved by O. Pelton. There are twenty-four illustrations in oval shapes on both, but the print styles of the maxims vary; upper- and lower-case is used in the older print, while all caps send the messages on the other. The backgrounds are incongruous as well. Less involved, the older is a puzzle sheet, whereas the newer is intended to be only a print in which the oval frames are separated by graceful sprigs of oak leaves and acorns. The engravings are almost identical . . . often it is only the most subtle of differences that challenges the reviewer.

Sources of prints are listed, as are placements of towns on the grid of a map. From left to right, columns are sequenced in alphabetical order from A through E. Rows are numbered 1 through 5 from the top down. A comparison of plates **(Figures R62, R64, R65, R67, and R68)** with the enlargements of segment A1 **(Figure R63)**, segment A2 **(Figure R66)**, and segment A3 **(Figure R69)** reveals some recreations to have been more faithful than others.

Teaching young Victorians the ethos of loving their labors as they licked their spoons utilized those precious hours of youthful energy, with diligence. The prolific number of plates that typify the self-help movement **(Figures R62 through R98)** needed also to include Charity **(Figure R99)**; not everyone could help themselves. (**Figure R99** is further discussed at the conclusion of "T Is for Transfers and Toybooks.")

Many other examples of children's tableware that feature messages of God, godliness, and dedicated energies may be found without alphabet borders. Their abundance is evidence of the importance of religion to the Victorians and the need for nourishment that fostered spiritual strengthening, lessons in ethics, and the motivation to join the reform rush toward self-help. Perhaps it was the influence of the new movement by the Church to educate for morality's sake, as the thrust of the Industrial Revolution forced the working class to move in crowded urban areas closer in proximity to the more fortunate; their "hardly gentrified" behavior lacked values. Perhaps, too, it was an effort to raise the level of competence of the workers as they faced industry's fast-appearing new technologies. Sunday Schools did what they could, though righteousness was better instilled than reading comprehension. From 1830 to 1870, reforms gradually championed the rights of every child to a guaranteed free and compulsory education. Isaac Watts would have burst forth with his immortal words of "The Sluggard," a hymn that rolled religion, reform, and reason into a rhyming homily that chastised the sleeper's scarce reading of his Bible, lost love of thinking, squander of time, waste of money, and, with no incentive to help himself, his sitting, aimlessly, with folded hands (see Appendix AR9). Work and worship were tied in these three R's that saved everyone's souls **(Figure R100)**.

"Poor Richard Illustrated. Lessons for the Young and Old on Industry, Temperance, Frugality, &c." by the artist, Robert Dighton. 17.37 x 24.25 in. Printed by T. O. H. P. Burnham of Boston, 1859. *Courtesy of the Library of Congress Print Collection.* Also shown as Figure R61 on page 277.

S Is for Sets

The search for printings that match ceramic designs (see "H Is for Hollowware" and "T Is for Transfers and Toybooks") is difficult, but even more so is the search for ceramic plates and drinking vessels that match one another in content and basic design. More than a dozen "settings" have emerged from this collection, though some do not match in transfer color and one of a "set" may not be overpainted. Only the estimated values of gathered items that completely match are given.

In large collections, sets will surface when plates and mugs are carefully itemized. Collectors are urged to keep thorough records to encourage the hunt for long-hidden plates that match mugs, mugs that match dishes, cups that match saucers, and even tall or rotund pitchers that match deep, decaled bowls. And it's the never-nding search for items that may never have been produced at all that both fascinates and frustrates the collector.

A quotation from *The Old China Book* "feels" it well. Moore remembers "a collector (who) was heard to remark that a ragged newspaper bundle made his heart beat and his wallet throb in his pocket" (Moore, 1903). Pray that what was wrapped was a match made in Heaven.

T Is for Transfers and Toybooks

Part I

It was the funniest of times, too. Charles Dickens, after a visit to the Copeland manufactory in Stoke in 1852, "penned an amusing sketch of what he was shown on the occasion of that visit." *Cox's Potteries Annual and Year Book of 1925* reprinted the humorous conversation between the writer and the plate . . . surely Dickens was impressed not only by the process of transferring a design upon a ceramic surface but by the "light-fingered damsel" who rubbed the back of the paper "prodigiously hard—with a long tight roll of flannel, tied up like a round of hung beef."

He called that transfer a paper impression. And it is that impression on an ABC plate that transports its admirer back to an earlier time to tell its tale . It's that transfer which is remembered as the phenomenon that reduced the huge costs of hand-decorated 18th- and 19th-century English ceramics. It was that flimsy piece of inked tissue that answered the call for mass-produced china services as tea was replacing beer and milk as the preferred beverage throughout the classes. And it was that impression that called the hand-painters to strike while it inched Staffordshire ever closer to the Industrial Revolution.

Before single-color transfers and their evolution into the art of photolithography in the 1940s came the making of the copper plates from which the transfers were taken. Though the true origin of printing from engraved metal is forever lost, 15th-century goldsmiths in Florence did cut designs into metal with gravers, small chisels with diamond-shaped cutting edges. Difficult and exacting, the process gave way to Jacques Callot's (1592-1635) ingenious method of digging into the metal with acid, though the process was not used for transfer-printing. Prints on paper were easily made from inked cut or etched plates, but the technology of transferring images from flat surfaces to the rounded surfaces of holloware had not yet come to be.

Transfer printings on enamels had been successful at the Battersea Enamel Factory (1753-1756) on snuffboxes and shoe buckles. But changes of fashion toward the end of the 18th century led to the decline in the enamel industry with the introduction of shoelaces. Battersea "stock and equipment were sold up by auction in June of 1756" (Little, 1969). The partners of the now defunct firm, Stephen Theodore Janssen, Henry Delamain, and John Brooks, teamed their expertise, says G. Bernard Hughes (1961), to accomplish the first practical application of the transfer process.

The first-named partner, Janssen, had been a London sta-

tioner whose knowledge of papers permitted him to begin work on a material that could be used to carry an image lifted from a copper plate and applied to a glazed ceramic surface. For this he made a substance from white linen cloth, straining the pulp repeatedly to make certain it would have no lint or holes; being totally nonabsorbent, the paper could then carry all of the enamel-oil ink from a copper engraving safely to an already glazed surface.

The second partner, Delamain, who had been a potter in Dublin and a manufacturer of Delft tiles, mixed finely ground enamels into a stiff paste in oil. These colors, after being lifted onto paper from the copper plate and set onto a glazed surface, would be fired at about 550° C. The oil would be burned away while the enameled lines of the design fused to the glaze. There is evidence that one Henry Delamain had presented a petition for a patent at the Irish House of Commons for this process of printing of earthenware in 1753.

The third partner, John Brooks, was an Irish mezzotint engraver. His contribution to the process was the engraving of copper plates in such a way that the ink, when worked into channels, held firmly until released onto transfer-paper when the copper plate and ink were warmed to the same temperature. Copper plates used for transfer printing had to be more thickly cut than those used for printing on paper. The depth of lines and dots was determined by trial and error; the deeper the engraving, the more the color and the darker the pattern. Of Brooks' three applications for patents, his first was at Birmingham in September of 1751, two years before his registration as a partner with Janssen and Delamain. It is to Brooks that, according to W. L. Little (1969), "credit for the first successful use of the (transfer printing) process must be awarded."

The three essentials of the transfer process—the tissue, the ink and the engravings—were then available. The techniques of overglaze printing from the enamel industry had been adapted to pottery. From Hughes (1961) comes a description of the early overglaze transfer-printing process:

> The process of transfer-printing began with engraving the design in such a way as to produce sharp clear lines or stipples on a thin copper plate. The engraved plate was warmed on a stove above a brisk fire and coated with colour mixed with thick boiled oil. Pigment was rubbed into the incised lines with a wooden tool and any excess was removed with a flexible steel knife and more completely with a beaver cushion (or "boss"). (Corduroy has been substituted for beaver skin since 1850.) A sheet of thin, strong "pottery tissue"

paper was made nonabsorbent by brush-coating with printer's size or soap and water. When dry, this paper was laid upon the prepared copper plate and subjected to the pressure of a printing press. Layers of flannel absorbed its moisture and helped to draw the color from the engravings. The paper, with its perfect impression of the plate, was then carefully drawn off and handed to the cutter, who removed the superfluous paper. The transfer, then set onto a glazed surface of soft-paste porcelain and rubbed gently with a flannel, was fired in a hardening-on kiln at a low temperature (Hughes 1956, 1961, 1968).

G. Bernard and Therle Hughes (*English Porcelain and Bone China*, 1968) suggest that it was the financial downfall of Janssen, Delamain, and Brooks that enabled engraver/printer John Sadler and his partner, Guy Green, both of Liverpool, to accomplish an unimaginable feat of transfer-printing. As stated in their famous affidavit dated 2nd August 1756, they did, in fact, accomplish the printing of more than twelve hundred earthenware tiles in only six hours on the 27th of July 1756. Perhaps, say the authors, Sadler had been interested in transfer making since he had seen children sticking waste prints onto broken earthenware. He and Green had attended the auction that finalized the end of the firm at Battersea only seven weeks before and had acquired Janssen's supply of transfer paper, prepared enamels, and engraved plates. The two may also have acquired a sudden urge to patent the process; the request was rejected as it obviously had repeated Janssen's work. In spite of the blotches and uneven lines typical of the early facsimiles, products from Longton Hall and Wedgwood's firm (W. L. Little, 1969) were sent to Messrs. Sadler and Green of Liverpool for decoration. (Sadler retired about 1770; Green continued printing until 1799.)

While overglaze transfer-printing was gathering interest, a second overglaze process, called *bat printing*, was originated by William Wynn Ryland in 1761, though it was seldom used after 1823. One Harry Baker, with the help of Liverpool engraver William Smith and Worcester printer Thomas Davis, perfected the technique about 1766.

Used in the earliest days mainly for adding small crests to earthenware dinner ware, bat printing was not used for larger-scale decoration until about 1803, when bone china tea wares were being made successfully in larger and larger quantities. The prints were generally about 4 inches square since the process involved the use of the operative's hand; the copper plate and the gelatin bat needed to be easily managed in the artist's palm. Delicate designs of dots, known as *stipple engraving*, were engraved into the copper and transferred onto a "bat," a 3-millimeter-thick flexible mat made of gelatin or of glue, treacle (a compound of molasses), and whiting (calcium carbonate, or chalk).

The fine design, transferred to the bat in oil, was dusted, using soft brushes, with a pulverized enamel mixed with Barbados tar. After the removal of excess color with cotton wool, the bat was pressed against the ware, and the design was set for its second firing.

There were strides in the art of transfer-printing with the efforts of Robert Hancock (1729-1816), whose whereabouts and possible credits remain somewhat hazy. Hancock, according to G. Bernard Hughes (1961), served as Janssen's engraver after an apprenticeship with engraver George Anderton at Birmingham in 1746. At Battersea, London, in 1753, he served as an engraver; after the closing of the firm he situated at Bow, east London. It is here, says Hughes (1961), that, "to the good fortune of English ceramic manufacturers, (Hancock) met the situation by introducing the (overglaze) transfer-printing process to Bow, then under the management of Thomas Frye. . . Bow porcelain is known to have been printed in four colours: brick red, black, a dull dark purple, and brown."

Hancock then moved to the Worcester Tonquin Manufactory in 1756 (7?), where he became director. Hughes (1961) says it "appears that" Hancock originated underglaze blue transfer-printing at the Worcester plant. Hancock's assistant at Worcester was Thomas Turner; after both resigned from Worcester, they eventually reunited at Turner's Caughley pottery (1775) in Stropshire. Here, at the Salopian Works, Turner was determined to develop blue underglaze transfer printing on porcelain; cobalt blue was used originally because only that color could withstand the high temperature of the glaze and not burn away. Though first attempts at underglaze were "blotchy and coarse," Turner further developed colors and glazes while Hancock worked at perfecting the techniques of engraving. The factory's engravers and printers were locked in for quiet and his colors were secretly prepared in a closed laboratory; four printing presses spelled success.

Hughes (1961) recounts the differences between the overglaze and underglaze processes; referring back to the description of the steps in making overglaze transfers, the process is the same until after the removal of the superfluous paper. The transferor then laid it upon the biscuit ware, rubbing first with a small piece of soaped flannel to fix it and afterwards furiously with a rubber formed of rolled flannel. The friction caused the color to adhere (evenly) to the biscuit. The piece was, after a few hours, immersed in cold water and the paper washed away; the color, full of oil, was unaffected. By placing the ware in a hardening-on-kiln heated only to 680 to 700° C (1250-1290° F), the oil was drawn off and the transfer affixed. As small a portion as possible was held by the dipper, who plunged the cooled piece into the cream-like glaze. By a dexterous jerk this "plunge" covered the entire surface with an opaque coat. Firing followed, once more revealing the transfer pattern. Certainly this style of printing, soon to be the product of so many Staffordshire manufactories, was more economical; it required one less firing.

The key potter for underglaze printing on earthenware, says Kathy Niblett (2001), was Stoke-upon-Trent's Josiah Spode, who, about 1784, saw great possibilities in the process of transferring designs in cobalt blue to his Pearlware biscuit. He spirited engraver Thomas Lucas and printer James Richards away from Caughly to further develop the printing process, and the master potter himself improved his own Pearlware and perfected a transparent glaze impervious to the assault of foods and forks (Hughes, 1961). But Spode's application of transfer-printing to bone china threatened his painters. He soothed their concerns by using underglaze outline transfers to guide their overglaze renderings. And from about 1820, parts of the designs were left entirely to the talented decorators for a more authentic "hand-painted" appearance; requiring one more firing at low temperatures, this early "print and tint" process allowed both the colors and their painters to retain their value.

Others also experimented with underglaze blue. One such was John Baddeley of Shelton, who was involved with the craft from about 1777. Assisted by Liverpool engraver William Smith and Worcester printer Thomas Davis, he became successful about 1782. It is possible that, according to Haggar, Mountford, and Thomas (1981), Spode may have used Baddeley's improvements in his own operations.

Talented individuals, other than potters, contributed to the new process as well. Because cobalt, which afforded many tints of the color, was in short supply, the French chemist Louis Jacques Thenard (1777-1857) invented an artificial ultramarine called Canton blue, Broseley blue, bamboo blue, or willow blue. Some say it was used in most of Staffordshire's underglaze transfer printing. The popularity of the blue prints began to wane after about thirty years, and soon other colors appeared. In 1828, it was found that when Barbados tar was combined with pulverized black, red, green, and yellow, the colors could be successfully used in underglaze printing. Combining transfers of varied colors was logically the next step toward the ultimate development of full-color images, but the firing of each separate color on a single item could not become a commercial reality (Hughes, 1961). In 1848, F. W. Collins and A. Reynolds, working in Hanley, solved the problem. They patented a process by which colored transfers were printed in register from two to three zinc plates onto sheets of tissue before their application to the surface of the ware in the traditional manner; the process was called *block printing*. This multicolored design was accomplished with a single firing, as the colored inks were prepared to "fix" at the same firing temperature. Brown and green were included from 1852. The process was used for decorating ornamental pottery and tiles from 1849 until the turn of the century (Haggar, Mountford, and Thomas, 1981).

Over time, new technologies emerged. About mid-century an application for a patent had been recorded in the *Pottery Gazette* announcing the discovery of a "dissolving" tissue, and an article from the same source dated September 1, 1896, advised the reader of a recent German patent dealing with an improved method of removing the transfer tissue. It read, mix "one part of clove oil . . . with 40 parts of 5 per cent carbolic acid solution—this being found the most satisfactory dilutent obtainable—at a fairly high temperature. The picture being applied to the ware, the surface of which is preferably covered with some adhesive lac, the back is brushed over with the diluted oil; in a short time the paper cover can be drawn off, and the piece is ready for immediate firing."

And there were developments in copper plate cutting techniques. The smudges resulting from cross-hatching were eliminated about 1800. The art of concealing surface imperfections in the ceramics resulted in bilious clouds above and watery pools at the foreground. As time passed and the quality of the transfer paper improved, engraved lines could be thinner and cutting lines, to different depths, yielded varieties of effects. Smoother gradations were the result of using both lines and stipples. "By adding the use of the burr to that of the graver, not only were fine-tone gradations in colour obtained, but completely new effects with shading covering nearly all the surface

of the design . . . (gave) the rich, soft effect of a water colour" (Little, 1969).

Talented engravers were employed by many companies . . . transfers tagged along with the artists when manufactories closed or were sold, or when their creators were spirited away to a competitor's firm. Potteries would sometimes purchase or trade copper plates among one another, and from the start of the 19th century on, the number of firms devoted to the production of transfers swelled. Similar transfers, with differing treatments, appeared on plates from the same companies and from different companies at the same time; often they were purposely changed to avoid copyright infringement (see **Figures V42 and V43** in "V Is for Variations on a Theme"). Spectacular examples of copied and somewhat changed transfers are **Figures N41 and N42**. The caption on the transfer, found in the Prints, Drawings and Paintings Department of The Victoria and Albert Museum in London, reads: "Ceramic transfer showing hunting scene(s), with lettering in reverse of Burmah hand; C. mid 19th-century (shelf number 8223:25, GJ1656)." The transfer was one of a handful left from the 19th-century potteries that were originally meant for a dinner service (the pattern name was Burmah). The pattern had been produced by Hope and Carter (1862-1880) at the Fountain Place Pottery, Burslem. Changes can be seen that avoided copyright infringement. Chapter "V Is for Variations on a Theme" describes other minimal differences in similar transfer designs, as well.

A new machine for making tissue paper made great advancements in the print quality. Fourdrinier produced a thin, strong tissue to replace the then used coarser papers. The Fourdriniers established the Ivy House Paper Mill in Hanley in 1827. Potters knew that if this improvement had not occurred, the clarity of impressions from the more detailed techniques of engraving would not have been possible.

And there was the mechanization of transfer production. Some of the history of the early printing machines comes from Gladstone's printing, *The Development of Ceramic Colours and Decorating Techniques in the Staffordshire Potteries* by Peter Freeman, 1977. Before the refining of the tissue-making process, there were two hollow cylinders between which a metal plate, which carried the engraving on copper, was moved. The plate had been heated on a stove to ensure that the color, which was mixed with thick oil, could penetrate into the smallest crevice of the engraved pattern. After tissue on reels became available, a patent was granted in 1831 to John Potts, Richard Oliver, and William Wainwright Potts, calico printers of New Mills Works near Derby, for a rotary press for printing transfer papers from revolving steel cylinders (Little, 1969). "These new machines were very much like mangles, the continuous reels of paper being passed between the two cylinders; the upper having the design engraved upon it" (Freeman, 1977). W. W. Potts was granted a second patent for multicolored printing, which, like the single-colored press, produced impressions in endless succession. In 1841, the process was enhanced with the use of John Lamb's (of Newcastle-under-Lyme) engraved copper rollers, which printed reels of transfers. Though they were not of the best quality, they did help to meet increased demands for products from North America. On newer presses, after the turn of the century, a side-lever was pulled down, sending an engraved copper plate under and out from a large, single cylinder. By the end of the century, steam-driven machines were employed in the printing process.

Whenever and however the design was applied onto the tissue, a cutter had to remove it. **Figure T1b** is an excellent illustration of how the cutter could, perhaps, save damaged designs. The lines of separation show tearing and skillful repair of the black transfer titled "The Flight into Egypt."

Traditionally, English ABC plates, which date through the 18th century, were produced with underglazed transfers applied to the once-fired biscuit ware and, if overpainted, were fired once more at low heat. It is that overpainting which gives the plate its character; actually painted or "splashed upon" by immature hands, decorated areas show brush marks and irregular edges that clearly distinguish them from the work of talented painters or the technologically advanced lithography. Though the cast alphabet was not usually overpainted, plates that featured single-letter transfers with non-ABC rims often sported edges of overpainted florals or dancing dots. And, though some blue transfers do appear to have "fuzzy" edges due both to the absorption of the blue color into the biscuit body and to the softening of the enamel by the glaze melting over it (Little, 1969), they are not to be confused with "flow-blue" (or "flown blue" or "flowing blue") designs, which display a slight flowing of the ink due to the presence of volatilizing agents such as lime of chloride or ammonia during the glost firing stags. To date, no flow-blue ABC plate has surfaced in texts, and leading flow-blue dealers have no knowledge of an item such as this. Other smudgy effects, brought about by the cross-hatching or closely cut horizontal lines on the copper plate, were effectively resolved by 1810.

Brightly colored decals were used on German hard-paste ware. According to Lindsay and Lindsay (1998), "since the decals were mechanically reproduced, the German china of a specific pattern has a cookie-cutter sameness, unlike the handmade English product." Called "decalomania," the lithographic process that produced decals (*Encyclopedia Britannica*, 1958) got its name from Greek roots; decal meant "off the paper" and mania, of course, translates to "craze." The process differed somewhat from ordinary lithography, which originated in France about 1860 and was quickly developed in Germany. Decals were, according to the encyclopedia (Volume 14), "printed on a very absorbent starch- or dextrine-coated paper. This coating material must afford both a smooth printing surface and one that will prevent the inks, lacquers, or varnishes from penetrating into the paper stock. It must also act as an adhesive." For application to ceramic surfaces, the decals were printed first with layers of white until enough ink had been laid to become a solid support for the actual design. After these basecoats had each been applied and dried, the colors followed, one by one, in a printing room where both temperature and humidity were controlled.

The wear patterns and scratches on many of the deep dishes shown in "D Is for Deep Dishes" indicate that the decals were applied on-glaze. Barbara Conroy (*Restaurant China, Volume 1,* Collector Books, 1998) explains that currently, decals can be applied directly onto the bisque, onto glaze-fired ware followed by a decoration firing of at least $2000+°$ F, which allows the decal to sink below the melted glaze surface. Or decals can be applied on-glaze and subjected to a decoration firing at a maximum of $1620°$ F. With that lower temperature,

the decal remains at the surface of the glaze; decals are somewhat rough to the touch and vulnerable to the wear and tear of acidic foods and spoon scrapes.

Not a transfer technique but a decorative treatment found on at least one ABC deep dish is the use of airbrushing; only one example is found in the collection. Though badly damaged, **Figure D85** represents a style of underglaze decoration that was known, at its start, as aerography. Invented by C. L. Burdick and patented in 1892, the aerograph worked as an atomizer with a valve system that enabled control over the shape and size of the ink-jet. Freeman (1977), for Gladstone, writes, "The main impact of a refined mechanical means of spraying (color) was on the glazing of pots but it also helped enormously two aspects of decorating: ground laying—the application of solid areas of flat colour which was a skilled and time consuming art, and shaded effects previously either brushed or blown onto the ware with a mouth blown diffuser." Conroy (1998) described a more modern process: "As a compressor supplies air pressure to the spray gun, a fine spray of color is applied to greenware, bisque and occasionally glaze fired ware. Always a smooth application, ware is sprayed lightly with fine color graduations for a soft effect or heavily for solid coverage." In the deep dish pictured, a shape was used as a stencil, likely overglaze.

Of course, the process that so brightly colored products of the Ohio Art Company was a lithographic process as well, one which is discussed in relation to **Figures M72 through M75** in "M Is for Metals."

Part II

Developments in the ceramic industry and the 19th-century surge of interest in children's literature flourished together; the growth of an industry devoted to the publication of works specifically designed to meet the developmental needs of children supplied the graphics that were copied for use on plates targeted to children's interests. A small percentage of these plates were rimmed with the letters of the alphabet. It is the collection of these plates and their original published transfer sources that highlight the history of children's literature.

Perhaps it was a tiny "thumb" Bible that sparked the phenomenon of writing strictly for youngsters, carried easily by peddlers, easily held by small hands, and captivating with engraved scenes of the saintly. It was righteous reading. Pious and pure, texts as far back as the 14th-century "personal devotional" primers were designed to save innocent souls from the poisonous world of sin should they suddenly be taken from their earthly sphere (see "R Is for Religion, Reform, and Reason"). Fear furthered education; children preparing for hovering catastrophes needed to be small adults "reading" centuries-old tales of martyrs who died with patience and courage. To help with reading, vowels and consonants were added in the 1700s. Books specifically designed for the learning of reading waited for the immortal Richard Harris (1686) to cross the Atlantic. In Boston he published his collections of religious and political verse as the *New England Primer*, which was revised yearly as theology and social sentiments evolved. It too carried riveting woodcuts of the righteous that "riveted" the attention of the children.

And tiny, illustrated, pocket-sized "tracts," published soon after the *New England Primer*, were printed on both sides of the Atlantic by the Religious Tract Society (1799) of London and the American Tract Society (1825). These editions were distributed door to door, conveniently available in whatever language was spoken there. Messages, through their overly dramatic texts, were clear: be the perfect, never sloppy or thoughtless or vain or drunk or . . . Be only the perfectly pious "goody-goody."

It was John Newbery (1713-1767), a man whose futuristic visions gave immortality to *Goody Two Shoes*, who produced twenty titles targeted to children. Newbery produced the first book to honestly meet the needs of young readers; other chap or toybooks may have frightened children into proper behavioral submission, as the vast majority of 18th-century literature was written for adults.

In varying sizes, pamphlet-like chapbooks were peddled by chapmen. Marketed for adults, they were appealing to youngsters as these books were a great relief from the thick, verbose classics crowded with tiny type. Like the messages on so many plates, the message of the early English printings was the "Godliness" of good habits soon after taught by the fables whose animated animals preached the moral lessons. Tales of travel were eagerly sought by those who had no chance of personally enjoying the world of the rich; travel diaries fed the need for adventure and allowed readers to share the rewards of new and exciting exploration. Chapbooks, printed in large 24-page sheets, were purchased from the printers. Readers might select the "penny" tales they wished to read; the pages were cut and the binding stitched by hand or cut from fabric and glued to strengthen the fold. First printed in France and England in the 16th and 17th centuries, the paper books were the primary texts for many just learning to read; their unsophisticated reading levels allowed them prolific distribution. A print from a chapbook that precedes a plate transfer is found as **Figure K11** in "K Is for Kitsch."

The transition from religious printings (see "R Is for Religion, Reform, and Reason") to instructive reading began slowly, starting with hornbooks and battledores, two- or three-leaved cards folded into a pocketbook shape. Religious tracts were sometimes replaced by the alphabet, numerals, and small illustrations and verse. Instruction on battledores was followed by an avalanche of ABC books that began mid-16th century, many with lovely hand-colored woodcuts or engravings.

ABC books were the stepping stones to reading; the first was printed in London in 1538 with religious instruction. "From 1538 to 1640, eight editions of ABC books were 'licensed' to be printed in England" (McCulloch, 1979). The influence of the church continued, though it waned as years went on; ABCs were focused not only on moralities but on historical events, animals, plants, occupations, names, traits, and random word choices that were combined into verses and nonsense rhymes. If letter sounds were to be tied to the first sound of a key word, the poetry was far beyond the comprehension of the little one who depended upon the adult, for it was the mother's responsibility to prepare her offspring for school. And preparation was often synonymous with memorization . . . lines recited and most often not understood.

It was in 1830, earlier in the century, that puzzle books, with formats designed to motivate question-and-answer parlor games, became popular (see "Q Is for Queries"). Puzzles were

instructive . . . and it was that yearning for instruction that pushed the presses. About 1837, a mother-daughter "dialogue-style" paper board book discussed hundreds of little-known topics of the day that its anonymous author thought would be useful throughout life. And McCulloch (1979) also writes about a chapbook, a *Museum of Foreign Animals*, published in New Haven (Connecticut), which introduces an engraving of a giraffe then called the "Cameleopard," a beast that looks like a leopard-spotted camel; see **Figure E120** for a transfer that just might have been taken from that source! Another exploration of the flora and fauna, this time related to biblical text, was published in 1852. That work was followed by a flood of toybooks which presented woodcut museums of animals, such as one by the famed woodcut artist Thomas Bewick, along with his series based on mathematics published a few years before. History and geography texts were issued and spellers were reprinted, and "improved editions" competed for selection, much as do our curriculum presses today.

Another aspect of instructive printing was information published for "young women going into service." The two transfers of Widow Green's good advice **(Figures T2, T3, and T4)**, from 1859 and 1862, were found as advertisements on the back of a Partridge Shilling Book. Noël Riley, in her *Gifts for Good Children* (1991), says, "The fact that this image was translated onto a child's plate is an interesting indication of the social groups towards which such china wares were being directed by the 1860s."

But it was a few years back, with Edward Lear's 1846 *Book of Nonsense*, that the idea of publishing a book solely for the purpose of enjoyment became a reality. The book was a no-nonsense landmark publication; it changed the attitudes of authors and publishers; it was now possible to publish a book with no hidden messages, moral overtones, or facts to memorize. Reading could be fun!

For enjoyment and enlightenment, short pieces written at gradually increasing reading levels and slowly reduced type sizes were published in wonderfully illustrated books. And hundreds of children's stories, some with religious overtones, taught life lessons of family unity, kindness, and hard work in beautifully illustrated magazines on both continents. They displayed the extraordinary engravings of George Cruikshank (see **Figure N88** in "N Is for 19th Century"), Thomas Bewick (see **Figure K11** in "K Is for Kitsch"), Louis Wain (see **Figure E157** in "E Is for Education"), Palmer Cox (see **Figure M45** in "M Is for Metals"), and others.

Not only were they beautifully illustrated, their covers were exquisite as well. An extraordinary history, titled *Victorian Illustrated Books, 1850-1870, The Heyday of Wood-Engraving* by Paul Goldman (1994), includes beautifully photographed designs of book exteriors that, he says, help readers to comprehend the text. **Figure T5** proves him correct. The exquisite binding is a fine example of the designs of the period . . . its brilliant colors invite readers to search its pages **(Figure T6)** and, perhaps, to dine from its dish **(Figure T7)**. Sadly, delicately tooled book covers, becoming too costly, gave way to cloth-covered spines and vulnerable paper-covered boards **(Figures T48, T54, and T57)**.

The designs the printer used as illustrations may well have been from other original and revised printings, stacks of transfers collected by engravers or printers, or purchased from shops that specialized in both original and pooled sources. It is the matching of transfers within books to those on plates with alphabet rims that makes the collection of ABC ware so enticing. The search for "transfer trails," the appearance of the identical graphics in varied sources, is the ABC plate collector's ultimate thrill.

From ABC books are whole alphabets applied to sets of mugs and plates, or single images that had been selected for publication in any one of the multitude of children's fiction, primers, or magazines, with or without modified text. Other prints were found matching those from books of rhymes and reason that postdated the production of the ceramics.

One alphabet book edition, whose religious engravings are found on the sides of drinking vessels, is the 1856 Darton publication called the *Alphabet of Virtues,* seen in **Figures H49 through H79** of "H Is for Hollowware." The transfers are sometimes accompanied by their poetry; several transfers carry an inappropriate letter, and some letter pairs are out of sequence.

Another illustrated alphabet featured in "H Is for Hollowware" is an early and undated set of illustrations, each designed around one alphabet letter. At least two of the graphics were turned into plate transfers, one with its original verbiage (**Figures T8 through T12**); in the hollowware chapter, some transfers (**Figures H24 through H42**) do not include their rhymes. Several of the transfers can also be seen in **Figures E8 through E13,** surrounded by nonalphabet dotted rims. The transfer series undoubtedly began its history in England. It was then published in *The Child's Treasure of Knowledge* by Wier and White of Boston. In the United States, it was published as *The Object Lesson ABC* by M. A. Donohue & Company, Chicago, Illinois (1931); see **Figure T8.** The transfer alphabet, with different accompanying poetry, was then replicated in Ruth Baldwin's book, *100 Rhyming Nineteenth Century Alphabets in English* published by the Southern Illinois University Press (Carbondale, Illinois, 1972).

A third ABC is the beautiful *Alphabet of Flowers* (**Figure T13**), included in *The Boys' and Girls' Illustrated Gift Book* published by George Routledge and Sons in London, 1864. Three of that series (**Figures T14, T16, and T18**) are pictured along with their plates (**Figures T15, T17 and T19**). The hand-colored book of floral poetry was also issued in Boston by Degen, Estes & Co. (n.d.). Aside from becoming transfers on ABC plates, at least one of the three ("L is the LILY, with leaves of bright green, / Which we'll wreathe round the head of our sweet Birthday Queen") was featured as a selected single letter in *Baby's Rhyme Book* (Richards, 1879). The rhyme there, however, read, "PRET-TY lit-tle Lil-y Bell, / Fresh, and sweet, and fair; / Lil-ies round her pret-ty feet, / Lil-ies in her hair. / Silver bells a ring-ing / In her sil-ver voice. / Of all the girls be-neath the sun, Lil-y Bell's my choice!" Similar histories follow other transfers, as "H is the HEATHER, red purple, and grey . . . ." can be seen in **Figure E27** of "E Is for Education."

Also published in 1862 was *The Mother's Picture Alphabet.* Magnificently illustrated by Henry Anelay and engraved by Ames Johnson, the work was published by S. W. Partridge, London. The book is the source of the transfer "K begins Kite / that we saw in the sky: / It vanished almost, / it was soaring so high." The illustration (**Figure T20**) is found on an overpainted plate manufactured by Edge Malkin (**Figure T21**).

In alphabetical order, the next print (**Figure T22**) and its coincident plate (**Figure T23**) found in the Anelay alphabet is

"N begins News-boy, / with papers to sell: / What a good thing it is / to learn to read well." Also found as **Figure N86** in "N Is for 19th Century," the 1862 engraving was replaced by a second rendering of a newsboy in the 1887 edition; the front-page news, readable there, tells about a great fire and reveals the name Babbage, undoubtedly the Charles Babbage of computer fame.

Another from the 1862 source is "R begins Rosa, how pleased she appears / To watch those plump Rabbits, with long, silky ears." Its history began with the 1862 printing in London (**Figure T24**) to be found later in the "Nursery," dated May 1887 (**Figure T25**). Here Rosa becomes Fanny, who, says the text, "takes the whole care of them, and they are very fond of her." In the later edition, "R begins Rosa" is newly engraved, though the rhyme remains the same. **Figure T26** carries the replicated image of Rosa (or Fanny) and her long-eared friends.

Last of these prints from *The Mother's Picture Alphabet* is the "transfer trail" of the "Two Girls Under an Umbrella." The verse told of their "Umbrella, that keeps us so dry, / When the heavy rain pours from the black angry sky." The 1862 print was seen soon after as a selected print that introduced eight spelling words, one of which was "rains"; it appeared in an 1864 publication of *The Primer or First Reader* by G. S. Hillard and L. J. Campbell, published by New York's Taintor Brothers, Merrill & Co. and Boston's William Ware & Co. The speller/reader (**Figures T27 and T28**), with only one religious message, is inscribed by Grace Appleby, 583 Maine Street, Providence. Its introduction to the text applauded it as being a unique tool for teachers who taught by sight as well as phonic strategies. The transfer (**Figure T29**) is then repeated on page 109 of *The Nursery, A Monthly Magazine for Youngest Readers*, published by John L. Shorey of Boston, April 1878. Two plates found with this transfer were made by Edge Malkin. The marks were different, one an impressed straight line accompanied by a garter mark, and the second an incised arc. A close inspection finds one print more detailed than the other (**Figures T30 and T31**).

Also found in a speller (**Figure T32**), the *Royal Road to Spelling and Reading* published by Edward N. Marks of London (1867), was a print of the "Pretty Child." A larger print in the authors' collection (**Figure T33**), framed in its original edging of painted cut paper, with no evidence of its source, is identical to the plate (**Figure T34**), which reads, "The pretty child on tiptoe stands to reach the piano with her hands." The plate, made by Elsmore and Forster (Foster?), was produced sometime between 1853 and 1871; the source may well have been the Royal Road.

Also echoed on plates, by Brownhills Pottery, are engravings from the wonderfully illustrated *Picture Alphabet of Nations of the World,* published by T. Nelson & Sons, London, 1874 (**Figures T35 through T45**). Reprints of the original text have been presented by Ruth Baldwin.

More personal than instructive is the alphabet series reprinted in Baldwin's book from *The Child's Picture Story Book,* "with Four Hundred Illustrations by Sir John Gilbert, R. A., J. D. Watson, W. M'Connell, W. Harvey, Harrison Weir and others." Engraved by the Brothers Dalziel, London, and printed by George Routledge and Sons, it was inscribed on June 27, 1886, with an earlier edition dated 1856. From this Pretty Name Alphabet comes the transfer (**Figures T46 and T47**) that calls the class's attention to "D is for DA-VID, the dunce of the school . . ." which has been reprinted here from The *Baby's Rhyme*

Book (Richards, 1879); see **Figures T48 and T49**. The plate celebrating David's nonperformance is undated **(Figure T50)**. One other of this series (I is for Is-A-Bel) has been seen on a plate with an alphabet edge.

Produced for H. C. Edmiston, an importer, is a fruit-dish whose print was found in a July 1880 edition of the "Nursery." The verse beneath it read, "Joanna and Josepha, / Janet and Dora dear, / Must take a morning airing / Whenever the day is clear" **(Figures T51 and T52)**. This plate, "Three Little Nurses," was produced sometime between 1902 and 1903, when Edmiston was in business in New York **(Figure T53)**.

Also from the unknown producer of plates for H. C. Edmiston comes the plate picturing a line drawing of Musicians, accompanied by a poem that reads, "We are Musicians three / As happy as can be, / Singing all the live long day / Songs and rhymes so merrily." The print is found on page 46 of *The Sailors* **(Figures T54 and T55)**, an instructive text of the alphabet letters, days of the week, and months of the year. This "non-fiction" release was published by the Juvenile Publishers and registered at the Library of Congress by J. P. Jones, presumably the editor. **Figure T56** copied the page three years later.

In the most recent volume, *Mother Goose Nursery Rhymes Complete,* published by the Homewood Publishing Company of Chicago in 1904 **(Figures T57 and T58)**, is a line drawing of "Tom, Tom, the piper's son, / He learned to play when he was young." Reminiscent of "The Pied Piper of Hamlin," the print is also found on a plate **(Figure T59)** produced by Elsmore and Forster (Foster?), whose Clayhills Pottery closed thirty-three years before the printing.

Given as well-earned prizes for performance and scholarship, both books and alphabet plates were treasured by 19th-century students. And now, highly treasured by collectors into the 21st century are those ABC plates whose designs match illustrations from any one of the prolific English and American 19th- and early 20th-century chapbooks, primers, collections of stories or poetry, and magazines, notably *The Nursery, A Monthly Magazine for Youngest Readers.*

Two matching graphics, "Lost," originally from *The Sunday Scholar's Companion*, August 1873, and "The Poor Boy and the Loaf" from *The Child's Companion*, October 1854, were identified through research at two eminent libraries but could not then be located for reproduction in this text; both can be seen in Riley's *Gifts for Good Children* (1991). Other captions presented in Riley are included here as well; a good example is the graphic of "The Cottage Girl," originally from the *Alphabet of Fruits*, an *Aunt Louisa's Toy Book*, Warne & Kronheim, London, 1875. In Riley, the text illustration and the coordinating plate can be found on pages 144 and 145. In this text, the plate can be found in **Figure N18** of "N Is for 19th Century."

A search through at least fifty volumes of *Nursery: A Monthly Magazine for Youngest Readers*, produced many of this chapter's prints; a search through the hundreds of other publications for children housed in libraries which protect special collections throughout the states and abroad would reveal others. A thorough accumulation of transfer-to-ABC plate transitions is most certainly a volume of its own and an area worthy of continued investigation.

U Is for Undersides

In this chapter are found the histories of firms that marked the undersides of flat plates (or the occasional fruit dish or cup-and-saucer set). Other chapters contain company histories as well. "D Is for Deep Dishes" presents the histories of those American, English, and German companies that produced cereal and soup bowls. "C Is for Commercialism" presents the stories of firms that produced any type of ceramic or metal that designed a product purely for commercial institutions (such as hotels) or included a company name (such as Lava Soap) or pictured characters designed purposely to popularize a product (such as Buster Brown Shoes) or a place (such as Holley, New York). "K Is for Kitsch" tells the story of the Kewpie dolls, a continuing commercial venture, produced as inexpensive statuettes and pictured on place settings to popularize those cute, chubby kids who sold Jell-O, endorsed the National Woman's Suffrage Association, posed for "cutouts," and cavorted through children's books and magazine adventures. Glass producers of ABC ware are discussed in "G Is for Glass," and mentions of metal industries are to be found in both "F Is for Flatware" and "M Is for Metals." Any history presented without its company's mark, such as Smith Phillips, has been included because it was mentioned in Lindsay's text. All items included in the Chalala collection are included in this text as well. A list of all marks in the text can be found on page 314, at the end of the Appendices.

The December 1, 1879, *Pottery Gazette* editorial looks back in reverie to the creativity and determination of the earlier potters, who, "knowing little of geology or chemistry, fought their way from sun-dried clay to the complicated substance of the finest porcelain. Only a few of them came to fame," the author says, "but their work has the stamp of individuality upon it." Artistically, of course. But the individual industrial stamps, which allow us to accurately identify these creative geniuses, are rarely found in 19th-century ware. Most marks in this collection are impressed into clay that "folds into them," and clear identification is often futile; it is the empty circle that typifies the period. And there are "chains" of marks. No matter how many graphics are recorded in a research source, it is safe to think there just might have been others. Some factories are known to have changed their marks each year, while some were consistent through the years, making their identification an easier task.

How fortunate it is when undersides do show some evidence of any one of the varied forms of markings. Printed, in relief or impressed, in full names or initials, in logos or on diamonds with letter codes, they are clues to the makers, whose

tales are often as unique as their plates themselves.

And how fortunate we are when a potter, after the 1884 call for itemizations, did register a piece. The importance of registering designs was the focus of a *Pottery Gazette* article dated April 1, 1889. In pleading tones it insisted that registration was of "utmost importance to the manufacturer to register his new designs and patterns, and so prevent any infringements of his rights." Justifiably, manufacturers lamented when their designs were copied but seemed to ignore their own abuse of the rights of competitors, whom they duplicated without qualms. And in the belief that they were being frugal, some submitted new items or designs before registration to determine their salability and were dismayed when copies appeared on others' shelves before the rightful registration could be accomplished.

A registration number, found after an "Rd" on the underside, will provide only the first date of manufacture, but it might have been used at any time later than that date. Consecutively, the numbers in 1884 began with 1. In 1885, numeration began with 19,756; in 1886, numbers began with 41,480, and so on. In January of 1989, the new sequence began at 2,000,000; in 1990, registration numbers started at 2,003,698 . . . and it has and will, surely, continue till the end of time. Registration numbers are listed at each figure site when known (see "Y Is for Yesteryear").

Certainly a registration number with a manufacturer's mark would be protective of designs on both sides of the Atlantic; some marked English goods were transfer-printed with a registration, a point of origin (Staffordshire, England), and no pottery identification. Almost amusing is the scolding directed to potters who sold their ware to shopkeepers who could not reorder items without makers' identification; the practice curtailed retail and wholesale sales, for there was no avenue for restocking. Certainly, with smaller pieces traveling the farthest, what might have been lucrative advertising netted nothing.

The estimate of registered articles was listed as 10%, which proved to be a well-educated guess for this collection. Often it is said that ABC plates were so "poor," they were not given the dignity of the maker's mark, but perhaps they were not singled out . . . it was simply not the marketing mind-set of the time. And perhaps, as the *Pottery Gazette* editorial dictates, it was carelessness, too, that prevented every potter from making certain that every workman stamped every article, rather than only the principal pieces. It was, after all, the infancy of advertising.

Pictured in this chapter are one, two, or three samples of

all marks of origin on the small, dinner-shaped plates that comprise the vast majority of ABC items. But identification is sometimes confusing. Errors are easily made when two or more firms' initials are identical. For example, H. Adams and H. Alcock, if listed as H. A., can be taken for each other. A substantial fragment of a mark on **Figure S10** may indicate either the firm of Henry Alcock at the Elder Pottery in Cobridge (1861-1910) or the firm of Harvey Adams of Longton **(Figure U3)**. Since the letters are handwritten on the published mark and on the "Goosey Gander" ceramic, it may be assumed that the mark was *possibly* produced by the Adams firm. The difference in the two marks kindles the issue of type styles and nuances of letter graphics in marks; they too must be considered as identifying clues. Though handwritten, the "A" on each mark is not exactly the same, and no crown appears on the plate mark. Continued comparison of the marks with replications in authoritative texts is essential.

A second illustration is the case of Elsmore & Forster vs. Elsmore & Foster. Both versions are listed in reference texts; Kowalsky and Kowalsky (*Encyclopedia of Marks*, Schiffer, 1999) say that "Foster" is a spelling error. Our three marks for the company are impressed rather than printed; ELSMORE & SON, ELSMORE & F-O-R-S-T-E-R, and ELSMORE & F-O-S-T-E-R are easily read. Would a reputable firm not correct the spelling of its name?

Unlike the available complex histories of glass producers, fewer tales of the potters are accessible. Geoffrey Godden, in his *Encyclopaedia of British Porcelain Manufacturers* (1988) and *Encyclopaedia of British Pottery and Porcelain Marks* (1991), has summarized information through every possible remaining source, from wine cellar to fire ash. Along with accounts of some makers found in Moore's *Old China Book* (1936), listings in a 1985 publication by the Department of Adult Education at the University of Keele titled *People of the Potteries, A Dictionary of Local Biography* (Stuart, 1985) were very helpful. Additional research and acquisition of some graphics have been facilitated by Kathy Niblett, former Senior Assistant Keeper of Ceramics at The Potteries Museum and Art Gallery in Stoke-on-Trent, who is now an esteemed author, researcher, and lecturer in The Potteries. The graphic of J. & G. Meakin has been contributed by Steven Birks, well known for his Web site (http://www.netcentral.co.uk/steveb), which offers absolutely everything anyone would ever want to know about The Potteries and more. What has been published of the information, with respect to all of those manufacturers who thoughtfully decorated the undersides of their ABC earthenware with identifying tags, is summarized here.

How many others should be included? Godden tells of records stored in a wine cellar that had long since turned to pulp. Perhaps it was just those chronicles, lying beneath all the others, that held accurate and complete lists. Each firm grew or failed with the business sense (or the luck) of its owners and innovative employees; microfilmed issues of the *Pottery Gazette* are filled with breathtaking numbers of their patent notices, each refining a technique or moving the state of the art a step or two ahead. And there really are records hidden in the fine print of those editions . . . the most-needed research tool is a detailed indexing of those printings.

William Adams & Sons (Figures U1 and U2)

First, listed in alphabetical order, is the Adams Pottery of

Tunstall, Staffordshire (1893-1917). The history of the Adams family of potters is extensive. The mark of William Adams & Sons of Tunstall most likely identifies William Adams, born in 1833. That son, the fourth William Adams, took over the Greenfield Works when his father passed away, and his brother, Thomas, took charge of the mines. After purchasing The Newfield Pottery, William was joined by two of his sons. Greengates Pottery was returned to its famous family by J. Meir in 1897, who had worked Greengates since c.1812. According to Batkin, the pottery produced a series of 1890s plates, each rimmed by vine-encircled letters. First produced by J. Meir & Sons, the metal plates, says Batkin (n.d.) "used for the prints were probably acquired by Adams when they took over the Greengates factory in about 1896." A plate from this pottery can be seen in **Figure S16** of "S Is for Sets."

Harvey Adams & Co. (Figure U3)

With this mark, which appears incomplete, accurate identification is inconclusive; the initials, H. A. & Co., may identify the Harvey Adams & Co. of Longton. From 1870 to 1885, the firm produced earthenware and china. The company was formerly Adams & Scrivener and subsequently Hammersley & Co. The mark pictured in Godden (1991) includes a crown with no enclosing shape, but the letters are handwritten as they are on the mark shown here. The mark may also have been that of Henry Aynsley & Company of Longton (1873-?), though the marks of this firm are far more fastidiously designed. Examples of items from this pottery can be seen in **Figure S10** of "S Is for Sets."

Charles Allerton & Sons (Figures U4 through U7)

Charles Allerton of Longton followed Allerton, Brough & Green at the Park Works on High Street at Longton, Staffordshire, which began in 1833 to produce both china and earthenware. With a workforce of 348 individuals and the monthly consumption of three tons of bones for the production of china, the factory must have been extensive. Becoming Charles Allerton & Sons in 1859 (1860?), the factory produced earthenware and china as well as silver and gold lustreware for export and local markets. After its founder's death sometime around June 1863, sons William, John Bill, Charles Bradbury, and Frederick James continued the company until the deaths of John and Frederick before August 1887, when Charles retired. In 1912, the firm, taken over by Cauldon Potteries Ltd., was called Allertons, Ltd; the mark C. A. & Sons, Ltd. and others identified the company until its closing in 1942. A plate from this pottery can be seen as **Figure A11** in "A Is for Americana."

H. Aynsley & Co. (Figures U8, U9, and U10)

H. Aynsley & Co., Longton, Staffordshire, was owned by Wooley and then by Chetham & Robinson until 1837. In the Chetham family for many years, the property became H. Aynsley & Company in 1873. According to Batkin (n.d.), Aynsley was advertising ABC muffins and toy wares in 1895. Registered in 1904, its series of plates bordered with hand signs proved its stand in the "hand-sign vs. lip-reading" approach to educating the hearing impaired. A plate from this pottery can be seen as **Figure E152** of "E Is for Education."

Bailey (and Ball?)

Though the partnership of John Bailey and Joseph Ball lasted from 1843 to December 18, 1849, the firm's name was still listed in Kelly's Post Office Directory of 1850. No marks have been found on items in this text, but ABC collectors immediately recognize the company's octagon-shaped earthenware (Figures E19 and E20). According to Godden (1988), the partnership at Stafford Street and Flint Street in Longton, Staffordshire, produced both china and earthenware. John Bailey continued to make pottery in his own name after the partnership ended at the same location until 1858.

Barkers & Kent Ltd. (Figure U11)

Barkers & Kent Ltd. of Fenton opened at Foley Potteries in 1889. "Ltd." was added to the name in 1898. The name of the pattern is inserted into the banner; the word "SCHOOL" runs across the globe, while the potter's initials, B & K L, stand below it. Reproductions of this brown transfer clock plate have been seen. Its photograph can be seen as Figure C6 of "C Is for Commercialism." The firm closed in 1941.

Britannia Porcelainworks (Figure U12)

Figure U12 names the M. B. (Moser Brothers) Britannia Porcelainworks of Meierhofen, Germany, which existed from 1898 until about 1925. It merged with the Brothers Benedikt Porcelain Factory, which had been in business since 1883 and ceased to exist after becoming part of the United Porcelain Factories of Meierhofen. Its ABC ware includes a cup, saucer, and pitcher, shown in Figure S17 of "S Is for Sets."

Brownhills Pottery Company (Figures U13 through U16)

The Brownhills (Brown Hills in the Chalala text) Pottery Company, founded in 1872 in Tunstall, Staffordshire, became Salt Brothers in 1896. Most marks are B. P. & Co., which may stand alone or be integrated into other designs. Preceding Brownhills was the Bowers firm, beginning with George Frederick Bowers (& Co.) from 1841; when the firm failed under his lead in 1871, it was purchased by James Eardley of Alsager and carried on under the name of The Brownhills Pottery Company. Many plates from this firm are included throughout the collection; one can be seen in Figure E140 of "E Is for Education."

E. Challinor & Co. (Figure U17)

Figure U17 is most likely the mark of an E. Challinor at the Pinnocks Works (Unicorn Pottery) in Tunstall from 1842 to 1867. There was another at Tunstall in 1851 and 1853-1854. A Fenton firm, E. Challinor & Co., became E. & C. Challinor in 1862 (to 1891) with the joining of Charles Challinor, a businessman with interests in several other potteries, collieries, the Railway Stilt Works, tileries, and flint and stone mills. With an interest in the community as well, Charles served on the Fenton Board of Health and became vice president of the North Staffordshire Infirmary. Sadly, this philanthropic spirit died following a steam engine accident at the Glebe Colliery. A plate from this pottery can be seen as Figure N94 of "N Is for 19th Century."

J. Clementson (Figure U18)

Joseph (J.) Clementson (1794-1871) began his career as a printer's apprentice in Shelton and a printers' overlooker at the Foley Pottery in Longton. About 1830, he crossed the Atlantic to assess the American and Canadian export market. From 1832 he established a seven-year partnership with Joseph Reed at the Phoenix Works, Shelton, Hanley. In 1839, Clementson became the sole proprietor of the works, bought another property, enlarged it, and added a new frontage on Broad Street. Research information differs here: one source says that in 1856, he occupied the nearby Bell Works, which he eventually purchased, while a second source maintains that he bought the Bell Works in 1856. From 1865 through 1916, the company was known as Clementson Brothers. A plate from this pottery can be seen as Figure N73 of "N Is for 19th Century."

Davenport (Figure U19)

Davenport of Longport was identified as the maker of the coveted frontispiece of Chalala's book; the lettered plate, with its blue feathered-edged design, must have been produced sometime after 1794. A plate in this collection, one that presents a sheep in green transfer, is clearly marked DAVENPORT in green transfer capital letters above an impressed mark of the Davenport anchor.

John Davenport, born in 1765, went to work shortly after his father's death in 1771. He became a partner of Thomas Wolfe until 1794, when he bought his own business and absorbed other potteries as he grew. In 1806, J. D. patented a method of ornamenting glass in imitation of engraving or etching (Stuart, 1985). (An interesting note in a biography published by the Keele University [Stuart, 1985] pictures the gentlemen and his manager [James Mawdesley] wearing glass hats in the victory parade of 1815!) About 1810, John Davenport acquired a pottery at Newport founded c.1795 by Walter Daniel and maintained, along with other acquisitions, by Davenport's sons after his retirement c.1830 (see Edge, Malkin and Company). The Davenport backstamps identify this maker of earthenware, creamware, porcelain, ironstone, and more. The anchor, seen in Figure U19, was used (in variations) to c.1860; the firm continued through 1887, when the last of the factories was sold to one Thomas Hughes. A plate from this pottery can be seen as Figure E23 in "E Is for Education."

Delinieres & Company (Figure U20)

The mark of an ABC item (a pink-lustred cup and saucer) made in France is marked by Delinieres & Company of Limoges, France, which produced ware between 1879 and 1900. The tea cup and saucer can be seen in Figure L21 of "L Is for Lustre."

Edge, Malkin & Co. (Figures U21 through U24)

The Newport Pottery, established by Walter Daniel, passed on to John Davenport in 1810; it became Cork and Edge from 1846 to 1860; Cork, Edge and Malkin from 1860 to 1871; and Edge, Malkin & Co. from 1871 until 1903. Joseph Edge began working as a confectioner, but by 1846, he was manufacturing earthenware with Benjamin Cork in Burslem. The firm's ware was exhibited at the Great Exhibition, and by 1875, a second firm, called Malkin, Edge & Company, turned out tiles for commercial properties. Joseph Edge had many business interests, which included the Staffordshire Tramway Company, the Waterworks, and the Gas Company. Committed to learning as well, he was the Superintendent of Wesleyan Methodist Schools in

Burslem and sat on the committee of the Wedgwood Memorial Institute. He died at eighty-eight at Wolstanton. A plate from this pottery can be seen as **Figure E138** of "E Is for Education."

Elsmore & Forster / Elsmore & Foster / Elsmore & Son (Figures U25, U26, and U27)

Elsmore & Forster (1853-1871) and the later 1872-1887 Elsmore & Son (England) are seen in Godden's writings. Elsmore & Foster is represented in this collection as well with two marks, one set on a horizontal baseline and the second set on a downturned arch. Forster and Foster are easily confused names with nearly identical spellings. References to both Forster and Foster are found in the text by the Chalalas, while the Lindsays refer only to Foster. A note in Kowalsky's *Encyclopedia of Marks* (Schiffer, 1999) alludes to a spelling error. But it is incredible to suppose that this significant firm would not replace a misspelled stamp over an extensive period of time, especially when the stamp was, in fact, redesigned. The manufacturer is noted as having produced earthenware and Parian ware at Clayhills (also listed as Clay Hills) in Tunstall, Staffordshire. Examples of plates backstamped in all three forms can be seen in "I Is for Infant to Infirm" as **Figure I20** marked Elsmore and Forster, **Figure I57** marked Elsmore and Foster, and **Figure E134** marked Elsmore and Son.

Thomas Godwin Burslem (Figure U28)

Thomas Godwin (1834-1854), says H. Moore, "confined himself chiefly to views of cities." His 18-inch platter brought from £15 to £20. Because his factory was established on Navigation Road in Burslem Wharf, Mr. G. marked his ware as T. or Thos Godwin New Wharf, leaving out the word "Burslem." The firm of Thoˢ Godwin Burslem was formerly T. & B. Godwin. A plate from this pottery can be seen as **Figure R21** of "R Is for Religion, Reform, and Reason."

W. H. Hackwood (Figure U29)

The Hackwood name occurs several times in the Godden encyclopedias, and the text reads, "Several potters of this name were working at Shelton or Hanley, Staffordshire, in the 19th century and it is difficult to attribute the 'Hackwood' . . . marks with certainty." Of the eight possible listings, it is known that W. H. Hackwood, who used the simple impression, "HACKWOOD," operated from 1827 to 1843. A plate from this pottery can be seen as **Figure E174** of "E Is for Education."

George Jones / George Jones & Sons (Figures U30 and U31)

The firm of George Jones is noted as a maker of ABC ware in the Godden collection. **Figure U31** marks this Burslem potter as the manufacturer of earthenware at Barnfield House. Some authors list the starting date at c.1861 (64?); "Sons" was added to the firm name in 1873. Noted for its large, lead-glazed majolica centerpieces and baskets, Jones operated both the Trent and Crescent Potteries in Stoke, where a design of an embellished monogram above a crescent moon identified its wares (earlier marks are impressed). George Jones died at seventy in December 1893, and the trade name disappeared in 1951 (7?). A plate from George Jones & Sons can be seen as **Figure R95** of "R Is for Religion, Reform, and Reason."

J. & G. Meakin (Figures U32 and U33)

A fortunate find in Staffordshire's *Pottery Gazette* dated March 2, 1885 (p. 293), was the obituary of James Meakin, who passed away on the 8th of February 1885 after a lingering illness. The firm of J. & G. Meakin was founded in 1851, when "Meakin Snr" (b. 1807) was joined by his two sons, James and George. Papa retired in 1852, handing the reins to "J. & G." George encouraged export sales to and from the United States and other British Colonies, while James managed the pottery works and shipping. Their new Eagle Pottery, a more up-to-date works, was built in Hanley in 1859 after absorbing the business of one Mr. Joseph Peake; the firm became "recognized as the largest producers of white granite ware in the world." Though the company owned other works in Cobridge and Burslem, it often asked the assistance of other potteries to meet its demands.

James was a philanthropic man, sharing his large fortune in support of all public and charitable movements in Hanley. Exalted were his contributions of £1,000 toward a free library at Hanley, £5,000 toward Hanley Park (1892-1897), land for the former St. Michael's Church, and the organ for Hanley's Victoria Hall. The community's sympathy for the family was intense and genuine; the firm was noted for its benevolent relationships with its employees. George passed away in 1891, and the business continued under the direction of the founder's grandsons until, in 1968, J. & G. Meakin joined with Midwinter. Two years later the company was absorbed by the Wedgwood Group, which currently administers its records. (Photo contributed by and used with permission of Steve Birks.) A plate from this pottery can be seen as **Figure I36** of "I Is for Infant to Infirm."

John Meir & Son (Figure U34)

John Meir of Tunstall, maker of earthenwares, occupied the Greengates Pottery (listed as Greengate in several sources) from 1812 through 1836. Adding "& Son" in 1837, the pottery continued at Greengates until 1897, when it was taken over by the Adams Pottery (see the Adams listing). A plate from this pottery can be seen as **Figure E114** of "E Is for Education."

W. E. Oulsnam & Sons (Figure U35)

W. E. Oulsnam & Sons was an identified producer of ceramic articles after 1860. Beginning his career as a tobacco dealer in Burslem, William Emmerson Oulsnam became an earthenware manufacturer in Tunstall under the name of Oulsnam and Holdcroft; Mr. M. Holdcroft left the firm in 1865. William went into partnership with one of his four sons at Furlong in 1880. The gentleman, whose establishment is listed in few texts, was a member of the Tunstall Board of Health for two years and served as chief bailiff in 1869. A plate from this pottery can be seen as **Figure V8** of "V Is for Variations on a Theme."

Podmore, Walker & Company (Figure U36)

Podmore, Walker & Company began in 1834 on Well Street in Tunstall. Several addresses were maintained for it (Well Street, Amicable Street, and Swan Bank) about the time when Enoch Wedgwood joined the firm. The initials P. W. & W. (from 1856 to 1859) signify that union. Feeling the name "Wedgwood" was more economically beneficial, Podmore, Walker & Wedgwood was renamed Wedgwood & Co. (1860-1965). **Figure V5**, a Pearl Stone Ware "Frolics of Youth" series edition, carries the imprint of Podmore, Walker & Company. The classic blue haze can be seen at the plate's edge.

Wedgwood & Co. is considered separately in this chapter. A plate with that mark is **Figure R13.**

Powell & Bishop (Figure U37)

Powell & Bishop began as Livesley, Powell & Co., 1851-1865(6), which became Powell & Bishop, 1866(7) to 1878, and evolved to Powell, Bishop, & Stonier (1878 to 1891). All produced earthenware at the Stafford Street Works and at other addresses in Hanley. Since the mark shown reads Powell & Bishop, the identified plates can be dated c.1866-1878. Mr. Bishop died on January 1st of 1900; James Bishop and John Stonier continued to make patterns for the home market, Canada, and the United States until the company's closure in 1939. Batkin lists many children's plates presented by the firm, but alphabet ware is not listed. A plate from this pottery can be seen as **Figure I41** of "I Is for Infant to Infirm."

Anthony (A.) Shaw & Son (Figure U38)

Most probably, the ABC plates and mugs were the work of A. SHAW of Staffordshire's Anthony Shaw & Company (Tunstall c.1851 to 1856 and Burslem from c.1860 to 1900), which manufactured goods especially designed for the United States, South America, and British colonies throughout the world. The firm was renamed Anthony (A.) Shaw & Son of Mersey Pottery in 1882; "& Co." replaced "& Son" in 1898, sixteen years after the plant was enlarged on an extensive scale. In 1900, the premises were sold to one A. J. Wilkinson. A plate from this pottery can be seen as **Figure E144** of "E Is for Education."

T. & H. (Figure U39)

No information is available concerning a T. & H. of Stoke-on-Trent. Godden's (1991) encyclopedia finds several firms whose initials are T. H. & Co. and TH (joined); no firms fit the pattern T. & H. in Stoke. One listing for a Taylor and Hopkinson of Shelton (Hanley) is available. Further research is required. A plate from this pottery can be seen as **Figure N4** of "N Is for 19th Century."

Josiah Wedgwood & Sons (Figure U40)

The story of Staffordshire's Wedgwood factory, the genius of Josiah and his influence upon late 18th-century industrial progress, is a tale immortal. The first Josiah Wedgwood was born in Burslem in 1730, the thirteenth child of Thomas and Mary Wedgwood. His family had been potters as early as Jacobean times. He was the great-grandson of mid-17th-century potter Gilbert Wedgwood. The old Churchyard Works served as his first classroom under the tutelage of his older brother, Thomas, with whom he entered a five-year apprenticeship in 1744. After a short partnership with John Harrison of Newcastle-under-Lyme, he became a junior partner of Thomas Whieldon of Fenton Hall in 1754. Beginning a firm for himself in 1759, he rented Burslem's Ivy House Works from Uncles John and Thomas. He expanded his firm to the Red Workhouses and the Brick House known as the Bell Works, and was famous for the way he summoned his workers and for his creamware, with which he charmed the good Queen Charlotte, wife of George III. Evidence of his seldom-mentioned rental at the Red Workhouses in Burslem is a rent account book archived at The Potteries Museum and Art Gallery at Stoke-on-Trent and quoted in Kathy Niblett's "A Useful Partner - Thomas Wedgwood, 1734-1788,"

as published in the *Northern Ceramic Society Journal* (Vol. 5, 1984, p. 3).

Josiah married and built new works at Etruria (1769), the start of an industrial village, where his white reliefs on matte-colored wares were created. To drive his mills, he installed Watts steam engines, and to drive materials to and from The Potteries more efficiently, he rallied for functional turnpike roads and canals before he died in 1795 at the age of sixty-five.

Josiah II succeeded his father as head of the pottery. The firm endured a decline in trade brought about by war and an economic depression, but being a man of integrity, he devoted his efforts to the production of translucent china. After enduring another down-spell, he gave up the London showrooms, but after he died his third son, Francis, carried the firm into the last quarter of the century with the successful production of bone china.

The firm continued at Etruria as Josiah Wedgwood and Sons. The export market, especially successful to American shores, was expanded. Under the leadership of Kennard, a fifth-generation Wedgwood, a magnificent 1,296-piece set of dinner china was sent to President Theodore Roosevelt to be used on state occasions.

The time between the two world wars proved the company's strength and vision. Though nearly bankrupt following the Wall Street crash, the company enjoyed the creative talents of Eric Ravilious, who was responsible for a design of ABC ware pictured on page 22 of Richard Dennis's *Ravilious & Wedgwood* (Dalrymple Press, 1986). The mug from this series of the 1930s was reissued fifty years later. Though not an antique, the mug and its mark are included here so that its graphic design may be compared with that of its original edition; the alphabet is completed on the mug's inner rim **(Figures U41, U42, and U43)**.

The bicentenary of the birth of Josiah Wedgwood was celebrated with a magnificent pageant in which the entire industry took part. Six years later, in 1936, the company negotiated a move from the cramped and unsuitable site at Etruria to a green field site in the countryside south of Stoke-on-Trent. The antiquated design of the old factory was no longer functional, the diggings of the Shelton Iron Works left their annoying residue on the premises, and Etruria Hall, which had not provided living quarters for the family since 1795, had become the offices for the iron and steel works. A 382-acre estate was bought at Barlaston. (Though Barlaston Hall was on the property, the hall was never used by the company, and no member of the Wedgwood family ever lived there.) The foundation stone of the modern premises was laid two years later, and in 1940, earthenware production was transferred from Etruria and continued throughout the war. The production of bone china and jasper ware was moved to Barlaston in 1950.

Modern times have seen the integration of at least eighteen well-known potteries under the Wedgwood umbrella, including three makers of ABC ware: William Adams & Sons in 1966, George Jones in 1967, and J. & G. Meakin Ltd. in 1970.

Wedgwood & Co. (Figure U44)

Though not an "antique," the Ravilious Mug is the only item in this collection that displays a Josiah Wedgwood firm mark; **Figure U44** might be confused for the famous firm's signature. This mark of Wedgwood & Co. (1860-1965) signifies the renaming of the Podmore, Walker Co. when, according to Gordon Lang

(1999), the firm was headed by Enoch Wedgwood. The Imperial Ironstone China works, which began in 1860 at the Unicorn and the Pinnox Works, survived in Tunstall until 1965. A plate from this pottery can be seen as **Figure R13** of "R Is for Religion, Reason, and Reform."

Wileman & Co. / James F. Wileman (Figure U45)

About 1857 saw the start of Henry Wileman's Foley China Works in Fenton. H. W. died seven years later and was succeeded by his sons, James Francis and Charles. The firm was then known as J. & C. Wileman until 1868(9), when the partnership dissolved; the firm was then headed by Charles only until his retirement in 1869(70). James returned and renamed the establishment J. F. W. for his own James Francis. **Figure U45** reads J. F. Wileman, which continued until 1872 (92?). Because there are conflicting dates of J. F.'s factory in reputable texts, dates on captions will read, 1869 (70?)-1872 (Godden, 1988) (1892?).

This industrial history concludes with the renaming of the firm to Wileman & Co. in recognition of its partnership with Joseph Ball Shelley, its subsequent turnover to Shelly Potteries Ltd. in 1925, and its more recent absorption into Royal Albert Ltd. from 1967. A plate from this pottery can be seen as **Figure E162** of "E Is for Education."

Enoch Wood & Sons (Figure U46)

Aside from the potter's marks, there were backstamps, which let the buyer know that the item was made solely for export to the United States. Enoch Wood & Sons used such a mark, which incorporated an American eagle. The son of Aaron Wood, Enoch Wood began independently in 1759 at Fountain Place in Burslem (see "P Is for Potters and Their Potteries") after a short-lived partnership with Ralph Wood II. From 1790 (92) to July 1818, he shared a partnership with James Caldwell, and called the firm Wood & Caldwell. From 1818 until 1846, the firm continued as Enoch Wood & Sons. Reverence for the work accomplished by this fine firm was shown by the deposits of its pottery into the foundations and walls of Burslem's Saint Paul's Church . . . a joining of the spirits of creation. A plate from this pottery can be seen as **Figure N92** of "N Is for 19th Century."

Others (Figures U47 through U51)

Other marks, called "Garter marks," gave different kinds of information. Garter marks of infinite varieties can be seen in the Kowalskys' encyclopedia (1999); they indicate the names of North American firms that brought ceramic goods across the Atlantic. But identifications can be confusing. Another example of coincident initials has been found on the list of importers. The mark pictured on **Figure U47** (and found in "T Is for Transfers and Toybooks" as **Figure T30)** may refer to the importing agencies of J. McD. and S., which, according to the Kowalskys (1999), could be the Jones, McDuffee and Stratton Company (c.1895) of Boston, Massachusetts. The firm imported goods from the potteries of William Adams, Josiah Wedgwood and Son, and Enoch Wood and Sons (Ltd.). Less likely, the initials may stand for John McDonald and Son of British Columbia (1840-c.1875), who represented both Edge Malkin and Podmore, Walker and Company. Further research would be needed to determine which of the two was indeed the importer of the ABC plate, since no pottery stamp is present along with the importer's identification. Unfortunately, the second garter design **(Figure U48)** from a firm whose initials are J. H. ?. & R. (and found in "E Is for Education" as **Figure E48**) could not be identified through Kowalskys' lists, though it is certain, from the initials B. & N. Y., that their offices were in both Boston and New York (City). Positive identifications of ceramic items cannot be determined from the list of joint ventures, but the list of potteries served by the importers does help to narrow the search for factory sources of items marked only with an exporter's mark (see Appendix AU1 for a merchant's ship tale).

Export businesses are joint-venture trade agreements. According to Kowalsky, these "connections" developed from the practice of auctioning earthenware destined for sale on U.S. and Canadian wharves during the late 18th and 19th centuries. "As towns and cities grew, so did an emerging network of importers, retailers and tradesmen who brought their wares to all areas of the expanding North American continent. Importers and retailers, as well as others, used china and earthenware as an advertising vehicle, as is evident by the printed backstamps of the American and Canadian Importer listing" (Kowalsky and Kowalsky, 1999).

Familiar family names of producers of ABC plates appear on the list of potteries that enlisted importers to assist in product distribution: Adams, Bridgwood, Challinor, Clementson, Davenport, Edge, Malkin, Meakin, Meir, Powell & Bishop, Shaw, Wedgwood, Wood, and others. For example, one importing agency for J. Clementson was A. J. Brown & Co. of Boston (c.1848); an agency for Sampson Bridgwood & Son was Rogers & Co., of Boston (c.1875); Enoch Wood & Sons were represented by John Gray of New York (c.1834-1845), etc. It is also interesting to note the names of importers that match the factories represented. For some, perhaps, it was all in the family; for example, the Meakin family of Boston represented J. & G. Meakin; J. Clementson was represented by Francis Clementson of St. John, New Brunswick; and Joseph Wedgwood of Montreal represented Josiah Wedgwood from 1816 through 1819. (Additional research would be needed for absolute verification of family ties.)

A different kind of importer stamp is seen in **Figure U49**, which reads, "Manufactured / H. C. Edmiston / England." Page 663 of the Kowalskys' encyclopedia lists "Hugh C. Edmiston / 25 West Broadway / New York (NYC) / c.1902-1903" in a list of "Importers, Wholesalers, Retailers, Auctioneers, English Imports 18th Century Through Early 20th Century United States." The section is noted as listing those firms for which "Printed backmarks . . . have not been recorded to date." The finding of this mark is indeed, then, a rarity. Though it is not a Garter design, it serves the same function. The individual represented by Edmiston is listed as Alfred Meakin, whose pottery was in Tunstall, Staffordshire (1875-1913). Before becoming Alfred Meakin, the firm was Pearson and Hancock. The Newfield Pottery was acquired by Meakin in 1930. By 1974, the Meakin holdings were bought by Myott & Son, Co. Ltd., and in 1982 the business was absorbed into the Churchill Group. No other marks from the firm of A. Meakin are found in this collection, and it is not certain that the plates marked Edmiston (David and Goliath and Little Miss Muffet) were, in fact, made by that Meakin pottery, since the editor of the encyclopedia states that the lists, as published, are yet incomplete. H. C. Edmiston might have served one or more potters, as well. A plate manufactured for H. C. Edmiston can be seen as **Figure E46** of "E Is for Education."

Only one example of a patent stamp for an item undoubtedly created in Staffordshire, with a patent applied for in the United States, has been found **(Figure U50)**. The backstamp, found on a plate featuring a graphic of the Administration Building at the Columbian Exposition **(Figure C17)**, was obviously manufactured for sale in Chicago, Illinois, in 1893. The Lindsays (1998) attribute the plate (also marked with this patent mark) to Charles Allerton & Sons.

General Staffordshire–England marks are often found that indicate only a point of origin similar to the German marks, which read "Germany" in all capital letters or in script of many colors. This unique stamp **(Figure U51)** presents both the point of origin and a Registry Number, which might allow another potter to investigate its factory source but does not provide much

information to the purchaser. A plate from this location can be seen as **Figure E31** of "E Is for Education."

How many potteries should have been included but for the placement of a potter's mark on an underside? Surely more than have been spoken for. And collectors might well find items identified with potters' marks not shown here, as varieties of indentations and transfers were concurrently applied. Dates, unless the diamond system or a Registry Number is displayed, can only be estimated even with information of the pottery's history. But identification increases the validity of the item and its value . . . surely the search for marks helps to find an ever widening market.

V Is for Variations on a Theme

Alphabet plates may be listed in varying sources by the same title and determined to be worth the same money, but they may actually be very different. The demand for large numbers of the same transfer required more than one engraving; because each was cut by hand, there were always variations. Additionally, there were differences in the colors of their final printings, their possible overpaintings, or excisions to avoid copyright disputes or to adjust to plate sizes. Also found are differences in borders, titles, captions, messages, plate sizes, etc. Worthy of mention as well are the inevitable differences in names currently created for plates with no written titles. Listings do vary among texts and other printings.

An inconspicuous difference, pervasive throughout all collections, is the placement of the transfer with respect to the position of the surrounding alphabet letters. Since transfers were always hand placed and set quickly, little notice of their positions with regard to their plate rims was taken; neither text nor photographs will call attention to these persistent differences.

In this chapter, plates will be pictured in sets of two or three, each demonstrating some variations of their common theme. Careful scrutiny may reveal "duplicates" to be singular examples of the ceramic industry's pre-assembly-line production.

• **Figures V1 and V2 - Like transfers; two colors; neither overpainted.** The 2-2-2 steam-train is pictured here from an illustration by Henry Anelay published in *The Mother's Picture Alphabet* (1862) under "T for Tunnel."

• **Figures V3 and V4 - Like transfers; two colors; one overpainted; one with edge; same size; same maker.** Both Crusoe plates were made by Brownhills Pottery. (**Figures R30 and R31** show like transfers, two colors, one overpainted, different makers.)

• **Figures V5 and V6 - Nearly-like transfers; two colors; one overpainted.** Obvious differences are seen when comparing faces and hairstyles, as well as other details, of the two "loosely copied" engravings.

• **Figures V7 and V8 - Like transfers; two colors; smaller overpainted; larger with edge-line trim.** Figure V8 is the largest in the collection. Other chapter items display edge-line differences also.

• **Figures V9 and V10 - Like transfers, two colors, two overpainted.** Each transfer eliciting its own "mood" through the painter's use of colors and patterns. The more intensely colored transfer "feels" more intimidating.

• **Figures V11 and V12 - Like transfers; one with background partially trimmed away. Figure V12** is a magnification of the excised area on "Baked Taters."

• **Figures V13, V14, V15, and V16 - Like prints and transfers; one print reversed. Figure V13** is a reprint of page "O" from *The Mother's Picture Alphabet* (1862). **Figures V14 and V15** are taken from it. **Figure V16** was found on page 49 of the 1867 edition of *The Nursery, A Magazine for Youngest Readers* by Fanny P. Seaverns. The mirror-image is captioned, ROBERT THE ORGAN-GRINDER. A turn-about such as this would occur if a "pull" from an engraving were copied, or if an engraver copied a reversed print as it appeared in a book. "Robert" evidently suffered one of the two. (For Robert's tale, see Appendix AV1.)

• **Figures V17 and V18 - Like transfers; differently molded ABC edges.** The larger dramatic scene has a delicate scallop below the molded letters.

• **Figures V19 and V20 - Like transfers; one non-alphabet molded edge.** The transfers are French/English translations of the word, La Lecture - Reading.

• **Figures V21, V22, and V23 - Like molds, different color distribution, with and without frosting.** The first Bo-Peep has a frosted rim and body with a painted blue image incised into the underside of the well. The second is a blue-rimmed deep dish with an uncolored frosted graphic. The third (lower image) is a clear pale yellow. (A fourth, clear with no color, is not shown.)

There are three different forms of verbiage on ABC plates: *titles*, *captions*, and *messages*. They may vary in different ways.

• **Titles: Figures V24 and V25 - Like transfers; one titled; neither overpainted.** ("Riddles" are in "Q Is for Queries.")

• **Titles: Figures V26 and V27 - Like transfers; one titled; smaller overpainted.** ("Riddles" are in "Q Is for Queries.)

• **Captions: Figures V28 and V29 - Like transfers; one captioned; larger overpainted.** Did the fox get away?

• **Captions: Figures V30 and V31 - Like transfers; one captioned; both overpainted**. All of the zebras are stripped of their stripes.

• **Captions: Figures V32, V33, V34, and V35 - Like transfers; partially like captions**. "Grapes" were more politically correct for northern American export. **Figure V35** highlights the rare, hand-printed caption.

• **Messages: Figures V36 and V37 - Like transfers; one with a message**. The illustration to "Keep thy shop . . ." is found on two differently sized rounds.

• **Messages: Figures V38 and V39 - Unlike transfers; partially like single message**. The first begins "For age and want . . . " and concludes with " . . . lasts all the day." The second concludes, " . . . lasts a whole day."

• **Messages: Figures V40 and V41 - Unlike transfers; partially like double messages**. Both remind the reader that, "Little strokes fell great Oaks" and "Little strokes fall great oaks." Additional message added on **Figure V41**.

Reviewing a mature collection can reveal extraordinary comparisons.

• **Figures V42 and V43 - Like transfers, each with one item removed to prevent copyright infringement**. On each mug, one of four dogs, perched upright on the brick wall, has been removed.

• **Figures V44 and V45 - Like transfers, possibly painted by the same hand**. Close examination of brushed shapes and their placements may provide sufficient evidence to consider that these two overpaintings may have been accomplished by one individual!

W Is for Worth

This text has valued more than one thousand plates. Those values have been determined with an acute sense of responsibility to both buyers and sellers. Since statements of worth, in texts such as this, may profoundly impact the retail marketplace, it is necessary that those who consult these estimates know that wholesale values and auction prices have not been investigated and that Internet sales have not been considered, as they do not always reflect the most common retail selling price.

Estimates of worth have been influenced by offerings at *current* cross-country shows and have been reviewed and contributed by knowledgeable specialists, reputable dealers, collectors from different areas of the United States and paper advertisements. Costs listed in published price guides, which reflected appropriate gains reflected from year to year and which seemed to have been based on consistent criteria, were considered as well. Certainly pieces have been sold both over and under the value ranges offered here; it is asked that neither the authors nor the publisher be considered liable for any losses incurred when using this list as the basis of any sale.

Ultimately, prices are assigned subjectively by vendors who reserve the right to consider their purchase investment and their intended profit. Then, to establish a reasonable retail value, their knowledge of the current common price range, their perceived demand of the item, their personal affinity for the item's history and its "charm," and the mitigating factors that are common to the assessment of any antique come into play.

Rather than attempt to assign definitive dollar values, then, costs have been spread into price ranges that allow for geographic and dealer differences. Very expensive items have been marked from $250+ to $500+. Ranges of prices in subject categories are fairly consistent. It is easy to recognize that many mixed-metal plates, priced in "M Is for Metals," have surpassed ceramic editions in value, and the costs of ABC ceramics mugs (listed in "H Is for Holloware") have increased at a faster pace than the plates that often match them. Glass alphabet plates have climbed in value, as most plate designs and Adams mugs are rarely seen.

The dollar value of an ABC plate or mug of any material depends primarily upon the when and where of its manufacture and a creditable identification of its maker. Backstamps can help to identify the age of an item. Comparisons of trademarks to drawn marks in classic texts can shed light upon the possible dates of a factory's existence and other clues, found in "Y Is for Yesteryear," can help to suggest dates of production.

Along with its provenance, a piece may have unique qualities that may differentiate it from most others. For instance, an earthenware plate that reflects a blue haze and shows a "puddling" of blue glaze at its border or under-rims is identified as highly prized Pearlware (for examples, see **Figures E91 and R100**). Recognition of this glaze can date the ceramic from about 1800-1825. Creamware, too, is very valuable. It is a lustre-trimmed, creamware mug **(Figure L8)** that displays the elegant design on the frontispiece of Riley's *Gifts for Good Children* (1991). Typically, creamware is lighter in weight than Pearlware and shows a greenish cast in the "puddling" areas. These two types of pieces would command high prices; their age and glazes would create serious interest among collectors.

Other factors contribute to estimations of value as well. Plates and mugs with well-executed overpainting are worth more than items whose transfers have not been embellished. And the value of ABC ware is also heightened by clearly cast and uniquely decorated borders, or by lustred rims (see "O Is for Ornamental Borders"). A plate becomes more interesting, too, if it is a published or unpublished member of a set (see "G Is for Glass"), if its transfer can be coordinated with a printed source, or if its engraver can be identified (see "H Is for Holloware" and "T Is for Transfers and Toybooks"). Sizes can weigh into the equation, as well; very large or rare miniature dishes of any material tend to be more costly (see "M Is for Metals"). Also very desirable are graphics that "cross over" collectors' areas of interest. For example, ABC plates which feature baseball currently command high prices from those interested in ABC ware and sports memorabilia.

Certainly a plate is an excellent investment and should cost more if perfect. *Prices in this chapter are, in fact, based upon plates in that excellent condition.* Most plates wear signs of passing years. Ceramic articles with damages from "mite bites" to badly glued breaks, enameled metals with heavily damaged edges, and mixed metal tea trays darkened with "age spots" and rusty flakes make it to the display tables. If a damaged piece is rare, completes a collector's set, or significantly expands a collection, the buyer is often forgiving. The "less perfect" can hold the place of one "more perfect" until it is found.

Some types of imperfections can be easily reversed to raise values. Severely darkened ceramics can be rejuvenated. Because so many plates were set into tin bonnets atop stoves, grease and gravies easily soaked through their glazes. With time and effort, a grease-laden plate can, after bleaching, be returned to its former glory. Dennis Berard, well-respected dealer of antiques from Fitzwilliam, New Hampshire, presents the process for bleaching ceramics in Appendix AW1.

Vendors can also enlist the services of professional restorers to ready items for sale. Plates may then be sold to vendors or clients, who may or may not know that their new "collectibles" have been renewed to recapture their value. Prices of commonly found pieces that have been restored, says well-respected Pasadena appraiser Bill Novotny, may slide to 50% of their "perfect" worth. Again, for rare finds, buyers are justifiably forgiving.

Of course there are those rare individuals to whom the cost of an item has no meaning. They are the aficionados for whom dealers of ABC plates may purchase select items with complete certainty. And there is the classic writing of N. Hudson Moore, whose words demean the purchase of any alphabet ware. The venerable Mooré, in his *Old China Book* (1936), ridicules our fondness and labels our precious earthenware as "old crockery or "old dishes." The potters, he says,

> . . . were so anxious to capture our market that every species of device . . . was seized upon. Many of Franklin's sayings were printed on cheap white ware with embossed borders, or the alphabet on the edge, chiefly for the use of children . . . . The plates come not only circular but octagonal as well, and the motto, or maxim is often illustrated by rude figures, printed in black and touched with colour. No list is given of these pieces as they speak for themselves . . . . Their only interest is their quaint character—for they have absolutely no beauty, and a collection of them is decidedly monotonous.

Despite Moore's lack of appreciation, we will list our treasures by their traditional picture-content categories for ease in finding their estimated values.

Advertisements

Buster Brown Shoes - Pouring Tea (J3)	100-150
Buster Brown Shoes - Toasting With Tea Cups (C44)	100-150
Campbell's Soup - Campbell's Kids - "Look-alike" with American Flag (C34)	100-150
Campbell's Soup - Campbell's Kids - Girl Holding Doll (Hotel) (C58)	100-150
Campbell's Soup - Campbell's Kids - Virginia (white plastic cereal) (C35)	50-75
Campbell's Soup - Campbell's Kids Deep Dish - Boy Holding Doll (C32)	150-200
Campbell's Soup - Campbell's Kids Deep Dish - Doll has Fallen (C33)	150-200
Campbell's Soup - Campbell's Kids Deep Dish - Girl Holding Doll (C31)	150-200
Cleverdon & Co. Halifax, N. S. (C46)	200-275
Disney Corp. - Mickey Mouse on a Train - Deep Dish (C85)	500+
Disney Corp. - Pluto - the Pup and Mickey Mouse - Deep Dish (C87 (J2) (Z6)	500+
Felix Cartoons - Felix the Cat - Now Felix, Keep on Walking - Deep Dish (C82)	275-300
Felix Cartoons - Felix the Cat - Please Felix, Don't Shoot - Deep Dish (C83)	275-300
Lava Soap - Here we go Round . . . . - Chromolithography (C37)	150-175
Lava Soap - Monkey on a Barrel - Chromolithography (C38)	150-175
Lava Soap - Playing at Driving Horses - Chromolithography (C36)	150-175
Lava Soap - Sailing Ship - Chromolithography (C40)	150-175
Lava Soap - Tom, Tom, ... - Chromolithography (C39)	150-175
Post Cereals - Beetleware - Donald Duck (C42)	60-80
Post Cereals - Beetleware - Mickey Mouse (C43)	60-80
Smith & Brown, Quebec - Pussy Cat, Pussy Cat, Where . . . . (C21)	150-175
Tomasini Hardware (C45) (D83)	150-200

Alphabet Letters

A - Apple, Ape, Air (E21)	275-325
A/B/C - Blind Man's Buff (E31)	275-325
A/B/C - Boy and Dog (E30)	275-325
A/Z - Goosey Gander Classroom - Plate/Mug listed in Sets (S10.)	listed
A/Z - Letter Border - Blue Letters/Animals - Plate/Pitcher listed in Sets (S14)	listed
A/Z - Letter Border - Blue-Green Letter Plate/Pitcher listed in Sets (S13) (O15)	listed
A/Z - Letter Border - Orange Letters/Animals- Varied items listed in Sets (S15)	listed
B - B is for Ball (E19)	275-325
B - B is for Bobby's Breakfast (E28)	275-325
B - Boat, Bat, Ball - 5.37 in. (E14)	275-325
B - Boat, Bat, Ball - 6.5 in. (E15)	275-325
C - C for Convolvulus (T15)	275-325
C - Cat, Carpet, Cup (E20)	275-325
C - Cow, Cat, Clown (E22)	275-325
D - D is for Da-vid, the Dunce (T50)	275-325
D/E/F - Boy with Bubble Pipe - Plate/Mug listed in Sets (S3)	listed
D/E/F - Shuttlecock (E32)	275-325
Dotted Rim Series - D is for Dash (E8)	275-325
Dotted Rim Series - H begins Horse (E9)	275-325
Dotted Rim Series - I is an Infant (E10)	275-325
Dotted Rim Series - R stands for Rabbit (E11)	275-325
Dotted Rim Series - V is a Violet (E12)	275-325
Dotted Rim Series - Y Is a Youth (E13)	275-325
E - E was an Eagle (E26)	275-325
E - Egg, Eye, Eel (E16)	275-325
F - F's for Fowls and the Farm (E29)	275-325
G - G stands for Gander (T10)	275-325
G/g - Getting Ready for a Walk - 5.37 in. (E24)	275-325
G/g - Getting Ready for a Walk - 7.18 in. (E25)	275-325
G/H/I - Boy on a Swing (E33)	275-325
H - Heather - Red Purple and Grey (E27)	275-325
J/K/L - Boy and Dog - Plate/Mug listed in Sets (S4)	listed
K - K begins Kite (T21)	275-325
K - Kitten. Kite. Key (E17)	275-325
L - L is the Lily (T17)	275-325
Letters at random - Saucer/Cup/Pitcher listed in Sets (S17)	listed
N - N begins News-boy or Newsie - 6 in. (N86)	275-325
N - N begins News-boy or Newsie - 8 in. (T23)	275-325
O - O begins Organ - 6.12 in. (V14)	275-325
O - O begins Organ - Allerton- 7.25 in. (V15)	275-325
P - Pig, Pigeon, Pins (E18)	275-325
P/Q/R - Flying a Kite (E34)	275-325
R - R begins Rosa (T26)	275-325
R - R stands for Rabbit (T12)	275-325
R - Red Riding Hood Meets the Wolf (E71)	275-325
R - Watch the bent of his . . . . - Pearlware (R100)	350+
S - Shee (p) (E23)	275-325
S/T/U - Going to School (E1)	275-325
T - T begins Tunnel - 5.12 in. (C1)	275-325

T - T begins Tunnel - 7 in. (V1)	275-325
T - T begins Tunnel - 7.25 in. (V2)	275-325
T - T is the Tulip (T19)	275-325
U - Also Umbrella that keeps us so dry . . . - 5.12 in. (T30)	275-325
U - Also Umbrella that keeps us so dry . . . - 6.25 in. (T31)	275-325
V/W/X - See-Saw (E35)	275-325
V/W/X - See-Saw - Plate/Mug listed in Sets (S5)	listed
Y - Y for Youth - Plate/Mug listed in Sets (S1)	listed
Y/Z/& - Snowballs - Plate/Mug listed in Sets (S6)	listed
Z - Z Comes the Last - Plate/Mug listed in Sets (S2)	listed

Americana-Early

Crossing the Plains (A4)	175-225
Landing Place of the Pilgrims (A2)	175-225
Native Americans - Candlefish (A1)	175-225
Native Americans - Chinonca Watching the Departure of the Cavalcade (A11)	175-225
Native Americans - Sioux Indian Chief (A12)	175-225
Philadelphia - Independence Hall (A7)	250+
Philadelphia - Public Buildings (A8)	250+
Washington, DC - The White House (A9)	250+
Washington, DC -The Capitol (A10)	250+

Animals - Domestic (See Horses listed in Horses)

Donkey (I61)	150-200
Fan Series - Donkey (E115)	150-200
Fan Series - Goat with Glasses (E116)	150-200
Fan Series - Horse (E113)	150-200
Fowls - Combat (N111)	75-125
Fowls - Death (N113)	75-125
Fowls - Exhibition of Prize Fowls (N112)	175-225
Sheep and Lamb (E118)	175-225

Animals - Wild

Brownhills - Bear with Cubs (E128)	275-350
Brownhills - Camel (E127)	275-350
Brownhills - Elephant (E123)	275-350
Brownhills - Kangaroo (E124)	275-350
Brownhills - Leopard (E126)	275-350
Brownhills - Lion (E125)	275-350
Brownhills - Stag (E129)	275-350
Brownhills - Tiger (E130)	275-350
Elephant (E121)	175-225
Fan Series - Stag - Fruit Shape (E114)	150-200
Fishing Elephant (E122)	175-225
Giraffe (May be Cameleopard) (E120)	175-225
Sly Fox (E119)	175-225
Wild Dog (E117)	175-225

Birds and Fowl

Bird among the Flowers (E144)	150-175
Bird among the Morning-glories (E145)	150-175
Birds in a Design (E149)	150-175
Birds in a Paisley Design (E148)	150-175
Birds of Paradise (E135)	175-225
Birds on a Limb (E146)	150-175
Brownhills - Chaffinch (reads CHFINCH) and Goldfinch (E136)	175-225
Brownhills - Robin - Plate/Mug listed in Sets (S9)	listed
Brownhills - Swallow (E139)	175-225
Brownhills - Titmouse (E140)	175-225
Brownhills - Wandering Pie (E132)	175-225
Bullfinch and Goldfinch (E137)	175-225
Chickens - Plate/Saucer/Cup listed in Sets (S18)	listed
Cock Fighter in Combat (N111)	75-125
Cock Fighter at Death (N113)	75-125
Fowl - Exhibition Prize Fowls (N112)	175-225
Hen and Her Chicks - Hotel - Not Shown	75-125
Heron and Two Frogs (E147)	150-175
House Sparrow (E138)	175-225
Kestral (E141)	175-225
Magpie (E133)	175-225
Owl - Hotel (C71)	75-125
Peacock (E134)	175-225
Robin - Hotel (C70)	75-125
Sky Lark (E143)	175-225

Campbell Kid's Collectibles

Campbell's Kids - Girl Holding Doll (Hotel) (C58)	100-150
Campbell's Kids - "Look-alike" with American flag (C34)	100-150
Campbell's Kids - Virginia (C35)	50-75
Campbell's Kids Deep Dish - Boy Holding Doll (C32)	150-200
Campbell's Kids Deep Dish - Doll has Fallen (C33)	150-200
Campbell's Kids Deep Dish - Girl Holding Doll (C31)	150-200

Cartoons (See other cartoons in Humor)

Disney Corp. - Donald Duck - Beetle Ware - Plastic cereal (C42)	60-80
Disney Corp. - Mickey Mouse - Beetle Ware - Plastic cereal (C43)	60-80
Disney Corp. - Mickey Mouse on a Train - Deep Dish (C85)	500+
Disney Corp. - Pluto - The Pup and Mickey Mouse - Deep Dish (C87) (J2) (Z6)	500+
Felix the Cat - Now Felix, Keep on Walking - Deep Dish (C82)	275-300
Felix the Cat - Please Felix Don't Shoot - Deep Dish (C83)	275-300
Goosey Gander Classroom - Dish/Mug listed in Sets (S10)	listed
Monkey School for Donkeys (E112)	150-200

Children's Activities (See other activities in Children and Animals, Farm Scenes, Fishing, Performing Arts, and Stages of Life)
Note - Titles integrated into transfers can increase item value

Archery (N115)	175-225
At the Zoo (N104)	150-175
Brother and Sister at Play (E2)	150-175
Dog Cart - Scene One (I15)	150-175
Dog Cart - Scene Two (I16)	150-175
Floral Coronation (I65)	150-175
Football (I46)	200-250
Garden Flower (I66)	150-175
Girl Teaching her Dog - Lustre (L4)	200-250
Hold Your Hand Out - 5 in. (V10)	175-225
Hold Your Hand Out - 8.25 in. (V9)	175-225
Ice Skating (N119)	175-225
Jousting (I38)	150-175
Jump Little Nag-Tail (I42)	175-225
Kite Flying (N114)	175-225
Leaf Frog (I40)	175-225

Leap Frog (I41)	150-175
Little Boys at Marbles Play (I33)	250+
Lost - 6.12 in. (V7)	150-175
Lost - 9.75 in. (V8)	300+
On a Swing (I28)	150-175
Playground (I47)	175-225
Playing at Lovers (I21)	175-225
Playing School (I26)	150-175
Playing Store (I17)	150-175
Playing with Scales (I14)	150-175
Raking the Garden (I63)	150-175
Reading Aloud (I7)	150-175
Ready for a Ride (T7)	150-175
Ship-building (I11)	150-175
Shuttlecock (I36)	175-225
Snowball Fight (I37)	150-175
Soldiers (I19)	150-175
Spelling Bee (C47)	175-225
Spinning Tops (I34)	175-225
Stacking Walnut Shells (I12)	150-175
Stilt Walking (I39)	150-175
Swing, Swung (I30)	150-175
Swinging (I29)	150-175
Tending the Garden (I64)	150-175
These cannons, Sir . . . . (I13)	150-175
This boy I think looks very grand . . . . (I18)	150-175
Three Little Nurses (T53)	150-175
Throwing a Ball (I45)	150-175
Tired of Play - 5 in. (I31)	150-175
Tired of Play - 6.87 in. (I32)	150-175
Top-Whipping (I35)	175-225
Two Girls Making Garlands (I67)	150-175
Very good fun is . . . . - 6.37 in. (I43)	150-175
Very good fun is . . . . - 7.5 in. (I44)	150-175
Writing in the Garden (I25)	150-175
Young Idea (I27)	150-175
Young Sergeant (I20)	150-175

Children and Animals (Moral Behaviors)

Catch it Carlo . . . . (I51)	150-200
Feeding the Donkey (I60)	150-200
Feeding the Geese (I58)	150-200
Guardian (I49)	150-200
New Pony (I54)	150-200
Oh Look Brother . . . . (I53)	150-200
Our Donkey and Foal (I62)	150-200
Pretty Poll, hold down your head . . . . (I57)	150-200
Pride of the Barnyard (I59)	150-200
That girl wants the pup away . . . . (I52)	150-200
These Children Trying . . . . (I50)	150-200
The Playfellows (I48)	150-200
Willie and his Rabbit (I56)	150-200

Children and Animals (Amoral Behaviors)

Don't Hurt It! (R59)	175-225
Cruel Boy (R58)	175-225
Stealing Apples (R60)	175-225

Clocks

A Ride on Carlo (C3)	200-250
A Wheelbarrow Ride (C4)	200-250
At the Seaside (C2)	200-250
Clock Face - Adams (C5)	75-100
Clock Face - Barkers & Kent (C6)	100-150
Clock Face - Enamel (M13)	125-175
Clock Face - Enamel GMT (M12)	125-175
Clock Face - Enamel Mikkimug (M14)	50-100
Clock Face - Enamel Orme (M15)	125-175
Clock Face - Glass (G16)	75-100
Clock Face - Glass - Days/Months/Alphabet (G39)	75-100
Clock Face - Glass Key Edge (G12)	75-100
Clock Face - Mixed Metal (M49)	100-150
Clock Face - Red - Dish/Mug listed in Sets (S16)	listed
Tea Tray, Clock Dials - Mixed Metal (M10)	75-125

Deep Dishes

At the Doghouse (D115)	150-200
Baby Bunting and Little Dog Bunch (D92)	150-200
Baby Bunting Runs Away (D96)	150-200
Batter Up! and coordinate patterns - Deep and Flat Dishes	
Batter-Up! and Football Player - USA Flat (D102)	75-100
Batter-Up! - German Deep Dish (D11)	150-200
Football Player - USA Deep Dish (D105)	150-200
Football Player and Skater - USA Flat (D103)	75-100
Bowled Over (D3)	200-250
Boy and Girl with a Basket (D55)	150-200
Boy and Three Girls Talking - 0-9 Surround (D60)	150-200
Boy and Three Girls Talking - A-Z Surround (D62)	150-200
Boy with a Hat and Girl with an Umbrella (D53)	150-200
Boy with a Wheelbarrow (D5)	150-200
Boy with Toys (D39)	150-200
Boy, Girl and Grey Dog (D38)	150-200
Boys with Paper Hats Threatening Bears (D15)	150-200
Campbell's Kids - "Look-alike" with American flag (C34)	100-150
Campbell's Kids - Virginia (C35)	50-75
Campbell's Kids Deep Dish - Boy Holding Doll (C32)	150-200
Campbell's Kids Deep Dish - Doll Has Fallen (C33)	150-200
Campbell's Kids Deep Dish - Girl Holding Doll (C31)	150-200
Cat in the Cradle - Animal Letter Border (D51) (J13)	150-200
Cat in the Cradle - Animal Letter Border - Heise (D9)	150-200
Children at the Puppet Stage (D57)	150-200
Children with Books (D40)	150-200
Clown Riding on a Pig (D13)	150-200
Franklin Plate -	
Constant Dropping wears/Little strokes fall . . . . (R77)	250-300
Cows at the Stream (D109)	150-200
Disney - Mickey Mouse on a Train (C85)	500+
Disney - Pluto - The Pup and Mickey Mouse (C87) (J2) (Z6)	500+
Dutch Boy and Girl Making a Wreath (D42)	150-200
Dutch Girl with a Basket (D32)	150-200
Elephants at Tennis (D46)	150-200
Feeding Teddy (D82)	150-200
Felix the Cat - Now Felix, Keep on Walking (C82)	275-300
Felix the Cat - Please Felix, Don't Shoot (C83)	275-300
First Lesson (D25)	150-200

Five Chickens (Tomasini gift) (D83) (C45)	150-200
Geography Lesson (D41)	150-200
Georgie Porgie, Pudding and Pie . . . . (D95)	150-200
Girl Feeding the Chicks (D7)	150-200
Girl with Pail and Shovel (D35)	150-200
Girl, Baby and Dog on a Swing (D44)	150-200
Good Luck Old Boy (D47)	150-200
Heres (no apostrophe on graphic) a little pig . . . . (D87)	150-200
Hey Diddle Diddle . . . . (D49)	
(See also D34 for smaller decal, 1 of 3)	150-200
Hickory, Dickory, Dock . . . . (D89)	150-200
Jack and Jill . . . . (D21)	150-200
Kewpie - One Holdfast Figure Running (K8)	150-200
Kewpie - One Holdfast Figure Standing (K7)	150-200
Kewpies - Five O'Neill Figures (K4)	175-225
Kewpies - Three Dresden Figures (K10)	150-200
Letter Border - Green Letters/Animals (D118)	50-100
Little Birdies in a Nest . . . . (D91)	150-200
Little Bo-Peep - Glass - Frosted Blue Floor (V21)	125-175
Little Bo-Peep - Glass - Frosted Blue Rim (V22)	125-175
Little Bo-Peep - Glass - Clear Yellow (V23)	125-175
Little Bo-Peep . . . . (D112)	150-200
Little Bo-Peep . . . . . - Schumann (D22)	
(See also D34 for smaller decal, 1 Of 3)	150-200
Little Bo-Peep . . . . (Lustre) (D72) (J15)	150-200
Little Boy Blue (D111)	150-200
Little Jack Horner (D117)	150-200
There came a big spider . . . . . - # 2 in a series (D101)	150-200
Little Polly Flinders . . . . (D71) (J14)	150-200
Little Red Riding Hood (D110)	150-200
Photographer (D114) (J16)	150-200
Playing Doctor - Soup Shape (D99)	150-200
Portraits of Two Children (D14)	150-200
Pussy Cat, Pussy Cat, where have . . . . (D94)	150-200
Pussy Cat, Pussy Cat, where have . . . . (Holdfast) (D88)	150-200
Reading (D116)	150-200
Regatta (D26)	150-200
Ride A Cock Horse (D90)	150-200
Ride in a Motorcar (D45)	150-200
Riding the Dog (D108)	150-200
Round Dance (D43)	150-200
Round Dance in the Garden (D77)	150-200
Sheriff Dog (D84)	150-200
Silhouette of a Girl Feeding a Lamb - 7.5 in. (D19)	150-200
Silhouette of a Girl Feeding a Lamb - 7.75 in. (D30)	150-200
Sitting Scottie (D85)	100-150
Stork - Carnival Glass (G11)	150-200
Sunbonnet Kids at Work (D98)	150-200
Sunbonnet Kids - National - I Love You (C79)	100-150
Sunbonnet Kids - National - T 4 2 or Tea For Two (C81)	100-150
Sunbonnet Kids - National - The Three of Us (C80)	100-150
Tea Party (D107)	150-200
There was an Old Woman . . . . (D67)	150-200
This is the cat that killed the rat . . . . (D24)	150-200
This is the cow with the crumpled horn . . . . (D74)	150-200
This little duck is out of luck . . . . (D120)	150-200
Three Children and a Goat (D17) (J12)	150-200
Three Dutch Children at the Seaside (D27)	150-200
Toddler and his Spoon (D69)	150-200
Toddler Reaching for a Pretzel (D58)	150-200
Tom, Tom, the Piper's Son . . . . (D79)	150-200
Tom, Tom, the Piper's Son . . . . (variation of D79) (D80)	150-200

Tortoise and the Hare (D65)	150-200
Two Children and a Cat (D37)	150-200
Two on a See-Saw (D113)	150-200

Double Alphabet Rims

Bird at its Nest (E5)	200-250
Blowing Bubbles (E7)	200-250
Farm Femme with Cow - 7.37 in. (E3) (O7) (N16)	200-250
Girl Feeding Chicks (E4)	200-250
Windmill at the Bridge (E6)	200-250

Farm Scenes (See farm scenes also in Children and Animals)

Corn is Taken Home (N5)	150-175
Cottage Girl (N18)	150-175
Family Feeding the Fowl (N13)	150-175
Farm Femme and her Cows (N15)	150-175
Farm Femme and her Sheep (N17)	150-175
Farm Femme Feeding the Chickens (N14)	150-175
Farm Femme with Cow - 7.37 in. (E3) (O7) (N16)	200-250
Field of Wheat (N2)	150-175
Gathering Cotton (A13) (V32) (V34)	250+
Gathering Grapes - Handwritten Caption (V33) (V35)	250+
Gleaners (N6)	150-175
Going to Market - J. & G. Meakin (N9)	150-175
Going to Market - (N10)	150-175
Harvest Home (N8)	150-175
Landowner Overseeing the Hay Wagon (N7)	150-175
Loading Straw onto the Donkey (N11)	150-175
Ploughing - J. & G. Meakin (N3)	150-175
Ploughing - T. & H. (N4)	150-175
Rest on the Hay (N12)	150-175
Seed in the Ground (N1)	150-175

Fishing

Angling (N130)	175-225
Father and Son Fishing (N129)	175-225
Fishing Elephant (E122)	175-225
Harry Baiting Is his Line (N128)	175-225
Fishing - G/Z - A through F to be found on matching cup (O16)	75-100

Flatware (See listings in "F Is for Flatware") listed

Franklin's Maxims

Constant dropping wears/Little strokes fall . . . . -	
Deep Dish (R77)	250-300
Constant droppings/And Little Strokes Fall . . . . (V41)	250-300
Dost thou love life/There will be . . . . (R72)	250-300
DR Franklin: It is hard for an empty bag . . . . (R88)	250-300
DR. Franklin's Maxim's:	
By diligence and/Diligence is the mother . . . . (R78)	250-300
DR. Franklin's Maxim's -	
Employ time/One day is/Since thou art . . . . (R75)	250-300
DR. Franklin's Maxim's:	
Industry needs not/There are no gains . . . . (R81)	250-300
DR. Franklin's Maxim's:	
Plow deep while/Work today for you . . . . (R98)	250-300
DR. Franklin's Maxim's:	
Want of care/For want of a . . . . - 7.25 in. (R70)	250-300

Employ time/God gives all things . . . . - 6.12 in. (R94)	250-300
Employ time/God gives all things . . . . - 7.37 in. (R95)	250-300
Employ time/Since thou art . . . . (R76)	250-300
Experience keeps a dear/But fools will learn . . . . - 6 in. (R82)	250-300
Experience keeps a dear/But fools will learn . . . . - 8.12 in. (R83)	250-300
Eye of the master . . . . (R87)	250-300
For Age and Want . . . . - Concludes, "lasts a whole day." (V39)	250-300
For Age and Want . . . . - Concludes, "lasts all the day." (V38)	250-300
Franklin's ProvBS: He that by the plough . . . . (R96)	250-300
Franklin's ProvBS:	
Three removes/A rolling stone . . . . - 6 in. (R86)	250-300
Franklin's ProvBS:	
Three removes/A rolling stone . . . . - 7 in. (R84)	250-300
Franklin's ProvBS:	
Three removes/A rolling stone . . . . - 8.12 in. (R85)	250-300
Franklin's Proverbs: Keep thy shop . . . . (V36)	250-300
Franklin's Proverbs: Make hay while the . . . . (R93)	250-300
Franklin's Proverbs: Silks and satins . . . . (R91)	250-300
He that hath a trade/At the working/	
Industry pays debts . . . . (R64)	250-300
He that hath a trade/Industry pays debts . . . . (R65)	250-300
If you would know the value/	
Creditors have better . . . - 6.25 in. (R79)	250-300
If you would know the value/	
Creditors have better . . . . - 8.5 in. (R80)	250-300
Keep thy shop . . . . - Graphic only (V37)	250-300
Little strokes fell . . . . (V40)	250-300
Not to oversee workmen is to leave . . . . (R90)	250-300
Now I have a cow and/Fly pleasure and . . . . (R67)	250-300
Plough deep while . . . . (R97)	250-300
Poor Richard's Maxim's:	
Fly pleasure/Now I have a sheep and . . . . (R68)	250-300
Poor Richard's Maxim's:	
He who saves not/A fat kitchen makes/Would you . . . . R74)	250-300
Poor Richard's Way to Wealth: Fly pleasures/	
The diligent spinner . . . . (R89)	250-300
Sloth like rust/God helps them that/Lost time is never . . . . (R62)	250-300
There are no gains/Then help hands for . . . . (R92)	250-300
Three removes/A rolling stone . . . . (R73)	250-300
Want of care/For want of a . . . . - 7.5 in. (R71)	250-300

Glassware

A through Z Mug (Christmas) (G6)	175-250
Bouquet (G10)	125-175
Christmas Eve (G45)	250-300
Clock Face (G16)	75-100
Clock Face - Days/Months/Alphabet (G39)	75-100
Clock Face - Key Edge (G12)	75-100
Dog at a Palm Tree (G15)	125-150
Ducks (or Doves) (G26)	125-150
Eight Pointed Star (G44)	75-100
Emblem of the United States of America (G4)	150-200
Emma (or Emmas) (G29)	200-250
Emma (or Emmas) - Detail of Trade Mark (G30)	200-250
Garfield, President James Abram (G17)	125-150
Hen and her Chicks - (G20)	100-125
Hen and her Chicks with Frosting (G21)	100-125
Ice Cream ABC Dishes - Round Plates - Six (G38) Price each	125-150
Ice Cream Dishes - Full Set (G38)	900+
Ice Cream Platter - Non ABC (G38)	150-200

Independence Hall, Philadelphia (G5)	150-200
Little Bo-Peep - Clear Yellow (V23)	125-175
Little Bo-Peep - Frosted - Blue Floor (V21)	125-175
Little Bo-Peep - Frosted Blue Rim(V22)	125-175
Milk Glass - Dutch Girl (G2)	50-75
Milk Glass - Plain alphabet (G1)	50-75
Milk Glass - Raised Colored Bird (G3)	150-200
Milk Glass - Santa Claus - Not Shown	150-200
Plain Star - (G33)	75-100
Plain Star - Vaseline (G34)	75-100
Plain Star - Vaseline - Detail of Trade Mark (G35)	75-100
Plain Star - Vaseline - View in Black Light (G36)	75-100
Platonite Bowls and Mugs (G37)	20-40
Repeated Design of Hexagrams (G43)	75-100
Repeated Design of Impressed Pyramid Shapes w/ Swags (G42)	75-100
Repeated Wave Design (G40)	75-100
Repeated Wave Design - Amber (G41)	75-100
Rover - Detail of Higby Bee Trademark on Rover (G31)	125-150
Rover - Detail of Smithsonian Institute	
Trade Mark on Rover (G32)	125-150
Running Deer (G8)	125-175
Running Rabbit (G23)	125-150
Sancho Panza and Dapple (G9)	125-175
Sitting Dog (G22)	100-125
Stork - Carnival Glass Deep Dish (G11)	150-200
Stork Standing (G24)	125-150
Stork Standing with Raised Leg (G25)	125-150
Thousand (1000) Eyes pattern (G7)	125-175
Three Riding in an Elephant's Howdah (G13)	125-150
Tumbler - Hubert at the Carnival - Mr. Peanut (G46)	10-16
Tumbler/s - Alphabet Animals (G48)	10-16

Hollowware in chapters other than "H Is for Hollowware"

Chapter C - Tea Cup and Saucer -	
High School/West Aurora, Illinois (C48)	150-200
Chapter D - Mug matching Deep Dishes D60 and D62 (D63)	65-80
Chapter G - Alphabet Mug (Christmas) (G6)	175-250
Chapter K - R is for Rendezvous (K17) (K18)	200-250
Chapter K - Tea Cup (Kewpie) (K6)	175-225
Chapter K - V/W/X Whipping (K19)	200-250
Chapter L - For a Good Girl (L8)	500+
Chapter L - Historical Scripture Alphabet Series -	
G was Goliath (L5)	350+
Chapter L - Historical Scripture Alphabet Series -	
K was the King (L6)	350+
Chapter L - Historical Scripture Alphabet Series -	
W was the Water (L7)	350+
Chapter L - Pink Lustre Cup and Saucer - French (L21)	125-175
Chapter L - Pink Lustre Cup and Saucer - German (L20)	100-125
Chapter M - Mixed Metal - A Good Girl (M96)	250-350+
Chapter M - Mixed Metal - For a Good Boy (M95)	250-350+
Chapter M - Mixed Metal - Four Line Stamping (M99)	250-300
Chapter M - Mixed Metal - Painted Finish (M97)	250-300
Chapter M - Mixed Metal - Three Line Stamping (M98)	250-300
Chapter M - Silver Plate (M100)	75-125
Chapter M - Silver Plate - Elephants, #470 (M103)	75-125
Chapter M - Sterling - Bing Crosby Family Heirloom (M104)	200+
Chapter O - Gothic Cup - A through L (O17)	75-100
Chapter S - Hollowware is included throughout listings of Sets.	listed
Chapter U - A through Z Ravilious Edition (U42) (U43)	75-100
Chapter V - Yellow Dogs - No 2nd Dog (V43)	200-250

Chapter V - Yellow Dogs - No 4th Dog (V42)   200-250

Hollowware in "H Is for Hollowware" (See Pitchers listed in Sets)

A/L - Gothic Letters (O17)   75-100
A/M at the rim and N-Z at the base - Three scenes (H125) 175-225
A/U - Portraits (H137)   100-150
A/Z - Alphabet in three Rows - Decorated Handle (H128)   250+
A/Z - Alphabet in a Cartouche (H134)   200-250
A/Z - Circus Rider - Alphabet Cast on Face (H135)   100-150
A/Z - Dog Chasing a Rabbit (H2)   200-250
A/Z - Elephants Serving Tea -
    Alphabet Cast on Rim and Face (H136)   100-150
A/Z - Farm House Scene (H130)   200-250
A/Z - Hummingbird (?) (H133)   175-225
A/Z - Kingfisher (H14)   250+
A/Z - Long-Billed Bird (H131)   175-225
A/Z - Manual Alphabet (H138)   500+
A/Z - Musicians - Decorated Handle (H129)   200-250
A/Z - Pet Lamb - Alphabet Cast on Rim (H126)   250+
A/Z - Rooster and Goat (H3)   200-250
A/Z - Samuel - Alphabet cast on rim (H106)   250+
A/Z - Slow Rolls the Churn (H127)   250+
A/Z - Who Killed Cock-Robin? (H132)   175-225
A/Z - Cats and Books (H13)   250+
A/Z Brownhills - Children on a Raft (blurred transfer) (H10) 250+
A/Z Brownhills - Coastal Scene (H4)   250+
A/Z Brownhills - Copenhagen (H11)   250+
A/Z Brownhills - Fishermen Carrying Nets (H6)   250+
A/Z Brownhills - Fishermen Emptying Fish Basket (H7)   250+
A/Z Brownhills - Greek Port Scene (H5)   250+
A/Z Brownhills - Little Jack Horner (H12)   250+
A/Z Brownhills - Rowboat at the Water's Edge (H8)   250+
A/Z Brownhills - Fishermen Boarding a Small Boat (H9)   250+
A/B - Animals/Bear (H107)   175-225
A/B - Apple/Ball (H24)   250+
A/B - Apple/Ball (with verbiage) (H43)   250+
A/B - Apple/Ball (with verbiage) (wavy rim) (H44)   250+
Alphabet of Virtues - A/B - Adoration/Benevolence (H51)   250+
Alphabet of Virtues - C - Charity (H53)   250+
Alphabet of Virtues - C/D - Charity/Devotion - Ht 2.62 in. (H54) 250+
Alphabet of Virtues - C/D - Charity/Devotion - Ht 2.75 in. (H55) 250+
Alphabet of Virtues - E - Economy (H57)   250+
Alphabet of Virtues - E/F - (Graphic error) Gratitude/Faith (H58) 250+
Alphabet of Virtues - E/G - Economy/Gratitude (H60)   250+
Alphabet of Virtues - H/I - Hope/Industry (H62)   250+
Alphabet of Virtues - I/J - Industry/Justice (H63)   250+
Alphabet of Virtues - K/L - Kindness/Love (H65)   250+
Alphabet of Virtues - M/N - Modesty/Noblemindedness (H67) 250+
Alphabet of Virtues - O/P - Obedience/Politeness (H69)   250+
Alphabet of Virtues - Q/R - Quietness/Repentance (H71)   250+
Alphabet of Virtues - S/T - Sobriety/Truth (H73)   250+
Alphabet of Virtues - U/V - Uprightness/Veneration (H75) 250+
Alphabet of Virtues - W/X - Wisdom/Letter Seldom Used (H77) 250+
Alphabet of Virtues - Y/Z - Yearn/Zeal (H79)   250+
B/C - Buffalo/Cat (H110)   250+
C/D - C Was a Captain/D Was a Drover (H87)   250+
C/D - C Was a Captain/D Was a Drunkard (H80)   250+
C/D - C Was a Councell_r/D Was a Drovier (H113)   250+
C/D - Cat/Dash (with verbiage) (H45)   250+
C/D - Cat/Dog (H108)   175-225
D - D is the Driver (H91)   300+

D/E/F - Flower Seller (H94)   200-250
E - E Stands for Elephant (H124)   200-250
E/F - E Was an Esquire/F Was a Farmer (H81)   250+
E/F - Elephant/Fox (with verbiage) (H46)   250+
E/F - Elephant/Fox - Height 2.62 in. (H25)   250+
E/F - Elephant/Fox - Height 2.75 in. (H26)   250+
F - F Was a Fiddler (H89)   250+
F - Fox - Simplification of Source Design (H27)   250+
G - G Is the Guard (H92)   300+
G/H - G for Goose/H for Horse (H123)   250+
G/H - G Was a Gamester/H Was a Hunter (H114)   250+
G/H - G Was a Gamester/H Was a Hunter
    (variation of H114) (H82)   250+
G/H - Goose/Horse (H28)   250+
G/H - Goose/Horse (with verbiage) (H47)   250+
G/H/I - At Tennis (H96)   200-250
G/H/I - Trap Bat & Ball (H95)   300+
G/S - Goose. Stork (H111)   250+
H - Horse. House. Hound. Horn. (H116)   250+
I/J - Infant/Jam (H29)   250+
J/K/L - For my Nephew (H97)   200-250
K/L - Kitten/Ladder (with verbiage) (H48)   250+
K/L - K Was a Knight/L Was a Lamplighter (H90)   250+
L/M - Lion/Mouse (H1)   200-250
L/R - Ladder/Rabbit (H30)   250+
M - Mil-ler Mill Mouse (H117)   250+
M/N/O - Whip Top (H98)   200-250
N - Nest- Simplification of Source Design (H31)   250+
N/O - N Was a Nobleman/O Was an Oystergirl (H83)   250+
O/P - O Is for Obadia/P Is for Peter (H104)   250+
O/P - Otter/Pig (H109)   175-225
P - Pug the Page (H122)   250+
P/H - Parrot/Horse (H32)   250+
P/Q - P Was a Parson/Q Was a Queen (H84)   250+
P/Q/R - Playing Hoops (H99)   200-250
P/Q/R - Pulling a Wagon (H100)   200-250
Q - Q the Queen. God bless Her. (H118)   400+
Q - Quail - Simplification of Source Design (H33)   250+
Q/R - Q Is the Queen/R Is for Ruth (H105)   250+
Q/R - Q Was a Quaker/R A Sly Ratcatcher (H121)   250+
Q/W - Queen Victoria/Wagon (H34)   400+
S - Silverlocks (H119)   250+
S/D - Stag/Dog (H112)   250+
S/T - Snail/Tiger (H35)   250+
S/T/U - Windmill (H101)   200-250
T - Four Masters/Tortoiseshell (H120)   250+
T - T Is the Tunnel (H93)   300+
T/V - T Was a Tinker/V Was a Vintner (H85)   250+
U - Uncle (H37)   250+
U/V - Uncle/Vulture (H36)   250+
V - Vulture (H38)   250+
V/W/X - Cricket (H102)   200-250
W - Wagon (H40)   250+
W/X - W Was a Watchman/X Was Expensive (H86)   250+
W/X - W Was a Watchman/X Was Expensive
    (Alternate Design of H86) (H115)   250+
W/X - Windmill/X Legged Table (H39)   250+
X - X Legged Table (H41)   250+
Y/Z - Y Was a Yeoman/Z Is a Zany (H88)   250+
Y/Z - Youth/Zebra (H42)   250+
Y/Z/& - Ice Skating (H103)   200-250

Horses

Drive (N48)	150-200
New Pony (I54)	150-200
Pony (I55)	150-200
Ride by the Sea (N46) (O14)	150-200
Rider with a Dog (N47)	150-200
Running Horse (N43)	150-200
Stable Yard (N44)	150-200
Walk (N45)	150-200

HOTEL (Manufactured by Harker and National China, East Liverpool, Ohio)

Baby Bunting and Bunch Went Out for a Walk- Harker look-alike (Brunt) (C54)	75-125
Baby Bunting and Bunch While Crossing a Log - Harker (C52)	75-125
Baby Bunting Lifts his Hat - Harker (C51)	75-125
Baby Bunting Runs Away - Harker - Not Shown	75-125
Campbell's Kids - Girl Holding Doll - Harker (C58)	100-150
Combat - National (N111)	75-125
Death - National (N113)	75-125
Dogs at the Doghouse - Harker (C65)	75-125
Dutch Children at the Seaside - Harker (C56)	75-125
Dutch Mother with Baby in Cradle - Harker - Not Shown	75-125
English Pointer - Harker (C63)	75-125
Great Expectations - Harker (C72)	75-125
Greyhound - Harker (C64)	75-125
Hen and her Chicks - Harker - Not Shown	75-125
Horse - Harker (C68)	75-125
Horse, Dog and Pups - Harker (C67)	75-125
Horses - Other Harker portraits bridled and unbridled not shown, price each	75-125
"It iss mutch better yet to shmile . . . ." - Harker (C55)	75-125
Kitten - Harker (C62)	75-125
Lions - Harker (C69)	75-125
Little Miss Muffet - Harker - Not Shown	75-125
Memories - Harker (C61)	75-125
Owl - Harker (C71)	75-125
Robin - Harker (C70)	75-125
Sunbonnet Kids - Harker - Candy for my Mandy (C75)	100-150
Sunbonnet Kids - Harker - Getting Acquainted - Not Shown	100-150
Sunbonnet Kids - Harker - I love you (C73).	100-150
Sunbonnet Kids - Harker - Kiss and Make Up (C76)	100-150
Sunbonnet Kids - Harker - Three of Us (C74)	100-150
Sunbonnet Kids - National - Deep Dish - I Love You (C79)	100-150
Sunbonnet Kids - National - Deep Dish - T 4 2 (Tea for Two) (C81)	100-150
Sunbonnet Kids - National - Deep Dish - Three of Us (C80)	100-150
Their First Day - Harker (C66)	75-125
There Came a Big Spider - Harker (C57)	75-125
This Little Duck is Out of Luck - Crown Hotel China (D120)	150-200
Tom, He was a Piper's Son - Harker - Not Shown	75-125
Tulips - Harker (C50)	75-125
Two Children on a Sled - Harker (C60)	75-125
Washing the Dog - Harker (C59)	75-125

Humor

Bull Comes Too Close (N34)	150-200
Diamond Series - Fisherman Trips on a Rope (N25)	150-200
Diamond Series - Fisherman's Hat is Blown Off (N24)	150-200

Diamond Series - Horse Returns Alone (N29)	150-200
Diamond Series - Horses for Hire (N27)	150-200
Diamond Series - Mounting (N26)	150-200
Diamond Series - Throwing the Rider (N28)	150-200
Dogs Stealing Food (N105)	150-200
Falling into the Hay (N33)	150-200
First Sitting (N107)	150-200
Fisherman Loses his Hat (N32)	150-200
Itinerant Musician (N108)	150-200
Leo Lion in the Fox's Barber Chair - Plate/Pitcher listed in Sets (S12)	listed
Monkey School for Donkeys (E112)	150-200
Rider Sitting in the Mud (N30)	150-200
Rider Walking in the Mud (N31)	150-200
Shave for a Penny (N106)	150-200
Stag Comes Too Close (N36)	150-200
Symptoms of Walking Made Easy (K12)	150-200
Timely Rescue (N35)	150-200
Who are you? (N109)	150-200

Hunting

At the Fox Hunt - 7.5 in. (V44)	150-200
At the Fox Hunt - Photo Detail (V45)	150-200
Buffalo Hunt (N39)	150-200
Chasing the Stag (N38)	150-200
Fox Hunt (V29)	150-200
Fox Hunt - Captioned (V28)	150-200
Hunting on Elephants for Leopards (N41)	200-250
Killing the Seals (N40)	150-200
Scottish Hunters (N23)	150-200
Shooting Quail (N20)	150-200
Showing the Kill (N22)	150-200
Stag Comes Too Close (N36)	150-200
Three Men and Two Dogs (N19)	150-200
Timely Rescue (N35)	150-200
Two Riders and Two Hounds (N21)	150-200
Wild Horse Hunt (N37)	150-200
Zebra Hunt (V31)	150-200
Zebra Hunt - Captioned (V30)	150-200

J - The Missing Letter (Last Letter of the Alphabet)

Blind Man's Buff (J6)	100-150
Bouquet (J11)	100-150
Buster Brown Pouring Tea (J3)	100-150
Cat in the Cradle (D51) (J13)	150-200
Flowering Plants - Majolica - Missing Letter (J1)	350+
Gnomes (J4)	100-150
Gnomes - Variant - Not Shown	100-150
Little Bo-Peep - Lustre (D72)	150-200
Little Polly Flinders, Lustre (D71) (J14)	150-200
Photographer (D114) (J16)	150-200
Pluto - The Pup and Mickey Mouse - Reversed I and J (C87) (J2) (Z6)	500+
Ring-a-Ring-a-Rosie (J7)	100-150
Tea Party for Cats and Kittens (J5)	100-150
Three Children and a Goat (D17) (J12)	150-200
Three Girls under One Umbrella (J9)	100-150
Three Girls With Fans (J10)	100-150
Training the Dog (J8)	100-150

Kewpies

Dresden- Three Kewpies - Deep Dish (K10)	150-200
Holdfast - One Kewpie Running - Deep Dish (K8)	150-200
Holdfast - One Kewpie Standing - Deep Dish (K7)	150-200
Rose O'Neill - Five Kewpies - Deep Dish (K4)	175-225
Rose O'Neill - Coordinating Tea Cup (K6)	175-225
Rose O'Neill - Three Kewpies (K3)	175-225
Rose O'Neill - Two Kewpies (K2)	175-225

Leaders - Political and Religious (See leaders of battle listed in Metal and War)

Flowers, Roswell Pettibone (C15)	100-150
Garfield, President James Abram (A36)	250+
Jordan, Reverend Richard (R14)	500+
Kossuth, Governor of Hungary - Mixed Metal (M62)	350+
Kossuth, General - Mixed Metal (M63)	350+
Lincoln, President Abraham (A30)	500+
Lincoln, Young President Abraham (A19)	500+
Mathew, Father Theobald (R20)	250+
Mathew, Father Theobald (M56)	350+
Peel, Sir Robert Bart (The Late) (N62)	500+
Penn, William (A3)	300+
Victoria & Albert, Portraits - Double Alphabet - Mixed Metal (M64)	400+
Victoria & Albert, Portraits - Floral Surround - Mixed Metal (M66)	400+
Victoria & Albert, Portraits - Mixed Metal (M65)	400+
Victoria & Prince Albert, Portraits - Mixed Metal (M67)	400+
Victoria, Queen, in Riding Habit (O18)	800+
Victoria, Queen (N65)	500+
Victoria, Queen - The Necklace (N64)	500+
Victoria, Queen - The Royal Favourite (N63)	500+
Wales, Prince/Princess of, in Carriage - Mixed Metal - 4.25 in. (M71)	400+
Wales, Prince/Princess of, In Carriage - Mixed Metal - 5.75 in. (M70)	400+
Wales, Prince/Princess of, Portraits - Mixed Metal (M69)	400+
Wales, Prince/Princess of, Portraits, Floral Surround - Mixed Metals (M68)	400+
Wales, Prince/Princess of, Married 10 March, 1863 (N66)	500+
Washington, George (A5)	500+
Washington, George - 6.12 in. (M58)	125-175
Washington, George - 5.62 in. (M59)	125-175

Literature - Adult Prose

Brownhills - Crusoe and his Pets (E78)	175-225
Brownhills - Crusoe at Work (E75)	175-225
Brownhills - Crusoe Finding the Footprints (E79)	175-225
Brownhills - Crusoe Making a Boat (blue) (V3)	175-225
Brownhills - Crusoe Making a Boat (V4) - Plate/Mug listed in Sets (S8)	175-225
Brownhills - Crusoe on the Raft (E73)	175-225
Brownhills - Crusoe Rescues Friday (E80)	175-225
Brownhills - Crusoe Teaching Friday- 6.37 in. (E81)	175-225
Brownhills - Crusoe Teaching Friday - 5.5 in. (E82)	175-225
Brownhills - Crusoe Viewing the Island (E76)	175-225
Grandville - Crusoe at his Tent (E77)	175-225
Grandville - Crusoe Milking the Goat (E74)	175-225
Paul and Virginia (N90)	175-225
Uncle Tom's Cabin - Vision of Uncle Tom (A18)	350+

Literature - Adult Poetry

But now your brow . . . . (Source: John Anderson My Joe/Burns) (I76)	300+
John Gilpin Pursued . . . . (Source : History of John Gilpin/Cowper) (N89)	300+
John Gilpin Starting . . . . (Source: History of John Gilpin/Cowper) (N87)	300+
From/Return Home (Source: History of John Gilpin/Cowper) - Lustre (L22)(Z4)	300+
Starting from London (Source: History of John Gilpin/Cowper) Not Shown	300+
Sire turns . . . . (Source: Cotter's Saturday/Burns) - 5.27 in. (I69)	300+
Sire turns . . . . (Source: Cotter's Saturday/Burns) - 6.5 in. (I70) (Z3)	300+
We kindly . . . . (Source: Cotter's Saturday/Burns) - 6.62 in. (I68)	300+
We kindly . . . . (Source: Cotter's Saturday/Burns) - 6.5 in. - Not Shown	300+

Literature - Children's Prose

Aesop's Fables - Cock and the Fox (E66)	200-250
Aesop's Fables - Dog and the Shadow (E58)	200-250
Aesop's Fables - Dog in the Manger (E61)	200-250
Aesop's Fables - Fox and the Goose (E59)	200-250
Aesop's Fables - Fox and the Grapes (E60)	200-250
Aesop's Fables - Fox and the Tiger (E65)	200-250
Aesop's Fables - Hare and the Tortoise (E64)	200-250
Aesop's Fables - Leopard and the Fox (E63)	300+
Aesop's Fables - Shepherd's Boy (E67)	300+
Aesop's Fables - Travellers (Old Spelling) and the Bear (E62)	200-250
Brownhills - Red Riding Hood and her . . . (E72)	200-250
Brownhills - Red Riding Hood Meets . . . (E70)	200-250
Brownhills - Red Riding Hood Starting (E69)	200-250
Brownhills Nursery Tales Series - Cinderella (E68)	200-250
Poggius Fable - The Man, the Boy and the Donkey - Scene One (E56)	175-225
Poggius Fable - The Man, the Boy and the Donkey - Scene Two (E57)	175-225
R - Red Riding Hood Meets the Wolf (E71)	275-325
Sunbonnet Kids - At Work (D98)	150-200
Sunbonnet Kids - Candy for My Mandy (C75)	100-150
Sunbonnet Kids - Getting Acquainted - Not Shown	100-150
Sunbonnet Kids - I Love You (C79)	100-150
Sunbonnet Kids - Kiss and Make Up (C76)	100-150
Sunbonnet Kids - T 4 2 or Tea For Two (C81)	100-150
Sunbonnet Kids - Three of Us (C80)	100-150

Literature - Children's Poetry (See listings in Deep Dishes)

Brownhills - Nursery Tales - Jack and Jill (E36)	200-250
Brownhills - Nursery Tales - Jack Horner (E38) - Plate/Mug listed in Sets (S7)	200-250
Brownhills - Nursery Tales - Old Mother Hubbard (E55)	200-250
Ding, Dong, Bell (E39)	225-275
DING, Dong, bell! . . . . - Dutch Scene - 6.62 in. (E40)	175-200
I'm Going a Milking . . . . (E48)	225-275
Little Bo-Peep - Scene One - Calling For her Sheep (E42)	225-275
Little Bo-Peep - Scene Three - Finding her Sheep (E43)	225-275
Little Bo-Peep - Scene Two - Running After her Sheep (E41)	225-275
Little Jack Horner (E37)	225-275
Little Miss Muffet (E46)	225-275

Nursery Rhyme Series - Hey Diddle Diddle (E45)	225-275
Nursery Rhyme Series - There Was a Crooked Man (E53)	225-275
Nursery Rhyme Series -Goosey, Goosey Gander (E51)	225-275
Old Mother Hubbard (E54)	225-275
See-Saw, Margery Daw . . . . (E52)	225-275
Simple Simon (E47)	225-275
This Is the Maiden - Fruit Shape (E44)	225-275
This Little Pig Went to Market (E50)	225-275
Tom, Tom the Piper's Son - 6.12 in. (T59)	225-275
Tom, Tom the Piper's Son - 7.75 in. (E49)	225-275

Lustre

Blue Lustre Border - Congressional Library - Washington, D. C. (C13)	150-200
Blue Lustre Border - Cup/Saucer - High School, West Aurora, Illinois (C48)	150-200
Blue Lustre Border - Flowers, Roswell P./Statue - Watertown, New York (C15)	100-150
Blue Lustre Border - Lincoln Monument - Springfield, Illinois - Not Shown	150-200
Blue Lustre Border - One Rooster and Two Hens (L10)	75-125
Blue Lustre Border - Post Office - Concord, New Hampshire (C16)	100-150
Blue Lustre Border - Union Station - Omaha, Nebraska (C14)	100-150
Deep Dish - Little Bo-Peep, Yellow Lustre (D72) (J15)	150-200
Deep Dish - Little Polly Flinders, Golden-Orange Lustre (D71) (J14)	150-200
Hollowware - Cup/Saucer - French Pink Lustre (L21)	125-175
Hollowware - Cup/Saucer - German Pink Lustre (L20)	100-125
Hollowware - Historical Scripture Alphabet - G/Goliath - Pink Lustre (L5)	350+
Hollowware - Historical Scripture Alphabet - K/King - Pink Lustre (L6)	350+
Hollowware - Historical Scripture Alphabet - W/Water - Pink Lustre (L7)	350+
Hollowware - Purple Lustre Rim - For a Good Girl - Creamware (L8)	500+
Orange Lustre Border - Diverting History of John Gilpin/Cowper (Z4) (L22)	300+
Pink Lustre Border - Children and a Dog, One Riding (L13)	75-125
Pink Lustre Border - Dutch Woman and Child (L16)	75-125
Pink Lustre Border - One Rooster and Two Hens (L9)	75-125
Pink Lustre Border - Round Dance (L12)	75-125
Pink Lustre Border - RS Style Portrait, Purple Petals (L17)	100-150
Pink Lustre Border - RS Style Portrait, Red Hair (L19)	100-150
Pink Lustre Border - RS Style Portrait, White Petals (L18)	100-150
Pink Lustre Border - See-Saw (L14)	75-125
Pink Lustre Border - Three Dutch Children (L15)	75-125
Pink Lustre Border - Two Roosters (L11)	75-125
Pink Lustre Paint - Cottage Design 1 - Flat Roof (L2)	200-250
Pink Lustre Paint - Cottage Design 2 - Flat Roof (L3)	200-250
Pink Lustre Paint - Cottage Design Peaked Roof - Drawn (L1)	200-250
Purple Lustre Border - Girl Teaching her Dog (L4)	200-250

Majolica

Flowering Plants - No Letter I (J1)	350+
Horseman in Armor - Not shown	350+

Mathematics

Decimals (E88)	300+
Interest (E87)	300+
Lecture on Long/Dry Measure - 7 in. (E85)	300+
Lecture on Long/Dry Measure - 8 in. (E86)	300+
Rule of Three (E83)	300+
Sum Total (E84)	300+

Metalware in Chapters other than "M Is for Metal" (See Flatware)

Chapter C - Lava Soap - Here we go Round . . . . Chromolithography (C37)	150-175
Chapter C - Lava Soap - Monkey on a Barrel - Chromolithography (C38)	150-175
Chapter C - Lava Soap - Playing at Driving Horses - Chromolithography (C36)	150-175
Chapter C - Lava Soap - Sailing Ship - Chromolithography (C40)	150-175
Chapter C - Lava Soap - Tom, Tom . . . . - Chromolithography (C39)	150-175
Chapter F - Flatware/Napkin Ring Designs in " F Is for Flatware."	listed
Chapter O - Miniature Pie Plate - Mixed Metal (M82) (O4)	200-250
Chapter O - Incomplete Alphabet - A/Q (M91) (O11)	150-200
Chapter O - Incomplete Alphabet - A/V (M90) (O12)	150-200
Chapter Z - Liberty with Reversal (Z7)	200-250
Chapter Z - Detail of Reversal (Z8)	200-250
Chapter Z - Liberty with Corrected Typeset (M94) (Z9)	200-250
Chapter Z - Detail of Corrected Graphics (Z10)	200-250
Chapter Z - Man on a Horse - Detail of reversed "Z" (Z5) (M93)	300+

Metalware in "M Is for Metal"

A/Z Block Border Design Mixed Metal (M34)	125-175
A/Z Border - Mixed Metal (M21)	50-100
A/Z Border - Mixed Metal (M22)	50-100
A/Z Border - Reverse of M22 (M23)	50-100
A/Z Border Detail: Z/Six Pointed Star/A - Mixed Metal (M33)	50-100
A/Z Border Detail: Z/&/./A - Mixed Metal (M30)	50-100
A/Z Border Detail: Z/&/./A - Mixed Metal (M31)	50-100
A/Z Border Detail: Z/&/A - Mixed Metal (M24)	50-100
A/Z Border Detail: Z/&/A - Mixed Metal (M25)	50-100
A/Z Border Detail: Z/&/Five Pointed Star/A - Mixed Metal (M26)	50-100
A/Z Border Detail: Z/&/Five Pointed Star/A - Mixed Metal (M27)	50-100
A/Z Border Detail: Z/&/Horizontal Diamond/A - Mixed Metal (M29)	50-100
A/Z Border Detail: Z/&/Pointing Hand/A - Mixed Metal (M28)	50-100
A/Z Border Detail: Z/Five Pointed Star/A - Silver Plate (M32)	50-100
A/Z Flourishes and Figures - Quadruple Plate (M35)	125-175
Chromolithography - After Supper run a Mile - Mixed Metal (M77)	150-175
Chromolithography - Circular Design - Mixed Metal (M76)	75-125
Chromolithography - Ohio Art - Girl on a Swing - 3.5 in. (M73)	50-70
Chromolithography - Ohio Art - Girl on a Swing - 8.25 in. (M72)	50-70
Chromolithography - Ohio Art - Kittens - 4.25 in. (M74)	50-70
Chromolithography - Ohio Art - Kittens - 6.25 in. (M75)	50-70
Enamel - Clock Face (M12)	125-175
Enamel - Clock Face (M13)	125-175

Enamel - Clock Face (M14)	50-100
Enamel - Clock Face (M15)	125-175
Enamel - Map of the British Isles (M11)	200-250
Hollowware/A Good Girl - Chromolithography - Mixed Metal (M96)	250-350
Hollowware/Baby Cup, Crosby Family Heirloom - Sterling (M104)	200+
Hollowware/Elephants #470 - Silver Plate (M103)	75-125
Hollowware/For A Good Boy - Chromolithography - Mixed Metal (M95)	250-350+
Hollowware/Painted Finish - Mixed Metal (M97)	250-300
Hollowware/Baby Cup- Silver Plate (M100)	75-125
Hollowware/Stamping, Four Lines - Mixed Metal (M99)	250-300
Hollowware/Stamping, Three Lines - Mixed Metal (M98)	250-300
Iron - An Iron Horse (M46)	300-350
Iron - Crystal Palace - 2.12 in. (M54)	200-250
Iron - Grant, General U. (M60)	300+
Iron - Hey Diddle Diddle - Flat Edge (M39)	100-150
Iron - Jumbo (M18)	125-175
Iron - Who Killed Cock Robin? (M43)	100-150
Iron - Who Killed Cock Robin? - Painted and Dated (M42)	100-150
Iron - Who Killed Cock Robin? I said the Sparrow . . . . (M44)	175-225
Mixed Metal - Incomplete Alphabet - A/Q (M91) (O11)	150-200
Mixed Metal - Incomplete Alphabet - A/V (M90) (O12)	150-200
Mixed Metal - Baby's Head (M85)	400+
Mixed Metal - Brass Horse (M47)	300-350
Mixed Metal - Brownies (M45)	175-225
Mixed Metal - Campbell, Sir Colin (M57)	350+
Mixed Metal - Clock Face (M49)	100-150
Mixed Metal - Crystal Palace - 2.78 in. (M53)	200-250
Mixed Metal - Crystal Palace - Queen's Imprimatur - Iron 96.3% (M52)	200-250
Mixed Metal - Crystal Palace - Queen's Imprimatur - Iron 97.9% (M51)	200-250
Mixed Metal - Double Alphabet - Upper and Lower Case (M36)	150-200
Mixed Metal - American Eagle (M48)	350+
Mixed Metal - Girl and Boy with Hoop (M83)	175-225
Mixed Metal - Grant, Lt. General U. S. (M61)	300+
Mixed Metal - Grinding Old into Young (M92)	300+
Mixed Metal - Hey Diddle Diddle - Rolled Edge (M38)	100-150
Mixed Metal - Horse (M86)	300+
Mixed Metal - Jenny Lind (M20)	250-300
Mixed Metal - Kossuth, General (M63)	350+
Mixed Metal - Kossuth, Governor of Hungary (M62)	350+
Mixed Metal - Liberty (M94)	200-250
Mixed Metal - Lion (M84)	350+
Mixed Metal - Little Jack Horner (M37)	125-175
Mixed Metal - Man on a Horse (M93) (Z5)	300+
Mixed Metal - Mary Had a Little Lamb (M40)	100-150
Mixed Metal - Mathew, Father (M56)	350+
Mixed Metal - Miniature Pie Plate (M82) (O4)	200-250
Mixed Metal - New Crystal Palace at Sydenham (M55)	200-250
Mixed Metal - Rooster (M89)	300+
Mixed Metal - Souvenir of Niagara Falls (M50)	100-150
Mixed Metal - Tom Thumb (M19)	250-300
Mixed Metal - Victoria/Albert, Portraits - Double Alphabet (M64)	400+
Mixed Metal - Victoria/Albert, Portraits (M65)	400+
Mixed Metal - Victoria/Albert, Portraits - Floral Surround (M66)	400+
Mixed Metal - Victoria/Albert, Prince, Portraits (M67)	400+
Mixed Metal - Wales, Prince/Princess of, in a Carriage (M71)	400+
Mixed Metal - Wales, Prince/Princess of, in a Carriage 5.75 in. (M70)	400+

Mixed Metal - Wales, Prince/Princess of, Portraits (M69)	400+
Mixed Metal - Wales, Prince/Princess of, Portraits - Floral Surround (M68)	400+
Mixed Metal - Washington, George 6.12 in. (M58)	125-175
Mixed Metal - Washington, George 5.62 in. (M59)	125-175
Mixed Metal - While I Live, I'll Crow (M87)	350+
Mixed Metal with Tin - Rooster (M88)	300+
Silver Plate - Simple Simon (M41)	75-125
Tea Tray - Clock Dials (M10)	75-125
Tea Tray - Design Eight (M9)	75-125
Tea Tray - Design Five (M6)	75-125
Tea Tray - Design Four (M5)	75-125
Tea Tray - Design One (M2)	75-125
Tea Tray - Design Seven (M8)	75-125
Tea Tray - Design Six (M7)	75-125
Tea Tray - Design Three (M4)	75-125
Tea Tray - Design Two (M3)	75-125
Toys - ABC Bank (M78)	250+
Toys - Miniature Candlestick - Iron (M79)	250+
Toys - Rattle, Mixed Metal (M81)	150-200
Toys - Toy Table - Mixed Metal (M80)	400+

Months

Browne Series - Summers Sun . . . . . - January (E89)	175-225
Browne Series - Summers Sun . . . . . - February (E90)	175-225
Browne Series - Summers Sun . . . . . - March (E91)	175-225
Browne Series - Summers Sun . . . . . - May (E92)	175-225
Browne Series - Summers Sun . . . . . - June (E93)	175-225
Browne Series - Summers Sun . . . . . - August (E94)	175-225
Browne Series - Summers Sun . . . . . - September (E95)	175-225
Browne Series - Summers Sun . . . . . - October (E96)	175-225
Browne Series - Summers Sun . . . . . - November (E97)	175-225
February (E98)	175-225
April (E99)	175-225
May (E100)	175-225
July (E101)	175-225
August (E102)	175-225
October (E103)	175-225
December - 5.87 in. (E104)	175-225
December - 7 in. (E105)	175-225

Mugs/Cups and their values are listed in Hollowware

Nations and Their Peoples

Brownhills - Greek (T37)	200-250
Brownhills - Italian (T38)	200-250
Brownhills - Japanese (T39)	200-250
Brownhills - Russian (T41)	200-250
Brownhills - Turk (T43)	200-250
Brownhills - Venetian (T44)	200-250
Brownhills - Wallachian (T45)	200-250
China - Chinese Boy (E109)	175-225
China - Chinese Gentleman (E107)	175-225
China - Chinese Girl (E108)	175-225
China - Chinese Lady (E106)	175-225
China - Chinese Villa (E111)	175-225
China - Three Chinese Figures (E110)	175-225
Holland - Deep Dish - Dutch Boy and Girl Making a Wreath (D42)	150-200
Holland - Deep Dish - Dutch Girl with a Basket (D32)	150-200

Holland - Deep Dish -
    Three Dutch Children at the Seaside (D27)   150-200
Holland - DING, Dong, bell! - Dutch Scene - (E40)   175-200
Holland - Dutch Boys - "It iss mutch better yet to
    shmile . . . ." (C55)   75-125
Holland - Dutch Children at the Seaside - Harker (C56) 75-125
Holland - Dutch Girl - Milk Glass (G2)   50-75
Holland - Dutch Language - Op Uw Geboortedag (E174)   200-250
Holland - Manual alphabet -
    Two Children Fearful of the Goose (E152)   300+
Holland - Manual alphabet on inner rim -
    Three Dutch Children (E153)   300+
Holland - Pink Lustre Border - Dutch Woman and Child (L16) 75-125
Holland - Pink Lustre Border - Three Dutch Children (L15)   75-125

Nineteenth Century - Milestones of Industrialization

Crystal Palace (N68)   200-250
Crystal Palace - Iron - 2.12 in. (M54)   200-250
Crystal Palace - Mixed Metal - 2.78 in. (M53)   200-250
Crystal Palace, Queen's Imprimatur -
    Iron 96.3% - 4.25 in. (M52)   200-250
Crystal Palace, Queen's Imprimatur -
    Iron 97.9% - 4.25 in. (M51)   200-250
New Crystal Palace at Sydenham - Mixed Metal (M55)   200-250
Penny Post (N67)   200-250
Thames Tunnel (N84)   200-250
The Great Eastern Paying Out the Cable (N85)   200-250

Occupations (See varied occupations listed in Hollowware)

Baked Taters All Hot - 7 in. (V12)   175-225
Baked Taters All Hot - 8.5 in. (V11)   175-225
Baker (N59)   175-225
Baker - One of a Series (N60)   175-225
Blacksmith, Village (N56)   175-225
Chairs to Mend (N57)   175-225
Diamond Series - The Artist Annoyed (N55)   175-225
Gathering Cotton (A13) (V32) (V34)   250+
Gathering Grapes - Handwritten Title (V33) (V35)   250+
Hold Your Hand Out - Teacher - 5 in. (V10)   175-225
Hold Your Hand Out - Teacher - 8.25 in. (V9)   175-225
Laundresses at the River Bank (N53)   175-225
London Dog Seller (N110)   175-225
Newsie - 8 in. (T23)   275-325
Newsie - 6 in. (N86)   275-325
Thrasher (N58)   175-225
What will you buy, my little dear? - The Bread Seller (N61) 175-225
Widow Green Wiping the Kitchen Table (T4)   175-225

Ornamental Borders with Letter Sequence Variances

Added Letters - Deep Dish with Inserted Letters to
    Fill a Space (O13) (D37)   150-200
Irregularly Set Letters - Large Green Letters - (O15) (S13) 75-125
Missing Letter - Buster Brown Pouring Tea - Missing J (J3)   100-150
Missing Letter - Cat in the Cradle - Missing J (D51) (J13)   150-200
Missing Letter - Flowering Plants - Majolica -
    Missing Letter I (J1)   350+
Missing Letter - Gnomes - Missing J (J4)   100-150
Missing Letter - Little Bo-Peep - Lustre - Missing J (D72) (J15) 150-200
Missing Letter - Photographer - Missing J (D114) (J16)   150-200

Missing Letter - Polly Flinders - Lustre - Missing J (D71) (J14) 150-200
Missing Letter - Three Children and a Goat -
    Missing J (D17) (J12)   150-200
Missing Letters - A/Q - Mixed Metal (M91) (O11)   150-200
Missing Letters - A/V - Mixed Metal (M90) (O12)   150-200
Missing Letters - Blind Man's Buff - Missing J, X, and Y (J6) 100-150
Missing Letters - Bouquet - Missing J, X and Y (J11)   100-150
Missing Letters - Fishing - G/Z (O16)
    A/F yet to be found on matching cup   75-100
Missing Letters - Gothic Cup - A/L (O17)
    M/Z yet to be found on saucer   75-100
Missing Letters - Ring-a-Ring-a-Rosie - Missing J, X, and Y (J7) 100-150
Missing Letters - Tea Party for Cats and Kittens -
    Missing J, X, and Y (J5)   100-150
Missing Letters - Three Girls under One Umbrella -
    Missing J, X, and Y (J9)   100-150
Missing Letters - Three Girls With Fans -
    Missing J, X, and Y (J10)   100-150
Missing Letters - Training the Dog - Missing J, X, and Y (J8) 100-150
Reversed Letters - Pluto - The Pup and Mickey Mouse -
    H-J-I-K- (C87) (J2) (Z6)   500+

Pearlware

Frolics of Youth - The Young Artist (V5)   350+
Singing the Scale (N92) (O6)   350+
Small hand-painted red petaled flower (Dedication)   350+
Watch the bent of his inclinations . . . . (R100)   350+

Performing Arts

Dance - Ballet Dance (N94)   175-225
Dance - Highland Dancers (N95)   175-225
Dance - Round Dance (N96)   175-225
Dance - Round Dance - Lustre (L12)   75-125
Dance - Two Girls with Fans - Fruit Shape (N93)   175-225
Instrument/s - At the Piano (N91)   175-225
Instrument/s - Boy with a Banjo (N99)   175-225
Instrument/s - Girls with Barrel-Organ and Tambourine (N97) 175-225
Instrument/s - Musicians (T56)   150-175
Instrument/s - Organ Grinder - 7.25 in. (V15)   275-325
Instrument/s - Organ Grinder - 6.12 in. (V14)   275-325
Instrument/s - Pretty Child (T34)   175-225
Instrument/s - Young Man Playing his Lute (N98)   175-225
Dramatic Performance - Billy Buttons (N103)   175-225
Dramatic Performance - Dog Circus (N102)   175-225
Dramatic Performance - Performing in Costume - 5.75 in. (V17) 175-225
Dramatic Performance - Performing in Costume - 8 in. (V18) 175-225
Dramatic Performance - Punch and Judy (N100)   175-225
Dramatic Performance - Punch and Judy with Dog Toby (N101) 175-225
Dramatic Performance - Punch and Judy With Frog -
    Plate/Mug listed in Sets (S11)   listed
Dramatic Performance - Peep-Show (N54)   175-225
Voice - Singing the Scale - Pearlware (N92) (O6)   350+

Places to Visit

Brownhills - New York City Hall/Mt. Vernon - 7.25 in. (C23) 200-250
Brownhills - New York City Hall/Mt. Vernon - 7.87 in. (A6) 200-250
Brownhills - Niagara Falls/White House (C24)   200-250
Brownhills - Ottawa, Canada, Parliament House/
    Post Office (C26)   200-250

Brownhills - Paris/Notre Dame (C27)	200-250
Brownhills - Quebec, Canada/Boston, Massachusetts State House (C25)	200-250
Chicago, Illinois - World's Columbian Exposition Administration Bldg. (C17)	200-250
Chicago, Illinois - World's Columbian Exposition Electrical Bldg. (C18)	200-250
Concord, New Hampshire, Post Office (C16)	100-150
Coney Island, New York - Brighton Beach Bathing Pavilion (C9)	175-225
Coney Island, New York - Evening Bathing/ Manhattan Beach (C7)	175-225
Coney Island, New York - Hotel Brighton & Concourse (C10)	175-225
Coney Island, New York - Iron Pier, West Brighton Beach (C11)	175-225
Coney Island, New York - Marine Railway, Manhattan Beach (C8)	175-225
Coney Island, New York - Oriental Hotel (C12)	175-225
Halifax, Nova Scotia Advertiser - Cleverdon & Co. (C46)	200-275
Holley (spelled HOLLY on plate), New York Souvenir - Bears at Tennis (C20)	150-175
Newport, New York Souvenir - Ride A Cock-Horse (C22)	150-175
Niagara Falls, New York - Niagara Falls (M50)	100-150
Omaha, Nebraska - Union Station (C14)	100-150
Philadelphia - Independence Hall (A7)	250+
Philadelphia - Public Buildings (A8)	250+
Quebec, Canada Advertiser - Pussy Cat (C21)	150-175
Springfield. Illinois - Lincoln Memorial -Not Shown	100-150
Washington D. C. - Capitol (A10)	250+
Washington D. C. - Congressional Library (C13)	150-200
Washington D. C. - White House (A9)	250+
Watertown, New York - Statue/Roswell P. Flowers (C15)	100-150
West Aurora, Illinois, High School - Cup/Saucer (C48)	150-200

Queries (Conundrums in numerical order)

Animated Conundrums - Title Plate (Q1)	250+
Conundrum Number One - Why is this poor little rabbit . . . (Q2)	250+
Conundrum Number Two - Why is this geometrical fishing . . . . (Q3)	250+
Conundrum Number Three - Why is the gentleman in cap and . . . . (Q4)	250+
Conundrum Number Four - Why are these boys wrong . . . . (Q5)	250+
Conundrum Number Five - Why would this pastry cook . . . . (Q6)	250+
Conundrum Number Six - What fruit does our sketch . . . . (Q7)	250+
Riddle - I ever live man's . . . . (Q8)	200-250
Riddle - Pray tell us ladies . . . . - 5.12 in. (Q10) (V24 - Titled)	200-250
Riddle - Pray tell us ladies . . . . - 6.12 in. (V25),	200-250
Riddle - Tis true I have both . . . . - 8.12 in. (Q9) (V27)	200-250
Riddle - Tis true I have both . . . . - 5.12 in. (V26 - Titled)	200-250

Religion - General

Going to Sunday School (R57)	250+
Classroom of the Missionary (R21)	250+
Students with the Missionary (R22)	250+
Reading the Bible (R2)	250+

Religion - Hymns

An Only Son - And can so kind a father frown . . . . (R13)	200-250
At twelve years old . . . . (R7)	200-250
Behold him rising from the grave . . . . (R6)	200-250
How doth the little busy bee . . . . (R8)	200-250
How glorious is our heavenly King . . . . (R4)	200-250
I lay my body down to sleep . . . . (R10)	200-250
The tulip and the butterfly . . . . (R9)	200-250

Religion - Lessons

Admonishing graphic - Don't hurt it! (R59)	175-225
Admonishing graphic - Stealing Apples (R60)	175-225
Admonishing graphic - The Cruel Boy (R58)	175-225
Flowers That Never Fade - Early Rising (R47)	250+
Flowers That Never Fade - Good Humor (R46)	250+
Flowers That Never Fade - Innocence (R48)	250+
Flowers That Never Fade - Liberty (R45)	250+
Flowers That Never Fade - Liberty (Three dimensional border) (O1a, O1b)	300+
Flowers That Never Fade - Meekness (R44)	250+
Flowers That Never Fade - Piety (R43)	250+
Happy Children - I thank the Goodness and . . . . (R11)	200-250
Importance of Punctuality - Indeed Sir, you are . . . . (R49)	200-250
Importance of Punctuality - Well here we are . . . . (R50)	200-250
Importance of Punctuality - You are behind . . . . (R51)	200-250
Lord's Prayer - Our Father, who art . . . . (R39)	200-250
Lord's Prayer - Thy Kingdom come, thy will . . . . (R40)	200-250
Morality - Let Brotherly Love Continue (R41)	200-250
Morality - Cherish your best hopes . . . . (R53)	200-250
Morality - Contentment makes the believer . . . . (R56)	200-250
Morality - Good thoughts should always . . . . (R52)	200-250
Morality - Keep Within Compass (R42)	200-250
Morality - Peace and Plenty - A good conscience . . . . (R55)	200-250
Morality - Poor Boy and the Loaf (R99)	200-250
Morality - Reason should guide . . . . (R54)	200-250
Morality - Remember the Sabbath Day to Keep it Holy (R1)	200-250
Mug - Alphabet of Virtues - A/B-Adoration/Benevolence (H51)	250+
Mug - Alphabet of Virtues - C - Charity (H53)	250+
Mug - Alphabet of Virtues - C/D-Charity/Devotion- Ht 2.62 in. (H54)	250+
Mug - Alphabet of Virtues - C/D-Charity/Devotion- Ht 2.75 in. (H55)	250+
Mug - Alphabet of Virtues - E-Economy (H57)	250+
Mug - Alphabet of Virtues - E/F (Graphic error) Gratitude/Faith (H58)	250+
Mug - Alphabet of Virtues - E/G-Economy/Gratitude (H60)	250+
Mug - Alphabet of Virtues - H/I-Hope/Industry (H62)	250+
Mug - Alphabet of Virtues - I/J-Industry/Justice (H63)	250+
Mug - Alphabet of Virtues - K/L-Kindness/Love (H65)	250+
Mug - Alphabet of Virtues - M/N-Modesty/Noblemindedness (H67)	250+
Mug - Alphabet of Virtues - O/P-Obedience/Politeness (H69)	250+
Mug - Alphabet of Virtues - Q/R-Quietness/Repentance (H71)	250+
Mug - Alphabet of Virtues - S/T-Sobriety/Truth (H73)	250+
Mug - Alphabet of Virtues - U/V-Uprightness/Veneration (H75)	250+
Mug - Alphabet of Virtues - W/X-Wisdom/ Letter Seldom Used (H77)	250+
Mug - Alphabet of Virtues - Y/Z-Yearn/Zeal (H79)	250+

R - Watch the bent . . . . - Pearlware (R100)	350+
Temperance - Band of Hope - Make our Temperance Army Strong (R16)	250+
Temperance - Band of Hope - The Mountain Rill (R15)	250+
Temperance - Father Mathew (R20)	250+
Temperance - Father Mathew - Mixed Metal (M56)	350+
Temperance - Jug and glass was filled again . . . . (R17)	250+
Temperance - Jug and glass we're done with you . . . . (R18)	250+
Temperance - The Drunkard's Progress - The Ruin'ed Family (R19)	250+
What blest examples do I find writ . . . . (R12)	200-250

Religion - Narratives

Brownhills, Bible Pictures Series - Daniel in the Lion's Den (R37)	200-250
Brownhills, Bible Pictures Series - Destruction of Pharaoh (R32)	200-250
Brownhills, Bible Pictures Series - Elijah Fed by the Ravens (R35)	200-250
Brownhills, Bible Pictures Series - Finding of Moses (R31)	200-250
Brownhills, Bible Pictures Series - Noah and the Ark (R24)	200-250
Brownhills, Bible Pictures Series - Samuel before Eli (R33)	200-250
Commandments - Thou Shalt Do no Murder (R23)	200-250
David and Goliath (R34)	200-250
Finding of Moses - Fruit Dish Shape (R30)	200-250
Flight into Egypt (T1a, T1b)	200-250
Hezekiah Beholding the Sun-Dial (R36)	200-250
Incidents in the Life of Our Blessed Savior - And they came . . . . (R38)	200-250
Joseph Interprets the Chief Butler's Dream (R28)	200-250
Mug - Chapter L - Historical Scripture Alphabet Series - G was Goliath (L5)	350+
Mug - Chapter L - Historical Scripture Alphabet Series - K was the King(L6)	350+
Mug - Chapter L - Historical Scripture Alphabet Series - W was the Water(L7)	350+
Mug - Samuel (H106)	250+
Sacred History of Joseph and his Brethren - Joseph's brethren . . . . (R29)	200-250
Sacred History of Joseph and his Brethren - Joseph's First Dream (R25)	200-250
Sacred History of Joseph and his Brethren - Potiphar's Wife . . . . (R27)	200-250
Sacred History of Joseph and his Brethren - Reuben Interceding . . . . (R26)	200-250

Romantic Scenes

Romantic Scene with Castles (C29)	150-200
Romantic Scene with Llamas (C28)	150-200

Royalty (See Leaders, Political and Religious)

Secondary Languages (Manual alphabet listed in Special Needs)

Dutch - Op Uw Geboortedag (E174)	200-250
French - Artistes/Artists (E167)	200-250
French - Baigneurs/Bathers (E168)	200-250
French - Candins/Dandies (E166)	200-250
French - Canotiers/Boatmen (E171)	200-250
French - Docteur/Doctor (E170)	200-250

French - Instituteur/Schoolmaster (E169)	200-250
French - Jockeys/Jockeys (E165)	200-250
French - Kabyles/Kabyles (E173)	200-250
French - L'exercice/Drill (E172)	200-250
French - La Lecture/Reading (Non-Alphabet border) (V19)	200-250
French - Lecture/Reading (V20)	200-250
Spanish Series - Carlota (E162)	200-250
Spanish Series - Michaelita (E164)	200-250
Spanish Series - Recuerdo (E163)	200-250

Sets (Articles placed together in matching or nearly matching "sets")

Blue Animal-Letter Surround - Plate/Pitcher (S14)	listed
Chickens - Plate/Saucer/Cup/Pitcher (S18)	listed
Crusoe Making a Boat - Plate/Mug (S8)	listed
D/E/F - Boy with Bubble Pipe - Plate/Mug (S3)	listed
Goosey Gander (Classroom) - Plate/Mug (S10)	listed
J/K/L - Boy and Dog - Plate/Mug (S4)	listed
Large green letter surround - Plate/Pitcher (S13) (O15)	listed
Leo Lion in the Fox's Barber Chair - Plate/Pitcher (S12)	listed
Little Jack Horner - Coordinate Plate/Mug (S7) (Plate E38)	listed
Orange Animal-Letter Surround - Varied Items (S15)	listed
Punch and Judy and Frog - Plate/Mug (S11)	listed
Red Clock - Plate/Bowl/Mug (Reissue?) - (S16)	listed
Robin - Plate/Mug (S9)	listed
Small Prints - Saucer/Cup/Pitcher (S17)	listed
V/W/X - See-Saw - Plate/Mug (S5)	listed
Y for Youth - Plate/Mug (S1)	listed
Y/Z/& - Snowballs - Plate/Mug (S6)	listed
Z for Zebra - Plate/Mug (S2)	listed

Sexually Suggestive Behavior

Children Caressing (K14)	400+
Children Caressing, One with hat (K16)	400+
Don't Tommy, Don't (K13)	200-250
Innocence (Photo displays auction price) - Do you see my . . . . (K20)	500+
Playing at Lovers (I21)	175-225
Two Children with Mustaches (K15)	400+
Hollowware - R for Rendezvous (K17)	200-250
Hollowware - R for Rendezvous - Detail of the Word (K18)	200-250
Hollowware - V/W/X - The Whipping (K19)	200-250

Special Needs

Ailment - Cold Water Cure - Not Shown	300+
Blind Girl (E159)	175-225
Braille Edged Ashtray - Cane (E160)	12-25
Braille Edged Ashtray - Guide Dog (E161)	12-25
Manual Alphabet - Felines Jumping Rope (E158)	300+
Manual Alphabet - Greeting (E157)	300+
Manual Alphabet - Hand Signs in a Circle (E150)	500+
Manual Alphabet - Owls at School (E155)	300+
Manual Alphabet - Rabbit Gent and Lady (E156)	300+
Manual Alphabet - Students at Study (E151)	300+
Manual Alphabet - The Tea Party (E154)	300+
Manual Alphabet - Three Dutch Children (E153)	300+
Manual Alphabet - Two Children Fearful of the Goose (E152)	300+
Manual Alphabet Hollowware (H138)	500+

Sports - Adult (Hunting scenes listed in Hunting)

Archery (N115)	175-225
Baseball: Running to First Base (N127)	500+
Baseball: Striker and Catcher (N126)	500+
Batter Up! and coordinate patterns - Deep and Flat Dishes	
Batter-Up! and Football Player - USA Flat (D102)	75-100
Batter-Up! German Deep Dish (D11)	150-200
Football Player - USA Deep Dish (D105)	150-200
Football Player and Skater - USA Flat (D103)	75-100
Boating - Ice Skating (N119)	175-225
Boating - Punting (N118)	175-225
Boating - Ready to Sail (N117)	175-225
Boating - Rowing (N116)	175-225
Cock Fighting or Breeding - Exhibition of Prize Fowls (N112)	175-225
Cock Fighting - Combat (N111)	75-125
Cock Fighting - Death (N113)	75-125
Cricket (N125)	200-250
Cricket - Meakin (N124)	200-250
Fishing - Father and Son Fishing (N129)	175-225
Football (N121)	200-250
Horsemanship - Horse Racing (N52)	200-250
Horsemanship - Sweepstakes (N51)	200-250
Horsemanship - Two Horses at the Steeplechase (N50)	150-200
Horsemanship - Two Horses at the Wall (N49)	150-200
Rugby - 7.37 in. (N123)	200-250
Rugby - 7.87 in. (N122)	200-250
Walking on the Bridge (N120)	150-200

Stages of Life

Early Years - And when my kite I wish to try . . . . (I5)	250+
Early Years - Christmas Day (I71)	350+
Early Years - Frolics of Youth - Don't I look like Papa (I22)	175-225
Early Years - Frolics of Youth - Now I'm Grandmother (I23) (Z1)	175-225
Early Years - Frolics of Youth - The Young Artist (V6)	175-225
Early Years - Frolics of Youth - The Young Artist - Pearlware (V5)	350+
Early Years - Grandpa's Hat (I24)	175-225
Early Years - Infancy (I1)	250+
Early Years - Playing at Lovers (I21)	175-225
Early Years - Toddler and Rocking Chair (I2)	175-225
Early Years - Who when he saw me . . . . (I6)	250+
Marriage - We kindly	
(Source: Cotter's Saturday/Burns) - 6.62 in. (I68)	300+
Middle Age - Grandmother (I10)	175-225
Middle Age - Manhood (I3)	250+
Middle Age - Mother and Children (I8)	175-225
Middle Age - Mother and daughter, dear to each . . . . (I9)	175-225
Middle Age - Wishes (I4)	175-225
Senescence - Taking Snuff (I75)	250+
Senescence - But now your brow	
(Source: John Anderson/Burns) (I76)	300+
Senescence - Gaping (I72)	250+
Senescence - Oh How Handsome! (I73)	250+
Senescence - Smoking (I74)	250+

Sunbonnet Kids (See Literature - Children's, Hotel, and Deep Dishes)

Temperance

Band of Hope - Make our Temperance Army Strong (R16)	250+
Band of Hope - The Mountain Rill (R15)	250+
Mathew, Father Theobald - Mixed Metal (M56)	350+
Mathew, Father Theobald (R20)	250+
Jug and glass was filled again . . . . (R17)	250+
Jug and glass we're done with you . . . . (R18)	250+
The Drunkard's Progress - The Ruin'ed Family (R19)	250+

Toys

ABC Bank - Chromolithography (M78)	250+
Miniature Candlestick - Iron (M79)	250+
Toy Table - Mixed Metal (M80)	400+
Rattle - Mixed Metal (M81)	150-200

War, Civil

Arrival of General McClellan (A24)	400+
Banks, Maj. Gen. N. P. (A28)	400+
Burnside, General (A26)	400+
Federal Generals (A21)	400+
Gathering Cotton (A13) (V32) (V34)	250+
Gillmore, Maj. Gen. Q. A. (A22)	400+
Go to sleep, my little picaninny . . . . (A35)	400
Grant, General U. (M60)	300+
Grant, Lt. General U. S. (M61)	300+
Grant, Maj. Gen. Ulysses S. (A29)	400+
Halleck, General (A23)	400+
Lincoln, President Abraham (A30)	500+
Lincoln, Young President Abraham - (A19)	500+
Meade, Maj. Gen. Geo. (A27)	400+
Union Troops in Virginia (A25)	400+
Vision of Uncle Tom (A18)	350+
Military Encounter (A20)	250+
Zouaves (A31)	400+

War, Crimean

Incidents of the War - Arrival of the Post (N69)	250+
Incidents of the War - Fight in the Trenches (N71)	250+
Incidents of the War - Foraging Party (N70)	250+
Incidents of the War - Wounded Sailors (N72)	250+

War, General Scenes

Awkward Squad (N81)	250+
Horseman in Armor - Majolica - Not Shown	350+
I'm sure in all the army list . . . . (N78)	250+
March - Rifleman (N80)	250+
Military Encounter - Allerton (N77)	250+
Partisan With Drawn Sword - (N83) (Z2)	250+
Quartermaster Serg I and Trumpeter (N75)	250+
Rifle Band (N82)	250+
Royal Standard - Riflemen (N79)	250+
Sailor (N73)	250+
Sleeping Soldier Unaware of his Portrait (N74)	250+
Whom are you for? (N76)	250+

X Is for Xenomania

The life of one afflicted with xenomania is always anxious. The root, *xeno*, is defined as "foreign" as in foreign things . . . items of unique interest from faraway places for which one may search. Having a mania, of course, means being hard-driven, devoted, and single-minded. Combine the two and there is the perfect definition of the totally absorbed collector who is always on the prowl . . . always in search of the perfect find, that one item with the most unique history or most allure. And those "finds" need not always be touchable. Even the stories of those whose lives have been similarly afflicted become part of the "collection." Every collector has his or her tales . . . tales that strengthen the soul.

Consider the soul of one H.W. In his *Old China Book* (1936), Mr. Moore pays homage to the late Henry Walpole, whose Gothic villa at Strawberry Hill housed England's greatest private china collection. He was, says the poem, "the prince."

> China's the passion of his soul;
> A cup, a plate, a dish, a bowl,
> Can kindle wishes in his breast,
> Inflame with joy or break his rest.

A casual sentence follows the poem: "He was so fond of his brittle treasures that he even washed them himself, though his poor hands were swollen and knotted with gout." It is easy to see that for the twenty-seven agonizing days of the auction of his estate, the tormented spectre of Horace Walpole shook its gnarled finger at the auctioneer whose hammer sent pieces of Walpole's coveted collection flying into a diaspora of rattling tea trays and tottering shelves. For twenty-seven days did he watch the coarse handling of his fragile treasures, jarred by the chilling clinks of edge-to-edge combat. It's over now, and we bid his anxious soul its rest. It is the anxiety in the poetry that quickly rekindles the spirit of this most venerable xenomaniac. It's the anxiety in the poetry that jangles each of our maniacal souls.

Of course, every collector's favorite place to find alphabet ware is in his or her own protected places. But most exciting finds may not be secured in personal stacks. We may have seen them, held them, even photographed them, but they "belong" only as thrilling memories. Anyone who has even thumbed through the late Mildred and Joseph Chalala's *Collector's Guide to ABC Plates, Mugs and Things* (1980) is familiar with the text's frontispiece, that very old Davenport plate framed by a blue feathered edge. Centered, with a blue rectangle housing

four rows of seven capital letters, the entire design is edged by three rows of tiny blue-rimmed circles. Holding that plate was the thrill of our collective lifetimes. Exciting, too, was lifting ABC ware from the dining room cabinet of Clara Barton's North Oxford, Massachusetts, home. It wasn't the design or the condition of the item that made the plate the "find." It was the link to America's past that made the moment a treasure. And for a most outstanding museum collection of children's mugs, the traveler can visit the Plantation Museum near Cape Cod. The quality of items is enthralling. Though not all ABC ware, the collection of English children's mugs there far outnumbers any collection in protected display encountered to date.

Sometimes "finds" are not there for the seeing. A somewhat obscure allusion to a third was found on page nine of *Louisa May Alcott, Determined Writer* (McGill, 1988), which quotes, "Running away was one of the delights of my early days . . . ." No wonder . . . the Alcotts moved continuously, but one early sojourn in Boston had a nostalgic connection for us. The description tells of when the "little woman" remembered being awakened from her perch on a friendly doorstep by the town crier calling, "Lost, a little girl, six years old, in a pink frock, white hat and new green shoes." "Why, that's me!" she recalled answering, and was soon enjoying "bread and molasses in a tin plate bordered with alphabet letters." Which tin plate of so many that fit that faded description? No matter. The connection was the find.

Reading the writings of those who have come upon special items or have increased their collections reveals the common thread of the passion and the sheer delight of being rewarded by sudden discoveries at the "hunt." It's the pure fun of it all, the separating of the spirit from the workaday world, the intrigue of clues that direct our interests from one vendor to another, the deals and arrangements we make to own precious items at future times, and the fascination of the sheer varieties of articles that have remained from days long gone that invigorates. For it is each new piece that connects the xenomaniac to those countless hands who have passed it from then to now, granting it, with every new home, a new life and a grand importance.

Xenomania is highly contagious . . . its symptoms include ever-widening goals, hunts that reach feverish intensities, and the limited abilities to focus only on those specific items needed to continue a sequence or set. The research that reveals the secrets behind the production of alphabet ware fuels the fire; the search for published prints in books and magazines that have echoed onto a ceramic treasure is intoxicating.

The sound of the auctioneer's hammer was a death knell at Pennsylvania's Strasburg Inn. In December of 1994, the Kovels wrote the obituary of the landmark collection dispersed at that early October auction The Chalalas' holdings were no longer theirs. Even the price of their book had been reduced long after it had been sold by rare book dealers at four times the publication price. But the pieces are now in the hands of new collectors or will soon catch the loving eye of searchers who will never know that their new treasure once held a respected place on the Chalalas' long stone mantel. By bringing new life to their own growing collections, they will have honored the memories of Millie and Joe Chalala, the original xenomaniacs!

Y Is for Yesteryear

Many general books about antiques have thorough chapters that present techniques for detecting the provenance of an item of pottery and porcelain, glass, or metal. This chapter will attempt to present the basics only of dating alphabet ware. Certainly clues presented by authentic factory marks most easily suggest production time periods, but because so few items are marked, there are other kinds of clues which must be investigated as well, to provide critical information. Throughout the text, the suggested dating of each item is included in each caption when "suspected."

Serious tracking of the evolution of potteries from remaining fragments of information shredded by time, fires, and insensitive disposals is the focus of at least three works authored by the esteemed Geoffrey Godden. Aside from factory histories, Godden's *Encyclopaedia of British Porcelain Manufacturers* (1988) provides lists of manufacturers by ten-year spans; several firms that produced ABC ware are found on this list. And samples of several "manufactory trees" are found on pages 258 through 264 of *Kovels' New Dictionary of Marks* by Ralph and Terry Kovel (1985). Information found in Volume I (there is no volume II) of Denis Stuart's *People of the Potteries*, published by the Department of Adult Education at the University of Keele, Staffordshire (1985), is another "gospel" from that bygone era. Both Lehner's *Encyclopedia of US Marks* and Gerald DeBolt's *Dictionary of American Pottery Marks* (1994) provide detailed histories of American factories and varieties of firm stamps, as well. Metal manufacturers are well represented in the *Encyclopedia of American Silver Manufacturers* by Dorothy Rainwater and Judy Redfield (1998), though there are few references to mixed-metal items in any text. For some manufacturers there are shelves of informative books, but with so many firms not yet fully represented in the literature, opportunities for research and writing abound.

The presence of a manufacturer's mark on an item tells that it was probably manufactured in or after 1800. It is understandable that not all trademark designs are published in all sources; a careful search of all resources helps to provide the missing links. Backstamps are pictured in "C Is for Commercialism," "D Is for Deep Dishes," "F Is for Flatware," and "K Is for Kitsch" and are the substance of "U Is for Undersides." Trademarks of silver-plate and sterling flatware and drinking mugs are clearly represented in the publication by Rainwater and Redfield. Some tips for using marks to help with dating include:

• A chronological review of a firm's designs will provide a term of origin. "Term of origin" refers here to a group of years within which the production took place.

• Chronological readings of firm histories provide the timelines of name changes. Name initials may vary. "Son" or "Sons" may be added or withdrawn, names of partners may be joined or deleted, and sometimes a city or landmark name is included, signifying either a move or a branch addition.

• Information varies concerning the addition of a "Ltd." or "Ld" or "Limited" to a potter's name; the addition of LTD. indicates a date subsequent to 1855. In practice, the letters did not appear generally for about twenty-five years.

• Some manufacturers—for instance, McNicol Pottery of East Liverpool—added an "x" beneath their backstamp to designate the "plant" of origin. Knowing the working period of the plant will indicate a time span of production.

• Rarely is the year printed within or adjacent to the trademark designs; in this collection, months and day notations (Dresden China and McNicol's Pottery) have been found beneath the marks on cereals (see "D Is for Deep Dishes"). Information of this nature should not be confused with dates of factory origins that may be included in the mark for all time (Buffalo Pottery).

• Most marks that include representations of the Royal Arms postdate 1800 (see "D Is for Deep Dishes"). Use of the term "Royal" in the firm name more than likely dates the manufacture to the mid-19th century.

• The word "trademark," according to Godden (1991), reveals manufacture after the Trade-Mark Act of 1862 and usually after 1872. The word "Registered" before "trademark" suggests the item to be of 20th-century origin.

• Ceramic marks that include the name of the country of origin were possibly made about 1887. The inclusion was mandated after the American McKinley Tariff Act of 1891 but the identification was not required by English law.

• Marks that include the words "Made in _____" indicate that the piece was made after 1914.

• Marks that indicate "Made for _____" or "Manufactured for _____" can sometimes be validated in the Kowalskys' impressive lists of importers who dispersed the items throughout the world. An example is the mark (see **Figure U51**) that informs the buyer that the item was made for H. C. Edmiston. That firm is listed as an importer in the Kowalskys' encyclopedia. It sold items made by A. Meakin from 1902 to 1903. Items bearing the mark could be listed as c.1903 with certainty. A more commonly seen mark of the importer is a variation of the "garter mark" introduced about 1840. An example of this type of transfer identification can be seen in **Figure U50**.

• Marks that indicate the material from which an item was made may ease a search. For example, a piece labeled "semi-vitreous" from the Buffalo China Company could be dated as "not before 1904" or "1904+," as it was then that the first semi-vitreous pieces were turned out by the factory. And, fortunately, some of the Buffalo China marks include the date as well as a picture of the thick-haired bovine.

Diamond-shaped British Registry Marks protected their item/shape for three years. As seen in **Figures Y2 and Y3**, there were two diamond designs, type A (**Figure Y2**) from 1842 through 1867 and the next, type B (**Figure Y3**), from 1868 through 1883. Each pointed angle represented information concerning the date of origin. The positions of the arcs rotated in the later design. An example of a diamond map from 1842-1867, the English Registry Mark type A (provided here by Ann and Dennis Berard), provides the following information:

• The bubble at the top of the diamond will always have the "IV" within it on both marks. (Number I indicates a metal item, II stands for glass, and III indicates a wood product.)

• The northern angle names the year by its appropriate initial:

1842 - X	1848 - U	1854 - J	1860 - Z	1866 - Q
1843 - H	1849 - S	1855 - E	1861 - R	1867 - T
1844 - C	1850 - V	1856 - L	1862 - O	
1845 - A	1851 - P	1857 - K	1863 - G	
1846 - I	1852 - D	1858 - B	1864 - N	
1847 - F	1853 - Y	1859 - M	1865 - W	

• The western angle will name the month identified by initials:

January = C
February = G
March = W
April = H
May = E
June = M
July = I
August = R
September = D
October = B
November = K
December = A

• The eastern angle will name the day of the month.

• The southern angle will name the parcel number.

While the Rd in the center consistently stood for "registered," the four angles of the type B diamond changed significance after 1867.

• The northern angle identified the day of the month.

• The western angle on the second plan identified the parcel number.

• The eastern angle told the year:

1868 - X	1874 - U	1880 - J
1869 - H	1875 - S	1881 - E
1870 - C	1876 - V	1882 - L
1871 - A	1877 - P	1883 - K
1872 - I	1878 - D	
1873 - F	1879 - Y	

• The southern point told the month (initials are the same on both).

January = C
February = G
March = W
April = H
May = E
June = M
July = I
August = R
September = D
October = B
November = K
December = A

• In 1884, the diamond-shaped schema was replaced by a simple registration number that followed the letters "Rd No," or Registry Number. All information was deleted but the year of registration; for example, the Brownhills Pottery Registry Number 154 **(Figure U15)** is indicative of an 1884 production (see Appendix AY1). Though there are no Registry Diamonds of the earlier "A" series in this collection of alphabet plates, **Figure Y2** and the interpretive information is included should they appear on an ABC item elsewhere.

Catalogue listings often (but *not* always) present a date of production for items pictured. Companies that manufactured metal (some sterling) ware provided detailed images of highly polished items (see "M Is for Metals"). But because old catalogues seldom include dates, the varying silver mark must be dated through volumes such as the Rainwater encyclopedia.

Other kinds of markings give clues to dates of manufacture. There are, for instance, names that advertise products, names that sell an item as a souvenir of special places, and names that honor a place, an individual, or an event.

• Dates are easily validated from message-marks indicating that an item was made as a firm's promotional. Such items can be quickly confirmed through area historical libraries that have phone books and lists of businesses/civic organizations, some from the last one hundred years. They are often able to provide personal contacts with a firm's family members who happily provide intimate details of "grandpa's" history. An example of this kind of research validated the dating of the "chicken plate" given to customers of the Tomasini Hardware Company of Petaluma, California, by the original owner of the firm (see "C Is for Commercialism").

• Items from major industries (such as Post cereals) can be dated by contacting the always-helpful company archivists, who have thorough records of advertising issues and specific names of products as they underwent changes throughout the years (see "C Is for Commercialism").

• An alphabet-surrounded picture of an individual on a statue or a historic piece of architecture leads to searches of "things to see" that are included in tour books similar to those distributed by the American Automobile Association. A graphic of a high school in Illinois, a train station in Nebraska, and a post office in New Hampshire were quickly dated by calls to a historical society, a railroad archivist, and a village clerk (see "C Is for Commercialism"). Phoning a city's Chamber of Commerce is an efficient route to information, as are Internet travel sites.

• Because pictures functioned as news releases, the content of the image would provide a time frame of about five years. For instance, pictures of the Crimean War would estimate production from 1854 to about 1858. Likewise, the plate memorializing Robert Peel would date from 1850, when he was tragically killed in a fall from his horse. Palmer Cox's Brownies, whose illustration is on a full sized, mixed-metal plate, made their debut in 1892; dates of publication can suggest years of production as well.

• Mugs that present only one transfer design are probably older than mugs with two designs, one on each side of the handle. Many mugs from the collection of Ann and Dennis Berard of Fitzwilliam, New Hampshire, show fine examples of single transfer vessels (see "H Is for Hollowware.").

• "T Is for Transfers and Toybooks" presents information concerning transfers, the approximate dates of their evolution, and many examples that identify their sources. The emergent date of source prints (in decorative prints, book illustrations, publications by religious societies, children's magazines or pennysheets, newspapers, etc.) provide reasonable production dates. For example, at least one of the well-known illustrators of *Robinson Crusoe* is featured on ABC plates. These illustrations were taken from J. J. Grandville's edition which, according to Noël Riley (1991), was published in French in 1853 **(Figure E74)**. Transfers would appear on plates on or after that date.

• Aside from transfers, hand-painted lustreware, which shone pink or purple, was probably made in the mid-19th century. Though Sunderland has been suggested as the area of origin of all pink lustreware, not all lustreware was made there.

• Transfer patterns do suggest the identification of their potters and their factory dates. For example, the bordered dinnerware manufactured by Hope and Carter of Burslem, 1862-1880, was identified by the factory initials incorporated into the border design of the transfer **(Figures N41 and N42)**. Immediately recognizable are the all-over diagonal letter backgrounds that were designed by Brownhills Pottery, etc.

• A comparison of pictured clothing trends or popular fads pictured that would correspond to changes in society's patterns help to estimate the starting dates of production. The earliest transfers showed finely dressed children with expensive possessions. Midcentury content was more relaxed . . . sports, pets, farm scenes, etc., were subjects more juvenile in their scope. Noted by the Kovels (1986) are "faddy" clues that can

be found in ABC ware . . . fish sets (1910), portraits (1880), Kewpie dolls (1912), and so on.

• Mixed-metal plates that displayed color lithography began after 1875, when the paper printing process was adapted to metals. One wonderfully illustrated source of information is Lisa Kerr's *Ohio Art - The World of Toys*, published by Schiffer Publishing Ltd. in 1998. Using technologies to authenticate dates is helpful.

• Comparison of one marked plate with another or with photos from a reliable published source can produce clues to sets and similar products made within a stated time frame. An illustration of this kind of discovery is discussed in "G Is for Glass." More critically, for example, finding artists' signatures on transfers or finding transfers that replicate artists' styles may suggest time spans **(Figure N88)**.

Without verbiage, the estimation of a date of manufacture can only be guessed at, but that guess can be an educated one. It might be well to consider the following:

• The molded alphabet rim may show less relief than molds cast earlier in the century. As the demand grew, the quality of items often diminished.

• The weight of a plate **may** hint at its date of manufacture . . . the heavier the item, when compared with others of similar size, the older it probably is.

• The undershape too may be a part of the detection. The "foot rim" around the bottom surface emerged at the start of the 1800s **(Figure Y1)**, and those that are glazed normally date after.

• The three marks on the face of the plate caused by the "spur" make an invisible triangle. They are the remainders of small "kiln furniture" used as supports and separators during firing. Though used heavily before 1825, they are not definitive daters because of their continued use on less valued items.

• Glazing techniques are genuine clues. "W Is For Worth" discusses the blue puddling on foot rims of plates and at the terminals of mugs, which indicates Pearlware, and the greenish puddling, which indicates creamware; both begin dating about the first quarter of the 19th century.

• A border, like the octagonal shape (registered in 1847 and produced through 1850 in Longton), can identify its maker, in this case Messrs. Bailey and Ball. Other castings can provide similar information.

Facilities such as CARC, the Computer Assisted Research Center at the Chicago Public Library, furnish countrywide sites where rare printings can be found; also rare book libraries house collections of children's literature whose graphics are found on alphabet ware. Worldwide library and museum sources provide reliable documentation difficult to find in popular sources.

• Contacting specialized institutions, such as the library at the Corning Glass Museum in Corning, New York, requires time and patience, but library personnel always do their best to answer questions in a timely manner. A thorough guide of national or international libraries and museums is accessible from the Internet. Helpful museum directors are eager to provide faxed source material and to suggest alternative options for research services.

• Source books that feature the history of particular item types are perhaps the most informative tools. Current authors present dissertations on narrowing categories, identifying their producers and explaining the sources of their designs. Sets of encyclopedias, relevant to the area in whose library they are stored, are more reliable and provide more definitive information than the popular sources. And so many rich references, no longer published, can be located by specialty bookstores and Amazon.com. Archival collections afford unique resources; un-

fortunately they are spread across the country and do not share their collections.

• Data provided by professional researchers are costly, but the accuracy of the historical information they present is invaluable. Personal contact with individuals who are authorities in the field provides a unique sense of confidence.

• Of course, Internet routes, though often circuitous, may produce immediate information saving weeks of library research; with Web sites continually evolving, it is advisable to frequently "re-search" for unanswered questions. Many Web sites invite personal questions, and much information and guidance has been gleaned through these very personable sources.

• Unfortunately, most ABC ware is unmarked . . . using the term *circa* or the initial c. estimates the date of an item, plus or minus a few years either way. An educated guess is the goal; seldom will we ever know how right we were!

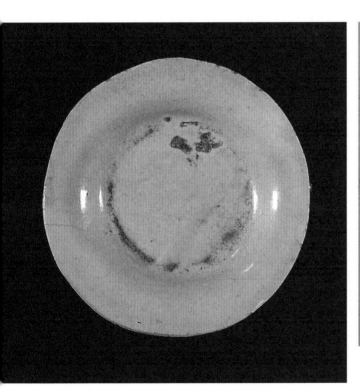

Figure Y1 - Underside of frontispiece. No mark. Pre-1800.

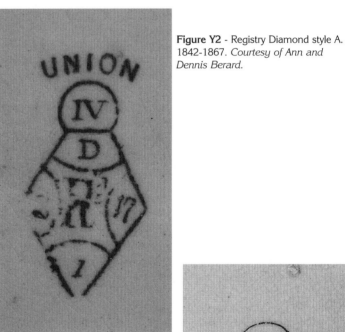

Figure Y2 - Registry Diamond style A. 1842-1867. *Courtesy of Ann and Dennis Berard.*

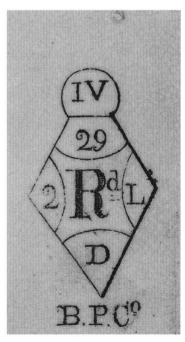

Figure Y3 - Registry Diamond style B. 1868-1883

Z Is for Ƨ and Other Reversals

It is always a "double find" when a plate includes one or more inadvertently placed letters. The examples shown in this chapter represent only a fraction of the ABC ware that display "turnabouts" in this collection. Molds, possibly made by the caring hands of nonreaders, may display letters horizontally reversed (as mirror images); errors may also occur in the sequence of alphabet letters and, in one instance, in the rotation of a whole word.

Of the alphabet letters, there are many that, if turned over horizontally, would still appear correct—A, H, I, M, O, T, U, V, W, X, and Y. The remaining letters are B, C, D, E, F, G, J, K, L, N, P, Q, R, S, and Z. Of these, only the N, Q, S, and Z are commonly seen to have been set incorrectly.

The tail of the Q, the clue to its position, is an easily transposed detail **(Figure Z1).** Cast in its mirror image, the reversal of the letter Q often goes unrecognized as it is small and castings are not always well defined.

S and Z are mirror images of one another and therefore visually bewildering. They are sometimes, though not necessarily, set improperly on the same rim. And from the viewpoint of one challenged by visual-spatial tasks, turning a capital Z on its side changes the letter immediately into an N. These lookalike positional confusions may add to the directional befuddlement of setting letters backward to become forward-facing letters when cast. The S-Z and Z-N pairs share spatially baffling elements, and, after a quick analysis, one finds their reversals to be consistent with forgivable mistakes made by students suffering from dyslexia. **Figure Z2** presents a sharp image of a mirror-image Z, which appears as Ƨ.

Figure Z3 displays the rim of a plate with two reversals; the S and the Z are reversed. **Figure Z4**, an orange-lustre-rimmed Cruikshank, boasts three mirror-image letters: Ͷ, Ƨ and Ƹ. Similar reversals are found on metals as well. On a tiny toy plate that features a gentleman astride a horse **(Figure M93)** is a mirror image Z **(Figure Z5)**, which completes the alphabet.

From the early 1930s comes the Disneyana plate of Mickey and Pluto. This impressive series, made in Bavaria and imported from the Schumann China Company, has skyrocketed in value. The undersides of these smooth, white, cereal bowls were clearly authorized by Walter E. Disney. The plate pictured reverses the I and J **(Figure Z6)**. The two letters may be visually confusing, and with the combined history of those elements of the alphabet (see "J Is for J, the Last Letter of the Alphabet") this error, too, may be completely understandable.

One whole-word rotation was neither easily photographed nor clearly read but was quite exciting to find. The word LIBERTY on one "Liberty" was rotated 180 degrees **(Figures Z7 and Z8)** and therefore incorrectly cast. The word is cast accurately on a similar plate, **Figure Z9**; a magnified view of that casting follows on **Figure Z10.** It appears upside down to the viewer, but is then correct from the perspective of the characters cast on the plate who are reading the print.

Because the rims of plates needed to be cast in reverse, the task of mold making would have become exponentially more difficult for illiterate workers or the spatially challenged. Just how many plates with ill-set letters were destroyed as items not suitable for sale will never be known. Certainly they were not effective teachers, but their occurrence contributes now to the effectiveness of any collection. Hunters of alphabet items might take the time to examine their private holdings for reversals or rotations. Surely they are there for the noticing.

Figures

A Is for Americana

Figure A4 - "Crossing The Plains." 8 in. No mark. $175-$225

Figure A1 - "Candlefish." 6.62 in. Charles Allerton & Sons. Longton, Staffordshire. Factory date: 1859-1942. Mark date: 1891-1912. $175-$225

Figure A2 - "Landing Place of the Pilgrims." 6.87 in. No mark. $175-$225
Figure A3 - "William Penn." 6.87 in. No mark. $300+

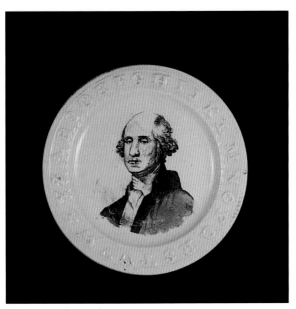

Figure A9 - "The White House." 8.37 in. No mark. $250+

Figure A5 - "George Washington." 6.75 in. No mark. *Courtesy of Irene and Ralph Lindsay.* $500+

Figure A6 - "New York City Hall and Mt. Vernon." 7.87 in. Brownhills Pottery Co. Tunstall, Staffordshire. Factory date: 1872-1896. Registry Mark #26734 date: 1885. $200-$250

Figure A10 - "The Capitol." 8.25 in. No mark. $250+

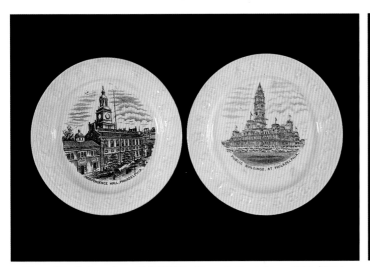

Figure A7 - "Independence Hall." 6.87 in. No mark. Event date: c.1886. $250+
Figure A8 - "Public Buildings in Philadelphia." 7 in. No mark. Event date: c.1886. $250+

Figure A11 - "Chinonca Watching the Departure of the Cavalcade." 7.27 in. Charles Allerton & Sons. Longton, Staffordshire. Factory date: 1859-1942. Mark date: 1891-1912. $175-$225
Figure A12 - "Sioux Indian Chief." 7.25 in. No mark. $175-$225

Figure A13 - "Gathering Cotton." 6 in. No mark. Event date: c.1860. This plate is also found as Figure V32 and V34 in "V Is for Variations on a Theme." $250+

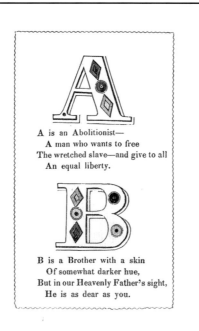

A is an Abolitionist—
A man who wants to free
The wretched slave—and give to all
An equal liberty.

B is a Brother with a skin
Of somewhat darker hue,
But in our Heavenly Father's sight,
He is as dear as you.

Figure A15 - Page 1 of *The Anti-Slavery Alphabet*, as noted in Figure A14. *Used with permission of the Huntington Library, San Marino, California.*

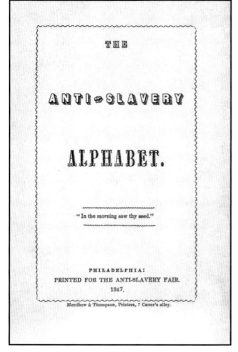

THE

ANTI-SLAVERY

ALPHABET.

" In the morning sow thy seed."

PHILADELPHIA:
PRINTED FOR THE ANTI-SLAVERY FAIR.
1847.

Merrihew & Thompson, Printers, 7 Carter's alley.

Figure A14 - Cover of *The Anti-Slavery Alphabet*. Merrihew & Thompson for the Anti-Slavery Fair, 1847. *Used with permission of the Huntington Library, San Marino, California.*

Aunt Chloe.—" Can't ye be decent when white folks come to see ye? Stop dat ar, now."

Figure A16 - Title Page of *Uncle Tom's Cabin or Negro Life in the Slave States of America.* London: Clark & Son, Foreign Booksellers. 1852.

Figure A17 - "Vision of Uncle Tom." *Uncle Tom's Cabin*, as noted in Figure A16.

Figure A18 - "Vision of Uncle Tom." 8 in. No mark. Event date: c.1852. Source: *Uncle Tom's Cabin*, as noted in Figure A16. $350+

Figure A19 - "Young President Abraham Lincoln." 6.75 in. No mark. Event date: c.1865. *Courtesy of Ann and Dennis Berard.* $500+

Figure A26 - "General Burnside." 6.12 in. No mark. Event date: c.1865. $400+

Figure A27 - "Maj. Gen. Geo. Meade." 5 in. No mark. Event date: c.1865. $400+

Figure A20 - "A Military Encounter." 8.75 in. No mark. Event date: c.1865. $250+

Figure A21 - "Federal Generals." 7 in. No mark. Event date: c.1865. $400+

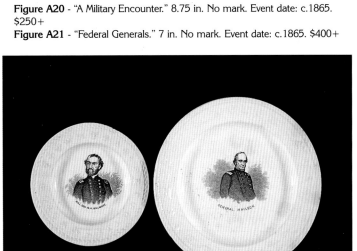

Figure A28 - "Major General N. P. Banks." 5 in. No mark. Event date: c.1865. $400+

Figure A29 - "Major Gen. Ulysses S. Grant." 5 in. No mark. Event date: c.1865. $400+

Figure A22 - "Maj. Gen. Q. A. Gillmore." 5 in. No mark. Event date: c.1865. $400+

Figure A23 - "General Halleck." 7 in. No mark. Event date: c.1865. $400+

Figure A30 - "President Abraham Lincoln." 5.06 in. Event date: c.1865. *Courtesy of Ann and Dennis Berard.* $500+

Figure A24 - "The Arrival of General McClellan." 7 in. No mark. Event date: c.1865. $400+

Figure A25 - "Union Troops in Virginia." 7 in. No mark. Event date: c.1865. $400+

Figure A31 - "Zouaves." 7 in. No mark. Event date: c.1865. *Courtesy of Dick and Elma Watson.* $400+

Figure A34 - Sheet Music Cover of "Little Alabama Coon." Hattie Starr. New York: copyright 1893 by Willis Woodward & Co. Copyright assigned 1932 to Edward B. Marks Music Corporation. *Used with permission of the John Hay Library, Brown University, Providence, Rhode Island.*

Figure A32 - Title Page of *The Union ABC.* Boston: Degan, Estes and Co. 1864. *Used with permission of the Department of Special Collections, Charles E. Young Research Library, University of California, Los Angeles.*

Figure A33 - Page of *The Union ABC*, as noted in A32. *Used with permission of the Department of Special Collections, Charles E. Young Research Library, University of California, Los Angeles.*

Figure A35 - "Go to sleep, my little picaninny . . . ." 7.27 in. Charles Allerton & Sons. Longton, Staffordshire. Factory date: 1859-1942. Event date: c.1893. $400

Figure A36 - "President James Abram Garfield." 7.75 in. No mark. Event date: c.1881. $250+

B Is for Bottle Ovens

Bottle Ovens

Figure B1 - "Skyline." Cover Photo from *Bottle Ovens* (leaflet), Wooliscroft, Terrence, contributor. Gladstone Working Museum. Longton, Staffordshire. n.d. *Courtesy of the Gladstone Working Museum, Longton, Staffordshire.*

Figure B3 - "Drawing a Trial." Photo from *Bottle Ovens* (leaflet), as noted in Figure B1, Page 4. *Courtesy of the Gladstone Working Museum, Longton, Staffordshire.*

Figure B4 - "The Clammins Broken Down." Photo from *Bottle Ovens* (leaflet), as noted in Figure B1, Page 4. *Courtesy of the Gladstone Working Museum, Longton, Staffordshire.*

Figure B2 - "Placing the Oven." Photo from *Bottle Ovens* (leaflet), as noted in Figure B1, Page 3. *Courtesy of the Gladstone Working Museum, Longton, Staffordshire.*

C Is for Commercialism

Figure C1 - "T begins Tunnel . . . ." 5.12 in. Edge Malkin & Co. Burslem, Staffordshire. Factory date: c.1871-1903. Source: *Mother's Picture Alphabet.* London: S. W. Partridge, 1862. $275-$325

Figure C7 - "Evening Bathing Scene at Manhattan Beach, Coney Island." 6.87 in. No mark. Event date: c.1880. $175-$225
Figure C8 - "Marine Railway Station, Manhattan Beach Hotel, Coney Island." 8.37 in. No mark. Event date: c.1880. $175-$225

Figure C2 - "At the Seaside." 7.25 in. Brownhills Pottery Co. Tunstall, Staffordshire. Factory date: 1872-1896. Registry Mark #253083 date: 1895. $200-$250
Figure C3 - "A Ride on Carlo." 7.5 in. Brownhills Pottery Co. Tunstall, Staffordshire. Factory date: 1872-1896. Registry Mark #253083 date: 1895. $200-$250
Figure C4 - "Wheelbarrow Ride." 7.25 in. Brownhills Pottery Co. Tunstall, Staffordshire. Factory date: 1872-1896. Registry Mark #253083 date: 1895. $200-$250

Figure C9 - "Brighton Beach, Bathing Pavilion, Coney Island." 7.17 in. No mark. Event date: c.1880. $175-$225
Figure C10 - "Hotel Brighton & Concourse, Coney Island." 6.75 in. No mark. Event date: c.1880. $175-$225
Figure C11 - "Iron Pier, Length 1000 Feet, West Brighton Beach, Coney Island." 6.87 in. No mark. Event date: c.1880. $175-$225

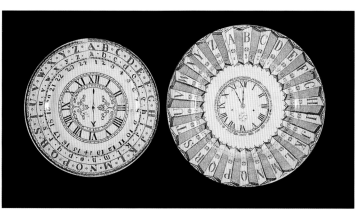

Figure C12 - "Oriental Hotel, Coney Island." 7.25 in. No mark. Event date: c.1880. $175-$225

Figure C5 - "Blue Clock Face." 5.75 in. William Adams & Sons. Tunstall and Stoke, Staffordshire. Matching mug not shown. Factory date: 1769+. Mark date: 1914-1940. $75-$100
Figure C6 - "Clock Face." 6.5 in. Barkers & Kent, Ltd. Fenton, Staffordshire. Factory date: 1889-1941. $100-$150

Figure C13 - "Congressional Library, Washington DC." Lustre. 6.50 in. Made in Germany. Event date: c.1897. $150-$200

Figure C19 - Mark: West End Pottery. East Liverpool, Ohio. Factory date: 1892 (3?)-1938. Mark date: 1893-1910.

Figure C20 - "Bears at Tennis." Souvenir: "Holly (correctly spelled, Holley), New York." 7 in. West End Pottery Co. East Liverpool, Ohio. Factory date: 1892 (3?)-1938. Mark date: 1893-1910. $150-$175

Figure C14 - "Union Station, Omaha, Nebraska." Lustre. 6.5 in. No mark. Event date: c.1899-1927. $100-$150

Figure C15 - "Statue of Roswell Pettibone Flowers, Watertown New York." Lustre. 6.5 in. Made in Germany. Event date: c.1900. $100-$150

Figure C16 - "Post Office, Concord, New Hampshire." Lustre. 6.5 in. No mark. Event date: 1889. $100-$150

Figure C21 - "Pussy Cat, Where Have you Been?" Commercial Message: "Smith and Brown, Quebec, Canada." 7.12 in. Holdfast, D. E. McNicol Pottery Co. East Liverpool, Ohio. Souvenir #2429. Factory date: 1892-c.1929. Mark date: c.1920. $150-$175

Figure C22 - "Ride A Cock-Horse." Commercial Message: Newport, New York. 7.12 in. Holdfast, D. E. McNicol Pottery Co. East Liverpool, Ohio. Factory date: 1892-c.1929. $150-$175

Figure C17 - "Administration Building, World's Columbian Exposition." 6.87 in. Trademark registered in US Patent Office (see information in "U Is for Undersides"). Event date: c.1893. $200-$250

Figure C18 - "The Electrical Building, World's Columbian Exposition." 6.87 in. No mark. Event date: c.1893. $200-$250

Figure C23 - "New York City Hall and Mt. Vernon." 7.25 in. Brownhills Pottery Co. Tunstall, Staffordshire. Factory date: 1872-1896. Registry Mark #26734 date: 1895. $200-$250

Figure C24 - "Niagara Falls and The White House, Washington, D.C." 7.25 in. Brownhills Pottery Co. Tunstall, Staffordshire. Factory date: 1872-1896. Registry Mark #26734 date: 1895. $200-$250

Figure C28 - "Romantic Scene with Llamas." 6.75 in. No mark. $150-$200
Figure C29 - "Romantic Scene with Castles." 6.75 in. No mark. $150-$200

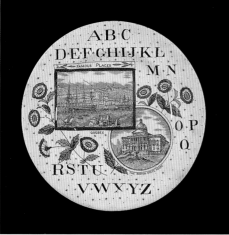

Figure C25- "Quebec and The Boston State House." 7.87 in. Brownhills Pottery Co. Tunstall, Staffordshire. Factory date: 1872-1896. Registry Mark #26734 date: 1895. $200-$250

Figure C30 - Mark: Semi-Vitreous: Buffalo Pottery. Buffalo, New York. Factory date: 1903+ Mark date: c.1907.

Figure C31 - "Campbell's Kids - the Girl is Holding the Doll." H-1.37 in. x D-7.62 in. Buffalo Pottery Semi-Vitreous, Buffalo, New York. Factory date: 1903+. Production date: 1917. $150-$200

Figure C26 - "Parliament House, Ottawa and The Post Office, Ottawa." 8.25 in. Brownhills Pottery Co. Tunstall, Staffordshire. Factory date: 1872-1896. Registry Mark #26734 date: 1895. $200-$250

Figure C27 - "Detail of "Paris and Notre Dame, Paris." 7.87 in. Brownhills Pottery Co. Tunstall, Staffordshire. Factory date: 1872-1896. Registry Mark #26734 date: 1895. $200-$250

Figure C32 - "Campbell's Kids - the Boy is Holding the Doll." H-1.37 in. x D-7.62 in. Buffalo Pottery Semi-Vitreous, Buffalo, New York. Factory date: 1903+. Production date: 1917. $150-$200

Figure C36 - "Playing at Driving Horses." Chromolithography. Assay: Iron 99.2%, Copper .2%, Nickel .5%, Chromium .01%, Trace elements .09% 6.12 in. Manufactured for Lava Soap Co., a Division of Proctor and Gamble. Cincinnati, Ohio. Production date: c.1930. *Courtesy of Ann and Dennis Berard.* $150-$175

Figure C33 - "Campbell's Kids - the Doll has Fallen." H-1.25 in. x D-7.37 in. Buffalo Pottery Semi-Vitreous, Buffalo, New York. Factory date: 1903+. Production date: 1917. $150-$200

Figure C37 - "Here We Go Round the Mulberry Bush." Chromolithography. Assay: Iron 99%, Copper .2%, Manganese .09%, Nickel .04%, Chromium .03%, Trace elements .64%. 6.12 in. Manufactured for Lava Soap Co., a Division of Proctor and Gamble. Cincinnati, Ohio. Production date: c.1930. *Courtesy of Ann and Dennis Berard.* $150-$175

Figure C34 - "Campbell's Kids Look-Alike with American Flag." Soup shape. H-1.25 in. x D-7.5 in. Crown Pottery & Co. Evansville, Indiana. Factory date: 1891-c.1955 (8?). Mark date: c.1936. $100-$150

Figure C38 - "Monkey on a Barrel." Chromolithography. Assay: Iron 99.5%, Copper .35%, Trace elements .15%. 6.12 in. Manufactured for Lava Soap Co., a Division of Proctor and Gamble. Cincinnati, Ohio. Production date: c.1930. *Courtesy of Ann and Dennis Berard.* $150-$175

Figure C35 - "Virginia (Campbell's Kids Cereal)." Cereal shape. Plastic. H-1.5 in. x D-6.25 in. No mark. Recent issue. $50-$75

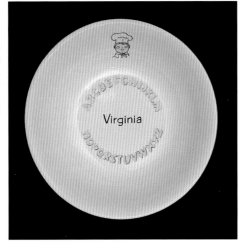

Figure C39 - "Tom, Tom the Piper's Son." Chromolithography. Assay: Iron 99%, Nickel 1%. 6.12 in. Manufactured for Lava Soap Co., a Division of Proctor and Gamble. Cincinnati, Ohio. Production date: c.1930. *Courtesy of Ann and Dennis Berard.* $150-$175

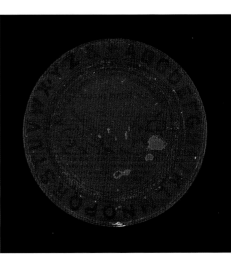

Figure C40 - "Sailing Ship." Chromolithography. Assay: Iron 99%, Copper .2%, Manganese .09%, Nickel .04%, Chromium .03%, Trace elements .64%. 6.12 in. Manufactured for Lava Soap Co., a Division of Proctor and Gamble. Cincinnati, Ohio. Production date: c.1930. *Courtesy of Ann and Dennis Berard.* $150-$175

Figure C44 - "Advertiser for Buster Brown Shoes - Buster Brown Toasting Tea Cups." 7 in. No mark. Production date: 1904+. $100-$150

Figure C41 - Mark: Beetleware - Advertiser for Post Cereals. Hemco Moulding, Division of the Bryant Electric Company. Bridgeport, Connecticut. Production date: 1935.

Figure C45 - Deep Dish also seen in Figure D83. Advertiser: "Compliments of Tomasini Hardware Co., Petaluma, California." $150-$200

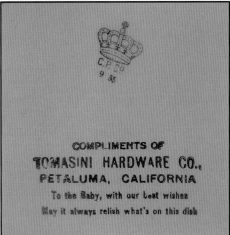

Figure C42 - "Donald Duck." Cereal shape. Plastic "Beetleware." H-1.5 in. x D-5.5 in. Manufactured for Post Cereals by Hemco Moulding, a Division of Bryant Electric Co. Bridgeport, Connecticut. Production date: 1935. $60-$80

Figure C43 - "Mickey Mouse." Cereal shape. Plastic "Beetleware." H-1.5 in. x D-5.5 in. Manufactured for Post Cereals by Hemco Moulding, a Division of Bryant Electric Co. Bridgeport, Connecticut. Production date: 1935. $60-$80

Figure C46 - "Advertiser for Cleverdon & Co. Halifax, Nova Scotia, below the ancient Coat of Arms." 5 in. No mark. Production date: 1860-1866. $200-$275

Figure C47 - "Spelling Bee." 6.25 in. No mark. $175-$225

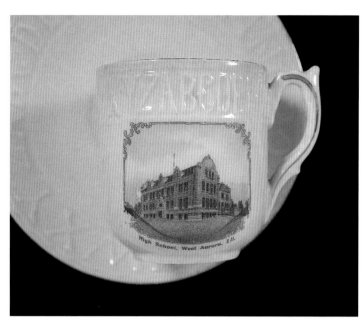

Figure C52 - "Baby Bunting and Bunch While Crossing a Log." 6.25 in. Hotel China, Harker Pottery Co. East Liverpool, Ohio. Factory date: c.1840-1972. Production date: 1890-1920. *Courtesy of William and Donna Gray.* $75-$125

Figure C48 - "High School, West Aurora, Illinois." Lustre. Saucer: 5 in. Cup: H-2.37 in. x D-2.5 in. No mark. Event date: c.1910. $150-$200

Figure C49 - Mark: Hotel China-Harker Pottery Co. East Liverpool, Ohio. Factory date: c.1840-1972. Production date: 1890-1920.

Figure C53 - Mark: William Brunt Pottery, East Liverpool, Ohio. Factory date: 1894 (2?)-1911. Mark date: 1900-1911.

Figure C50 - "Tulips." 6.25 in. Hotel China-Harker Pottery Co. East Liverpool, Ohio. Factory date: c.1840-1972. Production date: 1890-1920. *Courtesy of William and Donna Gray.* $75-$125

Figure C54 - "Baby Bunting and Bunch When (Went) Out for a Walk." 7 in. The William Brunt Pottery Company. East Liverpool, Ohio. Factory date: 1894 (2?)-1911. Mark date: 1900-1911. $75-$125

Figure C51 - "Baby Bunting Lifts his Hat." 6 in. Hotel China-Harker Pottery Co. East Liverpool, Ohio. Factory date: c.1840-1972. Production date: 1890-1920. *Courtesy of William and Donna Gray.* $75-$125

Figure C55 - "It iss mutch better yet to shmile . . . . " 6.12 in. Hotel China-Harker Pottery Co. East Liverpool, Ohio. Factory date: c.1840-1972. Production date: 1890-1920. *Courtesy of William and Donna Gray.* $75-$125

Figure C56 - "Dutch Children at the Seaside." 6 in. Hotel China-Harker Pottery Co. East Liverpool, Ohio. Factory date: c.1840-1972. Production date: 1890-1920. *Courtesy of William and Donna Gray.* $75-$125

Figure C60 - "Two Children on a Sled." 6.25 in. Hotel China-Harker Pottery Co. East Liverpool, Ohio. Factory date: c.1840-1972. Production date: 1890-1920. *Courtesy of William and Donna Gray.* $75-$125

Figure C57 - "There Came a Big Spider." 6 in. Hotel China-Harker Pottery Co. East Liverpool, Ohio. Factory date: c.1840-1972. Production date: 1890-1920. *Courtesy of William and Donna Gray.* $75-$125

Figure C61 - "Memories." 6.25 in. Hotel China-Harker Pottery Co. East Liverpool, Ohio. Factory date: c.1840-1972. Production date: 1890-1920. *Courtesy of William and Donna Gray.* $75-$125

Figure C58 - "Campbell's Kids - Girl Holding a Doll." 6 in. Hotel China-Harker Pottery Co. East Liverpool, Ohio. Factory date: c.1840-1972. Production date: 1890-1920. *Courtesy of William and Donna Gray.* $100-$150

Figure C62 - "Kitten." 6.25 in. Hotel China-Harker Pottery Co. East Liverpool, Ohio. Factory date: c.1840-1972. Production date: 1890-1920. *Courtesy of William and Donna Gray.* $75-$125

Figure C59 - "Washing the Dog." 6 in. Hotel China-Harker Pottery Co. East Liverpool, Ohio. Factory date: c.1840-1972. Production date: 1890-1920. *Courtesy of William and Donna Gray.* $75-$125

Figure C63 - "English Pointer." 6 in. Hotel China-Harker Pottery Co. East Liverpool, Ohio. Factory date: c.1840-1972. Production date: 1890-1920. *Courtesy of William and Donna Gray.* $75-$125

Figure C64 - "Greyhound." 6 in. Hotel China-Harker Pottery Co. East Liverpool, Ohio. Factory date: c.1840-1972. Production date: 1890-1920. *Courtesy of William and Donna Gray.* $75-$125

Figure C68- "Horse." 6 in. Hotel China-Harker Pottery Co. East Liverpool, Ohio. Factory date: c.1840-1972. Production date: 1890-1920. *Courtesy of William and Donna Gray.* $75-$125

Figure C65 - "Dogs at the Doghouse." 6.12 in. Hotel China-Harker Pottery Co. East Liverpool, Ohio. Factory date: c.1840-1972. Production date: 1890-1920. *Courtesy of William and Donna Gray.* $75-$125

Figure C69 - "Lions." 6.25 in. Hotel China-Harker Pottery Co. East Liverpool, Ohio. Factory date: c.1840-1972. Production date: 1890-1920. *Courtesy of William and Donna Gray.* $75-$125

Figure C66 - "Their First Day." 6 in. Hotel China-Harker Pottery Co. East Liverpool, Ohio. Factory date: c.1840-1972. Production date: 1890-1920. *Courtesy of William and Donna Gray.* $75-$125

Figure C70 - "Robin." 6 in. Hotel China-Harker Pottery Co. East Liverpool, Ohio. Factory date: c.1840-1972. Production date: 1890-1920. *Courtesy of William and Donna Gray.* $75-$125

Figure C67 - "Horse, Dog and Pups." 6 in. Hotel China-Harker Pottery Co. East Liverpool, Ohio. Factory date: c.1840-1972. Production date: 1890-1920. *Courtesy of William and Donna Gray.* $75-$125

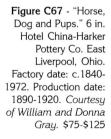

Figure C71 - "Owl." 6.25 in. Hotel China-Harker Pottery Co. East Liverpool, Ohio. Factory date: c.1840-1972. Production date: 1890-1920. *Courtesy of William and Donna Gray.* $75-$125

Figure C72 - "Great Expectations." 6.25 in. Hotel China-Harker Pottery Co. East Liverpool, Ohio. Factory date: c.1840-1972. Production date: 1890-1920. *Courtesy of Jean C. Rutter.* $75-$125

Figure C73 - "Sunbonnet Kids - I Love You." 6 in. Hotel China-Harker Pottery Co. East Liverpool, Ohio. Factory date: c.1840-1972. Production date: 1890-1920. *Courtesy of William and Donna Gray.* $100-$150

Figure C74 - "Sunbonnet Kids - The Three of Us." 6 in. Hotel China-Harker Pottery Co. East Liverpool, Ohio. Factory date: c.1840-1972. Production date: 1890-1920. *Courtesy of William and Donna Gray.* $100-$150

Figure C75 - "Sunbonnet Kids - Candy For My Mandy." 6 in. Hotel China-Harker Pottery Co. East Liverpool, Ohio. Factory date: c.1840-1972. Production date: 1890-1920. *Courtesy of William and Donna Gray.* $100-$150

Figure C76 - "Sunbonnet Kids - Kiss and Make Up." 6 in. Hotel China-Harker Pottery Co. East Liverpool, Ohio. Factory date: c.1840-1972. Production date: 1890-1920. $100-$150

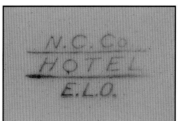

Figure C77 - Mark: National China Company. East Liverpool, Ohio. Factory date: c.1900-1929. Mark date: 1900-1911.

Figure C78 - Mark: National China Company. East Liverpool, Ohio. Factory date: c.1900-1929, Mark date: 1911-1920.

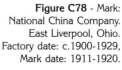

159

Figure C79 - "Sunbonnet Kids - I Love You." H-1.37 in. x D-6.5 in. National China Company. East Liverpool, Ohio. Factory date: c.1900-1929. Mark date: 1900-1911. $100-$150

Figure C83 - "Please Felix, Don't Shoot." H-1.5 in. x D-8 in. Holdfast-D. E. McNicol. East Liverpool, Ohio. Factory date: 1892-c.1929. Production date: c.1920. $275-$300

Figure C80 - "Sunbonnet Kids - The Three of Us." H-1.37 in. x D-6.5 in. National China Company. East Liverpool, Ohio. Factory date: c.1900-1929. Mark date: 1911-1920. $100-$150

Figure C84 - Mark: Carl Schumann Porcelain Factory. Arzberg, Bavaria. Factory date: 1881-1996. Registered and Authorized by Walter E. Disney.

Figure C81 - "Sunbonnet Kids - T 4 2 (Tea for Two)." H-1.37 in. x D-6.5 in. National China Company. East Liverpool, Ohio. Factory date: c.1900-1929. Mark date: 1900-1911. $100-$150

Figure C85 - "Mickey Mouse on a Train." H-1.5 in. x D-7. in. Carl Schumann Porcelain Factory. Arzberg, Bavaria. Factory date: 1881-1996. Registered and Authorized by Walter E. Disney. Production date: c.1930. $500+

Figure C86 - Mark: Carl Schumann Porcelain Factory. Arzberg, Bavaria. Factory date: 1881-1996. Registered and Authorized by Walter E. Disney.

Figure C82 - "Now Felix, Keep on Walking." H-1.5 in. x D-8 in. Holdfast-D. E. McNicol. East Liverpool, Ohio. Factory date: 1892-c.1929. Production date: c.1920. $275-$300

Figure C87 - "Pluto - the Pup and Mickey Mouse." H-1.5 in. x D-7.5 in. Carl Schumann Porcelain Factory. Arzberg, Bavaria. Factory date: 1881-1996. Registered and Authorized by Walter E. Disney. Production date: c.1935. This plate is also found as Figure J2, in "J Is for J, the Last Letter of the Alphabet," and Figure Z6 in "Z is for Σ and Other Reversals." $500+

D Is for Deep Dishes

Figure D1 - "Bowled Over!" Poster. Bethnal Museum of Childhood, Victoria and Albert Museum, London. *Used with permission of Victoria and Albert Museum, London.*

Figure D3 - "Bowled Over!" H-1.62 in. x D-6.87 in. Sampson Bridgwood & Son Pottery Co. Longton, Staffordshire. Factory date: 1853+. Production date: c.1920. $200-$250

Figure D4 - Pottery mark: "Made in Czechoslovakia."

Figure D2 - Advertisement for Sampson Bridgwood & Son Pottery Co. in the Pottery Gazette, Scott, Greenwood & Sons, London. n.d. *Used with permission of Tableware International, Surrey, England.*

Figure D5 - "Boy with a Wheelbarrow." H-1.5 in. x D-6.25 in. Made in Czechoslovakia. c.1930. $150-$200

Figure D6 - Mark: Arzberg Porcelain Factory. Arzberg, Bavaria. Factory date: 1927+

Figure D7 - "Girl Feeding Chicks." H-1.5 in. x D-6.75 in. Arzberg Porcelain Factory. Arzberg, Bavaria. Factory date: 1927+. $150-$200

Figure D8 - Mark: "Made in Germany." Heise Pottery Co. Berlin, Germany. Factory date: 1919+

Figure D9 - "Cat in the Cradle." H-1.27 in. x D-7.25 in. Heise Pottery Co. Berlin, Germany. Factory date: 1919+. $150-$200

Figure D10 - Mark: Possibly a variety of mark of the L. Hutschenreuther Porcelain Factory. Selb, Germany. Factory date: 1857+

Figure D11 - "Batter up!" H-1.5 in. x D-6.62 in. Possibly L. Hutschenreuther Porcelain Factory. Selb, Germany. Factory date: 1857+. $150-$200

Figure D12 - "Mark: C. A. Lehmann & Son. Leuchtenburg." Röntgen's listing found for C. A. Lehmann & Son locates the firm in Kahla, Thuringia, Germany. "Leuchtenburg" refers only to the castle which still stands above the city. Factory date: 1895-c.1935.

Figure D13 - "Clown Riding on a Pig." H-1.62 in. x D-6.87 in. C. A. Lehmann & Son. Leuchtenburg. Kahla, Thuringia, Germany. Factory date: 1895-c.1935. $150-$200

Figure D14 - "Portraits of Two Children." H-1.62 in. x D-5 in. C. A. Lehmann & Son. Leuchtenburg. Kahla, Thuringia, Germany. Factory date: 1895-c.1935. $150-$200.

Figure D15 - "Boys with Paper Hats Threatening Bears." H-1.5 in. x D-6.87 in. C. A. Lehmann & Son. Leuchtenburg. Kahla, Thuringia, Germany. Factory date: 1895-c.1935. $150-$200

Figure D16 - Mark: R. C. W. or Retsch & Co. Wunsiedel, Germany. Factory date: 1884+

Figure D17 - "Three Children and a Goat - Alphabet does not include the letter J." H-1.27 in. x D-6.75 in. R. C. W. or Retsch & Co. Wunsiedel, Germany. Factory date: 1884+. This plate is also found as Figure J12 in "J Is for J, the Last Letter of the Alphabet." $150-$200

Figure D18 - Mark: Royal Bavaria. Tettau, Bavaria. Factory date: 1957+ (?)

Figure D22 - "Little Bo-Peep." H-1.27 in. x D-6.62 in. Carl Schumann Porcelain Factory. Arzberg, Bavaria. Factory date: 1881-1996. $150-$200

Figure D19 - "Silhouette of a Girl Feeding a Lamb." H-1.27 in. x D-7.5 in. Possibly the mark of Royal Bayreuth. Tettau, Bavaria. Factory date: 1957+ (?). $150-$200

Figure D20 - Mark: Carl Schumann Porcelain Factory. Arzberg, Bavaria. Factory date: 1881-1996.

Figure D21 - "Jack and Jill." H-1.62. in. x D-7 in. Carl Schumann Porcelain Factory. Arzberg, Bavaria. Factory date: 1881-1996. $150-$200

Figure D23 - Mark: Three Crown Pottery. Listed in Danckert (1992) as "unknown."

Figure D24 - "This is the Cat that Killed the Rat." H-1.5 in. x D-6.75 in. Three Crown Pottery. $150-$200

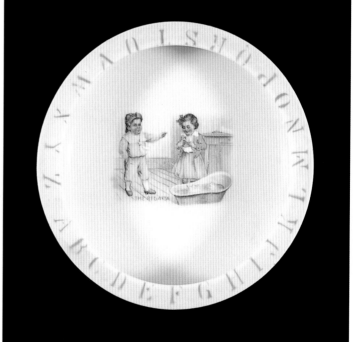

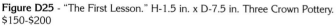

Figure D25 - "The First Lesson." H-1.5 in. x D-7.5 in. Three Crown Pottery. $150-$200

Center right: **Figure D26** - "The Regatta." H-1.5 in. x D-7.5 in. Three Crown Pottery. $150-$200

Bottom right: **Figure D27** - "Three Dutch Children at the Seaside." Dog dish shape. H-1.5 in. x D-7.27 in. Three Crown Pottery. $150-$200

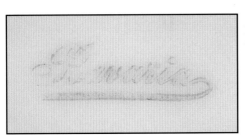

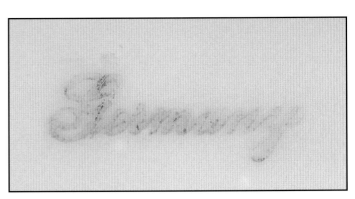

Figure D31 - Mark: Script Germany, Green.

Figure D29 - "Silhouette of a Boy Feeding the Birds." H-1.5 in. x D-7.75 in. Script Bavaria, Green. $150-$200

Figure D32 - "Dutch Girl with a Basket." H-1.5 in. x D-7.5 in. Script Germany, Green. $150-$200

Figure D30 - "Silhouette of a Girl Feeding a Lamb." H-1.5 in. x D-7.75 in. Script Bavaria, Green. $150-$200

Figure D33 - Mark: Script Germany, Blue.

Figure D34 - "Three graphics: Jack and Jill, Little Bo-Peep, and Hey Diddle Diddle." H-1.27 in. x D-7.62 in. Script Germany, Blue. $150-$200

Figure D37 - "Two Children and a Cat." Border of orange letter animals, A-Z and J-N. H-1.27 in. x D-7.27 in. Capital letters GERMANY, Orange. $150-$200

Figure D35 - "Girl With a Pail and a Shovel." H-1.5 in. x D-7.5 in. Script Germany, Blue. $150-$200

Figure D38 - "Boy, Girl, and Grey Dog." Border of blue letter animals, A-Z and T-X. H-1.27 in. x D-7.5 in. Capital letters GERMANY, Orange. $150-$200

Figure D36 - Mark: Capital letters GERMANY, Orange.

167

Figure D39 - "Boy with Toys." Border of blue letter animals, A-Z and J-N. H-1.5 in. x D-7.5 in. Capital letters GERMANY, Orange. $150-$200

Figure D43 - "Round Dance." Dog-dish shape. H-1.5 in. x D-7.5 in. Capital letters GERMANY, Orange. $150-$200

Figure D40 - "Children With Books." Border of blue letter animals, A-Z and D-H. H-1.5 in. x D-7.5 in. Capital letters GERMANY, Orange. $150-$200

Figure D44 - "Girl, Baby, and Dog on a Swing." Dog-dish shape. H-1.5 in. x D-7.5 in. Capital letters GERMANY, Orange. $150-$200

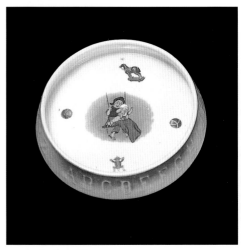

Figure D41 - "The Geography Lesson." Border of blue letter animals, A-Z and J-O. H-1.5 in. x D-7.5 in. Capital letters GERMANY, Orange. $150-$200

Figure D45 - "Ride in a Motorcar." H-1.5 in. x 7.5 in. Capital letters GERMANY, Orange. Non-alphabet matching items include a toy coffee pot, sugar, creamer, plates, cups, and saucers, not shown. Deep dish value: $150-$200.

Figure D42 - "Dutch Boy and Girl Making a Wreath." H-1.5 in. x D-7.5 in. Capital letters GERMANY, Orange. $150-$200

Figure D46 - "Elephant at Tennis." Dog-dish shape. H-1.5 in. x D-7.27 in. Capital letters GERMANY, Orange. $150-$200

Figure D47 - "Good Luck Old Boy." Dog-dish shape. H-1.5 in. x D-7.5 in. Capital letters GERMANY, Orange. $150-$200

Figure D51 - "Cat in the Cradle - Alphabet does not include the letter J." H-1.5 in. x D-7.62 in. Germany, Gold Arc. This plate is also found as Figure J13 in "J Is for J, the Last Letter of the Alphabet." $150-$200

Figure D48 - Mark: Script Germany, Blue and capital letters E(B or R)PHILA between circles, Green.

Figure D52 - Mark: Made in Germany, Circle shape, Orange.

Figure D49 - "Hey Diddle Diddle." H-1.5 in. x D-7.62 in. Script Germany, Blue and capital letters E(B or R)PHILA between circles, Green. $150-$200

Figure D53 - "Boy with a Hat and Girl with an Umbrella." H-1.5 in. x D-7.75 in. Made in Germany, Circle shape, Orange. $150-$200

Figure D50 - Mark: Germany, Gold Arc.

Figure D54 - Mark: Capital letters GERMANY between circles, Pink.

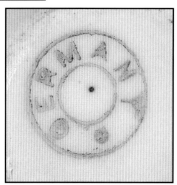

Figure D55 - "Boy and Girl with a Basket." H-1.5 in. x D-6.5 in. Capital letters GERMANY between circles, Pink. c.1930. $150-$200

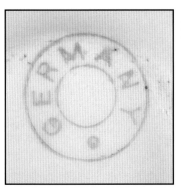

Figure D56 - Mark: Capital letters GERMANY between circles, Orange.

Figure D60 - "Boy and Three Girls Talking." Dog-dish shape. Numerals 0-9 surround. H-1.27 in. x D-6.12 in. Capital letters GERMANY between circles, Orange; numeral (manufacturer's mark) at center. $150-$200

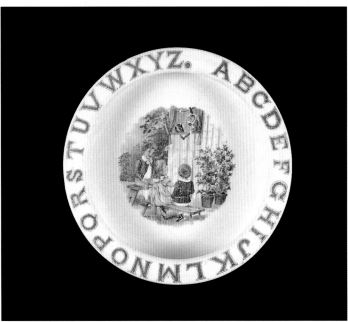

Figure D57 - "Children at the Puppet Stage." H-1.12 in. x D-6.62 in. Capital letters GERMANY between circles, Orange. $150-$200

Figure D61 - Mark: Capital letters GERMANY between circles, Green.

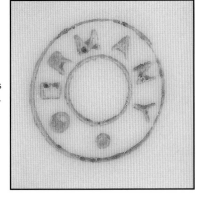

Figure D58 - "Toddler Reaching for a Pretzel." H-1.5 in. x D-6.62 in. Capital letters GERMANY between circles, Orange. $150-$200

Figure D62 - "A Boy and Three Girls Talking." Dog-dish shape. H-1.5 in. x D-6.12 in. Capital letters GERMANY between circles, Green. $150-$200

Figure D63 - "Mug Matching Deep Dishes D60 and D62." H-3.5 in. x D-3 in. No mark. $65-$80

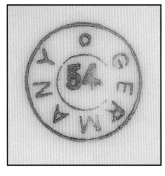

Figure D59 - Mark: Capital letters GERMANY between circles, Orange; numeral (manufacturer's mark) at center.

Figure D64 - Mark: Capital letters MADE IN AUSTRIA between circles, Orange.

Figure D68 - Mark: O (or D) G Germany (monogram).

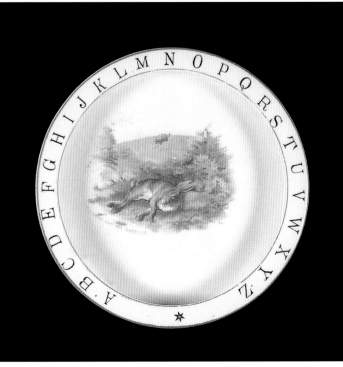

Figure D69 - "Toddler and his Spoon." Border of blue letter animals, A-Z and J-Q. H-1.5 in. x D-7.5 in. O (or D) G Germany. $150-$200

Figure D65 - "The Tortoise and the Hare." H-1.12 in. x D-7.25 in. Capital letters MADE IN AUSTRIA between circles, Orange. $150-$200

Figure D70 - Mark: G. W. Co. Germany.

Figure D66 - Mark: Script Germany, Blue and L. O. Co. New York export firm.

Figure D71 - "Little Polly Flinders - Alphabet does not include the letter J." Lustre. Alphabet and numeral surround. H-1.5 in. x D-7.62 in. G. W. Co. Germany. This plate is also found as Figure J14 in "J Is for J, the Last Letter of the Alphabet." $150-$200

Figure D67 - "There Was an Old Woman Who Lived under a Hill." H-1.5 in. x D- 7.5 in. Script Germany, Blue and L. O. Co. New York export firm. $150-$200

Figure D72 - "Little Bo-Peep - Alphabet does not include the letter J." Lustre. Alphabet and numeral surround. H-1.27 in. x D-6.62 in. G. W. Co. Germany. This plate is also found as Figure J15 in "J Is for J, the Last Letter of the Alphabet." $150-$200

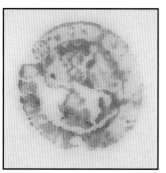

Figure D73 - Mark: Illegible mark (green).

Figure D77 - "Round Dance in the Garden." H-1.27 in. x D-7.25 in. Cochran & Fleming. Glasgow, Scotland. Factory date: 1896-1920. $150-$200

Figure D74 - "This is the Cow with the Crumpled Horn." H-1.27 in. x D-6.75 in. Illegible mark. $150-$200

Figure D78 - Mark: Swinnertons. Made in England. Hanley, Staffordshire. Factory date: 1906-1970 (1?). $150-$200

Figure D75 - Mark: Sampson Bridgwood & Son, Made in England. Longton, Staffordshire. Factory date: 1853+. (See Figures D1, D2, and D3.)

Figure D76 - Mark: C & F over G over England. Cochran & Fleming. Glasgow, Scotland. Factory date: 1896-1920.

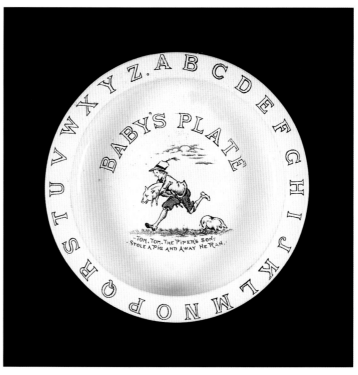

Figure D79 - "Tom, Tom the Piper's Son." H-1.75 in. x D-7.25 in. Swinnertons. Hanley, Staffordshire. Made in England. Factory date: 1906-1970 (1?). $150-$200

Figure D80 - "Tom, Tom the Piper's Son" (variation of D79). H-1.75 in. x D-7.25 in. Swinnertons. Made in England. Hanley, Staffordshire. Factory date: 1906-1970 (1?) $150-$200

Figure D84 - "Sheriff Dog." H-1.75 in. x D-7.5 in. Crown Potteries. Evansville, Indiana. Factory date: 1891-c.1955 (8?). Mark date: 1946. $150-$200

Figure D81 - Mark: Crown Potteries. Made in USA. Evansville, Indiana. Factory date: 1891-c.1955 (8?). Mark date: 1946.

Figure D85 - "Sitting Scottie." Air brush. H-1.75 in. x D-7.27 in. Crown Potteries. Evansville, Indiana. Factory date: 1891-c.1955 (8?). Mark date: 1936. $100-$150

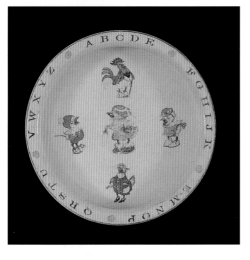

Figure D82 - "Feeding Teddy." H-1.5 in. x D-7.5 in. Crown Potteries. Evansville, Indiana. Factory date: 1891-c.1955 (8?). Mark date: 1946. $150-$200

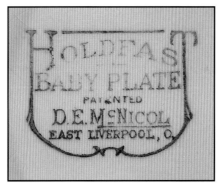

Figure D86 - Mark: Holdfast-D. E. McNicol Pottery Co. East Liverpool, Ohio. Factory date: 1892-c.1929. Mark date: c.1920.

Figure D83 - "Five Chickens." H-1.5 in. x D-7.5 in. Crown Potteries. Evansville, Indiana. Factory date: 1891-c.1955 (8?). Mark date: 1946. (See Figure C45 for information on reverse.) $150-$200

Figure D87 - "Heres a Little Pig Just as Hungry as Can Be." H-1.75 in. x D- 8 in. Holdfast-D. E. McNicol Pottery Co. East Liverpool, Ohio. Factory date: 1892-c.1929. Trademark date: c.1920. $150-$200

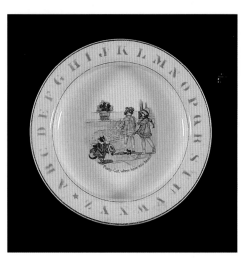

Figure D88 - "Pussy Cat, Where Have you Been?" H-1.5 in. x D-8.25 in. Holdfast-D. E. McNicol Pottery Co. East Liverpool, Ohio. Factory date: 1892-c.1929. Mark date: c.1920. $150-$200

Figure D92 - "Baby Bunting and Little Dog Bunch." H-2 in. x D-8.27 in. Holdfast-D. E. McNicol Pottery Co. East Liverpool, Ohio. Factory date: 1892-c.1929. Mark date: c.1920. $150-$200

Figure D89 - "Hickory, Dickory, Dock." H-2 in. x D-8.25 in. Holdfast-D. E. McNicol Pottery Co. East Liverpool, Ohio. Factory date: 1892-c.1929. Mark date: c.1920. $150-$200

Figure D93 - Mark: D. E. McNicol Pottery Co. East Liverpool, Ohio. Factory date: 1892-c.1929. Branch "X" Mark date: 1920-c.1928.

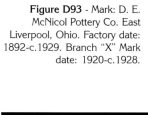

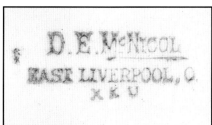

Figure D94 - "Pussy Cat, Pussy Cat, Where Have you Been?" H-2 in. x D-7.50 in. D. E. McNicol Pottery Co. East Liverpool, Ohio. Factory date: 1892-c.1929. Branch "X" Mark date: 1920-c.1928. $150-$200

Figure D90 - "Ride A-Cock-Horse." H-2 in. x D-8.62 in. Holdfast-D. E. McNicol Pottery Co. East Liverpool, Ohio. Factory date: 1892-c.1929. Mark date: c.1920. $150-$200

Figure D95- "Georgie Porgie, Pudding and Pie." H-1.87 in. x D-7.5 in. D. E. McNicol Pottery Co. East Liverpool, Ohio. Factory date: 1892-c.1929. Branch "X" Mark date: 1920-c.1928. $150-$200

Figure D91 - "Little Birdies In a Nest." H-2 in. x D-8 in. Holdfast-D. E. McNicol Pottery Co. East Liverpool, Ohio. Factory date: 1892-c.1929. Mark date: c.1920. $150-$200

Figure D96 - "Baby Bunting Runs Away." H-1.75 in. x D-7.5 in. D. E. McNicol Pottery Co. East Liverpool, Ohio. Factory date: 1892-c.1929. Branch "X" Mark date: 1920-c.1928. $150-$200

Figure D100 - Mark: ELPCO. Made in USA. China. East Liverpool Pottery Co. East Liverpool, Ohio. Factory date: 1884 (94?)-c.1901 (firm name initialized as E.L.P.CO. on some mark designs).

Figure D97 - Mark: D. E. McNicol Pottery Co. Clarksburg, West Virginia. Factory date: c.1914-1954. Mark date: probably before 1920 as the mark is undated.

Figure D101 - "There Came a Big Spider." H-1.5 in. x D-8.62 in. ELPCO. Made in USA. China. East Liverpool Pottery Co. East Liverpool, Ohio. Factory date: 1884 (94?)-c.1901. $150-$200

Figure D98 - "Sunbonnet Kids at Work." Soup bowl shape. H-1.62 in. x D-8.27 in. D. E. McNicol Pottery Co. Clarksburg, West Virginia. Factory date: c.1914-1954. Mark date: probably before 1920 as the mark is undated. $150-$200

Figure D102 - " A Baseball and Football Player (Design one)." Flat dish. 7 in. ELPCO. Made in USA. China. East Liverpool Pottery Co. East Liverpool, Ohio. Factory date: 1884 (94?)-c.1901. *Courtesy of Sunny Lenzner.* $75-$100

Figure D103 - "A Football Player and Skater (Design two)." Flat dish. 7 in. ELPCO. Made in USA. China. East Liverpool Pottery Co. East Liverpool, Ohio. Factory date: 1884 (94?)-c.1901. *Courtesy of Sunny Lenzner.* $75-$100

Figure D99 - "Playing Doctor." Soup bowl shape. H-1.25 in. x D-8.27 in. D. E. McNicol Pottery Co. Clarksburg, West Virginia. Factory date: c.1914-1954. Mark date: probably before 1920 as the mark is undated. $150-$200

Figure D104 - Mark: Dresden China Co. East Liverpool, Ohio. Factory date: 1875 (6?)-c.1927. Mark date: 1925.

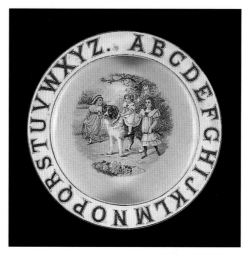

Figure D108 - "Riding the Dog." H-1.5 in. x D-7.5 in. No mark. $150-$200

Figure D105 - "The Football Player." Dog dish shape. Irregular placement of gold letters at perimeter. H-1.25 in. x D-7 in. Dresden China Co. East Liverpool, Ohio. Factory date: 1875 (6?)-c.1927. Mark date: 1925. $150-$200

Figure D109 - "Cows at the Stream." H-1.5 in. x D-7.5 in. No mark. $150-$200

Figure D106 - Mark: T. P. C-O. Co. SEMI-VIT. The Potter's Co-operative Co. East Liverpool, Ohio. Factory date: 1882-1925. Mark date: 1920-1925.

Figure D110 - "Little Red Riding Hood." H-1.25 in. x D-7.5 in. No mark. $150-$200

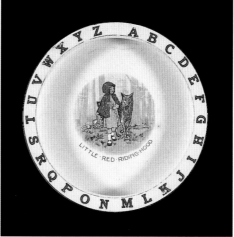

Figure D111 - "Little Boy Blue." H-1.25 in. x D-7.75 in. No mark. $150-$200

Figure D107 - "Tea Party." H-1.5 in. x D-7 in. T. P. C-O. Co. SEMI-VIT. The Potter's Co-operative Co. East Liverpool, Ohio. Factory date: 1882-1925. Mark date: 1920-1925. $150-$200

Figure D112 - "Little Bo-Peep." H-1.27 in. x D-7.5 in. No mark. $150-$200

Figure D116 - "Reading." H-1.27 in. x D-7.75 in. No mark. $150-$200

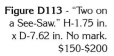

Figure D113 - "Two on a See-Saw." H-1.75 in. x D-7.62 in. No mark. $150-$200

Figure D117 - "Little Jack Horner." Dog dish shape. H-1.5 in. x D-7.5 in. No mark. $150-$200

Figure D114 - "The Photographer - Alphabet does not include the letter J." H-1.5 in. x D-7.62 in. No mark. This plate is also found as Figure J16 in 'J Is for J, the Last Letter of the Alphabet." $150-$200

Figure D118 - "Letters only." Border of green letter animals. H-1.25 in. x D-7. in. No mark. $50-$100

Figure D115 - "At the Doghouse." H-1.5 in. x D-7.5 in. No mark. $150-$200

Figure D119 - Mark: Crown Hotel China. Evansville, Indiana.

Figure D120 - "This Little Duck is Out of Luck." H-1 in. x D-7.5 in. Crown Hotel China. Evansville, Indiana. Firm unidentified (may be a mark of the Crown Pottery which reads: CROWN HOTEL WARE). $150-$200

E Is for Education

Figure E1 - "STU, Going to School." 5.75 in. No mark. $275- $325

Figure E4 - "Girl Feeding the Chicks (double alphabet)." 7.75 in. No mark. $200-$250

Figure E2 - "Brother and Sister at Play." 5.5 in. No mark. $150-$175

Figure E5 - "Bird at its Nest (double alphabet)." 7.25 in. No mark. $200-$250

Figure E6 - "Windmill at the Bridge (double alphabet)." 7.37 in. No mark. $200-$250

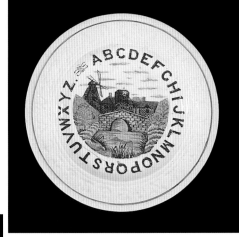

Figure E3 - "Farm Femme with Cow (double alphabet)." This plate is also found as Figure O7 in "O Is for Ornamental Borders." 7.37 in. No mark. $200-$250

Figure E7 - "Blowing Bubbles (double alphabet)." 7.25 in. No mark. $200-$250

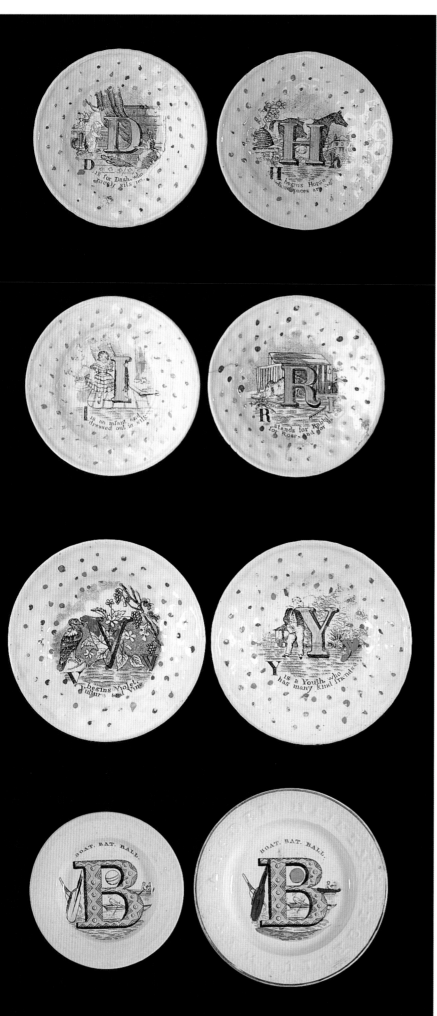

Figure E8 - "Dotted Rim Series - D is for Dash . . . ." 5.25 in. No mark. Sources: Baldwin, Ruth. *100 Nineteenth-Century Rhyming Alphabets in English.* Carbondale and Edwardsville, Illinois: Southern Illinois University Press, 1972. Originally published in the *Child's Treasury of Knowledge.* Boston: Wier & White. *Used with permission of Southern University Illinois Press. Courtesy of Ann and Dennis Berard.* Formerly of the Chalala Collection. $275-$325

Figure E9 - "Dotted Rim Series - H begins Horse . . . ." 5.25 in. No mark. Sources: *100 Nineteenth-Century . . . . as noted in E8. Courtesy of Ann and Dennis Berard.* $275-$325

Figure E10 - "Dotted Rim Series - I is an Infant . . . ." 5.25 in. No mark. Sources: *100 Nineteenth-Century . . . . as noted in E8. Courtesy of Ann and Dennis Berard.* Formerly of the Chalala Collection. $275-$325

Figure E11 - "Dotted Rim Series - R stands for Rabbit . . . ." 5.25 in. No mark. Sources: *100 Nineteenth-Century . . . . as noted in E8. Courtesy of Ann and Dennis Berard.* $275-$325

Figure E12 - "Dotted Rim Series - V is a Violet . . . ." 5.25 in. No mark. Sources: *100 Nineteenth-Century . . . . as noted in E8. Courtesy of Ann and Dennis Berard.* Formerly of the Chalala Collection. $275-$325

Figure E13 - "Dotted Rim Series - Y is a Youth . . . ." 5.25 in. No mark. Sources: *100 Nineteenth-Century . . . . as noted in E8. Courtesy of Ann and Dennis Berard.* Formerly of the Chalala Collection. $275-$325

Figure E14 - "B - Boat. Bat. Ball." 5.37 in. No mark. *Courtesy of Ann and Dennis Berard.* $275-$325

Figure E15 - "B - Boat. Bat. Ball." 6.5 in. No mark. *Courtesy of Ann and Dennis Berard.* $275-$325

Figure E16 - "E - Egg. Eye. Eel." 5.25 in. No mark. $275-$325
Figure E17 - "K - Kitten. Kite. Key." 5.25 in. No mark. $275-$325
Figure E18 - "P - Pig. Pigeon. Pins." 5 in. No mark. *Courtesy of Ann and Dennis Berard.* $275-$325

Figure E23 - "S - Shee (p)." Floral border. 6.5 in. Davenport (both transferred and impressed). Longton, Staffordshire. Factory date: c.1795-1887. Production date: 1871. *Courtesy of Ann and Dennis Berard.* $275-$325

Figure E19 - "B - B is for Ball . . . ." 5.25 in. (Identified by shape) Bailey and Ball or John Bailey. Longton, Staffordshire. Factory dates: 1843-1849 and 1849-1858. $275-$325
Figure E20 - "C - C begins Cat, Carpet, ..." 7.25 in. (Identified by shape) Bailey and Ball or John Bailey. Longton, Staffordshire. Factory dates: 1843-1849 and 1849-1858. *Courtesy of Ann and Dennis Berard.* $275-$325

Figure E21 - "A - Apple. Ape. Air." 6.37 in. No mark. *Courtesy of Ann and Dennis Berard.* $275-$325
Figure E22 - "C - Cow. Cat. Clown." 6.5 in. No mark. *Courtesy of Ann and Dennis Berard.* $275-$325

Figure E24 - "Getting Ready for a Walk." 5.37 in. No mark. *Courtesy of Ann and Dennis Berard.* $275-$325
Figure E25 - "Getting Ready for a Walk." 7.18 in. No mark. $275-$325

Figure E30 - "ABC - Boy and Dog." 5.75 in. No mark. $275-$325
Figure E31 - "ABC - Blind Man's Buff." 5.69 in. Staffordshire, England. *Courtesy of Ann and Dennis Berard.* $275-$325

Figure E26 - "E was an Eagle . . . ." Rococo, floral rim. 7.93 in. No mark. *Courtesy of Ann and Dennis Berard.* $275-$325
Figure E27 - "Heather - Red, Purple and Grey." Floral rim. 7.5 in. No mark. Source: Baldwin, Ruth. "The Alphabet of Flowers." *100 Nineteenth-Century Rhyming Alphabets in English.* Carbondale and Edwardsville, Illinois: Southern Illinois University Press, 1972. Originally published in *The Boys' and Girls' Illustrated Gift Book*, London: George Routledge & Sons, 1862. *Used with permission of Southern Illinois University Press.* $275-$325

Figure E32 - "DEF - Shuttlecock." 5.75 in. No mark. *Courtesy of Ann and Dennis Berard.* $275-$325
Figure E33 - "GHI - Boy on a Swing." 5.75 in. No mark. $275-$325

Figure E34 - "PQR - Flying a Kite." 5.62 in. No mark. $275-$325
Figure E35 - "VWX - See-Saw." 5.75 in. No mark. $275-$325

Figure E28 - "B is for Bobby's breakfast . . . ." 6.5 in. No mark. $275-$325
Figure E29 - "F's for the fowls and . . . ." 7.0 in. No mark. $275-$325

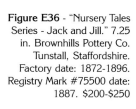
Figure E36 - "Nursery Tales Series - Jack and Jill." 7.25 in. Brownhills Pottery Co. Tunstall, Staffordshire. Factory date: 1872-1896. Registry Mark #75500 date: 1887. $200-$250

Figure E37 - "Little Jack Horner." 6.87 in. No mark. $225-$275
Figure E38 - "Nursery Tales Series - Little Jack Horner." 7.25 in. Brownhills Pottery Co. Tunstall, Staffordshire. Factory date: 1872-1896. Registry Mark #75500 date: 1887. This plate is also found as Figure S7 in "S Is for Sets." $200-$250

Figure E39 - "Ding, Dong, Bell." 6.37 in. No mark. $225-$275
Figure E40 - "DING, Dong, Bell!" . . . ." 6.62 in. No mark (possibly National China, East Liverpool, Ohio). $175-$200

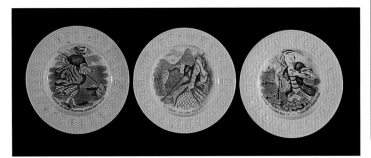

Figure E41 - "Little Bo-Peep, Running after her Sheep." 5.87 in. No mark. $225-$275
Figure E42 - "Bo-Peep, Calling for her Sheep." 5.75 in. No mark. $225-$275
Figure E43 - "Bo-Peep, Finding her Sheep." 5.87 in. No mark. $225-$275

Figure E44 - "This is the maiden . . . ." Fruit Shape. H-.75 in. x D-5.75 in. Germany. $225-$275

Figure E45 - "Nursery Rhyme Series - Hey, Diddle, Diddle." 7.5 in. No mark. $225-$275
Figure E46 - "Little Miss Muffet." 6.12 in. Manufactured in England for H. C. Edmiston, importer, New York. Firm date: 1902-1903. $225-$275

Figure E47 - "Simple Simon." 6.37 in. No mark. $225-$275

Figure E48 - "I'm going a milking, Sir, she said." 7.5 in. Importer's Garter mark: Boston & New York J. H. ?. & R. (Illegible). $225-$275
Figure E49 - "Tom the Piper's Son." 7.75 in. No mark. $225-$275

Figure E50 - "This Little Pig Went to Market." 7.12 in. No mark. $225-$275
Figure E51 - "Nursery Rhyme Series - Goosey Goosey Gander." 7.32 in. No mark. $225-$275

Figure E52 - "See-Saw Margery Daw." 7. in. No mark. $225-$275

Figure E56 - "The Man, the Boy, and the Donkey. Scene One." 7.62 in. No mark. $175-$225
Figure E57 - "The Man, the Boy, and the Donkey. Scene Two." 7.37 in. No mark. $175-$225

Figure E53 - "Nursery Rhyme Series - There was a Crooked Man." 7.5 in. No mark. $225-$275

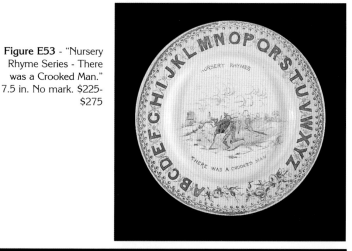

Figure E58 - "Aesop's Fables Series - The Dog and the Shadow." 8 in. No mark. $200-$250
Figure E59 - "Fox and Goose." 8 in. Elsmore & Son. Tunstall, Staffordshire. Factory date: (& Son)1872-1887. $200-$250

Figure E54 - "Old Mother Hubbard." 6.5 in. Mark illegible. $225-$275
Figure E55 - "Nursery Tales Series - Old Mother Hubbard." (Plate is included in this series although the tale is not composed in story form.) 7.25 in. Brownhills Pottery Co. Tunstall, Staffordshire. Factory date: 1872-1896. Registry Mark #75500 date: 1887. $200-$250

Figure E60 - "Aesop's Fables Series - The Fox and the Grapes." 6.37 in. No mark. Chalala dates production: 1875. $200-$250
Figure E61 - "Aesop's Fables Series - The Dog in the Manger." 6.25 in. No mark. Chalala dates production: 1875. $200-$250

Figure E62 - "Aesop's Fables Series - The Travellers (contemporary dictionaries spell the word as "travelers") and the Bear." 6.5 in. No mark. Chalala dates production: 1875. $200-$250
Figure E63 - "Aesop's Fables Series - The Leopard and the Fox." 6.5 in. No mark. Chalala dates production: 1834. $300+

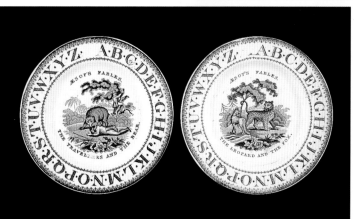

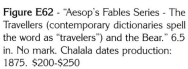

Figure E69 - "Red Riding Hood Starting." 7.25 in. Brownhills Pottery Co. Tunstall, Staffordshire. Factory date: 1872-1896. Registry Mark #149644 date: 1890. $200-$250

Figure E64 - "Aesop's Fables Series - The Hare and the Tortoise." 7.5 in. No mark. Chalala dates production: 1875. $200-$250

Figure E65 - "Aesop's Fables Series - The Fox and the Tiger." 7.35 in. No mark. Chalala dates production: 1875. $200-$250

Figure E66 - "Aesop's Fables Series - The Cock and the Fox." 5 in. No mark. Chalala dates production: 1875. $200-$250

Figure E67 - "Aesop's Fables Series - The Shepherd's Boy." 5.75 in. No mark. Sources (Riley, 1991): Croxall's Edition, Aesop's Fables. 1818. According to Riley (1991) an identical plate was marked T. & B. Godwin, New Wharf (#313). Factory date: 1809-1834. Chalala dates production: 1834. $300+

Figure E70 - "Red Riding Hood Meets . . . ." 7.25 in. Brownhills Pottery Co. Tunstall, Staffordshire. Factory date: 1872-1896. Registry Mark #149644 date: 1890. $200-$250

Figure E71 - "(Letter R) Red Riding Hood Meets . . . ." 7.25 in. No mark. $275-$325

Figure E68 - "Nursery Tales Series - Cinderella." 7.31 in. Brownhills Pottery Co. Tunstall, Staffordshire. Factory date: 1872-1896. Registry Mark #75500 date: 1887. $200-$250

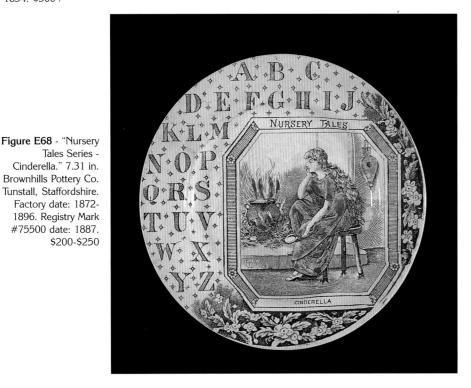

Figure E72 - "Red Riding Hood and her . . . ." 7.12 in. Brownhills Pottery Co. Tunstall, Staffordshire. Factory date: 1872-1896. Registry Mark #149644 date: 1890. $200-$250

Figure E77 - "Robinson Crusoe - Crusoe at his Tent." 5.12 in. No mark. Source: *Robinson Crusoe* as noted in E74. $175-$225

Figure E73 - "Robinson Crusoe Series - Crusoe on the Raft." 8. in. Brownhills Pottery Co. Tunstall, Staffordshire. Factory date: 1872-1896. Registry Mark #69963 date: 1887. $175-$225

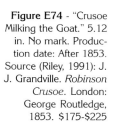

Figure E74 - "Crusoe Milking the Goat." 5.12 in. No mark. Production date: After 1853. Source (Riley, 1991): J. J. Grandville. *Robinson Crusoe*. London: George Routledge, 1853. $175-$225

Figure E78 - "Robinson Crusoe Series - Crusoe and his Pets." 8 in. Brownhills Pottery Co. Tunstall, Staffordshire. Factory date: 1872-1896. Registry Mark #69963 date: 1887. $175-$225

Figure E79 - "Robinson Crusoe Series - Crusoe Finding the Footprints." 8.12 in. Brownhills Pottery Co. Tunstall, Staffordshire. Factory date: 1872-1896. Registry Mark #69963 date: 1887. $175-$225

Figure E75 - "Robinson Crusoe Series - Crusoe at Work." 7.25 in. Brownhills Pottery Co. Tunstall, Staffordshire. Factory date: 1872-1896. Registry Mark #69963 date: 1887. $175-$225

Figure E76 - "Robinson Crusoe Series - Crusoe Viewing the Island." 7.12 in. Brownhills Pottery Co. Tunstall, Staffordshire. Factory date: 1872-1896. Registry Mark #69963 date: 1887. $175-$225

Figure E80 - "Robinson Crusoe Series - Crusoe Rescues Friday." 7.25 in. Brownhills Pottery Co. Tunstall, Staffordshire. Factory date: 1872-1896. Registry Mark #69963 date: 1887. $175-$225

Figure E81 - "Robinson Crusoe Series - Crusoe Teaching Friday." 6.37 in. Brownhills Pottery Co. Tunstall, Staffordshire. Factory date: 1872-1896. Registry Mark #69963 date: 1887. $175-$225

Figure E82 - "Robinson Crusoe Series - Crusoe Teaching Friday." 5.5 in. Brownhills Pottery Co. Tunstall, Staffordshire. Factory date: 1872-1896. Registry Mark #69963 date: 1887. $175- $225

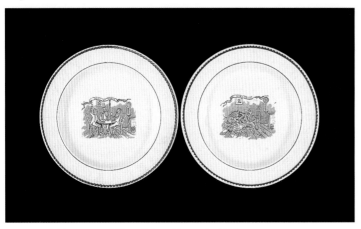

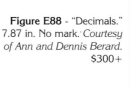

Figure E88 - "Decimals."
7.87 in. No mark. *Courtesy of Ann and Dennis Berard.*
$300+

Figure E83 - "Rule of Three." 8 in. No mark. $300+
Figure E84 - "The Sum Total." 8 in. No mark. $300+

Figure E85 - "Lecture in Long and Dry Measure." 7 in. No mark. $300+
Figure E86 - "Lecture in Long and Dry Measure." 8 in. No mark. $300+

Figure E89 - "Jane Browne Series - January . . . ." 6.37 in. No mark.
Source (Riley, 1991): Browne, Jane Euphemia (Aunt Effie). *Picture Scrap Book or Happy Hours at Home.* Religious Tract Society, c.1860. Second source: *Child's Companion and Juvenile Instructor.* Religious Tract Society, December, 1872. *Courtesy of Ann and Dennis Berard.* $175-$225
Figure E90 - "Jane Browne Series - February . . . ." 6.37 in. No mark. Source: *Picture Scrap Book . . . .* as noted in E89. *Courtesy of Ann and Dennis Berard.* $175-$225

Figure E87 - "Interest." 8 in. No mark. $300+

Figure E91 - "Jane Browne Series - March . . . ." 6.37 in. No mark. Source: *Picture Scrap Book . . . .* as noted in E89. *Courtesy of Ann and Dennis Berard.* $175-$225
Figure E92 - "Jane Browne Series - May . . . ." 6.37 in. No mark. Source: *Picture Scrap Book . . . .* as noted in E89. *Courtesy of Ann and Dennis Berard.* $175-$225

Figure E93 - "Jane Browne Series - June . . . . " 6.37 in. No mark. Source: *Picture Scrap Book* . . . . as noted in E89. *Courtesy of Ann and Dennis Berard.* $175-$225

Figure E94 - "Jane Browne Series - August . . . ." 6.37 in. No mark. Source: *Picture Scrap Book* . . . . as noted in E89. *Courtesy of Ann and Dennis Berard.* $175-$225

Figure E95 - "Jane Browne Series - September . . . ." 6.5 in. No mark. Source: *Picture Scrap Book* . . . . as noted in E89. *Courtesy of Ann and Dennis Berard.* $175-$225

Figure E96 - "Jane Browne Series - October . . . ." 6.31 in. No mark. Source: *Picture Scrap Book* . . . . as noted in E89. *Courtesy of Ann and Dennis Berard.* $175-$225

Figure E97 - "Jane Browne Series - November . . . ." 7.5 in. No mark. Source: *Picture Scrap Book* . . . . as noted in E89. *Courtesy of Ann and Dennis Berard.* $175-$225

Figure E98 - "February." 7 in. No mark. $175-$225
Figure E99 - "April." 5.75 in. No mark. $175-$225

Figure E100 - "May." 7.25 in. No mark. $175-$225
Figure E101 - "July." 7 in. No mark. $175-$225
Figure E102 - "August." 6.87 in. Impressed mark illegible. $175-$225

Figure E103 - "October." 7 in. No mark. $175-$225
Figure E104 - "December." 5.87 in. No mark. $175-$225
Figure E105 - "December." 7 in. No mark. $175-$225

Figure E106 - "Chinese Lady." 7.37 in. No mark. $175-$225
Figure E107 - "Chinese Gentleman." 7.37 in. No mark. $175-$225

Figure E108 - "Chinese Girl." 7.37 in. No mark. $175-$225
Figure E109 - "Chinese Boy." 7.37 in. No mark. $175-$225

Figure E110 - "Three Chinese Figures." 8.37 in. No mark. $175-$225

Figure E111 - "Chinese Villa." 5.5 in. No mark. $175-$225

Figure E112 - "Monkey School for Donkeys." 4 in. No mark. $150-$200

Figure E113 - "Fan Series - Horse." 7 in. W. Adams & Sons. Tunstall, Staffordshire. Factory date: 1769+ $150-$200
Figure E114 - "Fan Series - Stag." Fruit-dish shape. H-1.5 in. x D-6 in. John Meir & Son. Tunstall, Staffordshire. Factory date: 1837-1897. $150-$200

Figure E115 - "Fan Series - Donkey." 8.37 in. W. Adams & Sons. Tunstall, Staffordshire. Factory date: 1769+. Chalala dates production: 1891. $150-$200
Figure E116 - "Fan Series - Goat with Glasses." 8.25 in. W. Adams & Sons. Tunstall, Staffordshire. Factory date: 1769+ $150-$200

Figure E121 - "Elephant." 6.5 in. No mark. $175-$225
Figure E122 - "Fishing Elephant." 6.75 in. Impressed mark illegible. $175-$225

Figure E117 - "Wild Dog." 7.25 in. No mark. $175-$225
Figure E118 - "Sheep & Lamb." 7.5 in. No mark. $175-$225

Figure E123 - "Wild Animal Series - Elephant." 7.5 in. Brownhills Pottery Co. Tunstall, Staffordshire. Factory date: 1872-1896. Registry Diamond date: September 29, 1882. $275-$350
Figure E124 - "Wild Animal Series - Kangaroo." 6.37 in. Brownhills Pottery Co. Tunstall, Staffordshire. Factory date: 1872-1896. Registry Diamond date: September 29, 1882. Source (Riley, 1991): *The Picture Alphabet of Beasts*. London: T. Nelson & Sons. $275-$350

Figure E119 - "Sly Fox." 7 in. No mark. $175-$225
Figure E120 - "Giraffe (may be a 'Cameleopard')" 5 in. No mark. $175-$225

Figure E125 - "Wild Animal Series - The Lion." 7.5 in. Brownhills Pottery Co. Tunstall, Staffordshire. Factory date: 1872-1896. Registry Diamond date: September 29, 1882. $275-$350
Figure E126 - "Wild Animal Series - The Leopard." 7.25 in. Brownhills Pottery Co. Tunstall, Staffordshire. Factory date: 1872-1896. Registry Diamond date: September 29, 1882. $275-$350

Figure E127 - "Wild Animal Series - The Camel." 8.25 in. Brownhills Pottery Co. Tunstall, Staffordshire. Factory date: 1872-1896. Registry Diamond date: September 29, 1882. $275-$350

Figure E128 - "Wild Animal Series - Bear with Cubs." 7.25 in. Brownhills Pottery Co. Tunstall, Staffordshire. Factory date: 1872-1896. Registry Diamond date: September 29, 1882. $275-$350

Figure E132 - "Bird Series - Wandering Pie." 8.37 in. Brownhills Pottery Co. Tunstall, Staffordshire. Factory date: 1872-1896. Registry Mark #154 date: 1884. Source: as noted in E131. $175-$225

Figure E133 - "Magpie." 6.12 in. Edge, Malkin & Co. Burslem, Staffordshire. Factory date: 1871-1903. $175-$225

Figure E134 - "Peacock." 7 in. Elsmore & Son. Tunstall, Staffordshire. Factory date: 1872-1887. $175-$225

Figure E129 - "Wild Animal Series - The Stag." 8.37 in. Brownhills Pottery Co. Tunstall, Staffordshire. Factory date: 1872-1896. Registry Diamond date: September 29, 1882. $275-$350

Figure E130 - "Wild Animal Series - The Tiger." 6.5 in. Brownhills Pottery Co. Tunstall, Staffordshire. Factory date: 1872-1896. Registry Diamond date: September 29, 1882. $275-$350

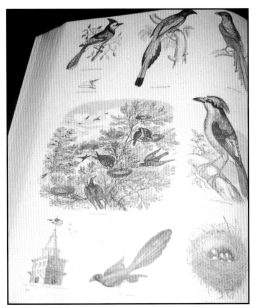

Figure E131 - "Photo of Figure E132: Page in *Knight's Pictorial Museum of Animated Nature* (1850)." Photographed in 1999 at the Yale University book storage facility; title is currently not listed in the university library's collection.

Figure E135 - "Birds of Paradise." 7.12 in. Edge, Malkin & Co. Burslem, Staffordshire. Factory date: 1871-1903. $175-$225

Figure E136 - "Bird Series - Chaffinch (verified) and Goldfinch." Patched transfer reads, "ch/finch and Goldfinch." 7.12 in. Brownhills Pottery Co. Tunstall, Staffordshire. Factory date: 1872-1896. Registry Mark #154 date: 1884. $175-$225
Figure E137 - "Bullfinch and Goldfinch." 6 in. No mark. $175-$225

Figure E138 - "House Sparrow." 6.12 in. Edge, Malkin & Co. Burslem, Staffordshire. Factory date: 1871-1903. $175-$225

Figure E141 - "Kestral." 8 in. No mark. $175-$225
Figure E142 - "The Reed Warbler." 8 in. No mark. $175-$225

Figure E139 - "Bird Series - Swallow." 8.35 in. Brownhills Pottery Co. Tunstall, Staffordshire. Factory date: 1872-1896. Registry Mark #154 date: 1884. $175-$225

Figure E143 - "Sky Lark (as identified by the National Audubon Society's *Sibley Guide to Birds*)." 6.23 in. Edge, Malkin & Co. Burslem, Staffordshire. Factory date: 1871-1903. $175-$225

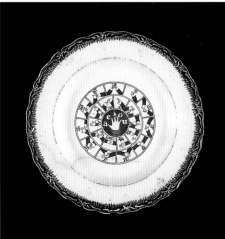

Figure E150 - "Manual Alphabet in a Circle." Scallop edge, shell ridges. Pearlware. 7.5 in. Possibly Leeds Pottery (?). 500+

Figure E144 - "Bird Among the Flowers." 7.25 in. A. Shaw & Son. Mersey Pottery. Burslem, Staffordshire. Factory date: 1882-1898. $150-$175

Figure E145 - "Bird Among the Morning Glories." 7.25 in. A Shaw & Son. Mersey Pottery. Burslem, Staffordshire. Factory date: 1882-1898. $150-$175

Figure E151 - "Manual Alphabet Series - Students at Study." Handsign inner rim. 8.25 in. H. Aynsley & Co. Longton, Staffordshire. Factory date: 1873+. Registry Mark #436673 date: 1904. 300+

Figure E146 - "Birds on a Limb." 7.25 in. No mark. $150-$175

Figure E147 - "Heron and Two Frogs." 7.25 in. No mark. $150-$175

Figure E152 - "Manual Alphabet Series - Two Children Fearful of the Goose." Handsign inner rim. 6.37 in. H. Aynsley & Co. Longton, Staffordshire. Factory date: 1873+. Registry Mark #436673 date: 1904. 300+

Figure E153 - "Manual Alphabet Series - Three Dutch Children." Handsign inner rim. 8.25 in. H. Aynsley & Co. Longton, Staffordshire. Factory date: 1873+. Registry Mark #436673 date: 1904. $300+

Figure E148 - "Birds in a Paisley Design." 5.5 in. No mark. $150-$175

Figure E149 - "Birds in a Design." 5.12 in. No mark. $150-$175

Figure E154 - "Manual Alphabet Series - The Tea Party." Handsign inner rim. 6.25 in. H. Aynsley & Co. Longton, Staffordshire. Factory date: 1873+. Registry Mark #436673 date: 1904. $300+

Figure E155 - "Manual Alphabet Series - Owls at School." Handsign inner rim. 7.25 in. H. Aynsley & Co. Longton, Staffordshire. Factory date: 1873+. Registry Mark #436673 date: 1904. $300+

Figure E160 - "Braille Edged Ashtray - Cane." 6.12 in. No mark. $12-$25
Figure E161 - "Braille Edged Ashtray - Guide-dog." 6.12 in. No mark. $12-$25

Figure E156 - "Manual Alphabet Series - Rabbit Gent and Lady [in the style of Louis Wain (1860-1939)]." Handsign inner rim. 6.5 in. H. Aynsley & Co. Longton, Staffordshire. Factory date: 1873+. Registry Mark #436673 date: 1904. $300+

Figure E157 - "Manual Alphabet Series - Greeting [in the style of Louis Wain (1860-1939)]." Handsign inner rim. 8.25 in. H. Aynsley & Co. Longton, Staffordshire. Factory date: 1873+. Registry Mark #436673 date: 1904. $300+

Figure E158 - "Manual Alphabet Series - Felines Jumping Rope [in the style of Louis Wain (1860-1939)]." Handsign inner rim. 6.5 in. H. Aynsley & Co. Longton, Staffordshire. Factory date: 1873+. Registry Mark #436673 date: 1904. $300+

Figure E159 - "The Blind Girl." 5.5 in. No mark. $175-$225

Figure E162 - "Spanish Name Series - Carlota." 4.87 in. J. F. Wileman. Fenton/Longton, Staffordshire. Factory date: 1869 (70?)-1872 (Godden, 1988) (1892?). $200-$250
Figure E163 - " Spanish Name Series - Recuerdo." 4.87 in. J. F. Wileman. Fenton/Longton, Staffordshire. Factory date: 1869 (70?)-1872 (Godden, 1988) (1892?). $200-$250
Figure E164 - " Spanish Name Series - Micaelita." 5 in. J. F. Wileman. Fenton/Longton, Staffordshire. Factory date: 1869 (70?)-1872 (Godden, 1988) (1892?). $200-$250

Figure E165 - "French/English Series - Jockeys = Jockeys." 7 in. No mark. $200-$250
Figure E166 - "French/English Series - Candins = Dandies." 6.87 in. No mark. $200-$250
Figure E167 - "French/English Series - Artistes = Artists." 7 in. No mark. $200-$250

Figure E168 - "French/English Series - Baigneurs = Bathers." 7 in. No mark. $200-$250
Figure E169 - "French/English Series - Instituteur = Schoolmaster." 6.37 in. Illegible mark. $200-$250
Figure E170 - "French/English Series - Docteur = Doctor." 7 in. No mark. $200-$250

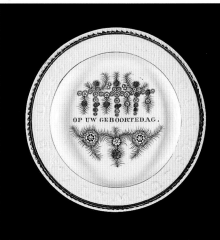

Figure E174 - "Op Uw Geboortedag = Dutch - Happy Day of Your Birth." 6.87 in. W. H. Hackwood (?). Hanley, Staffordshire. Factory date: 1827-1843. Trademark date: 1827-1843. $200-$250

Figure E171 - "French/English Series - Canotiers = Boatmen." 6 in. No mark. $200-$250
Figure E172 - "French/English Series - L'exercice = Drill." 5.75 in. J. F. Wileman. Fenton and Longton, Staffordshire. Factory date: 1869 (70?)-1872 (Godden, 1988) (1892?). $200-$250
Figure E173 - "French/English Series - Kabyles = Kabyles." 6. in No mark. $200-$250

F Is for Flatware

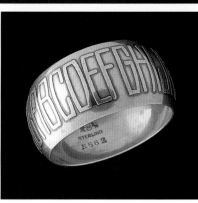

Figure F1 - Knife and Fork. Silver plate. Fork-5.12 in., Knife-6.5 in. ABC design on stems. Sheffield, England. $75-$125

Figure F2 - Napkin Ring #N662. Sterling. D-1.25 in. Reed & Barton. Taunton, Massachusetts. Factory date: 1840+. Made in or before 1928. $100-$150

Figure F3 - Detail of engraving of the Meriden Britannia Co. factory, Meriden, Connecticut, from the "Electro Gold and Silver Plate, Nickel Silver and White Metal" catalogue. 1882. *Used with permission of the Connecticut Historical Society Library, Hartford, Connecticut.*

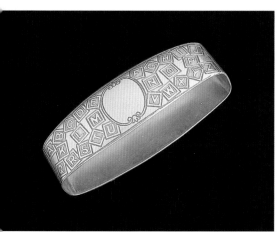

Figure F4 - Napkin Ring. Sterling. H-.87 in. x W-2.62 in. Meriden Britannia Co. Meriden, Connecticut. Factory date: 1852, merger with International Silver in 1898. June 15, 1913. $100-$150

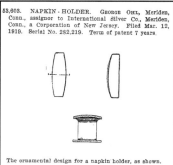

Figures F5a, F5b, F5c - Patent Office design patent #53603. Awarded to George Ohr of Meriden, Connecticut, July 15, 1919. Design for a napkin ring shape as seen in Figure F4: US Patent Title 241/49.

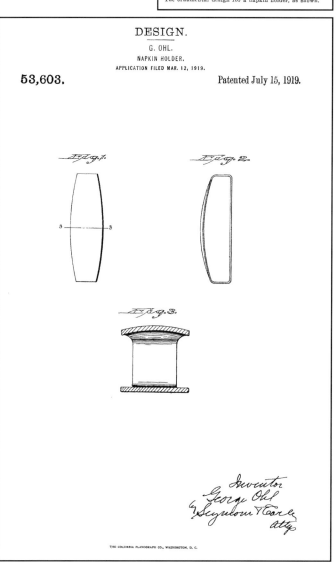

Figure F6 - Fork and Spoon with full alphabet design on stems. Sterling. Fork-4.18 in., Spoon-4.37 in. William Rogers Manufacturing Co. Hartford, Connecticut. Factory date: 1865-c.1898 when the firm was one of the original companies to form the International Silver Co. $200-$250 (pair)

Figure F7 - Fork, Spoon, and Loop-handled Spoon with cat-face design on stems. Sterling. Fork-4.31 in., Spoon-4.37 in., Loop-handled Spoon-3.19 in. G. K. Webster Company. North Attleboro, Massachusetts. Factory date: 1869-1950, when it became a subsidiary of Reed & Barton of Taunton, Massachusetts. $300-$350 (set)

Figure F8 - Fork, Spoon, and Loop-handled Spoon with cut-work ABC design on stems. Sterling. Fork-3.87 in., Spoon-4 in., Loop-handled Spoon-4.25 in. The Watson Company. Attleboro, Massachusetts. Factory date: 1874-1955. Trademark date: 1910-1955. $300-$350 (set)

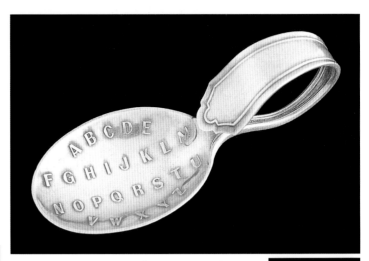

Figure F9 - Loop-handled Spoon with alphabet design on bowl. Sterling. 3 in. The Watson Company. Attleboro, Massachusetts. Factory date: 1874-1955. Trademark date: 1910-1955. $100-$150 (spoon)

Figure F10 - Fork with alphabet design in relief on black, scalloped stem. Sterling. 3.61 in. The Watson Company. Attleboro, Massachusetts. Factory date: 1874-1955. Engraved date 4-16-18 (1918). $100-$150 (fork)

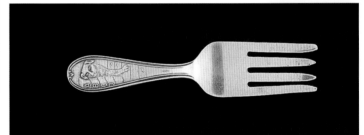

Figure F11 - Fork with sculptured dog and A, B, and C design on stem. Sterling. 3.6 in. Manchester Manufacturing Co. Providence, Rhode Island. Factory date: 1887-1980. $100-$150 (fork)

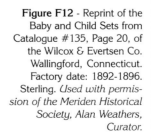

Figure F12 - Reprint of the Baby and Child Sets from Catalogue #135, Page 20, of the Wilcox & Evertsen Co. Wallingford, Connecticut. Factory date: 1892-1896. Sterling. *Used with permission of the Meriden Historical Society, Alan Weathers, Curator.*

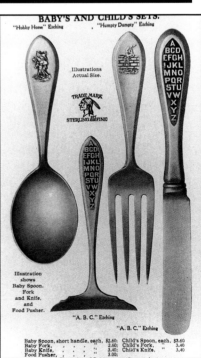

Figure F13 - Fork, Knife and Spoon with alphabet block design on stems. Malabar (Trademark) Assay: Tin 87.5%, Iron 12%, Lead .23%, Trace elements .23%. Fork-6.25 in., Knife-7.25 in., Spoon-5 in. Wallace Brothers. Wallingford, Connecticut. Factory date: 1875+. $225-$275 (set)

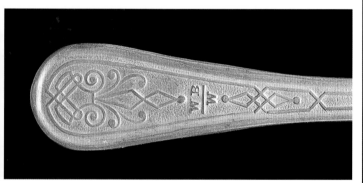

Figure F14 - Trademark of Wallace Brothers of Wallingford (WB over W) on reverse stem of F13.

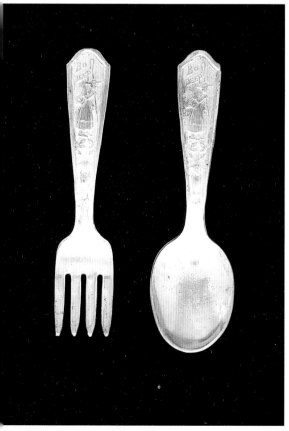

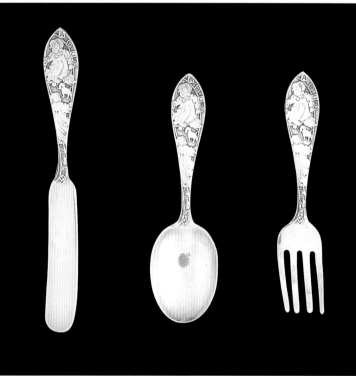

Figure F16 - Reverse stems of F15, spoon with A-M and fork with N-Z.

Figure F17- Fork, Knife and Spoon with baby and dog relief design on oxidized black; letters A-H only on stems. Sterling. Fork-4.12 in., Knife-5 in., Spoon-4.25 in. Paye and Baker Manufacturing Co. Attleboro, Massachusetts. Factory date: 1901-1952. $200-250

Figure F15 - Fork and Spoon with Bo-Peep design on stems. Assay: Tin 81%, Iron 16%, Copper 2%, Tungsten .6%, Lead .23%, Trace elements .2%. Fork-4 in., Spoon-4.25 in. Wallace Brothers. Wallingford, Connecticut. Factory date: 1875+. $150-$200 (pair)

Figure F18 - Fork, Knife and Spoon with dancing baby design on stems. Assay: Iron 88.65%, Manganese 8.1%, Copper 1.1%, Nickel .8%, Carbon .5%, Molybdenum .2%, Aluminum .1%, Sulphur .1% , Silicon .1%, Phosphorus .04%. Fork-6.25 in., Knife-7.1 in., Spoon-5.18 in. Mark: MADE IN U.S.A. n.d. $225-$275 (set)

Figure F19 - Spoon with Peter Rabbit design on stem. Assay: Iron 92.1%, Manganese 3.5%, Copper 1.7%, Carbon .9%, Nickel .8%, Sulphur .4%, Chromium .3%, Silicon .1%, Aluminum .1%, Phosphorus .07%. 4.18 in. Mark: MADE IN U.S.A. n.d. $75-$125 (spoon)

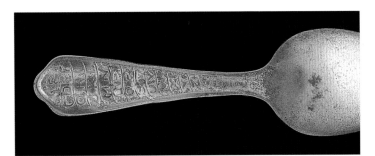

Figure F20 - Reverse stem of F19, with A-Z design.

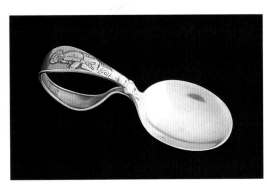

Figure F21 - Loop-handled spoon with ABC blocks and baby design on stem. Sterling. 3.37 in. Weidlich Sterling Spoon Co. Bridgeport, Connecticut. Factory date: c.1915-1952. Patent #103,304. March 30, 1915. $100-$150 (spoon)

Figure F22 - Spoon with stork and alphabet letter design on stem. Engraved bowl. Sterling. 5.5 in. Weidlich Sterling Spoon Co. Bridgeport, Connecticut. Factory date: c.1915-1952. $100-$150 (spoon)

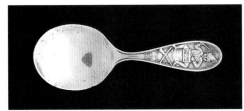

Figure F23 - Spoon with drummer boy design on stem. Sterling. 3.6 in. Weidlich Sterling Spoon Co. Bridgeport, Connecticut. Factory date: c.1915-1952. $100-150 (spoon)

Figure F24 - Reverse stem of F23 with full alphabet.

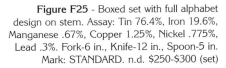

Figure F25 - Boxed set with full alphabet design on stem. Assay: Tin 76.4%, Iron 19.6%, Manganese .67%, Copper 1.25%, Nickel .775%, Lead .3%. Fork-6 in., Knife-12 in., Spoon-5 in. Mark: STANDARD. n.d. $250-$300 (set)

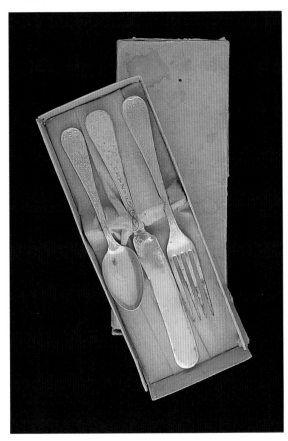

G Is for Glass

Figure G1 - "Plain alphabet." Milk Glass. 7 in. No mark. $50-75

Figure G2 - "Dutch Girl." Beaded edge. Gilt over molded letters. Milk Glass. 7 in. No mark. $50-$75

Figure G3 - Detail of "Raised Colored Bird." Milk Glass. 7 in. No mark. $150-$200

Figure G4 - "The Emblem of the United States of America." Clear. 6.27 in. Event date: c.1876. $150-$200
Figure G5 - "Independence Hall, Philadelphia." Clear. 6.75 in. No mark. Event date: c.1876. $150-$200

Figure G6 - "A/Z Mug (Christmas)." Clear. H-3 in. x D-1.5 in. Adams and Co. Pittsburgh, Pennsylvania. Factory date: 1851-1892. $175-$250

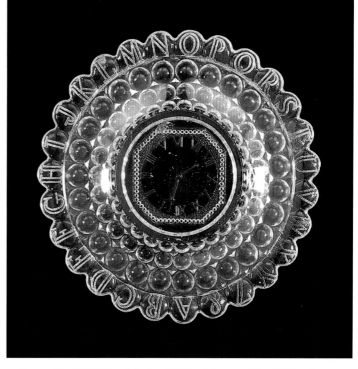

Figure G7 - "1000 Eyes." Amber. 6.25 in. Adams and Co. Pittsburgh, Pennsylvania. Factory date: 1851-1892. Production date (Husfloen, 1992): c.1880 as one of a dinner service. $125-$175

Figure G8 - "Running Deer." Clear and Frosted. 6 in. Gillinder and Sons Glass. Greensburg, Pennsylvania. Factory date: 1867-c.1900. Production date (Lechler, 1989): c.1885. $125-$175

Figure G12 - "Clock Face." Key design edge. Clear and Textured. 7.12 in. Ripley and Co. Pittsburgh, Pennsylvania. Factory date: 1866-1891 when Ripley joined U.S. Glass as Factory "F." Production date (Lechler, 1989): c.1890-1900. $75-100

Figure G9 - "Sancho Panza and Dapple." Clear and Frosted. 6 in. Gillinder and Sons Glass. Greensburg, Pennsylvania. Factory date: 1867-c.1900. Production date (Lechler, 1989): c.1885. $125-$175

Figure G13 - "Three Riding in an Elephant's Howdah." Clear. 6 in. Ripley and Co. Pittsburgh, Pennsylvania. Factory date: 1866-1891 when Ripley joined U.S. Glass as Factory "F." Production date (Lechler, 1989): c.1880-1895. $125-$150

Figure G10 - "The Bouquet." Clear and Frosted. 6 in. Gillinder and Sons Glass. Greensburg, Pennsylvania. Factory date: 1867-c.1900. Production date (Lechler, 1989): c.1885. $125-$175

Figure G14 - Detail of firm identification incorporated into Howdah.

Figure G11 - "The Stork." Carnival Glass. Amber. H-1.27 in., D-7.5 in. Belmont Glass. Bellaire, Ohio. Factory date: 1861 (or 1866)-1892. $150-$200

Figure G15 - "A Dog at a Palm Tree." Clear. 6 in. Ripley and Co. Pittsburgh, Pennsylvania. Factory date: 1866-1891 when Ripley joined U.S. Glass as Factory "F." Production date (Lechler, 1989): c.1880-1895. $125-$150

Figure G16 - "Clock Face." Clear. 6 in. U.S. Glass Co. (Ripley and Co.) Pittsburgh, Pennsylvania. Factory date: 1866-1891 when Ripley joined U.S. Glass as Factory "F." Production date (Lechler, 1989): c.1880-1895. $75-$100

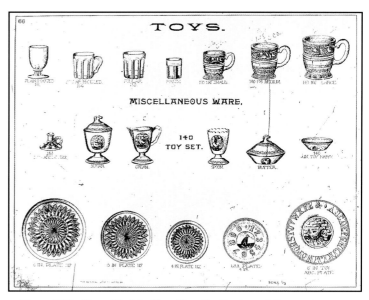

Figure G19 - "Page 66 of the King Glass Co. Catalogue." Factory date: 1869(?)-1891 when King joined U.S. Glass Company as Factory "K." Catalogue date: c.1880. Page shows spooner, sugar with lid, creamer and butter with lid; nappy with the Rooster design. *Courtesy of the Library of Congress, Microfiche Reproductions.*

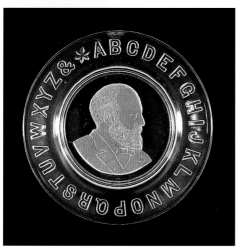

Figure G17 - "President James Abram Garfield." Clear. 6 in. Ripley and Co. Factory date: 1866-1891 when Ripley joined U.S. Glass as Factory "F." Production date (Lechler, 1989): 1880-1895. Maker may have been Campbell, Jones and Co. Pittsburgh, Pennsylvania. Factory date: 1865-1891. Event date: 1881. $125-$150

Figure G20 - "Hen and her Chicks." Clear. 6 in. King Glass Co. Pittsburgh, Pennsylvania. Factory date: 1869(?)-1891 when King joined U.S. Glass Company as Factory "K." Production date: c.1880. $100-$125

Figure G21 - "Hen and her Chicks." Clear and Frosted. 6 in. King Glass Co. Pittsburgh, Pennsylvania. Factory date: 1869(?)-1891 when King joined U.S. Glass Company as Factory "K." Production date: c.1880. $100-$125

Figure G18 - "Cover of the King Glass Co. Catalogue." Pittsburgh, Pennsylvania. Factory date: 1869(?)-1891 when King joined U.S. Glass Company as Factory "K." Catalogue date: c.1880. *Courtesy of The Library of Congress, Microfiche Reproductions.*

Figure G22 - "Sitting Dog." 0-9 surround. Clear. 4 in. King Glass Co. Pittsburgh, Pennsylvania. Factory date: 1869(?)-1891 when King joined U.S. Glass Company as Factory "K." Production date: c.1880. $100-$125

Figure G23 - "Running Rabbit." Clear and Frosted. 6 in. Crystal Glass Co. Pittsburgh, Pennsylvania. Factory date: 1869-c.1886. Production date: 1879-1884. $125-$150

Figure G27 - "Cover of the New Martinsville Glass Manufacturing Co. Catalogue." New Martinsville, West Virginia. Factory date: 1900-1944. Catalogue date: c. 1920-?

Figure G24 - "Standing Stork." Clear and Frosted. 6 in. Crystal Glass Co. Pittsburgh, Pennsylvania. Factory date: 1869-c.1887. Production date: 1879-1884. $125-$150

Figure G28 - "Miscellaneous" page of the New Martinsville Glass Manufacturing. Co. Catalogue." Factory date: 1900-1944. Catalogue date: c.1920-?

Figure G25 - "Standing Stork with Raised Leg." Clear and Frosted. 6 in. Crystal Glass Co. Pittsburgh, Pennsylvania. Factory date: 1869-c.1887. Production date (Lechler, 1989): c.1880-c.1884. $125-$150

Figure G29 - "Emma" or "Emmas." Clear. 6.27 in. J. B. Higbee Glass Co. Bridgeville, Pennsylvania. Factory date: 1907-1918. Production date: 1907-1918. $200-$250 (Plate with no mark is a current reproduction and, therefore, not shown.)

Figure G26 - "Ducks" or "Doves." Textured purple. 6 in. Crystal Glass Co. Pittsburgh, Pennsylvania. Factory date: 1869-c.1887. Production date (Lechler, 1989): c.1880-c.1884. $125-$150

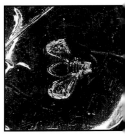

Figure G30 - Mark: Detail of Higbee "Bee" trademark as seen on Figure G29.

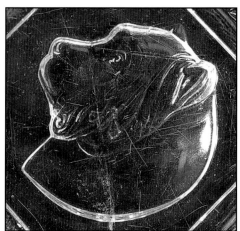

Figure G31 - Mark: Detail of Higbee "Bee" trademark as seen on "Rover," illustrated on Figure G28. ("Rover." 6.5 in. J. B. Higbee Glass Co. Bridgeville, Pennsylvania. Factory date: 1907-1918. Production date: c.1907-?) $125-$150

Figure G36 - "The Plain Star." Scallop Edge. Vaseline Glass (lime green) as seen under Black Light. 6.12 in. New Martinsville. Factory date: 1900-1944. Production date: c.1921-1928. *Courtesy of Wayne and Lola Higby.* $75-$100

Figure G32 - Mark: Detail of SI (Smithsonian Institution) trademark as seen on "Rover," illustrated on Figure G28. ("Rover." 6.5 in. New Martinsville Glass Manufacturing Co. New Martinsville, West Virginia. Factory date: 1900-1944. Production date: c.1921-1928.) $125-$150

Figure G33 - "The Plain Star." Scalloped and Beaded Edge. Clear. 6.12 in. Bryce, Higbee and Co. Bridgeville, Pennsylvania. Factory date: 1879-1907. Production date: c.1893-? $75-$100

Figure G34 - "The Plain Star." Scallop Edge, Lime Green Vaseline Glass. 6.12 in. New Martinsville Glass Manufacturing Co. New Martinsville, West Virginia. Factory date: 1900-1944. Production date: c.1921-1928. *Courtesy of Wayne and Lola Higby.* $75-$100

Figure G37 - "Platonite" mugs with painted animal figures; all measure H-3 in. x D-2.75 in. (marked HA) $20-$25 each. "H" Bowl measures H-2.5 x D-7.87 (no mark). $20-$25. Divided plate measures H-1.5 x D-6.62 in. (marked HA). $25-$30. Hazel-Atlas Glass Co. Wheeling, West Virginia. Factory date: 1902-1956. $40

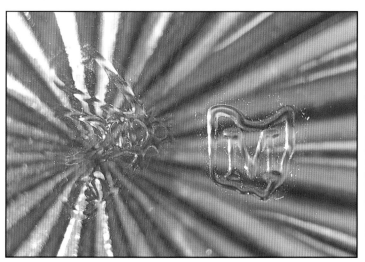

Figure G35 - Mark: Detail of combination Higbee "Bee" trademark and "M" New Martinsville trademark as seen in Figure G34. *Courtesy of Wayne and Lola Higby.*

Figure G38 - "ABC Ice Cream Set." Wabash Series. Clear. Platter W-5.5 in. H-4.5 in. Rounds 2.75 in. Federal Glass Co. Columbus, Ohio. Factory date: 1900-1980. Production date: c.1906-?. Complete set includes one platter and six rounds. Platter alone: $150-$200. Round plates: $125-$150. Total set $900+

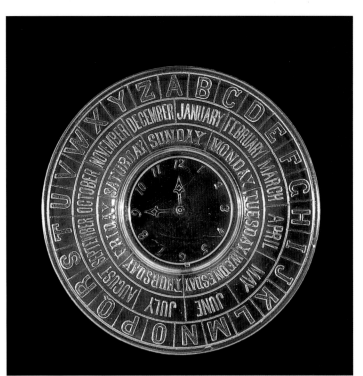

Figure G42 - "Repeated Design of Pyramid Shaped Triangles with Swags." Blue. 7 in. No mark. $75-$100

Figure G39 - "Clock Face with Days, Months, and Alphabet." Blue tint. 7 in. No mark. $75-$100

Figure G43 - "Repeated Design of Hexagrams." Clear. 6 in. No mark. $75-$100

Figure G40 - "Wave Design." Clear. 5.12 in. No mark. $75-$100
Figure G41 - "Wave Design." Amber. 5.12 in. No mark. $75-$100

Figure G44 - "Eight-Pointed Star." Clear. 6.25 in. No mark. $75-$100

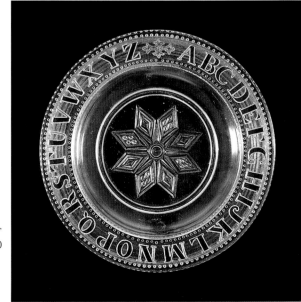

Figure G45 - "Christmas Eve" (photo computer enhanced). Clear. 6 in. No mark. *Courtesy of Irene and Ralph Lindsay.* $250-$300

Figure G47 - Mark: Hazel-Atlas Glass Co. Wheeling, West Virginia. Factory date: 1902-1956 (Mark from Platonite also, Figures G37 and G48).

Figure G48 - "Animal Alphabet Drinking Glasses, 6 oz. and 8 oz. Three designs." Hazel-Atlas Glass Co. Wheeling, West Virginia. Factory date: 1902-1956. $10-$16 each

Figure G46 - "Hubert at the Carnival - Mr. Peanut." Painted Drinking Glass. Alphabet and numeral surround. 12 oz. H-4.62 x 2.62 in. No mark. $10-$16

H Is for Hollowware

Figure H1 - "L/M - Lion/Mouse." Loop handle. H-3 in. x D-2.87 in. Adams, England. Factory date: 1769+. $200-$250

Figure H6 - "A/Z - Fishermen Carrying Nets." Loop handle. H-2.62 in. x D-2.87 in. Brownhills Pottery Co. Tunstall, Staffordshire. Factory date: 1872-1896. Registry Mark date: May, 1883. $250+

Figure H2 - "A/Z - Dog Chasing a Rabbit." Loop handle. H-3 in. x D-3 in. Charles Allerton & Sons. Longton, Staffordshire. Factory date: 1859-1942. $200-$250

Figure H7 - "A/Z - Fishermen Emptying Fish Basket." Loop handle. H-2.75 in. x D-2.87 in. Brownhills Pottery Co. Tunstall, Staffordshire. Factory date: 1872-1896. Registry Mark date: May, 1883. $250+

Figure H3 - "A/Z - Rooster and Goat." Loop handle. H-3 in. x D-3 in. Charles Allerton & Sons. Longton, Staffordshire. Factory date: 1859-1942. $200-$250

Figure H8 - "A/Z - Rowboat at the Water's Edge." Loop handle. H-2.62 in. x D-2.75 in. Brownhills Pottery Co. Tunstall, Staffordshire. Factory date: 1872-1896. Registry Mark date: May, 1883. $250+

Figure H4 - "A/Z - Coastal Scene." Loop handle. H-2.87 in. x D-2.87 in. (Assumed) Brownhills Pottery Co. Tunstall, Staffordshire. Factory date: 1872-1896. $250+

Figure H9 - "A/Z - Fishermen Boarding a Small Boat." Loop handle. H-2.75 in. x D-2.75 in. Brownhills Pottery Co. Tunstall, Staffordshire. Factory date: 1872-1896. Registry Mark date: May, 1883. $250+

Figure H5 - "A/Z - Greek Port Scene." Loop handle. H-2.87 in. x D-2.17 in. (Assumed) Brownhills Pottery Co. Tunstall, Staffordshire. Factory date: 1872-1896. $250+

Figure H10 - "A/Z - Children on a Raft (blurred transfer)." Loop handle. H-2.87 in. D-2.87 in. (Assumed) Brownhills Pottery Co. Tunstall, Staffordshire. Factory date: 1872-1896. $250+

Figure H11 - "A/Z - Copenhagen." Loop handle. H-2.5 in. x D-2.62 in. Brownhills Pottery Co. Tunstall, Staffordshire. Factory date: 1872-1896. Registry Mark #26734 date: 1885. $250+

Figure H12 - "A/Z - Little Jack Horner." Loop handle. H-2.75 in. x D- 2.5 in. (Assumed) Brownhills Pottery Co. Tunstall, Staffordshire. Factory date: 1872-1896. $250+

Figure H13 - "A/Z - Cats and Books." Loop handle. H-2.75 in. x D-2.81 in. (Assumed) Brownhills Pottery Co. Tunstall, Staffordshire. Factory date: 1872-1896. No mark. $250+

Figure H14 - "A/Z - Kingfisher." Loop handle. H-2.87 in. x D-2.87 in. A. Shaw & Son. Mersey Pottery. Burslem, Staffordshire. Factory date: 1882-1898. Production date: c.1898. $250+

Figure H16 - "D/E/F." Source: *Child's Treasury* . . . . as noted in Figure H15.

Figure H18 - "J/K/L." Source: *Child's Treasury* . . . . as noted in Figure H15.

Figure H15 - "A/B/C." Source: *Child's Treasury of Knowledge.* Boston: Wier & White. Reprinted in Baldwin, Ruth. *100 Nineteenth-Century Rhyming Alphabets in English.* Carbondale and Edwardsville, Illinois: Southern Illinois University Press, 1972. *Used with permission of Southern Illinois University Press.*

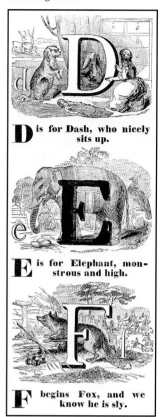

Figure H17 - "G/H/I." Source: *Child's Treasury* . . . . as noted in Figure H15.

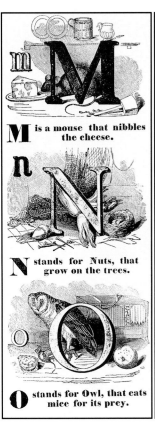

M is a mouse that nibbles the cheese.

N stands for Nuts, that grow on the trees.

O stands for Owl, that eats mice for its prey.

P stands for Parrots, some green and some grey.

Q stands for Quills, from the goose or the swan.

R stands for Rabbits, for Fanny or John.

S stands for Snail, with its house on its back.

T stands for Tiger, striped yellow and black.

U stands for Urn, to hold water for tea.

V is a Violet, which here you may see.

W is a Windmill, that turns with the wind.

X is a letter like this X, you will find.

Y is a Youth, who many kind frie[n]

Z comes the last, and it all ends.

Figure H19 - "M/N/O." Source: *Child's Treasury* . . . . as noted in Figure H15.

Figure H20 - "P/Q/R." Source: *Child's Treasury* . . . . as noted in Figure H15.

Figure H21 - "S/T/U." Source: *Child's Treasury* . . . . as noted in Figure H15.

Figure H22 - "V/W/X." Source: *Child's Treasury* . . . . as noted in Figure H15.

Figure H23 - "Y/Z." Source: *Child's Treasury* . . . . as noted in Figure H15.

Figure H24 - "A/B - Apple/Ball." Loop handle. H-2.5 in. x D-2.5 in. No mark. Source: *Child's Treasury* . . . . as noted in Figure H15. $250+

Figure H27 - "F - Fox (simplification of source design)." Flat-topped ear-shaped handle. H-2.62 in. x D-2.75 in. No mark. Source: *Child's Treasury* . . . . as noted in Figure H15. $250+

Figure H25 - "E/F - Elephant/Fox." Loop handle. H-2.62 in. x D-2.62 in. No mark. Source: *Child's Treasury* . . . . as noted in Figure H15. *Courtesy of Ann and Dennis Berard.* $250+

Figure H28 - "G/H - Goose/Horse." Spurred loop handle. H-2.75 in. x D-2.87 in. No mark. Source: *Child's Treasury* . . . . as noted in Figure H15. $250+

Figure H26 - "E/F - Elephant/Fox." Loop handle. H-2.75 in. x D-2.87 in. No mark. Source: *Child's Treasury* . . . . as noted in Figure H15. $250+

Figure H29 - "I/J - Infant/Jam." Loop handle. H-2.5 in. x D- 2.50 in. No mark. Source: *Child's Treasury* . . . . as noted in Figure H15. *Courtesy of Ann and Dennis Berard.* $250+

Figure H30 - "L/R - Ladder/Rabbit." Loop handle. H-2.50 in. x D-2.50 in. No mark. Source: *Child's Treasury* . . . . as noted in Figure H15. $250+

Figure H35 - "S/T - Snail/Tiger." Loop handle. H-2.75 in. x D-2.75 in. No mark. Source: *Child's Treasury* . . . . as noted in Figure H15. *Courtesy of Ann and Dennis Berard.* $250+

Figure H31 - "N - Nest (simplification of source design)." Flat-topped ear-shaped handle. H-2.62 in. x D-2.75 in. No mark. Source: *Child's Treasury* . . . . as noted in Figure H15. $250+

Figure H36 - "U/V - Uncle/Vulture." Loop handle. H-2.75 in. x D- 2.75 in. No mark. Source: *Child's Treasury* . . . . as noted in Figure H15. *Courtesy of Ann and Dennis Berard.* $250+

Figure H32 - "P/H - Parrot/Horse." Loop handle. H-2.62 in. x D-2.75 in. No mark. Source: *Child's Treasury* . . . . as noted in Figure H15. $250+

Figure H37- "U - Uncle." Flat-topped ear-shaped handle. H-2.75 in. x D-2.87 in. No mark. Source: *Child's Treasury* . . . . as noted in Figure H15. $250+

Figure H33 - "Q - Quail (simplification of source design)." Flat-topped ear-shaped handle. H-2.62 in. x D-2.37 in. No mark. Source: *Child's Treasury* . . . . as noted in Figure H15. $250+

Figure H38 - "V - Vulture." Triple ring base. Loop handle. Leaf terminals. H-2.50 in. x D-2.25 in. No mark. Source: *Child's Treasury* . . . . as noted in Figure H15. $250+

Figure H34 - "Q/W - Queen Victoria/Wagon." Spurred loop handle. H-2.75 in. x D-2.83 in. No mark. Source: *Child's Treasury* . . . . as noted in Figure H15. $400+

Figure H39 - "W/X - Windmill/X Legged Table." Loop handle. H-2.93 in. x D-2.5 in. No mark. Source: *Child's Treasury* . . . . as noted in Figure H15. *Courtesy of Ann and Dennis Berard.* $250+

Figure H40 - "W - Wagon." Flat -topped ear-shaped handle. H-2.75 in. x D-2.75 in. No mark. Source: *Child's Treasury* . . . . as noted in Figure H15. $250+

Figure H45 - "C/D - Cat/Dash (with verbiage)." Shaped base. Loop handle. H-2.75 in. x D-2.75 in. No mark. Source: *Child's Treasury* . . . . as noted in Figure H15. *Courtesy of Ann and Dennis Berard.* $250+

Figure H41 - "X - X Legged Table." Flat-topped ear-shaped handle. H-2.50 in. x D-2.75 in. No mark. Source: *Child's Treasury* . . . . as noted in Figure H15. $250+

Figure H46 - "E/F- Elephant/Fox (with verbiage)." Loop handle. H-2.37 in. x D-2.50 in. No mark. Source: *Child's Treasury* . . . . as noted in Figure H15. $250+

Figure H42 - "Y/Z - Youth/Zebra." Loop handle. H-2.62 in. x D-2.62 in. No mark. Source: *Child's Treasury* . . . . as noted in Figure H15. *Courtesy of Ann and Dennis Berard.* $250+

Figure H47- "G/H - Goose/Horse (with verbiage)." Loop handle. H-2.75 in. x D-2.75 in. No mark. Source: *Child's Treasury* . . . . as noted in Figure H15. $250+

Figure H43 - "A/B - Apple/Ball (with verbiage)." Shaped base. Loop handle. H-2.75 in. x D-2.75 in. No mark. Source: *Child's Treasury* . . . . as noted in Figure H15. *Courtesy of Ann and Dennis Berard.* $250+

Figure H48 - "K/L - Kitten/Ladder (with verbiage)." Loop handle. H-2.50 in. x D-2.87 in. No mark. Source: *Child's Treasury* . . . . as noted in Figure H15. *Courtesy of Ann and Dennis Berard.* $250+

Figure H44 - "A/B - Apple/Ball (with verbiage)." Wavy rim. Teacup shape. Spurred loop handle. H-3 in. x D-3.87 in. No mark. Source: *Child's Treasury* . . . . as noted in Figure H15. $250+

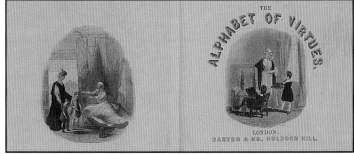

Figure H49 - "Frontispiece and Title Page of *The Alphabet of Virtues*." London: Darton & Co. June 20, 1856. *Used with permission of the Lilly Library, Indiana University, Bloomington, Indiana.*

Figure H50 - "A and B pages of *The Alphabet of Virtues*" as noted in Figure H49.

Figure H51 - "A/B - Adoration/Benevolence." Loop handle. H-2.5 in. x D-2.5 in. No mark. Production date: After 1856. Source: *The Alphabet of Virtues* as noted in Figure H49. *Courtesy of Ann and Dennis Berard.* $250+

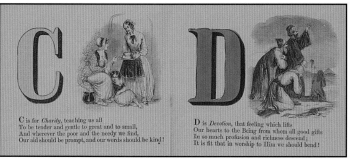

Figure H52 - "C and D pages of *The Alphabet of Virtues*" as noted in Figure H49.

Figure H53 - "C - Charity." Shaped base. Loop handle. Leaf terminal. H-2.75 in. x D-2.75 in. No mark. Production date: After 1856. Source: *The Alphabet of Virtues* as noted in Figure H49. $250+

Figure H54 - "C/D - Charity/Devotion." Loop handle. H-2.62 in. x D-2.5 in. No mark. Production date: After 1856. Source: *The Alphabet of Virtues* as noted in Figure H49. $250+

Figure H55 - C/D - Charity/Devotion." Loop handle. H-2.75 in. x D-2.75 in. No mark. Production date: After 1856. Source: *The Alphabet of Virtues* as noted in Figure H49. *Courtesy of Ann and Dennis Berard.* $250+

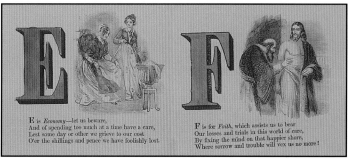

Figure H56 - "E and F pages of *The Alphabet of Virtues*" as noted in Figure H49.

Figure H57 - "E - Economy." Loop handle. Leaf terminals. H-2.75 in. x D-2.75 in. No mark. Production date: After 1856. Source: *The Alphabet of Virtues* as noted in Figure H49. $250+

Figure H58 - "E/F (Graphic with E is placed in error) - Faith." Loop handle. H-2.62 in. x D-2.62 in. No mark. Production date: After 1856. Source: *The Alphabet of Virtues* as noted in Figure H49. *Courtesy of Ann and Dennis Berard.* $250+

Figure H59 - "G and H pages of *The Alphabet of Virtues*" as noted in Figure H49.

Figure H64 - "K and L pages of *The Alphabet of Virtues*" as noted in Figure H49.

Figure H60 - "E/G - Economy/Gratitude." Shaped base. Loop handle. H-3.5 in. x D-3.5 in. No mark. Production date: After 1856. Source: *The Alphabet of Virtues* as noted in Figure H49. $250+

Figure H65 - "K/L - Kindness/Love." Loop handle. H-2.75 in. x D-2.75 in. No mark. Production date: After 1856. Source: *The Alphabet of Virtues* as noted in Figure H49. *Courtesy of Ann and Dennis Berard.* $250+

Figure H61 - "I and J pages of *The Alphabet of Virtues*" as noted in Figure H49.

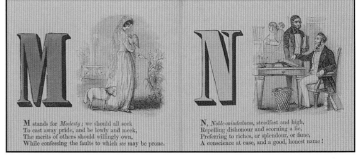

Figure H66 - "M and N Pages of *The Alphabet of Virtues*" as noted in Figure H49.

Figure H62 - "H/I - Hope/Industry." Loop handle. H-3 in. x D-2.87 in. No mark. Production date: After 1856. Source: *The Alphabet of Virtues* as noted in Figure H49. $250+

Figure H67 - "M/N - Modesty/Noble-mindedness." Loop handle. H-2.5 in. x D-2.62 in. No mark. Production date: After 1856. Source: *The Alphabet of Virtues* as noted in Figure H49. *Courtesy of Ann and Dennis Berard.* Formerly of the Chalala Collection. $250+

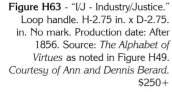

Figure H63 - "I/J - Industry/Justice." Loop handle. H-2.75 in. x D-2.75. in. No mark. Production date: After 1856. Source: *The Alphabet of Virtues* as noted in Figure H49. *Courtesy of Ann and Dennis Berard.* $250+

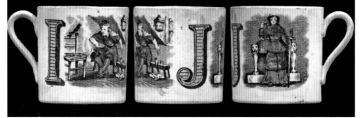

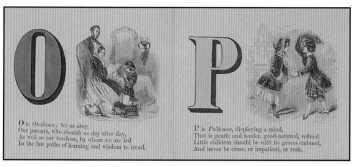

Figure H68 - "O and P Pages of *The Alphabet of Virtues*" as noted in Figure H49.

Figure H69 - "O/P - Obedience/Politeness." Loop handle. H-2.5 in. x D-2.5 in. No mark. Production date: After 1856. Source: The *Alphabet of Virtues* as noted in Figure H49. *Courtesy of Ann and Dennis Berard.* $250+

Figure H70 - "Q and R Pages of *The Alphabet of Virtues*" as noted in Figure H49.

Figure H71 - "Q/R - Quietness/Repentance." Loop handle. D-2.5 in. x D-2.5 in. No mark. Production date: After 1856. Source: *The Alphabet of Virtues* as noted in Figure H49. *Courtesy of Ann and Dennis Berard.* $250+

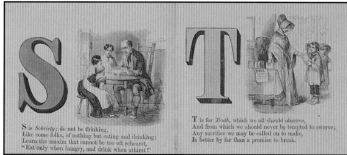

Figure H72 - "S and T Pages of *The Alphabet of Virtues*" as noted in Figure H49.

Figure H73 - "S/T - Sobriety/Truth." Loop handle. H-2.87 in. x D-2.87 in. No mark. Production date: After 1856. Source: *The Alphabet of Virtues* as noted in Figure H49. *Courtesy of Ann and Dennis Berard.* $250+

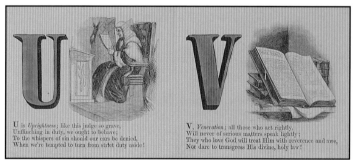

Figure H74 - "U and V Pages of *The Alphabet of Virtues*" as noted in Figure H49.

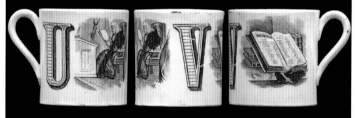

Figure H75 - "U/V - Uprightness/Veneration." Loop handle. H-2.75 in. x D-2.5 in. No mark. Production date: After 1856. Source: *The Alphabet of Virtues* as noted in Figure H49. $250+

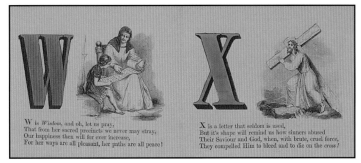

Figure H76 - "W and X Pages of *The Alphabet of Virtues*" as noted in Figure H49.

Figure H77 - "W/X - Wisdom/Letter Seldom Used." Loop handle. H-2.75 in. x D-2.5 in. No mark. Production date: After 1856. Source: *The Alphabet of Virtues* as noted in Figure H49. *Courtesy of Ann and Dennis Berard.* $250+

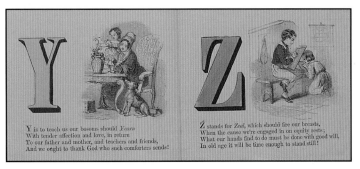

Figure H78 - "Y and Z Pages of *The Alphabet of Virtues*" as noted in Figure H49.

Figure H79 - "Y/Z - Yearn/Zeal." Loop handle. H-2.75 in. x D-2.75 in. No mark. Production date: After 1856. Source: *The Alphabet of Virtues* as noted in Figure H49. *Courtesy of Ann and Dennis Berard.* $250+

Figure H80 - "C was a Captain . . . D was a Drunkard . . . ." Tapered. Loop handle. H-2.75 in. x D-2.87 in. No mark. $250+

Figure H81 - "E was an Esquire . . . F was a Farmer . . . ." Loop handle. H-2.87 in. x D-2.75 in. No mark. $250+

Figure H82 - "G was a Gamester . . . H was a Hunter . . . ." Loop handle. H-2.87 in. x D-2.75 in. No mark. $250+

Figure H83 - "N was a Nobleman . . . O was an Oystergirl . . . ." Shaped base. Loop handle. H-2.5 in. x D-2.62 in. No mark. *Courtesy of Ann and Dennis Berard.* $250+

Figure H84 - "P was a Parson . . . Q was a Queen . . . ." Loop handle. H-2.87 in. x D-2.75 in. No mark. $250+

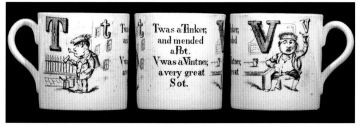

Figure H85 - "T was a Tinker . . . V was a Vintner . . . ." Loop handle. H-2.75 in. x D-2.62 in. No mark. $250+

Figure H90 - "K was a Knight . . . L was a Lamplighter . . . ." Loop handle. H-3 in. x D-3 in. No mark. $250+

Figure H86 - "W was a Watchman . . . X was Expensive . . . ." Loop handle. H-2.87 in. x D-2.75 in. No mark. $250+

Figure H91 - "D is the Driver . . . ." Loop handle. H-2.62 in. x D-2.75 in. No mark. Production date: After 1852. Source (Riley, 1991): *Cousin Chatterbox's Railway Alphabet.* Dean. c.1852. $300+

Figure H87 - "C was a Captain . . . D was a Drover . . . ." Shaped base. Loop handle. Leaf terminals. H-3 in. x D-2.87 in. No mark. $250+

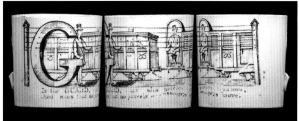

Figure H92 - "G is the Guard . . . ." Loop handle. H-2.62 in. x D-2.75 in. No mark. Production date: After 1852. Source (Riley, 1991): *Cousin Chatterbox's . . . .* as noted in Figure H91. *Courtesy of Ann and Dennis Berard.* $300+

Figure H88 - "Y was a Yeoman . . . Z is a Zany . . . ." Tapered shape. Loop handle. H-2.5 in. x D-3.12 in. No mark. $250+

Figure H93 - "T is the Tunnel . . . ." Loop handle. H-2.62 in. x D-2.75 in. No mark. Production date: After 1852. Source (Riley, 1991): *Cousin Chatterbox's . . . .* as noted in Figure H91. No mark. *Courtesy of Ann and Dennis Berard.* $300+

Figure H89 - "F was a Fiddler . . . ." Shaped base. Spurred loop handle. H-2.63 in. x D-2.75 in. No mark. $250+

Figure H94 - "D/E/F - The Flower Seller." Shaped base. Loop handle. Leaf terminals. H-3 in. x D-3 in. Staffordshire, England. $200-$250

Figure H95 - "G/H/I - Trap Bat & Ball." Shaped base. Loop handle. Leaf terminals. H-3.12 in. x D-3.12 in. No mark. $300+

Figure H100 - "P/Q/R - Pulling a Wagon." Tapered. Shaped base. Loop handle. Leaf terminals. H-2.87 in. x D-3 in. No mark. $200-$250

Figure H96- "G/H/I - At Tennis." Loop handle. H-3 in. x D-3. in. Staffordshire, England. $200-$250

Figure H101 - " S/T/U - Windmill." Loop handle. Leaf terminals. H-3 in. x D-3 in. No mark. $200-$250

Figure H97 - "J/K/L - For my Nephew." Shaped base. Loop handle. H-2.87 in. x D-2.87 in. Staffordshire, England. $200-$250

Figure H102 - "V/W/X - Cricket." Shaped base. Loop handle. Leaf terminals. H-3 in. x D-3 in. No mark. $200-$250

Figure H98 - "M/N/O - Whip-Top." Loop handle. Leaf terminals. H-2.75 in. x D-2.87 in. No mark. $200-$250

Figure H103 - "Y/Z/& - Ice Skating." Loop handle. Leaf terminals. H-3 in. x D-3 in. Staffordshire, England. No mark. $200-$250

Figure H99 - "P/Q/R - Playing Hoops." Loop handle. Leaf terminals. H-3 in. x D-3 in. Staffordshire, England. $200-$250

Figure H104 - "O/P - O is for Obadia . . . P is for Peter . . . ." Loop handle. H-2.75 in. x D-2.5 in. No mark. *Courtesy of Ann and Dennis Berard.* $250+

Figure H105 - "Q/R - Q is the Queen . . . R is for Ruth . . . ." Shaped base. Loop handle. H-2.62 in. x D-2.5 in. No mark. $250+

Figure H110 - "B/C - Buffalo/Cat." Loop handle. Leaf terminals. H-2.87 in. x D-2.87 in. No mark. $250+

Figure H106 - "A/Z - Samuel." (Alphabet cast on rim.) Tapered. Spurred loop handle. H-2.5 in. x D-2.62 in. No mark. $250+

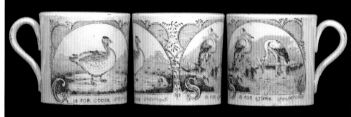

Figure H111- "G/S - Goose/Stork." Loop handle. H-2.75 in. x D-2.87 in. No mark. $250+

Figure H107 - "A/B - Animals/Bear (Filigree surround)." Loop handle. H-3 in. x D-3 in. No mark. $175-$225

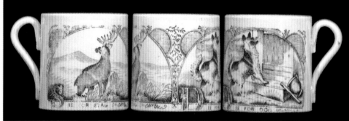

Figure H112 - "S/D - Stag/Dog." Loop handle. Leaf terminals. H-2.75 in. x D-2.62 in. No mark. $250+

Figure H108 - "C/D - Cat /Dog (Filigree surround)." Loop handle. H-3.12 in. x D-3.12 in. No mark. $175-$225

Figure H113 - "C/D - C was a Councell_r . . . D was a Drovier . . . ." Loop handle. H-2.7 in. x D-2.5 in. No mark. *Courtesy of Ann and Dennis Berard.* $250+

Figure H109 - "O/P - Otter/Pig (Filigree surround)." Shaped base. Loop handle. H-3.12 in. x D-3.12 in. No mark. $175-$225

Figure H114 - "G/H - G was a Gamester . . . H was a Hunter . . . ." Loop handle. H-2.5 in. x D-2.75 in. No mark. *Courtesy of Ann and Dennis Berard.* $250+

Figure H115 - "W/X - W was a Watchman . . . X was Expensive . . . ." Shaped base. Loop handle. H-2.87 in. x D-3.12 in. No mark. *Courtesy of Ann and Dennis Berard.* $250+

Figure H119 - "S - Silverlocks . . . ." Tapered, shaped base. Handle missing. H-2.75 in. x D-2.75 in. No mark. $250+

Figure H116 - "H - Horse. House. Hound. Horn." Shaped base. Loop handle. H-2.87 in. x D-2.87 in. No mark. $250+

Figure H120 - "T - The four masters . . . Tortoiseshell." Shaped base. Loop handle. H-2.62 in. x D-2.62 in. No mark. *Courtesy of Ann and Dennis Berard.* $250+

Figure H117 - "M - Mil-ler Mill Mouse." Loop handle. H-3 in. x D-3 in. No mark. $250+

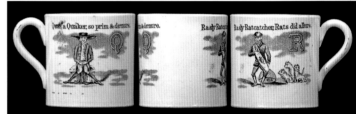

Figure H121 - "Q/R - Q was a Quaker . . . R a sly Ratcatcher." Loop handle. H-3 in. x D-3 in. No mark. $250+

Figure H118 - "Q - Q the Queen. God bless Her." Shaped base. Loop handle. H-2.75 in. x D-2.87 in. No mark. $400+

Figure H122 - "P - Pug the Page . . . ." Shaped base. Loop handle. H-2.75 in. x D-2.5 in. No mark. $250+

Figure H123 - "G/H - G - Goose . . . H - Horse . . . ." Loop handle. H-2.75 in. x D-2.75 in. No mark. *Courtesy of Ann and Dennis Berard.* $250+

Figure H127 - "A/Z - Slow rolls the churn . . . . (A-Z at inner rim)." Shaped base. Loop handle. Leaf terminals. H-2.5 in. x D-2.5 in. No mark. $250+

Figure H124 - "E Stands for Elephant . . . ." Flat-topped ear-shaped handle. H-3 in. x D-3 in. No mark. $200-$250

Figure H128 - "A/Z - Alphabet in Three Rows (Decorated handle)." Ear-shaped handle. H-2.25 in. x D-2.37 in. No mark. *Courtesy of Ann and Dennis Berard.* $250+

Figure H125 - "Three Scenes (A - M at top rim, N-Z at base)." Spurred loop handle. H-3 in. x D-2.75 in. No mark. $175-$225

Figure H129 - "A/Z - Musicians (Decorated handle)." Loop handle. H-2.87 in. x D-2.87 in. No mark. $200-$250

Figure H126 - "A/Z - Pet Lamb (A-Z cast at top rim)." Flared rim. Spurred loop handle. H-2.5 in. x D-2.75 in. No mark. *Courtesy of Ann and Dennis Berard.* $250+

Figure H130 - "A/Z - Farm House Scene." Spurred loop handle. Leaf terminals. H-2.75 in. x D-2.87 in. No mark. $200-$250

Figure H131 - "A/Z - Long-billed Bird." Loop handle. H-2.75 in. x D-2.75 in. No mark. $175-$225

Figure H135 - "A/Z - The Circus Rider." (Alphabet cast on face.) Demitasse shape. Flat-topped ear-shaped handle. H-2.5 in. x D-2.62 in. No mark. $100-$150

Figure H132 - "A/Z - Who Killed . . . ." Loop handle. H-2.75 in. x D-2.75 in. No mark. $175-$225

Figure H136 - "A/Z - Elephants Serving Tea." (Alphabet cast on rim and face.) Tapered. Flat-topped ear-shaped handle. H-3.12 in. x D-3.12 in. No mark. $100-$150

Figure H133 - "A/Z - Hummingbird (misnamed)." Loop handle. H-2.87 in. x D-2.75 in. No mark. $175-$225

Figure H137 - "A/U - Portraits." Spurred loop handle. H-2.87 in. x D-2.87 in. Germany. $100-$150

Figure H134 - "A/Z - Alphabet in a Cartouche." Loop handle. H-2.75 in. x D-2.75 in. No mark. $200-$250

Figure H138 - "A/Z - Manual Alphabet." Shaped base. Loop handle. H-2.75 in. x D-2.62 in. No mark. $500+

I Is for Infant to Infirm

Figure I1- "Stages of Life Series (untitled) - Infancy." 7.12 in. No mark. $250+

Figure I2 - "Toddler and Rocking Chair." 8.5 in. No mark. $175-$225

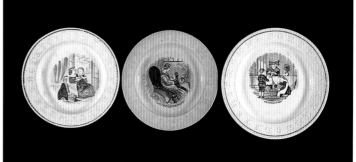

Figure I8 - "Mother and Children." 7.25 in. No mark. $175-$225

Figure I9 - "Mother and Daughter, dear to each . . . ." 7.5 in. No mark. $175-$225

Figure I10 - "Grandmother." 8 in. No mark. $175-$225

Figure I3 - "Stages of Life Series (untitled) - Manhood." 6 in. No mark. $250+

Figure I4 - "Wishes." 7 in. No mark. $175-$225

Figure I5 - "And when my kite I wish to try . . . ." 6.12 in. No mark. Source (Riley, 1991): Print from William Upton's illustrated poem, "My Grandfather." London: William Darton, Jr., 1812-1815. *Courtesy of Ann and Dennis Berard.* $250+

Figure I6 - "Who when he saw me . . . ." 6.06 in. No mark. Source (Riley, 1991): Print from William Upton's illustrated poem . . . ." as noted in Figure I5. *Courtesy of Ann and Dennis Berard.* $250+

Figure I11 - "Shipbuilding." 6.25 in. No mark. Sources (Riley, 1991): Print from *Aunt Friendly's Warne's Holiday Album.* c.1860, and 'W for Walnuts . . . .' *Alphabet of Fruits.* London: Frederick Warne & Co., 1875. $150-$175

Figure I12 - "Stacking Walnut Shells." 6.62 in. Charles Allerton & Sons. Longton, Staffordshire. Factory date: 1859-1942. Mark date: c.1859-1912. $150-$175

Figure I13 - "These cannons, Sir, are not the toys . . . ." 7.12 in. No mark. $150-$175

Figure I14 - "Playing with Scales." 8.25 in. No mark. $150-$175

Figure I19 - "Soldiers." 7 in. No mark. $150-$175

Figure I20 - "The Young Sergeant." 7 in. Elsmore & Forster / Foster. Tunstall, Staffordshire. Factory date: c.1853-1871. $150-$175

Figure I15 - "Dog-Cart, Scene One." 6.62 in. Charles Allerton & Sons. Longton, Staffordshire. Factory date: 1859-1942. Mark date: 1890+. $150-$175

Figure I16 - "Dog-Cart, Scene Two." 6.87 in. No mark. $150-$175

Figure I21 - "Playing at Lovers." 7.12 in. No mark. $175-$225

Figure I22 - "Frolics of Youth Series - Don't I look . . . ." 7.25 in. No mark. $175-$225

Figure I17 - "Playing Store." 5.75 in. Staffordshire. $150-$175

Figure I18 - "This boy, I think . . . ." 7.25 in. No mark. $150-$175

Figure I23 - "Frolics of Youth Series - Now I'm Grandmother . . . ." 7.5 in. No mark. Source (Riley, 1991): *Our Early Days*. No. 1. London: W. Clerk, c.1840. This plate is also found as Figure Z1 in "Z Is for Σ and Other Reversals." $175-$225

Figure I24 - "Grandpa's Hat." 7.87 in. Painted trademark illegible. $175-$225

Figure I25 - "Writing in the Garden." 5.31 in. No mark. $150-$175
Figure I26 - "Playing School." 6.12 in. J. & G. Meakin. Hanley, Staffordshire.
Factory date: 1851+. $150-$175

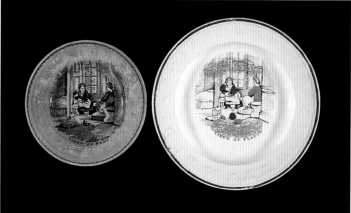

Figure I31 - "Tired of Play." 5 in. No mark. $150-$175
Figure I32 - "Tired of Play." 6.87 in. No mark. $150-$175

Figure I27 - "The Young Idea." 7.25 in. No mark. $150-$175

Figure I33 - "Little Boys at Marbles Play . . . ." 5.5 in. No mark. $250+

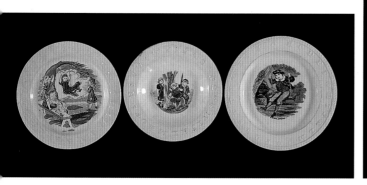

Figure I28 - "On a Swing." 7.5 in. No mark. $150-$175
Figure I29 - "Swinging." H-1.25 in. x D-6.87 in. No mark. $150-$175
Figure I30 - "Swing, Swung." Elsmore & Son. Tunstall, Staffordshire.
Factory date: 1872-1887. $150-$175

Figure I34 - "Spinning Tops." 7.1 in. No mark. Formerly of the Chalala
Collection. $175-$225
Figure I35 - "Top Whipping." 7.12 in. J. & G. Meakin. Hanley, Staffordshire.
Factory date: 1851+. $175-$225

Figure 136 - "Shuttlecock." 8 in. J. & G. Meakin, Hanley, Staffordshire. Factory date: 1851+. $175-$225

Figure 140 - "Leap Frog (captioned)." 6 in. No mark. $175-$225
Figure 141 - "Leap Frog." 5.12 in. Powell & Bishop. Hanley, Staffordshire. Factory date: 1866-1878. $150-$175
Figure 142 - "Jump Little Nag-Tail (captioned)." 6.87 in. No mark. $175-$225

Figure 137 - "Snowball Fight." 7.27 in. No mark. $150-$175

Figure 143 - "Very good fun is . . . ." 6.37 in. No mark. $150-$175
Figure 144 - "Very good fun is . . . ." 7.5 in. No mark. $150-$175

Figure 145 - "Throwing a Ball." 6.12 in. No mark. $150-$175
Figure 146 - "Football." 5.5 in. J. & G. Meakin. Hanley, Staffordshire. Factory date: 1851+. *Courtesy of Ann and Dennis Berard.* $200-$250

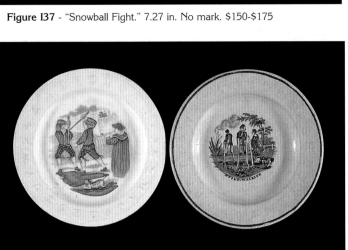

Figure 138 - "Jousting." 8.25 in. No mark. $150-$175
Figure 139 - "Stilt Walking." 8.25 in. Capital W. $150-$175

Figure 147 - "The Playground (captioned)." 6.12 in. No mark. $175-$225

Figure 153 - "Oh look brother . . . ." 6.87 in. No mark. $150-$200
Figure 154 - "The New Pony." 6.12 in. No mark. $150-$200
Figure 155 - "The Pony." 6.27 in. Ivory (mark). *Courtesy of Ann and Dennis Berard.* $150-$200

Figure 148 - "The Playfellows." 7.12 in. No mark. $150-$200
Figure 149 - "The Guardian." 7.12 in. Elsmore & Son. Tunstall, Staffordshire. Factory date: 1872-1887. $150-$200

Figure 156 - "Willie and his Rabbit." 6.25 in. No mark. $150-$200
Figure 157 - "Pretty, poll . . . ." 5.5 in. Elsmore and Foster / Forster. Tunstall, Staffordshire. Factory date: 1853-1871. $150- $200

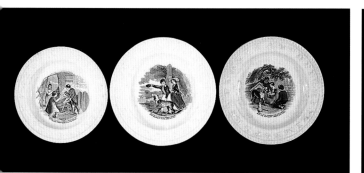

Figure 150 - "These children trying . . . ." 5.27 in. No mark. $150-$200
Figure 151 - "Catch it Carlo . . . ." 6 in. No mark. $150-$200
Figure 152 - "That girl wants . . . ." 6 in. E & F (Elsmore and Foster / Forster). Tunstall, Staffordshire. Factory date: 1853-1871. $150-$200

Figure 158 - "Feeding the Geese." 7 in. Elsmore & Son. Tunstall, Staffordshire. Factory date: 1872-1887. $150-$200
Figure 159 - "Pride of the Barn-Yard." 7 in. No mark. $150-$200

Figure 160 - "Feeding the Donkey." 7.12 in. No mark. $150-$200
Figure 161 - "The Donkey." 6.25 in. No mark. *Courtesy of Ann and Dennis Berard.* $150-$200
Figure 162 - "Our Donkey and Foal." 6 in. Elsmore & Son. Tunstall, Staffordshire. Factory date: 1872-1887. $150-$200

Figure 163 - "Raking the Garden." 5.87 in. No mark. $150-$175
Figure 164 - "Tending the Garden." 7.75 in. Staffordshire, England. Registry mark #153253 date: 1890. $150-$175

Figure 165 - "The Floral Coronation." 5.87 in. No mark. $150-$175
Figure 166 - "The Garden Flower." 7 in. Elsmore & Son - England. Tunstall, Staffordshire. Factory date: 1872-1887. $150-$175
Figure 167 - "Two Girls Making Garlands." 6.12 in. Powell & Bishop. Hanley, Staffordshire. Factory date: 1866-1878. $150-$175

Figure 168 - "We kindly welcome . . . ." 6.62 in. No mark. Source: *The Cotter's Saturday Night.* Poem published after 1786. $300+
Figure 169 - "The sire turns . . . ." 5.37 in. No mark. Source: *The Cotter's . . . .* as noted on Figure 168. This plate is also found as Figure Z3 in "Z Is for Σ and Other Reversals." $300+
Figure 170 - "The sire turns . . . ." 6.5 in. No mark. Source: *The Cotter's . . . .* as noted on Figure 168. $300+

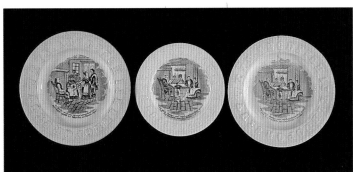

Figure 171 - "Christmas Day." 5 in. No mark. $350+

Figure 172 - "Gaping." 6.12 in. No mark. $250+
Figure 173 - "O How Handsome." 5.12 in. No mark. $250+

Figure 174 - "Smoking." 5.12 in. No mark. $250+
Figure 175 - "Taking Snuff." 7.25. in. No mark. $250+

Figure 176 - "But now your brow . . . ." 6.62 in. No mark. Source: Robert Burns. *John Anderson, My Jo.* Published in 1790. $300+

J Is for J, the Last Letter of the Alphabet

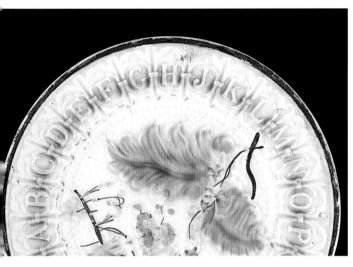

Figure J1 - "Majolica Flowering Plants (No letter I in sequence)." 7.5 in. No mark. 350+

Figure J2 - "Pluto - the Pup and Mickey Mouse (Reversed I and J in sequence)." H-1.5 in. x D-7.5 in. Carl Schumann Porcelain Factory. Arzberg, Bavaria. Trademark Registered and Authorized by Walter E. Disney. Bavaria. Factory date: 1881-1996. Production date: c.1935. This plate is also found as Figure C87 in "C Is for Commercialism" and as Figure Z6 in "Z Is for Σ and Other Reversals." 500+

Figure J4 - "Gnomes (No J in sequence)." 7 in. Germany #122. $100-$150

Figure J5 - "Tea Party for Cats and Kittens (No J, X, or Y in sequence)." 6 in. No mark. $100-$150

Figure J3 - "Advertiser for Buster Brown Shoes - Buster Brown Pouring Tea (No J in sequence)." 6.25 in. No mark. c.1904. $100-$150

Figure J6 - "Blind Man's Buff, cast design edge (No J, X, or Y in sequence)." 6.25 in. $100-$150

Figure J7 - "Ring-a-Ring-a-Rosie (No J, X, or Y in sequence)." Lustre. 6.12 in. No mark. $100-$150

Figure J8 - "Training the Dog (No J, X, or Y in sequence)." Rococo and lustre edge. 6.12 in. No mark. $100-$150

Figure J12 - Detail of Figure D17, "Three Children and a Goat," found in "D Is for Deep Dishes," showing exclusion of the J in the alphabet.

Figure J13 - Detail of Figure D51, "The Cat in the Cradle," found in "D Is for Deep Dishes," showing exclusion of the J in the alphabet.

Figure J9 - "Three Girls under One Umbrella (No J, X, or Y in sequence)." 5.37 in. No mark. $100-$150

Figure J10 - "Three Girls with Fans (No J, X, or Y in sequence)." 5.37 in. No mark. $100-$150

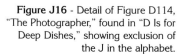

Figure J14 - Detail of Figure D71, "Little Polly Flinders," found in "D Is for Deep Dishes," showing exclusion of the J in the alphabet.

Figure J15 - Detail of Figure D72, "Little Bo-Peep," found in "D Is for Deep Dishes," showing exclusion of the J in the alphabet.

Figure J11 - "Bouquet (No J, X, or Y in sequence)." 6.25 in. No mark. $100-$150

Figure J16 - Detail of Figure D114, "The Photographer," found in "D Is for Deep Dishes," showing exclusion of the J in the alphabet.

K Is for Kitsch

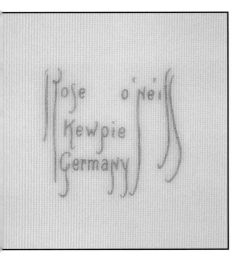

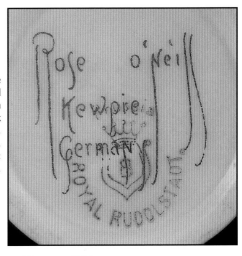

Figure K1 - Mark: Rose O'Neill. (Assumed Royal Rudolstadt Porcelain Factory a.k.a. New York & Rudolstadt. Rudolstadt, Thuringia, Germany. Factory date: 1882-1918.

Figure K5 - Mark: Rose O'Neill and Royal Rudolstadt Porcelain Factory a.k.a. New York & Rudolstadt. Rudolstsadt, Thuringia, Germany. Factory date: 1882-1918.

Figure K2 - "Two Kewpies." 6 in. Rose O'Neill. $175-$225

Figure K6 - "Teacup." H-2.75 in. x D-2.5 in. at top rim and 1.89 in. at base. Rose O'Neill and Royal Rudolstadt Porcelain Factory. Factory date: 1882-1918. $175-$225

Figure K3- "Three Kewpies." 6.89 in. Rose O'Neill. $175-$225

Figure K7 - "One Kewpie, Standing." H-1.89 in. x D-8.89 in. Holdfast Baby Plate. D. E. McNicol Pottery Co. East Liverpool, Ohio. Factory date: 1892-c.1929. Mark date: c.1920. $150-$200

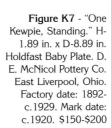

Figure K4 - "Five Kewpies." H-1.62 in. x D-7 in. Rose O'Neill. $175-$225

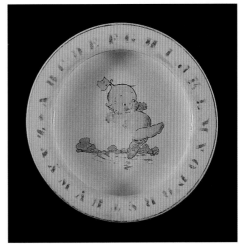

Figure K8 - "One Kewpie, Running." H-1.75 in. x D-8 in. Holdfast Baby Plate. D. E. McNicol Pottery Co. East Liverpool, Ohio. Factory date: 1892-c.1929. Mark date c.1920. $150-$200

Figure K9 - Mark: Dresden China Co. East Liverpool, Ohio. Factory date: 1875 (6?)-c.1927. Mark date: c.1926.

Figure K10 - "Three Kewpies." H-1.25 in. x D-8.62 in. Dresden China Co. Factory date: 1875 (6?)-c.1927. Mark date: c.1926. $150-$200

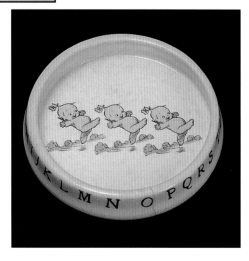

Figure K12 - "Symptoms of Walking Made Easy." 6.25 in. No mark. Source: "Drolleries of the Steam Engine" as noted in K11. $150-$200

108   BANBURY CHAP-BOOKS.

DROLLERIES OF THE STEAM ENGINE.

When Steam was first introduced it naturally called forth much 'text' and illustration. The above we believe to be designed by 'Cromek.' Miss Bewick spoke highly of him ; he was one of the 'Boys' or pupils in Bewick's School. He executed some choice vignettes for 'Burns's Poems,' much in Luke Clennell's style, Bewick's favourite pupil.

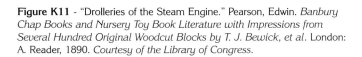

Figure K13 - "Don't Tommy, Don't." 7 in. No mark. $200-$250

Figure K11 - "Drolleries of the Steam Engine." Pearson, Edwin. *Banbury Chap Books and Nursery Toy Book Literature with Impressions from Several Hundred Original Woodcut Blocks by T. J. Bewick, et al.* London: A. Reader, 1890. *Courtesy of the Library of Congress.*

Figure K14 - "Children Caressing." 7 in. No mark. $400+

Figure K18 - Magnification of word "Rendezvous" as found on "R for Rendezvous."

Figure K15 - "Two Children with Mustaches." 7 in. No mark. *Courtesy of Dr. Joan George.* $400+

Figure K19 - Three letter mug: "VWX - The Whipping." H-2.5 in. x D-3 in. Pedestal base. Loop handle. Leaf terminals. No mark. $200-$250

Figure K16 - "Children Caressing, One with Hat." 7.5 in. No mark. *Courtesy of Dr. Joan George.* $400+

Figure K20 - "Innocence - Do you see my little Tommy?" (Irregular letter sequence due to computer enhancement) c. 7.5 in. No mark. *Original photo courtesy of Irene and Ralph Lindsay.* $500+

Figure K17 - "R for Rendezvous (Computer enhanced)." H-2.5 in. x D-2.3 in. Loop handle. No mark. $200-$250

L Is for Lustreware

Figure L1 - "Cottage Design - Peaked Roof." Pink lustre. 4.25 in. No mark. $200-$250

Figure L5 - "Historical Scripture Alphabet Series - G was Goliath, the Giant . . . ." Pink lustre. Shaped base. Loop handle. Leaf terminals. H-3.5 in. x D-3.5 in. No mark. $350+

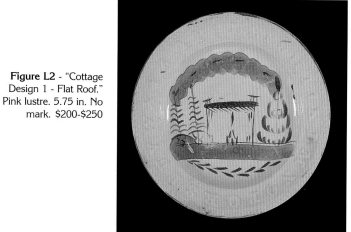

Figure L2 - "Cottage Design 1 - Flat Roof." Pink lustre. 5.75 in. No mark. $200-$250

Figure L6 - "Historical Scripture Alphabet Series - K was the King who gave Joseph command . . . ." Pink lustre. Shaped base. Loop handle. H-3 in. x D-3 in. No mark. $350+

Figure L7- "Historical Scripture Alphabet Series - W was the Water which sprang forth, when God . . . ." Pink lustre. Shaped base. Loop handle. H-2.87 in. x D-3 in. No mark. $350+

Figure L3 - "Cottage Design 2 - Flat Roof." Pink lustre. 7.25 in. No mark. $200-$250

Figure L8 - "For a Good Girl." Creamware. Purple lustre rim. Loop handle. Leaf terminals. H-2.5 in. x D-2.5 in. No mark. Source (Riley, 1991): Frontispiece. c.1800. *Courtesy of Ann and Dennis Berard.* Formerly of the Chalala Collection. 500+

Figure L4 - "Girl Teaching her Dog." 6.50 in. Purple lustre. No mark. $200-$250

Figure L9 - "One Rooster and Two Hens." Pink lustre rim. 5.25 in. No mark. $75-$125
Figure L10 - "One Rooster and Two Hens." Pale blue lustre rim. 5.25 in. No mark. $75-$125
Figure L11 - "Two Roosters." Pink lustre rim. 5.25 in. No mark. $75-$125

Figure L12 - "Round Dance." Wide pink lustre rim - inner gold edge. 7 in. No mark. $75-$125

Figure L17 - "R.S. Prussia Style Portrait (Purple petals)." Pink lustre. 6.37 in. No mark. $100-$150

Figure L18 - "R.S. Prussia Style Portrait (White petals)." Pink lustre. 6.37 in. No mark. $100-$150

Figure L19 - "R.S. Prussia Style Portrait (Red hair)." Pink lustre. 6.37 in. No mark. $100-$150

Figure L13 - "Children and a Dog, One Riding." Wide pink lustre rim. 7 in. No mark. $75-$125

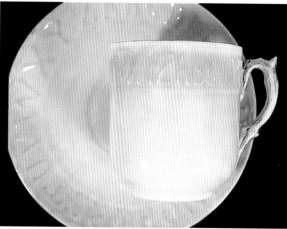

Figure L20 - "Cup/saucer - Pink lustre." Maker: Assumed German factory. Cup: Spurred ear-shaped handle. H-2.25 in. x D-2 in. No mark. Saucer: 4.75 in. No mark. $100-$125 (set)

Figure L14 - "See-Saw." Wide pink lustre rim - inner gold edge. 7 in. No mark. $75-$125

Figure L21 - "Cup/saucer - Pink lustre." Maker: Delinieres & Co. Limoges, France. Factory date: c.1879-1900. Cup: Loop handle. H-2.25 in. x D-2 in. Delinieres & Co. Limoges, France (now Bernardaud & Co.). Saucer: 4.75 in. Delinieres & Co. Limoges, France. $125-$175 (set)

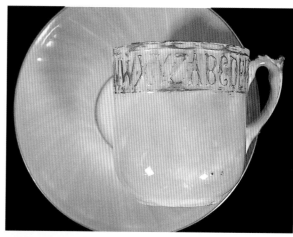

Figure L15 - "Three Dutch Children." Wide pink lustre rim - inner gold edge. 8 in. No mark. $75-$125

Figure L16 - "Dutch Woman and Child." Wide pink lustre - inner gold edge. 8 in. No mark. $75-$125

Figure L22 - "The Diverting History of John Gilpin - From and Return Home." Orange lustre. 7.25 in. This plate is also found as Figure Z4 in "Z Is for Ƨ and Other Reversals." $300+

M Is for Metals

Figure M1 - Alderman W. H. Jones, author of the *Story of the Japan, Tin Plate Working, and Iron Braziers' Trades, Bicycle and Galvanising Trades, and Enamel Ware Manufacture in Wolverhampton and District.* London: Alexander and Shepheard, Ltd., 1900. *Permission of the Wolverhampton Research Library, Wolverhampton, England.*

Figure M4 - "Tea Tray." 7.87 in. No mark. *Courtesy of Ann and Dennis Berard.* $75-$125

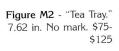

Figure M2 - "Tea Tray." 7.62 in. No mark. $75-$125

Figure M5 - "Tea Tray." 7.62 in. No mark. *Courtesy of Ann and Dennis Berard.* $75-$125

Figure M6 - "Tea Tray." 7.75 in. No mark. $75-$125

Figure M3 - "Tea Tray." 7.87 in. No mark. *Courtesy of Ann and Dennis Berard.* $75-$125

Figure M7 - "Tea Tray." 7.87 in. No mark. *Courtesy of Ann and Dennis Berard.* $75-$125

Figure M11 - "Map of the British Isles." Enamel. 7.87 in. No mark. $200-$250

Figure M8 - "Tea Tray." 8 in. No mark. *Courtesy of Ann and Dennis Berard.* $75-$125

Figure M12 - "Clock Face." Enamel. 7.87 in. GMT & Brothers. Germany. $125-$175

Figure M9 - "Tea Tray." 8.12 in. No mark. *Courtesy of Ann and Dennis Berard.* $75-$125

Figure M13 - "Clock Face." Enamel. 7 in. No mark. $125-$175

Figure M10 - "Tea Tray (Clock dials)." 7.5 in. No mark. *Courtesy of Marilyn Ross.* $75-$125

Figure M14 - "Clock Face." Enamel. 8.5 in. A Genuine MIKKIMUG. Hand Printed and Fired by Michael Wood, Uploders Bridport, Dorset, England (Information provided by dealer; no mark). n.d. $50-$100

Figure M15 - "Clock Face." Chromographic enamel. 7.87 in. Orme, Evans & Co., Ltd. Wolverhampton, England. Factory date: 1790-c.1940 (?). Catalogue date: 1926. $125-$175

Figure M18 - "Jumbo." Assay: Iron 100%. 6.12 in. Possibly Central Stamping Co. n.d. $125-$175

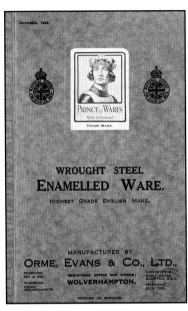

Figure M16 - "Cover of the Orme, Evans & Co., Ltd. Catalogue." Wolverhampton, England. 1926.

Figure M19 - "Tom Thumb." Assay: Iron 99.1%, Copper .9%. 2.87 in. No mark. Date source (Chalala): 1844. $250-$300

Figure M17 - "Page 16 of the Orme, Evans & Co., Ltd. Catalogue" as noted in M16.

Figure M20 - "Jenny Lind." Assay: Iron 98.8%, Carbon .8%, Silicon .4%. 4.25 in. No mark. *Courtesy of Ann and Dennis Berard.* $250-$300

Figure M21 - "ABC Border." Assay: Aluminum 99%, Trace elements 1%. 6.12 in. No mark. $50-$100

Figure M22 - "ABC Border." Assay: Aluminum 99%, Trace elements 1%. 6.12 in. Holdfast Junior Company. $50-$100

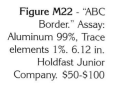

Figure M23 - Reverse of M22 showing table clamp, Patent #1177728.

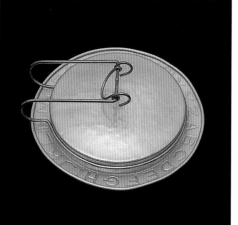

Figure M24 - "Border detail: Z/&/A." Assay: Iron 97.9%, Copper 2.1%. 6.12 in. No mark. $50-$100

Figure M25 - "Border detail: Z/&/A." Assay: Iron 99.3%, Copper .52%, Chromium .17%. 6.5 in. No mark. $50-$100

Figure M26 (upper plate) - "Border detail: Z/&/five pointed star/A." Assay: Iron 99.5%, Titanium .29%, Chromium .23%. 6.25 in. No mark. *Courtesy of Ann and Dennis Berard.* $50-$100

Figure M27 (lower plate): "Border detail: Z/&/five pointed star/A." Assay: Iron 98.9%, Cobalt .91%, Arsenic .13%. 6.5 in. No mark. $50-$100

Figure M32 - "Border detail: Z/five pointed star/A." Silver plated over white metal. 7 in. Reed & Barton, Taunton, Massachusetts. Factory date: 1840+ $50-$100

Figure M28 - "Border detail: Z/&/pointing hand/A." Assay: Iron 98.1%, Copper .85%, Titanium .85%, Chromium .21%. 6.12 in. No mark. *Courtesy of Ann and Dennis Berard.* $50-$100

Figure M33 - "Border detail: Z/six pointed star/A." Assay: Iron 90.2%, Beryllium 4.9%, Cobalt 4.27%, Arsenic .7%. 5.62 in. No mark. *Courtesy of Ann and Dennis Berard.* $50-$100

Figure M29 - "Border detail: Z/&/horizontal diamond/A." Assay: Iron 97.8%, Copper 2.2%. 6.25 in. No mark. $50-$100

Figure M30 (upper plate) - "Border detail: Z/&/./A." Assay: Iron 99.8%, Chromium .13%, Trace elements .07%. 5.62 in. No mark. $50-$100
Figure M31 (lower plate) - "Border detail: Z/&/./A." Assay: Iron 99.4%. Copper .56%. 5.89 in. No mark. *Courtesy of Ann and Dennis Berard.* $50-$100

Figure M34 - "Alphabet Block Border Design." Assay: Aluminum 94.5%, Silicon 4.5%, Beryllium .37%, Copper .26%, Iron .19%, Magnesium .1%, Arsenic .05%. Dog dish shape. 8.37 in. Underwood's Patent High Chair Baby Plate. Manufacturer's #242. $125-$175

Figure M35 - "Alphabet with Flourishes and Figures." Quadruple Plate. Dog-dish shape. 7.75 in. Van Bergh Silver Plate Co. Rochester, New York. 1892-1926 when it merged with Oenida. $125-$175

Figure M38 (left) - "Hey Diddle Diddle, Rolled Edge." Assay: Iron 99.5%, Nickel .37%, Copper .14%. 8.25 in. No mark. $100-$150

Figure M39 (right) - "Hey Diddle Diddle, Flat Edge." Assay: Iron 100%. 8.66 in. No mark. $100-$150

Figure M36 - "Double alphabet, Upper and Lower Case." Assay: Iron 99.2%, Copper .5%, Nickel .4%, Chromium .04%. 6.25 in. No mark. $150-$200

Figure M40 - "Mary Had a Little Lamb." Assay: Iron 99.7%, Nickel .27%. 8 in. No mark. $100-$150

Figure M41 - "Simple Simon." Silver plate. 6 in. Oneida Silversmiths. Sherrill, New York. Factory date: 1848+ $75-$125

Figure M37 - "Little Jack Horner." Assay: Aluminum 92.5%, Lead 1.8%, Manganese .4%, Copper 4.3%, Silicon .9%. 7.62 in. No mark. $125-$175

239

Figure M42 - "Who Killed Cock Robin (Owner Painted)?" Assay: Iron 100%. 7.62 in. No mark. Owner dated on reverse, 1897. Production date: c.1830-1899. $100-$150

Figure M43 - "Who Killed Cock Robin" Assay: Iron 100%. 7.75 in. No mark. Production date: c.1830-1899. $100-$150

Figure M47 - "A Brass Horse." Assay: Copper 82.2%, Iron 15.9%, Zinc .51%, Copper .37%. 5.5 in. No mark. *Courtesy of Ann and Dennis Berard.* $300-$350

Figure M44 - "Who Killed Cock Robin? I, said the Sparrow, with my bow and arrow." Iron 100%. 7.5 in. No mark. *Courtesy of Ann and Dennis Berard.* $175-$225

Figure M45 - "Brownies." Assay: Iron 99.4%, Nickel .7%, Copper .5%, Manganese .002%. 8.89 in. No mark. A Palmer Cox design. Patent date: February 11, 1896. $175-$225

Figure M48 - "American Eagle." Assay: Iron 99.8%, Chromium .14%. 6.25 in. No mark. *Courtesy of Ann and Dennis Berard.* $350+

Figure M49 - "Clock Face." Assay: Aluminum 99.5%, Iron .43%, Trace elements .07%. 8.12 in. Wolverhampton (trademark with comic wolverine and man-in-the-moon crescent, unidentified). Wolverhampton, England. $100-$150

Figure M46 - "An Iron Horse." Assay: Iron 100%. 5.62 in. No mark. $300-$350

240

Figure M50 - "Niagara Falls." Assay: Aluminum 99%, Iron .71%, Silicon .2%, Copper .12%. 6.25 in. No mark. *Courtesy of Ann and Dennis Berard.* $100-$150

Figure M54 - "The Crystal Palace." Assay: Iron 100%. 2.12 in. No mark. Event date: c.1851. $200-$250

Figure M51 - "The Crystal Palace." Assay: Iron 97.9%, Silicon .6%, Carbon 1.5%. 4.25 in. No mark. Queen's Imprimatur. Event date: c.1851.*Courtesy of Ann and Dennis Berard.* $200-$250

Figure M55 - "The New Crystal Palace at Sydenham." Assay: Iron 97.1%, Copper 2.4%, Silicon .3%, Carbon .2%. 5.78 in. No mark. Event date: c.1854. *Courtesy of Ann and Dennis Berard.* $200-$250

Figure M52 - "The Crystal Palace." Assay: Iron 96.3%, Copper 2.8%, Silicon .7%. 4.25 in. No mark. Queen's Imprimatur. Event date: c.1851. $200-$250

Figure M56- "Father Mathew (also spelled Matthew and Matthews)." Assay: 97.6%, Lead 1.07%, Cobalt 1.17%, Arsenic .17%. 6.37 in. No mark. c.1840. *Courtesy of Ann and Dennis Berard.* $350+

Figure M53 - "The Crystal Palace." Assay: Iron 95.2%, Copper 3.7%, Silicon .4%, Carbon .8%. 2.78 in. No mark. Event date: c.1851. *Courtesy of Ann and Dennis Berard.* $200-$250

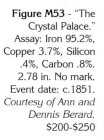

Figure M57 - "Sir Colin Campbell." Assay: Iron 95.6%, Copper 4.4%. 4.25 in. No mark. c.1855-1865. *Courtesy of Ann and Dennis Berard.* $350+

Figure M58- "Washington." Assay: Iron 99.2%, Nickel .14%, Copper .08%, Chromium .06%. 6.12 in. No mark. Event date assumed: c.1899 on the anniversary of his death. $125-$175

Figure M62 - "Kossuth, Governor of Hungary . . . ." Assay: Iron 99.2%, Copper .76%. 6 in. No mark. Event dates: London visit in 1851 and U.S. visit in 1852. *Courtesy of Ann and Dennis Berard.* $350+

Figure M59 - "Washington." Assay: Iron 99.8%, Nickel .2%. 5.62 in. No mark. Event date assumed: c.1899 on the anniversary of his death. $125-$175

Figure M63 - "General Kossuth." Assay: Iron 97.6%, Cobalt 2.1%, Arsenic .25%. 4.37 in. No mark. Event dates: London visit in 1851 and U.S. visit in 1852. *Courtesy of Ann and Dennis Berard.* $350+

Figure M60 - "General U. Grant." Assay: Iron 100%. 5.62 in. No mark. Event date: 1865-1885. $300+

Figure M64 - "Victoria and Albert, Portraits (double alphabet)." Assay: Aluminum 91.6%, Silicon 7.5%, Iron .83%, Zinc .017. 6.56 in. No mark. Event date: 1840-1861. $400+

Figure M61 - "Lt. General U. S. Grant." Assay: Iron 99.6%, Silicon .2%, Carbon .1%. 5.5 in. No mark. Event date: 1865-1885. $300+

Figure M65 - "Victoria and Albert, Portraits." Assay: Iron 97.1%, Copper 2.9. 4.25 in. No mark. Event date: 1840-1861. $400+

Figure M66 - "Victoria and Albert, Portraits, Floral Surround." Assay: Iron 99%, Copper .28%, Trace elements .7%. 6.25 in. No mark. Event date: 1840-1861. $400+

Figure M70 - "The Prince and Princes of Wales in a Carriage." Assay: Iron 100%. 5.75 in. No mark. Event date: March 10, 1863. *Courtesy of Ann and Dennis Berard.* $400+

Figure M71 - "The Prince and Princess of Wales in a Carriage." Assay: Iron 95.4%, Copper 4.6%. 4.25 in. No mark. Event date: March 10, 1863. *Courtesy of Ann and Dennis Berard.* $400+

Figure M67 - "Victoria and Prince Albert, Portraits." Assay: Iron 96.2%, Copper .8%, Trace elements 3%. 4.25 in. No mark. Event date: 1840-1861. *Courtesy of Ann and Dennis Berard.* $400+

Figure M68 - "The Prince and Princess of Wales, Portraits, Floral Surround." Assay: Iron 96.5%, Copper 3.5%. 4.25 in. No mark. Event date: March 10, 1863. $400+

Figure M69 - "The Prince and Princess of Wales, Portraits." Assay: Iron 97.5%, Copper 2.5%. 4.25 in. No mark. Event date: March 10, 1863. $400+

Figure M72 - "Girl on a Swing." Chromolithography. 8.25 in. Ohio Art Toy Company. Bryant, Ohio. 1918-1925. $50-$70

Figure M73 - "Girl on a Swing." Chromolithography. 3.5 in. Ohio Art Toy Company. Bryant, Ohio. 1918-1925. $50-$70

Figure M74 - "ABC Kittens." Chromolithography. 4.25 in. Ohio Art Toy Company. Bryant, Ohio. 1918-1925. $50-$70

Figure M75 - "ABC Kittens." Chromolithography. 6.25 in. Ohio Art Toy Company. Bryant, Ohio. 1918-1925. $50-$70

Figure M78 - "ABC Bank." Chromolithography. H-4.25 in. x W-3.5 in. x D-1.94 in. Burnett, Ltd. London. $250+

Figure M76 - "Circular Design." Chromolithography. Assay: Iron 99.8%, Nickel .3%, Copper .6%, Chromium .005%. 6 in. No mark. $75-$125

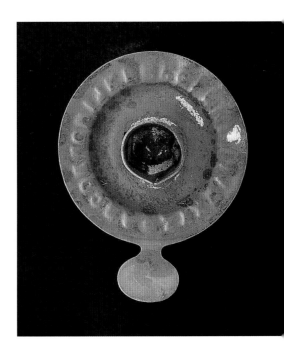

Figure M79 - "Miniature Candlestick." Assay: Iron 100%. Handle H-1.37 in. x Holder D-1.37 in. No mark. *Courtesy of William and Sandra Wassa.* $250+

Figure M80 - "Toy Table." Assay: Iron 97%, Lead 1.6%, Zinc 1.46%. H-2 in. x D- 2.75 in. No mark. $400+

Figure M77 - "After Supper, run a Mile." Chromolithography. Assay: Iron 99%. Trace elements 1%. 6.12 in. Kemp Manufacturing, Toronto, Canada. $150-$175

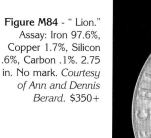

Figure M84 - " Lion." Assay: Iron 97.6%, Copper 1.7%, Silicon .6%, Carbon .1%. 2.75 in. No mark. *Courtesy of Ann and Dennis Berard.* $350+

Figure M81 - "Rattle." Assay: Iron 96.9%, Copper 3.1%. L-5.75 in. x W-1.87 in. x D-1 in. No mark. c.1825. Source: Weiss, Harry. *American Baby Rattles from Colonial Times to the Present.* Page 41. Plate VII. Item No. 32. 1941. Shown upside down so whistle holes can be seen. $150-$200

Figure M82 - "Miniature Pie Plate." Assay: Iron 98.6%, Copper 1.4%. 2.75 in. No mark. This plate is also found as Figure O4 in "O Is for Ornamental Borders." $200-$250

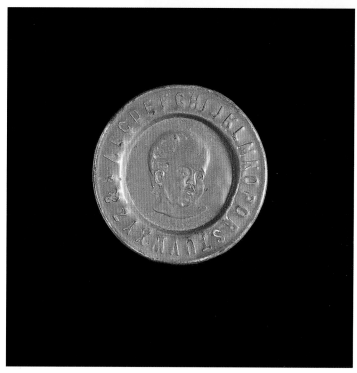

Figure M85 - "Baby's Head." Assay: Iron 98.3%, Copper 1.7%. 1.75 in. No mark. *Courtesy of Ann and Dennis Berard.* $400+

Figure M86 - "Horse." Assay: Iron 94.6%, Copper 5.4%. 2.25 in. No mark. $300+

Figure M83 - "Girl and Boy with Hoop." Assay: Iron 99%, Copper .19%, Manganese .15%, Nickel .12%. 2.87 in. No mark. $175-$225

Figure M87 - "While I Live, I'll Crow." Assay: Iron 97.8%, Copper 2.2%. 1.87 in. No mark. *Courtesy of Ann and Dennis Berard.* $350+

Figure M90 - "A through V - Geometric Design." Assay: Iron 51.5, Tin 40.5%, Copper 4%, Manganese 2%, Nickel 1%, Lead .4%, Trace elements .1%. 2.25 in. No mark. This plate is also found as Figure O12 in "O Is for Ornamental Borders." $150-$200

Figure M88 - "Rooster." Assay: Tin 56%, Iron 36.9, Cobalt 2.4%, Chromium 2.16%, Nickel 1.2%. Trace elements 2%. 2.12 in. No mark. $300+

Figure M91 - "A through Q." Assay: Lead 93.4%, Iron 5.9%, Gold .6%. 2.12 in. No mark. This plate is also found as Figure O11 in "O Is for Ornamental Borders." $150-$200

Figure M89 - "Rooster." Assay: Iron 95.5%, Copper 4.5%. 2.12 in. No mark. $300+

Figure M92 - "Grinding Old into Young." Assay: Tin 55.5%, Iron 41.3%, Cobalt 1.92, Nickel 1.1%, Lead .22%. 2.12 in. No mark. $300+

Figure M93 - "Man on a Horse." Assay: Iron 97.8%, Copper 1.5%, Manganese .6%, Lead .1%. 2.5 in. No mark. This plate is also found as Figure Z5 in "Z Is for Σ and Other Reversals." $300+

Figure M96 - "A Good Girl." Chromolithography. Colored handle. Assay: Iron 98.9 %, Copper 1.1%. H-2.25 in. x D-3 in. No mark. $250-$350

Figure M94 - "Liberty." Assay: Iron 99.4%, Copper .4%, Nickel .2%. 6.5 in. No mark. This plate is also found as Figure Z9 in "Z Is for Σ and Other Reversals." $200-$250

Figure M97 - "Mixed-Metal Cup, painted finish." Assay: Iron 98.1%, Copper 1.6%, Carbon .2%. H-2 in. x D-2.87 in. No mark. $250-$300

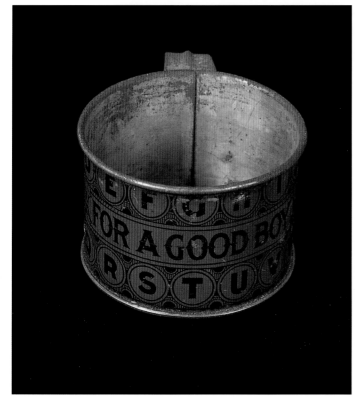

Figure M95 - "For A Good Boy." Chromolithography. Bare metal handle. Assay: Iron 98.9%, Copper 1.1%. H-2 in. x D-3 in. No mark. $250-$350+

Figure M98 - "Mixed-Metal Cup, three line stamping." Assay: Iron 97%, Copper 2.7%, Silicon .7%. H-1.75 in. x D-2.37 in. No mark. $250-$300

Figure M99 - "Mixed Metal Cup, four line stamping." Assay: Iron 89.8%, Tin 6.6%, Copper 2.7%, Silicon .7%. H-1.87 in. x D-2.87 in. No mark. $250-$300

Figure M100 - "Baby Cup #542." Silver Plate. H-2.5 in. x D-2.87 in. Forbes Silver Co. Meriden, Connecticut. Factory date: 1894-c.1900, when merged into International Silver. $75-$125

542 CHILD'S CUP — $2.50
Gold Lined
Chased

Figure M102 - "Display of M100, #542, as advertised by Forbes Silver Co." *Permission of the Connecticut Historical Society, Hartford Connecticut.*

Figure M103 - "Elephant Baby Cup, #470." Flat-topped floral handle. Silver Plate. H-2.37 in. x D-2.5 in. Wm. A. Rogers. Niagara Falls, New York. Factory date: 1894-1929. $75-$125

Figure M101 - "Cover of the Wm Rogers International Silver Catalogue of Silverplated Hollowware." Hand dated 1937. *Permission of the Connecticut Historical Society, Hartford, Connecticut.*

Figure M104 - "Baby Cup." Engraved: Mary Frances - with love - Lindsay - Xmas '59. Sterling. H-2.12 in. x D-2.87 in. Lebkuecher & Co. Newark, New Jersey. Factory date: 1896-1909. $200+

248

N Is for 19th Century

Figure N1 - "Detail of The Seed in the Ground." 7.5 in. No mark. $150-$175

Figure N5 - "The Corn is Taken Home." 5.12 in. No mark. $150-$175
Figure N6 - "The Gleaners." 5.5 in. No mark. $150-$175

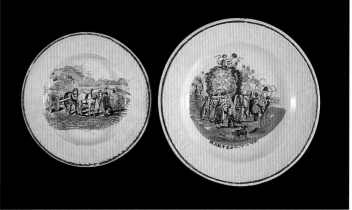

Figure N7 - "Landowner Overseeing the Hay Wagon." 5 in. No mark. $150-$175
Figure N8 - "Harvest Home." 6.12 in. Edge, Malkin & Co. Burslem, Staffordshire. Factory date: 1871-1903. $150-$175

Figure N2 - "A Field of Wheat." 7.5 in. No mark. $150-$175

Figure N9 - "Going to Market." 5 in. J. & G. Meakin. Hanley, Staffordshire. Factory date: 1851+. $150-$175
Figure N10 - "Going to Market." 7.37 in. No mark. $150-$175

Figure N3 - "Ploughing." 4.5 in. J. & G. Meakin. Hanley, Staffordshire. Factory date: 1851+. $150-$175
Figure N4 - "Ploughing." 5.25 in. T. & H. Stoke-on-Trent, Staffordshire. There is one listing for a Taylor & Hopkinson of Shelton (Hanley) in Godden (1988). Because the mark clearly names the location of the firm, further research is needed. $150-$175

Figure N18 - "Cottage Girl." 6.5 in. No mark. Source (Riley, 1991): *Alphabet of Fruits.* London: Warne and Kronheim, 1875. Reads: "N is the NECTARINE kind Jenny took / To the sick girl / Who'lived by the side of the brook." $150-$175

Figure N11 - "Loading Straw onto the Donkey." 4.87 in. No mark. $150-$175
Figure N12 - "A Rest on the Hay." 4.87 in. No mark. $150-$175

Figure N19 - "Three Men and Two Dogs." 5.62 in. No mark. $150-$200
Figure N20 - "Shooting Quail." 6.87 in. No mark. $150-$200

Figure N13 - "Family Feeding the Fowl." 7.12 in. No mark. $150-$175
Figure N14 - "Farm Femme Feeding the Chickens." 8 in. Brown print mark illegible. $150-$175

Figure N15 - "Farm Femme and her Cows." 5.12 in. No mark. $150-$175
Figure N16 - "Farm Femme with Cow (double alphabet)." 7.37 in. No mark. $200-$250
Figure N17 - "Farm Femme and her Sheep." 5.37 in. No mark. $150-$175

Figure N21 - "Two Riders and Two Hounds." 7.25 in. Staffordshire, England (after 1891). $150-$200
Figure N22 - "Showing the Kill." 7.25 in. No mark. $150-$200

Figure N23 - "Scottish Hunters." 6.93 in. No mark. $150-$200

Figure N28 - "Diamond Series - Throwing the Rider." 6.75 in. No mark. $150-$200
Figure N29 - "Diamond Series - Horse Returns Alone." 6.87 in. No mark. $150-$200

Figure N24 - "Diamond Series - Fisherman's Hat is Blown Off." 8.25 in. No mark. $150-$200
Figure N25 - "Diamond Series - Fisherman Trips on Rope." 8.37 in. No mark. $150-$200

Figure N30 - "Rider Sitting in the Mud." 7.37 in. No mark. $150-$200
Figure N31 - "Rider Walking in the Mud." 8 in. No mark. $150-$200

Figure N26 - "Diamond Series - Mounting." 7.5 in. Staffordshire, England (after 1891). No mark. $150-$200
Figure N27 - "Diamond Series - Horses for Hire." 6.75 in. No mark. $150-$200

Figure N32 - "Fisherman Loses his Hat." 7.12 in. Elsmore & Son. Tunstall, Staffordshire. Factory date: 1872-1887. $150-$200
Figure N33 - "Falling into the Hay." 6.75 in. Staffordshire, England (after 1891). $150-$200

251

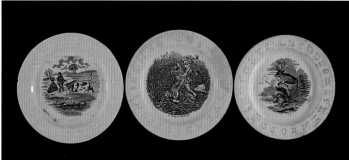

Figure N34 - "Bull Comes too Close." 7.27 in. No mark. $150-$200
Figure N35 - "A Timely Rescue." 7.37 in. Charles Allerton & Sons. Longton, Staffordshire. Factory date: 1859-1942. Mark date: 1890+. $150-$200
Figure N36 - " Stag Comes Too Close." 7 in. Elsmore & Son. Tunstall, Staffordshire. Factory date: 1872-1887. $150-$200

Figure N37 - "Wild Horse Hunt." 7.12 in. J. & G. Meakin. Hanley, Staffordshire. Factory date: 1851+. $150-$200
Figure N38 - "Chasing the Stag." 7.87 in. No mark. $150-$200

Figure N42 - "Source of N41: Burmah." Ceramic transfer pull of H&C: Hope & Carter. Burslem, Staffordshire. Factory date: 1862-1880. Source (Riley): One of four prints by Elisha Pepper. Shelton, Staffordshire. *Used with permission of the Prints, Drawings and Paintings Department of the Victoria & Albert Museum, London.*

Figure N39 - "Buffalo Hunt." 5.87 in. No mark. $150-$200
Figure N40 - "Killing the Seals." 7.5 in. Elsmore & Son. England. Tunstall, Staffordshire. Factory date: 1872-1887. $150-$200

Figure N43 - "Running Horse." 7 in. No mark. $150-$200
Figure N44 - "The Stable Yard." 8 in. No mark. $150-$200

Figure N45 - "The Walk." 7 in. No mark. $150-$200

Figure N46 - "Ride by the Sea." 5 in. No mark. This plate can also be found as Figure O14 in "O Is for Ornamental Borders." $150-$200

Figure N47 - "Rider with a Dog." 6 in. No mark. Source (Riley, 1991): Robinson, T. Illustrator. "Ride over the Farm." *The Picture Scrapbook*. Religious Tract Society, c.1860. $150-$200

Figure N48 - "The Drive." 6.87 in. No mark. $150-$200

Figure N53 - "Laundresses at the Riverbank." 6.87 in. No mark. $175-$225

Figure N54 - "Peep-Show." 6 in. No mark. $175-$225

Figure N49 - "Two Horses at the Wall." 7 in. No mark. $150-$200

Figure N50 - "Two Horses at the Steeplechase." 7.25 in. No mark. $150-$200

Figure N51 - "Sweepstakes." 5 in. No mark. $200-$250

Figure N52 - "Horse Racing." 6.5 in. Charles Allerton & Sons. Longton, Staffordshire. Factory date: 1859-1942. $200-$250

Figure N55 - "Diamond Series - The Artist Annoyed." 8.5 in. No mark. $175-$225

Figure N56 - "The Village Blacksmith." 7 in. No mark. $175-$225

Figure N57 - "Chairs to Mend." 8.37 in. No mark. $175-$225

Figure N59 - "The Baker." 7.12 in. No mark. $175-$225
Figure N60 - "The Baker." 5.25 in. No mark. $175-$225
Figure N61 - "What will you buy, my little dear? (The Breadseller)" 7.12 in. No mark. Source (Riley, 1991): Robinson, John Henry, Illustrator (1796-1871). *Child's Companion*. 1871. $175-$225

Figure N62 - "The Late Sir Robert Peel Bart." 5 in. No mark. c.1850. $500+

Figure N58 - "Thrasher." 5.25 in. No mark. Source (Riley, 1991): *The Progress of a Quartern Loaf* by Mary Belson Elliott. London: William Darton, 1820. Reads: "And see another Friend appears. / With active flail the corn to thrash. / To separate the clustering ears. / And clear the Grain from stalk & trash." $175-$225

Figure N68 - "Crystal Palace." 7.12 in. No mark. Event date: 1851. $200-$250

Figure N63 - "Royal Favourite." 5.12 in. No mark. c.1840. $500+
Figure N64 - "The Necklace." 7.12 in. No mark. c.1840. $500+

Figure N65 - "Queen Victoria." 6.25 in. No mark. c.1840. $500+
Figure N66 - "The Prince and Princess of Wales, Married 10 March, 1863." 6.63 in. No mark. c.1863. $500+

Figure N69 - "Incidents of the War Series - Arrival of the Post in the Army . . . ." 7.25 in. No mark. Event date: c.1854. $250+
Figure N70 - "Incidents of the War Series - Foraging Party . . . ." 7.25 in. No mark. Event date: c.1854. $250+

Figure N71 - "Incidents of the War Series - A Fight in the . . . ." 7.25 in. No mark. Event: c.1854. $250+
Figure N72 - "Incidents of the War Series - Wounded Sailors . . . ." 7.25 in. No mark. Event date: c.1854. $250+

Figure N67 - "The Penny Post. " 4.87 in. Edge, Malkin & Co. Burslem, Staffordshire. Factory date: 1871-1903. $200-$250

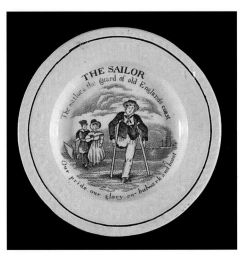

Figure N73 - "The Sailor." 5 in. J. Clementson. Shelton and Hanley, Staffordshire. Factory date: 1839-1864. $250+

Figure N77 - "A Military Encounter." 6.75 in. Charles Allerton & Sons. Longton, Staffordshire. Factory date: 1859-1942. $250+

Figure N74 - "The Sleeping Soldier Unaware of his Portrait." 8.25 in. Elsmore & Son. England. Tunstall, Staffordshire. Factory date: 1872-1887. Source (Riley, 1991): *The Good Boy's Soliloquy*. London: William Darton, 1811. Reads: "I must not ugly faces scrawl / With charcoal on a whitewashed wall." $250+

Figure N78 - "I'm sure in all the army list . . . ." 5 in. No mark. $250+

Figure N75 - "The Quartermaster Serg¹ and Trumpeter." 5.5 in. No mark. $250+
Figure N76 - "Whom Are You For?" 7 in. Edge, Malkin & Co. Burslem, Staffordshire. Factory date: 1871-1903. $250+

Figure N79 - "Royal Standard: Riflemen." 7.25 in. No mark. $250+
Figure N80 - "The March: Riflemen." 7.12 in. No mark. $250+

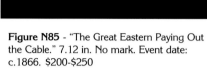

Figure N85 - "The Great Eastern Paying Out the Cable." 7.12 in. No mark. Event date: c.1866. $200-$250

Figure N81 - "Awkward Squad." 6 in. Edge, Malkin & Co. Burslem, Staffordshire. Factory date: 1871-1903. $250+

Figure N82 - "Rifle Band." 6.25 in. Edge, Malkin & Co. Burslem, Staffordshire. Factory date: 1871-1903. $250+

Figure N83 - "Partisan with Drawn Sword." 7.27 in. No mark. This plate can also be found as Figure Z2 in "Z Is for Σ and Other Reversals." *Courtesy of Ann and Dennis Berard.* $250+

Figure N86 - "N begins News-boy" or "The Newsie." 8 in. No mark. Source: *The Mother's Picture Alphabet.* Anelay, Henry, Illustrator. Johnson, Ames, Engraver. London: S. W. Partridge, 1862 (see Figure T23). $275-$325

Figure N84 - "The Thames Tunnel." 5.12 in. No mark. Event date: 1843. $200-$250

Figure N87 - "John Gilpin Starting from Ware." 5.75 in. No mark. Source: *The Diverting History of John Gilpin*. William Cowper (1731-1800). Illustrator: George Cruikshank. London: Charles Tilt, 1828. $300+

Figure N88 - "John Gilpin Pursued as a Highwayman." Source: "*The Diverting History . . . .*" as noted in N87. *Courtesy of the Beinecke Book and Manuscript Library, Yale University.*

Figure N89 - "John Gilpin Pursued as a Highwayman." 5.75 in. No mark. After 1828. $300+

Figure N90 - "Paul and Virginia." 7 in. Powell & Bishop. Hanley, Staffordshire. Factory date: 1866-1878. Source: De Saint-Pierre, Bernardin (1737-1814). *Paul and Virginia.* First printing: 1787. $175-$225

Figure N91 - "At the Piano."7.37 in. No mark. $175-$225

Figure N92 - "Singing the Scale." Pearlware. 7.5 in. Enoch Wood & Sons. Burslem, Staffordshire. Eagle mark for US export. Factory and mark dates: 1818-1846. *Courtesy of Ann and Dennis Berard.* This plate can also be found as Figure O6 in "O Is for Ornamental Borders." $350+

Figure N93 - "Two Girls with Fans." Fruit-dish shape. H-.87 in x D-4.5 in. William Adams & Co. Tunstall, Staffordshire. Factory date: c.1769+. Mark date: 1891+. $175-$225

Figure N94 - "Ballet Dance." 6.87 in. E. Challinor & Co. Fenton, Staffordshire. (See information at Figure U17 in "U Is for Undersides.") $175-$225

Figure N95 - "Highland Dancers." 5.25 in. No mark. $175-$225

Figure N96 - "Round Dance." 6.25 in. No mark. $175-$225

Figure N97 - "Girls with a Barrel-Organ and Tambourine." 7.12 in. Edge, Malkin & Co. Burslem, Staffordshire. Factory date: 1871-1903. Source (Riley, 1991): "Little Tambourine Player." *Peter Parely's Annual*. London: Darton & Co., 1858. $175-$225

Figure N98 - "Young Man Playing his Lute." 5.87 in. No mark. Source (Riley, 1991): Dawson & Co. Sunderland. Factory date: 1799-1864. $175-225

Figure N99 - "Boy with a Banjo." 6.75 in. No mark. $175-$225

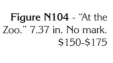

Figure N104 - "At the Zoo." 7.37 in. No mark. $150-$175

Figure N100 - "Punch and Judy." 7.75 in. Charles Allerton & Sons. Longton, Staffordshire. Factory date: 1859-1942. $175-$225

Figure N101 - "Punch and Judy with Dog Toby." 6.87 in. No mark. $175-$225

Figure N105 - "Dogs Stealing Food." 7 in. Elsmore & Son. England. Tunstall, Staffordshire. (England used here before 1891) 1872-1887. $150-$200

Figure N106 - "A Shave for a Penny." 6.62 in. No mark. Source: Monkey is reminiscent of an engraving in Bewick's *History of Quadrupeds*. "The monkey," he said, "imitates human actions with mischievous intent." $150-$200

Figure N102 - "A Dog Circus." 7.25 in. No mark. $175-$225

Figure N103 - "Billy Buttons." 7.87 in. No mark. $175-$225

Figure N107 - "The First Sitting." 5.12 in. No mark. $150-$200
Figure N108 - "The Itinerant Musician." 6.37 in. No mark. $150-$200
Figure N109 - "Who Are You." 6.25 in. No mark. $150-$200

Figure N114 - "Kite Flying." 6.37 in. J. & G. Meakin. Hanley, Staffordshire. Factory date: 1851+. $175-$225
Figure N115 - "Archery." 5.37 in. J. & G. Meakin. Hanley, Staffordshire. Factory date: 1851+. $175-$225

Figure N110 - "London Dog Seller." 7.12 in. No mark. $175-$225

Figure N116 - (top) "Rowing." 5.12 in. No mark. $175-$225
Figure N117 - (right) "Ready to Sail." 5.37 in. No mark. $175-$225
Figure N118 - (bottom) "Punting." 5.03 in. Edge Malkin & Co. Burslem, Staffordshire. Factory date: 1871-1903. $175-$225
Figure N119 - (left) "Ice Skating." 5.62 in. No mark. $175-$225

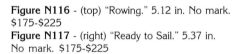

Figure N111 - "The Combat." 6.5 in. Hotel, National China Co. East Liverpool, Ohio. Factory date: 1900-c.1929. $75-$125
Figure N112 - "Exhibition of Prize Fowls (in the style of Harrison Weir)." 5 in. No mark. Source: Illustrations in the style of drawings found in the Harrison Weir sketch-book at the Victoria & Albert Museum, London. $175-$225
Figure N113 - "The Death." 6.5 in. Hotel, National China Co. East Liverpool, Ohio. Factory date: 1900-c.1929. $75-$125

Figure N120 - "Walking on the Bridge." 7.12 in. No mark. $150-$200

Figure N121 - "Foot-Ball." 5.37 in. J & G. Meakin. Hanley, Staffordshire. Factory date: 1851+. *Courtesy of Ann and Dennis Berard.* $200-$250

Figure N122 - "Rugby." 7.87 in. No mark. $200-$250
Figure N123 - "Rugby." 7.37 in. No mark. $200-$250

Figure N124 - "Cricket." 7.5 in. J. & G. Meakin. Hanley, Staffordshire. Factory date: 1851+. $200-$250
Figure N125 - "Cricket." 6.87 in. Staffordshire, England. $200-$250

Figure N126 - "American Sports: Baseball, Striker and Catcher." 7.12 in. No mark. Event date: 1842. *Courtesy of Ann and Dennis Berard.* $500+
Figure N127 - "American Sports: Baseball, Running to First Base." 8 in. No mark. Event date: 1842. *Courtesy of Ann and Dennis Berard.* $500+

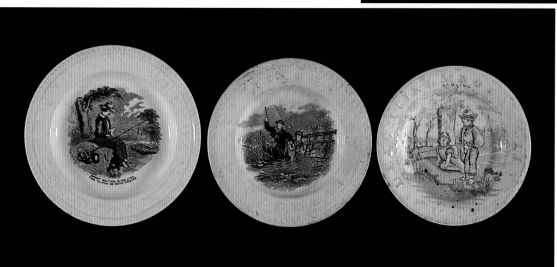

Figure N128 - "Harry Baiting Is his Line." 5.5 in. No mark. $175-$225
Figure N129 - "Father and Son Fishing." 5.12 in. No mark. $175-$225
Figure N130 - "Angling." 4.87 in. No mark. $175-$225

O Is for Ornamental Borders

Figures O1a, O1b - "Flowers That Never Fade - Liberty." A detail of the extraordinary border and a whole view. 7.9 in. No mark. $300+

Figure O3 - "Random grouping of transfer borders."

Figure O2 - "Random grouping of transfer borders."

Figure O4 - "Miniature mixed-metal toy plate showing outer perimeter baselines." H-.75 in. x D-2.75 in. No mark. This plate can also be found as Figure M82 in "M Is for Metals." $200-$250

Figure O5 - "Random grouping of painted and lustred edges."

Figure O7 - Double alphabet rim design. "Farm Femme and her Cow." 7.37 in. No mark. A second edition of this plate is also found as Figure E3 in "E Is for Education."

Figure O6 - "Detail showing blue tint on border of Pearlware plate." This plate can also be found as Figure N92 in "N Is for 19th Century."

Figure O8 - "Random grouping of transfer borders with flowers separating Z and A."

Figure O9 - Random letter selection on deep dish. "Three Scenes." No mark. This deep dish is also found as Figure D34 in "D Is for Deep Dishes."

Figure O11 - "Detail of A through Q." Assay: Lead 93.4%, Iron 5.9%, Gold .6%. 2.12 in. No mark. This dish is also found as Figure M91 in "M Is for Metals."

Figure O12 - "Detail of A through V, a Geometric Design." Assay: Iron 51.9, Tin 40.5%, Copper 4%, Manganese 2%, Nickel 1%, Lead .4%, Trace elements .1%. 2.25 in. No mark. This dish is also found as Figure M90 in "M Is for Metals."

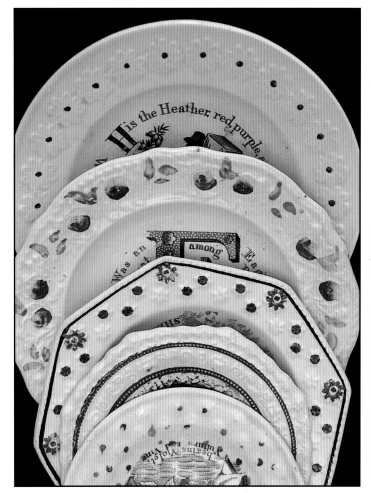

Figure O10 - "Random grouping of decorated nonalphabet borders (florals, dots, and lines)."

Figure O13 - "Example of transfer letters inserted to fill a void." This dish is also found as Figure D37 in "D Is for Deep Dishes."

Figure O14 - Example of imperfect border trim: "The Ride by the Sea." 6.12 in. No mark. This plate is also found as Figure N46 in "N Is for 19th Century."

Figure O15 - "Example of hand-set transfer letters L, M, N, and O with irregularities in baseline placements." This plate is also found as Figure S13 in "S Is for Sets."

Figure O18 - "Queen Victoria in Riding Habit." 6 in. No mark. c.1840. $800+

Figure O16 - "Fishing." Gothic G through Z: A through F to be found on matching cup. 6.25 in. Double gold circle, GERMANY. $75-$100

Figure O19 - "Detail of irregularly spaced letters as seen on Figure O18."

Figure O17 - "Gothic Cup." Gothic A through L: M through Z to be found on matching saucer. H-2.5 in. x D-2.5 in. No mark. $75-$100

Figure O20 - "Detail of irregularly spaced letters as seen on Figure O18."

P Is for Potters and Their Potteries

Figure P1 - "Marl Hole: Longton. 1920." Warrillow Collection, #332. *Photo used with permission of the Library at Keele University, Keele, Staffordshire.*

Figure P2 - "Itinerant Dealers in Staffordshire Ware." George Cruikshank. Source: *Eccentric Excursions.* London: G. M. Woodward, 1796. *Used with permission of the Yale Center for British Art, Paul Mellon Collection.*

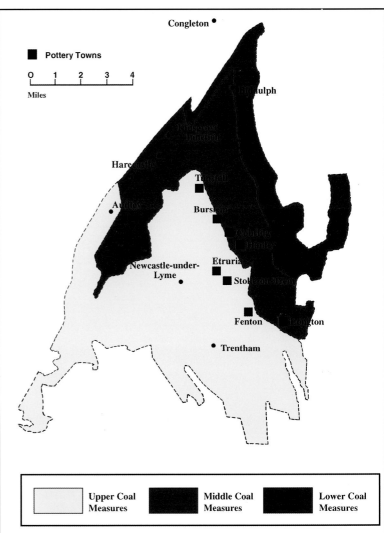

Figure P3 - "The Coal Areas of Staffordshire." Chart produced by Jeongsook Heo.

Figure P4 - "Frontispiece: *The Staffordshire Pottery. A Representation of the Manufactoring of Earthenware . . . .*" by Enoch Wood. 1827. *Print collection of Miriam and Ira D. Wallach Division of Art, Prints and Photographs. The New York Public Library. Astor, Lenox and Tilden Foundations. Used with permission of the New York Public Library.*

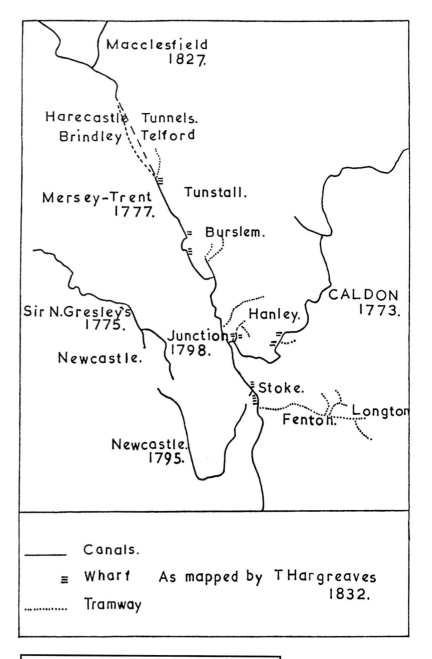

Macclesfield 1827.

Harecastle Tunnels.
Brindley Telford

Mersey-Trent 1777.

Tunstall.

Burslem.

Sir N. Gresley's 1775.

Newcastle.

Hanley.

CALDON 1773.

Junction 1798.

Stoke.

Longton

Fenton.

Newcastle. 1795.

_____ Canals.

= Wharf   As mapped by T Hargreaves 1832.

.... Tramway

Plan of Canals in North Staffordshire as mapped by T. Hargreaves, 1832.

Equivalent to One Mile

Figure P6 - "Map of the Canals of North Staffordshire." Source: Mapped by T. Hargreaves. 1832. Call number SP138.6. *Used with permission of the Potteries Museum, Stoke-on-Trent.*

Figure P5 - "A Pottery Town: Longton. c.1900." Warrillow Collection, #174. *Used with permission of the Library at Keel University, Keele, Staffordshire.*

A POTTERY TOWN LONGTON.

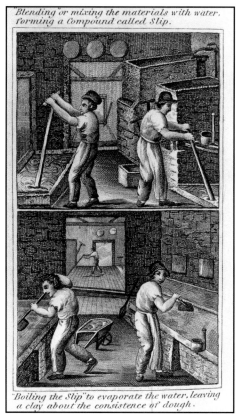

Blending or mixing the materials with water, forming a Compound called Slip.

"Boiling the Slip" to evaporate the water, leaving a clay about the consistence of dough.

Figure P7 - "1 - Blending . . . ." and "2 - Boiling the slip . . . ." Source: *A Representation of the Manufactoring of Earthenware . . . .* as noted in P4.

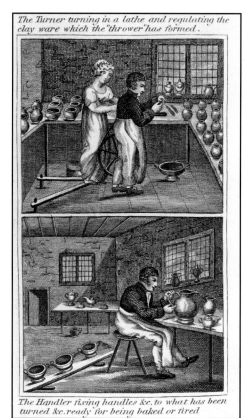

The Turner turning in a lathe and regulating the clay ware which the "thrower" has formed.

The Handler fixing handles &c. to what has been turned &c. ready for being baked or fired

Figure P9 - "5 - The Turner turning . . . ." and "6 - The Handler . . . ." Source: *A Representation of the Manufactoring of Earthenware . . . .* as noted in P4.

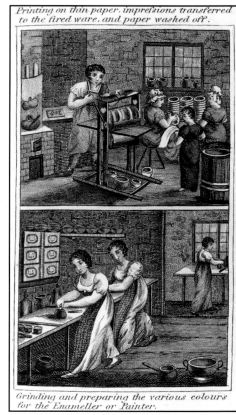

Printing on thin paper, impressions transferred to the fired ware, and paper washed off.

Grinding and preparing the various colours for the Enameller or Painter.

Figure P11 - "11 - Printing on . . . ." and "12 - Grinding and preparing . . . ." Source: *A Representation of the Manufactoring of Earthenware . . . .* as noted in P4.

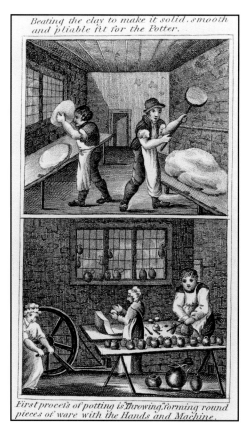

Beating the clay to make it solid, smooth and pliable fit for the Potter.

First process of potting is "Throwing" forming round pieces of ware with the Hands and Machine.

Figure P8 - "3 - Beating the clay . . . ." and "4 - Throwing . . . ." Source: *A Representation of the Manufactoring of Earthenware . . . .* as noted in P4.

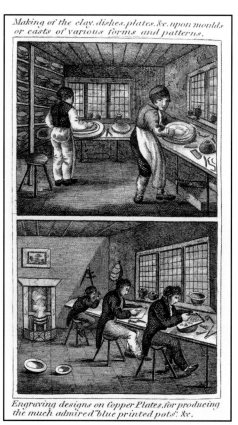

Making of the clay, dishes, plates, &c. upon moulds or casts of various forms and patterns.

Engraving designs on Copper Plates, for producing the much admired "blue printed pots" &c.

Figure P10 - "9 - Making the clay dishes . . . ." and "10 - Engraving. . . ." Source: *A Representation of the Manufactoring of Earthenware . . . .* as noted in P4.

Painting and Gilding China or Earthenware.

"Glazing" or dipping the ware in a prepared liquid, which produces the glossy surface.

Figure P12 - "13 - Painting . . . ." and "14 - Glazing or dipping . . . ." Source: *A Representation of the Manufactoring of Earthenware . . . .* as noted in P4.

Placing the "dipped" ware ready for its being fired or baked in the "Glazing" Oven.

A Potters Oven when firing or baking, the ware being therein placed in Safeguards, or "Saggers."

Examining and dressing the ware after its coming from the potters and glazing ovens.

Packing China and Earthenware in "Crates."

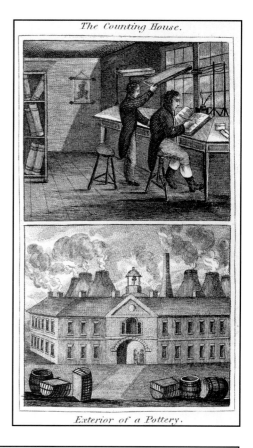

The Counting House.

Exterior of a Pottery.

Top left: **Figure P13** - "15 - Placing the dipped . . . ." and "16 - Baking the ware . . . ." Source: *A Representation of the Manufactoring of Earthenware . . . .* as noted in P4.

Top center: **Figure P14** - "17 - Examining and . . . ." and "18 - Packing . . . ." Source: *A Representation of the Manufactoring of Earthenware . . . .* as noted in P4.

Top right: **Figure P15** - "19 - the Counting House . . . ." and "20 - Exterior of a Pottery." Source: *A Representation of the Manufactoring of Earthenware . . . .* as noted in P4.

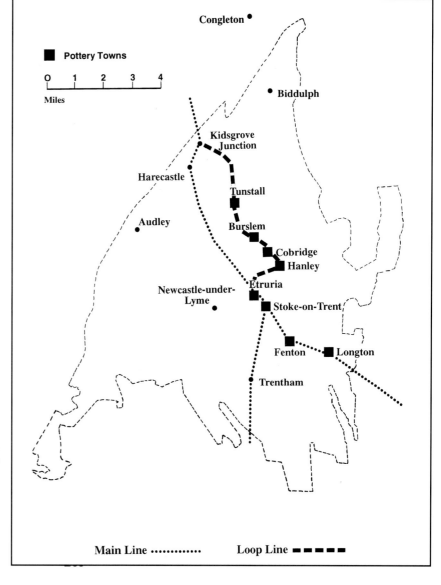

Figure P16 - "Map of the Loop Line, North Staffordshire Railway." Map produced by Jeongsook Heo.

Figure P17 - "Interior of Stoke Station c.1905." *Photo courtesy of Basil Jeuda, Guest Lecturer, Keele University. Keele, Staffordshire.*

Figure P18 - "Interior of Stoke Station c.1905." *Photo courtesy of Basil Jeuda, Guest Lecturer, Keele University. Keele, Staffordshire.*

Figure P19 - "Burslem Loop Line 1912." *Photo courtesy of Basil Jeuda, Guest Lecturer, Keele University. Keele, Staffordshire.*

Q Is for Queries

Figure Q1 - "Title Plate for Animated Conundrums." 6.12 in. No mark. $250+

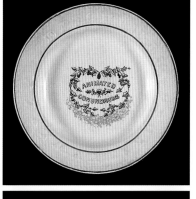

Figure Q2 - Conundrum #1 - "Why is this poor little rabbit so terribly frightened?" 6.12 in. No mark. $250+

Figure Q3 - Conundrum #2 - "Why is this geometrical fishing?" 6.12 in. No mark. $250+

Figure Q4 - Conundrum #3 - "Why is the gentleman in cap and gown the better logician of the two?" 5.12 in. No mark. $250+

Figure Q5 - Conundrum #4 - "Why are these boys wrong in their arithmetic?" 5 in. No mark. $250+

Figure Q6 - Conundrum #5 - "Why would this pastry cook make a good soldier?" 6 in. No mark. $250+

Figure Q7 - Conundrum #6 - "What fruit does our sketch represent?" 6 in. No mark. $250+

Figure Q8 - "Riddle - I ever live man's . . . ." 5.12 in. Impressed flower mark. Source (Riley, 1991): *Mrs. Child. The Girl's Own Book*. Thomas Tegg, 4th edition. 1832. $200-$250

Figure Q9 - "Riddle - Tis true I have both face and hands . . . ." 8.12 in. No mark. $200-$250

Figure Q10 - "Riddle - Pray tell us ladies if you can . . . ." 5.12 in. Impressed flower mark. $200-$250

R Is for Religion, Reform, and Reason

Figure R1 - "Remember the Sabbath Day to Keep it Holy." 5 in. No mark. $200-$250

Figure R4 - "How Glorious is Our Heavenly King." 5.37 in. J. & G. Meakin. Hanley, Staffordshire. Factory date: 1851+ Source: Watts, Isaac. *Divine and Moral Songs for Children.* London: Charles Tilt, 1832. $200-$250

Figure R2- "Reading The Bible." 5 in. J. & G. Meakin. Hanley, Staffordshire. Factory date: 1851+ $250+

Figure R5 - *Resurezione di Piero della Francesca. Permission of the Museo Civico San Sepulcro, Instituzioncultureale Biblioteca Museo della Citta'di San Sepolcro.*

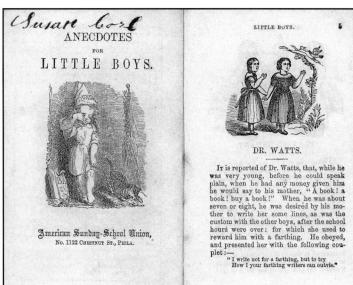

Figure R3 - Cover and interior plate of *"Anecdotes for Little Boys."* Philadelphia, Pennsylvania: American Sunday School Union., n.d.

Figure R6 - "Behold him rising from the grave." 5.25 in. Edge, Malkin & Co. Burslem, Staffordshire. Factory date: 1871-1903. Source: *Resurezione di Piero della Francesca.* $200-$250

Figure R7 - "At twelve years old he talk'd with men." 8.12 in. Edge, Malkin & Co. Burslem, Staffordshire. Factory date: 1871-1903. Source: Watts, Isaac. *Divine and Moral Songs for Children . . . .* as noted in R4. $200-$250

Figure R14 - "The Reverend Richard Jordan." 6.87 in. No mark. $500+

Figure R8 - "How doth the little busy bee . . . ." 5.62 in. No mark. Source: Watts, Isaac. *Divine and Moral Songs for Children . . . .* as noted in Figure R4. $200-$250
Figure R9 - "The tulip and the butterfly . . . ." 6.12 in. No mark. Source: Watts, Isaac. *Divine and Moral Songs for Children . . . .* as noted in Figure R4. $200-$250
Figure R10 - "I lay my body down to sleep . . . ." 7.12 in. J. & G. Meakin. Hanley, Staffordshire. Factory date: 1851+. Source: Watts, Isaac. *Divine and Moral Songs for Children . . . .* as noted in Figure R4. $200-$250

Figure R15 - "The Band of Hope - The Mountain Rill." 7.12 in. No mark. Source (Riley, 1991): A Dalziel illustration. *The Children's Friend.* S. W. Partridge, 1861. $250+
Figure R16 - "The Band of Hope - Make our Temperance Army Strong." 7 in. No mark. $250+

Figure R11 - "The Happy Children: I thank the goodness . . . ." 5 in. Mark "W." $200-$250
Figure R12 - "What blest examples do I find writ . . . ." 6.27 in. No mark. $200-$250
Figure R13 - "An Only Son: And can so kind a father frown . . . ." 4.27 in. Wedgwood & Co. Tunstall, Staffordshire. Factory date: 1860-1965. Source (Riley, 1991): Taylor, Jane and Ann. *Hymns for Infant Minds.* 1812. $200-$250

Figure R17 - "The jug and glass was filled again . . . ." 7.75 in. No mark. $250+
Figure R18 - "Now jug and glass we're done with you . . . ." 6.75 in. No mark. $250+

Figure R19 - "The Drunkard's Progress - The Ruin'ed Family." 5.25 in. No mark. $250+

Figure R25 - "Sacred History of Joseph and his Brethren Series - Joseph's First Dream." 7 in. No mark. $200-$250
Figure R26 - "Sacred History of Joseph and his Brethren Series - Reuben Interceding . . . ." 7.25 in. No mark. $200-$250

Figure R20 - "Father Theobald Mathew (sometimes spelled Matthew) of Cork, the Great Advocate." 5.25 in. No mark. $250+

Figure R27 - "Sacred History of Joseph and his Brethren Series - Potiphar's Wife Falsely . . . ." 7.12 in. No mark. $200-$250
Figure R28 - "Joseph Interprets the Chief Butler's Dream." 6.82 in. No mark. $200-$250

Figure R21 - "Classroom of the Missionary." 9.12 in. Thos Godwin, Stone China. Burslem, Staffordshire. Factory date: 1834-1854. $250+
Figure R22 - "Students with the Missionary." 9.12 in. Thos Godwin, Stone China. Burslem, Staffordshire. Factory date: 1834-1854. $250+

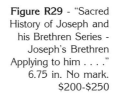

Figure R29 - "Sacred History of Joseph and his Brethren Series - Joseph's Brethren Applying to him . . . ." 6.75 in. No mark. $200-$250

Figure R23 - "The Commandments: Thou shalt do no murder." 5 in. No mark. $200-$250
Figure R24 - "Bible Pictures Series - Noah and the Ark." 6.25 in. Brownhills Pottery Co. Tunstall, Staffordshire. Factory date: 1872-1896. Registry mark #106738 date: 1888. $200-$250

Figure R30 - "The Finding of Moses." Fruit Shape. 4.75 in. Manufactured for H. C. Edmiston. New York. Firm listed: 1902-1903. Registry Mark #153253 date: 1890. $200-$250

Figure R31- "Bible Pictures Series - The Finding of Moses." 8.12 in. Brownhills Pottery Co. Tunstall, Staffordshire. Factory date: 1872-1896. Registry Mark #106738 date: 1888. $200-$250

Figure R36 - "Hezekiah Beholding the Sun-Dial." 7. in. No mark. $200-$250

Figure R37 - "Bible Pictures Series - Daniel in the Lion's Den." 8 in. Brownhills Pottery Co. Tunstall, Staffordshire. Factory date: 1872-1896. Registry Mark #106738 date: 1888. $200-$250

Figure R38 - "Incidents in the Life of Our Blessed Saviour: And they came with haste and found . . . ." 6.5 in. No mark. $200-$250

Figure R32 - "Bible Pictures Series - Destruction of Pharaoh." 7.12 in. Brownhills Pottery Co. Tunstall, Staffordshire. Factory date: 1872-1896. $200-$250

Figure R33 - "Bible Pictures Series - Samuel before Eli." 7.25 in. Brownhills Pottery Co. Tunstall, Staffordshire. Factory date: 1872-1896. $200-$250

Figure R39 - "The Lord's Prayer: Our Father, wh-h art in . . . ." 5.5 in. No mark. $200-$250

Figure R40 - "The Lord's Prayer: Thy Kingdom Come. Thy will . . . ." 6.25 in. No mark. $200-$250

Figure R34 - "David and Goliath." 6.25 in. Manufactured for H. C. Edmiston. New York. Firm listed: 1902-1903. $200-$250

Figure R35 - "Bible Pictures Series - Elijah Fed by the Ravens." 7.27 in. Brownhills Pottery Co. Tunstall, Staffordshire. Factory date: 1872-1896. Registry Mark #106738 date: 1888. $200-$250

Figure R41 - "Let Brotherly Love Continue." 5.87 in. No mark. *Courtesy of Ann and Dennis Berard.* $200-$250

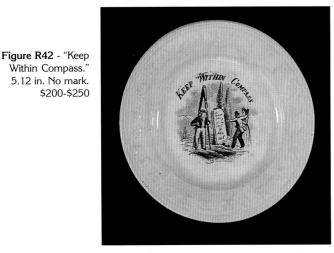

Figure R47 - "Flowers That Never Fade Series - Early Rising." 6.25 in. No mark. $250+

Figure R48 - "Flowers That Never Fade Series - Innocence." 7.25 in. No mark. $250+

Figure R42 - "Keep Within Compass." 5.12 in. No mark. $200-$250

Figure R49 - "The Importance of Punctuality Series - Indeed Sir, you are . . . ." 7.12 in. No mark. $200-$250

Figure R50 - "The Importance of Punctuality Series - Well here we are . . . ." 7.12 in. No mark. $200-$250

Figure R51 - "The Importance of Punctuality Series - You are behind . . . ." 7.12 in. No mark. $200-$250

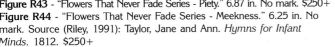

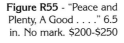

Figure R43 - "Flowers That Never Fade Series - Piety." 6.87 in. No mark. $250+

Figure R44 - "Flowers That Never Fade Series - Meekness." 6.25 in. No mark. Source (Riley, 1991): Taylor, Jane and Ann. *Hymns for Infant Minds.* 1812. $250+

Figure R52 - "Good thoughts should always . . . ." 6.27 in. No mark. $200-$250

Figure R53 - "Cherish your best hopes . . . ." 6.17 in. No mark. $200-$250

Figure R54 - "Reason should guide . . . ." 6.25 in. No mark. $200-$250

Figure R55 - "Peace and Plenty, A Good . . . ." 6.5 in. No mark. $200-$250

Figure R45 - "Flowers That Never Fade Series - Liberty." 6 in. No mark. $250+

Figure R46 - "Flowers That Never Fade Series - Good Humor." 6 in. No mark. Source (Riley, 1991): *Hymns for Infant Minds* as noted in Figure R44. $250+

Figure R56 - "Contentment makes the believer . . . ." 5 in. No mark. $200-$250

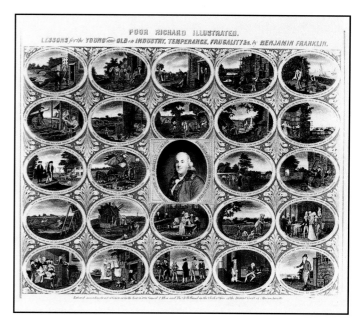

Figure R61 - "Poor Richard Illustrated. Lessons for the Young and Old on Industry, Temperance, Frugality, &c." by the artist, Robert Dighton. 17.37 x 24.25 in. Printed by T. O. H. P. Burnham of Boston, 1859. *Courtesy of the Library of Congress Print Collection.* See larger image on page 105.

Figure R57 - "Going to Sunday School." 5 in. No mark. $250+

Figure R62 - "Franklin Plate - Sloth like rust . . . . God helps them that . . . . Lost time is never . . . ." 6.62 in. No mark. Source: *Poor Richard's Illustrated Lessons . . .* as noted in Figure R61. $250-$300.

Figure R58 - "The Cruel Boy." 7.75 in. No mark. $175-$225

Figure R63 - Magnification of oval A-1 of *Poor Richard's Illustrated Lessons . . .* as noted in Figure R61. *Courtesy of the Library of Congress Print Collection, Washington, D. C.*

Figure R59 - "Don't Hurt It." 6 in. No mark. $175-$225
Figure R60 - "Stealing Apples." 6.75 in. No mark. $175-$225

Figure R64 - "Franklin Plate - He that hath a trade . . . . At the working man's . . . . Industry pays debts . . . ." 6.62 in. No mark. Source: *Poor Richard's Illustrated Lessons . . . .* as noted in Figure R61. $250-$300

Figure R65 - "Franklin Plate - He that hath a trade . . . . Industry pays debts . . . ." 6.12 in. No mark. Source: *Poor Richard's Illustrated Lessons . . . .* as noted in Figure R61. $250-$300

Figure R66 - Magnification of oval A-2 of *Poor Richard's Illustrated Lessons . . . .* as noted in Figure R61. *Courtesy of the Library of Congress Print Collection, Washington, D. C.*

Figure R67 - "Franklin Plate - Now I have a cow and a sheep . . . . Fly pleasure and it . . . ." 6.12 in. No mark. Source: *Poor Richard's Illustrated Lessons . . .* as noted in Figure R61. $250-$300

Figure R68 - "Poor Richard's Maxim's: Fly pleasure and it . . . . Now I have a sheep and a cow . . . ." 7.25 in. No mark. Source: *Poor Richard's Illustrated Lessons . . . .* as noted in Figure R61. $250-$300

Figure R69 - Magnification of oval A-3 of *Poor Richard's Illustrated Lessons . . . .* as noted in Figure R61. *Courtesy of the Library of Congress Print Collection, Washington, D. C.*

Figure R70 - "DR. Franklin's Maxim's: Want of care does us more . . . . For want of a nail . . . ." 7.25 in. No mark. Source: A4. *Poor Richard's Illustrated Lessons . . . .* as noted in Figure R61. $250-$300

Figure R71 - "Franklin Plate - Want of care does us more . . . . For want of a nail . . . ." 7.5 in. No mark. Source: A-4. *Poor Richard's Illustrated Lessons . . . .* as noted in Figure R61. $250-$300

Figure R72 - "Franklin Plate - Dost thou love life . . . .There will be . . . ." 6.62 in. No mark. Source: B-1. *Poor Richard's Illustrated Lessons . . . .* as noted in Figure R61. $250-$300

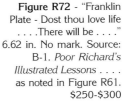

Figure R73 - "Franklin Plate - Three removes are as bad . . . . A rolling stone gathers . . . ." 7.5 in. No mark. Source: B-3. *Poor Richard's Illustrated Lessons . . .* as noted in Figure R61. $250-$300

Figure R77 - "Franklin Plate - Constant dropping wears . . . . And little strokes fall. . . ." Soup Shape. H-1.25 in. x D-7.37 in. No mark. Source: Variation of C-2. *Poor Richard's Illustrated Lessons . . . .* as noted in Figure R61. $250-$300

Figure R74 - "Poor Richard's Maxim's: He who saves not . . . . A fat kitchen makes . . . . Would you be rich . . . ." 6.12 in. No mark. Source: B-4. *Poor Richard's Illustrated Lessons . . . .* as noted in Figure R61. $250-$300

Figure R78 - "DR. Franklin's Maxim's: By diligence and . . . . Diligence is the mother . . . ." 5.75 in. No mark. Source: D-2. *Poor Richard's Illustrated Lessons . . . .* as noted in Figure R61. $250-$300

Figure R75 - "DR. Franklin's Maxim's: Employ time well . . . One day is worth . . . . Since thou art not sure . . . ." Rococo edge. 7.12 in. No mark: Source: B-5. *Poor Richard's Illustrated Lessons . . . .* as noted in Figure R61. $250-$300

Figure R76 - "Franklin Plate - Employ time well . . . . Since thou art not sure . . . ." 7.5 in. No mark. Source: B-5. *Poor Richard's Illustrated Lessons . . . .* as noted in Figure R61. $250-$300

Figure R79 - "Franklin Plate - If you would know the value . . . . Creditors have better . . . ." 6.25 in. No mark. Source: D-5. *Poor Richard's Illustrated Lessons . . . .* as noted in Figure R61. $250-$300

Figure R80 - "Franklin Plate - If you would know the value . . . . Creditors have better . . . ." 8.5 in. No mark. Source: D-5. *Poor Richard's Illustrated Lessons . . . .* as noted in Figure R61. $250-$300

Figure R81 - "DR. Franklin's Maxim's: Industry needs not . . . . There are no gains . . . ." 7.37 in. No mark. Source: E-1. *Poor Richard's Illustrated Lessons . . . .* as noted in Figure R61. $250-$300

Figure R87 - "Franklin Plate - The eye of the master will do more work than . . . ." 7.12 in. No mark. $250-$300
Figure R88 - "DR Franklin: It is hard for an empty bag . . . ." 7.25 in. No mark. $250-$300

Figure R82 - "Franklin Plate - Experience keeps a dear . . . But fools will learn . . . ." 6 in. No mark. Source: E-5. *Poor Richard's Illustrated Lessons . . . .* as noted in Figure R61. $250-$300
Figure R83 - "Franklin Plate - Experience keeps a dear . . . But fools will learn . . . ." 8.12 in. No mark. Source: E-5. *Poor Richard's Illustrated Lessons . . . .* as noted in Figure R61. $250-$300

Figure R89 - "Poor Richard's Way to Wealth: Fly pleasures and they will . . . . The diligent spinner has a . . . ." 8 in. No mark. $250-$300
Figure R90 - "Franklin Plate - Not to oversee workmen is to leave . . . ." 7.12 in. No mark. $250-$300

Figure R84 - "Franklin's ProvBS: Three removes are as bad . . . . A rolling stone gathers . . . ." 7 in. J. & G. Meakin. Hanley, Staffordshire. Factory date: 1851+ $250-$300
Figure R85 - "Franklin's ProvBS: Three removes are as bad . . . . A rolling stone gathers . . . ." 8.12 in. J. & G. Meakin. Hanley, Staffordshire. Factory date: 1851+ $250-$300
Figure R86 - "Franklin's ProvBS: Three removes are as bad . . . . A rolling stone gathers . . . ." 6 in. J. & G. Meakin. Hanley, Staffordshire. Factory date: 1851+ $250-$300

Figure R91 - "Franklin's Proverbs: Silks and satins scarlet and velvets put out the . . . ." 5.37 in. J. & G. Meakin. Hanley, Staffordshire. Factory date: 1851+ $250-$300
Figure R92 - "Franklin Plate - There are no gains . . . . Then help hands for . . . ." 6 in. No mark. $250-$300
Figure R93 - "Franklin's Proverbs: Make hay while the . . . ." 5.37 in. No mark. $250-$300

Figure R98 - "DR. Franklin's Maxim's: Plow deep while sluggards . . . . Work today for you . . . ." 6.75 in. No mark. $250-$300

Figure R94 - "Franklin Plate - Employ time well . . . . God gives all things . . . ." 6.12 in. No mark. $250-$300

Figure R95 - "Franklin Plate - Employ time well . . . . God gives all things . . . ." 7.37 in. George Jones & Sons. Stoke, Staffordshire. Factory date: 1873-1951. Mark date: 1874-1891. $250-$300

Figure R96 - "Franklin's ProvBS: He that by the plough . . . himself must either . . . ." 6.12 in. J. & G. Meakin. Hanley, Staffordshire. Factory date: 1851+ $250-$300

Figure R99 - "The Poor Boy and the Loaf." 6 in. No mark. Source (Riley, 1991): *The Child's Companion.* October, 1854. $200-$250

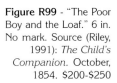

Figure R100 - "(Letter R) Watch the Bent of his Inclination . . . ." Pearlware. 4.62 in. No mark. *Courtesy of Ann and Dennis Berard.* $350+

Figure R97 - "Franklin Plate - Plough deep while sluggards . . . ." 7.25 in. No mark. $250-$300

S Is for Sets

Figure S1- "Y for Youth, Plate / Mug." Mismatch.
Maker: No marks
Plate: 6.25 in. $275-$325
Mug: Flat-topped ear-shaped handle. H-2.75 in. x D-3 in. $250+
Source: Baldwin, Ruth. *100 Nineteenth-Century Rhyming Alphabets in English.*
Carbondale and Edwardsville, Illinois: Southern Illinois University Press, 1972.

Figure S2 - "Z for Zebra or Z Comes the Last, Plate / Mug." Match.
Maker: No marks
Plate: 7.37 in. $275-$325
Mug: Loop handle. H-2.62 in. x D-2.87 in. $250+
Source: Baldwin, Ruth. *100 Nineteenth-Century Rhyming Alphabets in English* as noted in Figure S1. Estimated cost of set: $525-$600

Below: **Figure S3** - "DEF - Boy with Bubble Pipe, Plate / Mug." Mismatch.
Maker: No marks
Plate: 5.87 in. $275-$325
Mug: Footed base. H-2.75 in. x D-2.87 in. Loop handle. $250+

Figure S4 - "JKL - Boy and Dog, Plate / Mug." Mismatch.
Maker: No marks
Plate: 5.75 in. $275-$325
Mug: Loop handle. Leaf terminals. H-2.87 in. x D-3 in. $250+
Courtesy of Ann and Dennis Berard.

Figure S5 - "VWX - See-Saw, Plate / Mug." Mismatch.
Maker: No marks
Plate: 5.75 in. $275-$325
Mug: Loop handle. Leaf terminals. H-2.87 in. x D-3 in. $250+

Figure S6 - "YZ& - Snowballs, Plate / Mug." Mismatch.
Maker: No marks
Plate: 5.75 in. $275-$325
Mug: Loop handle. H-3 in. x D-3 in. $250+

Figure S7 - "Little Jack Horner, Plate / Mug." Mismatch.
Maker: Brownhills Pottery Co. Tunstall, Staffordshire (also found as Figure E38).
Factory date: 1872-1896.
Plate: 7.27 in. Registry Mark #69963 date: 1887. $200-$250
Mug: Loop handle. H-2.75 in. x D-2.87 in. Registry Mark #75500 date: 1887. $250+

Figure S10 - "Goosey Gander Classroom, Plate / Mug." Match.
Maker: Mark may identify Harvey Adams & Co. Longton, Staffordshire.
Factory date: 1870-1885 (inconclusive identification)
Plate: 7.25 in. $275-$325
Mug: Loop handle. H-3 in. x D-3 in. 250+
Estimated cost of set: $525-$600

Figure S8 - "Crusoe Making a Boat, Plate / Mug." Match.
Maker: Brownhills Pottery Co. Tunstall, Staffordshire.
Factory date: 1872-1896
Plate: 6.25 in. Registry Mark #69963 date: 1887. $175-$225
Mug: Footed base. Loop handle. H-3 in. x D-3 in. Registry Mark #69963 date: 1887. 250+
Estimated cost of set: $425-$500

Figure S11 - "Punch and Judy and Frog, Plate / Mug." Match.
Maker: Charles Allerton & Sons. England. Longton, Staffordshire.
Factory date: 1859-1942. Mark date: 1890+
Plate: 7.75 in. $175-$225
Mug: Loop handle. Leaf terminals. H-3 in. x D-3 in. $250+
Estimated cost of set: $425-$500

Figure S9 - "Robin, Plate / Mug." Match.
Maker: Brownhills Pottery Co. Tunstall, Staffordshire.
Factory date: 1872-1896
Plate: 6.5 in. Registry Mark #154 date: 1884. $175-$225
Mug: Loop handle. H-2.75 in. x D-2.87 in. Registry Mark #685 date: 1884. $250+
Estimated cost of set: $500

Figure S12 - "Leo Lion in Fox's Barber Chair, Plate / Pitcher." Match.
Maker: Made in Germany
Plate: 7.12 in. Gilt overpaint. $75-$125
Pitcher: A - N only. Loop handle. Leaf terminals. Small spurs. H-3 in. x D-3.62 in. $75-$125
Estimated cost of set: $150-$300

Figure S13 - "Green Letter Surround, Plate / Pitcher." Match.
Maker: Germany #188 (plate) and #184 (pitcher) (also found as Figure O15).
Plate: Shaped edge. Letters irregularly placed. 6.12 in. $75-$125
Pitcher: Flat-topped ear-shaped straight handle. H-3.25 in. x D-2.5 in. $75-$125
Estimated cost of set: $150-$300

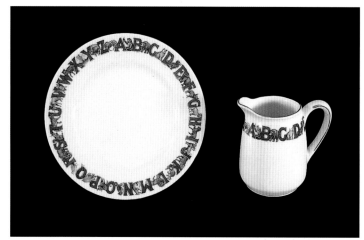

Figure S14 - "Blue Animal Surround, Plate / Pitcher." Match.
Maker: Germany with mark of J. B. & W. (Importer) New York.
Plate: 6.25 in. $75-$125
Pitcher: A through E and V through Z aside loop handle. H-3.5 in. x D-2.87 in. $75-$125
Estimated cost of set: $150-$250

Figure S15 - "Orange Animal Surround Items." Mismatch.
Maker: Germany
Demitasse Cup (A-I, not shown): H-2.50 in. x D-2.27 in. $30-$50
Demitasse Saucer (A-R, not shown): 4.50 in. $30-$50
Deep Dish (green lustre): H-7.5 in. x D-1.5 in. $150-$200
Plate (gold edge): 6.25 in. $75-$125
Plate (green lustre edge): 6.12 in. $75-$125
Pitcher: H-2.50 in. x D-2.62 in. $75-$125
Bowl: H-2.25 in. x D-5.12 in. $75-$125

Figure S16 - "Red Clock, Plate / Bowl / Mug." Match.
Maker: William Adams & Sons. Tunstall and Stoke.
Factory date: 1769+. Mark date: After 1962.
Plate: 6.87 in. $50-$75
Bowl: H-1.75 in. x D-5.75 in. $50-$75
Mug: Loop handle. H-3 in. x D-3.12 in. $50-$75
Estimated cost of set: $100-$150

Figure S17 - "Small Prints, Saucer / Mug / Pitcher." Match.
Maker: Moser Bros. Britannia Pottery Co. Meierhofen, Germany. Factory date: 1898-c.1925.
Saucer: 4.87 in. $75-$125
Mug: Flat-topped straight handle. H-2.5 in. x D-2.25 in. $75-125
Pitcher: H-3.75 in. x D-2.25 in. $75-$125
Estimated cost of set: $400

Figure S18 - "Chickens, Plate / Saucer / Cup / Pitcher." Match.
Maker: Germany
Plate: 7 in. $75-$125
Saucer: 5 in. No mark. $30-$50
Cup: Spurred loop handle. H-2.5 in. x D-2.75 in. $30-$50
Pitcher: Spurred loop handle. H-3 in. x D-3.12 in. $75-$125
Estimated cost of set: $250

T Is for Transfers and Toybooks

Figure T1a - "The Flight into Egypt." 5.25 in. No mark. Note repair of transfer. $200-$250
Figure T1b - Detail of "The Flight into Egypt."

Figure T4 - "The Widow Green Wiping the Kitchen Table." 4.5 in. No mark. c.1859. Sources: *The Widow Green and her Three Nieces* as noted in Figure T2 and/or Figure T3. $175-$225

Figure T2 - "The Widow Green Wiping the Kitchen Table." Source: Ellis, Sarah. *The Widow Green and her Three Nieces*. London: S. W. Partridge, 1862. Shelfmark: 1489e.4959. *Permission of the Bodleian Library, Oxford University, England.*

Figure T3 - "The Widow Green Wiping the Kitchen Table." Source: Ellis, Sarah. *The Widow Green and her Three Nieces*. London: S. W. Partridge, 1862. Shelfmark: 1489f.1667. *Permission of the Bodleian Library, Oxford University, England.*

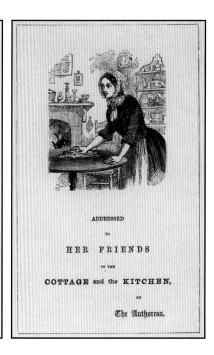

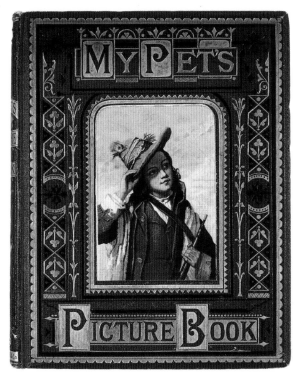

Figure T5 - "Cover of *My Pet's Picture Book*." Gilbert, Sir J., H. Anelay, H. Weir, etc., Illustrators. London: S. W. Partridge, 1873. Shelfmark: 12803.g.32. *Permission of the British Library.*

Figure T8 - "Cover of the *Object Lesson ABC*." Chicago: M. A. Donohue & Co., n.d. *Courtesy of Genevieve A. Krueger.*

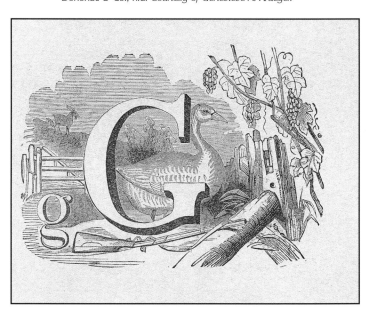

Figure T6 - "Ready for a Ride." *My Pet's Picture Book* as noted in Figure T5. *Permission of the British Library.*

Figure T9 - "G Stands for Gander . . . ." *Object Lesson ABC* as noted in Figure T8. *Courtesy of Genevieve A. Krueger.*

Figure T7 - "Ready for a Ride." 6.12 in. No mark. Source: *My Pet's Picture Book* as noted in Figure T5. $150-$175

Figure T10 - "G stands for Gander . . . ." 7.25 in. No mark. Sources: *Object Lesson ABC* as noted in Figure T8. Originally published in *The Child's Treasury of Knowledge.* Boston: Weir & White, n.d. $275-$325

Figure T11 - "R Stands for Rabbit . . . ." *Object Lesson ABC* as noted in Figure T8. *Courtesy of Genevieve A. Krueger.*

Figure T12 - "R Stands for Rabbit . . . ." 6.25 in. No mark. Sources: *Object Lesson ABC* as noted in Figure T8. Originally published in *The Child's Treasury of Knowledge.* Boston: Weir & White, n.d. $275-$325

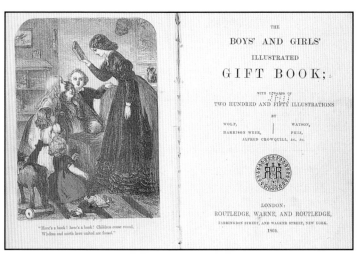

Figure T13 - "Frontispiece and Title Page of The Alphabet of Flowers." In *The Boy's and Girl's Illustrated Gift Book.* London: George Routledge & Sons, 1864. *Permission of The John Work Garrett Library of the Johns Hopkins University, Baltimore.*

Figure T14 - "C for Convolvulus." "The Alphabet of Flowers" as noted in Figure T13. *Permission of The John Work Garrett Library of the Johns Hopkins University, Baltimore.*

Figure T15 - "C for Convolvulus." 7.12 in. No mark. Source: "The Alphabet of Flowers" as noted in Figure T13. $275-$325

Figure T16 - "L is the Lily." "The Alphabet of Flowers" as noted in Figure T13. *Permission of The John Work Garrett Library of the Johns Hopkins University, Baltimore.*

Figure T17 - "L is the Lily." 7 in. No mark. Source: "The Alphabet of Flowers" as noted in Figure T13. $275-$325

Figure T18 - "T is the Tulip." "The Alphabet of Flowers" as noted in Figure T13. *Permission of The John Work Garrett Library of the Johns Hopkins University, Baltimore.*

Figure T21 - "K begins Kite." 6.87 in. No mark. c.1862. Source: *The Mother's Picture Alphabet* as noted in Figure T20. $275-$325

Figure T19 - "T is the Tulip." 7.12 in. No mark. Source: "The Alphabet of Flowers" as noted in Figure T13. $275-$325

Figure T22 - "N begins News-boy." or "The Newsie." *The Mother's Picture Alphabet* as noted in Figure T20. *Permission of the British Library.*

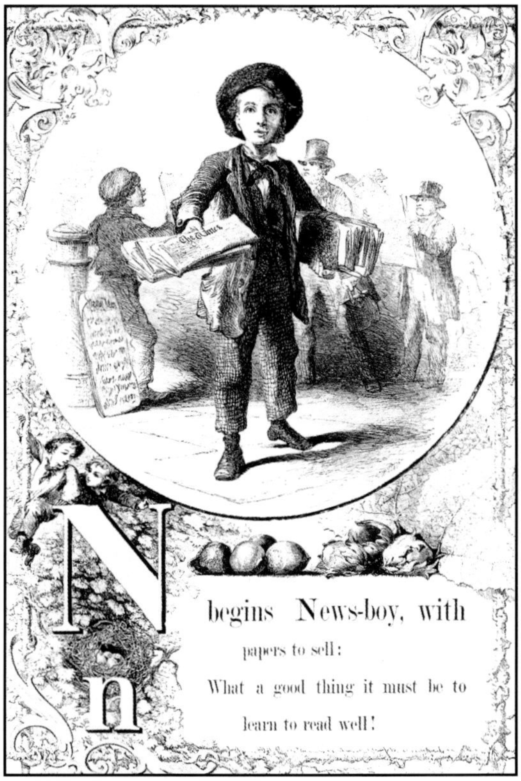

Figure T20 - "K begins Kite." *The Mother's Picture Alphabet*. Anelay, Henry, Illustrator. Johnson, Ames, Engraver. London: S. W. Partridge, 1862. Shelfmark: 12807.i.56. *Permission of the British Library.*

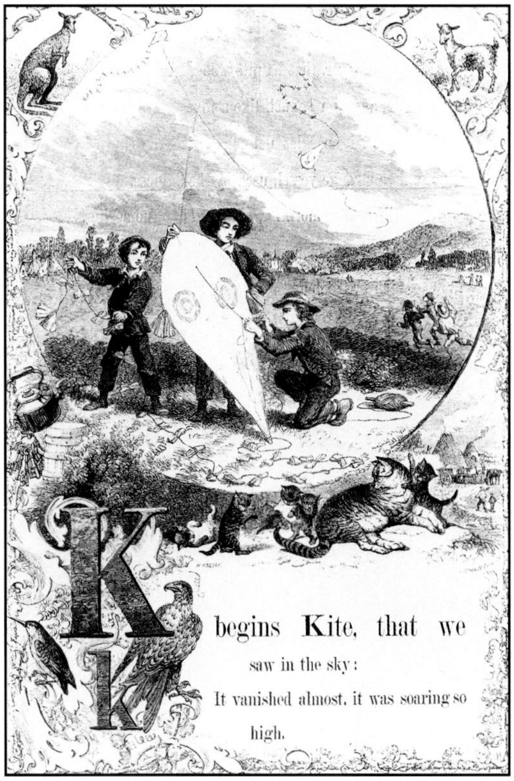

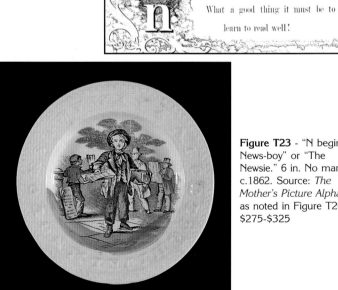

Figure T23 - "N begins News-boy" or "The Newsie." 6 in. No mark. c.1862. Source: *The Mother's Picture Alphabet* as noted in Figure T20. $275-$325

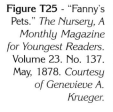

FANNY'S PETS.

ONE, two, three, four rabbits. One is white, with long gray ears. One is jet black. Two are gray, with white spots. These rabbits are Fanny's

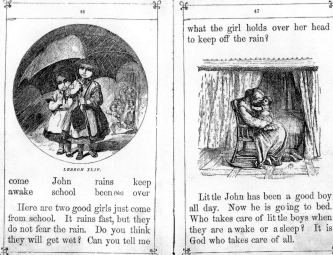

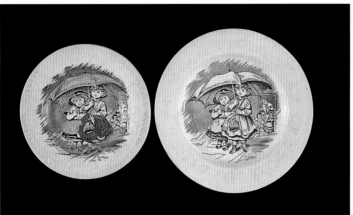

Figure T30 - "Girls Under an Umbrella or U for Umbrella That Keeps us so Dry." 5.12 in. Garter ring mark: Royal London Ironstone. J. McD. & S. (Possibly John McDonald and Son of Halifax, British Columbia, Importers for Edge, Malkin & Company.) Factory date: c.1871. Edge, Malkin & Company. Burslem, Staffordshire. Factory date: 1871-1903. Sources: *New Series Hillard's Primer* . . . . as noted in Figure T27 and/or *The Nursery* . . . . as noted in Figure T29. Originally published in *The Mother's Picture Alphabet* as noted in Figure T20. $275-$325

Figure T31 - "Girls Under an Umbrella or U for Umbrella That Keeps us so Dry." 6.25 in. No mark. Sources: as noted in Figure T30. $275-$325

Figure T32 - "Is this the right key?" *The Royal Road to Spelling and Reading*. London: Edward N. Marks, 1867. *Authors' collection.*

Center right: **Figure T35** - *The Picture Alphabet of the Nations of the World* (Set 1: A-F). In *100 Nineteenth Century Alphabets in English* from the Library of Ruth Baldwin. Carbondale and Edwardsville, Illinois: Southern Illinois University Press, 1972. Originally published in Edinburgh: T. Nelson & Sons, 1874. *Courtesy of the Southern Illinois University Press, Carbondale and Edwardsville, Illinois.*

Bottom right: **Figure T36** - *The Picture Alphabet of the Nations of the World* (Set 2: G-L) as noted in Figure T35. *Courtesy of the Southern Illinois University Press, Carbondale and Edwardsville, Illinois.*

Figure T33 - "Girl at the Piano." Engraving. 11 x 11 in. Glass framed with cut paper trims, glue and paper residue. *Authors' collection.*

Figure T37 - "The Greek." 7.25 in. Brownhills Pottery Co. Tunstall, Staffordshire. Factory date: 1872-1896. Registry Diamond date: December 14, 1883. Source: *The Picture Alphabet of the Nations of the World* as noted in Figure T35. $200-$250

Figure T38 - "The Italian." 6.25 in. Brownhills Pottery Co. Tunstall, Staffordshire. Factory date: 1872-1896. Registry Diamond date: December 14, 1883. Source: *The Picture Alphabet of the Nations of the World* as noted in Figure T35. $200-$250

Figure T41 - "The Russian." 6.5 in. Brownhills Pottery Co. Tunstall, Staffordshire. Factory date: 1872-1896. Registry Diamond date: December 14, 1883. Source: *The Picture Alphabet of the Nations of the World* as noted in Figure T35. $200-$250

Figure T42 - *The Picture Alphabet of the Nations of the World* (Set 4: T-Z) as noted in Figure T35. *Courtesy of the Southern Illinois University Press, Carbondale and Edwardsville, Illinois.*

Figure T39 - "The Japanese." 6.25 in. Brownhills Pottery Co. Tunstall, Staffordshire. Factory date: 1872-1896. Registry Diamond date: December 14, 1883. Source: *The Picture Alphabet of the Nations of the World* as noted in Figure T35. $200-$250

Figure T40 - *The Picture Alphabet of the Nations of the World* (Set 3: M-S) as noted in Figure T35. *Courtesy of the Southern Illinois University Press, Carbondale and Edwardsville, Illinois.*

Figure T43 - "The Turk." 8.25 in. Brownhills Pottery Co. Tunstall, Staffordshire. Factory date: 1872-1896. Registry Diamond date: December 14, 1883. Source: *The Picture Alphabet of the Nations of the World* as noted in Figure T35. $200-$250

Figure T44 - "The Venetian." 7.25 in. Brownhills Pottery Co. Tunstall, Staffordshire. Factory date: 1872-1896. Registry Diamond date: December 14, 1883. Source: *The Picture Alphabet of the Nations of the World* as noted in Figure T35. $200-$250
Figure T45 - "The Wallachian." 7.25 in. Brownhills Pottery Co. Tunstall, Staffordshire. Factory date: 1872-1896. Registry Diamond date: December 14, 1883. Source: *The Picture Alphabet of the Nations of the World* as noted in Figure T35. $200-$250

Figure T48 - "Cover of the *Baby's Rhyme Book*." Richards, Laura. Boston: Estes & Lauriat, 1879. Inscribed; Presented to Joseph E. Pottenger by his mother, Dec. 25, 1884. *Courtesy of Genevieve A. Krueger.*

Figure T46 - "Frontispiece of *The Pretty Name Alphabet*." In *100 Nineteenth-Century Rhyming Alphabets in English* from the Library of Ruth Baldwin. Carbondale and Edwardsville, Illinois: Southern Illinois University Press, 1972. Originally published in *The Child's Picture Story Book*. London: George Routledge and Sons, c.1886 (earlier edition, 1856). *Courtesy of the Southern Illinois University Press, Carbondale and Edwardsville, Illinois.*

Figure T49 - "Up on the dunce stool . . . ." *Baby's Rhyme Book* as noted in Figure T48. Originally published in *The Child's Picture Story Book* as noted in Figure T46. *Courtesy of Genevieve A. Krueger.*

ON THE DUNCE-STOOL.

UP on the dunce-stool. Poor lit-tle man!
Look-ing as wretch-ed as ev-er he can.
Eyes that look fix-ed-ly down on the floor,
Head that is droop-ing down low-er and low-er.

Up on the dunce-stool. Poor lit-tle dear!
Tell me, my lit-tle boy, what brought you here?
Ah! he must an-swer, in mourn-ful tone,
"No-bod-y's fault but just my own!"

Figure T47 - "D is for Da-vid." *The Pretty Name Alphabet* as noted in Figure T46. *Courtesy of the Southern Illinois University Press, Carbondale and Edwardsville, Illinois.*

D is for DA-VID, the dunce of the school,
Who wears the fool's cap while he stands on a stool.

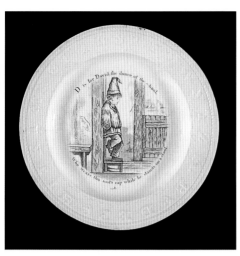

Figure T50 - "D is for David . . . ." 7.62 in. No mark. Sources: *The Pretty Name Alphabet* as noted in Figure T46 and *The Child's Picture Story Book* as noted in Figure T46. $275-$325

Figure T53 - "The Three Little Nurses." 4.75 in. Saucer shape. Manufactured (in England) for H. C. Edmiston. New York. c.1902-1903. Source: Possibly *The Nursery . . . .* as noted in Figure T51. $150-$175

Figure T54 - "Cover of *The Little Sailors, Merry Times for the Little Folks*." Jones, J. R. Juvenile Publishers, 1899. *Courtesy of Genevieve A. Krueger..*

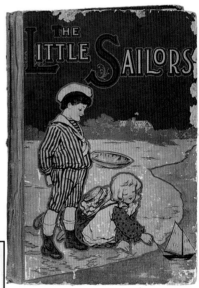

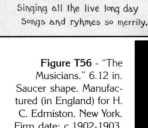

Figure T51 - "Cover of *The Nursery, A Monthly Magazine for Youngest Readers*." Boston: the Nursery Publishing Company, Vol. 28. No. 163. July, 1880. *Courtesy of Genevieve A. Krueger.*

Figure T55 - "The Musicians." *The Little Sailors, Merry Times for the Little Folks* as noted in Figure T54. *Courtesy of Genevieve A. Krueger.*

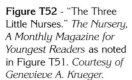

Figure T52 - "The Three Little Nurses." *The Nursery, A Monthly Magazine for Youngest Readers* as noted in Figure T51. *Courtesy of Genevieve A. Krueger.*

Figure T56 - "The Musicians." 6.12 in. Saucer shape. Manufactured (in England) for H. C. Edmiston. New York. Firm date: c.1902-1903. Possible Source: *The Little Sailors, Merry Times for the Little Folks* as noted in Figure T54. $150-$175

Figure T57 - "Cover of the *Mother Goose Rhymes Complete.*" Chicago: Homewood Publishing Co., 1904. *Authors' Collection.*

Figure T59 - "Tom, Tom the Piper's Son." 6.12 in. Elsmore and Foster / Forster. Tunstall, Staffordshire. Factory date: 1853-1871. Source: *Mother Goose Nursery Rhymes Complete* as noted in T57. $225-$275

Figure T58 - "Tom, Tom, the Piper's Son." *Mother Goose Nursery Rhymes Complete* as noted in T57. *Authors' Collection.*

Tom with his pipe did play with such skill
That those who heard him could never keep still;
Whenever they heard they began for to dance—
Even pigs on their hind legs would after him prance.

294

U Is for Undersides

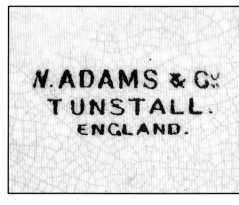

Figure U1 - Mark: William Adams & Co. at Greengates Pottery, etc. Tunstall, Staffordshire. Factory date: c.1769+.

Figure U4 - Advertisement for Allerton & Sons at Park Works, Longton, Staffordshire, as seen in the *Pottery Gazette*. Scott Greenwood & Sons, Lt. Est. 1875. London. c. 1890. *Used with permission of Tableware International, Surrey, England.*

Figure U7 - Mark: Charles Allerton & Sons at Park Works. Longton, Staffordshire. Factory date: 1859-1942. Mark date: c.1890-1912.

Figure U2 - Mark: William Adams & Co. at Greengates Pottery, etc. Tunstall, Staffordshire. Factory date: c.1769+.

Figure U5 - Mark: Charles Allerton & Sons at Park Works. Longton, Staffordshire. Factory date: 1859-1942. Mark date: c.1890-1912.

Figure U8 - Mark: H. Aynsley & Co. at Commerce Works. Longton, Staffordshire. Factory date: 1873+. Registry Mark #426673 date: 1904.

Figure U3 - Assumed mark: Harvey Adams & Co. at High Street and Sutherland Road, Longton, Staffordshire. Factory date: 1870-1885.

Figure U6 - Mark: Charles Allerton & Sons at Park Works. Longton, Staffordshire. Factory date: 1859-1942. Mark date: c.1890-1912.

Figure U9 - Mark: H. Aynsley & Co. at Commerce Works. Longton, Staffordshire. Factory date: 1873+. Registry Mark #426673 date: 1904.

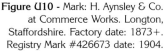

Figure U10 - Mark: H. Aynsley & Co. at Commerce Works. Longton, Staffordshire. Factory date: 1873+. Registry Mark #426673 date: 1904.

Figure U11 - Mark: Barkers & Kent Ltd. at Foley Pottery. Fenton, Staffordshire. Factory date: 1889-1941.

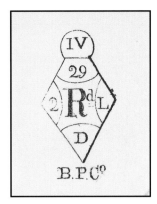

Figure U14 - Diamond Registry, Mark: Brownhills Pottery Co. at Brownhills China Works. Tunstall, Staffordshire. Factory date: 1872-1896. Diamond Marks used between 1842-1883; Registry Mark date: September 29, 1882.

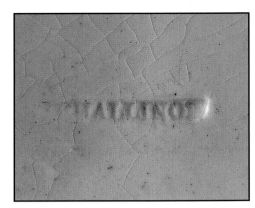

Figure U17 - Mark: E. Challinor & Co. at Pinnocks Works (Unicorn Pottery c.1862-1867). Tunstall, Staffordshire. Factory date: 1842-1867.

Figure U12 - Mark: M. B. Britannia at Moser Brothers Porcelain Works. Meierhofen, Germany (Bohemia, Czech Republic). Factory date: 1898-c. 1925.

Figure U15 - Mark: Brownhills Pottery Co. at Brownhills China Works. Tunstall, Staffordshire. Factory date: 1872-1896. Registry Mark #154 date: 1884.

Figure U18 - Mark: J. Clementson at Phoenix Works. Shelton, Staffordshire. Factory date: 1839-1864.

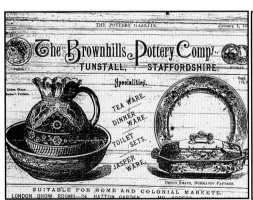

Figure U13 - Advertisement for Brownhills Pottery Co. at Brownhills China Works. Tunstall, Staffordshire, as seen in the *Pottery Gazette*, Scott Greenwood & Sons, Ltd. Est. 1875. London. January 1, 1890. *Used with permission of Tableware International, Surrey, England.*

Figure U16 - Mark: Brownhills Pottery Co. at Brownhills China Works. Tunstall, Staffordshire. Factory date: 1872-1896. Registry Mark #253083 date: 1895.

Figure U19 - Mark: W. Davenport & Co. Longport, Staffordshire. Factory date: 1793-1887. Mark date: 1871. Marks: transferred and impressed.

Figure U20 - Mark: Delinieres & Company. Limoges, France. Factory date: 1879-1900.

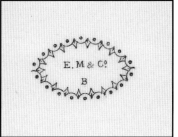

Figure U24 - Mark: Edge, Malkin & Co. at Newport and Middleport Works. Burslem, Staffordshire. Factory date: 1871-1903.

Figure U28 - Mark: Thomas Godwin at the Canal Works. Navigation Road, Burslem, Staffordshire. Factory date: 1834-1854.

Figure U32 - Aerial photo of J & G Meakin at Eagle Pottery. Hanley, Staffordshire. Factory date: 1851+. *Courtesy of Steve Birks, Stoke-on-Trent.*

Figure U21 - Advertisement for Edge, Malkin & Co. at Newport Works. Burslem, Staffordshire, as seen in the *Pottery Gazette.* Scott Greenwood & Sons, Ltd. Est. 1875. London. May 1, 1885. *Used with permission of Tableware International, Surrey, England.*

Figure U25 - Mark: Elsmore & Forster (Foster?) at Clayhills Pottery, Tunstall, Staffordshire. Factory date 1853-1871.

Figure U29 - Mark: William Hackwood Pottery. Hanley, Staffordshire. Factory date: 1827-1843.

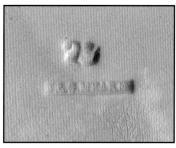

Figure U33 - Mark: J & G Meakin at Eagle Pottery. Hanley, Staffordshire. Factory date: 1851+

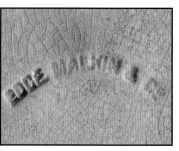

Figure U22 - Mark: Edge, Malkin & Co. at Newport and Middleport Works. Burslem, Staffordshire. Factory date: 1871-1903.

Figure U26 - Mark: Elsmore & Foster (Forster?) at Clayhills Pottery, Tunstall, Staffordshire. Factory date: 1853-1871.

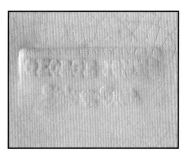

Figure U30 - Mark: George Jones at Trent Pottery. Stoke, Staffordshire. Factory date: c.1854 (64?)-1873.

Figure U34 - Mark: John Meir & Son at Greengates Pottery. Tunstall, Staffordshire. Factory date: c.1837-1897.

Figure U23 - Mark: Edge, Malkin & Co. at Newport and Middleport Works. Burslem, Staffordshire. Factory date: 1871-1903.

Figure U27 - Mark: Elsmore & Son, England at Clayhills Pottery. Tunstall, Staffordshire. Factory date: 1872-1887.

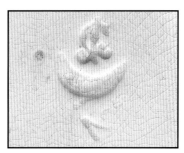

Figure U31 - Mark: George Jones & Sons at Crescent and Trent Potteries. Stoke, Staffordshire. Factory date: 1873-1951. Mark date: 1874-1891.

Figure U35 - Mark: William E. Oulsnam & Sons. Burslem, Staffordshire. Factory date: 1880 (?)-1892.

Figure U36 - Mark: Firm originally named Podmore, Walker & Co. from 1834-c.1856. Then Podmore, Walker & Wedgwood from c.1856-1859 and Wedgwood & Co. from 1860-1965. Tunstall, Staffordshire. Locations of mark: Amicable Street and Swan Bank Works.

Figure U40 - Line engraving of the Josiah Wedgwood Etruria Factory, c. 1850. *Courtesy of the Trustees of the Wedgwood Museum, Barlaston, Staffordshire, England.*

Figure U44 - Mark: Wedgwood & Co. Renamed from Podmore, Walker & Co. Tunstall, Staffordshire. Factory date: 1860-1965. Wedgwood & Co. is not connected with the firm of Josiah Wedgwood.

Figure U48 - Mark: J. H. ?. & R., Importer. Boston and New York. Identification unknown.

Figure U37 - Mark: Powell & Bishop at the Stafford Street Works. Hanley, Staffordshire. Factory date: 1866-1878.

Figure U41- Mark: Josiah Wedgwood & Sons. Factory dates: 1759+ in varied locations. Production date: c.1980 reissue of the Ravilious mug, 1937. Originally banded on white in golden orange, pink, blue, and vine green.

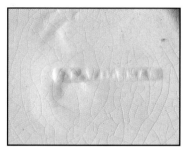

Figure U45 - Mark: James F. Wileman continued as Wileman & Co. at Foley China Works. Fenton, Staffordshire. Factory date: 1869 (70?)-1872 (Godden 1988) or 1892(?).

Figure U49 - Mark: Hugh C. Edmiston, Importer. New York, New York. Firm date: 1902-1903.

Figure U38 - Mark: A. Shaw from 1851-1856 in Tunstall and Burslem from 1860-1900. A. Shaw & Son at Mersey Pottery. Burslem, Staffordshire. Factory date: 1882-1898.

Figure U42 - Ravilious mug reissue as noted in Figure U41. $75-$100

Figure U46 - Mark: Enoch Wood & Sons at Fountain Place (and other locations). Burslem, Staffordshire. Factory date: 1818-1846. Export trademark date: 1818-1846.

Figure U50 - Trade Mark Registered in the US Patent Office.

Figure U39 - Mark: T & H: Godden (1991) finds no firm matching these initials, T & H, in Stoke-on-Trent. Godden does list a Taylor and Hopkinson of Shelton (Hanley). Further research is required.

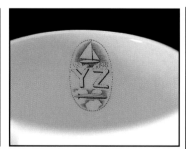

Figure U43 - Inner rim edge completion of the alphabet on Ravilious mug reissue as noted in Figure U41.

Figure U51 - Staffordshire, England. Registry Mark #153253 date: 1890.

Figure U47 - Mark: Jones, McDuffee & Stratton. Boston (c.1895) or John McDonald and Son, Halifax, Nova Scotia (1840-c.1875); both were importers.

V Is for Variations on a Theme

Figure V1 - Compare V1 with V2 for variations in transfer color and size. "T begins Tunnel . . . ." 7 in. Mark: England. Source: *The Mother's Picture Alphabet.* London: S. W. Partridge, 1862. $275-$325
Figure V2 - "T begins Tunnel . . . ." 7.25 in. No mark. Source: *The Mother's Picture Alphabet* as noted in Figure V1. $275-$325

Figure V7 - Compare V7 with V8 for significant size difference, color, and rim trim. "Lost." 6.12 in. No mark. Source (Riley, 1991) : "Little Margaret." *The Sunday Scholar's Companion.* August, 1873. $150-$175
Figure V8 - "Lost." 9.75 in. William E. Oulsnam & Sons - Ironstone. Burslem, Staffordshire. Factory date: 1880(?)-1892. Source: as noted in Figure V7. $300+

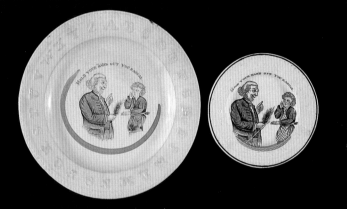

Figure V3 - Compare V3 with V4 for color, edge design, and maker. "Robinson Crusoe Series - Crusoe Making a Boat." 6.13 in. Brownhills Pottery Co. Tunstall, Staffordshire. Factory date: 1872-1896. Registry Mark #69963 date: 1887. $175-$225
Figure V4 - "Robinson Crusoe Series - Crusoe Making a Boat." 6.25 in. Brownhills Pottery Co. Tunstall, Staffordshire. Factory date: 1872-1896. Registry Mark #69963 date: 1887. This plate is also found in Figure S8. $175-$225

Figure V9 - Compare V9 with V10 for mood change through the use of color. "Hold Your Hand Out . . . ." 8.25 in. Edge Malkin & Co. Burslem, Staffordshire. Factory date: 1871-1903. $175-$225
Figure V10 - "Hold Your Hand Out . . . ." 5 in. No mark. $175-$225

Figure V5 - Compare V5 with V6 for line detail, color, and glaze. "Frolics of Youth Series - The Young Artist." Pearl Stone Ware. 7 in. Podmore, Walker & Co. Tunstall, Staffordshire. Factory date: 1834-1856. $350+
Figure V6 - "Frolics of Youth Series - The Young Artist." 7.25 in. No mark. $175-$225

Figure V11 - Compare with V12 for differences in background detail. "Baked Taters All Hot." 8.5 in. No mark. $175-$225

Figure V14 - Compare with V13 for details. "O begins Organ . . . ." 6.12 in. No mark. Source: *The Mother's Picture Alphabet* as noted in V13. $275-$325

Figure V12 - "Detail of "Baked Taters All Hot." 7 in. No mark. $175-$225

Figure V15 - Compare with V13 for details. "O begins Organ . . . ." 7.25 in. Charles Allerton & Sons. Longton, Staffordshire. Factory date: 1859-1942. Mark date: 1890-1912. Source: *The Mother's Picture Alphabet* as noted in V13. $275-$325

Figure V13 - Compare with V16 for image reversal. "O begins Organ . . . . " Source: *The Mother's Picture Alphabet.* Anelay, Henry, Illustrator. Johnson, Ames, Engraver. London: S. W. Partridge, 1862. Shelfmark: 12807.i.56. *Used with permission of the British Library.*

Figure V16 - Compare with V13 for image reversal. "Robert The Organ Grinder." Source*: The Nursery, A Magazine For Youngest Readers.* Boston: John Shorey, April, 1867. Originally printed in the reverse in *The Mother's Picture Alphabet* as noted in V13. *Courtesy of Genevieve A. Krueger.*

Figure V17 - Compare V17 with V18 for variance in molded edge. "Performing in Costume." 5.75 in. No mark. $175-$225
Figure V18 - "Performing in Costume." 8 in. No mark. $175-$225

Figure V19 - Compare V19 with V20 for ABC vs. non-ABC edge. (top) "French/English Series - La Lecture/Reading." Nonalphabet rim. 7.37 in. No mark. $200-$250
Figure V20 - (bottom) "French/English Series - Lecture/Reading." 6 in. No mark. $200-$250

Figure V26 - Compare V26 with V27 for inclusion of title and color. "Riddle, Tis True . . . . - Titled." 5.12 in. No mark. $200-$250
Figure V27 - "Riddle, Tis True . . . . " 8.12 in. No mark. $200-$250

Figure V28 - Compare V28 with V29 for inclusion of caption and color. "Fox Hunt - Captioned." 5.87 in. No mark. $150-$200
Figure V29 - "Fox Hunt." 7.12 in. Edge Malkin & Co. Burslem, Staffordshire. Factory date: 1871-1903. $150-$200

Figure V21 - Compare V21, V22, and V23 for variances in surfaces and colors. "Little Bo-Peep." H-1.5 in. x D-7.5 in. No mark. Frosted. Blue floor impress. $125-$175
Figure V22 - "Little Bo-Peep." H-1.5 in. x D-7.5 in. No mark. Frosted. Blue rim. $125-$175
Figure V23 - "Little Bo-Peep." H-1.5 in. x D-7.5 in. No mark. Clear. Yellow. $125-$175

Figure V30 - Compare V30 with V31 for inclusion of caption and color. "The Zebra Hunt - Captioned." 7.87 in. No mark. $150-$200
Figure V31 - "The Zebra Hunt." 6.25 in. No mark. $150-$200

Figure V24 - Compare V24 with V25 for inclusion of title. "Riddle, Pray Tell Us . . . - Titled." 5.12 in. Impressed flower mark. $200-$250
Figure V25 - "Riddle, Pray Tell Us . . ." 6.12 in. No mark. $200-$250

Figure V38 - Compare V38 with V39 for variance in concluding verbiage. "For Age and Want . . . ." 7.37 in. George Jones. Stoke, Staffordshire. Factory date: 1861 (64?)-1873. Concludes ". . . lasts all the day." $250-$300
Figure V39 - "For Age and Want . . . ." 5.5 in. Mark illegible. Concludes " . . . lasts a whole day." $250-$300

Figure V32 - Compare V32 with V33 for color and transfer type caption vs. handwritten caption. "Gathering Cotton." 6 in. No mark. This plate is also found as Figure A13 in "A Is for Americana." $250+
Figure V33 - "Gathering Grapes (handwritten caption)." 5.87 in. Elsmore & Son. Tunstall, Staffordshire. Factory date: 1872-1887. $250+

Figure V40 - Compare V40 with V41 for variances in message(s). "Little Strokes . . . ." 6.25 in. No mark. $250-$300
Figure V41 - "Constant Droppings . . . and Little Strokes . . . ," 7.5 in. No mark. $250-$300

Figure V34 - (bottom) Detail of caption (transfer) on V32, "Gathering Cotton."
Figure V35 - (top) Detail of caption (handwritten) on V33, "Gathering Grapes."

Figure V42 - Compare V42 with V43 for variance in images apparently for copyright protection. "Yellow-Dogs (two views only of mug)." H-2.75 in. x D-2.75 in. No mark. Note removal of fourth dog. $200-$250
Figure V43 - "Yellow-Dogs (one view of mug, at right)." H-2.75 in. x D-2.75 in. No mark. Note removal of second dog. $200-$250

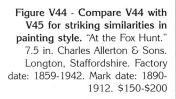

Figure V44 - Compare V44 with V45 for striking similarities in painting style. "At the Fox Hunt." 7.5 in. Charles Allerton & Sons. Longton, Staffordshire. Factory date: 1859-1942. Mark date: 1890-1912. $150-$200

Figure V36 - Compare V36 with V37 for inclusion of message. "Franklin's Proverbs - Keep Thy Shop . . . ." 7.87 in. J & G Meakin. Hanley, Staffordshire. Factory date: 1851+. $250-$300
Figure V37 - "Graphic Only - Keep Thy Shop . . . ." 4.37 in. Mark illegible. $250-$300

Figure V45 - "Detail of At the Fox Hunt." Detail taken from photo. $150-$200

Z Is for Z and Other Reversals

Figure Z1 - Reversed letter "Ɔ" on "Now I'm Grandmother." 7.37 in. No mark. This plate is also found as Figure I23 in "I Is for Infant to Infirm." $175-$225

Figure Z3 - Reversed letters "Ƨ" and "Ƨ' on "The sire turns . . . . " 5.75 in. No mark. This transfer and reversals are also found as Figures I69 and I70 in "I Is for Infant to Infirm." 300+

Figure Z2 - Reversed letter "Ƨ" on "Partisan with Drawn Sword." 7.27 in. No mark. *Courtesy of Ann and Dennis Berard.* This plate is also found as Figure N83 in "N Is for Nineteenth Century." $250+

Figure Z4 - Reversed letters "И," "Ƨ," and "Ƨ" on "The Diverting History of John Gilpin - From and Return Home." 7.25 in. Orange lustre rim. No mark. This plate is also found as Figure L22 in "L Is for Lustre." $300+

Figure Z5 - Reversed letter "Σ" on "Man on a Horse." This plate is also found as Figure M93 in "M Is for Metals." 300+

Figure Z6 - Reversed sequence of letters "J" and "I" on "Pluto - the pup and Mickey Mouse." H-1.5 in. x D-7.5 in. Carl Schumann Porcelain Factory. Arzberg, Bavaria. Factory dates: 1881-1996. Germany. Production date: c.1933. This plate is also found as Figure C87 in "C Is for Commercialism" and as Figure J2 in "J is for J, the Last Letter of the Alphabet." 500+

Figure Z7 - Rotation of word "LIBERTY" on "Liberty." Assay: Iron 99.6%, Copper .42%. 6.5 in. No mark. $200-$250

Figure Z8 - Detail of rotated word "LIBERTY" on Figure Z7.

Figure Z9 - "LIBERTY." 6.5 in. Iron 99.4%, Copper .4%, Nickel .2%. No mark. This plate is also found as Figure M94 in "M Is for Metals." $200-$250

Figure Z10 - Detail of corrected stamping on Figure Z9.

Appendices

Appendix AA1 - Little Alabama Coon

All words provided by the Library of Congress Web site but those of line five of the chorus; line five was inserted from a presentation of lyrics from the Special Collections Library of the University of South Florida in Tampa.

Words & music by Hattie Starr; New York: copyright 1893 by Willis Woodward & Co.; Copyright assigned 1932 to Edward B. Marks Music Corporation.

This song is based on an African American lullaby. Small bits of the melody can be heard in Dvorak's "New World Symphony," which was written much before Hattie Starr published her version. Words found on the ABC plate (**Figure A35**) are in bold type below.

One: I'se a little Alabama Coon! And I hasn't been born very long;
I 'member seein' a great big round moon! I member hearin' one sweet
song!
When dey tote me down to de cotton field, Dar I roll and I tumble in de sun!
While my daddy pick de cotton, Mammy watch me grow, And dis am de
song she Sung!

Chorus: Go to sleep, my little picaninny,
Brer' Fox'll catch you if yo' don't;
Slumber on de bosom of yo' ole mammy Jinny,
Mammy's gwine to swat yo' if you won't;
[swat! swat! swat! baby cry] sh! sh! sh!
Lula, lula lula lula lu!
Underneaf de silver southern moon; Rockaby! hushaby!
Mammy's little baby, Mammy's little Alabama Coon!

Two: Dis h'yar little Alabama Coon! Specks to be a growed up man some
day:
Dey's gwine to christen me hyar very soon! My name's gwine to be Henry Clay!
When I's big, I's gwine to wed a yellow gal, Den we'll hab picaninny's ob our own!
Den dat yellow gal shall rock'em on her bosom, And dis am de song she'll Croon!

Appendix AE1 - Apple Pie ABC

A was an apple pie, B bit it, C cut it, D dealt it, E eat it, F fought for it, G got it, H had it, J joined it, K kept it, L longed for it, M mourned for it, N nodded for it, O opened it, P peeped in it, Q quartered it, R ran for it, S stole it, T took it, V viewed it, W wanted it, and XYZ all wished a piece of it.

Or: A apple pie. B bit it. C cried for it. D danced for it. E eyed it. F fiddled for it. G gobbled it. H hid it. I inspected it. J jumped over it. K kicked it. L laughed at it. M mourned for it. N nodded for it. O opened it. P peeped into it. Q quaked for it. R rode for it. S skipped for it. T took it. U upset it. V viewed it. W warbled for it. Xerxes drew his sword for it. Y yawned for it. Z Zealous that all good boys and girls should be acquainted with his family, sat down and wrote the history of it.

Appendix AE2

Only the long verse for A will be provided here. A twelve-line verse is given for each of the twenty-six letters.

A begins Apple, Aunt, Annie, and Aim;
A is in master, and A is in dame.
A begins Archer, Ape, Arrow, and Arch;
A is in sugar, soap, treacle, and starch.
A begins Arthur, Ant, Andrew, and Axe;
A is in hammer, in nails, and in tacks.
A begins Alfred, Ann, Agnes, and Arm;
A is in meadow, lane, cottage, and farm.
A begins Anger, and Ankle, and Ache;
A is in custard, and mustard, and cake.
A begins Amy, and Ada, and Ass;
A is never in school, but is always in class.

Appendix AE3 - Rhymes to Remember

Because so much of "E Is for Education" focuses on transfers that select lines from the infant literature of nursery rhymes, the poems are reprinted, for reference, in their entirety. They are presented here in alphabetical order rather than in the text's chronological order. Most rhymes are quoted from sources more true to the period of the late 18th and 19th centuries than to current printings. Longer forms, when available, give interesting insights into the histories of the chants, whether found on the flat plates, deep dishes, or metal editions. Additional information concerning the histories of rhymes may be found in Iona and Peter Opie's *The Oxford Dictionary of Nursery Rhymes* published by Oxford University Press in 1997. A second invaluable source is Jean Harrowven's *Origins of Rhymes, Songs, and Sayings*, published by London's Kaye and Ward in 1977.

Ding Dong Bell
Pussy's in the well.
Who put her in?
Little Johnny Green,
Who pulled her out?
Little Tommy Stout.
What a naughty boy was that,
To try to drown poor pussy cat,
Who never did him any harm,
And killed the mice in his father's barn.

Georgie Porgie pudding and pie,
Kissed the girls and made them cry;
When the boys came out to play,
Georgie Porgie ran away.

Goosey Goosey Gander,
Whither shall I wander?
Upstairs and downstairs
And in my lady's chamber.
There I met an old man
Who would not say his prayers.
I took him by the left leg
And threw him down the stairs.

An earlier version ends:

Up stairs, down stairs, upon my Lady's window
There I saw a cup of Sack, and a race of Ginger.
Apples at the fire and nuts to crack,
A little Boy in the Cream Pot, up to his Neck.

Hey Diddle Diddle,
The cat and the fiddle.
The cow jumped over the moon;
The little dog laughed

To see such sport,
And the dish ran away with the spoon.

Hickory Dickory Dock
The mouse ran up the clock.
The clock struck one,
The mouse ran down,
Hickory, dickory, dock.

Jack and Jill went up the hill
To fetch a pail of water;
Jack fell down and broke his crown,
And Jill came tumbling after.
Up Jack got, and home did trot,
As fast as he could caper,
To old Dame Dob, who patched his nob
With vinegar and brown paper.

Little Bo-Peep has lost her sheep,
And can't tell where to find them;
Leave them alone, and they'll come home,
And bring their tails behind them.

Little Bo-Peep fell fast asleep,
And dreamt she heard them bleating;
But when she awoke, she found it a joke,
For they were still all fleeting.

Then up she took her little crook,
Determined for to find them;
She found them indeed, but it made her heart bleed,
For they's left their tails behind them.

It happened one day, as Bo-Peep did stray
Into a meadow hard by,
There she espied their tails side by side,
All hung on a tree to dry.

She heaved a sigh, and wiped her eye,
And over the hillocks went rambling,
And tried what she could, as a shepherdess should,
To tack again each to its lambkin.

Little Boy Blue,
Come blow your horn,
The sheep's in the meadow,
The cow's in the corn;
But where is the boy
Who looks after the sheep?
He's under a haycock,
Fast asleep.
Will you wake him?
No, not I,
for if I do,
He's sure to cry.

Little Jack Horner
Sat in the corner,
Eating a Christmas pie;
He put in his thumb,
And pulled out a plum,
And said, What a good boy am I!

Little Miss Muffet
Sat on her tuffet,
Eating her curds and whey;
There came a big spider
Who sat down beside her,
And frightened Miss Muffet away.

Little Polly Flinders
Sat among the cinders,
Warming her pretty little toes;
Her mother came and caught her,
And whipped her little daughter
For spoiling her nice new clothes.

Old Mother Hubbard
Went to the cupboard,
To fetch her poor dog a bone;
But when she came there

The cupboard was bare
And so the poor dog had none.

She went to the baker's
To buy him some bread;
But when she came back
The poor dog was dead.

She went to the undertaker's
To buy him a coffin;
But when she came back
The poor dog was laughing.

She took a clean dish
To get him some tripe;
But when she came back
He was smoking a pipe.

She went to the alehouse
To get him some beer;
But when she came back
The dog sat in a chair.

She went to the tavern
For white wine and red;
But when she came back
The dog stood on his head.

She went to the fruiterer's
To buy him some fruit;
But when she came back
He was playing the flute.

She went to the tailor's
To buy him a coat;
But when she came back
He was riding a goat.

She went to the hatter's
To buy him a hat;
But when she came back
He was feeding the cat.

She went to the barber's
To buy him a wig;
But when she came back
He was dancing a jig.

She went to the cobbler's
To buy him some shoes;
But when she came back
He was reading the news.

She went to the seamstress
To buy him some linen;
But when she came back
The dog was a-spinning.

She went to the hosier's
To buy him some hose;
But when she came back
He was dressed in his clothes.

The dame made a curtsy,
The dog made a bow;
The dame said, Your servant,
The dog said, Bow-wow.

Pussy Cat, Pussy Cat, where have you been?
I've been to London to look at the queen, (or: to see the great Queen.)
Pussy cat, pussy cat, what did you there?
I frightened a little mouse under her chair (or I saw a little mouse).

Ride (or Height) **a cock-horse to Banbury Cross,**
To see a fine lady upon a white horse;
Rings on her fingers and bells on her toes,
And she shall have music wherever she goes.
or:
Ride a cock-horse to Banbury Cross,
To buy little Johnny a galloping horse,

It trots behind and it ambles before,
And Johnny shall ride till he can ride no more.

See-saw, Margery Daw,
Jacky shall have a new master;
Jacky shall have but a penny a day,
Because he can't work any faster.

Simple Simon met a pieman,
Going to the fair;
Says Simple Simon to the pieman,
Let me taste your ware.

Says the pieman to Simple Simon,
Show me first your penny,
Says Simple Simon to the pieman,
Indeed I have not any.

Simple Simon went a-fishing,
For to catch a whale;
All the water he had got
Was in his mother's pail.

Simple Simon went to look
If plums grew on a thistle;
He pricked his finger very much,
Which made poor Simon whistle.

There was a crooked man, and he walked a crooked mile,
He found a crooked sixpence against a crooked stile;
He bought a crooked cat, which caught a crooked mouse,
And they all lived together in a little crooked house.

There was an old woman who lived in a shoe,
She had so many children she didn't know what to do;
She gave them some broth without any bread;
She whipped them all soundly and put them to bed.

An older version reads:

There was a little old woman, and she liv'd in a shoe,
She had so many children, she didn't know what to do.
She crumm'd 'em some porridge without any bread;
And she borrow'd a beetle, and she knocked 'em all o' the head,
Then out went th' old woman to bespeak 'em a coffin,
And when she came back, she found 'em all a-loffeing

There was an old lady who lived under a hill,
And if she's not gone, she lives there still.

The last stanza of the accumulative rhyme that includes the alphabet plate line, "**This is the maiden all forlorn,**" reads:

This is the farmer sowing his corn,
That kept the cock that crowed in the morn,
That waked the priest all shaven and shorn,
That married the man all tattered and torn,
That kissed the maiden all forlorn,
That milked the cow with the crumpled horn,
That tossed the dog,
That worried the cat,
That killed the rat,
That ate the malt
That lay in the house that Jack built.

This little pig went to market,
This little pig stayed home,
This little pig had roast beef,
This little pig had none,
And this little pig cried, Wee-wee-wee-wee-wee,
I can't find my way home.

Where are you going to, my pretty maid?
I'm going a-milking, sir, she said,
Sir, she said, sir, she said,
I'm going a-milking, sir, she said.

May I go with you, my pretty maid?
You're kindly welcome, sir, she said.

Say, will you marry me, my pretty maid?
Yes, if you please, kind sir, she said.

What is your father, my pretty maid?
My father's a farmer, sir, she said.

What is your fortune, my pretty maid?
My face is my fortune, sir, she said.

Then I can't marry you, my pretty maid,
Nobody asked you, sir, she said.

The older version, beginning with line three, reads:

I am going to the well, sweet Sir, she said,
For strawberry leaves make maidens fair.
Shall I go with thee pretty fair maid, he said
Do if you will, sweet Sir, she said
What if I do lay you down on the ground
I will rise up again, sweet Sir, she said
What if I do bring you with child
I will bear it, sweet Sir, she said
Who will you have for father for your child
You shall be his father, sweet Sir, she said
What will you do for whittles for your child
His father shall be a taylor, sweet Sir, she said &c.

Who killed Cock Robin?
I, said the Sparrow,
With my bow and arrow,
I killed Cock Robin.
Who saw him die?
I, said the Fly,
With my little eye,
I saw him die.

Who caught his blood?
I, said the fish,
With my little dish,
I caught his blood.
Who'll make the shroud?
I, said the Beetle,
With my thread and needle,
I'll make the shroud.

Who'll dig his grave?
I, said the Owl,
With my pick and shovel,
I'll dig his grave.

Who'll be the parson?
I, said the Rook,
With my little book,
I'll be the parson.

Who'll be the clerk?
I am said the Lark,
If it's not in the dark,
I'll be the clerk.

Who'll carry the link?
I, said the Linnet,
I'll fetch it in a minute,
I'll carry the link.

Who'll be chief mourner?
I, said the Dove,
I mourn for my love,
I'll be chief mourner.

Who'll carry the coffin?
I, said the Kite
If it's not through the night,
I'll carry the coffin.

Who'll bear the pall?
We, said the Wren,
Both the cock and the hen,
We'll bear the pall.

Who'll sing a psalm?
I, said the Thrush,
As she sat on a bush,
I'll sing a psalm.

Who'll toll the bell?
I, said the Bull,
Because I can pull,
I'll toll the bell.

All the birds of the air
Fell a-sighing and a-sobbing,
When they heard the bell toll
For poor Cock Robin.

Appendix AF1 - A Cut Above the Rest!

Rose Bradley, in *The English Housewife in the Seventeenth & Eighteenth Centuries* (Arnold, 1912), tells of the 17th-century duties of carving. In addition to covering the meat with paper to keep the food and the hand somewhat clean, it was the housewife's obligation to cut all the meat, serving the most-wanted cut to each individually. She might be assisted by another lady present who sat, with all the other women, at one end of the table. After William III had introduced the Dutch system of seating by alternate sexes, she was still obligated to do the job as she was painstakingly taught, at least three times a week, by a carving master to "thigh," "wing," "untack," "barb," "disfigure," or "string" by a set of procedures.

Appendix AH1 - A Word about Spelling

The word "hollow ware" is spelled as two words in many works on antiques and as "hollowware" in others, including publications by the respected Harry Abrams Press. (The definition, which originally seemed to relate only to metal objects, is now found broadened to vessels in all media.)

Appendices AI1, AI2, and AI3 - Parts of Poems by Robert Burns
AI1- The Cotter's Saturday Night - Verse VIII

With kindly welcome, Jenny brings him ben:
A strappan youth; he takes the Mother's eye;
Blythe Jenny sees the visit's no ill taen;
The Father cracks of horses, pleughs and kye.
The Youngster's artless heart o'erflows wi' joy,
But blate and laithfu', scarce can weel behave;
The Mother, wi' a woman's wiles, can spy
What makes the youth sae bashfu' and sae grave;
Weel-pleas'd to think her bairn's respected like the lave.

AI2 - The Cotter's Saturday Night - Verse XII

The cheerfu' Supper done, wi' serious face,
They, round the ingle, form a circle wide;
The Sire turns o'er, with patriarchal grace,
The big ha'-Bible, ance his Father's pride:
His bonnet rev'rently is laid aside,
His lyart haffets wearing thin and bare;
Those strains that once did sweet in ZION glide,
He wales a portion with judicious care;
'And let us worship God!' he says with solemn air.

AI3 - John Anderson, my jo

John Anderson, my jo, John,
When we were first acquent,
Your locks were like the raven,
Your bonnie brow was brent;
But now your brow is beld, John,
Your locks are like the snaw;
But blessings on your frosty pow,
John Anderson, my jo!
John Anderson, my jo, John,
We clamb the hill thegither;
And mony a canty day, John,
We've had wi'ane anither;
Now we maun totter down, John,
And hand in hand we'll go,
And sleep thegither at the foot,
John Anderson, my jo.

Selected Poems, K. Brown, Ed. Cambridge University Press, NY, 1998.

Appendix AM1 - Components of Metal Types

The compositions of metals as mentioned in the literature concerning 19th-century metal products:

Britannia metal: 91% tin, 7% antimony, 2% copper
Pewter: tin and lead
Nickel silver: 65% copper, 20% nickel, 15% zinc
German silver: same as nickel silver
Silver solder: silver, copper, zinc
Sheffield plate: copper with silver laminate

Appendix AM2 - The Pedlar's Caravan

Poem author: William Brighty Rands
Source: *The Posey Ring, A Book of Verse for Children*
Book Editors: Kate Douglas Wiggin and Nora Archibald Smith
Publisher: New York: McClure, Phillips & Company,1903

I wish I lived in a caravan,
With a horse to drive like a pedlar-man,
Where he comes from nobody knows,
Or where he goes to, but on he goes!

His caravan has windows too,
And a chimney of tin that the smoke comes through;
He has a wife, with a baby brown,
And they go riding from town to town.

Chairs to mend and delf to sell!
He clashes the basins like a bell;
Tea-trays, baskets ranged in order,
Plates with the alphabet round the border!

The roads are brown, and the sea is green,
But his house is just like a bathing machine;
The world is round, and he can ride,
Rumble and splash, to the other side!

With the pedlar-man I should like to roam,
And write a book when I came home;
And the people would read my book,
Just like the travels of Captain Cook!

Appendix AN1 - British Colonies

Colonies are divided by world areas: Africa, Asia (including the Middle East); colonies in the Caribbean, Central America and the South Atlantic; colonies in Europe including the Mediterranean; former British colonies in North America; and British colonies in the Pacific.

Areas (by modern names) colonized in Africa include Sudan, Lesotho, Botswana, Cameroon, South Africa, Egypt, The Gambia, Ghana, Kenya, Mauritius, South Africa, Nigeria, Zambia, Malawi, Seychelles, Sierra Leone, Zimbabwe, Somalia, Namibia, Swaziland, Tanzania, Ghana, and Uganda.

Areas (by modern names) colonized in the Middle East include Yemen, Bahrain, Malaysia (Sabah), Brune, Myanmar, Sri Lanka, Hong Kong, India, Pakistan, Bangladesh, Iraq, Kuwait, Maldives, Qatar, Israel, Singapore, and Jordan.

Areas (by modern names) colonized in the Caribbean, Central America, and the South Atlantic include Anguilla, Antigua and Barbuda, Ascension, Bahamas, Barbados, Bermuda, Guyana, Belize, British Virgin Islands, Cayman Islands, Dominica, Falkland Islands, Grenada, Jamaica, Montserrat, St. Kitts-Nevis, St. Helena, St. Lucia, St. Vincent and the Grenadines, South Georgia, South Sandwich Islands, Trinidad and Tobago, Tristan da Cunha, and the Turks and Caicos Islands.

Areas (by modern names) colonized in the Europe and the Mediterranean include Cyprus, Gibraltar, Germany, Greece, Malta, and Spain.

Areas (by modern names) colonized in North America include The Thirteen Colonies, British Columbia, Hudson's Bay Territories, Newfoundland, Nova Scotia, Ontario, Prince Edward Island, Quebec, and Vancouver Island.

Areas (by modern names) colonized in the Pacific include: Fiji, Tuvalu, Kiribati, Nauru, Papua New Guinea, Vanuatu, Australia, New Zealand, Pitcarin, Solomon Islands, Tonga, and Western Samoa.

JOHN GILPIN was a citizen,
Of credit and renown;
A train-band captain eke was he,
Of famous London town.

John Gilpin's spouse said to her dear,
"Though wedded we have been
These twice ten tedious years, yet we
No holiday have seen.

"To-morrow is our wedding-day,
And we will then repair
Unto the "Bell" at Edmonton,
All in a chaise and pair.

"My sister, and my sister's child,
Myself, and children three,
Will fill the chaise; so you must ride
On horseback after we."

He soon replied, "I do admire
Of womankind but one,
And you are she, my dearest dear,
Therefore it shall be done.

"I am a linendraper bold,
As all the world doth know,
And my good friend, the calender,
Will lend his horse to go."

Quoth Mrs. Gilpin, "That's well said;
And for that wine is dear,
We will be furnished with our own,
Which is both bright and clear."

John Gilpin kissed his loving wife;
O'erjoyed was he to find,
That though on pleasure she was bent,
She had a frugal mind.

The morning came, the chaise was brought,
But yet was not allowed
To drive up to the door, lest all
Should say that she was proud.

So three doors off the chaise was stayed,
Where they did all get in;
Six precious souls, and all agog
To dash through thick and thin.

Smack went the whip, round went the wheels,
Were never folks so glad!
The stones did rattle underneath,
As if Cheapside were mad.

John Gilpin at his horse's side
Seized fast the flowing mane,
And up he got, in haste to ride,
But soon came down again.

For saddletree scarce reached had he,
His journey to begin,
When, turning round his head, he saw
Three customers come in.

So down he came' for loss of time,
Although it grieved his sore,
Yet loss of pence, full well he knew,
Would trouble him much more.

'Twas long before the customers
Were suited to their mind,
When Betty screaming came downstairs,
"The wine is left behind."

"Good luck!" quoth he, "yet bring it me,
My leathern belt likewise,
In which I bear my trusty sword
When I do exercise."

Now Mistress Gilpin (careful soul!)
Had two stone bottles found,
To hold the liquor that she loved,
And kept it safe and sound.

Each bottle had a curling ear,
Through which the belt he drew,
And hung a bottle on each side,
To make his balance true.

Then over all, that he might be
Equipped from top to toe,
His long red cloak, well brushed and neat,
He manfully did throw.

Now see him mounted once again
Upon his nimble steed,
Full slowly pacing o'er the stones,
With caution and good heed.

But finding soon a smoother road
Beneath his well-shod feet,
The snorting beast began to trot,
Which galled him in his seat.

"So, fair and softly!" John he cried,
But John he cried in vain.
That trot became a gallop soon,
In spite of curb and rein.

So stopping down, as needs he must
Who cannot sit upright.
He grasped the mane with both his hands,
And eke with all his might.

His horse, who never in that sort
Had handled been before,
What thing upon his back had got,
Did wonder more and more.

Away went Gilpin, neck or nought;
Away went hat and wig;
He little dreamt, when he set out,
Of running such a rig.

The wind did blow, the cloak did fly
Like streamer long and gay,
Till, loop and button failing both,
At last it flew away.

Then might all people well discern
The bottles he had slung;
A bottle swinging at each side,
As hath been said or sung.

The dogs did bark, the children screamed,
Up flew the windows all;
And every soul cried out, "Well done!"
As loud as he could bawl.

Away went Gilpin – who but he?
His fame soon spread around;
"He carries weight! He rides a race!
'Tis for a thousand pound!"

And still as fast as he drew near,
'Twas wonderful to view,
How in a trice the turnpike-men
Their gates wide open threw.

And now, as he went bowing down
His reeking head full low,
The bottle twain behind his back
Were shattered at a blow.

Down ran the wine into the road,
Most piteous to be seen,
Which made the horse's flanks to smoke
As they had basted been.

But still he seemed to carry weight,
With leathern girdle braced;
For all might see the bottle-necks
Still dangling at his waist.

Thus all through merry Islington
These gambols he did play,
Until he came unto the wash
Of Edmonton so gay;

And there he threw the wash about
On both sides of the way,
Just like unto a trundling mop,
Or a wild goose at play.

At Edmonton his loving wife
From the balcony spied
Her tender husband, wondering much
To see how he did ride.

"Stop, stop, John Gilpin! Here's the house!"
They all at once did cry;
"The dinner waits, and we are tired;"
Said Gilpin – "So am I!"

But yet his horse was not a whit
Inclined to tarry there;
For why? – his owner had a house
Full ten miles off, at Ware.

So like an arrow swift he flew,
Shot by an archer strong;
So did he fly – which brings me to
The middle of my song.

Away went Gilpin out of breath
And sore against his will.
Till at his friend, the calender's,
His horse at last stood still.

The calender, amazed to see
His neighbor in such trim,
Laid down his pipe, flew to the gate,
And thus accosted him:

"What news?" what news? your tidings tell;
Tell me, you must and shall –
Say why bareheaded you are come,
Or why you come at all?"

Now Gilpin had a pleasant wit,
And loved a timely joke;
And thus unto the calendar
In merry guise he spoke:

"I came because your horse would come;
And, if I well forebode,
My hat and wig will soon be here;
They are upon the road."

The calendar, right glad to find
His friend in merry pin,
Returned him not a single word,
But to the house went in;

Whence straight he came with hat and wig,
A wig that flowed behind;
A hat not much the worse for wear,
Each comely in its kind.

He held them up, and in his turn
Thus showed his ready wit.
"My head is twice as big as yours.
They therefore needs must fit.

"But let me scrape the dirt away,
That hangs upon your face;
And stop and eat, for well you may
Be in a hungry case."

Said John, "It is my wedding-day,
And all the world would stare
If wife should dine at Edmonton,
And I should dine at Ware."

So turning to his horse, he said,
"I am in haste to dine;
'Twas for your pleasure you came here,
You shall go back for mine."

Ah! luckless speech, and bootless boast!
For which he paid full dear;
For while he spake, a braying ass
Did sing most load and clear;

Whereat his horse did snort, as he
Had heard a lion roar,
And galloped off with all his might,
As he had done before.

Away went Gilpin, and away
Went Gilpin's hat and wig;
He lost them sooner than at first,
For why – they were too big.

Now Mistress Gilpin, when she saw
Her husband posting down
Into the country far away,
She pulled out half-a-crown;

And thus unto the youth she said
That drove them to the "Bell,"
"This shall be yours when you bring back
My husband, safe and well."

The youth did ride, and soon did meet
John coming back amain;
Whom in a trice he tried to stop,
By catching at his rein;

But not performing what he meant
And gladly would have done,
The frighted steed he frighted more,
And made him faster run.

Away went Gilpin, and away
Went postboy at his heels,
The postboy's horse right glad to miss
The lumbering of the wheels.

Six gentlemen upon the road,
Thus seeing Gilpin fly,
With postboy scampering in the rear,
They raised the hue and cry:

"Stop thief! stop thief! a highway man!"
Not one of them was mute;
And all and each that passed that way
Did join in the pursuit.

And now the turnpike-gates again
Flew open in short space;
The toll-men thinking, as before,
That Gilpin rode a race.

And so he did, and won it, too,
For he got first to town;
Nor stopped till when he had got up,
He did again get down.

Now let us sing, Long live the King,
And Gilpin, long live he;
And when he next doth ride abroad,
May I be there to see.

Appendix AN3 - The Cock Fight

From Lydia M. Fish's *The Folklore of the Coal Miners of the Northeast of England,* Norwood Editions, 1975.

Come all ye colliers far and near,
I'll tell of a cock-fight, when and where.
Out on the moors I heard them say,
Between a black and our bonny grey.

Chorus: With the silver breast and the silver wing,
He's fit to fight in front of the king.
Hip hooray, hooray, hooray!
Away we carried our bonny grey.

First come in was the Oldham lads;
They come with all the money they had.
The reason why they all did say:
"The black's too big for the bonny grey."

It's into the pub to take a sup,
The cock-fight it was soon made up.
For twenty pound these cocks will play.
The charcoal-black and the bonny grey.

The Oldham lads stood about in round:
"I'll lay ye a quid to half a crown,
If our black cock he gets fair play,
He'll make mincemeat of the bonny grey!"

So the cocks they at it, and the grey was tossed,
And the Oldham lads said: "Bah, you've lost!"
Us collier lads we went right pale,
And wished we'd fought for a barrel of ale.

And the cocks they at it, one, two, three.
And the charcoal-black got stuck in the eye.
They picked him up, but he would not play,
And the cock-fight went to our bonny grey.

Appendix AP1 - Watery Graves

The marl holes and old mine shafts were as rich in secrets as they were in raw materials. Wound through the sleuthing fiction written by Staffordshire's Roy Whitfield (Whitfield, 1997) are passages which cast a black light on these remnants of industry. Whitfield writes,

A marlhole was the legacy of the pottery industry's quest for the raw materials to make the pottery articles. When the marl (clay) was exhausted, the vast holes were left to fill with water and most were over a hundred feet deep. Many a poor soul had ended their miserable lives in the murky depths. The local lads used the filthy waters to swim in after wading through the maggoty dead dogs and cats littering the water's edge. More than one young life was lost through getting entangled in the debris hidden under water, apart from the diseases which killed no end . . . . Rumors abounded about unwanted pregnancies ending up in the filthy waters . . . (T)hese poor little scraps of mans' inhumanity to man were often found having been partially gnawed by the vermin infesting these God forsaken holes . . . (A)nd there is even a cart-horse and cat down there. Poor bugger went down when tipping pottery shards . . . (P)it shafts . . . long since abandoned . . . were surrounded by twenty feet high walls and looked like square fortified towers of some ancient castle . . . What was disposed of in the confines of the shafts was anybody's guess.

Appendix AP2 - A Snippet on the *Gazette*

Hundreds of elegantly written informative columns, announcements of new inventions and patents, charming vignettes of the industry's ambitious characters, records of exports safely strapped in barrels and parts and pieces of the industry's day-to-day ups and downs tied the people of the industry together. The small-print pages of the *Pottery Gazette* were a vehicle, too, for the advertisements—many of which provided pictures of factories that no longer exist. A few of those prints, reprinted in this text, recalled some of the factories that produced ABC plates; their streaks are typical of images taken from microfilms of *Pottery Gazettes* in the library in Stoke. They are reprinted with the permission of Tableware International.

A tedious search of the *Gazettes* afforded no mention of alphabet plates in particular . . . they were not items of pride or planning. Though among the first mass produced wares of the Industrial Revolution, these darkened, rough, heavy earthenware vessels were not affordable by those who made them. (Pottery families still tell of stealing items under long skirts or stowing items in the river to make these or any other products of the manufactories more affordable.)

Appendix AP3 - Arnold Bennett

Born into poverty in Halley, 1867, Bennett wrote plays and novels. If he hadn't failed his bar examinations, we might never have seen his novels serialized for television.

Appendix AQ1 - Answers to the Conundrums

1. Because he is not game.
2. Because it is a triangle.
3. Because he has beaten his antagonist in argument.
4. Because two and one cannot make four.
5. Because he seems to stand fire well.
6. A pear (pair)

Appendix AR1 - Recipes for Infant Meals

Contributed by Muriel Z. Motola, Member, the American Collectors of Infant Feeders, York, Pennsylvania.

Posset: A spiced drink of hot sweetened milk or cream, eggs, and curdled with wine or ale, it was sometimes medicated with herbs. Traditionally, the recipe was administered for respiratory discomfort.

Pap: Flour or bread crumbs soaked in water or milk make this luscious treat. Sometimes a little beer or wine was added. Water pap was made of bread and baked flour . . . it proved so successful that other foods were introduced. Weak broth was offered with the first tooth and with the second, the minced wing of a chicken to celebrate. Sugar was added, being given with bread boiled in water.

Gruel: Flour or bread crumbs, soaked in water, became a thin, watery porridge. Corn meal or any cereal might have been added to pulverized walnuts for richness.

Caudle: Mainly a drink for invalids or women in childbirth, this warm beverage was given to ailing persons. It consisted of wine or ale mixed with sugar, eggs, bread, and various spices. It might also have been made of oatmeal mixed with hot wine or beer, then sweetened and spiced.

Penada: Penada was a sort of cereal made of flour, bread, and perhaps a little butter or milk, all cooked in vegetable and meat broth. Sugar, beer, or wine was sometimes added. One recipe for penada called for steeping bread in water for six hours, pressing it through a cloth, and boiling it with sufficient water for eight hours. It was to be stirred from time to time and diluted with warm water. For seasoning, 59 grains of anise and an ounce of sugar for each pound of bread were used. Finally the whole thing was passed through a hair sieve. The user was cautioned to take care to reheat each time only the necessary quantity to be used.

Sillabub: This was a drink made of cream or milk curdled by wine or cider and sweetened with sugar. And, of course, there was Porridge, which was the broth of meat or chicken, the traditional healer.

Appendix AR2

Source: A General Song of Praise to God. *Divine Songs*, Song I (Watts, 1832).

HOW glorious is our heavenly King,
Who reigns above the sky!
How shall a child presume to sing
His dreadful majesty!

How great his power is none can tell,
Nor think how large his grace;
Not men below, not saints that dwell
On high before his face.

Not angels that stand round the Lord
Can search his secret will;
But they perform his heavenly work,
And sing his praises still.

Then let me join this holy train,
And my first offerings bring;
The eternal God will not disdain
To hear an infant sing.

My heart resolves, my tongue obeys
And angels shall rejoice
To hear their mighty Maker's praise
Sound from a feeble voice.

Appendix AR3

Source: Praise Be to God for Our Redemption, *Divine Songs*, Song III
(Watts, 1832).

BLESS'D be the wisdom and the power,
The justice and the grace,
That join'd in council to restore.
And save our ruin'd race.

Our father ate forbidden fruit,
And from his glory fell;
And we his children thus were brought
To death, and near to hell.

Bless'd be the Lord, that sent his Son
To take our flesh and blood;
He for our lives gave up his own,
To make our peace with God.

He honour'd all his Father's laws,
Which we have disobey'd;
He bore our sins upon the cross,
And the full ransom paid.

Behold him rising from the grave,
Behold him raised on high;
He pleads his merits there to save
Transgressors doom'd to die.

There on a glorious throne he reigns,
And by his power Divine,
Redeems us from the slavish chains
Of Satan and of sin.

Thence shall the Lord to judgment come,
And, with a sovereign voice,
Shall call and break up every tomb,
While waking saints rejoice.

Oh may I then with joy appear
Before the Judge's face;
And, with the bless'd assembly there,
Sing his redeeming grace.

Appendix AR4

Source: Examples of Early Piety, *Divine Songs*, Song XIV (Watts, 1832).

WHAT bless'd examples do I find
Writ in the word of truth,
Of children that began to mind
Religion in their youth!

Jesus, who reigns above the sky,
And keeps the world in awe,
Was once a child as young as I,
And kept his Father's law.

At twelve years old he talk'd with men,
(The Jews all wondering stand;)
Yet he obey'd his mother then,
And came at her command.

Children a sweet hosanna sung,
And bless'd their Saviour's name;
They gave him honour with their tongue,
While scribes and priests blaspheme.

Samuel, the child, was wean'd, and brought
To wait upon the Lord;
Young Timothy betimes was taught
To know his holy word.

Then why should I so long delay
What others learned so soon?
I would not pass another day
Without this work begun.

Appendix AR5

Source: Against Idleness and Mischief, *Divine Songs*, Song XX (Watts,
1832).

HOW doth the little busy bee
Improve each shining hour,
And gather honey all the day
From every opening flower!

How skillfully she builds her cell,
How neat she spreads the wax!
And labours hard to store it well
With the sweet food she makes!

In works of labour, or of skill,
I would be busy too,
For Satan finds some mischief still
For idle hands to do.

In books, or work, or healthful play,
Let my first years be past;
That I may give for every day
Some good account at last.

Appendix AR6

Source: Against Pride in Clothes, *Divine Songs*, Song 22 (Watts, 1832).

WHY should our garments, made to hide
Our parents' shame, provoke our pride?
The art of dress did ne'er begin,
Till Eve, our mother, learn'd to sin.

When first she put the covering on,
Her robe of innocence was gone;
And yet her children vainly boast
In the sad marks of glory lost.

How proud we are, how fond to show
Our clothes, and call them rich and new,
When the poor sheep and silkworm wore
That very clothing long before!

The tulip and the butterfly
Appear in gayer coats than I:
Let me be dress'd fine as I will,
Flies, worms, and flowers exceed me still.

Then will I set my heart to find
Inward adornings of the mind;
Knowledge and virtue, truth and grace,
These are the robes of riches dress.

No more shall worms with me compare.
This is the raiment angels wear;
The Son of God, when here below,
Put on this bless'd apparel too.

It never fades, it ne'er grows old,
Nor fears the rain, no moth, nor mould;
It takes no spot, but still refines;
The more 'tis worn, the more it shines.

In this on earth should I appear,
Then go to heaven, and wear it there;
God will approve it in his sight,
'Tis his own work and his delight.

Appendix AR7

Source: An Evening Song, *Divine Songs*, Song XXVI (Watts, 1832).

AND now another day is gone,
I'll sing my Maker's praise;

My comforts every hour make known
His providence and grace.

But how my childhood runs to waste!
My sins, how great their sum!
Lord, give me pardon for the past,
And strength for days to come.

I lay my body down to sleep,
Let angels guard my head,
And through the hours of darkness keep
Their watch around my bed.

With cheerful heart I close mine eyes,
Since thou wilt not remove:
And in the morning let me rise
Rejoicing in thy love.

Appendix AR8 - Ode of Welcome - Tune - God Save the Queen (Tayler, 1946)

Welcome to join our Band,
Welcome with us to stand,
In this pure cause.
Welcome the pledge to take,
Welcome those vows to make,
And for sweet Temperance' sake
To keep her laws.

As pledged in truth you stand,
Angels, a heavenly band,
Take up the song;
"Welcome, your souls, to be,
In vows of purity,
From dark temptation free,
In virtue strong.

"Welcome! we bend in love
From the bright heaven above,
And bid you come.
Our love, with tireless wing,
Shall strength and blessing bring,
Until in heaven we sing
Your welcome home."

Then welcome to our Band,
And with us, hand in hand,
Welcome to go;
To give our cause success,
And with the Pledge to bless,
Bring health and happiness,
And banish woe.

Welcome to joy and peace,
To virtue's sure increase,
And wisdom's ways.
And may we ever be
From the destroyer free,
To sing our victory,
In love and praise.

Appendix AR9

Source: The Sluggard, *Moral Songs* (Watts, 1832).

TIS the voice of the sluggard; I heard him complain,
"You have waked me too soon, I must slumber again."
As the door on its hinges, so he on his bed,
Turns his sides, and his shoulders, and his heavy head.

"A little more sleep, and a little more slumber;
Thus he wastes half his days, and his hours without number:
And when he gets up he sits folding his hands,
Or walks about saunt'ring, or trifling he stands.

I pass'd by his garden, and saw the wild brier,
The thorn and the thistle grow broader and higher:
The clothes that hang on him are turning to rags;
And his money still wastes, till he starves or he begs.

I made him a visit, still hoping to find
He had took better care for improving his mind.
He told me his dreams, talk'd of eating and drinking;
But he scarce reads his Bible, and never loves thinking.

Said I then to my heart, "Here's a lesson for me,
This man's but a picture of what I might be;
But thanks to my friends for their care in my breeding,
Who taught me betimes to love working and reading."

Appendix AU1 - Proof Positive of Exported ABC Ware

Proof positive of exported alphabet ware is found in a captivating article presented in the Winter, 2002, edition of *The ABC Collectors' Circle, A Newsletter for Collectors of Educational China*, edited by Dr. Joan George. Titled "Plates from a Ship Wreck," the text tells of two ABC plates and the fragment of a third which were but a few of the ten thousand artifacts rescued from the drowned *Principessa Margherita di Piemonte*. The vessel began her journey from Naples, Italy. She stopped to load stacks of stoneware and pottery from Plymouth, England, before crossing the sea, only to sink not far from her Delaware port. Displayed in the DiscoverSea Museum on Fenwick Island in Delaware, the three plates are titled, "The Dancing Master," "The New Pony," and "The Village Blacksmith;" the last can be seen as **Figure N56** of "N Is for Nineteenth Century."

Appendix AV1 - The Tale of Robert, the Organ Grinder

Most interesting is the change of verbiage that accompanied transfers as they appeared in different publications. In this case, where the figure of the organ grinder originally had a short poem beneath it ("O begins Organ; / the tune is so gay, ..."), the *Nursery* wrote a short tale of the brave music maker who lost his right hand in the war. Since Robert could no longer farm, he was given, says the story, a hand-organ by the rich Mr. Wilson. Mothers were grateful to this new organ-grinder who earned his living by entertaining troops of little ones with his high spirits and merry melodies.

Appendix AW1 - Dennis Berard's Recipe for Bleaching Ceramics

Dennis Berard's procedure for bleaching plates is simple and the equipment needed is easily acquired.

Needed are: a gallon of commercial 35% hydrogen peroxide, a plastic container with an airtight cover, and a pair of rubber gloves. After pouring the hydrogen peroxide into the plastic container, the plate (or mug) can be immersed using rubber gloves. Its length of stay depends upon its degree of stain. (Darker stains may soak for several weeks!) The need to check progress each day is vital; a ceramic coming out of the solution may not necessarily look clean . . . it must then be washed in soap and soft water and dried thoroughly. The next phase requires baking the item for 45 minutes at 175-200 degrees (F). The heat will extract a film of dirt or a layer of orange grease which can be quickly washed away. Whether the article is "clean enough" is now a judgment call. The entire process may be repeated but a second soak may fade the overpainting which will, ultimately, be devaluing. The last step calls for a thorough drying to prevent the appearance of a grey-brown fuzz from the crazing; molding demands the repeat of the process.

Appendix AY1 - English Pottery Registration Numbers by Years

Details of the registrations for 1 to 54820 are in the process of being moved to the Public Record Office, Ruskin Avenue in Kew from the Design Registry , Room 1124A, State House, High Holburn, London, WC2A 1AY.

1884	1
1885	19756
1886	40480
1887	64520
1888	90483
1889	116648
1890	141273
1891	163767
1892	185713
1893	205240
1894	224720
1895	246975
1896	268392
1897	291241
1898	311658

1899	331707
1900	351202
1901	368154
1902	385180

Continuation of this list through 1965 can be found on the Internet: http://www.stoke.gov.uk/museums/gladstone/gpminf17.htm

Appendix A/Combined Chapter List - All marks seen in this text

The following is a list, grouped by countries of origin and alphabetically, of the ceramic and glass marks found throughout the text. Marks of silver plate and sterling flatware, as noted in "F Is for Flatware" and "M Is for Metals" are not included here but are noted in the *Encyclopedia of American Silver Manufacturers, Revised Fourth Edition* by Dorothy T. Rainwater and Judy Redfield, Schiffer Publishing, Ltd. Atglen, Pa. 1998. Marks on mixed metal flatware are included when possible **(see Figure F14)** and the mark of the only mixed metal plate that carries a maker's identification is seen on the face of **Figure M15**, a clock face manufactured in Wolverhampton, England.

American Pottery
Beetleware. Hemco Moulding Co. Bridgeport, Connecticut. C41
Buffalo Pottery. Buffalo, New York. C30
William Brunt Pottery. East Liverpool, Ohio. C53
Crown Hotel China. Evansville, Indiana. D119
Crown Potteries. Evansville, Indiana. D81
Dresden China Co. East Liverpool, Ohio. D104, K9
ELPCO. East Liverpool, Ohio. D100
Harker Pottery Co. Hotel China. East Liverpool, Ohio. C49
D. E. McNicol.
       Holdfast Baby Plate Design. D86
       East Liverpool, Ohio. D93
       Clarksburg, West Virginia. D97
National China Co. East Liverpool, Ohio. C77, C78
T.P.C.-O. Co. East Liverpool, Ohio. D106
West End Pottery. East Liverpool, Ohio. C19

American Glass Manufacturers
Hazel Atlas Glass Co. Wheeling, West Virginia. G47
J. B. Higbee Glass Co. Bridgeville, Pennsylvania. G30, G31
Combined Marks: Higbee "Bee" and New Martinsville Glass Mfg.
      Co. "M." New Martinsville, West Virginia. G35
SI (Smithsonian Institution) mark on "Rover." New Martinsville Glass Mfg.
      Co. New Martinsville, West Virginia. G32

Czechoslovakian Pottery Mark
Made in Czechoslovakia. D4

United Kingdom Pottery Marks
William Adams & Co. Tunstall, Staffordshire. U1, U2
Harvey Adams & Co. (assumed) Longton, Staffordshire. U3
Charles Allerton & Sons. Longton, Staffordshire. U5, U6, U7
H. Aynsley & Co. Longton, Staffordshire. U8, U9, U10
Barkers and Kent Co. Fenton, Staffordshire. U11
Sampson Bridgwood. Longton, Staffordshire. D75
Brownhills Pottery. (See listings for Registry Marks)
C & F over G over England. Glasgow, Scotland. D76
E. Challinor. Tunstall, Staffordshire. U17
Joseph Clementson. Shelton, Staffordshire. U18
W. Davenport & Co. Longport, Staffordshire. U19
Edge, Malkin & Co. Burslem, Staffordshire. U22, U23, U24
Elsmore &
      Forster. Tunstall, Staffordshire. U25
      Foster. Tunstall, Staffordshire. U26
      Son. Tunstall, Staffordshire. U27
Thomas Godwin at the Canal Works. Burslem, Staffordshire. U28
William Hackwood Pottery. Hanley, Staffordshire. U29
George Jones at
      Trent Pottery. Stoke, Staffordshire. U30
      (& Sons) at Crescent and Trent. Stoke, Staffordshire. U31
J & G Meakin. Hanley, Staffordshire. U33
John Meir & Son. Tunstall, Staffordshire. U34
William E. Oulsnam & Sons. Burslem, Staffordshire. U35
Podmore, Walker & Co. Tunstall, Staffordshire. U36
      or Podmore, Walker & Wedgwood Co. Tunstall, Staffordshire

or Wedgwood & Co. Tunstall, Staffordshire. U44
Powell & Bishop. Hanley, Staffordshire. U37
A. Shaw at Tunstall, Staffordshire. (1851-1856)
      or at Burslem, Staffordshire. (1860-1900)
      or at Burslem, Staffordshire. (1882-1898) U38
Swinnertons. Hanley, Staffordshire. D78
T & H – further research needed. U39
Josiah Wedgwood & Sons. Etruria and Barlaston, Staffordshire. U41
Wedgwood & Co. (See listing for Podmore, Walker & Co.) U44
James Wileman & Co. Fenton, Staffordshire. U45
Enoch Wood & Sons. Burslem, Staffordshire. U46

English Pottery Importer Marks
May be: Jones, McDuffe and Stratton. Boston, Massachusetts.
      or John McDonald and Son. Halifax, Nova Scotia. U47
J. H. ?. & R. Boston, Massachusetts and New York, New York. U48
Hugh C. Edmiston. New York, New York. U49
Trade Mark Registered in the US Patent Office. U50

English Pottery Registry Marks
Registry Mark - Brownhills Pottery. U14
Registry Mark - Brownhills Pottery. U15
Registry Mark - Brownhills Pottery. U16
Registry Mark # 153253 - Staffordshire, England. U51.
Registry Diamond Style A. Staffordshire. Y2
Registry Diamond Style B. Staffordshire. Y3

French Pottery Mark
Deliniers & Company. Limoges, France. U20

German/Bavarian Pottery Marks
Arzberg Porcelain Factory. Arzberg, Bavaria. D6
M. B. Britannia Porcelain Works. Meierhofen, Germany. U12
Disney Authorized
      Carl Schumann Porcelain. Arzberg, Bavaria. C84
      Carl Schumann Porcelain. Arzberg, Bavaria. C86
G. W. Co. Germany. D70
Heise Pottery. Berlin, Germany. D8
Variant of L. Hutschenreuther Porcelain Factory. Selb. Germany. D10
C. A. Lehman at Leuchtenberg. Kahla. Thuringia, Germany. D12
O (or D) G (monogram). Germany. Unidentified. D68
Retsch & Co. (or R. C. W.) Wunsiedel, Germany. D16
Rose O'Neill. Rudolstadt, Germany. K1
Combined Marks: Rose O'Neill and Royal Rudolstadt Porcelain
      Factory. Rudolstadt, Germany. K5
Royal Bavaria. Tettau. Bavaria. D18
Carl Schumann Porcelain Factory. Arzberg, Bavaria. D20
Three Crown Pottery. Unknown. D23
Unknown and illegible mark. D73

German Marks: Point of Origin (Bavaria/Austria)
Capital Letter GERMANY between circles. Green. D61
Capital Letter GERMANY. Orange. D36
Capital Letter GERMANY between circles. Orange. D56
Capital Letter GERMANY between circles with numeral. Orange. D59
Capital Letter GERMANY between circles. Pink. D54
Capital Letter MADE IN AUSTRIA between circles. Orange. D64
Circle Shaped Made in Germany. Orange. D52
Lower Half-circle Shaped Germany. Metallic Gold. D50
Script *Bavaria*. Green. D28
Script *Germany*. Green. D31
Script *Germany*. Blue. D33
Combined Marks: Script *Germany*. Blue and L. O. Co. New York
      export firm. D66
Combined Marks: Script *Germany*. Blue and Capital letters E
      (B/R)PHILA between two circles. Green. D48

German Pottery Export Firms
L. O. Co. New York, New York. D67
Carl Schumann Porcelain Factory, Arzberg, Bavaria. For Disney.
      C84 and C86
New York & Rudolstadt (a.k.a. Royal Rudolstadt). Thuringia,
      Germany. For Rose O'Neill. K5

Bibliography

A. B. C., "Fanny's Pets." *The Nursery, A Monthly Magazine for Youngest Readers*, Vol. XXIII, No. 137., April 1878.

Alphabet of Virtues, London: Darton & Co., c.1856.

Altman, Violet, and Seymour Altman. *The Book of Buffalo Pottery.* Atglen, Pa.: Schiffer Publishing Ltd., 1987.

American Pottery and Glassware Reporter, December 11, 1879.

Anecdotes for Little Boys, No. 308 (pamphlet). Philadelphia, Pa.: American Sunday-School Union, n.d.

Anelay, Henry, illustrator. *The Mother's Picture Alphabet.* London: S. W. Partridge, 1862.

Anthony, John. *Women Against Slavery, The Story of Harriet Beecher Stowe.* New York: Thomas Crowell, 1978.

Anti Slavery Alphabet. Philadelphia: Merrihew & Thompson, 1847.

Armitage, Shelly. *Kewpies and Beyond.* Jackson, Miss.: University Press of Mississippi, 1994.

Arthur's Alphabet, Aunt Mayor's Toy Books [series]. London: Routledge, Warne & Routledge, 1887.

Bagdade, Susan, and Al Bagade. *Warman's English & Continental Pottery and Porcelain,* 2nd ed. Radnor, Pa.: Wallace-Homestead Book Co., 1991.

Baldwin, Ruth. *100 Nineteenth-Century Rhyming Alphabets in English.* Carbondale and Edwardsville, Ill.: Southern Illinois University Press, 1972.

Ball, A. *Collecting Pottery.* Burton upon Trent, Staffordshire: M. A. B. Publishing, 1979.

Batkin, Maureen. *Gifts for Good Children, The History of Children's China, 1890-1900.* Somerset: Richard Dennis, n.d.

Baynton, Douglas. *Forbidden Signs.* Chicago: University of Chicago Press, 1996.

Bedford, John. *Old English Lustre Ware.* New York: Walker and Co., 1968.

Bennett, Arnold. *Anna of the Five Towns; A Novel.* Plainview, N.Y.: Books for Libraries Press, 1975.

Bettelheim, Bruno. *The Uses of Enchantment, the Meaning and Importance of Fairy Tales.* New York: Vintage Books, 1977.

Bibby, Mark, and Simon Henderson. *Potteries Men in the Crimean War.* Hanley, England: Hanley Library, n.d.

A Biographical Memoir of Richard Jordan. York, U.K.: Alexander & Son, 1828.

Bishop, Robert, and Patricia Coblentz. *The World of Antiques, Art and Architecture in Victorian America.* New York: E. P. Dutton, 1979.

Bloom, Ken. *American Song, the Complete Musical Theatre Companion.* New York: Schirmer Books, 1949.

Bly, John. *Miller's Silver and Sheffield Plate Marks.* London: Octopus Publishing Group, Ltd., 1993.

Boatner, Mark May III. *The Civil War Dictionary.* New York: David McKay Co., Inc., 1959.

Bologna, Gianfranco. *Simon & Schuster's Guide to Birds of the World.* New York: Simon and Schuster, 1978.

Bottle Ovens (leaflet). With the assistance of Terence Woolliscroft and others. Longton: The Gladstone Working Pottery Museum, n.d.

Bowers, Sharon, Sue Closser, and Kathy Ellis. *Czechoslovakian Pottery: "Czeching" out America.* Marietta, Ohio: The Glass Press, Inc., 1999.

Boys' and Girls; Illustrated Gift Book. London: Routledge, 1872.

Bradley, Rose. *The English Housewife in the 17th and 18th Centuries.* London: Edward Arnold, 1912.

Briggs, John. *A History of Longton.* Keele, England: University of Keele Press, 1982.

Bronowski, J. *The Ascent of Man.* Boston: Little, Brown & Co., 1973.

Brown, Ivar. *Dickens in His Time.* London: Thomas Nelson and Sons, Ltd., 1965.

Brown, Kenneth, 1998. *Robert Burns, Selected Poems.* Cambridge, Mass.: Cambridge University Press.

Brühl, Georg. *Porzellan-figuren, Zierde des Bürgerlichen Salons.* München: Germany: Georg D. W. Callwey, 1989.

Buehr, Walter. *Home Sweet Home in the Nineteenth Century.* New York: Thomas Crowell, 1965.

Bulwer, John. *Deafe and Dumbe Man's Friend.* London: Humphrey Moseley, 1648.

Burton, Elizabeth. *The Early Victorians at Home, 1837-1861.* London: Longman Group, Ltd., 1972a.

_____. *The Pageant of Early Victorian England.* New York: Charles Scribner's Sons, 1972b.

Byrne, Tom. *Tales from the Past.* Newcastle under Lyme: Remploy, 1977.

Calhoun, W. A. *Early Clay Industries of the Upper Ohio Valley.* Library of the Ohio Archaeological and Historical Society, n.d.

Calvocoressi, Peter. *Who's Who in the Bible.* New York: Penguin Books, 1990.

Carroll, Lewis. *Alice in Wonderland.* New York: Grosset & Dunlap, 1963.

Cavendish, Richard, ed. *Man, Myth & Magic.* New York: Marshall Cavendish Corporation, 1970.

Chalala, Mildred. "ABC Plates." *The Antique Trader.* December 1986.

Chalala, Mildred, and Joseph Chalala. *Collector's Guide to ABC Plates, Mugs and Things.* Lancaster, Pa.: Pridemark Press, 1980.

Charleston, Robert J., ed. *World Ceramics and Illustrated History.* New York: McGraw-Hill Book Company, 1968.

Chase, Mark, and Michael Kelly. *Collectible Drinking Glasses.* Paducah, Ky.: Collector Books, 1996.

Chase, Sara Hannum. *The First Book of Silver.* New York: Franklin Watts, Inc., 1969.

Chavarria, Joaquim. *The Big Book of Ceramics.* New York: Watson-Guptill Publications, 1994.

Cheadle, Dave. *Victorian Trade Cards.* Paducah, Ky.: Collector Books, 1997.

Child J. *The Staffordshire Potteries as an Empire Asset and Illustrated Souvenir of the Royal Visit.* Manchester: Manchester Courier, Ltd., 1913.

Child, Mrs. *The Girl's Own Book,* 4th ed. London: Thomas Tegg, 1832.

Childhood's Happy Hours. London: Warne and Kronheim, 1865.

Child's Picture Story Book, The. London: George Routledge and Sons, c.1886.

Child's Treasury of Knowledge, Boston: Wier and White, n.d.

Christensen, James C. *Rhymes and Reasons–An Annotated Collection of Mother Goose Rhymes.* Shelton, Conn.: The Greenwich Workshop Press, 1997.

Christiansen, Rex, and R. W. Miller. *The North Staffordshire Railway.* Devon: David & Charles Publishers, Ltd., 1971.

Cieslik, Jurgen, and Marianne Cieslik. *The German Doll Encyclopedia,* 1800-1939. Cumberland, Md.: Hobbyhouse Press, 1985.

Cleaver, James. *History of Graphic Art.* New York: Philosophical Library, 1963.

Clements, Paul. *Marc Isambard Brunel.* Harlow: Longmans, 1970.

Clinton, Margery. *Lustres.* The Complete Potter Series. London: B. T. Batsford Ltd., 1991.

Coffin, Margaret. *The History & Folklore of American Country Tinware, 1700-1900.* New York: Galahad Books, 1968.

Cohen, Mortimer J. *Pathways Through the Bible.* Philadelphia, Pa.: The Jewish Publication Society of America, 1953.

Coleman, Dorothy S., Elizabeth A. Coleman, and Evelyn J. Coleman. *The*

Collector's Encyclopedia of Dolls. New York: Crown Publishers, 1968.

Collier, Christopher, and James Lincoln. *The American Revolution*. New York: Marshall Cavendish (Benchmark), 1998.

Comic Adventures of Old Mother Hubbard and Her Dog: London: J. Harris, 1805.

Conroy, Barbara. *Restaurant China*. Volume I. Paducah, Ky.: Collector Books, 1998.

Cowper, William. *The Diverting History of John Gilpin*. London: Charles Tilt, 1828.

Danckert, Ludwig. German Edition of *Handbook of European Porcelain Marks*. Munich: Prestel, 1992.

DeBolt, Gerald. *Dictionary of American Pottery Marks, Whiteware & Porcelain*. Paducah, Ky.: Collector Books, 1994.

Defoe, Daniel. *Robinson Crusoe*. George Cruikshank, illustrator. London: George Routledge, 1840.

De Saint-Pierre, Bernardin. *Paul and Virginia*. Chicago: A. C. McClurg & Co., 1907.

Dennis, Richard. *Ravilious and Wedgwood*. Somerset, England: Dalrymple Press, 1986.

Dennison, Carmel. *Burslem, People and Buildings, Buildings and People*. Stoke on Trent: Ray Johnson Productions, 1996

Digby, Ann, and Peter Searby. *Children, School and Society in Nineteenth Century England*. London: Macmillan Publishers, 1981.

Dolan, J. R. *Yankee Peddlers of Early America*. New York: C. N. Porter, 1964.

Douglas, Norman. *London Street Games*. London: Ghatto and Windus, 1931.

Dover Stamping Co. *1869 Illustrated Catalog*. Mendham, N.J.: Astragal Press, 1994.

Drimmer, Frederick, ed. *The Illustrated Encyclopedia of Animal Life*. New York: Greystone Press, 1961.

DuPree, Marguerite W. *Family Structure in the Staffordshire Potteries*. Oxford: Clarendon Press, 1995.

DuVall, Nell. *Domestic Technology*. Boston: J. K. Hall & Co., 1988.

Edwards, Bill, and Mike Carwile. *The Standard Encyclopedia of Pressed Glass, 1860-1930*. Paducah, Ky.: Collector Books, 1999.

_____. *The Standard Encyclopedia of Carnival Glass*. Edition 7. Paducah, Ky.: Collector Books, 2000.

Faust, Patricia L. *Historical Times Illustrated Encyclopedia of the Civil War*. New York: Harper and Row, 1986.

Fay, Ida. "The Summer Shower." *The Nursery, A Monthly Magazine for Youngest Readers*, Vol. XXIII, No. 136, April 1878.

Fish, Lydia M. *Folklore of the Coal Miners of the Northeast of England*. England: Norwood Editions, 1975.

Fisher, Trevor. *Prostitution and the Victorians*. New York: St. Martin's Press, 1997.

Flick, Pauline. *Old Toys*. Album #147. Buckinghamshire: Shire Publications, Ltd., 1985.

Fox and the Geese, The. An Ancient Nursery Tale. London: Joseph Cundall, 1845.

Franklin, Benjamin. *Poor Richard's Almanack*. Benjamin Smith, ed. New York: The Century Co., 1898.

Franklin, Linda. *300 Years of Kitchen Collectibles*. Iola, Wisc.: Krause Publications, 1997.

Freeman, Peter. *The Development of Ceramic Colours and Decorating Techniques in the Staffordshire Potteries* (leaflet). Longton: The Gladstone Working Pottery Museum, 1977.

Fröebel, Friedrich. *Mother's Songs, Games and Stories*. London: William Rice, 1890.

Gardner, Helen. *Art Through the Ages*. New York: Harcourt Brace & Co., 1948.

Gaston, Mary. *Collector's Encyclopedia of R. S. Prussia*. Fourth Series. Paducah, Ky.: Collector Books, 1995.

Gates, William C., Jr., and Dana E. Ormerod. *The East Liverpool, Ohio, Pottery District: Identification of Manufacturers and Marks*. Published in book form by the *Journal of the Society for Historical Archaeology* as Volume 16, Numbers 1 & 2, 1982.

Gates, William C. *The City of Hills and Kilns: Life and Work in East Liverpool, Ohio*. East Liverpool, Ohio: East Liverpool Historical Society, 1984.

George, Dr. Joan, Ed. *The ABC Collectors' Circle, A Newsletter for Collectors of Educational China*. Old Bridge, New Jersey.

Giblin, James Cross. *From Hand to Mouth*. New York: Thomas Crowell, 1987.

Gibson, Michael. *19th Century Lustreware*. Wrappingers' Falls, N.Y.: Antique Collector's Club, Ltd., 1999.

Glass Collector's Digest, Vol. 1, No. 4, December-January, 1988.

Godden Geoffrey. *British Pottery and Porcelain. 1780-1850*. London: Arthur Barker, Ltd., 1963.

_____. *British Pottery, An Illustrated Guide*. London: Barrie & Jenkins, 1974

_____. *Encyclopaedia of British Porcelain Manufacturers*. London: Barrie & Jenkins, 1988.

_____. *Collecting Lustreware*. London: Barrie & Jenkins, 1991a.

_____. *Encyclopaedia of British Pottery and Porcelain Marks*. London: Barrie & Jenkins, 1991b.

Godden, Geoffrey, and Michael Gibson. *Collecting Lustreware*. London: Barrie & Jenkins, 1991.

Goldberg, Rabbi Nathan. *Passover Haggadah*. New York: Ktav Publications, 1973.

Goldman, Paul. *Victorian Illustrated Books, 1850-1870*. Boston: David R. Godine, 1994.

Gomme, Lady Alice Bertha. *A Dictionary of British Folk-Lore, Part I, Traditional Games, Volume II*. London: David Nutt, 1898.

Greenslade, M. W. *A History of Burslem*. Staffordshire: Staffordshire County Library, Reprint, 1983a.

_____. *A History of Hanley*. Staffordshire: Staffordshire County Library, Reprint, 1983b.

_____. *A History of Stoke*. Staffordshire: Staffordshire County Library, Reprint, 1983c.

_____. *A History of Tunstall*. Staffordshire: Staffordshire County Library, Reprint, 1983d.

Guzzetti, Paula. *The White House*. Parsippany, N.J.: Dillon Press, 1996.

Halfpenny, Pat. "Joseph Clemenson, A Potter, Remarkable for Energy of Character." *Northern Ceramic Society Journal*, Vol. 5, 1984.

Haggar, R. G., A. R. Mountford, and J. Thomas. *The Staffordshire Pottery Industry*. Staffordshire: Staffordshire County Council, 1981.

Hakim, Joy. *History of the U.S.—Making Thirteen Colonies*. Volume 2. New York: Oxford University Press, 1993.

_____. *History of the U.S.—War, Terrible War*. Volume 6. New York: Oxford University Press, 1999.

Haley, Allan. *The History, Evolution and Design of the Letters We Use Today*. New York: Watson-Guptill Publications, 1995.

Harris, Neil. *Humbug, The Art of P. T. Barnum*. Chicago: University of Chicago Press, 1973.

Harrowen, Jean. *Origins of Rhymes, Songs and Sayings*. London: Kaye & Ward, 1977.

_____. *Origins of Festivals and Feasts*. Kent: Pryor Publications, 1980.

Heaivilin, Annise Doring. *Grandma's Tea Leaf Ironstone —A History and Study of English and American Potteries*. Lombard, Ill.: Wallace Homestead Book Co., 1981.

Hedges, Ernest Sydney. *Tin in Social and Economic History*. New York: St. Martin's Press, 1964.

Heide, Robert, and John Gilman. *Disneyana, Classic Collectibles*. New York: Hyperion, 1994.

Henry Francis du Pont Winterthur Museum Trade Catalogues, 1750-1980. Compiled by E. Richard McKinstry. New York: Garland Publishers, 1984.

Hibbert, Christopher. *Queen Victoria in Her Letters and Journals*. Gloucestershire: Sutton Publishing, 1984.

Higby, Lola, and Wayne Higby. *Bryce, Higbee and J. B. Higbee Glass*. Marietta, Ohio: The Glass Press, Inc., 1998.

Hillard, G. S., and L. J. Campbell. *The Primer or First Reader*. New York: Taintor Brothers, Merril & Co., 1864.

Holland, Rupert S. *Historic Poems and Ballads*. Freeport, N.Y.: Books for Libraries Press, 1970.

Hollinan, Lincoln. *The Shire Book—Royal Commemoratives*. Buckinghamshire: Cromwell House, 1997.

Hood, Thomas. *Puzzledom—An Original Collection of Charades, Conundrums, Puzzles and Games*. Philadelphia, 1886.

Hughes, G. Bernard. *Victorian Pottery and Porcelain*. London: Spring Books, 1959.

_____. *English and Scottish Earthenware, 1660-1860*. New York: Macmillan Company, 1961.

Hughes, G. Bernard, and Therle Hughes. *The Collector's Encyclopaedia of English Ceramics*. London: Lutterworth Press, 1956.

_____. *English Porcelain and Bone China, 1743-1850*. London: Lutterworth Press, 1968.

Hughes, Thomas, *Tom Brown's Schooldays*. Oxford: Oxford University Press, 1999.

Husfloen, Kyle. *Collector's Guide to American Pressed Glass. 1825-1915*. Iola, Wisc.: Krause Publications, 1992.

Jenkins, J. G. *A History of Fenton*. Staffordshire: Staffordshire County Council Reprint, 1985.

Jenks, Tudor. *The Country World Fair Book for Boys and Girls,* New York: Century Co., 1893.

Jeuda, Basil. Personal communication, July 2000.

Johnston, Joyce J. "Christmas, 1879." *Glass Collectors Digest,* Vol. 1, No. 4., Dec./Jan. 1988.

Jones, J. B. *The Little Sailors—Merry Times for the Little Folks.* Juvenile Publications, 1899.

Jones, Alderman W. H. *Story of the Japan, Tin Plate Working, and Iron Braziers' Trades, Bicycle and Galvanising Trades, and Enamel Ware Manufacture in Wolverhampton and District.* London: Alexander and Shepheard, Ltd., 1900.

Jordan, Thomas E. *Victorian England.* Albany, N.Y.: State University of New York Press, 1987.

Julian (D. D.), John. *A Dictionary of Hymnology.* London: John Murray, 1915.

Kamm, Minnie Watson. *An Eighth Pattern Glass Book.* Gross Pointe, Mich.: Kamm Publications, 1970.

Kerr, Lisa, and Jim Gilcher. *Ohio Art—The World of Toys.* Atglen, Pa.: Schiffer Publishing Ltd., 1998.

King Glass Co. (Catalogue). Pittsburgh: King Glass Co., 1888-1891.

Knight, Charles. *Knights Pictorial Museum of Animal Nature.* 1850.

Kowalsky, Arnold, and Dorothy E. Kowalsky. *Encyclopedia of Marks of American, English, and European Earthenware, Ironstone, and Stoneware, 1780-1980.* Atglen, Pa.: Schiffer Publishing Ltd., 1999.

Kovel, Ralph, and Terry Kovel. *Kovels' New Dictionary of Marks.* New York: Crown Publishers, 1985.

Lang, Kathleen. "Dishing Up A Taste of Childhood." *The Country Home Magazine,* April 1988.

Laver, James. *Victorian Vista.* London: Hulton Press, 1954.

Lawrence-Smith, Kathleen. *Tales of Old Staffordshire.* Berkshire: Countryside Books, 1992.

Lechler, Doris Anderson. *Children's Glass Dishes China and Furniture.* Paducah, Ky.: Collector Books, 1985.

_____. *Toy Glass.* Marietta, Ohio: Antique Publications, 1989.

Lee, Angela. Personal communication, July 2000.

Lehner, Lois. *Lehner's Encyclopedia of US Marks on Pottery, Porcelain & Clay.* Paducah, Ky.: Collector Books, 1988.

Lewis, R. A., advisor. *Children in the Potteries, I and II.* Hanley, England: Staffordshire County Council, Education Department, 1975.

_____. *Children in the Mines.* Hanley, England: Staffordshire County Council Education Department, 1981a.

_____. *Staffordshire Pottery Industry (Gr. 4).* Stafford: Staffordshire County Council Education Support Unit, 1981b.

_____. *Victorian School Days.* Staffordshire Study Book B. Stafford: Staffordshire County Council Education Department, December 1981c.

_____. *Education since 1700 (History Unit H1).* Stafford: Staffordshire County Council, Education Department, January 1984.

Lewis, Roy. *Pottery Workers in Staffordshire. A Portrait in Old Picture Postcards.* Sussex: S. B. Publications, 1995.

Lindsay, Irene, and Ralph Lindsay. *ABC Plates & Mugs.* Paducah, Ky.: Collector Books, 1998.

Lindsey, Bessie. *American Historical Glass.* Rutland, Vt.: Charles E. Tuttle Co., 1967.

Liston, Robert A. *By These Faiths, Religions for Today.* New York: Julian Messner, 1978.

Little, W. L. *Staffordshire Blue—Underglaze Blue Transfer—Printed Earthenware.* New York: Crown Publishers, 1969.

Liungman, Carl G. *Dictionary of Symbols.* New York: W. W. Norton & Company, 1991.

Livingston, Anna. *The Nursery, A Magazine For Youngest Readers,* Volume II, 1867.

Long, E. B., with Barbara Long. *The Civil War Day by Day.* New York: Doubleday, 1971.

Louisa's Apple Pie, London Toy Books (series). London: Frederick Warne and Kronheim, c.1865.

Ludwig, Stephanie. "Hersteller heute." *Puppengeschirr in Vergangen und Gegenwart (Doll Dishes Past and Present),* n.d.

"Manufacture of Ceramic Transfers." *Ceramics,* Vol. II, No. 13, March 1950.

McClellan, Marilyn, Personal communication, November 2000.

McCulloch, Lou. *Children's Books of the 19th Century.* De Moines, Iowa: Wallace-Homestead Book Co., 1979.

McCullough, Edo. *Good Old Coney Island.* New York: Charles Scribner's Sons, 1957.

McGill, M. *The Story of Louisa May Alcott, Determined Writer.* New York: Benton Doubleday Dell, Parachute Press, 1988.

Measell, James. *New Martinsville Glass.* Marietta, Ohio: Antique Publications, 1994.

Mitchell, Sally. *Daily Life in Victorian England.* Westport, Conn.: Greenwood Press, 1996.

Moore, N. Hudson. *The Old China Book.* New York: Tudor Publishing Co., 1936.

Moreland, Bill. "Kid Cogs." *Staffordshire Magazine,* February 1980.

Mother Goose Nursery Rhymes. Chicago: Homewood Publishing Co., 1904.

Motola, Muriel. "Invalid Feeders." Paper presented at The Southern California Collectors Association Conference, Claremont College, Claremont, Ca., June 1-2, 1996.

Mother's Picture Alphabet. London: S. W. Partridge, 1887.

Mountford, Arnold. *Illustrated Guide to Staffordshire Salt-Glazed Stoneware.* New York: Praeger Publications, 1971.

Mundey, Alfred. *Tin and the Tin Industries.* London: Sir Isaac Pitman and Sons, 1926.

Munsey, Cecil. *Disneyana: Walt Disney Collectibles.* New York: Hawthorne Books, 1974.

Mysteries of the Bible (film, 50 minutes). New York: A&E Television Networks, 1995.

Myths of the Vampires (film, 50 minutes). New York: A&E Television Networks, 1997.

New Martinsville Glass Manufacturing Co. Catalogue. New Martinsville, Va.: New Martinsville Glass Manufacturing Co., c.1901-1944.

Newbery, John. *Goody Two-Shoes, a facsimile reproduction of the edition of 1766.* Detroit: Singing Tree Press, 1970.

Niblett, Kathy. Personal communication, 2000-2001.

_____. "A Useful Partner - Thomas Wedgwood." *Northern Ceramic Society Journal,* Vol. 5., 1984, p. 3.

North, C. *History of Berlin, Connecticut.* New Haven, Conn.: Tuttle, Morehouse and Taylor Co., 1916.

Oaklander, Violet. *Windows to our Children.* Moab, Utah: Real People Press. 1978.

Object Lesson ABC. Chicago: M. A. Donohue & Co., n.d. (1912-1931).

Ogg, Oscar. *The 26 Letters.* New York: Thomas Crowell, Co., 1971.

Old Nursery Rhymes from Mother Goose. New York: McLoughlin Bros., n.d.

Opie, Iona, and Peter Opie. *The Oxford Dictionary of Nursery Rhymes.* Oxford, England: Oxford University Press, 1997.

Osterwalder, Marcos. *Dictionary des Illustrateurs.* Paris: Hubschmid & Bouret, 1983.

Pearsall, Ronald. *Collapse of Stout Party, Victorian Wit and Humor.* London: Widenfeld and Nicolson, 1975.

Pearson, Edwin. *Banbury Chap Books and Nursery Toy Book Literature with Impressions from Several Hundred Original Woodcut Blocks by T. J. Bewick, et. al.* London: A. Reader, 1890.

Penner, Lucille R. *Eating the Plates.* New York: Macmillan Publishing Co., 1991.

Perugini, Mark Edward. *Victorian Days and Ways.* London: Jarrolds, 1932.

Petroski, Henry. *The Evolution of Useful Things.* New York: Alfred A, Knopf, 1992.

Picture Alphabet of Nations of the World. London: T. Nelson & Sons, 1847.

Picturesque Primer. London: Griffith, Farran, Okeden & Welsh, c.1880.

Pottery Gazette and Glass Trades Review. London: Scott, Greenwood & Sons, Ltd. Est. 1875. Now incorporated into the *Tableware International,* Surrey, England.

Powers, Bernice F. and Olive Floyd. *Early American Decorated Tinware.* New York: Hastings House Publishers, 1957.

Priestley, J. B. *Victoria's Heyday.* London: Wm Heinemann, Ltd., 1972.

Pullan, Mrs. *The Book of Riddles.* Holborn Hill, England: Darton & Co., 1855.

Rainwater, Dorothy, and Judy Redfield. *Encyclopedia of American Silver Manufacturers.* Atglen, Pa.: Schiffer Publishing Ltd., 1998.

Ray, Delia. *A Nation Torn.* New York: Puffin Books, 1996.

Read, G. W., and Frederick A. Read. *Staffordshire Pots and Potters.* London: Hutchinson and Co., 1906.

Reader, W. J. *Victorian England.* New York: G. P. Putnam & Sons, 1973.

Rhodehamel, John. *The Great Experiment.* New Haven, Conn.: Yale University Press, 1998.

Richards, Laurie, ed. *Baby's Rhyme Book—with Pretty Pictures.* Boston: Estes & Lauriat, 1879.

Riley, Noël. *Gifts for Good Children—the History of Children's China 1790-1890.* Somerset, England: Richard Dennis, 1991.

Rinker, Harry. "Romantic Staffordshire, The Perfect Reflection of Victorian Taste." *Inside Antiques,* August 1944.

Roe, F. Gordon. *The Victorian Child.* London: Phoenix House, Ltd., 1959.

Röntgen, Robert. *Marks on German, Bohemian and Austrian Porcelain—*

1710 to the Present. Atglen, Pa.: Schiffer Publishing Ltd., 1997.

Royal Road to Spelling and Reading. London: Edward N. Marks, 1867.

Scarratt, William. *Old Times in the Potteries*. London: S. R. Publications, Ltd., 1969.

Seekers, David. *Popular Staffordshire Pottery*. London: Michael Joseph Publishers, 1977.

Sellers, Charles, and Henry May. *A Synopsis of American History*. Chicago: Rand McNally, 1963.

Shaw, Charles. *When I Was a Child*. London: Caliban Books, 1986.

Shaw, Peter. *The Autobiography and Other Writings by Benjamin Franklin*. New York: Bantam Books, 1989.

Shaw, Simeon. *History of the Staffordshire Potteries*. Hanley: G. Jackson, 1829.

Sibley, David Allen. *National Audubon Society: The Sibley Guide to Birds*. New York: Alfred A. Knopf, 2000.

Sifakis, Stewart. *Who Was Who in the Civil War*. New York: Facts on File Publications, 1988.

Smiles, Samuel. *Self-Help*. London: John Murray, 1882. Also http://www.fordham.edu/halsall/mod/1882smiles.html

Smith, Robin, and Bill Younghusband. *American Civil War Zouaves*. Elite Series. Oxford: Osprey Publishing Co., 1996.

Some Landmarks in the History of the Staffordshire Pottery Industry 1600-1900 (leaflet). Longton: Gladstone Working Pottery Museum, 1978.

Sterry, Iveagh Hunt, and William H. Garrigus. *They Found a Way*. Brattleboro, Vt.: Stephen Daye Press, 1938.

Stowe, Harriet Beecher. *Uncle Tom's Cabin* or *Negro Life in the Slave States of America*. London: Clarke & Son, 1852 (first edition).

Strachey, Lytton. *Queen Victoria*. New York: Harcourt Brace & Co., 1949.

Strong, Michael. *Language Learning and Deafness*. Cambridge: Cambridge University Press, 1988.

Stuart, Denis., ed. *People of the Potteries*. Keel, England: University of Keele, 1985.

Swindall, David. *David*. Dallas, Tex.: Word Publishing, 1997a.

_____. *Joseph*. Dallas, Tex.: Word Publishing, 1997b.

Tayler, Robert. *The Hope of the Race*. London: Hope House, 1946.

Taylor, Isaac. *The History of the Alphabet*. New York: C. Scribners & Sons, 1899.

Taylor, Jane, and Ann Taylor. *Hymns for Infant Minds, 1812.*

Thomas, John. *The Rise of the Staffordshire Potteries*. Bath: Adams & Dart, 1971.

"Transfers and Transfer Printing," *Cox's Potteries Annual and Year Book*. Liverpool: Publishers and Advertisers Ltd., 1925.

Transport in the Potteries 1750-1950. Longton, Staffordshire: Working Pottery Museum, n.d.

Truman, Charles., ed. *Southeby's Concise Encyclopedia of Silver*. London: Conran Octopus, 1996.

Uncle Charles. "Robert the Organ Grinder." *The Nursery Magazine for Youngest Readers*, Vol II., 1867.

Uncle George. *Parlour Pastimes for the Young*. London: James Blackwood, 1857.

Union ABC. Boston: Degen, Estes and Co., 1864.

Van Loon, Henrik. *The Story of Mankind*. New York: Garden City Publishing Co., 1938.

Van Rose, Susanna. *Earth*. Eyewitness Science Series. London: Dorling Kindersley, 1994.

Vicinus, Martha. *Suffer and Be Still, Women in the Victorian Age*. Bloomington: Indiana University Press, 1972.

Vose, Z. Pope. *The Band of Hope Ritual Together with a Form of Constitution and Rules*. Boston: Samuel W. Hodges Publisher, 1872.

Wakefield, Hugh. *Victorian Pottery*. New York: Nelson, 1963.

Walker, Kizer. Personal communication, October, 2000.

Ward, Geoffrey C., and Ken Burns. *Baseball—An Illustrated History*. New York: Alfred A. Knopf, 1994.

Ward, John. *The Borough of Stoke-Upon-Trent*. Yorkshire: S. R. Publishers, Ltd., 1969.

Ware, George W. *German and Austrian Porcelain*. New York: Crown Publishers, 1963.

Warrillow, Ernest J. D. *Sociological History of Stoke-on-Trent*. Stoke-on-Trent, Staffordshire: Etruscan Publishers, 1960.

Watney, Bernard. *Longton Hall Porcelain*. London: Faber and Faber, 1957.

_____. *English Blue and White Porcelain of the Eighteenth Century*. New York: Faber and Faber, 1963.

Watts, Isaac. *Divine and Moral Songs for Children*. London: Charles Tilt, 1832.

Wedgwood, Josiah C. *Staffordshire Pottery and Its History*. New York: McBride, Nast & Co., 1913.

Weiss, Harry Bischoff. *American Baby Rattles from Colonial Times to the Present*. Trenton, N.J.: Priv. Pub., 1941.

Welker, John, and Elizabeth Welker. *Pressed Glass in America: Encyclopedia of the First Hundred Years 1825-1925*. Ivyland, Pa.: Antique Acres Press, 1985.

White, R. W. *From Peterloo to the Crystal Palace*. London: Heinemann Educational Books, 1972.

_____. *Life in Regency England*. New York: G. P. Putnam's Sons, 1969.

White House—An Historical Guide. Washington, D.C.: White House Historical Association, 1966.

Whitmeyer, Margaret, and Ken Whitmeyer. *Children's Dishes*. Paducah, Ky.: Collector Books, 1984.

Who's Who, Historical Volume (1607-1896). Chicago: Who's Who, Incorporated, 1967.

Whitfield, Roy. *Potters Rot*. Staffordshire: Whitfield, 1997.

Wiggin, Kate Douglas, and Nora Archibald. *The Posey Ring, a Book of Verse for Children*. New York: McClure, Phillips & Co., 1903.

Wilhelmina. "The Three Little Nurses." *The Nursery, a Monthly Magazine for Youngest Readers*, Vol. XXVII., 1880. No. 163.

Wohl, Anthony. *The Victorian Family, Structure and Stresses*. New York: St. Martin's Press, 1978.

Wolfman, Peri, and Charles Gold. *Forks, Knives & Spoons*. New York: Clarkson Potter Publishers, 1994.

Wood, Hamish. Personal communication, August 9, 1999.

Yates, Raymond, and Marguerite Yates. *Early American Crafts and Hobbies*. New York: Wilfred Funk, 1954.

Young, Barbara, and J. G. Jenkins. *A History of Longton*. Stafford: Staffordshire County Library, 1985.

Young, David, and Micki Young. *Campbell's Soup Collectibles*. Iola, Wisc.: Krause Publications, 1998.

Web Sites

Campbell's Soups Community Center:
http://www.campbellsoup.com

Canals: http://www/canals.org.uk/rootsandroutes/pages/nwest/t+m.htm

People for the Ethical Treatment of Animals:
http://www.peta-online.org

Felix The Cat: http://www.felixthecat.com

London Labour and the London Post:
http://www.uoguelph.ca/englit/victorian/html/caster.html

Morrell, Virginia, "Africa's Wild Dog," International Wildlife Magazine:
http://www.nwf.org/internationalwildlife/wilddog.html

Orme, Evans & Co. Ltd:
http://www.localhistory.scit.wlv.ac.uk/Museum/metalware/general/orme.htm

The Poem Finder: http://www.poemfinder.com

Kewpie dolls: http://www.wwwisions.com/craftbb/antique/3474.html

Stoke-on-Trent, Pottery and Ceramics, Web site of Steve Birks:
http://www.netcentral.co.uk/steveb

The Missing J:
http://www.planetkc.com/stm/missingj.htm

Tin Pages/Printing Processes:
http://www.wickedlady.com/tins/processes.html

US Patents Database Patent Full-Text and Bibliographic site:
http://www.uspto.gov/patft

The Victorian Web: Social History, Public Health.

Watts' Hymns:
http://www.ccel.org/w/watts/psalmshymns/TOC.htm

Index